Reading About Language

Reading
About
Language

edited by

Charlton Laird
Emeritus, University of Nevada

Robert M. Gorrell
University of Nevada

Harcourt Brace Jovanovich, Inc.
New York / Chicago / San Francisco / Atlanta

COVER ART by Petie Brigham

ISBN: 0–575535–8

Library of Congress Catalog Card Number: 71-152585

PRINTED IN THE UNITED STATES OF AMERICA

Acknowledgments and Copyrights

For permission to use material in this book the editors wish to thank the following publishers and individuals.

TEXTUAL MATERIAL

AMERICAN HERITAGE PUBLISHING CO., INC.   For the selections from *The American Heritage Dictionary of the English Language,* © copyright 1969, 1970 by American Heritage Publishing Co., Inc. Reprinted by permission.

AMERICAN NAME SOCIETY.   For the selection from "Salt-Derived Place Names in the Ohio Valley" by John A. Jakle from *Names,* Vol. 16 (1968). For the selection from "Bible Belt Onomastics or Some Curiosities of Anti-Pedobaptist Nomenclature" by Thomas Pyles from *Names,* Vol. 7 (1959).

AMERICAN SCIENTIST.   For the selection from "What Is Semantics?" by Anatol Rapoport from *American Scientist,* Vol. 40 (1952).

ELLSWORTH BARNARD.   For a letter to the editor of *The Reporter* by Ellsworth Barnard, January 24, 1957.

BARNES & NOBLE, INC.   For the selection from *The Origin of English Surnames* by P. H. Reaney.

BASIC BOOKS, INC., PUBLISHERS.   For Chapter 24, with deletions, by Robert P. Stockwell, of *Linguistics Today,* edited by Archibald C. Hill, © 1969 by Basic Books, Inc., Publishers, New York.

ROBERT H. BENTLEY.   For "On Black Dialects, White Linguists, and the Teaching of English," not previously published.

BLACKWELL & MOTT LTD.   For the selection from *The Growth and Structure of the English Language,* 9th ed., by Otto Jespersen.

THE BODLEY HEAD.   For the selection from *Grammar Without Tears* by Hugh Sykes Davies.

CURTIS BROWN, LTD.   For the selection from *Semantics, The Nature of Words and Their Meanings* by Hugh R. Walpole. Copyright © 1941 by Hugh R. Walpole.

Reprinted by permission of Curtis Brown, New York. For the selection from Caxton, *Mirror of Fifteenth-Century Letters* by Nellie Slayton Aurner. Reprinted by permission of Curtis Brown Ltd., London.

JONATHAN CAPE LTD. For two excerpts from *A Farewell to Arms* by Ernest Hemingway. Copyright 1929 by Charles Scribner's Sons; renewal copyright © 1957 by Ernest Hemingway. Reprinted by permission of Jonathan Cape Ltd. and the Executors of the Estate of Ernest Hemingway.

THE CENTER FOR CURRICULUM DEVELOPMENT, INC. For the selection from *Introductory Linguistics* by Robert A. Hall, Jr.

THE CLARENDON PRESS. For the selection from *A Dictionary of Modern English Usage,* Second Edition, by H. W. Fowler, revised by Sir Ernest Gowers. For the selection from *The Oxford Dictionary of English Etymology,* edited by C. T. Onions, et al. Both reprinted by permission of The Clarendon Press, Oxford.

COLUMBIA UNIVERSITY PRESS. For the selection from *Headlines and Deadlines* by Robert E. Garst and Theodore M. Bernstein. For the selection from "What Is College Slang?" by Henry Kratz from *American Speech* (1964).

CONTROLLER OF HER BRITANNIC MAJESTY'S STATIONERY OFFICE. For the selection from *Plain Words: Their ABC* by Sir Ernest Gowers.

DONALD P. COSTELLO. For "The Language of *The Catcher in the Rye*" by Donald P. Costello from *American Speech* (1959).

THOMAS Y. CROWELL COMPANY, INC. For the selection from Lester V. Berrey and Melvin Van den Bark: *American Thesaurus of Slang.* Copyright 1942, 1947, 1953 by Thomas Y. Crowell Company, Inc., New York, publishers. For the selections from Harold Wentworth and Stuart B. Flexner: *Dictionary of American Slang.* Copyright © 1967, 1960 by Thomas Y. Crowell Company, Inc., New York, publishers.

THE JOHN DAY COMPANY, INC. For the selection from *Grammar Without Tears* by Hugh Sykes Davies. Copyright © 1951 by Hugh Sykes Davies, and reprinted by permission of The John Day Company, Inc., publisher.

FUNK & WAGNALLS. For the selection from *Current American Usage* by Margaret Bryant. Copyright © 1962 by Funk & Wagnalls Company, Inc. All rights reserved. Printed by permission of Funk & Wagnalls, New York.

GROSSMAN PUBLISHERS, INC. For the selection from *An Exaltation of Larks or, The Veneral Game* by James Lipton. Copyright © 1968 by James Lipton. All rights reserved. Reprinted by permission of Grossman Publishers, Inc.

HARCOURT BRACE JOVANOVICH, INC. For the selections from *Aspects of Language* by Dwight Bolinger. Copyright © 1968 by Harcourt Brace Jovanovich, Inc. For the selection from *Language and Its Structure* by Ronald W. Langacker. Copyright © 1967, 1968 by Harcourt Brace Jovanovich, Inc. For the selection from *The Origins and Development of the English Language,* Second Edition, by Thomas Pyles. Copyright © 1964, 1971 by Harcourt Brace Jovanovich, Inc. For the selection from *Language* by Edward Sapir. Copyright 1921 by Harcourt Brace Jovanovich, Inc.; renewed 1949 by Jean V. Sapir. For the selection from *Introduction to Linguistic Structures* by Archibald A. Hill. Copyright © 1958 by Harcourt Brace Jovanovich, Inc. All reprinted by permission of the publisher.

HARPER & ROW, PUBLISHERS, INC. For the selection abridged from pp. 37–43 in *Understanding English* by Paul Roberts. Copyright © 1958 by Paul Roberts. Reprinted by permission of Harper & Row, Publishers, Inc.

HARPER'S MAGAZINE, INC. For the selection from "Western Half-Acre" by Thomas

Hornsby Ferril. Copyright © 1946 by Harper's Magazine, Inc. Reprinted from the July, 1946, issue of *Harper's Magazine* by permission of the author.

GEORGE G. HARRAP & COMPANY LIMITED. For the selection from *American Thesaurus of Slang* by Lester V. Berrey and Melvin Van den Bark. For the selections from *Dictionary of American Slang* by Harold Wentworth and Stuart B. Flexner.

HARVARD UNIVERSITY PRESS. For the selections from *Philosophy in a New Key* by Susanne K. Langer. Cambridge, Mass.: Harvard University Press. Copyright 1942, 1951, 1957 by the President and Fellows of Harvard College; 1970 by Susanne K. Langer. Reprinted by permission of the publishers.

HOLT, RINEHART AND WINSTON, INC. For the selection from Chapter 2, from *Language* by Leonard Bloomfield. Copyright 1933 by Holt, Rinehart and Winston, Inc. Copyright © 1961 by Leonard Bloomfield. For the selection from *Semantics and Common Sense* by Louis B. Salomon. Copyright © 1966 by Holt, Rinehart and Winston, Inc. Both reprinted by permission of Holt, Rinehart and Winston, Inc.

HOUGHTON MIFFLIN COMPANY. For the selection from *The Works of Geoffrey Chaucer*, edited by F. N. Robinson.

MRS. ALDOUS HUXLEY. For the selection from *Words and Their Meanings* by Aldous Huxley.

INDIANA UNIVERSITY PRESS. For the selection from *Tough, Sweet & Stuffy: An Essay on Modern American Prose Styles* by Walker Gibson. Copyright © 1966 by Indiana University Press. Reprinted by permission of the publisher.

JOHN A. JAKLE. For the selection from "Salt-Derived Place Names in the Ohio Valley" by John A. Jakle from *Names*, Vol. 16 (1968).

MARGOT JOHNSON AGENCY. For the selection from "Bottom's Dream: The Likeness of Poems and Jokes" by Howard Nemerov from *The Virginia Quarterly Review* (Autumn, 1966).

EDWARD H. KELLY. For "A 'Bitch' by Any Other Name Is Less Poetic" by Edward H. Kelly from *Word Study* (October, 1969).

ALFRED A. KNOPF, INC. For the selection from *Plain Words: Their ABC* by Sir Ernest Gowers. Copyright 1954 by The Controller of Her Britannic Majesty's Stationery Office. For the selection from *A New Handbook for Writers* by Sumner Ives. Copyright © 1960 by Sumner Ives. For the selection from *The American Language,* 4th ed., abridged, by H. L. Mencken; Raven I. McDavid, Jr. and David W. Maurer, editors. Copyright 1936 by Alfred A. Knopf, Inc. and renewed 1964 by August Mencken and Mercantile Safe Deposit Trust Co. Copyright © 1963 by Alfred A. Knopf, Inc. All reprinted by permission of Alfred A. Knopf, Inc.

SVEN LILJEBLAD. For "A Primitive Language?" by Sven Liljeblad.

THE MACMILLAN COMPANY. For the selection from *Psycholinguistics: Selected Papers* by Roger Brown. Copyright © 1970 by The Free Press, a Division of The Macmillan Company. For the selection from *Naming Day in Eden* by Noah Jonathan Jacobs. Copyright © by Noah Jonathan Jacobs, 1958, 1969. For the selection from *Origins* by Eric Partridge. Copyright © 1958 by The Macmillan Company. All reprinted with the permission of The Macmillan Company.

ALBERT H. MARCKWARDT. For the selection from *Facts About Current English Usage* by Albert H. Marckwardt and Fred G. Walcott.

MCGRAW-HILL BOOK COMPANY. For a quotation from *The Ape and the Child* by W. N. Kellogg and L. A. Kellogg. Copyright 1933. For the selection from *The Joys of Yiddish* by Leo Rosten. Copyright © 1968 by Leo Rosten. Both used with the permission of McGraw-Hill Book Company.

G. & C. MERRIAM COMPANY. For "A 'Bitch' by Any Other Name Is Less Poetic" by Edward H. Kelly from the October issue of *Word Story*, © 1969 by G. & C. Merriam Co., Publishers of the Merriam-Webster Dictionaries. By permission.

THE M.I.T. PRESS. For the selection from *Language, Thought, and Reality* by Benjamin Lee Whorf. Copyright © 1956 by The Massachusetts Institute of Technology. Reprinted by permission of The M.I.T. Press, Cambridge, Massachusetts.

NATIONAL COUNCIL OF TEACHERS OF ENGLISH. For "Sequence of Tenses, or Was James Thurber the First Transformational Grammarian?" by David DeCamp from *College Composition and Communication* (February, 1967). For the selection from "Where Our Grammar Came From" by Karl Dykema from *College English* (April, 1961). For the selection from "Connotation in Dictionary Definition" by David B. Guralnik from *College Composition and Communication* (May, 1958). For the selection from "Doctrines of English Usage" by Charles V. Hartung from *English Journal* (December, 1956). For the selection from "Regionalism in American English" by Hans Kurath from *The English Language in the School Program*. For the selection from "Literature As Sentences" by Richard Ohmann from *College English* (January, 1966). For "Bi-Dialectalism: The Linguistics of White Supremacy" by James Sledd from *English Journal* (December, 1969). For "Stratificational Grammar: A New Theory of Language" by John White from *College Composition and Communication* (October, 1969). All reprinted with the permission of the National Council of Teachers of English and the authors.

NORTH-HOLLAND PUBLISHING COMPANY. For "Linguistics, Stylistics; Criticism?" by Roger Fowler from *Lingua XVI* (1966).

W. W. NORTON & COMPANY, INC. For the selection from *Semantics, The Nature of Words and Their Meanings* by Hugh R. Walpole. By permission of W. W. Norton & Company, Inc. Copyright 1941 by W. W. Norton & Company, Inc. Copyright renewed 1968 by Rupert Hart-Davis.

PENGUIN BOOKS LTD. For the selection from *Our Language* by Simeon Potter.

KENNETH L. PIKE. For the selection from *Linguistic Concepts: An Introduction to Tagmemics,* an unpublished manuscript by Kenneth L. Pike.

PRENTICE-HALL, INC. For the selection from *The Development of Modern English,* Second Edition, by Stuart Robertson and Frederic G. Cassidy. Copyright © 1954. Reprinted by permission of Prentice-Hall, Inc., Englewood Cliffs, New Jersey.

PSYCHOLOGY TODAY. For the selection from "Language and the Mind" by Noam Chomsky. Reprinted from *Psychology Today* Magazine (February, 1968). Copyright © Communications/Research/Machines, Inc.

RANDOM HOUSE, INC. For the selection from *A Dictionary of Contemporary American Usage* by Bergen Evans and Cornelia Evans. Copyright 1957 by Bergen Evans and Cornelia Evans. All rights reserved under International and Pan-American Copyright Conventions.

THE REPORTER. For a letter to the editor by Ellsworth Barnard (January 24, 1957). Copyright 1957 by The Reporter Magazine Company. For "For Who the Bell Tolls," a Reporter *Note* (December 27, 1956). Copyright 1956 by The Reporter Magazine Company.

ILLUSTRATIVE MATERIAL

FOLGER SHAKESPEARE LIBRARY. For facsimiles on pages 403–04.

HARCOURT BRACE JOVANOVICH. For map on page 292 from *Aspects of Language* by Dwight Bolinger. Copyright © 1968 by Harcourt Brace Jovanovich, Inc. (As adapted from Hans Kurath, *A Word Geography of the Eastern United States,* Ann Arbor, Michigan: University of Michigan Press, 1949.) For art on page 371 from *The Origins and Development of the English Language,* Second Edition, by Thomas Pyles. Copyright © 1964, 1971 by Harcourt Brace Jovanovich, Inc., and reproduced with their permission.

THE MACMILLAN COMPANY. For art on page 44 from *Psycholinguistics: Selected Papers* by Roger Brown. Copyright © 1970 by The Free Press, a Division of The Macmillan Company. Used with the permission of The Macmillan Company.

THE M.I.T. PRESS. For Figure 1, page 66, adapted from *Language, Thought, and Reality* by Benjamin Lee Whorf, by permission of The M.I.T. Press, Cambridge, Massachusetts. Copyright © 1956 by The Massachusetts Institute of Technology.

NATIONAL COUNCIL OF TEACHERS OF ENGLISH. For Figure 1, page 231, and art on pages 228, 229, and 230 from "Stratificational Grammar" by John White from *College Composition and Communication,* XX (1969). Copyright © 1969 by the National Council of Teachers of English. Adapted by permission of the publisher and John White.

PSYCHOLOGY TODAY. For Figure 2, page 81, adapted from *Language and the Mind* by Noam Chomsky. Adapted from *Psychology Today* Magazine (February, 1968). Copyright © Communications/Research/Machines, Inc.

THE RONALD PRESS COMPANY. For art on pages 212, 213, 214, and 215 from *The Structure of American English* by W. Nelson Francis. Copyright © 1958 The Ronald Press Company, New York.

THE WORLD PUBLISHING COMPANY. For Table 1, page 188, and Table 2, page 189, adapted by permission of The World Publishing Company from *An Introduction to English Linguistics* by Joseph H. Friend.

Preface

The English language is the accretion and growth of every dialect, race, and range of time . . . it stands for Language in the largest sense, and is really the greatest of studies. It involves so much; is indeed a sort of universal absorber, combiner, and conqueror.
WALT WHITMAN, Slang in America

The most difficult step in the study of language is the first step. Again and again, scholarship has approached the study of language without actually entering upon it.
LEONARD BLOOMFIELD, Language

The last quarter-century has seen a revolution in thinking about language, perhaps especially about grammar, but also about usage, meaning, the role of language in society, and the relationship between language and literature. Never has there been so much healthy controversy in the field in so many areas. *Reading About Language* aims to help the student making his first step in language study. It seeks to direct him beyond the immediate practical concerns of "correct" grammar and usage to an understanding of the fundamental questions that have been asked and are being asked about the nature of language, about the way language works and the way it changes, and about the importance of language in modern society.

We believe that it is both more exciting and more instructive to hunt than to be handed a trophy, particularly if the hunter is a student and the quarry a subject like language. This book is intended to encourage pursuit. The selections within each part have been arranged primarily to encourage inductive thinking; those at the beginning of a part usually provide concrete evidence, whereas those at the end present general statements. For example, Part 5, on dialect, begins with Thomas Kochman's essay "'Rapping' in the Black Ghetto," which includes numerous examples of a particular black dialect, and ends with Dwight Bolinger's remarks on dialect and language, in which he defines dialect and distinguishes between dialects and linguistic codes. Many selections do not make direct statements about language but illustrate different uses of language so that students may make their own generalizations. Part 7, for instance, includes passages from Orm to Shakespeare intended to suggest how the English language changed between 1200 and 1600.

The introductions to the parts raise questions that are explored in the selections and thus promote speculative reading. At the end of each selection are suggestions for discussion and written work, which attempt to help students reach their own conclusions about the selection and to prepare them for the readings that follow. The exercises also suggest subjects for further investigation and discussion.

We have tried to make the collection exciting, not ponderous. Nothing was included solely because it is authoritative. We were pleased to find readable statements from many of the great thinkers on language, from Wilhelm von Humboldt and William Dwight Whitney, through Bloomfield, Cassirer, and Whorf, to Noam Chomsky and Kenneth Pike. The selections reflect the excitement, vitality, and scope of the field. Among the discussions of recent developments is Roger Brown's report in Part 1 on the progress Allen and Beatrice Gardner have made in teaching sign language to a chimpanzee. Part 4 illustrates the wealth of current ideas about grammar, the area of linguistics in which there is the greatest activity and perhaps the greatest disagreement. The pressing problem of the treatment of dialect in language teaching is considered in Part 5. Finally, these selections are particularly meaningful because students are able to evaluate them on the basis of their own understanding of language—an understanding gained in large part from working with language.

We are grateful to Richard Hendrickson for reading and commenting on the manuscript. We would also like to thank Ronald Campbell and Patricia Stoltz of Harcourt Brace Jovanovich, whose personal attention and concern far exceeded their editorial duties.

Charlton Laird
Robert M. Gorrell

Contents

Part 2 Words and Names

Part 3 Language and Meaning

Part 4 From Use into Grammar

Part 5   Dialect and Dialects 256

Part 8   Language, Literature, and Style   428

Reading About Language

introduction

Some Thoughts About Language

The "talkative animal," as William Entwistle once called man, has long admired his talk and has wondered about it. In primitive societies men looked with awe at language: they endowed words with magical powers, used as names words for qualities they hoped to find in their offspring, and made words for death and illness taboo in the hope of protecting themselves from the unpleasantness the words symbolized. Cantrips, curses, and spells have largely disappeared, but word magic, the confusion of words and things, is still practiced in much advertising and in other types of propaganda. Our word babel reflects an early conviction that men can be confounded by confounding their language. Modern controversies about usage, about the treatment of social dialects, and about the responsible use of language in politics demonstrate that the conviction persists.

Accompanying the popular preoccupation of the talkative animal with his language is a long tradition of more scholarly thought about the nature and origin of language and its significance in society. The following selections are only a sample of the thousands of such comments that have appeared over the centuries.

1

The Origin of Language

Lucretius

Men have puzzled over the question of the origin of language from very early times. In the first century B.C. the Roman philosopher Lucretius speculated on it in On the Nature of Things, *from which the following passage is taken.*

But the diverse sounds of the tongue nature constrained men to utter, and use shaped the names of things, in a manner not far other than the very speechlessness of their tongue is seen to lead children on to gesture, when it makes them point out with the finger the things that are before their eyes. For every one feels to what purpose he can use his own powers. Before the horns of a calf appear and sprout from his forehead, he butts with them when angry, and pushes passionately. But the whelps of panthers and lion-cubs already fight with claws and feet and biting, when their teeth and claws are scarce yet formed. Further, we see all the tribe of winged fowls trusting to their wings, and seeking an unsteady aid from their pinions. Again, to think that any one then parcelled out names to things, and that from him men learnt their first words, is mere folly. For why should he be able to mark off all things by words, and to utter the diverse sounds of the tongue, and at the same time others be thought unable to do this? Moreover, if others too had not used words to one another, whence was implanted in him the concept of their use; whence was he given the first power to know and see in his mind what he wanted to do? Likewise one man could not avail to constrain many, and vanquish them to his will, that they should be willing to learn all his names for things; nor indeed is it easy in any way to teach and persuade the deaf what it is needful to do; for they would not endure it, nor in any way suffer the sounds of words unheard before to batter on their ears any more to no purpose. Lastly, what is there so marvellous in this, if the human race, with strong voice and tongue, should mark off things with diverse sounds for diverse feelings? When the dumb cattle, yea and the races of wild beasts are wont to give forth diverse unlike sounds, when they are in fear or pain, or again when their joys grow strong. Yea verily, this we may learn from things clear to see. When the large loose lips of Molossian dogs start to snarl in anger, baring their hard teeth, thus drawn back in rage, they threaten with a noise far other than when they bark and fill all around with their clamour. Yet when they essay fondly to lick their cubs with their tongue, or when they toss them with their feet, and making for them with open mouth, feign gently to swallow them, checking their closing teeth, they fondle them with growling voice in a way far other than when left alone in the house they bay, or when whining they shrink from a beating with cringing body. Again, is not neighing seen to differ likewise, when a young stallion in the flower of his years rages among the mares, pricked by the spur of winged love, and from spreading nostrils snorts for the fray, and when, it may be, at other times he whinnies with trembling limbs? Lastly, the tribe of winged fowls and the diverse birds, hawks and ospreys and gulls amid the sea-waves, seeking in the salt waters for life and livelihood, utter at other times cries far other than when they are struggling for their food and fighting for their prey. And some of them change their harsh notes with the weather, as the long-lived tribes of crows and flocks of rooks, when they are said to cry for water and rains, and anon to summon the winds and breezes. And so, if diverse feelings constrain animals, though they are dumb, to utter diverse sounds, how much more likely is it that mortals should then have been able to mark off things unlike with one sound and another.

WORKING WITH THE SELECTION

Lucretius' argument that language grew up naturally through human experiment rests partly on an analogy; what is the analogy? Does Lucretius' argument imply that animals are able to use language?

2

Lucretius Refuted

James Beattie

Lucretius' speculations on the origin of language retained enough vitality so that 1800 years later the Scottish philosopher and rhetorician James Beattie (1735–1803), writing his Theory of Language *(1788), felt impelled to refute him.*

Other absurdities in [Lucretius'] account of the origin of society I may possibly touch upon hereafter. At present I would only observe, that *speech* could not have been invented in the way here described. For to animals in this state of brutality I have already remarked, that language could not be needful: and it is hardly to be supposed, that dumb and beastly creatures would apply themselves to the cultivation of unnecessary arts, which they had never felt any inconvenience from the want of, and which had never been attempted by other animals. To which I may add, what is clear from some of the preceding observations, that Speech, if invented at all, must have been invented, either by children, who were incapable of invention, or by men, who were incapable of speech. And therefore reason, as well as history, intimates, that mankind in all ages must have been speaking animals; the young having constantly acquired this art by imitating those who were elder. And we may warrantably suppose, that our first parents must have received it by immediate inspiration.

As the first language, whatever it was, must therefore have been perfect; and liable to no depravation from a mixture of foreign idioms; and held in reverence by those who spoke it, that is, by all mankind, on account of its divine original; we may believe, that it would continue unaltered for many ages. Accordingly Scripture informs us, that when the building of Babel was begun, about eighteen hundred years after the fall, the whole earth was of one speech. And, had no miraculous interposition taken place, it is probable, that some traces of it would have remained in every language to this day. For, though, in so long a time, many words must have been changed, many introduced, and many forgotten, in every country, yet men being all of the same family, and all deriving their speech from the only one primitive tongue, it may be presumed, that some of the original words would still have been in use throughout the whole earth: even as in all the modern languages of Europe some Greek, and some Hebrew, and a great deal of Latin, is still discernible. But Providence thought fit to prevent this; and, by confounding the language of the builders of Babel, to establish in the world a variety of primitive tongues.

This miracle could not fail to be attended with important consequences. Those men only would remain in the same society who understood one another: and so the human race would be broken into a number of small tribes or nations, each of which would keep together, and consequently at some distance from the rest. A general dispersion would follow: and in this way it is probable, that the whole world would be sooner inhabited, than if all the species had remained united in one great nation. And the distinctions of friend and stranger, of citizen and foreigner, would now take place: whence rivalship would arise; than which nothing more effectually promotes industry, and the various arts of life.

WORKING WITH THE SELECTION

1. How much of Beattie's refutation of Lucretius is sound? Does Lucretius, as Beattie seems to suggest, assume that animals invented speech? Granting Beattie's earlier assumptions, is the final sentence of the first paragraph logically sound?

2. What benefits to mankind does Beattie see in what happened at Babel (Genesis 11:1-9)? Reconstruct Beattie's argument. *variety of primitive tongues*

3

Adam and Eve and Language

Noah Webster

In the Preface to his American Dictionary of the English Language *(1828), the great American lexicographer Noah Webster (1758–1843) discussed the tradition of attributing language to the benevolence of a supreme being.*

We read, in the Scriptures, that God, when he had created man, "Blessed them and said to them, be fruitful and multiply and replenish the earth and subdue it; and have dominion over the fish of the sea, &c." God afterwards planted a garden, and placed in it the man he had made, with a command to keep it, and to dress it; and he gave him a rule of moral conduct, in permitting him to eat the fruit of every tree in the garden, except one, the eating of which was prohibited. We further read, that God brought to Adam the fowls and beasts he had made, and that Adam gave them names; and that when his female companion was made, he gave her a name. After the eating of the forbidden fruit, it is stated that God addressed Adam and Eve, reproving them for their disobedience, and pronouncing the penalties, which they had incurred. In the account of these transactions, it is further related that Adam and Eve both replied to their Maker, and excused their disobedience.

If we admit what is the literal and obvious interpretation of this narrative, that vocal sounds or words were used in these communications between God and the progenitors of the human race, it results that Adam was not only endowed with intellect for understanding his Maker, or the signification of words, but was furnished both with the faculty of speech, and with speech itself, or the knowledge and use of words, as signs of ideas, and this before the formation of the woman. Hence we may infer that language was bestowed on Adam, in the same manner as all his other faculties and knowledge, by supernatural power; or in other words, was of divine origin; for supposing Adam to have had all the intellectual powers of any adult individual of the species, who has since lived, we cannot admit as probable, or even possible, that he should have invented and constructed even a barren language, as soon as he was created, without supernatural aid. It may even be doubted, whether without such aid, men would ever have learnt the use of the organs of speech, so far as to form a language. At any rate, the invention of words, and the construction of a language must have been a slow process, and must have required a much longer time, than that which passed between the creation of Adam and of Eve. It is therefore probable that *language* as well as the faculty of speech, was the *immediate gift of God*. We are not however to suppose the language of our first parents in paradise to have been copious, like most modern languages; or the identical language they used, to be now in existence. Many of the primitive radical words may and probably do exist in various languages; but observation teaches that languages must improve and undergo great changes as knowledge increases, and be subject to continual alterations, from other causes incident to men in society.

WORKING WITH THE SELECTION

On the whole does Webster agree with Lucretius or Beattie? Can you think of any reasons why? Both Webster and Beattie accept the statement in the first chapter of Genesis as the basic truth from which to begin. How do they differ in what they make of it?

4

Another View of Genesis

Frederic William Farrar

The English clergyman and philologist Frederic William Farrar (1831–1903) opposed those who believed language had a divine origin, as the following selection from his Language and Languages *(1878) reveals. Farrar regarded the "theory of onomatopoeia as the only discovered or discoverable basis of language."*

The assertors of revealed language distinctly contradict the very book to which, in their desire to usurp the keys of all knowledge, they groundlessly appeal as a scientific authority. For what does the Jehovist say? 'And out of the ground the Lord God formed every beast of the field, and every fowl of the air; and brought them unto Adam *to see what he would call them: and whatsoever Adam called every living creature, that was the name thereof. And Adam gave names* to all cattle, and to the fowl of the air, and to every *beast of the field*' (Gen. ii. 19, 20). When we remember the invariable tendency of the Semitic intellect to overlook in every instance all secondary causes, and to attribute every result *directly* to the agency of superior beings, it is clear that by no possibility could the writer have given more unmistakeable expression to his view that language was the product of the human intelligence, and had no origin more divine than that which is divine in man.

Nature with its infinity of sweet and varied sounds was ringing in the ears of primal man. 'Heavens!' exclaims Herder, 'what a schoolroom of ideas and of speech! Bring no Mercury or Apollo as a *Deus ex machina* from the clouds to earth. The whole many-sounding godlike nature is man's language-teacher and Muse. She leads all her creatures before him; each carries its name upon its tongue, and declares itself vassal and servant to this veiled yet visible god! It delivers to him its markword into the book of his sovereignty, like a tribute, in order that he may by this name remember it, and in the future use and call it. I ask whether this truth, viz., that the understanding, whereby man is lord of nature, was the source of a living speech which he drew for himself from the sounds of creatures, as tokens whereby to distinguish them—I ask whether this dry truth could in Oriental fashion be more nobly or beautifully expressed than by saying that God led the animals to him to see what he would name them, and the name that he would give them, that should be the name thereof? How, in Oriental poetic fashion, can it be more distinctly stated that man discovered speech for himself out of the tones of living Nature, as a sign of his ruling intelligence? and that is the point which I am proving.'

WORKING WITH THE SELECTION

How do Webster and Farrar differ in their uses of Genesis? Compare Farrar's view of the origin of language with that of Lucretius. Have any of the writers you have read so far looked at language itself for evidence? On what do they base their arguments?

5

Language and General Terms

John Locke

The English philosopher John Locke (1632–1704) saw in language evidence of the nature of the human mind; the following selection is from his Essay Concerning Human Understanding (*1690*).

All things that exist being particulars, it may perhaps be thought reasonable that words, which ought to be conformed to things, should be so too; I mean in their signification: but yet we find quite the contrary. The far greatest part of words, that make all languages, are general terms; which has not been the effect of neglect or chance, but of reason and necessity.

First, It is impossible that every particular thing should have a distinct peculiar name. For the signification and use of words, depending on that connexion which the mind makes between its ideas and the sounds it uses as signs of them, it is necessary, in the application of names to things that the mind should have distinct ideas of the things, and retain also the particular name that belongs to every one, with its peculiar appropriation to that idea. But it is beyond the power of human capacity to frame and retain distinct ideas of all the particular things we meet with: every bird and beast men saw, every tree and plant that affected the senses, could not find a place in the most capacious understanding. If it be looked on as an instance of a prodigious memory, that some generals have been able to call every soldier in their army by his proper name, we may easily find a reason, why men have never attempted to give names to each sheep in their flock, or crow that flies over their heads; much less to call every leaf of plants, or grain of sand that came in their way, by a peculiar name.

Secondly, If it were possible, it would yet be useless; because it would not serve to the chief end of language. Men would in vain heap up names of particular things, that would not serve them to communicate their thoughts. Men learn names, and use them in talk with others, only that they may be understood: which is then only done, when by use or consent the sound I make by the organs of speech, excites in another man's mind, who hears it, the idea I apply it to in mine, when I speak it. This cannot be done by names applied to particular things, whereof I alone having the ideas in my mind, the names of them could not be significant or intelligible to another, who was not acquainted with all those very particular things which had fallen under my notice.

Thirdly, But yet granting this also feasible (which I think is not) yet a distinct name for every particular thing would not be of any great use for the improvement of knowledge: which, though founded in particular things, enlarges itself by general views: to which things reduced into sorts under general names, are properly subservient. These, with the names belonging to them, come within some compass, and do not multiply every moment, beyond what either the mind can contain, or use requires: and therefore, in these, men have for the most part stopped; but yet not so as to hinder themselves from distinguishing particular things, by appropriated names, where convenience demands it. And therefore in their own species, which they have most to do with, and wherein they have often occasion to mention particular persons, they make use of proper names; and there distinct individuals have distinct denominations.

WORKING WITH THE SELECTION

In the light of Locke's comments about the need for general terms, can you account for the fact that the language of the Eskimos has individual names for various sorts or conditions of snow, such as snow falling and snow packed in drifts, but no general term like English *snow?*

6

Slang in America

Walt Whitman

In an article published in The North American Review, *141 (1885), the American poet Walt Whitman (1819–92) revealed his interest in the vitality of language.*

Viewed freely, the English language is the accretion and growth of every dialect, race, and range of time, and is the culling and composition of all. From this point of view, it stands for Language in the largest sense, and is really the greatest of studies. It involves so much; is indeed a sort of universal absorber, combiner, and conqueror. The scope of its etymologies is the scope not only of man and civilization, but the history of Nature in all departments, and of the organic Universe, brought up to date; for all are comprehended in words, and their backgrounds. This is when words become vitalized, and stand for things, as they unerringly and very soon come to do, in the mind that enters on their study with fitting spirit, grasp, and appreciation.

Slang, profoundly considered, is the lawless germinal element, below all words and sentences, and behind all poetry, and proves a certain freedom and perennial rankness and protestantism in speech. As the United States inherit by far their most precious possession—the language they talk and write—from the Old World, under and out of its feudal institutes, I will allow myself to borrow a simile even of those forms farthest removed from American Democracy. Considering Language then as some mighty potentate, into the majestic audience-hall of the monarch ever enters a personage like one of Shakspere's clowns, and takes position there, and plays a part even in the stateliest ceremonies. Such is Slang, or indirection, an attempt of common humanity to escape from bald literalism, and express itself illimitably, which in highest walks produces poets and poems, and doubtless in pre-historic times gave the start to, and perfected, the whole immense tangle of the old mythologies. For, curious as it may appear, it is strictly the same impulse-source, the same thing. Slang, too, is the wholesome fermentation or eructation of those processes eternally active in language, by which froth and specks are thrown up, mostly to pass away; though occasionally to settle and permanently crystallize.

To make it plainer, it is certain that many of the oldest and solidest words we use, were originally generated from the daring and license of slang. In the processes of word-formation, myriads die, but here and there the attempt attracts superior meanings, becomes valuable and indispensable, and lives forever. Thus the term *right* means literally only straight. *Wrong* primarily meant twisted, distorted. *Integrity* meant, oneness. *Spirit* meant breath, or flame. A *supercilious* person was one who raised his eyebrows. To *insult* was to leap against. If you *influenced* a man, you but flowed into him. The Hebrew word which is translated prophesy meant to bubble up and pour forth as a fountain. The enthusiast bubbles up with the Spirit of God within him, and it pours forth from him like a fountain. The word *prophecy* is misunderstood. Many suppose that it is limited to mere prediction; that is but the lesser portion of prophecy. The greater work is to reveal God. Every true religious enthusiast is a prophet. . . .

Daring as it is to say so, in the growth of Language it is certain that the retrospect of slang from the start would be the recalling from their nebulous conditions of all that is poetical in the stores of human utterance. Moreover, the honest delving, as of late years, by the German and British workers in comparative philology has pierced and dispersed many of the falsest bubbles of centuries; and will disperse many more. It was long recorded that in Scandinavian mythology the heroes in the Norse Paradise drank out of the skulls of their slain enemies. Later investigation proves the word taken for skulls to mean *horns* of beasts slain in the hunt. And what reader had not been exercised over the traces of that feudal custom, by which *seigneurs* warmed their feet in the bowels of serfs, the abdomen being opened for the purpose? It now is made to appear that the serf was only required to submit his unharmed abdomen as a foot cushion while his lord supped, and was required to chafe the legs of the seigneur with his hands.

WORKING WITH THE SELECTION

Is Whitman being consistent with the general point of his essay when he says at the end of the third paragraph that "the word *prophecy* is misunderstood"?

7

Language as Change

Wilhelm von Humboldt

In a pioneering work, On the Structural Variety of Human Language and Its Influence on the Intellectual Development of Mankind *(1836), the German philologist Wilhelm von Humboldt (1767–1835) set forth his views on the relationship of language and society—views that have had increasing influence on modern linguists.*

Since language . . . always possesses only an ideal existence in the heads and spirits of men, never a material one—even when engraved on stone or bronze —and since the force of the languages which are no longer spoken depends largely on the strength of our own capability to revivify them, to the extent in which we can still perceive them, in the same way there can never be a moment of true standstill in language, just as little as in the ceaselessly flaming thought of men. By nature it is a continuous process of development under the influence of the actual intellectual force of the speaker. Two periods which must be definitely distinguished arise of course in this process: the one in which the sound-creating force of the language is still in growth and living activity; the other in which an apparent standstill takes place after complete formation of at least the external form of language and then a visible decline of that creative, sensual force follows. But even from the period of decline new principles of life and new successful reformations of language can develop. . . .

Humboldt attached great importance to change. If one accepts his statement, how does one regard earlier arguments, even those of a profound thinker like Locke?

8

Animal Sounds and Human Speech

William Dwight Whitney

William Dwight Whitney (1827–94) was one of the first important American scholars of Sanskrit and comparative philology and he served as editor-in-chief of the monumental Century Dictionary *(1889–97). In the following selection from* The Life and Growth of Language *(1877) he attempts to distinguish between natural expression and language.*

The essential difference, which separates man's means of communication in kind as well as degree from that of the other animals, is that, while the latter is instinctive, the former is, in all its parts, arbitrary and conventional. That this is so, the whole course of our exposition has sufficiently shown. It is fully proved by the single circumstance that for each object, or act, or quality, there are as many names as there are languages in the world, each answering as good a purpose as any other, and capable of being substituted for another in the usage of any individual. There is not in a known language a single item which can be truly claimed to exist φύσει, 'by nature;' each stands in its accepted use θέσει, 'by an act of attribution,' in which men's circumstances, habits, preferences, will, are the determining force. Even where the onomatopoeic or imitative element is most conspicuous—as in *cuckoo* and *pewee,* in *crack* and *whiz*—there is no tie of necessity, but only of convenience: if there were a necessity, it would extend equally to other animals and other noises; and also to all tongues; while in fact these conceptions have elsewhere wholly other names. No man can become possessed of any existing language without learning it; no animal (that we know of) has any expression which he learns, which is not the direct gift of nature to him. We are not less generously treated in this latter respect than the animals; we have also our "natural" expression, in grimace, gesture, and tone; and we make use of it: on the one hand, for communication where the usual conventional means is made of no avail—as between men of different tongue, or those who by deafness are cut off from the use of speech—and, on the other hand, for embellishing and explaining and enforcing our ordinary language: where it is of a power and value that no student of language can afford to overlook. In the domain of feeling and persuasion, in all that is intended to impress the personality of the communicator upon the recipient, it possesses the highest consequence. We say with literal truth that a look, a tone, a gesture, is often more eloquent than elaborate speech. Language is harmed for some uses by its conventionality. Words of sympathy or affection can be repeated parrot-like by one whose heartless tone takes all value from them; there is no persuasion in a discourse which is given as if from a mere animated speaking-machine. And herein comes clearly to light the true sphere of natural expression; it indicates feeling, and feeling only. From the cry and groan and laugh and smile up to the lightest variations of tone and feature which the skilled elocutionist uses, it is emotional, subjective. Not a tittle of evidence has ever been brought forward to show that there is such a thing as the natural expression of an intellectual conception, of a judgment, of a cognition. It is where expression quits its emotional natural basis, and turns to intellectual uses, that the history of language begins.

WORKING WITH THE SELECTION

Do Whitney's assumptions about animal communication differ from those of Lucretius and Beattie?

9

The Use of Language

Leonard Bloomfield

Leonard Bloomfield (1887–1949) is known as the major American figure in the development of structural linguistics. In the following selection from Language *(1933) he defines a linguist's concerns with language.*

The most difficult step in the study of language is the first step. Again and again, scholarship has approached the study of language without actually entering upon it. Linguistic science arose from relatively practical preoccupations, such as the use of writing, the study of literature and especially of older records, and the prescription of elegant speech, but people can spend any amount of time on these things without actually entering upon linguistic study. As the individual student is likely to repeat the delays of history, we may do well to speak of these matters, so as to distinguish them from the subject of our study.

Writing is not language, but merely a way of recording language by means of visible marks. In some countries, such as China, Egypt, and Mesopotamia, writing was practised thousands of years ago, but to most of the languages that are spoken today it has been applied either in relatively recent times or not at all. Moreover, until the days of printing, literacy was confined to a very few people. All languages were spoken through nearly all of their history by people who did not read or write; the languages of such peoples are just as stable, regular, and rich as the languages of literate nations. A language is the same no matter what system of writing may be used to record it, just as a person is the same no matter how you take his picture. The Japanese have three systems of writing and are developing a fourth. When the Turks, in 1928, adopted the Latin alphabet in place of the Arabic, they went on talking in just the same way as before. In order to study writing, we must know something about language, but the reverse is not true. To be sure, we get our information about the speech of past times largely from written records—and for this reason we shall, in another connection, study the history of writing—but we find this to be a handicap. We have to use great care in interpreting the written symbols into terms of actual speech; often we fail in this, and always we should prefer to have the audible word.

Literature, whether presented in spoken form or, as is now our custom, in writing, consists of beautiful or otherwise notable utterances. The student of literature observes the utterances of certain persons (say, of a Shakspere) and concerns himself with the content and with the unusual features of form. The interest of the philologist is even broader, for he is concerned with the cultural significance and background of what he reads. The linguist, on the other hand, studies the language of all persons alike; the individual features in which the language of a great writer differs from the ordinary speech of his time and place, interest the linguist no more than do the individual features of any other person's speech, and much less than do the features that are common to all speakers.

The discrimination of elegant or "correct" speech is a by-product of certain social conditions. The linguist has to observe it as he observes other linguistic phenomena. The fact that speakers label a speech-form as "good" or "correct," or else as "bad" or "incorrect," is merely a part of the linguist's data concerning this speech-form. Needless to say, it does not permit him to ignore part of his material or to falsify his records: he observes all speech-forms impartially. It is part of his task to find out under what circumstances the speakers label a form in one way or the other, and, in the case of each particular form, why they label it as they do: why, for example, many people say that *ain't* is "bad" and *am not* is "good." This is only one of the problems of linguistics, and since it is not a fundamental one, it can be attacked only after many other things are known. Strangely enough, people without linguistic training devote a great deal of effort to futile discussions of this topic without progressing to the study of language, which alone could give them the key.

A student of writing, of literature or philology, or of correct speech, if he were persistent and methodical enough, might realize, after some waste of effort, that he had better first study language and then return to these problems.

WORKING WITH THE SELECTION

Explain Bloomfield's assertion that one can study writing, literature, and usage "without actually entering upon linguistic study." What, according to Bloomfield, is the linguist's attitude toward distinctions between "correct" and "incorrect" speech or writing?

10

Language and Thinking

Edward Sapir

Edward Sapir (1884–1939) is known for both his extensive work on American Indian languages and his imaginative theories about relationships among languages, many of which are recorded in Language *(1929), from which the following selection is taken.*

Most people, asked if they can think without speech, would probably answer, "Yes, but it is not easy for me to do so. Still I know it can be done." Language is but a garment! But what if language is not so much a garment as a prepared road or groove? It is, indeed, in the highest degree likely that language is an instrument originally put to uses lower than the conceptual plane and that thought arises as a refined interpretation of its content. The product grows, in other words, with the instrument, and thought may be no more conceivable, in its genesis and daily practice, without speech than is mathematical reasoning practicable without the lever of an appropriate mathematical symbolism. No one believes that even the most difficult mathematical proposition is inherently dependent on an arbitrary set of symbols, but it is impossible to suppose that the human mind is capable of arriving at or holding such a proposition without the symbolism. The writer, for one, is strongly of the opinion that the feeling entertained by so many that they can think, or even reason, without language is an illusion. The illusion seems to be due to a number of factors. The simplest of these is the failure to distinguish between imagery and thought. As a matter of fact, no sooner do we try to put an image into conscious relation with another than we find ourselves slipping into a silent flow of words. Thought may be a natural domain apart from the artificial one of speech, but speech would seem to be the only road we know of that leads to it. A still more fruitful source of the illusive feeling that language may be dispensed with in thought is the common failure to realize that language is not identical with its auditory symbolism. The auditory symbolism may be replaced, point for point, by a motor or by a visual symbolism (many people can read, for instance, in a purely visual sense, that is, without the intermediating link of an inner flow of the auditory images that correspond to the printed or written words) or by still other, more subtle and elusive, types of transfer that are not so easy to define. Hence the contention that one thinks without language merely because he is not aware of a coexisting auditory imagery is very far indeed from being a valid one. One may go so far as to suspect that the symbolic expression of thought may in some cases run along outside the fringe of the conscious mind, so that the feeling of a free, non-linguistic stream of thought is for minds of a certain type a relatively, but only a relatively, justified one. Psycho-physically, this would mean that the auditory or equivalent visual or motor centers in the brain, together with the appropriate paths of association, that are the cerebral equivalent of speech, are touched off so lightly during the process of thought as not to rise into consciousness at all. This would be a limiting case —thought riding lightly on the submerged crests of speech, instead of jogging along with it, hand in hand. The modern psychology has shown us how powerfully symbolism is at work in the unconscious mind. It is therefore easier to understand at the present time than it would have been twenty years ago that the most rarefied thought may be but the conscious counterpart of an unconscious linguistic symbolism.

One word more as to the relation between language and thought. The point of view that we have developed does not by any means preclude the possibility of the growth of speech being in a high degree dependent on the development of thought. We may assume that language arose pre-rationally —just how and on what precise level of mental activity we do not know— but we must not imagine that a highly developed system of speech symbols worked itself out before the genesis of distinct concepts and of thinking, the handling of concepts. We must rather imagine that thought processes set in, as a kind of psychic overflow, almost at the beginning of linguistic expression; further, that the concept, once defined, necessarily reacted on the life of its linguistic symbol, encouraging further linguistic growth. We see this complex process of the interaction of language and thought actually taking place under our eyes. The instrument makes possible the product, the product refines the instrument. The birth of a new concept is invariably foreshadowed by a more or less strained or extended use of old linguistic material; the concept does not attain to individual and independent life until it has found a distinctive linguistic embodiment. In most cases the new symbol is but a thing wrought from linguistic material already in existence in ways mapped out by crushingly despotic precedents. As soon as the word is at hand, we instinctively feel, with something of a sigh of relief, that the concept is ours for the handling. Not until we own the symbol do we feel that we hold a key to the immediate knowledge or understanding of the concept. Would we be so ready to die for "liberty," to struggle for "ideals," if the words themselves were not ringing within us? And the word, as we know, is not only a key; it may also be a fetter.

WORKING WITH THE SELECTION

What does Sapir mean by "the failure to distinguish between imagery and thought"? What does he mean by "the product refines the instrument"?

part 1

Man, Mind, and Language

Modern man is a product of biological evolution, but he is also a product of language. Over millions of years, man evolved, slowly, haltingly, from the single-celled protozoa through a vast number of increasingly complex creatures, whose ability to survive was great but whose ability to think was meager, into an animal capable of developing speech and culture. So long as the evolution of modern man relied on biological change, it was slow; but when human development came to rely more on social change than on biological change, more on new knowledge and new ways of thinking than on more brain cells and opposable thumbs, man evolved faster and faster. Man can now think more than he has before because he has more to think with and more to think about. The knowledge explosion proceeds at a dizzying speed. There are more great scientists and scholars living today than in all the previous centuries combined, and more highly literate men than in any previous society. And the pace is accelerating.

Through science, technology, education, and communication, man is increasing and refining culture in all parts of the world, and his basic tool is language. Obviously, then, we must know more about language, the invention with which man made himself "human." We must know more as students of language and as citizens of the modern world, for language is both a subject of study in itself and the means of gathering, analyzing, and disseminating information in all fields.

For centuries, men have asked fundamental questions about the nature of language and its relation to them. Some of these questions are perhaps unanswerable—at least they have not yet been answered—but they are not therefore less important or less interesting or less likely to provoke continuing speculation. What is the origin of language? How does one learn language? Do animals other than man use language? Can animals learn to use language? Can one think without language, or is language essential to thought? Does logic or reason exist independently, or does it only describe patterns for manipulating language? Do the distinguishing characteristics of a language grow from the culture in which it develops? Does a language help mold the culture in which it is used? These questions, and others like them, involving the relationship between man and his mind and his language, are the concern of the selections in Part 1.

1

What Is Language?

Archibald A. Hill

Since we all know when we are using language, many writers have not tried to define it. It is easy to recognize but hard to define; nevertheless, trying to define it may help us to think about it. The following selection is an attempt by Archibald A. Hill, professor of English and linguistics at the University of Texas at Austin, in his Introduction to Linguistic Structures *(1958).*

Linguists can offer a set of five defining characteristics which serve to set off language from other forms of symbolic behavior and to establish language as a purely human activity. Often animal communication will have one or more of these five characteristics, but never all of them.

First, language, as has been said, is a set of sounds. This is perhaps the least important characteristic, since the communication of mammals and birds is also a set of sounds. On the other hand, the system of communication which is in some ways most strikingly like language, that of bees, is a set of body movements, not sounds. It would be easy, further, to imagine a language based on something else than sound, but no human language is so constructed. Even the manual language of the deaf is derived from the pre-existent spoken language of the community.

Second, the connection between the sounds, or sequences of sounds, and objects of the outside world is arbitrary and unpredictable. That is to say, a visitor from Mars would be unable to predict that in London a given animal is connected with the sound sequence written *dog,* in Paris with the sequence *chien,* in Madrid with *perro.* The arbitrary quality of language symbols is not infrequently denied, for a number of reasons. Sometimes the denial is based on nothing more than the notion that the forms of one's native language are so inevitably right that they must be instinctive for all proper men. Sometimes the denial is more subtle. <u>It is often maintained that all language, even though now largely arbitrary, must once have been a systematic imitation of objects by means of sound.</u> It is true that there are some imitative words in all languages, but they are at best a limited part of the vocabulary. It is easy to imitate the noise of a barking dog, for instance, but difficult if not impossible to imitate a noiseless object, such as a rainbow. Though imitative words show similarity in many languages, absolute identity is rare. A dog goes "bow-wow" in English, but in related languages he often goes "wow-wow" or "bow-bow." The imitative words do not, after all, entirely escape from the general arbitrariness of language. The imitative origin of language appears, therefore, at worst unlikely and at best unprovable. The same injunction holds for theories of language origin which speculate that it is an imitation of facial or other gestures.

If it is assumed that language is arbitrary, what is meant by the statement? Just that the sounds of speech and their connection with entities of experience are passed on to all members of any community by older members of that community. Therefore, a human being cut off from contact with a speech community can never learn to talk as that community does, and cut off from all speech communities never learns to talk at all. In essence, to say that language is arbitrary is merely to say that it is social. This is perhaps the most important statement that can be made about language.

In contrast, much of animal communication is instinctive rather than social. That is to say, all cats mew and purr, and would do so even if they were cut off from all communication with other cats. On the other hand, some animal communication seems to share the social nature of human speech and is therefore learned activity. A striking example is the barking of dogs, which is characteristic only of the domesticated animal, not of dogs in the wild state. Similarly, the honey dances of bees may not be altogether without an arbitrary element. It is also likely that when more is known of the cries and chatterings of the great apes in the wild state, a considerable social element in their communication may be found. Nor should it be thought that all human communication is social. A part of our communication consists of instinctive reactions which accompany language, like the trembling of fear or the suffusion of blood which accompanies anger. Yet even in the nonlinguistic accompaniments of speech, the tones of voice and the gestures, it is now clear that there is more of arbitrary and socially learned behavior than had at one time been supposed.

Third, language is systematic. I cannot hope to make this statement completely clear at this point, since the whole of this book is devoted to an exposition of the system of language. However, some observations may now be made about the system of language. As in any system, language entities are arranged in recurrent designs, so that if a part of the design is seen, predictions can be made about the whole of it, as a triangle can be drawn if one side and two angles are given. Suppose there is an incomplete sentence like "John ——s Mary an ——." A good deal about what must fill the two blanks is obvious. The first must be a verb, the second a noun. Furthermore, not all verbs will go in the first blank, since it requires a verb whose third person singular is spelled with -s and which can take two objects (that is, not such a verb as *look* or *see*). Nor will all nouns fit in the second place, since an initial vowel is required, and the noun must be one which takes an article. There is no difficulty in deciding that the sentence could be either "John gives Mary an apple" or "John hands Mary an aspirin," but not "John *gaves* Mary an *book*."[1]

[1] In this book, an asterisk placed before a form means that it is believed to be impossible.

Another observation that can be made about language systems is that every occurrence of language is a substitution frame. Any sentence is a series of entities, for each of which a whole group of other entities can be substituted without changing the frame. Thus the sentence "John gives Mary an apple" is such a substitution frame. For *John* there can be replacements like *he, Jack, William, the man, her husband,* or many others. For the verb, entities like *buys, takes, offers,* as well as the alternatives *hands* or *gives,* may be used. This characteristic of extensive substitutability for all parts of any language utterance is of some importance in that it enables us to say that parrots, no matter how startlingly human their utterances may be, are not carrying on language activity. A parakeet may produce the sentence "Birds can't talk!" with human pitch, voice tones, and nearly perfect sounds. But the bird never says "Dogs can't talk!" or "Birds can't write!" His utterance is a unit, not a multiple substitution frame.

Still another characteristic of language systems is that the entities of language are grouped into classes, always simpler, more predictable, and more sharply separated than the infinite variety of objects in the world. For instance, a whole series of objects is grouped under the single word *chair,* and *chair* is put into the large class of nouns. In dealing with objects in the outside world it may be difficult to decide whether something is a chair, a stool, or merely a rock. In language, we think of nouns and verbs as quite separate and are apt to say that the one class represents things, the other events. But in the outside world, as the physicists tell us, it is often hard to decide whether an object is best described as thing or as event.

To return once more to the defining characteristics of language, the fourth characteristic is that it is a set of symbols. That is to say, language has meaning. In this form the statement is a platitude and does not distinguish language from other activities which are also symbolic. The nature of language symbols turns out to be rather different from the symbols of other types of communication. The simplest nonlinguistic symbol can be defined as a substitute stimulus. Pavlov's famous dogs, fed at the sound of a bell, eventually began to drool at the sound of the bell even when no food was present. The dogs were responding to a substitute stimulus. Nonlinguistic symbols can also be substitute responses, and these can also be taught to animals. A dog who learns to "speak" at the sight of food has learned such a substitute response. In human speech, however, one of the most striking facts is that we can talk about things which are not present, and we can talk about things which ordinarily produce a strong physical reaction without experiencing that reaction. For instance, I can talk about apples even though there are none in the room, and I can talk about them without always making my mouth water, even when I am hungry. This type of language, which occurs without an immediately present stimulus or response, is called "displaced speech," and it is obviously of great importance. It is what enables man to

---

In historical treatments of language, on the other hand, an asterisk before a form indicates that it has been reconstructed by comparison but is not actually recorded. These two uses of the asterisk should not be confused.

know something of the past and of the world beyond the limited range of his vision and hearing at a given moment.

The crucial fact in producing this almost miraculous and purely human effect seems to be that a given language entity can be both substitute stimulus and substitute response, and can also be a stimulus for further language responses or a response to other language stimuli. I can talk about apples when they are absent because "something reminds me of them." That is, I can make language responses to what is before me, and these language responses can stimulate the further response *apple* without any direct physical stimulus to my vision, touch, or smell. *Apple* can call forth still further language entities, like *pear* or *banana,* in an endless chain; these entities are also both stimuli and responses. When human speakers do this, they are setting up what philosophers call a "universe of discourse." The ability to make connected discourse within the symbol system is what enables men to talk at length, and profitably, about things they have never seen. By means of language men make elaborate models of distant experience and eventually test their accuracy by acting upon them. All that is known of animal communication leads to the supposition that precisely what is absent from it is the kind of symbolic activity here described, symbolic activity connected not merely with experience but with all parts of the symbol system itself. We believe, in short, that animals are incapable of displaced speech.

The paragraphs above are rather general, so that a concrete example may be helpful. Let us suppose that two speakers of English are together in a room. One of them is cold. A direct response for him would be to close the window.

Instead of this he can use the substitute response, which is also substitute stimulus: "John, please close the window for me." John can either close the window or reply with a further substitute: "Just a minute. Wait until I finish this page." Such a reply may produce acceptance or may lead to a discussion of John's procrastinating character, of the fact that his parents did not discipline him properly in youth and that modern young people are generally rebellious and unmannerly. To all of this John may reply that modern times are marked by progress and the disappearance of old taboos. In the meantime the window may have been quietly closed, or completely forgotten in the warmth of discussion. What is important is that each speaker has begun reacting, not to the immediate situation, but to the other speaker's language and to his own. And in so doing, each has been building a model of general social conditions, of wide scope and ultimately of some value, even in a random and unchecked conversation of the sort described.

We are now ready to turn to the last defining characteristic of language, the fact that it is complete. By this is meant that whenever a human language has been accurately observed, it has been found to be so elaborated that its speakers can make a linguistic response to any experience they may undergo. This complex elaboration is such a regular characteristic of all languages, even those of the simplest societies, that linguists have long ago accepted it as a universal characteristic. Nevertheless, in early books about language, and in the descriptions by linguistically untrained travelers today, there are statements that tribe X has a language with only two or three hundred words in it, forcing the tribe to eke out its vocabulary by gesture.[2] Linguists maintain that all such statements are the product of lack of knowledge, and are false. Skepticism about such statements is borne out by the fact that in all instances where it was possible to check on tribe X, its language proved to be complete as usual, whereupon the statement was transferred to tribe Y, whose language was as yet unknown. The statement that human language is complete once again serves to distinguish it from animal activity. In the communication of bees, for instance, the subjects of systematic discourse are severely limited. Bees cannot, apparently, make an utterance equivalent to "The beekeeper is coming."

The statement that human language is always complete should not be interpreted to mean that every language has a word for everything. Obviously the ancient Greeks had no words for automobiles or atom bombs, and probably the modern Yahgan of Tierra del Fuego lack them as well. The completeness of language lies rather in the fact that a speaker of ancient Greek would have been perfectly capable of describing an automobile had he seen one, and further that had automobiles become important in ancient Greece, the speakers of Greek would have been perfectly capable of coining a word for them. It is a characteristic of vocabulary that, except in languages which have gone out of use, it is always expansible, in spite of the fact that resistance to new forms may frequently appear. Since language enables the user to make appropriate responses to all things and since vocabulary is thus characteristically "open," differences in vocabulary between two languages are not an accurate measure of the difference in efficiency or excellence of the two tongues. The fact that Eskimo does not have as highly developed a vocabulary of philosophy as does German merely indicates that the Eskimos are less interested in philosophy; on the other hand, Eskimo has a highly developed vocabulary for various kinds of snow, indicating that snow is important in Eskimo society. The completeness of human language and the openness of vocabulary make a groundless chimera of the occasionally expressed fear that a language might so degenerate as to become useless.

We can now attempt a definition of language, though the definition will

---

[2] A typical recent statement of this sort was reported by Leonard Bloomfield in "Secondary and Tertiary Responses to Language," *Language,* XX, 1944, p. 49 *n.*

"A physician, of good general background and education, who had been hunting in the north woods, told me that the Chippewa language contains only a few hundred words. Upon question, he said that he got this information from his guide, a Chippewa Indian. When I tried to state the diagnostic setting, the physician, our host, briefly and with signs of displeasure repeated his statement and then turned his back to me. A third person, observing this discourtesy, explained that I had some experience of the language in question. This information had no effect."

For a good general account of the completeness of primitive languages and the use of gesture as a substitute among mutually unintelligible language groups, consult Ralph L. Beals and Harry Hoijer, *An Introduction to Anthropology,* Macmillan, New York, 1956, pp. 508–11.

be cumbersome. Language is the primary and most highly elaborated form of human symbolic activity. Its symbols are made up of sounds produced by the vocal apparatus, and they are arranged in classes and patterns which make up a complex and symmetrical structure. The entities of language are symbols, that is, they have meaning, but the connection between symbol and thing is arbitrary and socially controlled. The symbols of language are simultaneously substitute stimuli and substitute responses and can call forth further stimuli and responses, so that discourse becomes independent of an immediate physical stimulus. The entities and structure of language are always so elaborated as to give the speaker the possibility of making a linguistic response to any experience. Most of the above can be paraphrased by saying that every language is a model of a culture and its adjustment to the world.

WORKING WITH THE SELECTION

1. Hill discusses what he calls "five defining characteristics" of language. In *The English Language: An Introduction* (1965), W. Nelson Francis discusses "observations about language" under four headings; according to Francis, every language is arbitrary, conventional, culturally transmitted, and characterized by multiple structure. Does Francis' list of characteristics differ significantly from Hill's? Are the characteristics in Hill's and Francis' lists incorporated in the following summary definition from Dwight Bolinger's *Aspects of Language* (1968): "Human language is a system of vocal-auditory communication using conventional signs composed of arbitrary patterned sound units and assembled according to set rules, interacting with the experiences of its users"?

2. Robert A. Peters of Western Washington State College, writing in *A Linguistic History of English* (1968), defines language as follows: "Language is an arbitrary system of articulated sounds used by human beings to carry on the social affairs of their society." On the basis of this definition he then makes the following ten statements: (1) Language is speech; (2) language is human activity; (3) language is a form of communication; (4) language is a system; (5) language is an arbitrary system; (6) language is noninstinctive; (7) language is a form of social behavior; (8) language is subject to change; (9) language is adequate to its culture; and (10) there is no universal language.

   Do Peters' statements in any way contradict those of Hill and Francis? Does he add anything of importance that either Hill or Francis does not mention? (One should notice, of course, that Hill and Francis were trying to be helpful, not comprehensive, and for simplicity they doubtless omitted much they might have said.)

3. Probably the most widely known definition of language is that by Edward Sapir. Central to it is the following passage:

   > Language is a purely human and non-instinctive method of communicating ideas, emotions, and desires by means of a system of voluntarily produced symbols. These symbols are, in the first instance, auditory and they are produced by the so-called "organ of speech." There is no dis-

cernible instinctive basis in human speech as such, however much instinctive expressions and the natural environment may serve as a stimulus for the development of certain elements of speech, however much instinctive tendencies, motor and other, may give a predetermined range or mold to linguistic expression. Such human or animal communication, if "communication" it may be called, as is brought about by involuntary, instinctive cries is not, in our sense, language at all.

Does Sapir's statement differ essentially from the other definitions you have examined?

4. Describing the second characteristic of language, Hill remarks, "To say that language is arbitrary is merely to say that it is social." He then observes, "This is perhaps the most important statement that can be made about language." Offhand, this may not seem to you a very important observation. Can you suggest any reasons why it may be?

5. You will have noticed that various writers have insisted that language is human speech, that the attempts of animals to communicate is not language. You may want to raise this question again when you read the following selection by Roger Brown.

Apes and Wild Children

Susanne K. Langer

Susanne K. Langer has taught at a number of major American colleges and universities and has been professor emeritus of philosophy at Connecticut College since 1961. Her comments on language reflect the breadth of her learning— knowledge of philosophy, psychology, anthropology, and linguistics. The following selection from one of her significant books, Philosophy in a New Key *(1942), is only a brief part of her discussion of "the function of symbolic transformation as a natural activity, a high form of nervous response, characteristic of man among the animals." It introduces some of the problems of determining how language is acquired.*

Language is, without a doubt, the most momentous and at the same time the most mysterious product of the human mind. Between the clearest animal call of love or warning or anger, and a man's least, trivial *word,* there lies a whole day of Creation—or in modern phrase, a whole chapter of evolution. In language we have the free, accomplished use of symbolism, the record of articulate conceptual thinking; without language there seems to be nothing like explicit thought whatever. All races of men—even the scattered, primitive denizens of the deep jungle, and brutish cannibals who have lived for centuries on world-removed islands—have their complete and articulate language. There seem to be no simple, amorphous, or imperfect languages, such as one would naturally expect to find in conjunction with the lowest cultures. People who have not invented textiles, who live under roofs of pleated branches, need no privacy and mind no filth and roast their enemies for dinner, will yet converse over their bestial feasts in a tongue as grammatical as Greek, and as fluent as French! [1]

[1] There are several statements in philological and psychological literature to the effect that certain primitive races have but a rudimentary language, and depend on gesture to supplement their speech. All such statements that I have found, however, can be traced back to one common source, namely Mary H. Kingsley's *Travels in West Africa* (London, 1897). This writer enjoyed so high a reputation in other fields than philology that her casual and apparently erroneous observations of native languages have been accepted rather uncritically by men as learned as Sir Richard Paget, Professor G. F. Stout, and Dr. Israel Latif. Yet Miss Kingsley's testimony is very shaky. She tells us (p. 504) that "the inhabitants of Fernando Po, the Bubis, are quite un-

Animals, on the other hand, are one and all without speech. They communicate, of course; but not by any method that can be likened to speaking. They express their emotions and indicate their wishes and control one another's behavior by suggestion. One ape will take another by the hand and drag him into a game or to his bed; he will hold out his hand to beg for food, and will sometimes receive it. But even the highest apes give no indication of speech. Careful studies have been made of the sounds they emit, but all systematic observers agree that none of these are denotative, i.e. none of them are rudimentary words.[2] Furness, for instance, says: "If these animals have a language it is restricted to a very few sounds of a general emotional signification. Articulate speech they have none and communication with one another is accomplished by vocal sounds to no greater extent than it is by dogs, with a growl, a whine, or a bark."[3] Mr. and Mrs. Yerkes, who are very reluctant to abandon the search for pre-human speech-functions in simians, come to the conclusion that "although evidence of use of the voice and of definite word-like sounds to symbolize feelings, and possibly also ideas,

---

able to converse with each other unless they have sufficient light to see the accompanying gestures of the conversation." But in an earlier part of the book she writes, "I know nothing of it [the Bubi language] myself save that it is harsh in sound," and refers the reader to the work of Dr. Baumann for information about its words and structure; Baumann gives a vocabulary and grammar that would certainly suffice a European to carry on any ordinary conversation in the dark. (See O. Baumann, "Beiträge zur Kentniss der Bubesprache auf Fernando Póo," *Zeitschrift für afrikanische Sprachen,* I, 1888, 138–155.) It seems plausible, therefore, that the Bubis find such conversation personally or socially "impossible" for some other reasons. Her other example is no surer. "When I was with the Fans they frequently said, 'We will go to the fire so we can see what they say,' when any question had to be decided after dark . . ." (p. 504). It is strange that a language in which one can make, in the dark, so complex a statement as: "We will go to the fire so we can see what they say," should require gesture to complete other propositions; moreover, where there is a question to decide, it might be awkward for the most civilized congress to take a majority vote without switching on the lights.

I am inclined, therefore, to credit the statement of Edward Sapir, that "the gift of speech and a well-ordered language are characteristic of every known group of human beings. No tribe has ever been found which is without language and all statements to the contrary may be dismissed as mere folklore." After repudiating specifically the stories just related, he concludes: "The truth of the matter is that language is an essentially perfect means of expression and communication among every known people." (From Article "Language," in *Encyclopedia of the Social Sciences,* by permission of The Macmillan Company, publishers. Cf. Otto Jespersen, *Language: its Nature, Development and Origin,* London, 1922, p. 413.)

[2] In 1892 R. L. Garner published a book in New York, *The Speech of Monkeys,* which aroused considerable interest, for he claimed to have learned a monkey vocabulary of about forty words. The book, however, is so fanciful and unscientific, and its interpretations so extravagant, that I think it must be discounted *in toto,* especially as more careful observations of later scientists belie its findings.

[3] W. H. Furness, "Observations on the Mentality of Chimpanzees and Orang-Utans," *Proceedings of the American Philosophical Society,* LV (1916), 281–290.

becomes increasingly abundant from lemur to ape, no one of the infra-human primates exhibits a systematization of vocal symbols which may approximately be described as speech." [4]

If the apes really used "definite word-like sounds to *symbolize* feelings and possibly also ideas," it would be hard to deny their power of speech. But all descriptions of their behavior indicate that they use such sounds only to *signify* their feelings, perhaps their desires. Their vocal expressions of love are *symptoms* of an emotion, not the name of it, nor any other symbol that represents it (like the heart on a Valentine). And true language begins only when a sound keeps its reference beyond the situation of its instinctive utterance, e.g. when an individual can say not only: "My love, my love!" but also: "He loves me—he loves me not." Even though Professor Yerkes's young apes, Chim and Panzee, met their food with exclamations like "Kha!" or "Nga!" these are like a cry of "Yum-yum!" rather than: "Banana, to-day." They are sounds of enthusiastic assent, of a very specialized emotional reaction; *they cannot be used between meals to talk over the merits of the feast.*

Undoubtedly one reason for the lack of language in apes is their lack of any tendency to babble. Professor and Mrs. Kellogg, who brought up a little chimpanzee, Gua, for nine months exactly as they were bringing up their own child, observed that even in an environment of speaking persons "there was no attempt on Gua's part to use her lips, tongue, teeth and mouth-cavity in the production of new utterances; while in the case of the human subject a continuous vocalized play was apparent from the earliest months. . . . There were no 'random' noises to compare with the baby's prattle or the spontaneous chatter of many birds. On the whole, it may be said she never vocalized without some definite provocation, that is, without a clearly discernible external stimulus or cause. And in most cases this stimulus was obviously of an emotional character." [5] She had, indeed, what they called her "food-bark," and a pathetic "Ooo-oo" of fear; the bark was extended to signify assent in general, the "Ooo" to express dissent. That is as near as she came to language. The child, too, used only a few words before the comparative experiment ended, but it is noteworthy that they were not "yes" and "no," but were *denotative words*—"din-din," "Gya" (Gua), and "Daddy." The use of true vocables for "yes" and "no" is apt to be late in children. Their interest in words centers on *names* for things and actions.

If we find no prototype of language in our nearest simian relatives, the apes, how can we conceive of a beginning for this all-important human function? We might suppose that speech is man's distinguishing instinct, that man is by nature the Linguistic Primate. Horatio Hale expressed this view

[4] R. M. Yerkes and A. W. Yerkes, *The Great Apes* (New Haven: Yale University Press, 1929), p. 569.

[5] W. N. Kellogg and L. A. Kellogg, *The Ape and the Child* (New York: McGraw-Hill Book Co., 1933), p. 281. This passage [is] reproduced by permission of the McGraw-Hill Book Co., publishers.

in a presidential address to a learned society, many years ago.[6] He was deeply impressed with a phenomenon that occurs every so often—the invention of a spontaneous, individual language by a child or a pair of children, a language unrelated to the tongue spoken in the household. Some children will persist up to school age, or even a little beyond it, in this vagary. Such observations led him to believe that man is by nature a language-making creature, and learns his "mother tongue" merely by the overwhelming force of suggestion, when he hears a ready-made language from earliest infancy. Under the primitive conditions of nomadic family life, he thought, it might well happen that a group of young children would be orphaned, alone in the wilderness; and where the climate was warm and food abundant, such a little company might survive. The younger children's language would become the idiom of the family. Rather ingeniously he develops this notion as an explanation of the many utterly unrelated languages in the world, their distribution, and the mystery of their origin. But the interesting content of his paper in the present connection is his underlying assumption that man makes languages instinctively.

"The plain conclusion," he says, "to which all examples point with irresistible force, is that the origin of linguistic stocks is to be found in what may be termed the language-making instinct of very young children." [7]

After citing a case of two children who constructed an entirely original language, he comments: "There is nothing in the example which clearly proves that the children in question would have spoken at all if they had not heard their parents and others about them communicating by oral sounds —*though we may, on good grounds* (as will be shown), *believe that they would have done so.*" [8]

The last part of his statement embodies the "instinct theory"; and that, so far as we know, is—*mere* theory. What do we know of children who, without being deaf and therefore unaware even of their own voices, have grown up without the example of people using speech around them? We know very little, but that little serves here to give us pause.

There are a few well-authenticated cases on record of so-called "wild children," waifs from infancy in the wilderness, who have managed to survive by their own precocious efforts or the motherly care of some large animal. In regions where it was (or is) customary to expose undesired infants, babes in the wood are not a nine days' wonder. Of course they usually die of neglect very soon, or are devoured; but on a few known occasions the maternal instinct of a bear or a wolf has held the foundling more sacred than did man's moral law, and a child has grown up, at least to pre-adolescence, without human influence.

[6] "The Origin of Languages and the Antiquity of Speaking Man," *Proceedings of the American Association for the Advancement of Science,* XXXV (1887), 279–323.
[7] *Ibid.,* p. 285.
[8] *Ibid.,* p. 286. Italics mine.

The only well-attested cases are Peter the Wild Boy, found in the fields near Hanover in 1723;[9] Victor, known as "the Savage of Aveyron," captured in that district of Southern France in 1799;[10] and two little girls, Amala and Kamala, taken in the vicinity of Midnapur, India, in 1920.[11] Several other "wild children" have been reported, but all accounts of them require considerable sifting, and some—like Lukas the Baboon Boy—prove to be spurious. Even of the ones here mentioned, only Victor has been scientifically studied and described. One thing, however, we know definitely about all of them: *none of these children could speak in any tongue, remembered or invented*. A child without human companions would, of course, find no response to his chattering; but if speech were a genuine instinct, this should make little difference. Civilized children talk to the cat without knowing that they are soliloquizing, and a dog that answers with a bark is a good audience; moreover, Amala and Kamala had each other. Yet they did not talk. Where, then, is "the language-making instinct of very young children"?

It probably does not exist at all. Language, though normally learned in infancy without any compulsion or formal training, is none the less a product of sheer learning, an art handed down from generation to generation, and where there is no teacher there is no accomplishment. Despite the caprices of the children cited by Professor Hale, it is fairly certain that these little inventors would *not* have talked at all if they had not heard their elders speaking. Whatever talent it is that helps a baby to learn a language with three or four times (or any number of times!) the ease of an adult, this talent is apparently not a "speech instinct." We have no birthright to vocabularies and syntaxes.

This throws us back upon an old and mystifying problem. If we find no prototype of speech in the highest animals, and man will not say even the first word by instinct, then how did all his tribes acquire their various languages? Who began the art which now we all have to learn? And why is it not restricted to the cultured races, but possessed by every primitive family, from darkest Africa to the loneliness of the polar ice? Even the simplest of practical arts, such as clothing, cooking, or pottery, is found wanting in one human group or another, or at least found to be very rudimentary. Language is neither absent nor archaic in any of them. . . .

[Here Langer quotes two paragraphs from Sapir, the gist of which is implied in the next sentence.]

If it is true that a vocal actualization of "the tendency to see reality symbolically" is the real keynote of language, then most researches into the roots of the speech-function have been misdirected. Communication by sound is what

---

[9] See Henry Wilson, *Wonderful Characters,* 2 vols. (London, 1821), vol. II; also J. Burnett, Lord Monboddo, *Of the Origin and Progress of Language,* 6 vols. (Edinburgh, 1773), vol. I.

[10] See E. M. Itard, *The Savage of Aveyron* (English translation, London, 1802).

[11] The story of these children is told in their guardian's diary, published in *Wolf Children and Feral Man,* by J. A. L. Singh and R. M. Zingg (New York and London: Harper and Bros., 1942).

we have looked for among the apes; a *pragmatic use of vocables* is the only sign of word-conception that we have interpreted to their credit, the only thing we have tried to inspire in them, and in the "wild children," to pave their way toward language. What we should look for is *the first indication of symbolic behavior,* which is not likely to be anything as specialized, conscious, or rational as the *use* of semantic. Language is a very high form of symbolism; presentational forms are much lower than discursive, and the appreciation of meaning probably earlier than its expression. The earliest manifestation of any symbol-making tendency, therefore, is likely to be a mere *sense of significance* attached to certain objects, certain forms or sounds, a vague emotional arrest of the mind by something that is neither dangerous nor useful in reality. The beginnings of symbolic transformation in the cortex must be elusive and disturbing experiences, perhaps thrilling, but very useless, and hard on the whole nervous system. It is absurd to suppose that the earliest symbols could be *invented;* they are merely *Gestalten* furnished to the senses of a creature ready to give them some diffuse meaning. But even in such rudimentary new behavior lies the first break with the world of pure signs. Aesthetic attraction, mysterious fear, are probably the first manifestations of that mental function which in man becomes a peculiar "tendency to see reality symbolically," and which issues in the *power of conception,* and the life-long habit of speech.

WORKING WITH THE SELECTION

1. What are Langer's arguments against the theory that man is "by nature the Linguistic Primate"?

2. On what basis does Langer say in the final paragraph that "most researches into the roots of the speech-function have been misdirected"?

3. In what ways does animal communication as described by Langer fail to meet the requirements for language specified by Hill?

4. Dogs can readily be trained to distinguish between words like *heel, sit, speak, roll over,* and *play dead.* Are the dogs using language?

3

Teaching Sign Language to a Chimpanzee

Roger Brown

The most recent extensive experiment in teaching language to a chimpanzee was begun in 1966 by R. Allen and Beatrice T. Gardner, psychologists at the University of Nevada, whose significant accomplishments through the use of sign language are described in part in the following selection. Roger Brown, professor of psychology at the University of Michigan, has been one of the most active contributors to the new discipline of psycholinguistics. The following selection is from "The First Sentences of Child and Chimpanzee," in Psycholinguistics *(1970). Brown based his analysis of the chimpanzee's use of language on reports up to June, 1968, when Washoe was about three years old. Since that time —at this writing the project is in its fifth year—Washoe has continued to develop her skills. For example, she has learned names for some colors—red, white, and black—and applies them to different objects, although not always accurately. She has demonstrated ability to generalize the applications of words, using the sign* meat *for sausage, ham, or stew, the sign* string *for thread and rope, and the sign* leaf *for various kinds of leaves, including lettuce and cabbage. She has also greatly increased her use of combinations of signs, sometimes using three- or four-sign combinations as well as the two-sign groups considered by Brown.*

Once again, and for the third time in this century, psychology has a home-raised chimpanzee who threatens to learn language. Washoe, named for Washoe county in Nevada, has been raised as a child by Allen and Beatrice Gardner of the University of Nevada since June of 1966 when she was slightly under one year old. At this writing the materials available consist of summaries of Washoe's Diary extending to the age of 36 months.

The first of the home-raised chimps was Gua, also a female, raised by the Winthrop Kelloggs nearly 40 years ago. Gua gave some evidence of understanding English utterances, she responded distinctively and appropriately to about 70, but Gua did not speak at all. Viki, the second chimp to be adopted by a human family and also a female, learned to make four sounds that were recognizable approximations to English words. Viki was given intensive training by her foster parents, Keith and Cathy Hayes, but the four word-like sounds seemed to mark the upper limit of her productive linguistic capacity.

Both Viki and Gua were asked to learn one particular form of language —speech—which is not the only form. The essential properties of language can be divorced from articulation. Meaning or "semanticity" and grammatical productivity appear not only in speech but in writing and print and in sign language. There is good reason to believe that the production of vowels and consonants and the control of prosodic features is, simply as a motor performance, something to which chimpanzees are not well adapted. The chimpanzee articulatory apparatus is quite different from the human, and chimpanzees do not make many speech-like sounds either spontaneously or imitatively. It is possible, therefore, that Viki and Gua failed not because of an incapacity that is essentially linguistic but because of a motoric ineptitude that is only incidentally linguistic. The Gardners thought the basic experiment was worth trying again, but with a change that would eliminate the articulatory problem. They have undertaken to teach Washoe the American Sign Language, the language of the deaf in North America. What is required on the motoric level is manual dexterity, and that is something chimps have in abundance. They skillfully manipulate so many of man's inventions that one naturally wonders whether they can also move their fingers in the air—to symbolize ideas.

Why does anyone care? For the same reason, perhaps, that we care about space travel. It is lonely being the only language-using species in the universe. We want a chimp to talk so that we can say: "Hello, out there? What's it like, being a chimpanzee?"

I have always been very credulous about life on other planets and talking animals, and so I have been often disappointed. Remembering the disappointments of Gua and Viki I was slow to take an interest in Washoe. From the beginning of their study the Gardners sent out periodic summaries in diary form to psychologists who might be expected to take an interest. I glanced over the first 4 of these and noticed that Washoe seemed to understand quite a large number of signs and that she was producing a few—in what appeared to be a meaningful way. This much Gua and Viki, between them, had also done, and it seemed likely that Washoe's linguistic progress would soon come to an end, but little advanced beyond that of her forerunners. Then, on the first page of the 5th summary, which covers the period when Washoe was estimated to be between 28 and 32 months old, I read the following: "Since late April, 1967, Washoe has used her signs—at that time there were six—in strings of two or more as well as singly. We have kept records of all occurrences of combinations in the period covered by the previous diary summaries, and found that Washoe used 29 different two-sign combinations and four different combinations of three signs."

It was rather as if the seismometer left on the moon had started to tap out "S-O-S." I got out the earlier diaries and studied them carefully and I read with the greatest interest the subsequent diary installments as they came along, and then the Gardners' article "Teaching Sign Language to a Chimpanzee" which appeared in *Science* in 1969. In the spring of 1969 the Gardners themselves paid us a visit at Harvard for two days, showing films of Washoe and discussing her achievements with a group here that studies the development of language in children. We were particularly interested in comparing Washoe's early linguistic development with that of three children whom we have followed for a number of years. In the literature these children are named: Adam, Eve, and Sarah.

From an evolutionary point of view the important thing about language is that it makes life experiences cumulative; across generations and, within one generation, among individuals. Everyone can know much more than he could possibly learn by direct experience. Knowledge and folly, skills and superstitions, all alike begin to accumulate and cultural evolution takes off at a rate that leaves biological evolution far behind. Among the various defining features of language there are two that are peculiarly important in making experience cumulative. They are semanticity or meaningfulness and productivity or openness.

Semanticity occurs in some degree in the natural communication systems of many kinds of animal society but productivity does not. Productivity is the capacity to generate novel messages for every sort of novel meaning. Languages have this property because they have grammars which are rules for the compositional expression of meaning, rules which create meanings from words and patterns. Signs in sequence suggest grammar, and so it was a momentous day when Washoe began to produce them. For grammar has heretofore been an exclusively human preserve.

WASHOE'S SIGNING PROGRESS

The signs of the American Sign Language (ASL) are described in Stokoe, Casterline, and Croneberg (1965) and a transformational grammar of the language has been written by McCall (1965).

There are two basic forms of ASL: finger-spelling and signing proper. In finger-spelling there is a distinct sign each letter of the alphabet and the signer simply spells in the air. This system, like our alphabetic writing, is entirely dependent on knowledge of the spoken language. In signing proper, as opposed to finger-spelling, the configurations and movements produced refer directly to concepts. Some such signs are iconic, which is to say that the sign suggests its sense. The sign for *flower* in American Sign Language is created by holding the fingers of one hand extended and joined at the tips, like a closed tulip, and touching the tip first to one nostril and then another—as if sniffing a flower. That is a good icon. Many other signs are arbitrarily related to their references. Most deaf Americans use some combination of directly semantic signs and finger-spelling. The Gardners only attempted to teach Washoe the directly semantic signs.

The Gardners are not deaf and did not know sign language at the start of their experiment. They learned it from books and from a teacher, but do not yet count themselves really fluent. They and their associates, when with Washoe, and someone is with her all day long, sign, as one would with a child, the names of actions and things; they sign questions and requests and they just chatter. In addition to providing this rich opportunity for incidental learning Washoe's human tutors have induced her to imitate signs and have used instrumental conditioning (with tickling as reward) to train her to sign appropriately for objects and pictures in books.

In the first seven months of the project Washoe learned to use four signs with some degree of appropriate semanticity. The *come-gimme* sign was directed at persons or animals and also at objects out of reach. The *more* sign, made by bringing the fingertips together overhead, seemed to ask for continuation or repetition of pleasurable activities and also to ask for second helpings of food. *Up* was used when Washoe wanted to be lifted and *sweet* was used at the end of a meal when dessert was in order. In the next seven months 9 more signs were added, and by the end of 22 months, when Washoe was about three years old, she seemed to control 34 signs.

In the spring of 1969 the Gardners showed a group of us at Harvard a film of Washoe looking at a picture book and making appropriate signs as a tutor pointed and signed "What's this?" On a first showing the performance was rather disappointing. The viewer is not entirely sure that he has seen the signs since there is so much action going on. However, this changes on a second viewing. The signs of sign language are not, at first, perceptual segregates for the uninitiated, but even a single viewing makes them very much more "visible." And, probably because so many of them are iconic, one very rapidly learns about 10–20 of them. I now do not doubt that Washoe produces the signs.

In the diary reports one can trace the semantic generalization of each sign and this generalization, much of it spontaneous, is quite astonishingly child-like. To appreciate the accomplishment it is necessary to recover a certain innocence in connection with some thoroughly familiar abstractions. Consider the notion connected with the English word *more* when it is used as a request. Washoe started out signalling *more* with the specific sense of more tickling. Far from adhering to a particular context the sign rapidly generalized to hairbrushing and swinging and other processes involving Washoe which Washoe enjoyed. And then it generalized further to "second helpings" of dessert and soda pop and the like. And then to performances of another which only involved Washoe as a spectator—acrobatics and somersaults. Human children regularly use the word *more* as a request over just this same range. And when they start to make two-word sentences with *more* they use nouns to request additional helpings (e.g., *More milk, More grapefruit juice*), but also verbs to request that processes and exhibitions be repeated (e.g., *More write, More swing*).

The semantic accomplishments are remarkable, but it is the evidence of syntax that most concerns us. Table 1 sets out some of Washoe's strings or sentences; they are drawn from the Gardners' fifth and sixth summaries which appeared in 1968, and I have selected examples which, in English,

Table 1 Some of Washoe's sign sequences as classified by the Gardners.

A. Two Signs.
    1. Using "emphasizers" (*please, come-gimme, hurry, more*).
    Hurry open.
    More sweet.
    More tickle.
    Come-gimme drink.

    2. Using "specifiers."
    Go sweet (to be carried to fruitbushes).
    Listen eat (at sound of supper bell).
    Listen dog (at sound of barking).

    3. Using names or pronouns.
    You drink.
    You eat.
    Roger come.

B. Three or More Signs.
    1. Using "emphasizers."
    Gimme please food.
    Please tickle more.
    Hurry gimme toothbrush.

    2. Using "specifiers."
    Key open food.
    Open key clean.
    Key open please blanket.

    3. Using names or pronouns.
    You me go-there in.
    You out go.
    Roger Washoe tickle.

look very much like sentences. The classification into combinations using "emphasizers," "specifiers," and "names or pronouns" is the Gardners' own. In Table 1 we have sign sequences which translate into English as *Hurry open, Go sweet, You eat, Open key clean, You me go-there in,* and so on. How do these multi-sign sequences compare with the first multi-word combinations produced by children learning American English and other languages? . . .

COMPARISON OF WASHOE AND CHILD

How do Washoe's Sign Sequences (Table 1) compare with the sentences of Table 2? [Table 2 analyzes two-word ("Stage I") sentences recorded in various descriptions of children's language learning.] *More sweet* and *More tickle* look like expressions of Recurrence. *Go sweet* (to be carried to the fruitbushes) seems to be an Action-Locative construction; *You eat* an Agent-Action construction; and *Gimme please food* an Action-Object construction. The sentences with *key* appear to express an Instrumental relation which also occasionally appears in Stage I child speech. Several of Washoe's three-term sequences look like instances of the three-term relations that appear at the end of Stage I for children; *Roger Washoe tickle* could be an Agent-Action-Object sentence and *You out go* an Agent-Action-Locative. In sum, the strings of Table 1 look very much the same as a sample of early child speech.

However, there is more to syntax than sequences or strings. The deeper question is whether Washoe was simply making signs distributed in time or whether the signs were *in construction*. What is the difference? As a first approximation, a sequence may simply name a series of ideas which succeed one another in time but do not combine cognitively, whereas a construction puts ideas into one or another structural relation.

In two superficial respects Washoe's combinations seem to be constructions and not simply sequences. Before one can make a grammatical analysis of child speech it must be segmented into utterances which mark off just those words that are "in construction" with one another. Segmentation proves to be very easily done, for the reason that children, when they begin to make combinations, already control several of the prosodic patterns that adults use to mark off sentences. One easily hears in child speech the "declarative" pattern, with high pitch and stress near the end and a final fall and fade, as well as the interrogative pattern that ends with a rising pitch. An adult who uses sign language also has devices for marking off sentences. Stokoe *et al.* (1965) say that in the declarative case the hands of the signer return to the position of repose from which they started when he began to sign. In the interrogative case the hands remain, for a perceptible period, in the position of the last sign or even move out toward the person being interrogated. When we talked with the Gardners we asked whether Washoe used such "terminal" or "juncture" signs. Not having been interested in this particular feature they were not quite sure, but since then Allen Gardner has written to me: "Once we started to look for it, it was very clear that Washoe's segmentation (and our own, of course) is very much the same as that described by Stokoe, *et al.* . . . It is such a natural aspect of signing that we just were not aware that both Washoe and her friends were doing this all along. As in the case of speech contours it is so obvious that you don't notice it until you worry about it."

There is a second surface feature of Washoe's combinations which suggests that they are constructions rather than sequences. In child speech the very slow rise over time in utterance length seems to represent an increase of information-processing power. The fact that the child at I produces subject and object without any verb surely means that he operates under some kind of complexity limitation. Now it also is the case that Washoe's sequences gradually increase. Two signs are common before three and three precede four. Why should that be so if the sign combinations are not constructions? If they were only signs strung out in time and not interacting semantically and grammatically then one would think they might be of any length at all, and that there would be no reason for them to start short and become long.

The presence of terminal contours in child speech suggests that certain words are in construction but not what the constructions are; there are no contours to mark off the various relations and operations of Table 2. What is there in child speech to suggest that these structural meanings are being expressed and, specifically to the present point, is there anything not also found in Washoe's sign sequences? What there is in child speech, most generally, is the order of the words. The order, generally, is appropriate to the structural meaning suggested by the non-linguistic situation.

Consider the two drawings of Figure 1. An adult might say of the one on the left "A dog is biting a cat" and of the one on the right "A cat is biting a dog." In both pictures just the same creatures and process are involved. The difference is that the arguments of the verb, the agent and object, are coordinated with different nouns in the two cases. It is the structure of the total situation that changes, and in English the changes are expressed by word order, by the order agent-action-object. What would a child of Stage I say in the two cases? Concerning the picture on the left he might

Figure 1 Pictures illustrating agent-object relations.

say: *Dog bite* (agent-action); *Bite cat* (action-object), or *Dog-cat* agent-object). In effect, any two of the three terms in correct relational order. Of the picture on the right he might say: *Cat bite* (agent-action); *Bite dog;* or *Cat-dog.* The two sets of pairs are different; there is no overlap. It is this kind of discriminating response, discriminating with respect to the order of elements, that justifies the inference that the child distinguishes structural meanings. What should we say of a child who in connection with either picture simply produced all possible combinations and permutations of two content words: *Dog bite; Bite dog; Cat bite; Bite cat; Dog cat;* and *Cat dog.* We should say that there was no evidence that the structural meanings were understood. This, it turns out, is approximately what Washoe does.

The Gardners have kept careful records of all the occurrences of each combination of signs, and in their 5th and 6th diary summaries they report that the signs in a combination tend to occur in all possible orders. And that order often changes when there is no change in the non-linguistic circumstances. It appears, then, that we do not yet have evidence that Washoe's sequences are syntactic. Because syntax is not just sign-combination but is sign combination employed to express structural meanings. If Washoe does not intend structural meanings, if *Go sweet* and *Sweet go* are not action-object expressions, then what does she intend? What would her stream of ideas be like? It may be that it is a stream of conceptions having no relation beyond order in time. Having thought of "go" she next thinks of "sweet." Washoe's signs may be something like the *leitmotiven* in Richard Wagner's operas. Wagner, especially in the *Ring,* used short musical "motives" with a certain degree of semanticity, enough to enable musicologists to label them with names like *Valhalla, Curse of the Ring, Nibelungen gold, Renunciation of love,* and so on. In given passages the motives succeed one another, and the related ideas may be called to mind in the listener, but they do not enter into relations like agent-object and action-object. They do, of course, enter into musical relationship. . . .

While I am prepared to conclude that Washoe has not demonstrated that she intends the structural meanings of Table 2 I do not conclude that it has been demonstrated that she lacks these meanings. Appropriate word order can be used as evidence for the intention to express structural meanings, but the lack of such order does not establish the absence of such meanings. It does not do so because appropriate word order is not strictly *necessary* for purposes of communication for either the Stage I child or the Stage I chimpanzee. Let us look again at the pictures of Figure 1. If the child uses correct orders for the two pictures it is likely that he distinguishes the meanings. But, suppose we were parents in the presence of the action pictures on the left and the child used an inappropriate order: *Cat bite* or *Cat dog* or *Bite dog.* We should still understand him and would mentally make the switches to *Dog bite* and *Dog cat* and *Bite cat* which fit the situation. The structure being supplied by our perception of the situation we can receive the words in any order and understand them as the situation dictates. Even when we are unacquainted with the situation our knowledge of what is possible in the world enables us to set right some sentences such as *Nose blow* and *Balloon throw* and *Garbage empty.* It follows, therefore, that there is little or no communication pressure on either children or Washoe to use the right word order for the meanings they intend. In their world of very simple sentences, which are usually clarified by concurrent circumstances and which often have only one sensible reading in any case, they will be understood whether the order is right or not.

They will be understood, at least, until they begin to want to say things like *I tickle you* and *You tickle me* or *Mommy call Daddy* and *Daddy call Mommy* or *Car hit truck* and *Truck hit car;* and to say these outside of a clarifying action context. In terms of real-world possibilities the paired propositions are on the same footing. If the propositions do not refer to ongoing actions but to actions at another time, then the listener or viewer, if he is to understand the message correctly, must be given structural signals, of order or of some other kind, to indicate who or what is in each semantic role. In general, as sentences become more complex and more varied and become "displaced" in time from their references the need to mark attributives, possessors, locatives, agents, objects, and the like grows greater. The capacity for "displacement" is, like the properties of semanticity and productivity, universal in human languages and we notice now that experience cannot become truly cumulative until it is possible to report on events not concurrent with the act of communication.

My conclusion, therefore, is that the question of Washoe's syntactic capacity is still quite open. If she fails to mark structures distinctively when a real communication-necessity develops then we shall conclude that she lacks real syntactic capacity. If, on the other hand, when her sentences become complex and displaced in reference from the immediate context, Washoe begins to mark structure with whatever means is available to her in the sign language—why then. . . . Then, there is a man on the moon, after all.

WORKING WITH THE SELECTION

1. How does the decision of the Gardners to use ASL rather than vocal English relate to the comments in the final paragraph of Langer's discussion?

2. Why did the Gardners decide that everyone associated with Washoe should use only ASL in the chimpanzee's presence?

3. Horses have been taught to "count" by lifting a hoof the required number of times; are they using the same kind of communication being attempted with Washoe?

4. What tendency discussed by Brown is illustrated when Washoe spontaneously uses the sign *brush,* formerly applied only to hairbrushes, to designate a paintbrush and applies the sign *pencil-write* to crayons and chalk? Does this ability of Washoe reinforce Locke's argument on the need for general words?

5. What are some of the considerations involved in answering the question, Does Washoe have language? How well does Washoe's "language" fulfill the criteria provided by Hill?

6. Brown says that he is interested primarily in evidence of syntax in Washoe's language. Why?

7. Does Brown seem justified in his conclusion that "the question of Washoe's syntactic capacity is still quite open"? The following phrases, combinations of signs, are some of those Washoe has used since Brown's analysis:

> *Sorry sorry please good out* (when she has been sent to a corner for punishment).
> *Key open out blanket hurry.*
> *You me go out hurry.*
> *Help help more up go chair ride* (when she is in her wagon asking for a push).

Do phrases like these have any significance for the kinds of conclusions Brown reaches about Washoe's capacity for syntax?

4

Babbles, Games, and Language Learning

Charlton Laird

Charlton Laird is professor emeritus of English at the University of Nevada. In the following selection, from The Range of English: NCTE Distinguished Lectures for 1968, *Laird relates how his granddaughter acquired language.*

She is a good-natured, outgoing, chattery child, and by [the time she was one year old] she had learned to jabber extensively in what I take to be pure babble, incomprehensible to a second party and probably without meaning. She would babble at anyone to whom she had become accustomed. In line with my general belief that children should be treated like human beings and as much like adults as possible, I talked with her, using words and constructing sentences, since I did not trust myself to speak naturally other-wise. During this process I noticed that we were carrying on a conversation. Hanna would ask a question, in her babble sounds, which I would answer in English. Of course I did not know what the question concerned, because Hanna had used nothing in these discourses that could be recognized as English words, but I postulated a subject for her question and answered as I would have answered that question under the circumstances. I would then ask her a question, a real question, to which she would reply sometimes promptly, sometimes with a show of deliberation, using the sentence pat-terns of what were obviously various sorts of answers in modern English.

This intrigued me, and I started listening to Hanna's speech as phonemic patterns. By this time she had acquired many of the segmented sounds of modern English, both vowels and consonants, but I observed nothing that could be called a morpheme or a word used with any consistency for any purpose.[1] Her grammatical patterns, on the other hand, were unmistakable, and she commanded all of the more common ones without hesitation and

---

[1] My amateur observations here seem to be confirmed by many careful studies of sound acquisition. Perhaps the classic work is Roman Jakobson, *Kindersprache, Aphasie und allgemeine Lautgeschichte* (1941), translated in *Selected Writings* (The Hague: Mouton and Company, 1962), I, 328–401. For bibliography and a survey of scholar-ship, see Ruth H. Weir, "Some Questions of the Child's Learning of Phonology" [in *The Genesis of Language in Children and Animals: A Psycholinguistic Approach,* ed. Frank Smith and George A. Miller (Cambridge, Mass.: M.I.T. Press, 1966)], pp. 153–172.

with no evidence of difficulty. Obviously she was having fun; in fact, she used her language only when she was happy. Any kind of distress led only to silence or wails, but when she was enjoying herself she could command all the sentence patterns adequate to her life. She could greet you, saying the equivalent of "Hi, Bud," or a somewhat more restrained "Hello, nice you came." She could attract attention ("Hey, see what I'm doing") and make expository observations, some of them rather lengthy and accompanied with pauses, as though she were thinking. As I have observed above, she could ask and answer questions, and she could distinguish, using pitch, stress, and juncture patterns, the differences between various sorts of imperatives. What I took to be the equivalent of "Give me a bottle" shared something with an imperative like "Notice that my sister is really very funny" but was also distinguished from it. She could even "read" a book; that is, she could chatter while turning the pages of a book, but so far as I could observe she was much less sure of herself when "reading," probably because she heard less reading than speaking and because the various members of the family who read to her did so in quite different speech patterns.

This "language" of Hanna's gave evidence of being a self-contained system, although it must have grown from the sentence patterns she had heard in her home, which would have been mainly adult patterns.[2] Her sisters are

---

[2] Here I am at variance with most previous writers, although by no means with all of them. [John B. Carroll, "Language Development in Children," in *Encyclopedia of Educational Research,* ed. Chester Harris, 3rd ed. (New York: Macmillan, 1960)], p. 335, apparently relying especially on Lewis and Jakobson, concludes as follows: "Despite the fact that phonetic diversity noted during the period of babbling increases considerably, these phenomena have little specific relevance for the development of true language. It is as if the child starts learning afresh when he begins to learn to utter meaningful speech." Carroll, however, noted that grammatical patterns had been too little studied among the very young, adding that "investigators . . . have almost completely overlooked such features of language as intonation patterns, which are very likely among the first items distinguished, as Lewis has observed." Ruth H. Weir based her excellent study, *Language in the Crib* (The Hague: Mouton and Company, 1962), on observations beginning in the third year of the child's life, but in her last paper before her untimely death in 1965 she was studying smaller children; see Smith and Miller, pp. 153–172, especially p. 157. She concludes: "1. At an early stage (before the infant is about nine months old) the child shows discrimination, in a broad way, among different patterns of expression in intonation. 2. . . . at first the intonational rather than the phonetic form dominates the child's response. 3. Then the phonetic pattern becomes the dominant feature in evoking the specific response; but while the function of the intonational pattern may be considerably subordinated, it certainly does not vanish." My own observations are quite in accord with Weir's, and, although I too noticed the apparent reduction in language use as the child begins to generate syntactic patterns, my explanation, as will appear below, differs from those of observers surveyed by Carroll. Apparently Walburga von Raffler Engel has been interested in the early acquisition of sound patterns; Professor William J. Griffin has kindly called the following to my attention: *Il Prelinguaggio Infantil* (Brescia: Paideia Editrice, 1964); "Appunti sul Linguaggio Infantil," *Scuola e Citta* (December 1964), pp. 660–663. Suggestions along these lines by Otto Jespersen, John Dewey, P. Guillaume, and F. H. Champneys were not very zealously pursued.

respectively some ten and twelve years older than she, of much more than average literacy for their ages; and at that time she was not regularly seeing children of her own age. So far as I could observe, her use of her language patterns was impeccable. She was never at a loss for grammatical sequences, and she seemed to use them with a high degree of consistency—granted, of course, that one did not usually know what she meant to say. Obviously, her imitative powers were very great, especially, it would seem, in her ability to reproduce pitch, stress, and juncture unconsciously. All the sounds she used in her language were involved within these patterns. Meanwhile, she was beginning to use a few words. I heard *Mommy* and *bobbu* (for bottle), but these she never used in her babble language. They were isolated cries, not much more than signs, occasioned by immediate need.

In general the situation seems clear enough. In the first year of her life Hanna had learned a considerable number of what probably amounted to segmental phonemes—at least she had learned sounds, and she seemed to use them phonemically. She was still having difficulty with many sounds she had heard, and her ability to imitate isolated sounds was limited, partly no doubt because of short verbal memory, and partly because she as yet had too little control of her tongue to make possible the sounds requiring agile and precise tongue movement. She could make combinations of sound, but it is doubtful that any sounds, whether individual or combined, represented much more than material she could put into patterns. Meanwhile, she had learned pitch, stress, and juncture with remarkable accuracy and some variety, and these included all of the common patterns that she heard regularly in her home.

During the next few months, I observed some increase in the complexity of the sentence patterns Hanna employed. She had learned simple coordination and would coordinate what appeared to be nouns, modifiers, and clauses, the latter often with pauses between them. I suspect that she was here imitating, even to the apparently thoughtful breaks, her eldest sister, a speculative youngster who would sometimes offer quite mature observations. She had learned subordination before the noun; she could say the equivalent of *an old man*, but I did not isolate patterns like *a very decrepit, pitiful old man*, presumably because the conversation in the household did not much run to extensive subordinational patterns. Naturally, with only one adult in the home and the remaining members relatively young, Hanna heard only simple structures with any consistency, but her facility in acquisition was such that one must assume she would have learned any pattern, however complex, if she had heard it enough.

Meanwhile, Hanna's mother and her sisters were deliberately teaching her words. A sister would say, "See the kitty, Hanna. Say 'kitty.'" "Kitty." "What is that, Hanna?" No answer. "It's a kitty. Say 'kitty,' Hanna." "Kitty." That is, by now Hanna could say most brief words in immediate, direct imitation, but she could say these words only by repeating them immediately after someone. They did not enter into her language, and they were never said with the sentence patterns of conversation. She would say "kitty" with the sentence pattern that her sister had used in "Say 'kitty,' Hanna," never with the pattern "The kitty wants some milk."

During the next few months, until Hanna was nearly a year and a half old, she was developing at least four aural systems simultaneously. One answered to immediate need; limited in vocabulary and almost innocent of grammar, it consisted of cries, more or less urgent. The original *Mommy* and *bobbu* had been joined by a few others—her sisters' names, for example, along with *read* and *dinner*—but this system grew very slowly both in extent and complexity. The others Hanna had made into games, which I shall call for convenience the Whazzat Game, the Ritual Game, and the Playing Grown-up Game. The first of these games probably grew out of the "Say 'kitty' " pattern. Hanna had now learned the names of various objects around the home, particularly those that could be observed in children's books or in mail order catalogues, and during this period any adult who appeared would be set upon by Hanna, dragging a picture book or a catalogue.

To play the Whazzat Game, Hanna sat on the adult's lap—or stood nearby if she was not certain of the adult—and both looked at the book. If Hanna said "Whazzat?" the adult was supposed to name the object. If the adult pointed to a man and said, "What's that?" Hanna would answer, "Daddy," or "clock," or "fish," or whatever might be appropriate. She would reply promptly if she had a word for the object, and part of the game seemed to be to answer as quickly as possible. She used the pattern of her sister in "Say 'kitty,' " and she would do this interminably with great delight. In fact, she seemed to prefer the mail order catalogues because they permitted the interlocutor to point to twenty clocks in succession, and she could say "clock" almost instantaneously. Never, however, did she use the pattern that she would have used had she been saying "The clock has stopped." This was a game with its own rules, and it had nothing to do with either her cries in need or her babble-language, that is, with the quite separate activity which I have called the game of Playing Grown-up. She used the pattern of "Say 'kitty,' " which was the pattern associated with this game, no matter who was doing the pointing. During this game she was not averse to learning to respond to previously unknown objects, to a shotgun or a swimming suit, but clearly she preferred the same object available in many variations, so that she could respond with zealous rapidity to a series of clocks or to a sequence of clocks and daddies pointed at alternately.

Hanna's use of clues and her playing of the Whazzat Game suggest that she had as yet no working concept of vocabulary, but they also suggest that she was developing a rudimentary understanding of signs and symbols which she would later turn to use when she developed a vocabulary. In view of the paucity of her general understanding, her grasp of what she conceived to be the central idea behind a group of related and nameable objects was amazing. She could recognize a cooked fish at the dinner table, a photograph of a fish, a painting of a fish, a caricature of a fish, a fish design on an ashtray (even though it was no more than a fishlike blob), and jewelry in a form suggestive of a fish. Presented with a fishlike form in a medium strange to her she might hesitate a bit, but she seldom missed, and she was apparently pleased with herself when she recognized a fish under a strange guise, as though this was part of the game and she was winning. This was a game using answers, and it had nothing to do with communication, but it does give evidence that Hanna had the concept of a fish as symbol, or at least as a generalized sign; and, considering the importance that linguists now attach to a symbol in the origin and growth of language, this seems to me an observation of some importance.

A set of responses somewhat similar to those in the Whazzat Game I have included in what I call the Ritual Game, although this complex was not a game in the sense represented in the Whazzat Game and the Grown-up Game. This activity was a game in the sense that Hanna had fun with it, but she did not require another player, except that she had to use an adult for the original imitation. The activity combined set phrases, apparently repeated as a ritual associated with action, especially her action. The Ritual Game was like the Whazzat Game in that it used words and linguistic patterns to accompany an action, but it differed in that it was much more varied in the patterns it employed and in that she played it alone, although she may have been acutely aware of her observers. This game was like the others in that it seemed to constitute its own system. I did not hear either the words or the patterns involved in the Ritual Game appearing in any other context; Hanna had learned them as wholes, and she used them as wholes—and only in the context with which she associated them.

For example, there is, in the living room of Hanna's home, a chair that rocks so readily that, if rocked hard enough, it will go over backward, dumping a frightened Hanna on the floor. This chair, perhaps because it seemed to be playing a game with her, intrigued Hanna, so that she would frequently try to climb into it, whereat her mother would say, "Careful." Soon Hanna was saying "Careful," with her mother's pitches and stresses, whenever she climbed into the chair. Of course she was not being careful, and she seemed to have no notion of what *careful* was intended to imply. To her, *careful* was the accompaniment of scrambling into that chair, repeated with the tones she had learned, as a sort of ritual. Similarly, when she fell

31

down, her mother would say, "oh-oh," /o ə/, in the hope of suggesting that this was no more than an amusing joke, nothing that warranted weeping calculated to gain sympathy. Soon Hanna was saying "oh-oh," with her mother's pitch and stress, whenever she fell down.

Thus this version of the Whazzat Game was providing Hanna with slight variations upon patterns she already knew, and in association with words, although she did not necessarily understand these words. As soon as it had occurred to me that I was observing activities of some linguistic interest, I made my gesture to science by taking tapes of Hanna's speech. To distract her and also to keep her near the microphone, my wife called Hanna's attention to the revolving reels and said, "See. It goes round and round." Hanna took this up at once, saying "round and round"—although she reduced it to *ronaron*—with the stress, pitch, and juncture my wife had used in saying "It goes round and round." This became the family name for a tape recorder, and Hanna associated the name with the whole object. She would start pointing and shouting *ronaron*, still using the speech pattern my wife had used in a sentence, whenever I got out of the car carrying the tape machine. Clearly she did not associate *round and round* with the action of the reels and was somewhat disturbed when the cover was taken off the machine and placed in another part of the room, since there now seemed to be two round-and-rounds.

Meanwhile, Hanna had continued her imaginary conversations in what I have called the Playing Grown-up Game, and I so name it because, although without any real proof, I conceive that this activity was direct imitation of what she supposed adults were doing. I have the impression that she associated me particularly with this game; at least she would seize upon me and we would start playing the game at once. No doubt her mother and her sisters had to endure a good bit of this sort of thing, and they probably occasionally evinced their boredom—after all, they were exposed to it much more than was I, and they did not have any reasons for listening to apparently meaningless chatter. By now Hanna was "talking" more volubly, I assume because she was gaining better control of her vocal mechanisms, and partly because she remembered me better—when she was younger, if I happened not to see her for a couple of weeks, she had apparently forgotten me. Her sounds were increasing somewhat, but I made no careful analysis of these sounds since that subject has already been well researched. The complexity of her sentence structure had apparently increased, but I have inadequate evidence to say very precisely how the patterns were developing, although one could notice that both coordination and subordination were more extensive.

What struck me was that she was now learning grammar relatively slowly, compared with the rapidity with which she had learned it during the first twelve months of her life. In that period she had learned all the basic patterns, but in the next six months, during which her use of sounds increased rapidly, she seemed to be learning relatively few new patterns. She may have been learning more grammar at this time than appeared, but if my conclusions are valid I must assume that she was now hearing few sentence patterns she did not already know, that the new ones she did hear appeared infrequently enough so that they did not much impinge upon her, and that, in any event, she already had most of the patterns that would have seemed to her to be any good. The other patterns she heard were not needed in either her cries or her games.

Perhaps the most notable development was that although Hanna was by now beginning to link vocabulary associated with her cries with vocabulary that was growing out of the Whazzat Game and its variations, I could detect no influence of either of these upon the Ritual Game or the Playing Grown-up Game. I did not during this time hear her say anything in the

Grown-up Game suggestive of the words she used as cries, as part of a ritual, or as replies in the Whazzat Game.

Shortly before Hanna was two she began fusing her various aural systems into one and associating this one system with a true understanding of language. Words from the Whazzat Game or from her cries would now occasionally appear in the Grown-up Game, usually with some hesitation. Why she hesitated I am not sure; she may have felt unsure of herself, or she may have doubted the propriety of introducing part of one game into another; in support of this last thesis I note that she was uncommonly sensitive to any adverse comment; the mildest word of rebuke would so chasten her that she would lie down on her stomach and shut out the world by hiding her face.

At about twenty months, her mother reported that Hanna had generated her first sentence, "See the flower." I doubt that she was as yet using grammar in association with words she had learned. I did not hear her doing so then, but I have many times heard her sisters, in a laudable attempt to promote a sense of beauty, saying "See the flower, Hanna." I suspect that this "sentence" is of a piece with "careful" and "oh-oh," a ritual to be performed under certain circumstances. I was not so fortunate as to hear this locution, but I would be fairly confident that it was uttered with the pedagogical pitch patterns of Hanna's older sisters, not with the conversational patterns she used when playing the Grown-up Game.

By the time Hanna was two her "sentences" had greatly increased in number and variety, if not much in length. I suspect that most of them were still imitations of locutions she had heard, with the pitch patterns associated—"go bed now," "go pottie," "have dinner"—and by now apparently the sentence patterns she had used in the Grown-up Game were coalescing with the words she had learned in her cries, since now the cries used some of the Grown-up Game patterns. At some time during this period, the last few months before she was two, so far as I could observe, Hanna did begin to generate sentences. The grammar was very simple, and one did not always know what she was saying. An initial sound plus a word with the interrogative pattern might be intended for "Is it yellow?" "It's yellow?" "It yellow?" "Is yellow?" or something else, but clearly she now had the concept of vocabulary and grammar as the ingredients of communication. That is, she had developed the essential concept of language.[3]

[3] The timing here accords with that of many observers whose collection of material was more systematic than mine. Hanna started generating sentences relying exclusively on words in her third year, perhaps a little earlier. This period was marked by an apparent reduction of her use of linguistic activity, but I suspect that this reduction is more apparent than real, that she was fusing her various sorts of linguistic activity into a new game that was genuine language, with which she did not as yet feel sure of herself. I doubt, as other observers have suggested, that she was learning all over again. I suspect that she continued to learn, but she used her linguistic abilities less, in audible form, because she was now outgrowing the linguistic complexes in which she had an easy competence and was combining her linguistic skills in a way not as yet second nature to her.

In the subsequent months—my subject is, at this writing, somewhat more than two and a half—Hanna has grown rapidly in linguistic sophistication. By now she has a considerable vocabulary, and she is addicted to observations that convulse the family. She has ceased entirely to play the Grown-up Game: just when, we are not sure. The family, of course, was interested in her learning to talk, not in her ceasing to babble, and it is easier to notice when things start than when they stop. All the family agrees, however, that she has not played the game for some months. Her mother confirms my impression that she went on playing the game a little when she was tired or frustrated, and this indulgence continued somewhat after the time when she had played it at every opportunity. I assume she wanted to do something with adults but could not quite face the problem of using words.

Meanwhile, her other baby games declined, although with no consistency. For a time she played the Whazzat Game with continuing zeal and growing competence. Her identifications speeded up, and she apparently used "Whazzat" more frequently because she wanted the information more than she had earlier. Now, however, she plays Whazzat less frequently and is apparently trying to learn to read. She will still present any visitor with a book or magazine, but if I try to play the Whazzat Game with her she loses interest. As for her cries and her ritualistic expressions, they blended readily with the patterns used in the Grown-up Game, and if there was any marked change here I did not notice it. . . .

Since I am more interested in pure than in applied linguistics, I surmise that we can learn something from Hanna about the nature and history of language. Here I recall that we have never been able to agree upon the origin of language; we have devised many possible origins for language or parts of language: that it started from cries of need or fear, from imitation of natural sounds, from the rhythm of bodily movements, from the desire to have fun making noises, and the like, but none of these seem to account for all of language or to be such a good explanation that it has displanted all the others. Now, observing Hanna, I am constrained to wonder if we have failed to find the origin of language because it never had a single origin but resulted from the coalition of various activities, each non-linguistic or semi-linguistic in character. Of course we cannot be sure that ontogeny repeats phylogeny, that the experience of the individual reflects the experience of the race, but we do have evidence that something of this sort is true, and certainly language in Hanna developed only some time after she had learned sound as cries, sound as ritual, and sound as various sort of fun. Hanna may be, among other things, a toddling explanation of the origin of language.

1. Compare Laird's observations of the development of language in a child with Brown's report of a chimpanzee's communication. In what ways did the child and the chimpanzee behave alike; in what ways differently? How, for example, do experiences with transfer compare? The reports were written when the child was somewhat younger than the chimpanzee; which had progressed more?

2. In the introduction to his lecture, not included here, Laird says that he is "making no pretense to being scientific." In what ways is Laird's observation less scientific than that of the Gardners as reported by Brown? Does his method of observation have any advantages, however, in producing reliable information?

3. In another part of the lecture not included here, Laird points out that Hanna "learned grammar before she learned vocabulary; she had learned grammatical structures before she had anything but nonsense syllables with which to flesh those skeletons." What is the evidence in his report that supports this conclusion?

4. If you have had an opportunity to observe the language behavior of a very young child, compare your experiences with Laird's. Do your observations confirm or contradict his view of the language-learning process? Laird suggests that animals probably learn to deal with human speech very much as children do, by recognizing tones of voice and patterns of sound. If you have not observed a child carefully, you may have trained a pet and noticed how it learned to respond to your voice.

5

The Key to Language

Helen Keller

Deaf and blind from infancy Helen Keller (1880–1968) managed, with the help of her remarkable teacher, Anne Mansfield Sullivan, to overcome her handicaps, graduate from Radcliffe College in 1904, and pursue an active career as writer and lecturer. The following selection is from one of her best-known books, The Story of My Life (1902).

The morning after my teacher came she led me into her room and gave me a doll. The little blind children at the Perkins Institution had sent it and Laura Bridgman had dressed it; but I did not know this until afterward.

When I had played with it a little while, Miss Sullivan slowly spelled into my hand the word "d-o-l-l." I was at once interested in this finger play and tried to imitate it. When I finally succeeded in making the letters correctly I was flushed with childish pleasure and pride. Running downstairs to my mother I held up my hands and made the letters for doll. I did not know that I was spelling a word or even that words existed; I was simply making my fingers go in monkey-like imitation. In the days that followed I learned to spell in this uncomprehending way a great many words, among them pin, hat, cup and a few verbs like sit, stand and walk. But my teacher had been with me several weeks before I understood that everything has a name.

One day, while I was playing with my new doll, Miss Sullivan put my big rag doll into my lap also, spelled "d-o-l-l" and tried to make me understand that "d-o-l-l" applied to both. Earlier in the day we had had a tussle over the words "m-u-g" and "w-a-t-e-r." Miss Sullivan had tried to impress it upon me that "m-u-g" is *mug* and "w-a-t-e-r" is *water*, but I persisted in confounding the two. In despair she had dropped the subject for the time only to renew it at the first opportunity. I became impatient at her repeated attempts and, seizing the new doll, I dashed it upon the floor. . . .

We walked down the path to the well-house, attracted by the fragrance of the honeysuckle with which it was covered. Someone was drawing water and my teacher placed my hand under the spout. As the cool stream gushed over one hand she spelled into the other the word water, first slowly, then rapidly. I stood still, my whole attention fixed upon the motions of her fingers. Suddenly I felt a misty consciousness as of something forgotten—a thrill of returning thought; and somehow the mystery of language was revealed to me. I knew then that "w-a-t-e-r" meant the wonderful cool something that was flowing over my hand. That living word awakened my soul, gave it light, hope, joy, set it free! There were barriers still, it is true, but barriers that could in time be swept away.

I left the well-house eager to learn. Everything had a name, and each name gave birth to a new thought. As we returned to the house every object which I touched seemed to quiver with life. That was because I saw everything with the strange, new sight that had come to me. On entering the door I remembered the doll I had broken. I felt my way to the hearth and picked up the pieces. I tried vainly to put them together. Then my eyes filled with tears; for I realized what I had done, and for the first time I felt repentance and sorrow.

I learned a great many new words that day. I do not remember what they all were; but I do know that mother, father, sister, teacher were among them—words that were to make the world blossom for me, "like Aaron's rod, with flowers." It would have been difficult to find a happier child than I was as I lay in my crib at the close of that eventful day and lived over the joys it had brought me, and for the first time longed for a new day to come. . . .

I had now the key to all language, and I was eager to learn to use it. Children who hear acquire language without any particular effort; the words that fall from others' lips they catch on the wing, as it were, delightedly, while the little deaf child must trap them by a slow and often painful process. But whatever the process, the result is wonderful. Gradually from naming an object we advance step by step until we have traversed the vast distance between our first stammered syllable and the sweep of thought in a line of Shakespeare.

At first, when my teacher told me about a new thing I asked very few questions. My ideas were vague, and my vocabulary was inadequate; but as my knowledge of things grew, and I learned more and more words, my field of inquiry broadened, and I would return again and again to the same subject, eager for further information. Sometimes a new word revived an image that some earlier experience had engraved on my brain.

I remember the morning that I first asked the meaning of the word, "love." This was before I knew many words. I had found a few early violets in the garden and brought them to my teacher. She tried to kiss me; but at that time I did not like to have anyone kiss me except my mother. Miss Sullivan put her arm gently around me and spelled into my hand, "I love Helen."

"What is love?" I asked.

She drew me closer to her and said, "It is here," pointing to my heart, whose beats I was conscious of for the first time. Her words puzzled me very much because I did not then understand anything unless I touched it.

I smelt the violets in her hand and asked, half in words, half in signs, a question which meant, "Is love the sweetness of flowers?"

"No," said my teacher.

Again I thought. The warm sun was shining on us.

"Is this not love?" I asked, pointing in the direction from which the heat came, "Is this not love?"

It seemed to me that there could be nothing more beautiful than the sun, whose warmth makes all things grow. But Miss Sullivan shook her head, and I was greatly puzzled and disappointed. I thought it strange that my teacher could not show me love.

A day or two afterward I was stringing beads of different sizes in symmetrical groups—two large beads, three small ones, and so on. I had made many mistakes, and Miss Sullivan had pointed them out again and again with gentle patience. Finally I noticed a very obvious error in the sequence and for an instant I concentrated my attention on the lesson and tried to think how I should have arranged the beads. Miss Sullivan touched my forehead and spelled with decided emphasis, "Think."

In a flash I knew that the word was the name of the process that was going on in my head. This was my first conscious perception of an abstract idea.

1. How did Helen Keller's discovery of the meaning of the word *think* differ from her discovery of the meaning of *water?* Why would most children have less difficulty learning the meaning of *water?*

2. Which of the learning processes described by Brown was Miss Sullivan trying to promote when she gave Helen a second doll and tried to make her apply the word *doll?*

3. Keller finds the "key to all language" in her discovery that everything has a name. Hill denies that every language has a name for everything. Can this apparent contradiction be resolved?

4. In what ways did Helen Keller's language-learning differ from that of Laird's granddaughter? Do the differences suggest that Laird's conjectures are wrong?

6

Language and Thought

Ronald W. Langacker

Edward Sapir expressed the opinion that "the feeling entertained by so many that they can think, or even reason, without language is an illusion." In the following selection from Language and Its Structure *(1968), linguist Ronald W. Langacker, who teaches at the University of California at San Diego, explores in more detail the relations between thought and language.*

The fact that language can be used to express our thoughts gives rise to some interesting questions. How are language and thought related? Can we think without language? Is our thinking molded by the structure of our language? These are very difficult questions, questions that we cannot hope to answer definitively without a much better understanding of human psychological structure than we presently have. Conflicting opinions have been advanced. The following observations carry no guarantee that all linguists or psychologists would agree with them.

If we define thought as conscious mental activity, we can observe first that thought, or at least certain kinds of thought, can take place completely independently of language. The simplest example is that of music. We have all had the experience of being absorbed in listening to an instrumental work or mentally running through a familiar tune. Language is simply not involved. (The existence of music with lyrics is of course beside the point.) Musical composition is in no way dependent on language, so far as the actual process of creation is concerned, and the same would seem to be true of various other forms of creative or problem-solving activity. The sculptor at work is in no significant sense guided by language. He may, of course, receive much of his instruction through language, talk about his creations, and even entertain himself with an internal verbal soliloquy as he chips away with hammer and chisel. But such verbalization does not appear to be instrumental in his creative activity. There may be many stretches of time during which he is so busy conceptualizing forms and techniques that words disappear entirely from his thoughts. Much the same is true of a person engrossed in solving a jigsaw puzzle. Suddenly perceiving that two independently completed sections belong together is in no way a linguistic accomplishment, although one may subsequently exclaim "Aha! This must go over here!" It is thus hard to understand why some people have maintained that thought without language is impossible. They have probably been construing thought quite narrowly to mean something like propositional thought. If thought is construed too narrowly, the claim becomes a tautology; it is not very informative to learn that thought which involves language is impossible without language.

A further argument for the existence of thought without language is the common experience of wishing to express some idea but being unable to find a satisfactory way to put it into words. If thought were impossible without language, this problem would never arise.

Nevertheless, much of our thought clearly does involve language, some of it in an essential way. The problem of assessing the influence of language on thought, however, deserves to be treated with great caution. It is all too easy to lament the tyranny of language and to claim that the world view of a person or community is shaped by the language used. Certainly people have sometimes been misled by a blind reliance on words, but we can recognize such cases and set the record straight; if language were all that tyrannical, we would be unable to perceive that it sometimes leads us into error when we are not being careful. Furthermore, we must entertain the possibility that much of what passes for linguistically conditioned thought is not molded by language at all; there may be a more general human cognitive capacity at play, for which language merely serves as a medium, just as music serves as a medium for the composer's creative powers.

Scholars generally agree that words greatly facilitate certain kinds of thinking by serving as counters, or symbols, that can easily be manipulated. We all have a fairly good idea of what arithmetic is; we know how to add, subtract, multiply, and divide. We also know the word *arithmetic,* which serves as a label for this conceptual complex. When we think about arithmetic (how it fits into the rest of mathematics, how it is taught in our schools, whether our children are good at it, whether we like it, how hard it is), we can use the word *arithmetic* as a symbol in our thought processes. It is much easier to manipulate the word *arithmetic* in our thoughts than to operate with the entire conceptual complex that this word symbolizes. The use of verbal symbols thus makes thought easier in many cases. One might even argue that some kinds of thinking would be impossible without the existence of these convenient counters to operate with.

Verbal labels are particularly important in the realm of abstract ideas. *Justice, democracy, liberty, communism,* and *education* are familiar terms, yet it would be very hard to pin down their meaning precisely. *Justice* does not evoke a concrete image in the way *table* does. We can usually agree on whether or not something is a table, but how sure can we ever be about justice? When is something correctly labeled *obscene?* Does the word *liberty* have any real significance? We certainly have at least a vague idea of what is meant by these terms, but their meanings tend to be quite elusive and to vary considerably from person to person. These concepts probably would not exist at all if there were no words for them, serving to gather and hold together a number of vague, not too coherent notions. Because they are abstract, words like these are quite loosely tied to reality. In a sense, they are almost empty. If one is not careful, they can become emotionally charged labels functioning only to brand someone or something as good or bad. It is unfortunately very easy to call someone a *communist* or to do something *in the name of liberty,* and it is very easy to be misled by the empty use of words.

What is the relation between our thought processes and the structure of our language? Is language a tyrannical master, relentlessly forcing our thinking to follow certain well-worn paths, blinding us to all other possibilities? Is our conception of the world crucially conditioned by the language we speak, as some people have claimed? These questions can be posed with respect both to words and to grammatical structures.

We have seen that a word can be helpful in forming, retaining, or operating with the concept it designates. We have also seen that no two languages match precisely in the way in which they break up conceptual space and assign the pieces to words as meanings; recall that English distinguishes between *green* and *blue* while other languages use a single word to designate this entire range of the spectrum, and that the Eskimos use a number of words to designate different kinds of snow where English has the single word *snow.* Differences like these extend throughout the vocabulary and will be found no matter what two languages are compared. Our question, then, is to what extent these differences in the linguistic categorization of experience are responsible for corresponding differences in thought.

There is little doubt that lexical differences have some effect on thought, at least in the sense that it is easier to think about things we have words for. We are accustomed to labeling some colors with the term *red* and others with the term *blue.* When presented with a typically red or blue object, we can quickly name its color; the terms *red* and *blue* are readily available to us, for we have had lifelong experience in calling some things red and others blue. We will have little trouble remembering the color of a red or blue object. Suppose, however, that you are presented with an object that is an extremely dark shade of brown, so dark that it is almost black. There is no common term in English for this particular color. Most likely you will hesitate to call it either *brown* or *black*, because it is not typical of the colors usually called *brown* or *black*. Eventually you may resort to a phrase like *very dark brown* or *brownish black*, but such a phrase will probably not come to mind as quickly and readily as *red* or *blue*. We are not so accustomed to distinguishing shades of brown from one another as we are to distinguishing red from blue. It will prove harder to remember a particular shade of brown (as opposed to other shades of brown) than to remember the color of a typically red object. If our language, on the other hand, had a separate word for this very dark shade of brown and if we were accustomed to categorizing objects of this color by describing them with this word, there would be no such difficulties.

Our thinking is thus conditioned by the linguistic categorization of experience in that it is easier to operate with concepts coded by single words than with concepts for which no single term is available. The way in which one's language breaks up conceptual space thus has at least a minimal effect on thought. But there is absolutely no evidence to suggest that this influence is in any significant way a tyrannical or even a powerful one. We are perfectly capable of forming and mentally manipulating concepts for which no word is available. We can make up imaginary entities at will and, if we so choose, proceed to name them. For example, imagine a unicorn with a flower growing out of each nostril. No word exists for such an entity, but it is easy to think about it nevertheless. We could dream up a name for it, but we do not have to.

What about the grammatical structures of a language? Do they force our thinking into certain customary grooves to the exclusion of other possibilities? Do they determine our way of viewing the world, as many scholars have maintained?

Overtly, languages sometimes display very striking differences in grammatical structure. (We will see later, however, that upon deeper examination languages appear to be very similar to one another grammatically.) For example, what we express in English with adjectives is expressed in some other languages with the equivalent of intransitive verbs. The word-for-word translation of the sentence meaning 'The tree is tall' would thus be *The tree talls*. To say that the river is deep, one would say literally *The river deeps*. Much more commonly, languages differ in the grammatical categories that are obligatorily represented in sentences. One such category is gender. In French, for instance, every noun is classified as either masculine or feminine, and in the singular the article meaning 'the' appears as *le* if its noun is masculine but as *la* if its noun is feminine. Whereas in English we say *the cheese* and *the meat*, in French one makes a distinction and says *le fromage* but *la viande*. In German, there is a three-way distinction. *Der Käse* 'the cheese' is masculine; *die Kartoffel* 'the potato' is feminine; and *das Fleisch* 'the meat' is neuter. In other languages, there are even more gender categories requiring agreement. (These distinctions, by the way, are grammatical ones; they have nothing very directly to do with sex.)

Gender is of course only one example. Number, case, tense, and aspect are other categories often found in familiar European languages. And many languages mark categories that seem more exotic to speakers of English. It is not unusual for the plural to be marked differently depending on whether the objects involved are close together or scattered about. Certain Navaho verbs of handling, meaning such things as 'drop' or 'pick up,' vary in form depending on the shape of the thing that is handled. Thus one form will be used if the object is round or amorphous in shape, another form will be used if it is long, slender, and rigid, and so on. Sentences in the Siouan languages contain markers indicating the speaker's estimation of the veracity of what is expressed.

No one denies that these overt grammatical differences exist. If two languages are different enough in structure, a literal, item-by-item translation of a sentence from one language into the other can seem most bizarre to speakers of the second language. It is quite another thing, however, to claim that these differences in grammatical structure entail significant differences in the thought processes of the speakers. No evidence has ever been presented to support this claim. Grandiose assumptions about one's world view being determined by the structure of one's language have never been shown to be anchored in fact. There is absolutely no reason to believe that the grammatical structure of our language holds our thoughts in a tyrannical, vise-like grip.

It is not really surprising that no such evidence has been found. The claims are based on really very superficial aspects of linguistic structure. If French nouns are divided into two gender classes while English nouns are not, so what? No valid psychological conclusions follow from this arbitrary, rather uninteresting grammatical fact. If, in your native language, you were brought up to say the equivalent of *The flower reds, The tree talls,* and *The river deeps,* it would not follow that you lived in an especially exciting mental world where colors were actions on the part of objects, where trees continually participated in the activity of tallness, where rivers stretched themselves vertically while flowing horizontally. These ways of expressing yourself, being customary, would not strike you as poetic, as they strike a speaker of English. You would live in the same world you live in now.

WORKING WITH THE SELECTION

1. What does Langacker mean near the end of the second paragraph by "propositional thought"? Explain what he means in the next sentence by "the claim becomes a tautology."

2. Consider the validity of Langacker's argument in the third paragraph. Is a thought that one cannot satisfactorily put into words necessarily a thought that has developed without language?

3. How do the second and third paragraphs of Langacker's discussion depend on his definition of thought? Does his definition differ from that of Sapir in the Introduction?

4. Some languages have names for individual types of trees—palm, gum, and banyan—but no general word equivalent to the English *tree*. What is the significance of this difference? Does it show that language places different restrictions on the way people can think?

5. Consider Langacker's example of imagining a unicorn with a flower in each nostril. Although we have no name for the creature, do we use language in thinking about it?

6. Langacker suggests that language cannot prevent thinking. Can it promote thinking? The wealth of a surgeon's words for diseases helps him to talk precisely about disease. Would it be likely that this same wealth of language helps him to think more precisely about disease?

7

English and Nootka

Benjamin Lee Whorf

Like his teacher Edward Sapir, Benjamin Lee Whorf (1897–1941), used his extensive researches in American Indian languages as the background for broader speculations about the relations between language and culture. Observing dramatic differences between Indian languages and Indo-European languages, Sapir and Whorf supported the hypothesis that differences in language reflect differences in a society's view of the world, and that language habits influence cultural development. The brief selection that follows, from a longer essay Languages and Logic, *which appeared in* Languages, Thought, and Reality (1956), *shows Whorf presenting one of his many examples of differences between English and other languages.*

As I said in the April 1940 *Review,* segmentation of nature is an aspect of grammar—one as yet little studied by grammarians. We cut up and organize the spread and flow of events as we do, largely because, through our mother tongue, we are parties to an agreement to do so, not because nature itself is segmented in exactly that way for all to see. Languages differ not only in how they build their sentences but also in how they break down nature to secure the elements to put in those sentences. This breakdown gives units of the lexicon. "Word" is not a very good "word" for them; "lexeme" has been suggested, and "term" will do for the present. By these more or less distinct terms we ascribe a semifictitious isolation to parts of experience. English terms, like "sky, hill, swamp," persuade us to regard some elusive aspect of nature's endless variety as a distinct THING, almost like a table or chair. Thus English and similar tongues lead us to think of the universe as a collection of rather distinct objects and events corresponding to words. Indeed this is the implicit picture of classical physics and astronomy—that the universe is essentially a collection of detached objects of different sizes.

The examples used by older logicians in dealing with this point are usually unfortunately chosen. They tend to pick out tables and chairs and apples on tables as test objects to demonstrate the object-like nature of reality and its one-to-one correspondence with logic. Man's artifacts and the agricultural products he severs from living plants have a unique degree of isolation; we may expect that languages will have fairly isolated terms for them. The real question is: What do different languages do, not with these artificially isolated objects but with the flowing face of nature in its motion, color, and changing form; with clouds, beaches, and yonder flight of birds? For, as goes our segmentation of the face of nature, so goes our physics of the Cosmos.

Here we find differences in segmentation and selection of basic terms. We might isolate something in nature by saying "It is a dripping spring." Apache erects the statement on a verb *ga:* "be white (including clear, uncolored, and so on)." With a prefix *nō-* the meaning of downward motion enters: "whiteness moves downward." Then *tó,* meaning both "water" and "spring" is prefixed. The result corresponds to our "dripping spring," but synthetically it is "as water, or springs, whiteness moves downward." How utterly unlike our way of thinking! The same verb, *ga,* with a prefix that means "a place manifests the condition" becomes *gohlga:* "the place is white, clear; a clearing, a plain." These examples show that some languages have means of expression—chemical combination, as I called it—in which the separate terms are not so separate as in English but flow together into plastic synthetic creations. Hence such languages, which do not paint the separate-object picture of the universe to the same degree as English and its sister tongues, point toward possible new types of logic and possible new cosmical pictures.

The Indo-European languages and many others give great prominence to a type of sentence having two parts, each part built around a class of word —substantives and verbs—which those languages treat differently in grammar. As I showed in the April 1940 *Review*, this distinction is not drawn from nature; it is just a result of the fact that every tongue must have some kind of structure, and those tongues have made a go of exploiting this kind. The Greeks, especially Aristotle, built up this contrast and made it a law of reason. Since then, the contrast has been stated in logic in many different ways: subject and predicate, actor and action, things and relations between things, objects and their attributes, quantities and operations. And, pursuant again to grammar, the notion became ingrained that one of these classes of entities can exist in its own right but that the verb class cannot exist without an entity of the other class, the "thing" class, as a peg to hang on. "Embodiment is necessary," the watchword of this ideology, is seldom STRONGLY questioned. Yet the whole trend of modern physics, with its emphasis on "the field," is an implicit questioning of the ideology. This contrast crops out in our mathematics as two kinds of symbols—the kind like 1, 2, 3, x, y, z and the kind like $+$, $-$, $\div$, $\sqrt{}$, log $-$, though, in view of 0, $\frac{1}{2}$, $\frac{3}{4}$, π, and others, perhaps no strict two-group classification holds. The two-group notion, however, is always present at the back of the thinking, although often not overtly expressed.

Our Indian languages show that with a suitable grammar we may have intelligent sentences that cannot be broken into subjects and predicates. Any attempted breakup is a breakup of some English translation or paraphrase of the sentence, not of the Indian sentence itself. We might as well try to decompose a certain synthetic resin into Celluloid and whiting because the resin can be imitated with Celluloid and whiting. . . .

When we come to Nootka, the sentence without subject or predicate is the only type. The term "predication" is used, but it means "sentence." Nootka has no parts of speech; the simplest utterance is a sentence, treating of some event or event-complex. Long sentences are sentences of sentences (complex sentences), not just sentences of words. In Fig. 1 we have a simple, not a complex, Nootka sentence. The translation, "he invites people to a feast," splits into subject and predicate. Not so the native sentence. It begins with the event of "boiling or cooking," *tl'imsh;* then comes *-ya* ("result") = "cooked"; then *-'is* "eating" = "eating cooked food"; then *-ita* ("those who do") = "eaters of cooked food"; then *-'itl* ("going for"); then *-ma,* sign of third-person indicative, giving *tl'imshya'isita'itlma,* which answers to the crude paraphrase, "he, or somebody, goes for (invites) eaters of cooked food."

The English technique of talking depends on the contrast of two artificial classes, substantives and verbs, and on the bipartitioned ideology of nature, already discussed. Our normal sentence, unless imperative, must have some substantive before its verb, a requirement that corresponds to the philosophical and also naïve notion of an actor who produces an action. This last might not have been so if English had had thousands of verbs like "hold," denoting positions. But most of our verbs follow a type of segmentation that isolates from nature what we call "actions," that is, moving outlines.

Following majority rule, we therefore read action into every sentence, even into "I hold it." A moment's reflection will show that "hold" is no action but a state of relative positions. Yet we think of it and even see it as an action because language formulates it in the same way as it formulates more numerous expressions, like "I strike it," which deal with movements and changes.

We are constantly reading into nature fictional acting entities, simply because our verbs must have substantives in front of them. We have to say "It flashed" or "A light flashed," setting up an actor, "it" or "light," to per-

Figure 1 Here are shown the different ways in which English and Nootka formulate the same event. The English sentence is divisible into subject and predicate; the Nootka sentence is not, yet it is complete and logical. Furthermore, the Nootka sentence is just one word, consisting of the root *tl'imsh* with five suffixes.

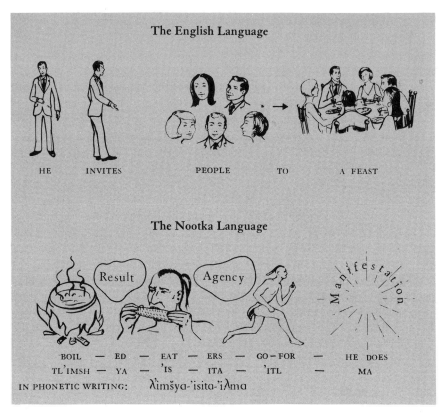

form what we call an action, "to flash." Yet the flashing and the light are one and the same! The Hopi language reports the flash with a simple verb, *rehpi*: "flash (occurred)." There is no division into subject and predicate, not even a suffix like *-t* of Latin *tona-t* "it thunders." Hopi can and does have verbs without subjects, a fact which may give that tongue potentialities, probably never to be developed, as a logical system for understanding some aspects of the universe. Undoubtedly modern science, strongly reflecting western Indo-European tongues, often does as we all do, sees actions and forces where it sometimes might be better to see states. On the other hand, 'state' is a noun, and as such it enjoys the superior prestige traditionally attaching to the subject or thing class; therefore science is exceedingly ready to speak of states if permitted to manipulate the concept like a noun. Perhaps, in place of the 'states' of an atom or a dividing cell, it would be better if we could manipulate as readily a more verblike concept but without the concealed premises of actor and action.

1. What is the major difference between English and Nootka described by Whorf?

2. In the third paragraph Whorf suggests that the Apache way of expressing the English notion "It is a dripping spring" represents an entirely different way of thinking. Explain his argument. Does it seem plausible?

3. Review the last four paragraphs of the Langacker selection. How do Langacker's views differ from those of Whorf?

4. The hypothesis of Sapir and Whorf might be criticized in the following way as circular logic: "Different cultures have different languages because they have different ways of looking at the world. We know that different cultures have different ways of looking at the world because they have different languages." Does this criticism seem to you to apply to Whorf's discussion here?

8

A Primitive Language?

Sven Liljeblad

Sven Liljeblad, formerly a scholar at Uppsala University in Sweden, is widely recognized in Europe as a folklorist. In this country he is known mainly among specialists, especially for his elaborate study, continued for some thirty years, of the dialects and languages used by American Indians in a section of the western United States known as the Great Basin. He has taught at a number of American universities, including Idaho State, where he delivered the following piece, not previously printed, as a Sigma Xi lecture in 1969. The title, one can infer, was suggested to him.

A primitive language? Is there such a thing? If there were, and since human thought and human language no doubt are more or less identical phenomena, we would be obliged to ask ourselves the useless question: What is primitive thought?

Of course, there are highly specialized languages, as for example mathematical language, esoteric languages that we would hesitate to call primitive. But all known so-called natural languages are esoteric inasmuch as they are regulated by means of an extremely complicated and comprehensive code, a system of rules that we call a grammar. A particular grammar. Can any one grammar, any so-called natural-language grammar, be primitive in any possible sense of the word? It cannot. Without using a single word in the lexicon of a particular language, the grammar of this language can in itself be clearly and precisely stated in its totality in mathematical language.

What do people mean, then, by the term *primitive* in regard to language? The question is legitimate since we meet it all the time, some of us almost daily. Could it be that a language would be regarded as primitive that has never been recorded in written form, whereas a language that for some reason or other happens to exist in both oral and written form would be the opposite of primitive? If so, most languages existing today would be primitive, and a few languages spoken several thousand years ago and now extinct would be nonprimitive. Otherwise there would be no principal difference.

Another question: Could it be that *primitive* in regard to language would mean something outdated, something left behind in the evolution of man, something without any long and well-known history?

The answer is: The history—or the prehistory, rather—of a contemporary language is known at the most for three or four thousand years and in a most elementary way. But all existing languages, that is, all human speech, must have a history, albeit so far unknown, of some two million years or so. And why do we say prehistory rather than history for the few thousand years that we know something about the predecessors, the parent languages, of for example the Semitic languages or the Indo-European languages? Because the lifetime of a language as spoken at a certain time can be no longer than some eight hundred years.

A third and final question: Could it be, then, that a primitive language would be a very elementary one, simple in its structure as compared to a language with a much more developed and complex structure?

The answer is: As far as has been observed, there is no such difference. This answer may warrant illustration. Although this has not been explicitly requested, I take it for granted that here tonight what more specifically is meant by a *primitive language* would be Paiute as spoken by some less than one thousand impoverished Indians in the immediate area; and by contrast, a nonprimitive language would be English. Let us then compare a couple of very common terms in these two languages, terms with the same meaning but quite different as to linguistic construction.

We have in the English lexicon two words, two root words, rather, that can stand by themselves and that cannot be grammatically reduced into smaller parts, namely *go* and *walk*. The Paiute lexicon contains only one root word for both meanings, *mia-*. But this root word never occurs in isolation, that is, *mia* is actually never uttered in just that simple form. By adding a glottal catch to the stem *mia-*, resulting in something like *miʔá*, the meaning 'to go' is verbalized. In contrast, by adding the suffix *-kkai* to the same stem, *miákkai*, the meaning 'to walk' is verbalized. The suffix *-kkai* actually expresses continuative movement: *miákkai*, then, means 'to go continuously,' that is, 'to walk.' The verbalization power of the two languages is equally strong in expressing this contrast in meaning, the discreet contrast between 'to go' and 'to walk.' The only difference is that English uses selectively two different stems, whereas Paiute uses one stem, which is differently inflected in order to express the difference in meaning.

Let us take another and more striking example. In English we say *my brother* regardless of whether a man is speaking about *his* brother or a woman is speaking about *her* brother, and regardless of whether my brother is *older* than I am or *younger* than I am. It is always *my brother*. In Paiute only a woman can use a holophrastic term in this meaning, that is, one single unqualified word *brother*. A Paiute-speaking woman can use *samú* to refer to any one of her male siblings: *isamú* 'my brother.' When speaking about a brother of his, a man cannot use the term *samú*, which means simply a sibling of the opposite sex from the viewpoint of a woman. When verbalizing the meaning 'brother,' a man must necessarily in order to be understood use either the word *pabíʔi*, which means 'brother older than the speaker,' or *waŋŋáʔa*, which means 'brother younger than the speaker.' For a male speaker there is no holophrastic term *brother* just as in English there is none telling relative order of age.

How, then, can a Paiute speaker possibly verbalize the plural meaning *brothers—my brothers*—since he must refer simultaneously to the plural of both *pabíʔi* and *waŋŋáʔa* unless he happens to be the very oldest one or the very youngest one? In English, as we know, the process of forming the plural of nouns is very simple indeed: we add to the stem *brother* the plural suffix, of which there are several quite different phonetic representations: to the stem *brother* we add /-ᴢ/ and get *brothers* just as we add the variant form /-s/ to the stem *cat* and get *cats*. But English can, of course, mark plural in nouns by adding to the stem other phonetic variants of the same suffix. One can add the variant /-ən/ to the stem *ox* and get *oxen,* or one can add the variant *zero* to the stem *sheep* and get the plural form *sheep*.

But what in the world can the poor Paiute speaker do in order to generate the plural term meaning 'brothers' from the two singular forms *pabíʔi* 'older brother' and *waŋŋáʔa* 'younger brother'? This would seem an almost hopeless dilemma. But he does it in a most convincing way. There is in the language a prefix /na-/ with reflexive meaning, that is, /na-/ plus a nominal or verbal stem means 'oneself,' or 'each other,' or 'mutually,' or 'together,' all depending on what the stem in itself means. For example, *aataʔa* means 'several sit.' There is no single stem, no holophrastic term, with the general meaning 'to sit.' The singular meaning, 'one sits,' is verbalized in the root word *katý;* the dual meaning, 'two sit,' is represented by the verb *jykwí;* and the plural meaning, 'more than two sit,' is present in the verb *aataʔa*. This stem together with the prefix /na-/ is used, for example, in the sentence *tammí naátaʔa,* which means 'we (more than two) sit together'. However, in the contemporary idiomatic usage of the sentence *tammí naátaʔa* we get a shift of meaning, namely 'we sit together being drunk'; that is, the present-day idiomatic meaning of *naáta?a* 'several sit together' represents the plural of 'to be drunk.'

But now, let us go back to the Paiute terms for brotherhood in a more strict sense than being drunk together. With the limited Paiute lexicon we have at this moment we do know that *pabí?i* means 'older brother' and that *waŋŋá?a* means 'younger brother.' By combining the prefix /na-/ with the stem *waŋŋá?a* we get the form *nawaŋŋa?a*, which literally means 'younger brother together.' In depth the construction means 'two brothers one of whom is younger than the other.' This form is a dual derived from the singular stem. If we now reduplicate the prefixed element, that is, transform it from /na-/ to /nanna-/, we obtain another derived form of *waŋŋá?a*, namely *nannawaŋŋa-*, which has a plural meaning. This is, however, a form that cannot be uttered without the addition of the plural suffix /-my/. If we add this suffix to the derived base *nannawaŋŋa-*, we get the final form *nannáwaŋŋamy*, meaning literally 'younger brothers together.'

Younger brothers together—what is the underlying meaning? It is as follows: 'more than two male siblings form a unit of which all but one is younger than this one,' in other words, one is the oldest and all the others are his younger brothers together. This, now, is what *nannáwaŋŋamy* means in the deep structure of the language, and we can be reasonably sure that this linguistic usage reflects a social order that once must have dominated Paiute society even if it today is obsolete and forgotten. Popularly translated into English, *nannáwaŋŋamy* means 'brothers,' the plural form of both *waŋŋá?a* and *pabí?i*. This is an elegant and economic construction forming a common plural of two singular nouns having related meaning but contrastive shapes.

Just one more example in order to show the difference in surface structure between two languages where there is a clearly discernible common meaning in depth. In English we say *my brother's knife*. Marking the possessive case we add the suffix /-z/ to the nominal stem representing the possessor, and we say that we inflect the noun for possessive case by this simple means: on the one hand we have *my brother*, and on the other hand we have *the knife*, and saying in the most convenient way that the first is the owner of the latter we add /-z/ to the stem *brother*. A Paiute speaker does exactly the opposite. He says *iwaŋŋá?a* 'my younger brother,' and he says *wihí* 'knife.' But for *my younger brother's knife* he says *iwaŋŋá kwihí*. That is, he changes the nominal stem *wihí* 'knife' to *kwihí* in order to say that the knife is owned by somebody, that it is possessed. We can say that English marks possessive case in the noun representing the possessor, but that Paiute marks possessive case in the noun representing the possession, the possessed thing.

Now, I wonder, is there any difference? Yes, on the surface there is a difference, of course. In the sentence, as it occurs in the actual utterance, there is a difference. But the basic idea is the same. In depth there is the idea of somebody possessing something. More precisely, both the English phrase *my younger brother's knife* and the Paiute phrase, literally translated *my younger brother, the knife is possessed*, go back to a common idea that contains two different propositions: (1) I have a younger brother, and (2) he has a knife. This is the precise and particular statement contained in the underlying deep structure of the sentence in either language. It is this underlying structure that determines the meaning of the phonetic sequence on the surface. "I have a younger brother. He has a knife." That is what we think. "My younger brother's knife." That is what we say. The sequence of words immediately underlying the phonetic utterance is the result, the end product of a process of thought on a deep level of construction that the speaker himself is not aware of, for below it, on an even deeper level, there is the very base of this particular statement, namely, a noun possesses a noun which in turn possesses a third noun.

This now is grammar as we think of it today. Every language has a grammar consisting of a set of rules governing the process of changing a thought, an idea into an utterance—of making speech out of thought. Every individual speaker of a language has a grammar of his own: his individual system of linguistic rules, by necessity a bit eclectic or, at any rate, less complete than the highly complex and comprehensive grammatical model of the total speech community, but in every essential detail conforming to it.

Would there then, behind the various grammars of all human languages, be a grammar that would be comprehensive enough to include them all, but at the same time narrow enough to present a finite system of general rules so contrived that out of it the grammar of any particular language so far known could be generated? What we now inquire about is nothing less than a universal grammar. Thus, if anything, a universal grammar, would be the goal of all the studies there have been and will be of all languages there are —be they primitive or not. And this, now, will be the theme of the rest of our discussion tonight.

This certainly is a somewhat ambitious topic for a half-hour after-dinner talk, and attempting to put some sugar on the hard-digested little cake, I now wish to tell a little story. Although it contains only fifty-four words, I should think that next to Alice in Wonderland it is the best-known little story in the world. It was written about 1930 by the great American linguist Leonard Bloomfield. It reads as follows:

> Suppose that Jack and Jill are walking down a lane. Jill is hungry. She sees an apple in a tree. She makes a noise with her larynx, tongue, and lips. Jack vaults the fence, climbs the tree, takes the apple, brings it to Jill, and places it in her hand. Jill eats the apple.

What Bloomfield wanted to illustrate with his story is the following:
Every act of speech must have a reason. Just as any other act of human behavior is triggered by a stimulus of some kind and constitutes the response to this stimulus, so the act of speech is the response to a stimulus of some kind. Usually, of course, man, like all other animals, reacts to a stimulus with a physical response of some kind, or as Bloomfield himself preferred to call it, with "a practical reaction" to the stimulus. The situation in the story can

most easily be analyzed into three events: (1) the practical event preceding the act of speech, (2) the act of speech, and (3) practical events following the act of speech. Jill was hungry. She saw the apple and wanted to have it. These details taken together constitute the stimulus. The response to this stimulus, the practical reaction, would be that Jill would have reacted by getting the apple herself the best she could. But she had Jack at her side and reacted instead by talking. This Bloomfield called *the speaker's linguistic substitute response,* quite another thing than any practical response. The sound waves of Jill's speech reached Jack's ears. The message encoded in Jill's speech was decoded in Jack's brain, and he got the meaning of Jill's message. This Bloomfield called *the hearer's linguistic substitute stimulus,* which, in turn, would lead to the final practical response, in this case executed by Jack.

The point of the story is that man, in contrast to every other animal, is capable of reacting to a stimulus not only in a practical way but also—and fundamentally—by the act of speech.

Behind Bloomfield's little story we sense the empirically based psychology of the time, the *behaviorism* that dominated the thinking of the 1920's and 1930's. Bloomfield published his book *Language* in 1933. Perhaps there is no work in modern linguistic science that meant more and exercised a greater influence than this book did for many years. In fact, it dominated linguistic studies until quite recently—and it still makes its weight felt. Bloomfield was not alone, though, far from it. In the early years of the century there was a Swiss scholar, Ferdinand de Saussure, who was a most important forerunner. After de Saussure's death, his students published in 1915 the lectures he had delivered at the University of Geneva in a famous book entitled *Cours de linguistique générale.* The general theme in this famous book is quite clear. Speech, the sounds we hear and react to—at least in our minds— the sum of the acoustic elements we perceive, is one sort of thing. For this de Saussure used the term *la parole,* but let us just call it speech, the act of speech. It is the instrument of language, the instrument we play upon when we talk. But it is not language itself. Quite another thing, according to de Saussure, is the pattern underlying speech, the system of sound symbols common to all speakers of a language together with a particular lexical inventory. All this de Saussure called *la langue,* that is, language *per se.*

Now all the linguists in the world got busy, and in the course of half a century they worked out the sound systems of a large number of languages, both languages that had never before been recorded (and, incidentally, these were the languages they were mainly interested in) and languages like Latin, or Arabic, or English, or Chinese that had been taught in schools for centuries and millennia. Under the influence of de Saussure and Bloomfield and the Russian linguist Trubetskoi, students of language found to their surprise that out of the enormous mass of possible sounds that the human physical speech mechanism is capable of producing, only very few discrete sounds are actually employed in each language. The number of distinctive sounds in a given language as they are identified by the linguist varies slightly according to the principles of discovery he applies, that is to say, how he divides the possible inventory. But in any case, they are very few. In languages in general, there are from about fifteen to about forty-five phonemes or units of distinctive sounds. On this basis the linguists worked out highly detailed descriptive grammars of a number of languages, not only in regard to the sound system but in regard to all the possible combinations of the constituent parts of a sentence, that is, the combination power of all the root words and prefixes and suffixes and other classes of smallest possible meaningful units in any given language.

This state of affairs went on until about fifteen years ago, until the midst of the 1950's. Then, almost over night, the linguists began to wonder: Is there nothing but all these little stimuli and responses in the brains of people who already at the age of four or five are capable of handling such a tremendously complicated instrument of communication as a grammar is? Bloomfield and his followers—and they are here to this day—had made it a virtue to make linguistics into an exact science on a "mechanistic" ground, as Bloomfield used to call it, on the principle that nothing could be in the mind unless it had first been in the senses. He rejected what he called a "mentalistic" approach to the study of language. The linguists of the day did not want to conduct their work on the premise that, eventually, the human mind inherently possesses a frame, an innate ability corresponding to a universal grammar, and all that would be needed is to fill this frame with a content consisting of the rules a particular grammar entails. Today we do accept this premise. There must be an innate linguistic ability in the human mind that no other creature possesses. As soon as it masters the rules of one grammatical system, we call this ability *linguistic competence*.

The mechanism of linguistic competence, the rules according to which a sentence can be formed and understood in any particular language, was first tentatively worked out by a young linguist at Massachusetts Institute of Technology, Noam Chomsky, in a famous treatise entitled "Syntactic Structures," published in 1957. The effect of this publication in the linguistic world was very great. It came, one might say, like a gust of wind in a slackened sail. Since that date, Chomsky himself and many linguists with him have formulated the rules—or the classes of rules—underlying linguistic competence, a notion he introduced. From this quite recent revolution in linguistic theory there is no return.

But the idea is by no means new. In the seventeenth century when modern philosophy and, indeed, modern science took the first steps, Cartesian philosophy postulated the independence of the mind of physical accidents and stressed the creative aspect of language entirely on what Bloomfield called a mentalistic principle. These views resulted in the "Port-Royal Grammar" of 1660, written by Claude Lancelot and Antoine Arnauld and entitled *Grammaire générale et raisonnée,* a monumental work in linguistic philosophy that every student of language has heard about but very few have read. The principle of this grammar as discussed by Chomsky is clear and convincing: a phrase in the language relates to an idea in the mind, an idea that might be quite complex. A sentence is automatically subdivided into simple phrases and the phrases into the individual words that make up the utterance. The forms actually spoken represent what Chomsky calls the surface structure of the sentence. As an example of those used in the Port-Royal Grammar, Chomsky calls to mind the sentence *Invisible God created the visible world*. On the surface, this sentence contains the subject *invisible God* and the predicate *created the visible world*. In various ways this analysis is insufficient in order to explain the structural growth of the underlying meaning. But the Port-Royal Grammar formally recognized what Chomsky calls a deep linguistic structure in the mind of the speaker but unknown to him. For the sentence *invisible God created the visible world* three propositions necessary in order to reach the meaning underlying this sentence were postulated: (1) God is invisible, (2) God created the world, and (3) the world is visible. Essentially it is this idea Chomsky has revived and developed after three hundred years of slumber. You may read about it yourself in a most exciting new little book by Chomsky. It is entitled *Language and Mind* and written in nontechnical language.

Very briefly stated Chomsky's reasoning is as follows.

The deep structure of the sentence determines the meaning of its surface structure, ultimately to be represented in speech sounds. This act of rapport between the meaningful deep structure and the final string of speech sounds on the surface level is carried out by means of certain mental operations in modern terminology called grammatical transformations. The grammar of each particular language can be regarded as a set of definite rules by means of which the deep-lying meaning is transformed step by step into phrases and phrases into words. The final string of words in the particular order that the rules provide for conveys the underlying meaning. Thus, the deep structure of a sentence represents the complete meaning of the utterance. Hence, the semantic content of the utterance has to be traced to the deep level underlying the order of the words actually uttered, which constitute the surface structure.

The competent speaker of a language knows subconsciously the rules that constitute his grammar, and in his speech he intuitively applies these rules. Yet, nobody will have the time and the opportunity to produce or even hear more than a limited part of the entire language that potentially is his and that is limitless and enables him to produce correct sentences that he has not heard before.

Now, finally, in order to show how this works not only in theory but in reality, I wish to tell another little story, but not one by Bloomfield this time—a true story that happened to me.

Many years ago my wife and I took an Indian friend, a very old Paiute-speaking lady with us on a trip. We were out for a whole day and made a campfire and cooked our food the Indian way after the old lady's directions. The fourth person in the party was little Joe, the son of one of my colleagues. In honor of the day little Joe had dressed himself in feathers and a fringed skin-shirt and acted Indian. Some time later the old lady asked me about little Joe. With a smile in her wrinkled face she then uttered the following sentence: *symýtabinonymyjow*. The remarkable thing about this sentence is that it is not only a sentence, it is a single word, but it is so skillfully composed and so beautifully phrased that it reads like a little poem.

Now we need to know four root words in the Paiute lexicon and two suffixes in the Paiute grammar. These forms are as follows: (1) *manai* 'to be' (actually, 'to do by and for oneself'), (2) *nymy* 'Indian,' (3) *symy* 'one,' (4) *tabi-* 'to be daylight,' (5) *-no* nominalizing to verbal stems denoting time (*tabino* 'day'), (6) *-su* 'only.' Instantly we will then know that the Paiute phrase *symýtabinonymyjow* means 'one-day-Indian-Joe.' This phrase is a compound, one single word, composed of the nominal stem *symy* 'one,' the derived noun *tabino* 'day,' the noun *nymy* 'Indian,' and still another noun, Joe.

It is highly unlikely that this utterance had ever been heard before. Still, it is completely grammatical. But it is far removed from the deep structure of the Paiute language, and it is not how a Paiute speaker in general would have expressed the idea. For one thing, in a Paiute sentence a verb is needed, just as in an English sentence, or in a full sentence of any known language. This, then, would be the requirement of universal grammar: $S \rightarrow NP + VP$, that is, the sentence is to be rewritten as noun phrase plus verb phrase.

Let us assume that the deep structure underlying the compound *symý-tabinonymyjow* would require the full sentence **jow nymy manai symy tabinosu*, which literally translated into English would mean 'Joe Indian be one daylight-be-NOMINALIZING-only.' The actual mental operation whereby the abstraction $S \rightarrow NP + VP$ is transformed into the five words contained in our sentence is certainly not understood even today. But in a formal way it can easily be retraced, the first step being $NP \rightarrow jow$; that is, the noun phrase is rewritten as *Joe* resulting in the immediate form $S \rightarrow jow + VP$. The turn now comes to the predicate, *VP*, which has a quite complicated structure, and which we now simplify a bit merely for clarity: $VP \rightarrow N + V_m + Adv$, that is, a noun plus a verb that we might call "middle," since it is neither active nor passive, plus an adverbial complement. The immediate result we obtain is $VP \rightarrow nymy \; manai + Adv$. The adverbial part of the sentence contains a bare stem meaning 'one' of a class that we simply call number; further, a verbal noun, and finally an enclitic ending /-su/, meaning 'only,' which might be freely added to a noun or to a verb indiscriminately. Accordingly we may write $Adv \rightarrow n + VN + c$ with the immediate result $Adv \rightarrow symy + VN + c$.

The rules we have so far followed are called phrase structure rules, since they assign to the sentence the proper phrase constituents. We now have to apply a rule of another class, the so-called transformational rules, with the power of rearranging, changing, adding, or deleting the elements of a phrase. Thus, by adding the nominalizing suffix /-no/ to the stem *tabi-* we obtain the meaning 'day' and the transformation $VN \rightarrow tabino + c$. The construction now reads $S \rightarrow jow \; nymy \; manai \; symy \; tabino + c$. By another transformational rule we insert the enclitic element /-su/, which is required in an adverbial complement following V_m (a verb signifying the middle voice) if the intended meaning of singularity is to be represented, and we obtain the final form $S \to \check{j}\acute{o}w\ nym\acute{y}\ man\acute{a}i\ sym\acute{y}\ tab\acute{\imath}nosu$.

However, this in itself complete and final sentence is never uttered. We are still on the level of deep structure. Another transformational rule of a kind we may call permutation rules is required in order to lift the sentence from its full deep-structure form up to the level of surface structure. The order of the verb and the adverb must be inverted, and we obtain the final string $S \to \check{j}\acute{o}w\ sym\acute{y}\ tab\acute{\imath}nosu\ nym\acute{y}\ man\acute{a}i$. This is how a Paiute speaker would ordinarily express the idea. But this was not what the old lady said. In order to produce an utterance more eloquent and less commonplace than the expected form, she applied a transformational rule that allows for the deletion of the verb in an attributive verb phrase but at the same time requires that if this deletion takes place the order between the noun phrase and the reduced verb phrase be reversed. Actually, of course, this statement must be resolved by two different rules. But what we now get is the following: $S \to sym\acute{y}\ tab\acute{\imath}nosu\ nym\acute{y}\ \check{j}\acute{o}w$. In order to transform this sentence into a compound under one accent only, still another transformation is necessary: the enclitic /-su/ is not tolerated within a compound and must be deleted by another deletion rule, and we finally obtain the single word the old lady uttered: $S \to sym\acute{y}tab\acute{\imath}non\check{y}myj\check{o}w$.

From the original deep structure of the sentence, $S \to NP + VP$ (sentence rewritten as noun phrase plus verb phrase) to the final string of meaningful units, 'One-day-Indian-Joe,' we have accounted for nine operations necessary to generate this one word. And yet, this is not all. For the sake of convenience we have allowed ourselves to make a few short cuts. Still, it is a big order for generating a word uttered in less than three seconds.

Without hesitation the old lady instantly produced her one-word witty little remark happily unaware of the fact that it would require a full page and at least nine grammatical rules to make her utterance comprehensible in terms of the deep structure of the sentence she had in mind. In order to write the full wording of the sentence in its deep structural form, twenty-four symbols are required for the final string. In order to write the surface structure sentence that the old lady actually used with such delight, only seventeen symbols are required.

There was simplicity in the brief utterance old Lizzi produced in this moment of ingenuity, a simplicity that was intended, a style characteristic of interlocutory art in her community and one that the grammar provides for in the surface structure rules. Such a manner of speaking is an open field to anybody who has the talent and inclination to handle the necessary rules productively. And now we leave it to everybody's own discretion whether we should call this simplicity primitive or artistic or, eventually, both.

WORKING WITH THE SELECTION

1. Do Liljeblad's examples indicate that Paiute is a "primitive" language in the sense that it is elementary, simple in its structure?

2. In what sense are Paiute and English alike in their handling of possessive forms? In what sense different?

3. Would Liljeblad's interpretation of the differences between English and Paiute agree or disagree with Whorf's interpretation?

4. Liljeblad says that speakers of a language know its grammatical laws subconsciously. Does this statement seem to explain or to contradict Laird's observations about Hanna's use of language?

5. How does the view Liljeblad describes of "an innate linguistic ability in the human mind which no other creature possesses" compare with Langer's attitude toward "the language-making instinct of very young children"?

6. What is meant by a *universal grammar* as Liljeblad uses the term?

9

Language and the Mind

Noam Chomsky

Noam Chomsky, Ferrari P. Ward Professor of Modern Languages and Linguistics at Massachusetts Institute of Technology, is recognized as one of the most significant contemporary linguists, not only for his development of transformational grammar but also for his comments on the nature of language and language learning. In the following selection from an essay in Psychology Today, *1 (February, 1968), Chomsky relates transformational grammar to its backgrounds in psychology and philosophy, thinking of how language works as part of how the mind works.*

How does the mind work? To answer this question we must look at some of the work performed by the mind. One of its main functions is the acquisition of knowledge. The two major factors in acquisition of knowledge, perception and learning, have been the subject of study and speculation for centuries. It would not, I think, be misleading to characterize the major positions that have developed as outgrowths of classical rationalism and empiricism. The rationalist theories are marked by the importance they assign to *intrinsic* structures in mental operations—to central processes and organizing principles in perception, and to innate ideas and principles in learning. The empiricist approach, in contrast, has stressed the role of experience and control by environmental factors.

The classical empiricist view is that sensory images are transmitted to the brain as impressions. They remain as ideas that will be associated in various ways, depending on the fortuitous character of experience. In this view a language is merely a collection of words, phrases, and sentences, a habit system, acquired accidentally and extrinsically. In the formulation of Williard Quine, knowledge of a language (and, in fact, knowledge in general) can be represented as "a fabric of sentences variously associated to one another and to nonverbal stimuli by the mechanism of conditioned response." Acquisition of knowledge is only a matter of the gradual construction of this fabric. When sensory experience is interpreted, the already established network may be activated in some fashion. In its essentials, this view has been predominant in modern behavioral science, and it has been accepted with little question by many philosophers as well.

The classical rationalist view is quite different. In this view the mind contains a system of "common notions" that enable it to interpret the scattered and incoherent data of sense in terms of objects and their relations, cause and effect, whole and part, symmetry, gestalt properties, functions, and so on. Sensation, providing only fleeting and meaningless images, is degenerate and particular. Knowledge, much of it beyond immediate awareness, is rich in structure, involves universals, and is highly organized. The innate general principles that underlie and organize this knowledge, according to Leibniz, "enter into our thoughts, of which they form the soul and the connection . . . although we do not at all think of them."

This "active" rationalist view of the acquisition of knowledge persisted through the romantic period in its essentials. With respect to language, it achieves its most illuminating expression in the profound investigations of Wilhelm von Humboldt. His theory of speech perception supposes a generative system of rules that underlies speech production as well as its interpretation. The system is generative in that it makes infinite use of finite means. He regards a language as a structure of forms and concepts based on a system of rules that determine their interrelations, arrangement, and organization. But these finite materials can be combined to make a never-ending product.

In the rationalist and romantic tradition of linguistic theory, the normal use of language is regarded as characteristically innovative. We construct sentences that are entirely new to us. There is no substantive notion of "analogy" or "generalization" that accounts for this creative aspect of language use. It is equally erroneous to describe language as a "habit structure" or as a network of associated responses. The innovative element in normal use of language quickly exceeds the bounds of such marginal principles as analogy or generalization (under any substantive interpretation of these notions). It is important to emphasize this fact because the insight has been lost under the impact of the behaviorist assumptions that have dominated speculation and research in the twentieth century.

In Humboldt's view, acquisition of language is largely a matter of maturation of an innate language capacity. The maturation is guided by internal factors, by an innate "form of language" that is sharpened, differentiated, and given its specific realization through experience. Language is thus a kind of latent structure in the human mind, developed and fixed by exposure to specific linguistic experience. Humboldt believes that all languages will be found to be very similar in their grammatical form, similar not on the surface but in their deeper inner structures. The innate organizing principles severely limit the class of possible languages, and these principles determine the properties of the language that is learned in the normal way.

The active and passive views of perception and learning have elaborated with varying degrees of clarity since the seventeenth century. These views can be confronted with empirical evidence in a variety of ways. Some recent work in psychology and neurophysiology is highly suggestive in this regard. There is evidence for the existence of central processes in perception, specifically for control over the functioning of sensory neurons by the brain-stem reticular system. Behavioral counterparts of this central control have been under investigation for several years. Furthermore, there is evidence for innate organization of the perceptual system of a highly specific sort at every level of biological organization. Studies of the visual system of the frog, the discovery of specialized cells responding to angle and motion in the lower cortical centers of cats and rabbits, and the somewhat comparable investigations of the auditory system of frogs—all are relevant to the classical questions of intrinsic structure mentioned earlier. These studies suggest that there are highly organized, innately determined perceptual systems that are adapted closely to the animal's "life space" and that provide the basis for what we might call "acquisition of knowledge." Also relevant are certain behavioral studies of human infants, for example those showing the preference for faces over other complex stimuli.

These and other studies make it reasonable to inquire into the possibility that complex intellectual structures are determined narrowly by innate mental organization. What is perceived may be determined by mental processes of considerable depth. As far as language learning is concerned, it seems to me that a rather convincing argument can be made for the view that certain principles intrinsic to the mind provide invariant structures that are a precondition for linguistic experience. In the course of this article I would like to sketch some of the ways such conclusions might be clarified and firmly established.

There are several ways linguistic evidence can be used to reveal properties of human perception and learning. In this section we consider one research strategy that might take us nearer to this goal.

Let us say that in interpreting a certain physical stimulus a person constructs a "percept." This percept represents some of his conclusions (in general, unconscious) about the stimulus. To the extent that we can characterize such percepts, we can go on to investigate the mechanisms that relate stimulus and percept. Imagine a model of perception that takes stimuli as inputs and arrives at percepts as "outputs." The model might contain a system of beliefs, strategies for interpreting stimuli, and other factors, such as the organization of memory. We would then have a perceptual model that might be represented graphically.

Figure 1 Model for perception. Each physical stimulus, after interpretation by the mental processes, will result in a percept.

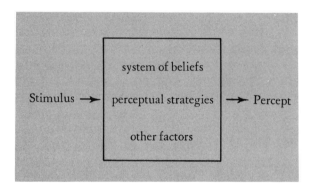

Consider next the system of beliefs that is a component of the perceptual model. How was this acquired? To study this problem, we must investigate a second model, which takes certain data as input and gives as "output" (again, internally represented) the system of beliefs operating in the perceptual model. This second model, a model of learning, would have its own intrinsic structure, as did the first. This structure might consist of conditions on the nature of the system of beliefs that can be acquired, of innate inductive strategies, and again, of other factors such as the organization of memory.

Under further conditions, which are interesting but not relevant here, we can take these perceptual and learning models as theories of the acquisition of knowledge, rather than of belief. How then would the models apply to language? The input stimulus to the perceptual model is a speech signal, and the percept is a representation of the utterance that the hearer takes the signal to be and of the interpretation he assigns to it. We can think of the percept as the structural description of a linguistic expression which contains certain phonetic, semantic, and syntactic information. Most interesting is the syntactic information, which best can be discussed by examining a few typical cases.

The three sentences in the example [below] seem to be the same syntactic structure. Each contains the subject *I*, and the predicate of each consists of a verb (*told, expected, persuaded*), a noun phrase (*John*), and an embedded predicate phrase (*to leave*). This similarity is only superficial, however—a

Figure 2 Model for learning. One's system of beliefs, a part of the perception model, is acquired from data as shown above.

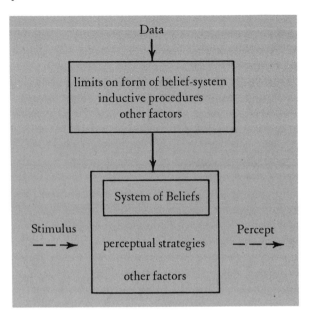

similarity in what we may call the "surface structure" of these sentences, which differ in important ways when we consider them with somewhat greater care.

(1)   I told John to leave
(2)   I expected John to leave
(3)   I persuaded John to leave

First Paraphrase:

(1a)   What I told John was to leave (ACCEPTABLE)
(2a)   What I expected John was to leave (UNACCEPTABLE)
(3a)   What I persuaded John was to leave (UNACCEPTABLE)

Second Paraphrase:

(1b)   It was told by me that John would leave (UNACCEPTABLE)
(2b)   It was expected by me that John would leave (ACCEPTABLE)
(3b)   It was persuaded by me that John would leave (UNACCEPTABLE)

(4)   I expected the doctor to examine John
(5)   I persuaded the doctor to examine John

Passive replacement as paraphrase:

(4a)   I expected John to be examined by the doctor (MEANING RE-
       TAINED)

(5a) I persuaded John to be examined by the doctor (MEANING CHANGED)

The differences can be seen when the sentences are paraphrased or subjected to certain grammatical operations, such as the conversion from active to passive forms. For example, in normal conversation the sentence "I told John to leave" can be roughly paraphrased as "What I told John was to leave." But the other two sentences cannot be paraphrased as "What I persuaded John was to leave" or "What I expected John was to leave." Sentence 2 can be paraphrased as: "It was expected by me that John would leave." But the other two sentences cannot undergo a corresponding formal operation, yielding: "It was persuaded by me that John would leave" or "It was told by me that John should leave."

Sentences 2 and 3 differ more subtly. In Sentence 3 *John* is the direct object of *persuade,* but in Sentence 2 *John* is not the direct object of *expect.* We can show this by using these verbs in slightly more complex sentences: "I persuaded the doctor to examine John" and "I expected the doctor to examine John." If we replace the embedded proposition *the doctor to examine John* with its passive form *John to be examined by the doctor,* the change to the passive does not, in itself, change the meaning. We can accept as paraphrases "I expected the doctor to examine John" and "I expected John to be examined by the doctor." But we cannot accept as paraphrases "I persuaded the doctor to examine John" and "I persuaded John to be examined by the doctor."

The parts of these sentences differ in their grammatical functions. In "I persuaded John to leave" *John* is both the object of *persuade* and the subject of *leave.* These facts must be represented in the percept since they are known, intuitively, to the hearer of the speech signal. No special training or instruction is necessary to enable the native speaker to understand these examples, to know which are "wrong" and which "right," although they may all be quite new to him. They are interpreted by the native speaker instantaneously and uniformly, in accordance with structural principles that are known tacitly, intuitively, and unconsciously.

These examples illustrate two significant points. First, the surface structure of a sentence, its organization into various phrases, may not reveal or immediately reflect its deep syntactic structure. The deep structure is not represented directly in the form of the speech signal; it is abstract. Second, the rules that determine deep and surface structure and their interrelation in particular cases must themselves be highly abstract. They are surely remote from consciousness, and in all likelihood they cannot be brought to consciousness.

A study of such examples, examples characteristic of all human languages that have been carefully studied, constitutes the first stage of the linguistic investigation outlined above, namely the study of the percept. The percept contains phonetic and semantic information related through the medium of syntactic structure. There are two aspects to this syntactic structure. It consists of a surface directly related to the phonetic form, and a deep structure that underlies the semantic interpretation. The deep structure is represented in the mind and rarely is indicated directly in the physical signal.

A language, then, involves a set of semantic-phonetic percepts, of sound-meaning correlations, the correlations being determined by the kind of intervening syntactic structure just illustrated. The English language correlates sound and meaning in one way, Japanese in another, and so on. But the general properties of percepts, their forms and mechanisms, are remarkably similar for all languages that have been carefully studied.

Returning to our models of perception and learning, we can now take up the problem of formulating the system of beliefs that is a central component in perceptual processes. In the case of language, the "system of beliefs" would now be called the "generative grammar," the system of rules that specifies the sound-meaning correlation and generates the class of structural descriptions (percepts) that constitute the language in question. The generative grammar, then, represents the speaker-hearer's knowledge of his language. We can use the term *grammar of a language* ambiguously, as referring not only to the speaker's internalized, subconscious knowledge but to the professional linguist's representation of this internalized and intuitive system of rules as well.

How is this generative grammar acquired? Or, using our learning model, what is the internal structure of the device that could develop a generative grammar?

We can think of every normal human's internalized grammar as, in effect, a theory of his language. This theory provides a sound-meaning correlation for an infinite number of sentences. It provides an infinite set of structural descriptions; each contains a surface structure that determines phonetic form and a deep structure that determines semantic content.

In formal terms, then, we can describe the child's acquisition of language as a kind of theory construction. The child discovers the theory of his language with only small amounts of data from that language. Not only does his "theory of the language" have an enormous predictive scope, but it also enables the child to reject a great deal of the very data on which the theory has been constructed. Normal speech consists, in large part, of fragments, false starts, blends, and other distortions of the underlying idealized forms. Nevertheless, as is evident from a study of the mature use of language, what the child learns is the underlying ideal theory. This is a remarkable fact. We must also bear in mind that the child constructs this ideal theory without explicit instruction, that he acquires this knowledge at a time when he is not capable of complex intellectual achievements in many other domains, and that this achievement is relatively independent of intelligence or the particular course of experience. These are facts that a theory of learning must face.

A scientist who approaches phenomena of this sort without prejudice or dogma would conclude that the acquired knowledge must be determined in a rather specific way by intrinsic properties of mental organization. He would then set himself the task of discovering the innate ideas and principles that make such acquisition of knowledge possible.

It is unimaginable that a highly specific, abstract, and tightly organized language comes by accident into the mind of every four-year-old child. If there were not an innate restriction on the form of grammar, then the child could employ innumerable theories to account for his linguistic experience, and no one system, or even small class of systems, would be found exclusively acceptable or even preferable. The child could not possibly acquire knowledge of a language. This restriction on the form of grammar is a precondition for linguistic experience, and it is surely the critical factor in determining the course and result of language learning. The child cannot know at birth which language he is going to learn. But he must "know" that its grammar must be of a predetermined form that excludes many imaginable languages.

The child's task is to select the appropriate hypothesis from this restricted class. Having selected it, he can confirm his choice with the evidence further available to him. But neither the evidence nor any process of induction (in any well-defined sense) could in themselves have led to this choice. Once the hypothesis is sufficiently well confirmed, the child knows the language defined by this hypothesis; consequently, his knowledge extends vastly beyond his linguistic experience, and he can reject much of this experience as imperfect, as resulting from the interaction of many factors, only one of which is the ideal grammar that determines a sound-meaning connection for an infinite class of linguistic expressions. Along such lines as these one might outline a theory to explain the acquisition of language. . . .

[A discussion of bracketing of deep and surface structures has been omitted.]

Recent studies have sought to explore the ways in which grammatical structure of the sort just described enters into mental operations. Much of this work has been based on a proposal formulated by George Miller as a first approximation, namely, that the amount of memory used to store a sentence should reflect the number of transformations used in deriving it. For example, H. B. Savin and E. Perchonock investigated this assumption in the following way: they presented to subjects a sentence followed by a sequence of unrelated words. They then determined the number of these unrelated words recalled when the subject attempted to repeat the sentence and the sequence of words. The more words recalled, the less memory used to store the sentence. The fewer words recalled, the more memory used to store the sentence. The results showed a remarkable correlation of amount of memory and number of transformations in certain simple cases. In fact, in their experimental material, shorter sentences with more transformations took up more "space in memory" than longer sentences that involved fewer transformations.

Savin has extended this work and has shown that the effects of deep structure and surface structure can be differentiated by a similar technique. He considered paired sentences with approximately the same deep structure but with one of the pair being more complex in surface structure. He showed that, under the experimental conditions just described, the paired sentences were indistinguishable. But if the sequence of unrelated words precedes, rather than follows, the sentence being tested, then the more complex (in surface structure) of the pair is more difficult to repeat correctly than the simpler member. Savin's very plausible inference is that sentences are coded in memory in terms of deep structure. When the unrelated words precede the test sentence, these words use up a certain amount of short-term memory, and the sentence that is more complex in surface structure cannot be analyzed with the amount of memory remaining. But if the test sentence precedes the unrelated words, it is, once understood, stored in terms of deep structure, which is about the same in both cases. Therefore the same amount of memory remains, in the paired cases, for recall of the following words. This is a beautiful example of the way creative experimental studies can interweave with theoretical work in the study of language and of mental processes.

In speaking of mental processes we have returned to our original problem. We can now see why it is reasonable to maintain that the linguistic evidence supports an "active" theory of acquisition of knowledge. The study of sentences and of speech perception, it seems to me, leads to a perceptual theory of a classical rationalist sort. Representative of this school, among others, were the seventeenth-century Cambridge Platonists, who developed the idea that our perception is guided by notions that originate from the mind and that provide the framework for the interpretation of sensory stimuli. It is not sufficient to suggest that this framework is a store of "neural models" or "schemata" which are in some manner applied to perception (as is postulated in some current theories of perception). We must go well beyond this assumption and return to the view of Wilhelm von Humboldt, who attributed to the mind a system of rules that generates such models and schemata under the stimulation of the senses. The system of rules itself determines the content of the percept that is formed.

We can offer more than this vague and metaphoric account. A generative grammar and an associated theory of speech perception provide a concrete example of the rules that operate and of the mental objects that they construct and manipulate. Physiology cannot yet explain the physical mechanisms that affect these abstract functions. But neither physiology nor psychology provides evidence that calls this account into question or that suggests an alternative. As mentioned earlier, the most exciting current work in the physiology of perception shows that even the peripheral systems analyze stimuli into the complex properties of objects, and that central processes may significantly affect the information transmitted by the receptor organs.

The study of language, it seems to me, offers strong empirical evidence that empiricist theories of learning are quite inadequate. Serious efforts have been made in recent years to develop principles of induction, generalization, and data analysis that would account for knowledge of a language. These efforts have been a total failure. The methods and principles fail not for any superficial reason such as lack of time or data. They fail because they are intrinsically incapable of giving rise to the system of rules that underlies the normal use of language. What evidence is now available supports the view that all human languages share deep-seated properties of organization and structure. These properties—these linguistic universals—can be plausibly assumed to be an innate mental endowment rather than the result of learning. If this is true, then the study of language sheds light on certain long-standing issues in the theory of knowledge. Once again, I see little reason to doubt that what is true of language is true of other forms of human knowledge as well.

There is one further question that might be raised at this point. How does the human mind come to have the innate properties that underlie acquisition of knowledge? Here linguistic evidence obviously provides no information at all. The process by which the human mind has achieved its present state of complexity and its particular form of innate organization are a complete mystery, as much of a mystery as the analogous questions that can be asked about the processes leading to the physical and mental organization of any other complex organism. It is perfectly safe to attribute this to evolution, so long as we bear in mind that there is no substance to this assertion —it amounts to nothing more than the belief that there is surely some naturalistic explanation for these phenomena.

WORKING WITH THE SELECTION

1. What is the distinction between the empiricist and the rationalist view of language? Summarize Humboldt's views as Chomsky describes them.

2. Examine Chomsky's argument that the mind has "innate restrictions on the form of grammar" it accepts. Is his argument convincing? Is there any disagreement between Chomsky's view and the view expressed by Langer, beginning in the fifth paragraph of her selection?

3. Does Whorf's view agree with Chomsky's comment that "the general properties of percepts, their forms and mechanics, are remarkably similar for all languages that have been carefully studied"?

4. Chomsky says that what a child first learns is the "underlying ideal theory" of language. Does this view seem consistent with the observations of Laird?

5. We can be fairly sure that individual languages and language as a human activity reflect the human mind, at least within limits. We can probably assume also that languages affect minds, although perhaps less than Whorf believed. No one knows, very certainly, just what these relationships are, but you might ask yourself, and record your conclusions in a statement, what we apparently know, what we can plausibly surmise, and what we can only guess at. Since Whorf, Liljeblad, and Chomsky cannot agree, you are not likely to solve all problems, but recording your best observations will help clarify your thoughts and prepare you for the more particular discussions to come.

part 2

Words
and
Names

When a literate person uses language, he seems to begin with words, which in turn suggest names or extensions of names. A child appears to begin using language by learning names for the things and people around him. When he learns to read, he learns meanings and uses of words; and when he writes, he tries to think of words to express his ideas. Actually, language and using language are not so simple as these statements imply. The child learns sounds, and probably basic grammar, before he learns words, even though parents tend to be impressed mainly by the first mama *or* dada. *Language is so complex that no single aspect of it can be isolated as fundamental. In fact, many linguists, observing that the word* word *cannot be strictly defined, find the concept of the word unsuitable for some kinds of serious language study. These scholars prefer to break language into minimum units of distinctive sounds, called phonemes, and minimum units of meaning or use, called morphemes.*

But the word is an accepted convention, at least in English and in most other languages Americans are likely to know; and in anything so conventional as language, we must respect convention. Literate users of the English language are accustomed to consulting wordbooks and to accepting the symbols they find there as units of language; they gain much of their knowledge by listening to sounds and observing printed symbols that they accept as standing for words, and they expect to communicate by stringing one word after another.

The selections in Part 2 consider mainly some of the ways in which words come into being; later parts include discussions of how words have meaning and how they work together in grammatical patterns.

1

Adam Engages in Onomastics

Noah Jonathan Jacobs

Seldom have wit and wisdom been more engagingly blended with broad learning than in the following selection from Naming Day in Eden, *rev. ed. (1969), by Noah Jonathan Jacobs. Jacobs is well grounded in both the Hebraic and the Western European traditions and has taught in this country and in the Near East. In* Naming Day in Eden, *Jacobs is concerned at least as much with man's mind and his culture as he is with his ostensible subject, onomastics, or the study of the origin and meaning of names.*

ADAM NAMES THE ANIMALS

How did it dawn on first man to use his invisible breath to express the ideas stirring within him? Spirit alone is formless and empty; language alone seduces us from the truth with its syntax and euphony. Which of the two mandates did Adam follow? The problem was how to introduce opaque language into spirit without obscuring it. How did the sounds Adam uttered capture the essence of the animals that passed before him in review? Was the conjunction of the airy concept and the palpable intuition fortuitous? Were the animal names invented for the occasion or were they stored up in some divine greenhouse waiting to be selected by Adam's brooding mind? Did the bewildered beasts fall noiselessly into place when their master's voice fell upon them and slip into their names as if into preexisting garments? And if Adam created these garments a priori, on what principles were the patterns cut? Would another man differently disposed have created other designs? Did man aim his arrowy words at the target's center or was his bow struck at a venture? And if shot from his primal brain in happy ignorance, how did those random verbal darts find their fleshy marks to brand them forever? But our Great Progenitor proceeded confidently and with an air of strong assurance. He himself seems to have set high store on his performance. After he had reviewed the Parade, we see him pacing to and fro, soliloquizing on the import of his linguistic feat, which he straightway made the subject of a panegyric:

> I named them as they passed, and understood
> Their nature; with such knowledge God endued
> My sudden apprehension. . . .
>
> *Paradise Lost*, Book VIII, ll. 352–354

What *was* the nature of that "sudden apprehension"? Of the infinity of natural sounds ringing in his ears, which did Adam choose to render the essence of the tabanid horsefly, the piebald magpie, the aciculated hedgehog, the wanton lapwing, and all the animals which in that brief review frolicked before him on the green? Was the name he gave the elephant, for example, a faithful reproduction of its roaring (the bow-wow theory) or of some mystic harmony between it and the sound that its vast trunk emitted when struck (the ding-dong theory)? Was the name a rhythmic chant designed to raise its flagging spirit as man goaded it on to do his work (the yo-heave-ho-theory) or a vocal reflex signifying his displeasure (the pooh-pooh theory)? It may be that Adam's tongue unwittingly reproduced some typical elephantine gesture, an oral replica of the beast's lithe proboscis, the texture of its wrinkled bulk or the swish of its flapping tail (the ta-ta or the wig-wag theory). Or, to take a more modest example, how did Adam name the bat? Which characteristic impressed him at the moment of naming? Did its blindness move him to call it *murciélago* (Sp.), its baldness *chauve-souris* (Fr.), its shyness *pipistrello* (It.), its leathery skin *Laderlapp* (Dan.) or *böregér* (Hung. from *bör*, leather; *egér*, mouse), its preference for the night *nukteris* (Gr.), its resemblance to the mouse *Fledermaus* (Ger.) or *letutsaya mysh* (Rus.), the sound of its flapping wings *watwat* (Arab.), its winglike hands *chiroptera* (Lat. from Gr. *chir*, hand, plus *pteron*, wing), its resemblance to a lily (!) *liliac* (Rum.), its reputed love of bacon *bat* (OE *backe*, bacon)? The Chinese have conferred a number of laudatory names on this mouselike mammal, such as *embracing wings, heavenly rat, fairy rat, night swallow,* and use it as a symbol of happiness and long life because its name *fu* in Chinese happens to be a homonym which means both *bat* and *prosperity.*

The truth of the matter seems to be that in the short time at his disposal, roughly about thirty minutes, Adam was obliged to employ a number of linguistic devices. The beasts had first to be divided into hoofed and clawed, and the former subdivided into cloven and noncloven hoofed. The question of gender then obtruded itself, and this Adam solved by composition (*she-elephant, nanny goat*), by addition of a suffix (*lioness, tigress*), by inverse deduction, deriving the male from the female (*goose-gander, duck-drake, cat-tomcat*); and by suppletion, that is, by supplying new forms (*ram-ewe, boar-sow, dog-bitch*). Where the mode of propagation escaped detection because of its rapidity or obscurity, making a responsible decision impossible (as in the case of the rabbit, the turtle and the elephant), Adam disregarded the distinction of sex. The other criteria at his disposal were:

a) place of origin: the *great Dane*, the *Pekingese, Scotty, spaniel* (Spain) and the *tarantula* (Lat. Tarentum, now Taranto in Sicily);
b) size: the *horsefly*, the *bumblebee*, the *bug* (akin to *big?*), and the *chameleon* (Gr. *khamaí*, dwarf, plus *léon*, lion);
c) means of sustenance: the *linnet* which feeds on the seeds of flax and hemp (Lat. *linum*, flax), the *anteater* and the *fish crow;*

d) characteristic sounds emitted: the *bullfrog*, whose croak resembles a bull's roar; the *catbird*, whose call is like the mewing of a cat; and the *partridge* (Gr. *pérdix*, applied to one who expels wind), from the sound it makes when rising;

e) shape: the *ringworm*, the *spoonbill duck*, the *crossbill* and the *fiddler crab*, which holds its large claw as a fiddler his bow;

f) method of locomotion: the *grasshopper, adelopodes* (animals whose feet are hidden), *reptiles* (Lat. *repere*, to creep), *dromedary* (Gr. *dromas*, running—about nine miles an hour), *bustard* (OF *bistarde*, from Lat. *avis tarda*, slow-walking bird), *duck* (from *ducking*) and *dove* (from *diving*);

g) color: the *redbreast*, the *hare* (related to *hazy, gray*), the *oppossum* (Algon. *apasum*, white beast), the *penguin* (Welsh *pen*, head, plus *gwyn*, white), the *pygarg*, a kind of antelope with white hindquarters (Gr. *pugé*, rump, plus *argós*, white), *albatross* (corruption from Lat. *albus*, white, plus Port. *alcatras*, cormorant) and *beaver* (OE *beofor*, brown);

h) odor exuded: the *muskrat* (from its musky smell), the *pismire*, from the urinous smell of an anthill (ME *pissemyre*, from *piss*, plus *mire*, ant), and the Ger. *Stinktier*, skunk;

i) facial expression: the *dodo* (Port. *doudo*, stupid);

j) mode of scratching: *racoon* (Algon. *arathcone*, he scratches with his hands);

k) mode of excretion: the *butterfly*, whose excrement resembles butter, and the *shitepoke heron*, because of the way it empties its bowels when frightened by a shot.

When confronted with two or more criteria, demanding a split decision, Adam adopted more than one name: *turkey* (Turkey) and Fr. *coq d'Inde* (India); *pewit*, from its cry, or *lapwing*, from its motion (OE *hleápan*, to leap, plus *winc*, to totter); the name of the *owl*, which he at first mistook for a feathered cat, he derived from its doleful hooting (Eng. owl, (h)owl; Lat. *ulula*, Swah. *babewatoto*) and also from its glaring eyes (Gr. *glauks* from *glaúkos*, blue, gray, hence glaring); Finn. *pöllö*, owl = staring eyes, *pöllö-pää*, to gape; the *lynx* received its name from its light color or from its sharp eyes. An additional factor which complicated Adam's task was the relative distance between the animals and himself. This determined the length of the vowels in the name because the tongue, in accordance with a theory now associated with the name of Piaget but which goes back to Aulus Gellius and Nigidius Figulus, instinctively imitates the space relation of the namer's body to the object, so that the vowels made with the shortened tongue are attached to the animals close by, as the *hen*, the *lamb* or the *squirrel*, and those made with the protruding tongue are extended to those farther removed, as the *mole*, the *cow* and the *owl*.

Adam did not permit himself to be diverted by deceptive sounds or arbitrary combinations at the expense of good sense as did poets of a later age. He did not exploit "apt alliteration's artful aid" to suggest the clatter of hoofbeats (Virgil), hissing serpents (Racine) or the progress of rats (Browning's "The Pied Piper"). Sound alone, which beguiles the ear without engaging the mind, is an unreliable vehicle for thought. The commonplace must not be made alluring by tawdry adornment; the mule's head need not be hung with tinkling bells. Adam called the horse a horse and not Pegasus, the lion a lion and not the father of roaring, the camel a camel and not the ship of the desert. His aim was not to copy reality in every detail in the manner of the "material imitation" of the pre-Platonic philosophers who regarded language as a passive stamp of reality, every sound having an innate quality which makes it suitable to represent certain ideas; he followed Plato's theory of "ideal imitation" where a word expresses the inner essence of a thing, the meaning behind the ever changing object. This view is rejected by those who hold to the "convention theory" according to which words acquire meaning not from their sounds but by common agreement. A word merely provides an appropriate mode of conveying our thoughts, and its meaning is defined by custom and mutual agreement. The sound of a word tells us as little about its meaning as a key about the contents of a room or a seashell about the marine life that haunts the deep. Adam could have given different names to the same creature (Eng. *ewe*, Arab. *najat*) or the same name (Eng. *ewe*, Hung. *juh*); or two different animals could have received the same name (Eng. *dog*, Heb. *dag*, fish). This is the ever recurrent argument advanced against the theory of "ideal imitation" since the days of the Sophists when Democritus refuted Heraclitus: there is no natural connection between a word and the thing it designates. But Adam's names could not have been submitted to anyone for agreement by the very nature of the case. They rang true of their own accord because his speech was a reflection of his reason, his *oratio* flowed from his *ratio*. That is, his basic agreement did not come from the arbitrary corroboration of mortal men but from God who inspired him with the breath of life and who vouched for his speech, as we shall see in the next chapter.

THE JOUST WITH THE DEVIL

A rabbinic legend which has come down to us represents the naming scene in the Garden as a verbal contest or spelling bee among Adam, the angels and the Devil. The angels, of course, were the first to be eliminated, for angels are notoriously poor linguists. They are too conceited (that is, conceptual), and since they speak to God face to face, their diaphanous words are defecated of all opaqueness. Their sensuous functions have been extinguished so that they have no idea of sensible images, metaphor, tones or gestures. They have no need in their noumenal sphere of these seductive and puzzling artifices. Their penchant for unashamed abstraction is the deepest strain in their make-up. The thick facts in the redundant realm of feeling are totally foreign to the angelic mood. Eliminated in the very first round, the angels retired behind the Lord to watch the principals from the background. On the other side, infant History, still unoccupied, was wistfully awaiting the incubation of the second creation. We now see Adam emerging from the wings of the green stage, skipping his way amid the fragrant foliage. The Devil then entered from the north on horseback, as is his custom. Adam, though chaste and vigorous, was no match for the Devil, whose impetuous mind, unburdened by moral scruples and sharpened in the struggle with virtue, was fit to rend into pieces the most recalcitrant material. He was even then an expert in language, a past master of polyptoton, epanados, opomnemonysis, anacoenosis and persiflage, and could quote Scripture by heart. He knew the hang of things in this hurly-burly world of illusion and deception. His aggressive mind hankered after concrete ideas in the world of flesh. He never lost sight of the innumerable portents of mortality in the stubborn world of sense, the material base that lies at the root of words— the eye in *daisy* (OE *daeges éage,* day's eye), the ass in *easel* (Dut. *ezel,* ass), the groove in *delirium* (Lat. *de* plus *lira,* furrow, that is, not in the groove), the buttocks in *recoil* (Lat. *re* plus *culus,* the posteriors) and the testicles in *orchid* (Gr. *órkhis,* testicle). The Devil, unlike the angels, was at home in the world of phenomena. He knew how to combine pure concepts with empirical intuitions, the sound with the inner form, which is the basic principle of linguistic creation. No wonder he was self-assured and confident of victory.

The Lord then passed before the contestants the ox, the camel and the ass, in the order named. A Midrashic footnote informs us that only *one* animal, namely, the ox, was presented, since the Hebrew text gives only the singular form: "And the Lord brought *it* to Adam to see what he would call *it*." This, however, could only mean that Adam was still unfamiliar with the plural number. The dual number was first devised by Noah, according to the available linguistic data, when he reviewed the animals two by two as they embarked. To Adam, however, the animals were presented one by one until the zoological parade was completed, with the exception of the pig and the cat, which were created later in Noah's Ark, the pig being formed from the elephant's trunk in order to dispose of the accumulated garbage and the cat being sneezed forth by the lion so as to rid the boat of rats. In any case, the Devil, heckled by the unfriendly spectators, became rattled and failed to give the proper names to the first three animals presented. Thereupon Adam, without hesitation, pronounced the right names and was hailed victor. How did he contrive to win the contest against such superior odds?

At this point a rabbinic tradition comes to our rescue with an amazing particular not generally known; namely, that this verbal duel had been previously "fixed" by the Lord, who deliberately revealed to Adam the proper answers by a mnemonic device concealed within the question; that is, the Divine Interlocutor framed the questions in such a manner that the first letter of the first word of the question was the same as the first letter of the name of the animal under consideration. The Devil had hoped for little sympathy but he was not prepared for this unscrupulous ruse. It turned his enthusiasm to bitterness. As soon as he detected the unethical stratagem, he retired to the shades vowing vengeance. His chagrin spurred him to undertake the most arduous tasks. After he had planned and executed the Fall, he was condemned to the confines of the netherworld. He managed to escape later by hiding behind the donkey when it was taken into the Ark before the Deluge. Since then the Devil has had his tail in everything. He has invented paper money, dabbled in chemistry and has learned to play all the instruments in the orchestra, although having a marked preference for the French horn. He is also credited with the authorship of the largest Bible in existence, the so-called Devil's Bible, which is preserved in the Royal Library of Stockholm. The Manichean heretics were impressed with these achievements, and concluded that he had created at least half of the world and that we are all made in his image. His cleverest ruse, however, has been to convince the moderns (except the Scots, who claim to possess his tomb at Kirkcaldy, the birthplace of Adam Smith) that he does *not* exist. If true, this would be a great blow to the theologians. The Devil himself, however, has recorded that he loves humanity more than man who has outdeviled him a hundredfold (compare Leonid Andreyev's *Satan's Diary* for a moving account of his torments at the hands of men).

Now, from this divine Intervention at the very dawn of human history we can gain a number of linguistic and pedagogical insights of prime importance. In the first place it is evident that Adam in naming the animals applied a priori principles not derived from his own meager experience. That is, the God-given rational principle, which is the *conditio sine qua non* of all knowledge, was already part of man's mind and operative in the spiritual activity of naming, else he would not have understood God's promptings. Abravanel of Portugal, the last of the Jewish Aristotelians at the time of Columbus, formulated this principle as follows: "God created language according to nature; and when He created man, He created in him the principles of language." This formulation is based on the phrase "and man became a living soul" (Genesis 2:7), which in the Aramaic translation, obviously influenced by the Stoics, is rendered "and the breath of life became in man a speaking spirit." Corroboration for this rational conviction has been found by exegetes in the verb *to see* in our text (Genesis 2:19), from which they deduce that the Lord was watching Adam during the contest, just as a teacher watches his pupil, *to see* whether the lesson had been learned well. From this we learn that God is the Author of language, that He imparted it to Adam when He prompted him to name the animals He presented to his gaze, and that man "caught on" because God had condescended to breathe the breath of life into the dust He had formed so that He could speak to man on common ground. This divine Whispering holds things together in the perceptual world and is the guarantee of the validity of human communication. Prayer precedes speech, and words have meaning only in relation to the Word. The collaboration between the human and the divine gives language its substance. Adam thus becomes the Interpreter of the divine, which is the proper function of the prophet.

The Devil, with all his prodigious learning, could not withstand this sagacious division of labor. He knew the law, but Adam knew the Judge of whose protection he was assured: "And I have put my words in thy mouth, and I have covered thee in the shadow of mine hand, that I may plant the heavens and lay the foundations of the earth" (Isaiah 51:16). The animals could have been named by the Lord, but He relegated the task to Adam for pedagogical reasons, to summon him to use his reason, to make him responsible in a dialogic situation and to give him the opportunity for re-creation. Though God could have prompted Adam with the entire name of the animal in question, He preferred to give him only the first letter, a mere hint. For each man must appropriate the truth on his own as a free act of ethical choice. Repetition by rote deprives the student of the challenge to make decisions by increasing his dependence upon the teacher. A teacher's precepts should be deliberately vague, since the circumstances in life are too varied and intricate for the arbitrary application of specific rules. The function of the teacher is to present problems, not solutions; to give yeast, not bread. Truth does not fall into the student's mouth like a ripe apple. Thus did God convey His purposes to Adam in this first lesson. God was the coining master, but Adam had to learn the value of money through his own responsible labors.

WORKING WITH THE SELECTION

1. Beneath his surface brilliance, Jacobs seems to be concerned with fundamental principles and basic understandings. Locate at least one place in the text in which he seems to imply each of the following ideas:
    a. The giving of names is basic in the growth of language.
    b. The widespread notion that all words reflect in their sound the objects they name is silly.
    c. If a person is ever to understand language he must work with it.
    d. The nature of language must somehow grow out of the nature of man.
    e. However we define divinity, there must be something divine in language.

2. Early settlers in the New World were a little like Adam; they found the continent full of strange plants, animals, fish, and even strange insects. How did they solve the problem of needing names for new things? A good place to look for the answer is in any standard dictionary of Americanisms, such as *A Dictionary of American English* or *A Dictionary of Americanisms.* You might try looking up common words, such as *duck, grass,* and even *red.* Try also some unusual words, such as *woodchuck, quahog,* and *menhaden.*

2

Getting Named in the Bible Belt

Thomas Pyles

Whenever a child is born, the parents assume in a limited way the godlike powers of name-giving, but not always do they approach this portentous event with the self-imposed dignity that Jacobs attributes to Adam, or at least so much is suggested by Thomas Pyles in "Bible Belt Onomastics or Some Curiosities of Anti-Pedobaptist Nomenclature," Names: Journal of the American Name Society, 7 *(June, 1959), from which the following selection is taken. Pyles, professor of English and linguistics at Northwestern University, is perhaps best known for* Words and Ways of American English *(1952) and* The Origins and Development of the English Language, 2nd ed. *(1971).*

In a youth agreeably misspent *in partibus infidelium,* I was little conscious of the tendencies in name-giving with which I am here concerned. It is true that names which were thought strange or amusing did in those days occasionally come to one's attention, but they were almost invariably cited as curiosa and equated with naïveté, inferior social standing, and ignorance. They were more or less sporadic even on the social level at which they were believed most likely to occur and were regarded as the creations of those who led drab and lowly lives—the onomastic *bijouterie* of the underprivileged.

It was not indeed until my translation, fairly late in life, first to the southwestern and later to the southeastern sector of the Bible Belt—in Mencken's classic definition, as utilized by M. M. Mathews in the *Dictionary of Americanisms,* "those parts of the country in which the literal accuracy of the Bible is credited and clergymen who preach it have public influence"—that I first became aware of such names in high places. To what extent the onomastic mores with which I am here concerned have become nationwide I do not really know. Mr. Thomas L. Crowell in *American Speech* (XXIII [1948], 265–272) contributes some very fruity specimens from Washington, a city which has a more or less transient population, and has collected similar examples in New York City. Mencken also cites a good many from outside the Bible Belt. It is likely that the isoglosses demarcating the Fancy Names Belt have by now spread considerably beyond the limits of the Bible Belt. Two World Wars have brought hosts of anti-pedobaptists from the hills to the towns and cities, where their fecundity has shown no signs of abating.

Their places of worship have moved from deserted stores to gaudy, neon-illuminated erections and, among the more sophisticated, to tabernacles of neo-Gothic and colonial meeting-house architecture. But the moral, social, and ecclesiastical customs of the rural Bethels linger on, as do also the naming habits of the remoter areas, despite increasing prosperity, superficial sophistication, and considerable distinction in business, politics, and the professions on the part of many. In the towns of the inland South and even to a large extent in the cities, the pastors of these formerly more or less obscure religious bodies[1] have retained much of the public influence which they and their predecessors had in the hill country, but unlike the pedobaptist men of God whom they have displaced in prestige, they exert no influence over the name-giving habits of those committed to their charge. The naming of Christians is no part of their ghostly office. . . .

The effect of these circumstances peculiar to our American religious life in the matter of name-giving is obvious. Where name-giving is no part of the sacrament of baptism, and where consequently a clergyman with some sense of traditional onomastic decorum has no say, individual taste and fancy may run riot—and usually do. It is highly unlikely that any man of God, even though the canons of his church were not explicit in the matter, would consent in the course of his sacerdotal duties to confer upon hapless infants such names as Buzz Buzz, Coeta, Merdine, Aslean, La Void, Arsie, Phalla, and Raz—all legal names borne by Bible Belters of repute. And it is certain that Ima Hogg, the *grande dame* of Houston society, whose father was once governor of Texas, was so named without the connivance of any anointed priest.

One result of the increasing numbers and prestige of anti-pedobaptists has thus been, ironically enough, the decline of the Christian name in what is certainly the most self-consciously and vocally Christian of all lands, where God's name is minted into the very currency and He runs on all sides of every political campaign. It has also, incidentally, given rise to a new type of urban Christianity, quite unlike anything ever known in Europe and probably never before known even in this nation under God.

The proud bearers of the names which I shall shortly begin to cite are all, unless otherwise specified, Christian Caucasians of good standing in their communities—people of sufficient importance that their engagements, their marriages, their parturitions, and, alas, their deaths are recounted fairly fully

---

[1] The Baptists were of course never obscure in American life. But there are now, according to my friend and former student, the Reverend James Sims, himself a Baptist pastor, at least 117 other anti-pedobaptist denominations among the 272 listed in the 1956 *World Almanac*. (Of still others he was not sure.) The groups most prominent in the inland South, in addition to the various Baptist bodies, are the Assemblies of God, the Churches of Christ, the Disciples of Christ, Jehovah's Witnesses, the Churches of God, the Pentecostal Assemblies, and the Church of the Nazarene.

on "society" pages and in full-length obituaries in the newspapers,[2] which are a veritable onomastic treasure-trove. Other important sources have been class lists, yearbooks, official lists of voters and of property owners, telephone directories, and commencement programs. These last have provided entertainment and instruction during many commencement addresses by atomic physicists, business executives, industrialists, generals, and presidents of neighboring colleges and universities panting after yet another honorary doctorate to add to their string. Many of my handsomest specimens were collected under such otherwise depressing circumstances. It should be obvious that the names culled from these sources are not those of the underprivileged, the economically depressed, or whatever the current term for "poor and lowly" happens to be. Nor are such names to be regarded as nicknames, since they appear in formal and dignified surroundings—those in the commencement programs being obviously the same as those which appear in Old English calligraphy on diplomas.

The formal and official use of diminutives by adults is quite common in the Belt. The most popular of these diminutives is Billy (with "clear" *l*), usually masculine, though considered perfectly appropriate for women also, with Bobby, Johnny, and Jimmy—also bisexual—running slightly behind. In a single year (1950), no fewer than eighteen Billys, including two Billy Joes, two Billy Genes, and one feminine Billye, received degrees from the University of Oklahoma. In addition, there were four Willies.[3] At the University of Florida in the same year, three Billys graduated from a single college, Business Administration.

So prestigious is Billy, in fact, that one of Florida's representatives in Congress, Hon. Donald Ray Matthews, has adopted the name, using the official style D. R. (Billy) Matthews. It is unlikely that many of his constituents are even aware that *Billy* is a *nom de guerre*. For similar reasons doubtless, Rev. Dr. Billy Graham long ago abandoned the full form of his name, which happens really to be William. ("We don't put on airs in God's family.") Diminutive forms occur frequently in combination with clipped forms, as in the previously mentioned Billy Joe and Billy Gene, and with non-hypocoristic forms, as in Billy Donald, Larry Leroy, and Jerry Roscoe.

I have collected scores of printed instances of diminutives and apparent diminutives used as legal names by adults, some of them adults of advanced years, some recently gone to their Great Reward. Most of these are commonplace enough (like Dannie, Davie, and Maxie), most are bisexual, and some are diminutives by virtue of their endings, without being necessarily derivative. Only Zippie (Mrs. Billy), Sippie, Vandie, Watie, Beadie, Lamie, Collie, Cossie, Ossie, Carlie (Mrs. Bobby), Omie (f.), Fonzy, Lonzie, Lokie, Mammie, Toppy, Schiley, Mealy, Bussie, Jadie Obie (m.), Nicy, Dicey, Ledgie,

[2] Among my richest sources are the Oklahoma City *Daily Oklahoman*, the Norman (Okla.) *Transcript*, the Jacksonville *Florida Times-Union*, and the Gainesville (Fla.) *Sun*.

[3] The preferred spelling of the *W*-form seems to be *Willie* rather than *Willy*.

Raffie, Dilly, Coarsey, Sugie, Urksey, Skeety, and Ripsie seem to me particularly noteworthy, though I confess to a personal fondness for the comparatively conventional Early Bill and Jody Elijah.

. . . Often a hypocoristic name becomes so closely identified with a person that it is customarily inserted in parentheses after his legal given names or initials. This retention of what in some instances must be by-names acquired in school is by no means confined to the Bible Belt though it is probably of more frequent occurrence in anti-pedobaptist civilization than in the Sodoms and Gomorrahs of the Atlantic Coast. I must confess that I was brought up suddenly by the following item from the Gainesville *Sun* (Oct. 1, 1952, p. 5): "Friends of Mr. A. W. (Poopy) Roundtree, Sr., will be interested to know that he is recuperating following an operation in Lake City." Similar, if less colorful, specimens, all taken from printed sources, are Tootie, Tucky, Bus, Tiny (male principal of an elementary school), and Lefty. . . .

I am convinced that such forms as Buddy, Bubba, Bud, Buck, Sonny, Bunnie, and Buster, which occur with an almost nauseating frequency, are legal names, not merely alternate names like those cited just previously, since they appear alone in formal connotations without quotation marks. They are frequently preceded by honorifics, as in an account of a reception following a large church wedding at which Mrs. Buddy was "floor hostess"—whatever that is—and Mrs. Buster greeted guests. (*Times-Union*, Feb. 20, 1949, p. 11.) The ceremony might have been performed either by Rev. Buck or by Rev. Buddy, both of whom are in my files, but I regret to say that it was not. A third-generation Buddy is indicated in "A.O.M. 2-c. Buddy E. C. Kelly III, son of Mrs. Clara Kelly and the late Mr. Buddy E. C. Kelly, Jr." [4] A new trend may be indicated by the fact that a Mr. and Mrs. Buddy named their son Ronald Eugene (*Times-Union*, Aug. 18, 1958, p. 22) and a Mr. and Mrs. Sonny named theirs Randy Allen (*loc. cit.*). . . .

Because they share a certain indefinable folksy quality which is highly regarded in the inland South, I have grouped the following names, some of them derivative forms, together; all are borne by substantial citizens: Lum, Dub, Teet, Quince, Zack, Zeph, Zeb, Clem, Wash, and Sim. Had I never been privileged to live in the Bible Belt, I should have thought to this day that their only existence was in the literature of backhouse humor. *Ish,* though it had no previous associations for me, seems to me nevertheless to have the same homely, down-to-earth flavor. It is borne by Hon. Ish W. Brant, Superintendent of Public Instruction of Duval County, Florida (the county seat of which is Jacksonville), who has the additional distinction of being governor of the Florida District of Kiwanis International. When Hon. Ish was merely a candidate for the political office which he now holds with grace and distinction, his campaign slogan was "Ish Is Everybody's Wish." His opponents were Mr. Coke L. Barr and Mrs. Iva Sprinkle. . . .

I hasten to cite a few miscellaneous whimsicalities, all full names, which

---

[4] This gem appeared in the Gainesville *Sun*. The cutting is in my possession, but I carelessly neglected to take down the date.

have appealed to me for one reason or another: Oleander Lafayette Fitz-gerald III, Ed Ek, Shellie Swilley, Early Hawaiian McKinnon, Sandy Gandy, Earl Curl, Jr., Percy Nursey, Rev. Fay de Sha (m.), Lovie Slappey, Esperanza LeSocke, Pamela Gay Day, Staff-Sgt. Mehogany Brewer, Girlie Burns, Fawn Grey Trawick Dunkle, Alure Sweat (f., sister of Alfa, Alta, Sabry, and the late Cleveland Sweat [*Times-Union,* Feb. 12, 1958, p. 22]), Bloomer Bedenbaugh, Martha Magdalene Toot, Okla Bobo, and Melody Clinkenbeard. The last-cited given name may be bisexual, for a fellow towns-man of Miss Clinkenbeard's is Hon. Melody Reynolds, an officer of the Veterans of Foreign Wars in Norman, Oklahoma. The same bisexuality seems to be characteristic of Memory: Hon. Memory Martin is lieutenant governor of division 6, Florida Kiwanis district, as well as a former school teacher and principal; my files also disclose Memorie Frances Griner, whom I take to be female from the spelling of the second name. Hon. Cowboy Pink Williams, former Lieutenant Governor of Oklahoma, was defeated to succeed himself in 1958 despite a style which should have endeared him to all Southwesterners. It is possible that Cowboy Pink is merely a *nom de guerre,* but the hon. gentleman is so listed in the 1958 *World Almanac* and in the *Britannica* Yearbook.

WORKING WITH THE SELECTION

1. Many American parents name their offspring for an ancestor or for a person they admire; sometimes they choose a name just because they like the sound of it. This has not always been the fashion, if we can rely on earlier records and the evidence names themselves provide. Sort the following common given names into categories; then try to derive from the categories some of the prin-ciples that seem to have affected name-giving. If you do not know the meaning of a name, a good dictionary should provide the information.

John	Ruth	Margarite	Mark
Joe	Rose	Lily	Dora
Jo	Charlotte	Dorothy	Gary
Dorothea	Edmund	Toni	Gerald
Opal	Edgar	Ruby	Caroline
Diana	Dolly	Marjorie	William
Bruce	Grant	Graham	Sarah
Faith	Robert	Douglas	Jacob
Charles	Helen	Elizabeth	Jane
Jake	Daisy	Mary	James
Violet	Pearl	Matthew	Dave
Edward	Tony	Paul	Esther
Charity	Hope	Dot	Minerva

2. Which biblical names have been popular, and why? Mary is probably the most popular name for girls. Jesus is not often used for boys in English-speaking countries, though it is in many Spanish-speaking parts of the world. The reason for this contrast may be both social and psychological, and not easy to

determine, but the reasons behind many other choices are obvious. John is popular in many languages, appearing also as Johannes, Hans, Ivan, Jan, Jean, and Ian, in the girl's names Jeanne, Joanna, and Joan, and probably in the surnames Jones and Evans. The name John means 'Yahweh is gracious.' What can be said about some other religious names? Tige, a common name for the Devil, is given to dogs but not to men.

3. What have been recent trends in name-giving? Sharon and Jennifer are much more common than they used to be; Celeste and Eugenia are much less popular. Try comparing lists like those Pyles used; for example, compare the names of seniors in an old yearbook with those in a recent one, or the names of the brides on the society page with those of their mothers.

3

Surnames from Occupations

P. H. Reaney

Given names, as the phrase implies, are given by somebody, but surnames often grow naturally and tend to be inherited. In the following selection from The Origin of English Surnames (*1967*), *P. H. Reaney describes the kinds of names that grew from occupations on an English manor. The contemporary authority on names in English, Reaney is the editor of* A Dictionary of British Surnames (*1961*) *and the author of* The Origin of English Place Names (*1961*) *and many studies concerned with local English history.*

The *Bailiff* or *Bailey,* with *Bayliss* (OFr *bailif* (acc.), *baillis* (nom.), later *bailli*) or sergeant, whatever his title, was a free man of importance as the mouthpiece of the lord by whom he was appointed. At Droxford he received £6 per annum as compared with the ploughman's 8*s.* and the shepherd's 4*s.* He lived in the manor-house at the lord's expense and was the general supervisor of agricultural policy. It was his duty to see that the services due were not evaded or ill-performed and to direct and determine the men's work. Originally meaning 'carrier', later 'manager, administrator', the term was also used of the public administrator of a district, the chief officer of a hundred or of an officer of justice under a sheriff, a warrant officer, pursuivant and a catchpoll.

Beadle or constable, messor or hayward—it is impossible to separate their duties for the terms were interchangeable. He was either chosen by the lord or elected by the homage, one of the lesser men of the village. He had to make all summonses ordered by the hallmote, levy distresses, take pledges, make attachments and collect fines. In fact, he acted as the village policeman. The surname survives in various forms. *Beadel* and *Beedle* may be from either OFr *bedel* or OE *bydel*. The latter has also given *Biddell, Biddle, Buddell* and *Buddles*. Other possible meanings are 'messenger of justice, under-bailiff, tipstaff', 'apparitor', 'mace-bearer', 'crier or usher of a law-court', 'town-crier'. The alternative *Sargeant* (OFr *sergent, seriant*) was a very common surname, probably in general 'servant', latinised as *serviens*. It was commonly used of the king's sergeants, tenants by military service under the rank of a knight and of officers of justice, e.g. William Roculf bailiff of Worcester (1320 Pat) and John de Halteby constable of Ipswich (1315 Pat). *Constable* (OFr *cunestable,* from Lat *comes stabuli* 'count of the stable') may also denote 'the chief officer of the household or court', 'governor of a royal fortress', 'military officer' and 'parish constable'.

Of all the manorial officers, the two most important were the hayward and the reeve. The original duties of the former seem to have been to protect the fences round the Lammas lands when enclosed for hay (Coulton), hence his name, OE *heȝe-weard* 'guardian of the fence or hedge'. This *heȝe* was a dead hedge easily erected and removed, forming an enclosure (OE *(ge)hæg*) from which, to judge from the early and regular variation between *heiward* and *haiward,* and from his more general duties of preventing cattle from breaking through into the enclosed fields and growing crops, the hayward seems also to have been called *(ge)hægweard* 'enclosure-protector'; cf. (from *Piers Plowman*): 'Canstow . . . have an horne and be haywarde, and liggen oute a nyghtes, And kepe my corn in my croft fro pykers and þeeues?' It was his duty to see that breaches in the hedges were repaired and straying cattle impounded, to serve under certain conditions as an officer of the hallmote, to levy distresses, make attachments and collect fines. *Hayward* is a very common surname; its Latin equivalent *Messer* (OFr *messier, messer* 'harvester', from Low Lat *messarius* 'hayward'), frequent in the Middle Ages, is now rare.

The *Reeve* was 'only a little less important as one of the management of a manor than he was as the chief officer of a village'. He was of servile origin, usually elected by the villeins for a year at Michaelmas, though his term of office was frequently extended. Men paid fines to escape the onerous duties involved. Though a villein, he was a man of substance, holding a yardland, strictly accountable to the lord for all that concerned the manorial economy. As reeve, he was quit of all or a large part of the services due and was often paid a stipend with such perquisites as a horse in the lord's stable or a special piece of land as reeve. He ate at the lord's table in the manor house from Lammas to Michaelmas (i.e. during harvest) and was responsible (with the bailiff or sergeant) for the management of the lord's demesne farm, especially for overseeing work-services owed by villeins. He had to see 'that the keepers of all kinds of beasts do not go to fairs, or markets, or wrestling-matches, or taverns, whereby the beasts may go astray without guard or do harm to the lord or another, but they must ask leave and put keepers in their places that no harm may happen'. Some collected the lord's rents, took over tenements which had escheated to the lord, distrained men to do homage and fealty, had power of giving permission to villeins' daughters to marry outside the manor and had custody of the rolls of the hallmote. More often than not it was the reeve and not the bailiff who accounted every year for the income and outgo of the manor-rents, profits of courts, sales of corn and stock and all expenditure. In Northumbria the term used was ONorthumb *græfa,* originally 'governor of a province', later 'overseer, manager, head-workman on a farm, farm-bailiff', surviving as *Grieve(s).* In Yorkshire we have ME *greyve,* from ON *greifi* 'steward', 'a person in charge of property', the origin of the modern *Grave(s).*

Although not, strictly speaking, surnames of office, manorial tenants often held their land on condition of performing particular duties. In the Durham *Boldon Buke* of 1183 it is frequently the work required which names the tenement, not that of the tenant, e.g. *Quidam carbonarius* 'charcoal-burner' (now *Collier*) holds one toft, a croft and four acres and finds the coal for making the iron-work of the ploughs. Similarly, the smith and the miller held their land in return for specific services. The *Miller* was commonly one of the most considerable men of the village. The lord had a monopoly of the village mill and the villeins were compelled to take their corn to his mill to be ground. The revenue of the mill came from the multure, that share of the flour which the miller kept in payment for his services. The mill was usually let to farm to the miller, the village capitalist, who was always suspected of adding to his gains by sharp practice, by using false measures and other frauds. He was forbidden to water or change corn sent to him or to give worse for better. He was not to keep hogs or more than three hens and a cock; 'gluttonous geese' especially were forbidden. The miller was also known as *Milner* and *Millward, Millard* and *Mellard* and, less commonly, by the French terms *Mulliner, Mullender* and *Mullinger* (OFr *molinier*).

The frequency of *Smith,* our most common surname, is due chiefly to the blacksmith who was ubiquitous. We find him on every manor and in the towns where the smiths congregated in such streets as Smythen Street in Exeter, but partly to workers in other metals who could also be called simply *smith.* OE *smiþþe,* too, has contributed to the name, Robert *atte Smyth* 1332 SRSx, 'worker at the smithy'. The surname is even more common than would appear for it survives also in the Lat *Faber* and the French *Feaver* (OFr *fevere*) and *Ferrar* and *Farrer* (OFr *ferreor* 'worker in iron') which has also become *Farrow.* In the manor, the smith was of less substance than the miller. He might be a free-holder or a villein and he held his land in return for his work. At Aldingbourne in Sussex, for example, the smith's widow held four acres of land and in return rendered 100 horseshoes a year to the lord's chamber, 50 with eight holes and 50 with six, without nails, for which she received 25*d*. She had to shoe the steward's hackney at all his comings if needed and for this she had 1*d*. for the four shoes. She also had to shoe the sergeant's horse and the carter's horse all the year at

1d. for the four shoes. In addition, she was to make of the lord's iron and mend and sharpen the irons of two ploughs all the year and to charge nothing, to mend the irons of the other two ploughs when needed and for this the lord was to pay. She had her coals of the lord's wood at the three terms and her dinner while the lord stayed on the manor. The lord was to plough all her land till sowing was done.

Just as the peasant was not allowed to grind his corn where he wished, so he was forbidden to bake his bread at home or anywhere save in a special oven constructed for the purpose and belonging to the lord. Many peasants had no means of baking at home. The lord's oven was generally rented to an individual or to the peasants as a body. The village oven or bakehouse was a communal convenience. Hence we have not only the common surnames *Baker* and *Baxter* but also *Ovens,* John *Attenouene* 1276 AssSo, from OE *ofen* 'oven', *Backhouse, Bacchus, Backus,* Robert *atte bachus* 1289 NorwDeeds, 'worker at the bakehouse', with the French *Bullinger, Pullinger* and *Pillinger* (OFr *boulengier* 'baker'), *Furner* and *Fournier* (OFr *furnier*), and *Pester, Pistor* (AFr *pestour, pistour,* Lat *pistor*). . . .

Such surnames as *Shepherd, Swinerd* or *Swinnard* 'swine-herd' and *Nothard* or *Nutter* (ON *naut* 'beast, ox', neat-herd) may be something more than mere occupational-names. They may refer to a specific office or service undertaken for the benefit of the community. More often than not, perhaps, each family designated one of its members to be shepherd for its own sheep. Many custumals stipulate that no tenement need send its shepherd to reap and carry the lord's corn: he could not be spared from his job of keeping the sheep on the fallows and out of the corn. It was also common for the men of a village to choose village neatherds, village shepherds and village swineherds, to keep the stock of all the village and the neighbours assessed themselves for the wages of the common herdsmen; cf. *Tunnard* (OE **tūn-hierde*) 'guardian of the village or town animals'.

Among the lesser officers of the manor, we may note *Granger* 'one in charge of a grange or outlying farm', farm-bailiff; *Parker* 'keeper of the park', usually a deer-park; *Warrener* or *Warner,* the officer employed to watch over game in a park or preserve, and the *Pinder,* responsible for impounding stray beasts on the manor.

WORKING WITH THE SELECTION

1. Many occupational names are obvious—Gardner and Bookbinder, for example —but some that seem obvious are not: a farmer was a tax collector before he became one who paid fees on land "farmed out." The origin of many names is obscure, however, because the occupation has declined or the appearance of the word for it is unfamiliar, having changed or come from a language other than English. Some names derive from more than one source; Bower can mean a maker of bows, or it can be an English spelling of German *Bauer* 'farm laborer.' Look up the following names in a dictionary of names and explain their most commonly accepted origins.

Brewster	Fletcher	Mercer	Stewart
Chaucer	Fuller	Palmer	Waner
Clark	Knight	Potter	Webster
Cooper	Leech	Sherman	Wright

Think of other names whose origin is obvious, like Fisher and Hunter; the suffix -er means something like 'one who does.' If you know a foreign language, you will know why some names—Fischer, Müller (or Moller), and Marchant, for example—are spelled as they are.

2. Surnames do not come only from occupations, of course. There are many ways in which a man or a family can get a surname. One common one is through family relationships. Presumably, the Wilsons got their name, directly or indirectly, from somebody who was Will's son, as the Larsons got theirs from Lars's son, the Nelsons from Nels's son. But several other syllables that have gone into surnames also mean 'son': fitz (Anglo-Norman, that is, French in England); Mc, Mac, and Mak (Scottish and Irish); vitch, vich, and vic (Slavic languages, including Russian and Polish); and ap (Welsh). Thus Macmillan presumably means 'son of the shaveling,' whether the bald person was a tonsured divine or a shaved servant.

3. Many given names have become surnames: John, Johns, James, George, Peter, Williams, Henry. Some given names have been obscured; Jones and Evans are presumably Welsh forms of John or Johnson. Can you turn up others?

4. Some cultures have produced but few occupational names. Among these are most tribes of North American Indians. Can you imagine why?

4

Salt-Derived Place Names in the Ohio Valley

John A. Jakle

Professor of geography at the University of Illinois, John A. Jakle is a linguistic geographer with a special interest in onomastics. In the following selection, from an article that appeared in Names: Journal of the American Name Society, 16 (March, 1968), *Jakle offers one example of a kind of name-giving that has occurred with many variations in many lands since the dawn of language.*

During the late eighteenth and early nineteenth centuries settlers in the Ohio Valley found their salt supply a critical economic concern. Most pioneer farmers pursued a subsistence agriculture, but cattle-raising as a commercial endeavor was equally important. Through the sale of beef or pork, either salted or on the hoof, the western farmer obtained cash to purchase powder, iron goods, and other necessities and to pay his annual tax bill as well. Yet without adequate salt livestock could not survive on the western frontier; nor could animals deprived of the vital salt element be slaughtered, for such activity necessitated salt-curing.

After 1783 a commercial salt industry developed at many of the Valley's larger salt springs,[1] but several attempts to monopolize the salt trade in Kentucky and strict governmental control of salines in Ohio, Indiana, and Illinois greatly restricted salt manufacture. Farmers forced to subsistence salt production as well as land speculators, eager for premium land prices, searched the Valley for the necessary springs from which individual families or even whole neighborhoods could produce a limited salt supply. A rich place name heritage derived from this activity.

The first settlers to utilize the Valley's salt springs were hunters for bison, deer, and elk, once attracted to the salines to lick the salt-encrusted earth, and particularly vulnerable to the well concealed rifleman. Thus salt springs were initially characterized and named for the attractive influence which they exerted over game animals. Gilbert Imlay, an early geographer of the Trans-Appalachian West, wrote, "A salt spring is called a Lick, from the earth about them being furrowed out, in a most curious manner, by the buffalo and deer, which lick the earth on account of the saline particles with which it is impregnated."[2] This term, applied by the hunters, continued in the popular usage long after a farming population came to dominate the region.

These salt licks varied in size from marshes encompassing several acres to small incrustations measured in feet or in inches. Most frequently, however, the lick was actually a spring where saliferous brines derived from entrapped sea-water evaporated on reaching the surface to precipitate deposits of sodium chloride. The Ohio Valley was once covered by an inland sea in which sand, lime, and organic material accumulated to depths of several thousand feet. Under pressure, these buried sediments were consolidated and connate water was entrapped in the interstices between the mineral grains. From

---

[1] The following salines gained pre-eminence in the Ohio Valley between 1783 and 1800: Bullitt's, Mann's, Lower Blue, Big Bone, Drennon's, Ohio, and May's Licks (all in Kentucky) as well as the Muskingum Saline in Ohio and the Saltville Saline in Virginia. After 1800 the Kanawha Saline in West Virginia, the Wabash Saline in Illinois, the Scioto Saline in Ohio, and the Little Sandy and Clay County Salt Works in Kentucky came to dominate the Valley's salt industry.

[2] Gilbert Imlay, *A Topographical Description of The Western Territory of North America* (London: J. Debrett, 1792), pp. 46–47.

these aquifers "fossil sea water" rose (as it does today) along zones of disconformity by way of deep seated faults and fissures to the surface.[3]

The great majority of the Valley's salt springs were known only locally and few were ever recorded even by local antiquarians, so insignificant were their brines considered. Surviving place names such as "lick," "licking," "mahoning," "salt," and "saline" represent for many districts the only evidences of salt availability in the past. . . .

The term "lick" is the most extensively used place name of salt derivation in the Ohio Valley; yet its present usage varies somewhat from its original context. Today the term usually identifies a river or lesser hydrologic feature along which a salt lick had in the past been discovered. Since brines were usually exposed in valley bottoms, it was quite common for settlers to use individual licks in identifying adjacent streams. Thus the term usually appears as a part of a compound specific name, e.g. "Elk Lick Branch," and sometimes, but less frequently, as a pure generic term, e.g. "Elk Lick."[4] In the latter usage "lick" appears as the equivalent of other generic place names, e.g. "branch," "creek," and "run," as these terms serve to identify water courses generally.

The place names "salt" and "saline" were usually applied to large rivers and creeks and were, therefore, less frequently employed. In addition, these place-designations enjoyed more popular usage after 1800 than before; therefore, they are relatively more common in Illinois, Indiana, Ohio, and Tennessee, in areas opened to settlement after the turn of the century. Perhaps the term "saline" was more appropriately applied to springs utilized for commercial salt making purposes, but this generalization is not valid south of the Ohio River where even the largest salt works were more traditionally known as "licks." Indeed, even in the north the infrequent use of the place names "salt" and "saline" reflected the pervasive popularity of the older and more traditional "lick" terminology.

The terms "mahoning" and "licking" were also descriptive of the Valley's salt resource. "Mahoning," derived from the Delaware Indian word "M'hoani," signified "a salt lick."[5] The term "licking" is also of Delaware derivation;[6] however, it is certain that most American settlers attached this place name to the landscape not as an Indian word, but as a corruption of

[3] Paul H. Price, et al., "Springs of West Virginia," *West Virginia Geological Survey,* VI, 1936, pp. 7–8; Gerald C. Gambs and George W. White, "Ohio's Mineral Resources; Salt Reserves," *Ohio State University Studies, Engineering Experiment Station Circular,* No. 49, XV, 1946, p. 4; and Wilbur Stout, et al., "Brines of Ohio," *Ohio Geological Survey Bulletin,* Series 4, No. 37, 1932, p. 15.

[4] Wilbur Zelinsky, "Some Problems in the Distribution of Generic Terms in the Place-Names of the Northeastern United States," *Annals of the Association of American Geographers,* XVL, 1955, p. 324.

[5] August C. Mahr, "Indian River and Place Names in Ohio," *Ohio Archaeological and Historical Quarterly,* LXVI, 1957, p. 143.

[6] *Ibid.*

the term "lick." Today these designations appear infrequently in the Valley, but, since major rivers carry both place names, these terms enjoy a certain degree of notoriety. "Mahoning" appears almost exclusively in the old Delaware region of northwestern Pennsylvania and northeastern Ohio, while "licking" enjoys a somewhat broader usage in Pennsylvania, Ohio, and Kentucky.

It is interesting to note that other place names may have reflected salt's availability. In Indiana, for example, the "Blue," "White," and "Whitewater" Rivers probably received their respective names as well as their distinctive coloration from dissolved saliferous material.[7] So also were the ubiquitously distributed "White," "Paint," and "Blue" Licks appropriately named. Water courses carrying place names depicting white and blue coloration are frequently found on the Valley's topographic maps as tributary, stem, and neighboring streams to water courses carrying specific designations of salt-derivation.

Taken in the aggregate, salt-derived place names, although common throughout the Ohio Valley, appear in greater density in southern Appalachia. There structural discordance has produced a profusion of saline occurrences, and a rash of place names indicative of this salt availability has obviously resulted. Throughout the flatlands of Ohio, Indiana, and Illinois, where a general lack of outcropping bedrock and a preponderance of glacially-derived overburden did not foster a widespread occurrence of surface brines, such place names do not appear in great density. . . .

After 1840, place names reflecting salt availability were attached less frequently to the land. The stimulus to salt exploration had all but disappeared, for the Ohio Valley's economy had rapidly matured. A high quality, low cost, commercial salt product had eliminated the need for subsistence salt production and, since the woodlands and prairies had been largely converted to agriculture, the opportunities to hunt in and about the licks had declined as well. As the Ohio Valley matured, her population turned increasingly to an urbanized commercial economy; in the process an active place name tradition was lost.

WORKING WITH THE SELECTION

1. The land is strewn with place names having generic words that, like *saline* and *lick* in the Ohio Valley, reflect physical features of the region or ways the land is used. Obvious examples are Chesapeake Bay, Niagara Falls, Port Huron, and Jackson Hole. Often these generic words are not readily recognized because they appear in a foreign language or in an obsolete form: *sault*, as in Sault St. Marie, is a French word for *falls; down*, as in Piltdown, is an old form of *dune;* and *hoo*, as in Sutton Hoo, is an old form of *height.* One of the most common combinations of this sort includes a word meaning

[7] David Thomas, *Travels Through the Western Country in the Summer of 1816* (Auburn, New York: David Rumsey, 1819), p. 134.

'dwelling site' or 'enclosed place,' such as *-grad* in Stalingrad and Leningrad. An older form of *-grad* appears in Novgorod 'new town.' A common equivalent in French is *-ville*, as in Deauville, and in German, *-burg*, as in Hamburg. English is rich in such forms, which include variations of the word *town*, such as *-ton*, *-den*, and *-don* (although the last may also represent *dune*). Variations of Old English *burh*, a cognate of German *Burg*, appear as *-burg*, *-burrough*, *-boro*, *-bury*, and the like; variants of Old English *stede*, as in the word *homestead*, can appear as *-sted* or *-stead*. Similar terms borrowed from other languages include *-by* from Old Norse, *-ville*, *-vil*, and *city* from French, and suffixes derived from Latin *castra*, which usually appear as *-caster* or *-chester*. Try to find at least one place name having each of these suffixes or generic terms. For most of them, a map of England will be best; for *-vil*, *-ville*, and *city* you will probably need a map of the United States. Can you guess why? See if you can find any names that mean 'town-town.' For example, if there were a place named Ingtonbury, it could mean 'town-town-town,' since *ing* is also an Old English term for place.

2. Other natural phenomena and uses of land are reflected in place names. What would you make of the following: Hilton, Portsmouth, Cornhill, Cruikshaven, Ravenswood, Fall River, Westlake, Oxford, Newcastle, Bridgewater?

3. Obviously, a place can be named for a person and a person can be named for a place, and this sort of thing can work back and forth. The state of Washington was presumably named for George Washington, but the Washington family must have got the name in part from a place, since *-ing* and *-ton* probably meant something like 'place' and 'farm,' respectively. Lincoln, Nebraska, got its name from Abraham Lincoln, but the Lincoln family presumably got theirs from Lincoln, England. The word *Lincoln*, partly Latin, partly Celtic, means something like '(Roman) colony by the water.' Find twenty more surnames that might have come from place names. Of course you cannot be sure that your guesses are correct; a name can grow in any of several ways. You might guess, for example, that the name Lovelock comes from somebody named Love who lived on a *loch* 'lake.' Actually, the name was probably descriptive of dandified Anglo-Saxons who wore part of their hair curled into lovelocks. Guessing will do no harm, so long as you do not accept the results without first checking them against a good dictionary of names.

4. Look at a map of southern England. Are there many place names with the suffix *-ford*? From this body of names, what would you infer about the drainage system of the area? About the prevalence of bridges during the Middle Ages? What does the scarcity of names like Cambridge suggest?

5. Notice some of the impact of words for flowing water. An Old English word for a stream was *burna*, often appearing as *bourne*, and a Celtic word was *ouse*; a Celtic word for a meandering stream was *cam*. Do you find these words used for rivers and habitations associated with rivers in England? Do you find them much used in place names in the United States? What are the common words, aside from *river*, on the North American continent?

6. Rivers can be explored downstream from the source to the mouth or upstream from mouth to source. Many American rivers and their tributaries were given their names when they were first explored. Study the names of

rivers on the western slope of the Appalachian mountains, in western Pennsylvania and West Virginia and in eastern Kentucky and Tennessee. You will find a few streams called forks or branches, but very few. Compare the names of rivers in California, Oregon, and Washington flowing west out of the Rockies and Sierra Nevadas. Many of these streams are called forks or branches. What difference in exploration does this difference in naming reveal?

5

From Names to Language

Ernst Cassirer

Ernst Cassirer (1874–1945), who spent most of his life teaching at various European universities, was one of the most widely respected modern philosophers. A student of the history of philosophy, he wrote on Kant, Rousseau, Einstein, and many others. He is best known among linguists for his Language and Myth *(1946). The following selection is from* An Essay on Man *(1944).*

"By the beginning of the twenty-third month," says D. R. Major, "the child had developed a mania for going about naming things, as if to tell others their names, or to call our attention to the things he was examining. He would look at, point toward, or put his hand on an article, speak its name, then look at his companions."[1] Such an attitude would not be understandable were it not for the fact that the name, in the mental growth of the child, has a function of the first importance to perform. If a child when learning to talk had simply to learn a certain vocabulary, if he only had to impress on his mind and memory a great mass of artificial and arbitrary sounds, this would be a purely mechanical process. It would be very laborious and tiresome, and would require too great conscious effort for the child to make without a certain reluctance since what he is expected to do would be entirely disconnected from actual biological needs. The "hunger for names" which at a certain age appears in every normal child and which has been described by all students of child psychology[2] proves the contrary.

---

[1] David R. Major, *First Steps in Mental Growth* (New York, Macmillan, 1906), pp. 321f.

[2] See, for instance, Clara and William Stern, *Die Kindersprache* (Leipzig, 1907), pp. 175ff.

It reminds us that we are here confronted with a quite different problem. By learning to name things a child does not simply add a list of artificial signs to his previous knowledge of ready-made empirical objects. He learns rather to form the concepts of those objects, to come to terms with the objective world. Henceforth the child stands on firmer ground. His vague, uncertain, fluctuating perceptions and his dim feelings begin to assume a new shape. They may be said to crystallize around the name as a fixed center, a focus of thought. Without the help of the name every new advance made in the process of objectification would always run the risk of being lost again in the next moment. The first names of which a child makes conscious use may be compared to a stick by the aid of which a blind man gropes his way. And language, taken as a whole, becomes the gateway to a new world. All progress here opens a new perspective and widens and enriches our concrete experience. Eagerness and enthusiasm to talk do not originate in a mere desire for learning or using names; they mark the desire for the detection and conquest of an objective world.[3]

We can still when learning a foreign language subject ourselves to an experience similar to that of the child. Here it is not sufficient to acquire a new vocabulary or to acquaint ourselves with a system of abstract grammatical rules. All this is necessary but it is only the first and less important step. If we do not learn to think in the new language all our efforts remain fruitless. In most cases we find it extremely difficult to fulfill this requirement. Linguists and psychologists have often raised the question as to how it is possible for a child by his own efforts to accomplish a task that no adult can ever perform in the same way or as well. We can perhaps answer this puzzling question by looking back at our former analysis. In a later and more advanced state of our conscious life we can never repeat the process which led to our first entrance into the world of human speech. In the freshness, in the agility and elasticity of early childhood this process had a quite different meaning. Paradoxically enough the real difficulty consists much less in the learning of the new language than in the forgetting of a former one. We are no longer in the mental condition of the child who for the first time approaches a conception of the objective world. To the adult the objective world already has a definite shape as a result of speech activity, which has in a sense molded all our other activities. Our perceptions, intuitions, and concepts have coalesced with the terms and speech forms of our mother tongue. Great efforts are required to release the bond between words and things. And yet, when we set about to learn a new language, we have to make such efforts and to separate the two elements. Overcoming this difficulty always marks a new and important step in the learning of a language. When penetrating into the "spirit" of a foreign tongue we invariably have the impression of approaching a new world, a world which has an intellec-

---

[3] For a more detailed discussion of this problem see Cassirer, "Le langage et la construction du monde des objets," *Journal de Psychologie,* XXXe Année (1933), pp. 18–44.

tual structure of its own. It is like a voyage of discovery in an alien land, and the greatest gain from such a voyage lies in our having learned to look upon our mother tongue in a new light. "*Wer fremde Sprachen nicht kennt, weiss nichts von seiner eigenen* [He who is not acquainted with some foreign tongue knows nothing about his own]," said Goethe.[4] So long as we know no foreign languages we are in a sense ignorant of our own, for we fail to see its specific structure and its distinctive features. A comparison of different languages shows us that there are no exact synonyms. Corresponding terms from two languages seldom refer to the same objects or actions. They cover different fields which interpenetrate and give us many-colored views and varied perspectives of our experience.

This becomes especially clear if we consider the methods of classification employed in different languages, particularly in those of divergent linguistic types. Classification is one of the fundamental features of human speech. The very act of denomination depends on a process of classification. To give a name to an object or action is to subsume it under a certain class concept. If this subsumption were once and for all prescribed by the nature of things, it would be unique and uniform. Yet the names which occur in human speech cannot be interpreted in any such invariable manner. They are not designed to refer to substantial things, independent entities which exist by themselves. They are determined rather by human interests and human purposes. But these interests are not fixed and invariable. Nor are the classifications to be found in human speech made at random; they are based on certain constant and recurring elements in our sense experience. Without such recurrences there would be no foothold, no point of support, for our linguistic concepts. But the combination or separation of perceptual data depends upon the free choice of a frame of reference. There is no rigid and pre-established scheme according to which our divisions and subdivisions might once for all be made. Even in languages closely akin and agreeing in their general structure we do not find identical names. As Humboldt pointed out, the Greek and Latin terms for the moon, although they refer to the same object, do not express the same intention or concept. The Greek term (*mēn*) denotes the function of the moon to "measure" time; the Latin term (*luna, luc-na*) denotes the moon's lucidity or brightness. Thus we have obviously isolated and focused attention on two very different features of the object. But the act itself, the process of concentration and condensation, is the same. The name of an object lays no claim upon its nature; it is not intended . . . to give us the truth of a thing. The function of a name is always limited to emphasizing a particular aspect of a thing, and it is precisely this restriction and limitation upon which the value of the name depends. It is not the function of a name to refer exhaustively to a concrete situation, but merely to single out and dwell upon a certain aspect. The isolation of this aspect is not a negative but a positive act. For in the act of denomination we select, out of the multiplicity and diffusion of our sense data, certain fixed centers

[4] Goethe, *Sprüche in Prosa*, "Werke," XLII, Pt. II, 118.

of perception. These centers are not the same as in logical or scientific thought. The terms of ordinary speech are not to be measured by the same standards as those in which we express scientific concepts. As compared with scientific terminology the words of common speech always exhibit a certain vagueness; almost without exception they are so indistinct and ill-defined as not to stand the test of logical analysis. But notwithstanding this unavoidable and inherent defect our everyday terms and names are the milestones on the road which leads to scientific concepts; it is in these terms that we receive our first objective or theoretical view of the world. Such a view is not simply "given"; it is the result of a constructive intellectual effort which without the constant assistance of language could not attain its end.

WORKING WITH THE SELECTION

1. Observing that at a certain age a child experiences a "hunger for names," Cassirer points out that naming is important because it helps one to form concepts, to "come to terms with the objective world." Making use of materials collected while dealing with the four previous selections, try writing a discussion of the need for naming and the way in which naming contributes to the ordering of one's surroundings. For example, consider the Pilgrims landing in New England, confronted with strange flora and fauna. How did a system of naming help them? Consider the problem of pioneers moving west, going down the Ohio River and up the Missouri, trying to survive and to make a living in surroundings different from the Atlantic seaboard, much different from Europe. How did naming help them to order a wild, new world? What do you know of the areas man is now exploring—the moon, the polar regions, the deep sea? What is naming doing to these areas, to the men engaged in lunar and marine exploration, and to those other people who must be concerned with the problems presented by new sorts of terrain —scientists, business men, journalists, governmental officers, even lawyers and doctors—all of whom need means of communication about areas that even now have few names.

2. Select a place moderately difficult to find—a certain room in one of the buildings on the campus, your favorite fishing spot, the best place in town to buy records, or something of the sort. Tell a friend how to get there. Then try to repeat these directions without using any place name. Or try to describe the flora or fauna that might be encountered in a given place—a salt marsh, a farm, a nearby forest—without using the name for any plant or animal, such as *rhododendron* or *cow*.

3. Some places on your campus are named, some are not. Most buildings are named, few sidewalks, some stretches of grass or asphalt. Can you determine why some places are named and some are not?

6

An Exaltation of Larks

James Lipton

James Lipton is not a professional student of language, and in spite of the moral and esthetic purposes he attributes to himself, his book An Exaltation of Larks *(1968) is, appropriately, perhaps more a* jeu d'esprit *than a labor of love or duty. Among recent fads in language is concern with what Lipton calls terms of venery—a pod of whales, a raft of ducks, a gaggle of geese if the fowl are traipsing on the ground but a skein if they are stretched out in flight—and with coining more such phrases. Lipton was moved to write a book about such locutions, from which the following selection is taken.*

The fact that many [words like *pride* for a family of lions] have slipped out of our common speech can only, I think, be described as lamentable. There is little enough poetry in our speech (and lives) to continue to ignore a vein as rich as this. The purpose of this book is to try, in an admittedly modest measure, to redress the balance. The thesis of this book can be summed up very simply: when a group of ravens flaps by, you should, if you want to refer to their presence, say, "There goes an unkindness of ravens." Anything else would be wrong.

The reader may have noticed that, until this moment, I have avoided giving a single, comprehensive collective term to these collective terms. That is because there isn't any. Oddly enough, the compilers of the numerous lists of these words, though obviously enthusiastic philologists, have never felt compelled to settle on a group term for them. The explorer in this field will find these words variously referred to as "nouns of multitude," "company terms," "nouns of assemblage," "collective nouns,"[1] "group terms," and "terms of venery." This last seems to me best and most appropriate, and itself warrants some explanation.

"Venery" and its adjective, "venereal," are most often thought of, of course, as signifying love, and more specifically physical love. From *Venus* we have the Latin root *ven* which appears in the word *venari,* meaning "to hunt game." Eric Partridge, in his etymological dictionary *Origins,* asserts that the *ven* in *venari* has its original meaning: "to desire (and therefore)

---

[1] I hold this to be a misnomer since, obviously, it can be confused with the strictly grammatical term referring to such words as "majority." The same may be said of "nouns of multitude."

116

to pursue," and he sees a close connection between it and the word "win," from the Middle English *winnen,* and even the Sanskrit *vanoti,* "he conquers." It is in this sense that venery came to signify the hunt, and it was so used in all the early works on the chase, including the earliest known on the subject of English hunting, *Le Art* [sic] *de Venery,* written in Norman French in the 1320's by the huntsman of Edward II, Master William Twici.

So, if all the earlier and far greater experts in this field have left it to someone of the twentieth century to select the proper term for these proper terms, I (cautiously and with boundless and well-founded humility) pick up the gauntlet and declare for "terms of venery"; if for no more cogent reason than that it allows of such disingenuous derivative delights as "venereal," "venerealize," and "veneralization" (*vide* Part III of this book).

So be it. Henceforward we are talking about terms of venery or venereal terms.

Before beginning the list of the authentic venereal terms themselves, a word is in order on the various *types* of terms. Etymologically speaking, the order of venereal terms seems to me to break down into six families, according to the apparent original inspiration for the term. I would list the six families as:

1: *Onomatopoeia:* for example, A MURMURATION OF STARLINGS, A GAGGLE OF GEESE.
2: *Characteristic:* A LEAP OF LEOPARDS, A SKULK OF FOXES. This is by far the largest family.
3: *Appearance:* A KNOT OF TOADS, A BOUQUET OF PHEASANTS.
4: *Habitat:* A SHOAL OF BASS, A NEST OF RABBITS.
5: *Comment* (pro or con, reflecting the observer's point of view): A RICHNESS OF MARTENS, A COWARDICE OF CURS.
6: *Error* (resulting from an incorrect transcription by a scribe or printer, faithfully preserved in the corrupted form by subsequent compilers): A SCHOOL OF FISH, originally "shoal.". . .

So you see, by 1486 the venereal game was already in full swing. There are examples of it in most of the early manuscripts. The first *Harley Manuscript* gives GAGGLE OF GOSSIPS, and the very early book *The Hors, Shepe, & the Ghoos* contributes A PITY OF PRISONERS and A HASTINESS OF COOKS. The extreme importance of these books in the fifteenth century is indicated by the fact that the last named was one of the first printed by William Caxton in the year that he introduced printing to England. And if we are still inclined to think of the social terms of venery as frivolous, C. E. Hare asserts that A BLAST OF HUNTERS and its fellows "were all probably in use at one time or another." There is of course no law or canon of usage that gives any of these terms sole possession of the field, but clearly they were once considered well enough established to take their places with A FLOCK OF SHEEP and A SCHOOL OF FISH.

But, that the codifiers of these terms knew they were playing a word game is equally clear, from the terms themselves—and the history of the game in the centuries since Caxton. It has never stopped. The reader of this book may already know the popular philological story that usually takes Oxford as its locale. In it, four dons, each representing a different academic discipline and therefore a different viewpoint, were flapping along the Oxford High when their path was crossed by a small but conspicuous group of prostitutes. The quickest of the dons muttered, "A jam of tarts." The second, obviously a fellow in Music, riposted, "No, a flourish of strumpets." From the third, apparently an expert on nineteenth-century English literature, came, "Not at all . . . an essay of Trollope's." The fourth—Modern English Literature—said, "An anthology of pros." (I have heard versions that included "a peal of Jezebels," "a smelting of ores" and even "a troop of horse," but this begins to be flogging a dead one.)

WORKING WITH THE SELECTION

1. Try your hand at coining new examples of what Lipton calls terms of venery. Assuming you do not care much for the book you are reading, how might the contributors be designated—*a ululation of linguists, an apiary of onomasts, a paradigm of grammarians?* What might the faculty of a department be called? Should English teachers have a different term from that for physics teachers or psychologists? What should a sorority of women students be called, except that? What should a body of student militants be called? And what about the students who violently oppose the militants? What should a meeting of deans be called? Or you make up the categories.

2. The following are some of the terms of venery recorded or coined by Lipton. Can you improve on any of them?

a sentence of judges	a wrangle of philosophers
an impatience of wives	a flush of plumbers
a boast of soldiers	an odium of politicians
an eloquence of lawyers	a column of accountants
a foresight of housekeepers	a shrivel of critics
a skulk of thieves	a tantrum of decorators
a pontificality of prelates	a slant of journalists
a wince of dentists	a twaddle of public speakers

7

Word Creation

Simeon Potter

Simeon Potter, Baines Professor of English at the University of Liverpool in England, has not propounded startling theories, as has Noam Chomsky, or explored vast new areas, as did Otto Jespersen, but for good reasons he is one of the most respected and most widely read of contemporary students of language. He is well known outside English-speaking areas, having lectured at the University of Brno in Czechoslovakia and at the University of Aarhus in Denmark —both centers of language study—and he keeps in touch with what is happening throughout the world, including the United States, an area sometimes neglected by European scholars. The following selection is from one of his many popular books, Our Language *(1950).*

At all periods in the history of a language a new word may suddenly appear as if from nowhere, or a new word may be deliberately created by one man who tells the world exactly what he is doing. Echoic words like *bang, pop,* and *whizz* or nonsense-syllables like *ta-ra-ra-boom-de-ay* and *a-heigh-and-a-ho-and-a-heigh-nonny-no* form yet a third class, and they are easily accounted for.

Let us take *dog* and *pig* as examples of the first class. The old word for 'dog' is *hound*. So far as is known, *dog* is first recorded in its genitive plural for *docgena*, glossing Latin *canum*, in a twelfth-century manuscript. Its previous origin and history are quite unknown. Not many years later *pig* makes its first appearance in the *Ancrene Riwle*. The old word was *swine*. Other common words of unknown provenance are *bad, big, cut, fog, lad,* and *lass,* which were first employed in the thirteenth and fourteenth centuries; *bet, crease, dodge, gloat,* and *jump* in the sixteenth; *blight, chum, fun, hump,* and *job* in the seventeenth; *bore* (in the sense 'ennui'), *donkey* (first pronounced 'dunkey'; perhaps a pet form of Duncan), *fun, hoax,* and *jam* in the eighteenth. In the nineteenth century we first encounter *slum* and *loaf* in the sense 'to spend time idly'. According to *The Oxford Dictionary* the last word was first used in *Charcoal Sketches* (1838) by Joseph Neal, who evidently regarded it as colloquial or slang because he placed it within inverted commas—'One night, Mr Dabbs came home from his 'loafing' place—for he 'loafs' of an evening like the generality of people—that being the most popular and the cheapest amusement extant'. A few years later it was used by Dickens in *Martin Chuzzlewit* and by Mrs Beecher Stowe in

Uncle Tom's Cabin. No one knows its origin. Lowell conjectured that it might come from *lofen,* a dialectal variant of German *laufen* 'to run', which, as we saw in Chapter I, is related to our *leap.* This is a mere guess and yet, though the difference in meaning is so strongly against it, it has been adopted as a plausible etymology by many English and American dictionaries. *The Oxford Dictionary* is more guarded. It mentions Lowell's surmise, but it marks the word as 'of obscure origin'. Under *loafer* 'one who spends his time in idleness' the possibility is mooted that this substantive may be the source of the verb by 'back-formation'. That is all. In nineteenth-century American may be found for the first time *blizzard* (from the storm of 1880), *bogus,* and *rowdy.*

Among the many notable word-creations in the second class let us consider just four: *gas, paraffin, vaseline,* and *blurb.* These certainly have strange appearances, but no lexicographer, however cautious, need add *etym. dub.* 'etymology dubious' or *of obscure origin* to his account of them, since precise facts are known. In his *Ortus Medicinae* or *Rise of Medicine* (1652) the Dutch chemist J. B. Van Helmont states that he invented the form *gas* on the basis of the Greek *chaos,* the *ch-* or χ- of Greek and the *g-* of Dutch both alike being pronounced as a fricative similar to the *-ch* in Scottish *loch.* As for *paraffin,* this artificial mixture of hydrocarbons was first discovered by the German physicist Karl von Reichenbach in 1830 and he was very much impressed at the time by the remarkably *small affinity* (Latin *parum* 'little'-*affinis* 'having relationship, partaking, sharing') that it possessed with other bodies. Von Reichenbach took these two Latin words, cut off their terminations, and joined them together! It was as simple as that! Some forty years or so later (1872) Robert A. Chesebrough concocted the trade and proprietary name *vas-el-ine* for soft petroleum jelly by adding the suffix *-ine* to the initial syllables of German *Wasser* (*w*—pronounced *v-*) and Greek *élaion* 'oil'. In 1907 the American journalist Gelett Burgess hit upon the bright idea of calling the publisher's 'puff' or eulogy, printed on a book-jacket, the *blurb.* A long and detailed account of the frivolous occasion may be found in the First Supplement (1945) to H. L. Mencken's work on *The American Language.*

Even ancient words may have been compounded on specific occasions, the details of which are known. The Greek thinker Pythagoras resented being called *sophistés* 'wise man, wizard' and so he persuaded his friends to name him *philósophos* 'lover of wisdom' instead. We now use both words in slightly modified forms, *sophist* and *philosopher.* Cicero formed *qualitas* and *indolentia* to render Aristotle's *poiótēs* and *apátheia,* and these have become *quality* and *indolence* in English. *Apathy* means, in the first place, 'insensibility to suffering', but it may still be said to imply 'indolence of mind'.

Chaucer not only imported hundreds of words into English: he also created hundreds. So, too, did the Elizabethan poets, Shakespeare above all. In his *Pseudodoxia Epidemica* or *Vulgar Errors* Sir Thomas Browne introduced ponderous words like *antediluvian, hallucination, incontrovertible, insecurity, precarious,* and *retrogression.* Sir Isaac Newton was the first to use *centrifu-*

gal and *centripetal*. Indeed, many words may be traced to individual writers in Newton's century: *central, circuitous, decorous, fortuitous,* and *freakish* to the Cambridge Platonist Henry More; *attitude, balustrade, cascade, contour, monochrome, opera, outline,* and *pastel* to the diarist John Evelyn; and *corpuscle, intensity, pathological,* and *pendulum* to the natural philosopher and chemist Robert Boyle. Edmund Burke was responsible for *colonial, colonization, diplomacy, electioneering, expenditure, federalism, financial,* and *municipality*. Coleridge introduced *intensify, pessimism,* and *phenomenal;* and, in *Biographia Literaria,* he first referred to the period of Queen Elizabeth as 'our golden *Elizabethian* age', Carlyle modifying the epithet to *Elizabethan* in *Heroes and Hero-Worship*. Jeremy Bentham was the first, in the phrase 'the good of the community', to apply the term *community* to the people of a country as a whole. He it was who first used the adjectives *detachable, dynamic, exhaustive, unilateral,* and *international,* the last with a sincere apology! The term *international,* he pointed out in his *Principles of Morals and Legislation* (1780), is 'a new one; though, it is hoped, sufficiently analogous and intelligible. It is calculated to express, in a more significant way, the branch of law which goes commonly under the name of the *law of nations'*. William Whewell likewise apologized for indulging in such unheard-of word-formations as *physicist* and *scientist* in his *Philosophy of the Inductive Sciences* (1840). 'The terminations *-ize, -ism,* and *-ist'*, he claimed, 'are applied to words of all origins: thus we have to *pulverize,* to *colonize; witticism, heathenism; journalist, tobacconist.* Hence we may make such words when they are wanted. As we cannot use *physician* for a cultivator of *physics,* I have called him a *physicist*. We need very much a name to describe a cultivator of science in general. I should incline to call him a *scientist.'* George Eliot was once asked, 'Are you an optimist or a pessimist?' 'Neither,' came the reply, 'I am a *meliorist.'* Macaulay apologized for using *constituency,* but his contemporary Carlyle, that intrepid word-coiner, saw no need to express regret for his word-creations, however eccentric or exotic they might be. Some of his combinations, like *mischief-joy,* translating *Schadenfreude,* are intelligible only to those of his readers who know German. Like Scott, however, he brought such Scottish words into English as *feckless, lilt* (with the meaning of 'cadence'), and *outcome,* and made them current. The now common words *decadent, environment,* and *self-help* seem to have been Carlyle's own. Shaw translated Nietzsche's *Übermensch* as *superman*—others had previously rendered it *beyondman* and *overman*—and set the fashion in *super* words, especially in America, where linguistic exuberance has produced *super-colossal, super-maximum, super-ultra, super-superlative,* and even *super-super.* . . . .

The wealth and resourcefulness of English in the formation of derivatives may be illustrated by a study of all the words springing from the native root *bear* and the Latin *ced*. Some forty other words, ranging from *birth* to *overburdensome,* have been formed from *bear* during the course of ten centuries. The Latin root *ced* 'go from', with its participial form *cess-* and its related French form *cease,* has been yet more prolific and has produced no fewer than eighty derivatives. Many of these have been formed by means of classical and native affixes which, for the most part, still live and thrive.

Let us consider, for example, the various prefixes that may still be used to express negation. There is, first of all, the Greek *a-*, or 'privative alpha,' as in *amorphous, apathetic,* and *atheist;* becoming *an-* before vowels as in *anaemia, anaesthesia, anarchy, anodyne,* and *anonymous.* Then there is the Latin *in-* as in *inaccessible, inaudible, incorrect, incredible, intangible,* and *invisible;* becoming *il-, im-,* and *ir-* before certain consonants as in *illegal, illegible,* and *illicit; immature, immediate* 'not separated by any intervening medium', and *immortal; irrational, irremediable,* and *irresponsible.* Further, Latin and French *non-* is used in *nonchalance* and *nonpareil,* as well as *noncombatant, nonconductor, nondescript,* and *nonjuring.* Germanic *un-*, as in *ungodly, unjust, unkind, unknowable,* and *unutterable,* is probably the commonest negative prefix of all, but it should be dissociated from the other *un-* prefix of quite different origin which denotes reversal or deprivation as in *unbind, unbutton, uncover, undo, unlock,* and *unpack.* Old English *ne-,* becoming *n-* before vowels, is manifest in *neither, never, none,* and *nor;* whereas Modern English *no-* appears in *no-ball, no-confidence,* and *no-thoroughfare.* Having such an abundance of prefixes to choose from, people sometimes vacillate between two forms. It is, after all, usage alone that determines us in saying *inexpressible* but *unexpressive, impracticable* but *unpractical, irresponsible* but *unresponsive.* Northern children still say *unpossible* and they are liable to be rebuked by their elders for using an expression that is 'vulgar' or 'substandard'. This was, in fact, the commoner form from Langland to Dryden and it was the only form in the King James Bible, having been silently changed to *impossible* in later editions of the Authorized Version. It is interesting to observe that in current philosophical writings we find three living prefixes still competing for recognition in the terms *amoral, unmoral,* and *nonmoral.* To the student of ethics or moral science these adjectives all mean the same thing, namely 'beyond the sphere of morals, unconcerned with morality', as distinct from the more general term *immoral* 'opposed to morality, morally evil, vicious'. . . .

Apart from inherited formative elements new words are daily created in scores of other ways. The pleasing antiphony of *ding-dong, ping-pong,* and *sing-song* is varied in *dingle-dangle, dilly-dally, fibble-fabble* (from *fibble-fable,* a playful elaboration of *fable,* whence our *fib*), *flim-flam, flip-flop, riff-raff,* Shakespeare's *skimble-skamble, shilly-shally* (probably from the old subjunctive *shill I* alternating with the old indicative *shall I*), *tittle-tattle,* and *zig-zag.* The playful iterations with change of initial consonant in *hoity-toity* and *namby-pamby* (from Ambrose Philips) are extended to *hanky-panky* and *higgledy-piggledy.* Words may be blended as in *blotch* from *blot* and *botch, blurt* from *blare* and *spurt, chump* from *chunk* and *lump, flaunt* from *flout* and *vaunt, flurry* from *fly* and *hurry, grumble* from *growl* and *rumble, splutter* from *splash* and *sputter,* and *twirl* from *twist* and *whirl.* By the most natural process in the world a word may by *aphesis* lose an initial unstressed syllable and assume a new meaning. Thus, for example, to *disport* oneself 'to carry oneself in a different direction from one's ordinary business' becomes *sport; a dispenser* 'a steward or butler who dispenses the household provisions' becomes *Spenser* or *Spencer; defend, defender,* and *defence* become, at different times and independently, *fend, fender,* and *fence; amend, attend, distain,* and *envy,* take on new ways as *mend, tend, stain,* and *vie; acute, alive* (on life), and *alone* (all one) give *cute, live* (as in 'live wire'), and *lone; assize, despite,* and *example* become *size, spite,* and *sample.* By the contrary process of *apocope* words may shed their final unstressed syllables. When people started calling a *cabriolet* a *cab* they showed a natural predilection for the snappy monosyllable. In colloquial speech they call a *perambulator* a *pram* and a *prefabricated house* a *prefab.* They go to the *Zoological Gardens* or the *Zoo* and to the *Promenade Concerts* or the *Proms.* Similarly a *chapman* has become a *chap* or 'merchant of any kind, good or bad', a *quacksalver* has become a *quack,* and a veterinary surgeon is affectionately referred to as a *vet.*

WORKING WITH THE SELECTION

1. Most English words in use today have a long history: some came into English from other languages; others grew from words used in an earlier form of English. As Potter demonstrates, however, there are also words that seem to have appeared suddenly as if from nowhere, and a few we know were deliberately coined. Do you know any such words aside from those given by Potter? *Quiz* is one. There are guesses about its origin of course; one is that the word came from Latin *quis* or *quid* or both, but nobody knows just how. And there are stories; one is that an Irish producer of plays, presumably well-liquored after dinner, bet that he could so juggle language that by the next morning every adult in Dublin would have uttered a word he did not know the meaning of. After the dinner he summoned his employees who distributed handbills for the theater and told them to go through the town scrawling *quiz* on walls or any other vacant spot. He is said to have won the bet, but the story may be apocryphal; even if it is not, it may not have started the word. Incidentally, words like *hippie* are out of bounds; it presumably comes from *hip* in one of its meanings.

2. One of the paragraphs omitted from Potter's chapter has the following topic sentence: "Another prefix which has been resuscitated in recent years is Latin *semi-.*" What examples might Potter have included in this paragraph?

3. Potter makes very little use of words devised by adding suffixes, probably because he considers many of them essentially unchanged. What is the effect of adding the following suffixes to words: *-ly, -ize, -ness, -like, -ous, -ity?*

8

Borrowing from the Normans

Otto Jespersen

Without question the Dane Otto Jespersen (1860–1943) was one of the great students of English, and in some ways he was the first of the great modern students of language. He was trained as a lawyer, and found his way into linguistics through a consuming, though at first amateur, interest in language, becoming in time a philologist of the rank of W. W. Skeat, H. C. Wyld, and Henry Sweet. He wrote one standard work after another, including Language, Its Nature, Development, and Origin *(1922) and his monumental* Modern English Grammar *(6 vols., 1904–42). The following selection is from what is perhaps his best-known work, many times reprinted,* Growth and Structure of the English Language, *9th ed. (1938).*

The Normans became masters of England, and they remained masters for a sufficiently long time to leave a deep impress on the language. The conquerors were numerous and powerful, but the linguistic influence would have been far less if they had not continued for centuries in actual contact and constant intercourse with the French of France, of whom many were induced by later kings to settle in England. We need only go through a list of French loan-words in English to be firmly convinced of the fact that the immigrants formed the upper classes of the English society after the conquest, so many of the words are distinctly aristocratic. It is true that they left the old words *king* and *queen* intact, but apart from these nearly all words relating to government and to the highest administration are French; see, for instance, *crown, state, government* and to *govern, reign, realm* (OFr. realme, Mod. Fr. royaume), *sovereign, country, power, minister, chancellor, council* (and *counsel*), *authority, parliament, exchequer. People* and *nation,* too, were political words; the corresponding OE. *þeod* soon went out of ordinary use. Feudalism was imported from France, and with it were introduced a number of words, such as *fief, feudal, vassal, liege,* and the names of the various steps in the scale of rank: *prince, peer, duke* with *duchess, marquis, viscount, baron.* It is, perhaps, surprising that *lord* and *lady* should have remained in esteem, and that *earl* should have been retained, *count* being chiefly used in speaking of foreigners, but the earl's wife was designated by the French word *countess,* and *court* is French, as well as the adjectives relating to court life, such as *courteous, noble, fine* and *refined. Honour* and *glory* belong to the French, and so does *heraldry,* while nearly all English expressions relating to that difficult science (*argent, gules, verdant,* etc.) are of French origin, some of them curiously distorted.

The upper classes, as a matter of course, took into their hands the management of military matters; and although in some cases it was a long time before the old native terms were finally displaced (*here* and *fird,* for instance, were used till the fifteenth century when *army* began to be common), we have a host of French military words, many of them of very early introduction. Such are *war* (ME. werre, Old North Fr. werre, Central French guerre) and *peace, battle, arms, armour, buckler, hauberk, mail* (chain-mail; OFr. maille 'mesh of a net'), *lance, dart, cutlass, banner, ensign, assault, siege,* etc. Further, *officer, chieftain* (*captain* and *colonel* are later), *lieutenant, sergeant, soldier, troops, dragoon, vessel, navy* and *admiral* (orig. *amiral* in English as in French, ultimately an Arabic word). Some words which are now used very extensively outside the military sphere were without any doubt at first purely military, such as *challenge, enemy, danger, escape* (scape), *espy* (spy), *aid, prison, hardy, gallant, march, force, company, guard,* etc.

Another natural consequence of the power of the Norman upper classes is that most of the terms pertaining to the law are of French origin, such as *justice, just, judge; jury, court* (we have seen the word already in another sense), *suit, sue, plaintiff* and *defendant,* a *plea, plead,* to *summon, cause, assize, session, attorney, fee, accuse, crime, guile, felony, traitor, damage, dower, heritage, property, real estate, tenure, penalty, demesne, injury, privilege.* Some of these are now hardly to be called technical juridical words, and there are others which belong still more to the ordinary vocabulary of everyday life, but which were undoubtedly at first introduced by lawyers at the time when procedure was conducted entirely in French;[1] for instance, *case, marry, marriage, oust, prove, false* (perhaps also *fault*), *heir,* probably also *male* and *female,* while *defend* and *prison* are common to the juridical and the military worlds. *Petty* (Fr. petit, was, I suspect, introduced by the jurists in such combinations as *petty jury, petty larceny, petty constable, petty sessions, petty averages, petty treason* (still often spelt *petit treason*), etc., before it was used commonly. The French *puis né* in its legal sense remains *puisne* in English (in law it means 'younger or inferior in rank,' but originally 'later born'), while in ordinary language it has adopted the spelling *puny,* as if the *-y* had been the usual adjective ending.

Besides, there are a good many words that have never become common property, but have been known to jurists only, such as *mainour* (to be taken with the mainour, to be caught in the very act of stealing, from Fr. manœuvre), *jeofail* ('an oversight,' the acknowledgment of an error in pleading,

---

[1] From 1362 English was established as the official language spoken in the courts of justice, yet the curious mongrel language known as 'Law French' continued in use there for centuries; Cromwell tried to break its power, but it was not finally abolished till an act of Parliament of 1731. On the position of the French language in England, see J. Vising, *Anglo-Norman Language and Literature* (London, 1923).

from je faille), *cestui que trust, cestui (a) que vie* and other phrases equally shrouded in mystery to the man in the street. *Larceny* has been almost exclusively the property of lawyers, so that it has not ousted *theft* from general use; such words as *thief* and *steal* were of course too popular to be displanted by French juridical terms, though *burglar* is probably of French origin. It is also worth observing how many of the phrases in which the adjective is invariably placed after its noun are law terms, taken over bodily from the French, e.g. *heir male, issue male, fee simple, proof demonstrative, malice prepense* (or, Englished, *malice aforethought*),[2] *letters patent* (formerly also with the adjective inflected, *letters patents*, Shakesp. R2, II, 1, 202), *attorney general* (and other combinations of *general*, all of which are official, though some of them are not juridical).

As ecclesiastical matters were also chiefly under the control of the higher classes, we find a great many French words connected with the church, such as *religion, service, trinity, saviour, virgin, angel* (OFr. angele, now Fr. ange; the OE. word engel was taken direct from Latin), *saint, relic, abbey, cloister, friar* (ME. frère as in French), *clergy, parish, baptism, sacrifice, orison, homily, altar, miracle, preach, pray, prayer, sermon, psalter* (ME. sauter), *feast* ('religious anniversary'). Words like *rule, lesson, save, tempt, blame, order, nature*, which now belong to the common language and have very extensive ranges of signification, were probably at first purely ecclesiastical words. As the clergy were, moreover, teachers of morality as well as of religion they introduced the whole gamut of words pertaining to moral ideas from *virtue* to *vice: duty, conscience, grace, charity, cruel, chaste, covet, desire, lechery, fool* (one of the oldest meanings is 'sensual'), *jealousy, pity, discipline, mercy*, and others.

To these words, taken from different domains, may be added other words of more general meaning, which are highly significant as to the relations between the Normans and the English, such as *sir* and *madam, master* and *mistress* with their contrast *servant* (and the verb to *serve*), further, *command* and *obey, order, rich* and *poor* with the nouns *riches* and *poverty; money, interest, cash, rent*, etc.

It is a remark that was first made by John Wallis[3] and that has been very often repeated, especially since Sir Walter Scott made it popular in *Ivanhoe*, that while the names of several animals in their lifetime are English (*ox, cow, calf, sheep, swine, boar, deer*), they appear on the table with French names (*beef, veal, mutton, pork, bacon, brawn, venison*). This is generally explained from the masters leaving the care of the living animals to the lower classes, while they did not leave much of the meat to be eaten by them. But it may with just as much right be contended that the use of the French words here is due to the superiority of the French *cuisine*, which is shown by a great many other words as well, such as *sauce, boil, fry, roast, toast, pasty, pastry, soup, sausage, jelly, dainty;* while the humbler *breakfast* is

[2] Cf. also *lords spiritual* and *lords temporal;* the *body politic*.
[3] *Grammatica Linguae Anglicanae* (1653).

English, the more sumptuous meals, *dinner* and *supper,* as well as *feasts* generally, are French. . . .

The following table shows the strength of the influx of French words at different periods; it comprises one thousand words (the first hundred French words in the New English Dictionary for each of the first nine letters and the first 50 for *j* and *l*) and gives the half-century to which the earliest quotation in that Dictionary belongs.[4] After + I add the corresponding numbers found by A. Koszal[5] for those volumes of NED. which had not appeared when I worked up my statistics. It should be remembered that many or even most of these words, at any rate the more popular ones, had probably been in use some time before these quotations. Even if, however, the average age of French words is say fifty years greater than here indicated, the table retains its value for the comparative chronology of the language:

			carried forward:	581 + 526
Before 1050	2 +	0	1451–1500	76 + 68
1051–1100	2 +	1	1501–1550	84 + 80
1101–1150	1 +	2	1551–1600	91 + 89
1151–1200	15 +	11	1601–1650	69 + 63
1201–1250	64 +	39	1651–1700	34 + 48
1251–1300	127 +	122	1701–1750	24 + 32
1301–1350	120 +	118	1751–1800	16 + 33
1351–1400	180 +	164	1801–1850	23 + 35
1401–1450	70 +	69	1851–1900	2 + 14
	581 +	526		1000 + 988

The list shows conclusively that the linguistic influence did not begin immediately after the conquest, and that it was strongest in the years 1251–1400, to which nearly half of the borrowings belong. Further, it will be seen that the common assumption that the age of Dryden was particularly apt to introduce new words from French is very far from being correct.

WORKING WITH THE SELECTION

1. Jespersen's table at the end of the selection makes clear that borrowing from French did not increase immediately after the Norman conquest in 1066, but did increase as a result of the Norman occupation that followed the conquest.

---

[4] I have followed the authority of the same Dictionary also in regard to the question of the origin of the words, reckoning thus as French some words which I should, perhaps, myself have called Latin. Derivative words that have certainly or probably arisen in English (e.g. *daintily, damageable*) have been excluded, as also those perfectly unimportant words for which the NED. gives less than five quotations. Most of them cannot really be said to have ever belonged to the English language. Cf. also R. Mettig, *Die franz. Elemente im Alt- und Mittelengl.,* Engl. St., 41, 176ff.

[5] *Bulletin de la Faculté des Lettres de Strasbourg* (Jan., 1937). The letters Q, U, and W did not yield a full hundred.

What does this seem to mean for the popular notion that more words in English have been borrowed from French than from any other language because the French conquered England? What may it mean about the common notion that language is spread mainly by war? Can you find evidence elsewhere that seems to confirm or contradict this testimony?

2. Examine Jespersen's table further, noticing when French borrowings were numerous, when less so. Knowing what you do of English and French history, how can you account for these changes?

3. In every language there are words that have not been borrowed from a foreign language, but have descended within the language from an earlier form. These may be called native words. Such words in English were present in the language in the earliest form we have of it, that is, in Old English, a term for the form of English that was used until about A.D. 1100. The two lists below contain words for things you might see if you looked around a classroom or laboratory and for things you might see on the street. The words that are borrowed are marked B, and those that are native are marked N.

wall	N	wheel	N
floor	N	man	N
thermometer	B	woman	N
electric lamp	B	automobile	B
window	N	exhaust	B
door	N	motorcycle	B
book	N	hat	N
spectrometer	B	dungarees	B
fountain pen	B	shoe	N
pencil	B	suit	B
eraser	B	bicycle	B
teacher	N	library	B
professor	B	house	N

4. The preceding lists may not be representative. Try writing down the first twenty-five words you think of in connection with a particular pastime or profession. Look up the etymologies in a dictionary. Do you get the same conclusions as in 3, above, or different conclusions?

5. Write down a number of words that reveal grammar in English, words like *who, or, since,* and *up.* Now write down a number of words used in discussing grammar, terms like *preposition, predicate,* and *grammar* itself. By consulting your dictionary, find out which are native words and which are borrowed. What can you conclude from your results?

6. The following words are terms in music; the native terms are marked N and are undated, since they have been in English or an ancestor of English for an undated time. The borrowed words are marked with the date given in *The Oxford English Dictionary* as the first known occurrence in English, and the language from which each word was borrowed is indicated.

song	N	giterene, Old French, 1381 (date from *Middle English*
horn	N	*Dictionary*)

```
play   N     psaltery (often spelled something like sawter), Latin
pipe   N         through Old French, c. 1400
harp   N     rebeck or ribibe, Old French from Arabic, 1450
             dulcimer, Old French, 1475
             roundeley or roundlet, Old French, 1589
             fugue, French from Latin, 1597
             recorder, Anglo-French, 1598
             sonata, Italian, 1694
             concerto, Italian, 1730
             pianoforte (shortened to piano), Italian, 1767
             scherzo, Italian, 1862
             violoncello (shortened to cello), Italian, 1881
             Klavierstück, German, partly through French and Latin,
                 19th century (not in OED)
             hillbilly, American English, 20th century (not in OED)
```

On the basis of this information attempt to write a very brief history of the development of music in England.

7. Write down twenty-five words that pertain to a pastime or profession as you did in 4, above. Using *The Oxford English Dictionary*—or if it is not available *The Oxford Universal Dictionary*—along with your own desk dictionary, determine which words are native, which borrowed and from what languages, and date the borrowing. Then summarize what this evidence allows you to infer.

8. Consider what you have learned from the evidence in exercises 1–7, and draw the most important conclusions you can about borrowing into English and borrowing as a phenomenon in language.

part 3

Language
and
Meaning

As Helen Keller discovered, things can be named. It is relatively simple to designate a particular person by the name Jack or a specific book by its title. But language is seldom so simple. Even the chimpanzee Washoe began fairly early to change her signs to symbols by transferring them from particular objects to classes of objects. Names, then, develop meanings. The proper name Jack became the word for a manual laborer and for a device to raise heavy objects. Furthermore, meanings change. Fond meant 'foolish' in Shakespeare's time, and ecstasy meant 'madness.' Words also become associated with particular kinds of circumstances and develop emotional significances; some are even outlawed at a particular time in a particular society. And not all words begin as names.

Language, of course, does not communicate solely through the meanings of individual words—words make sense only as parts of grammatical structures—but problems of meaning can be isolated for study. The discipline of semantics has developed to study the meaning of meaning. The nature of meaning is obscure, complex, and subtle; it is also fascinating. The readings in Part 3 indicate how extensively considerations of meaning may range. They include speculation about the mind of man and about man as a symbol-using animal, discussion of the vagaries of individual words and groups of words and problems of defining them, and consideration of the ways in which choices among words, the handling of meaning, can influence the workings of our society.

1

Semantic Change

One of the relatively few determinable facts about meaning is that it changes. For example, many English words adopted from foreign languages have moved a long way from their originals; dilapidated, *from the Latin* lapis *'stone,' is not applied exclusively to stone structures;* candidate *has lost the meaning of its origin in Latin,* candidus *'white.' Though meaning changes are usually unpredictable, they tend often to follow regular patterns. The first of the following two selections describes some of these patterns; it is from a standard history,* The Development of Modern English *(1954), written by Stuart Robertson (1893–1940), formerly a professor at Temple University, and revised by Frederic G. Cassidy, professor of English and American language at the University of Wisconsin and director of an ongoing survey of American usage that is the most extensive ever attempted. The second selection is from William Dwight Whitney,* The Life and Growth of Language, *rev. ed. (1897).*

Generalization and Specialization

Stuart Robertson and Frederic G. Cassidy

One very common type of change is that in which the "area" of the meaning is changed. When a word that has referred broadly or inclusively begins instead to refer narrowly or exclusively, this is an example of "specialization" of meaning; the contrary is called "generalization." Interestingly enough, the same word may undergo both processes at different stages of the development of its meaning. *Go,* for example, is a verb of motion that seems as general as possible in meaning, and presumably this is also the basic meaning; early in its history in English, however, it must have specialized, for Old English *gān* sometimes means "walk," and in Middle English *ryde or gon* (ride or walk) is a familiar formula. Although the present meaning is the generalized one, the specialization "walk" was still possible in the late seventeenth century, as we see in these phrases from Bunyan: "I am resolved to run when I can, to go when I cannot run, and to creep when I cannot go." [1]

Borrowed words are quite as likely as native ones to undergo such trans-

---

[1] Quoted by Bradley, *The Making of English*, p. 182.

formations in meaning. *Virtue*[2] is connected with Latin *vir* (man). Thus, *virtue* first meant "manliness" in general; but its meaning later specialized to stand for the manly quality most in demand in the military state, namely "fortitude" or "warlike prowess"—the meaning familiar in Cæsar's *Commentaries*. But a still later Latin meaning is more comprehensive, and it was this very general meaning that was attached to *virtue* when it was borrowed in English through French. One possible specialization was "power," as in "Virtue had gone out of him," or even "magical power," as in "the virtue of the spell" or Milton's "virtuous ring and glass." More commonly, however, the word in English retained a general sense of "noble quality"—though more and more with reference to moral rather than to mental or physical characteristics. But another specialization limits its application to women; for example, "All the sons were brave, and all the daughters virtuous," where *virtuous* is equivalent to "chaste." "A woman's virtue" will today be interpreted in only the last sense. A curious evolution, indeed, when one recalls that the etymological meaning is "manliness."

The foregoing are particularly striking examples, but hundreds of others could be cited. We find generalization in such everyday words as *picture*, once restricted, as the etymology would suggest (compare: the *Picts*, "painted ones"), to a *painted* representation of something seen, but now applicable to photograph, crayon drawing, and so forth; *butcher*, who once slew one animal only, the goat (French *bouc*); the verb *sail*, which has been transferred to *steam* navigation, just as *drive* has been transferred to self-propelled vehicles; *injury*, which once was limited to "injustice"; *zest*, which meant "bit of lemon-peel"; *chest*, which usually meant "coffin"—"He is now deed and nayled in his cheste";[3] *pen*, which meant "feather," but which is now much more likely to mean a writing implement tipped with metal than a quill; *quarantine*, from which the original meaning of a "forty" days' isolation has quite disappeared; and *companion*, which has likewise lost the etymological sense of "one who (shares) bread with" another.

But generalization of meaning does not always stay within bounds; under some conditions the meaning becomes so broad that, in extreme cases, there is hardly any meaning left. We have a whole set of words, used conversationally when we either do not know, or cannot remember, or perhaps will not take the trouble to search for a more precise term: the *what-you-may-call-it* kind of word—*thingumabob, doohickie, jigger,* and so on.[4] Not so long ago *gadget* was imported into the U.S. from England, and has found a very hearty welcome into this company.

Another type, in which generalization goes even farther, has aroused strong opposition from guardians of literary style, who realize that empti-

[2] This history is given in greater detail in Greenough and Kittredge, *Words and Their Ways in English Speech*, pp. 241–242.

[3] Chaucer's clerk, speaking of Petrarch (*Clerk's Prologue*, line 30).

[4] Louise Pound has collected more than 100 such terms now current in popular speech: "American Indefinite Names," *American Speech*, Vol. VI, No. 4 (April 1931), pp. 257–259.

ness and "jargon" result from the indiscriminate use of "words that mean little or nothing, but may stand for almost anything":[5] such words are *thing, business, concern, condition, matter, article, circumstance.* As we all recognize at once, these are words that have a fairly exact sense, but which also have acquired the ability to fit into a wide variety of everyday contexts, in which their meaning becomes extremely vague—in fact, almost wholly dependent on the context. The word *deal* is the current American favorite in this group, its gamut of meaning running all the way from perfectly favorable ("Your job sounds like a pretty fine deal") to thoroughly unfavorable ("I won't take part in any of his deals"). This word serves the purpose, and is going through the same general sort of development, that *proposition* did a generation ago.

Even more frequent than generalization, and even more readily illustrated in numberless familiar instances, is the opposite process of specialization. *Steorfan* is an Old English word, cognate with the German *sterben,* which meant "die"; but the standard Modern English meaning ("starve") is a specialized one, namely "die from hunger." Another specialization, "die from cold," is found in certain Modern English dialects: "[he] . . . bid her come . . . sit close by the fire: he was sure she was starved" is from the Yorkshire dialect of *Wuthering Heights* (Chapter XXX). The older meaning of *meat* was "food" in general, as one might suspect from the archaic phrase *meat and drink* and from the compound *sweetmeat.* For the meaning "meat," the older term was *flesh* or *flesh meat.* It is interesting to observe, incidentally, that the German cognate for *flesh, Fleisch,* suggests first of all the specialized sense of "meat"; this is the present meaning, too, of French *viande,* while the English *viands* retains the general sense of "food." *Coast* is a borrowing, through French, from a Latin word for "side" or "rib" (compare Modern English *intercostal*), and once meant "border" or "frontier"—the "coast of Bohemia" was not always an absurdity. But *coast* in present use not only has the usual specialization "seashore"; as employed in the eastern United States, it means specifically "Pacific coast." *Shore,* on the other hand, means, in parts of the east at any rate, "Atlantic shore."[6] In some of the same localities, however, "eastern shore" means what elsewhere would have to be expanded into "eastern shore of the Chesapeake in Maryland," just as in part of New England "the cape" means definitely "Cape Cod." *Token* formerly had the broad meaning "sign," but was long ago specialized to mean a physical thing that is a sign (of something)—as in *love token,* or the metal tokens used on streetcars or busses.

An *undertaker* once could undertake to do anything; nowadays he only undertakes to manage funerals. So, to people in general, *doctor* stands only for *doctor of medicine. Liquor,* which once was synonymous with *liquid,*

---

[5] Greenough and Kittredge, *op. cit.,* p. 235.
[6] In Philadelphia it is often used in a still more specific sense, "southern New Jersey shore"; it sometimes bears a yet more localized signification: "Atlantic City," which occurs repeatedly in the headlines of Philadelphia newspapers.

is now definitely specialized. *Reek,* like the German *rauchen,* once had the broad meaning "smoke," as it still has in the Scotch dialect; but the standard Modern English use limits it quite definitely to unpleasant exhalations. *Disease* meant "discomfort"—"lack of ease" in general. *Girl* meant "young person (of either sex)." The limitation of *corpse* to "*dead* body" made it necessary to re-borrow the word in its Modern French form *corps* for another possible meaning of "body," and to make occasional use of the original Latin, *corpus,* for still another sense, "complete collection of writings." *Corn,* in general American use, will be immediately understood as "Indian corn" or "maize." But the word itself once meant simply "grain," and so, in other parts of the English-speaking world, it is differently specialized [7]—in Scotland, to mean "oats," and in England "wheat." Keats' allusion to "Ruth amid the alien corn" probably calls up, to many American readers, a very different picture from what the poet had in mind.

What are the factors that account for specialization of meaning? One is, of course, that localities and groups of people have their own specialized associations for words that otherwise may convey a broader meaning. It has been well remarked that "every man is his own specializer." [8] *Pipe,* for example, calls up different ideas in the mind of the smoker, the plumber, and the organist. *Ring* may be thought of in connection with jewelry, opera, politics, or pugilism—even though, in the last connection, the "squared circle" has long since superseded the original truly circular shape. Quite apart from particular or local specializations, however, there are a great many words whose meaning has become specialized for nearly everybody. A second factor that helps to account for both generalization and specialization is the fading of the etymological significance of the word. Thus, to illustrate the one point, *arrive* [< Lat. *ad* (to) + *ripa* (shore)] originally applied to the end of a voyage only, and was used without the preposition, since this was included in the word. Milton's "ere he arrive the happy isle" illustrates a use that is in strict accord with the etymology of the word. When, however, consciousness of the Latin parts that made up the word was weakened, it was no longer used transitively, but in the phrase "arrive at," and with the more generalized application to the end of any journey.

Yet another factor is the competition among synonymous words. The borrowing of the Latin *animal* and the French *beast* meant that, with the native *deer,* English would have possessed three exactly synonymous terms for one idea; it is obviously in the interests of economy that *deer* should have specialized to mean one particular species of animal rather than "animal" in general, and that *beast* should have acquired connotations that limit its sphere. *Bird* and *fowl, dog* and *hound, boy* and *knave, chair* and *stool* are further instances of words that were once synonyms but that have been

---

[7] In other Germanic languages, the cognate word has still different specializations in various places: "barley" in Sweden, "rye" in north Germany, and "spelt" in south Germany. (Jespersen, *Mankind, Nation, and Individual,* p. 212.)

[8] Quoted by Greenough and Kittredge, *op. cit.,* p. 251.

differentiated in meaning here by the specialization of the second term of each pair.

A further remark about generalization and specialization is suggested by some of the words just alluded to. The degree of specialization which a language exhibits seems to depend on cultural need. In a culture in which the coconut is essential—as in Polynesia—an extremely complex vocabulary is said to have grown up, with different terms for many stages or ripeness of the fruit. So also, the Eskimos have different terms for falling snow, snow on the ground, snow packed hard like ice, slushy snow, wind-driven flying snow, and other kinds.[9] Many similar examples could be cited, for the languages of peoples of undeveloped culture appear to be particularly rich in specialized terms. At one time in the course of the English language it must have seemed desirable to speakers to make verbal distinctions in connection with groups of animals—mostly those of interest to farmers and hunters. An elaborate set of what are called "company terms" was accordingly developed, some (but by no means all) of which survive today. The better known ones include a *herd* or a *drove* of cattle, but of a *flock* of sheep (or birds), a *school* of fish, a *pack* of wolves (or hounds), a *covey* of partridges, and a *swarm* of bees. But there are others far more esoteric,[10] such as *nye* of pheasants, *cete* of badgers, *sord* of mallards, *wisp* of snipe, *doylt* of tame swine, *gaggle* of geese, *harras* of horses, and *kennel* of raches. There is a similar profusion of names for the same animal (*cow, heifer, bull, calf, steer,* and *ox*), the young of various animals (*puppy, kitten, kid, calf, colt, lamb,* and so forth), and the male and female of the same species (*gander* and *goose, drake* and *duck, horse* and *mare, cock* and *hen, dog* and *bitch*).[11] The need for a generic term is of course particularly felt here, and it is supplied, not quite satisfactorily, by the convention of making either the name of the male (*horse* and *dog*) or of the female (*cow, duck,* and *goose*), or even that of the young of the species (*chicken* and *pig*), perform a larger duty.

[9] See B. L. Whorf, "Science and Linguistics," *The Technology Review,* Vol. XLII, No. 6 (April 1940), reprinted in *Four Articles on Metalinguistics,* Washington, D.C. (Foreign Service Institute), 1950, p. 6. For further examples see also Jespersen, *Language,* pp. 429–431.

[10] These, and many others, are mentioned in an editorial comment in the *New York Times* for November 20, 1930. All but *doylt* are recorded in the *Oxford Dictionary.*

[11] McKnight, *English Words and Their Background,* p. 239, calls attention in greater detail to the lack of generalizing terms in the animal kingdom, and suggests further that the variety of names for sea craft (*sloop, schooner, brig, ship, boat, dinghy, bark,* and so on) is a similar survival of primitive habits of thought.

Figurative Language

William Dwight Whitney

The extension of a name's application, however, involves a great deal more that is far less plain and legitimate than [generalization and specialization]. Not only a true accordance in generic character, but relations of an infinitely looser kind, are used to tie together classes that go under one name. . . .

Since fruit is apt to be green when not fully ripe, *green* becomes a synonym for 'unripe' (and so we can commit the familiar linguistic paradox that *black*berries are *red* when they are *green*); and then, in less elegant diction, it is again shifted to signify 'immature, not versed in the ways of the world.' Such transfers we are wont to call figurative; they rest upon an apprehended analogy, but one generally so distant, subjective, fanciful, that we can hardly regard it as sufficient to make a connected class. Instances of this kind lie all about us, in our most familiar words; and this department of change is of so conspicuous importance in language-history that we must dwell upon it a little longer. Our minds delight in the discovery of resemblances, near and remote, obvious and obscure, and are always ready to make them the foundation of an association that involves the addition of a new use to an old name. Thus, not only an animal has a *head,* but also a pin, a cabbage. A bed has one, where the head of its occupant usually lies—and it has a *foot* for the same reason, besides the four *feet* it stands on by another figure, and the six *feet* it measures by yet another. More remarkable still, a river has a *head:* its highest point, namely, where it *heads* among the highlands—and so it has *arms;* or, by another figure, *branches;* or, by another, *feeders;* or, by another, *tributaries;* and it has a right and left *side;* and it has a *bed,* in which, by an unfortunate mixture of metaphors, it *runs* instead of lying still; and then, at the farthest extremity from the head, we find, not its *foot,* but its *mouth.* Further, an army, a school, a sect, has its *head.* A class has its *head* and its *tail;* and so has a coin, though in quite a different way. A sermon has its *heads,* as divided by their different *headings;* and we can beg to be spared anything more "on that *head.*" A sore comes to a *head;* and so, by one step further away from literalness, a conspiracy or other disorder in the state, the *body* politic, does the same. We give a horse his *head,* which he had before our donation; and then we treat in the same way our passions—that is to say, if by their overmastering violence we lose our *heads.* And so on, *ad infinitum.*

These side or figurative uses of a word do not perplex us; they do not even strike us as anything out of the way; they are part and parcel of the sphere of application of the word. For it is an important item in this process of transfer that we gradually lose our sense of the figure implied, and come to employ each sign as if it had always been the simple and downright representative of its idea. Here we see again the willingness, which has been already pointed out, and which is essential to the prosperous development of a language, to forget the origin of a name when once it is won, to let drop the old associations and suggestions which belonged to it in virtue of its etymology, and invest it with a new set appertaining to its present use. Perhaps there is in English hardly a more striking example of this than our word *butterfly,* a name of utterly prosaic and trivial origin, but which has become truly poetic and elegant, as we think in connection with it of the beautiful creatures it designates, and not one in a thousand has ever had come into his head the idea that it literally means 'a *fly* of *butter*-color.' The relics of forgotten derivations, of faded metaphors, are scattered thickly through every part of our vocabulary. It is, to our apprehension, in the nature of a word to have its figurative as well as its literal uses and applications; we inherited our vocabulary in that condition; and, by new discoveries of analogies and new transfers of meaning, we are all the time adding to the confusion—if it were a confusion. Sometimes the connection between the different senses is obvious on the least reflection; sometimes, again, it is so obscure that we cannot find it, or that we conceive it wrongly; ordinarily, we do not concern ourselves about the matter; we use each word as we have learned it, leaving to the lexicographer to follow up the ramifications to their source in its primitive or etymological meaning.

A conspicuous branch of the department of figurative transfer, and one of indispensable importance in the history of language, is the application of terms having a physical, sensible meaning, to the designation of intellectual and moral conceptions and their relations. It is almost useless to attempt to illustrate this; the examples would come crowding in too numerously to be dealt with: we will merely notice a few of those which happen to be offered in the preceding paragraph. *Perplex* means 'braid together, intertwine.' *Simple* is 'without fold,' as distinguished from what is *double,* or 'two-fold;' in *simplicity* and *duplicity* we have a moral contrast more distinctly brought to view; *application* contains the same root, and denotes an actual physical 'folding or bending to' anything, so as to fit it closely; while *imply* intimates a 'folding in.' *Important,* means 'bringing in, *importing,* having conferred *import* or consequence.' *Apprehension* signifies literally the 'taking hold' of a thing. *Relation* is a 'carrying back,' as *transfer* is a 'carrying across' in Latin, and *metaphor* nearly the same thing in Greek. To *invest* is to 'put into clothes;' to *develop* is to 'unwrap.' *Trivial* is what is found 'at the street-crossings;' anything is *obvious* which meets us 'in the way,' which *occurs* to, or 'runs against' us. *Derivation* involves the curiously special idea of drawing off streams of water from a *river,* for irrigation or the like. To *suggest* is to 'carry under,' or supply, as it were, from beneath, not conspicuously —and so on. All these are from the Latin part of our language, which furnishes examples in the greatest abundance, because our philosophical and scientific vocabulary comes mainly from that source; but there is plenty like it in the Saxon part also. *Wrong* is *'wrung'* or 'twisted,' as its opposite *right* is 'straight;' and *downright* involves the same figure as *upright,* as having nothing oblique or indirect about it. A *striking* example needs no comment. To *forget* is the opposite of to *get*, but signifies only a mental loss. We *see* things that never come before our bodily eyes. And *point out, let drop, follow up, lay down, come into the head, out of the way*, are instances of phrases that show plainly a similar shift of application. In fact, our whole mental and moral vocabulary has been gained precisely in this way; the etymologist feels that he has not finished tracing out the history of any one of its terms until he has hunted it back to the physical conception in which, by the general analogies of language, it must have had its origin.

WORKING WITH THE SELECTIONS

1. In the thirteenth century, the French word *perisse* 'to cease' was borrowed into Middle English; a century or so later it had developed the specialized meaning 'to die,' becoming our word *perish*. How may its introduction have affected the development of *starve*?

2. Look up the word *radical*. Do the meanings recorded all conform to your usual interpretation of the word today? Do earlier senses survive in some uses of the word?

3. Robertson and Cassidy cite the profusion of names for the same animal (*cow, heifer, bull, calf, steer, ox*) as possible examples of a cultural need in an agricultural society. Can you list similar groups of specialized names for horses or pigs or other animals? For styles of automobiles?

4. Sometimes a general word can specialize and become standard English quite rapidly. A very recent dictionary defines *Establishment* as "an exclusive group of powerful people who rule a government or society by means of private agreements and decisions." See if you can find this use in any dictionary published prior to 1965; you probably will not. What word—exclusive of slang, which is treated later—is the fastest growing today?

5. List three or four words like *deal* that seem to you examples of words generalized to the point of vagueness.

6. Look up the following words and describe how the meaning of each has changed. For a borrowed word, notice changes from meanings in the original language as well as changes since the word's introduction into English. The words may show the effects of generalization or specialization or of figurative change; some words may illustrate two or three kinds of semantic change.

spill	manuscript
estate	ambition
wretch	divan
mammoth	mug

7. Whitney offers a number of examples of figurative English containing the word *head*. What examples can you give with *foot*? Try some other parts of

the body, *arm, tooth, phalanges, pituitary*. Why do you find more figurative uses of some words than others?

2

Emotive Association, Euphemism, Taboo

Louis B. Salomon

Arguments about the "right" definition of a word are futile for several reasons, but partly because meaning involves more than direct reference between symbol and idea. Meaning, or at least the total effect of a word, includes a variety of subtle implications affected by the feelings and attitudes of both speaker and listener. The following discussion of some of the emotional ingredients of meaning is a chapter of Semantics and Common Sense *(1966) by Louis B. Salomon, professor of English at Brooklyn College of the City University of New York.*

THE EMOTIVE COMPONENT OF MEANING

If the human mind were a strictly logical device like a calculating machine, it would deal with words simply as names of categories, and with categories as essential tools for imposing order and system on a universe which otherwise presents itself as an unsorted chaos of sense stimuli. But human reaction to words, like much other human behavior, is also motivated by irrational impulses such as those we label *love, hate, joy, sorrow, fear, awe,* and so forth; and, whenever the users of a language evince a fairly uniform emotional response to a given word, that response becomes part of the connotation, therefore part of the standard meaning of the word in that language. While the bulk of the vocabulary doubtless consists of words that carry little or no perceptible emotional charge (*lamp, book, read, subtract, through*), there are nevertheless a good many that produce reactions of various colors and shades, with voltages ranging from mild to knockout force.

Not that it is always easy to distinguish the emotional response to a word itself from the emotional response to the class of things or concepts the word names. A rose or a skylark's song by any other names would smell or sound as sweet, and a dungheap or a subway train's wheel-screech by any other names would be a stench in the nostril or a pain in the eardrum; but many words are undoubtedly "loaded" with the speaker's or hearer's feelings, independent of any observable attributes in the class of objects named. When someone says "Watch your language!" he is usually not attacking your right to refer to the thing(s) you are referring to, but only urging you to abstain from an expression that *in itself*, quite apart from its denotation and linguistic connotation, is offensive to his ear or eye. There are, as Professor Hayakawa puts it, words that snarl and words that purr—and, of course, there are innumerable gradations in between. An informer and an informant deliver the same confidential information; selective service and the draft impose identical duties on young male citizens; sweat and perspiration produce the same demand for deodorant—but the different words have different odors too, and the nose that is insensitive to their scent is apt to end up a punched nose; the ear that does not hear their harmonies and discords, a cauliflower ear.

In *Romeo and Juliet,* for example, when hot-blooded Tybalt meets Mercutio and Benvolio, the friends of the man he is seeking, he might say to Mercutio, "Thou knowest [*or* art a friend of, *or* often accompaniest] Romeo;" instead, he begins, doubtless maliciously, "Mercutio, thou consort'st with Romeo—." Mercutio immediately bridles in anger at the choice of a word which, being then associated with bands of wandering minstrels, could only in contempt be applied to noblemen: "Consort! What, dost thou make us minstrels? . . . Zounds, consort!" A few moments later Tybalt has "made worm's meat" of Mercutio, Romeo has slain Tybalt, and the train of circumstances leading to the tragic deaths of the two young lovers has been irrevocably set in motion. Today, although the minstrel connection no longer operates to arouse such a violent sense of insult, the word *consort* still has a somewhat derogatory flavor (compare the phrase "consorting with known criminals") as compared with the almost completely neutral *associate,* though both terms have the same denotation and the same linguistic connotation.

Sometimes even slightly different forms of the same basic verbal symbol will carry widely variant emotive charges, as, for example, *informer* and *informant,* already cited. If you wanted to compliment a man on his virility of appearance or behavior you would speak of him as *manly,* certainly not as *mannish* (a derogatory term applied mostly to women) or *manlike* (usually a neutral term divorced from value judgment, as in "The carvings included several manlike figures"). The same emotive distinctions are to be found in the usage of *womanly, womanish, womanlike;* the form *childly* never appears, but *childish* and *childlike* convey respectively denigration and mild praise.

At first glimpse it might appear that this emotive component occurs only in the passion-sullied vocabulary of common speech, that judiciously selected diction—above all, scientific terminology—carries no such inflammatory charge. While this is hopefully true of the use of terms in technical discussion among trained scientists, there is nothing whatever to prevent a "scientific" word from being taken into the popular vocabulary, or, once there, from developing an aura of feeling that may all but obliterate its original denotation and linguistic connotation. The word *science* itself furnishes a striking instance: one of the most potent bits of ritual incantation in the repertoire of present-day spellbinding is "Science says. . . ." This being the case, as people with things or ideas to sell are well aware, any word that even sounds or looks like a scientific term carries a quasi-magical charge that makes blood tingle and cash registers tinkle. You have probably never seen, and hopefully never will see, an advertisement reading "This mouthwash contains megatherium"; but if you look at the "Atomic" entries in the 1964–65 Manhattan telephone directory you will find, along with Atomic Energy Commission, such other nuclear-oriented enterprises as Atomic Cleaners and Dyers, Atomic Dress Co., Atomic Handbag Co., Atomic Music Co., Atomic Neckware Mfg. Co., Atomic Trucking Corp., and Atomic Undergarment Co.

"SHADES" OF MEANING

Since the emotive component of meaning reflects so much of the current technological-sociological-moral climate, it is subject to more rapid and unpredictable change than are the denotation and linguistic connotation—so much so, indeed, that in extreme cases observations on particular specimens may sound as dated as last year's slang.[1] Even at any one time the emotive connotation of a given term may vary a great deal in both kind and intensity from one group of speakers to another, or among the same group in different circumstances. Some words acceptable at stag smokers cause raised eyebrows in mixed company in a drawing room; some that are appropriate in addressing a college class will sound pompous or stuffy in haranguing the same college students at a campus football rally; some are allowable in printed books and on the stage but not in radio or television broadcasts or in "family" magazines. Perhaps this kaleidoscopic shiftiness becomes most painfully apparent when you try to acquire a real working knowledge of a foreign language, that is, a mastery of the subtle nuances that make one phrase courteous and another, perhaps only slightly different, offensive. Even in your own language you may run into problems enough, particularly if you move from one social or cultural milieu to another—as many young men have found on entering the armed services, and then again on reentering civilian life.

The term *nuances* may be misleading, since it suggests that two or more terms really mean the same thing apart from a trivial shade of feeling they

[1] Compare Shakespeare's Doll Tearsheet, disputing Pistol's claim to the title of captain: "A captain! God's light, these villains will make the word as odious as the word 'occupy,' which was an excellent good word before it was ill sorted."

arouse. But we have defined symbolic meaning as the totality of what is conveyed by its symbol; hence, no two words are exactly synonymous, regardless of what they denote or what defining qualities they connote, as long as any tinge of emotive association, however minuscule, differentiates them. Consider, for example, the supply of simple adjectives at your disposal for indicating that a person's figure is noticeably below the national norm in weight. If it is someone whose feelings you particularly want to spare (yourself, for instance), you might use *slender;* if you want to sound patronizing, even a trifle acid, you might say *thin* or *lanky;* if you really want to leave a sting you might try *skinny* or *scrawny*—leaving still, for intermediate shades, *slim, spare, delicate, underweight, lean, emaciated.* For the opposite weight pattern, you could make your selection among *plump, well-rounded, portly, fleshy, overweight, stout, pudgy, chubby, fat, corpulent, obese,* and *bloated.* The abundance of such word choices makes possible an instructive little exercise, proposed many years ago by Bertrand Russell under the name "conjugation of adjectives." Examples (playing the game without too rigid adherence to rules) might go: "I am careful, you are timid, he is afraid of his shadow"; "I am interested, you are inquisitive, he is a snooper"; "I am a social drinker, you may be overindulging, he is a lush."

In the rough-and-tumble of actual use, however, synonym-juggling is anything but a game—unless Russian roulette is also a game. The differences between a fair trade practices law and a minimum price law, between senior citizens and old people, between underprivileged areas and slums, between extra crews and featherbedding, between a quarantine and a naval blockade: these are differences measurable in such units as sales figures, vote-getting, and bloodletting. The bloody draft-law riots of 1863 may or may not have been avoidable; but it is sobering to reflect that there have never been any selective-service-law riots. The modern public relations specialty known as motivation research has a heavy stake in identifying the hidden, perhaps subconscious resonances of contempt or reverence, aggression or longing, archetypal dread or narcissistic self-love which are likely to be stirred by verbal symbols at a given time and place, because without this information an advertising program or a political campaign might founder on an insidiously loaded synonym like a ship on a submerged reef.

TABOO AND EUPHEMISM

The dyslogistic connotations of a good many words, to be sure, are matters openly acknowledged and widely agreed upon, and whenever a common word gathers so heavy a load of taboo or social disapproval that many speakers hesitate to use the word at all, a process known as euphemism sets in. Most people, that is, employ another expression (either a new coinage or a new application for one already familiar) to symbolize the class to which the taboo word normally refers. Some speakers, on the other hand, resist such substitutions as semantically unjustifiable, and speak with pride of "calling a spade a spade," implying that the symbol *spade* is the one and eternally right name for the well-known digging tool, hence any other must be a shilly-shallying evasion. Without taking sides, this book will merely observe that for certain classes of objects, actions, and ideas (not, ordinarily, including spades) there are often two or more expressions with the same denotation and the same linguistic connotation, and that in general the shortest, simplest (and, historically, oldest) word tends to be more or less taboo, while a longer word or phrase, often originally metaphorical as a substitute for the taboo word, has gentler overtones or is socially more acceptable. Naturally this phenomenon occurs oftenest in connection with concepts that in themselves produce a sense of uneasiness in the minds of the users of the language—whether because of religious or sociological pressures peculiar to a certain culture or because of deep-rooted psychological impulses common to virtually the entire human race.

A few examples of this gentling-down process will suffice to suggest many others:

1. The idea of death is so painful that most speakers (including undertakers and life insurance salesmen, who of all people have occasion to talk about it most matter-of-factly) shun the three-letter verb in favor of euphemisms like *pass away, pass on, pass out of the picture, be no longer with us,* and so on. *expire*

2. Serious diseases of the heart or the mind sound somehow less forbidding as *heart condition, mental case.*

3. Because the use of the deity's name and other theological terms, except in solemn and reverent discussion, is regarded as blasphemous by many religious sects, we have (for nontheological discourse) near approximations in sound: *gosh, golly, gad* for *God; darn, dang, dash* for *damn; heck* for *hell*—or, in writing, the omission of one or more letters, as in *G—d* for *God.*

4. Names of the physiological functions of sex and excretion, and of the external parts of the body most closely associated with these, of course have spawned an assortment of euphemistic expressions, the use of which reflects wide variation in level of taboo from one cultural epoch to another. In mid-Victorian England, even legs became *limbs,* and all articles of underclothing *unmentionables.*

It is worth noting that the law of diminishing returns governs the value of any given euphemism just as inexorably as it does that of a factory machine, and the more commonly the euphemistic term appears in speech and writing, the more it tends to gather to itself the same stigma of taboo that is associated with whatever word or words it displaced. The word *undertaker,* for example, though once about as neutral a term as could be found for a person whose professional *raison d'être* we prefer not to be reminded of, is now giving way to *mortician* or *funeral director* because *undertaker* sounds too callously frank. Or take the name of that ingenious bathroom fixture which disposes of the waste products of the human body: the nearest approach to a plain, direct name for it in present-day standard American English is *toilet*—originally a euphemism of a very metaphorical order, stemming from the French *toile* ("cloth"). Once this euphemism came into very general use, however, it became *the* name for a thing which many people still prefer to mention only obliquely, and for which any reader can easily supply a half-dozen substitute expressions currently in vogue. The phrase *to make one's toilet,* referring to purely cosmetic activity, has all but been driven out of circulation, and the modern reader of *The Rape of the Lock* feels a sense of almost grotesque incongruity when, in a setting as urbane as any in English verse, he comes to the line introducing Belinda's dressing table: "And now, unveiled, the Toilet stands displayed."

From one culture or social stratum or chronological era to another, the kind and number of words subject to taboo, and hence generative of euphemistic substitutes, swings between wide extremes. At almost any time and place, however, there will be found a few words so heavily frowned upon that by large elements of the population their use, whether in speech or in writing, is regarded as a gross breach of decorum or morals, or both. Indeed, many legal prosecutions for obscenity have been based not on the subject-matter of a book or play but merely on the fact that it employed one or more of these words.[2] Even in the relatively permissive linguistic climate of the time in which this book has been written, there is a small handful of short, pungent English words which, though they are found liberally scrawled on walls and sidewalks, even printed in works of fiction or poetry issued by highly reputable publishers, the present writer feels constrained to mention only by proxy, as it were, in order to avoid giving offense.

These words, all with pedigrees of great antiquity, are used in two very different ways. First, they have denotation and linguistic connotation related to sex or excrement, and are so employed, either simply and naturally by speakers to whom these are symbols untainted by taboo, or self-consciously by a sophisticated class of men and women bent on demonstrating their emancipation from middle-class standards of respectability. But taking a statistical rather than a normative view one finds that in the vast majority of their occurrences these highly charged words point to no referents and no defining qualities at all, but are called upon to serve merely as rhetorical intensifiers, attention-getters, corresponding in function to gestures, changes of vocal intonation, or writing-devices like italics or exclamation points. This is true to some extent of all taboo words, and hence may be illustrated with

---

[2] The term *obscenity* usually is reserved for language that violates the sexual and excremental taboos, blasphemy for those that violate the religious taboos. *Profanity* seems to take in both categories. *Pornography,* commonly defined as writing designed to appeal to the prurient interest, often makes use of no words that in themselves are taboo; for example, consider the polished, even flowery diction of *Fanny Hill,* as contrasted with *Lady Chatterley's Lover,* the objection to which was based very largely on its use of taboo words.

examples that, hopefully, will not bruise any reader's sensibilities. Consider the meanings of the following phrases: *a good-looking girl, a damned good-looking girl, a goddamned good-looking girl;* or, conversely, *a homely girl, a damned homely girl, a goddamned homely girl; a hell of a fine play, a hell of a flop; Who the hell do you think you are? Hi, there, how the hell are you?* Obviously, the taboo words in these contexts do not refer to anything, but are simply another way of saying "very" or "Listen to this" or "Hey, this is important!" or pounding on the table. What is being made use of is the shock value of the taboo itself, and any expressions with a strong-enough dyslogistic charge would do equally well.

Two other curiosities may be observed about this divorcing of emotive connotation entirely from the other components of meaning. In the first place, it is not necessary that any of the highly taboo words themselves, or even near-homophones of them, be physically present as long as it is somehow suggested that their intensifying effect is what is intended. Devices traditionally used by the more finicky to produce the same effect include the spoken *so-and-so* or *blankety-blank,* the written asterisks or dashes, which permit the hearer or reader to supply his own verbal intensifiers or not, as he likes; the question of what is *meant* by the dashes has little to do with what words, if any, the reader chooses to imagine in their place.

Second, the law of diminishing returns operates here too in a way to give pause even to those who scorn to let social or moral pressures circumscribe their vocabulary. Setting aside any possible considerations deriving from squeamishness, and merely weighing the effect in the passionless scale of the efficiency expert, one can easily see that in a passage such as "How the ——— are you? I sure as ——— wish, ——— ——— it, you'd quit reading that ——— ——— book and give me the ——— low-down on what the ——— ——— you've been doing since I saw you at that ——— party at the boss's ——— ——— country place," and so forth, the attention-getting force of each successive three-em line, or whatever taboo expression it may replace, is less than that of the preceding one. If anyone speaks habitually in a shout, his decibels soon become merely monotonous, and only a sudden drop to a whisper will bring his audience up with a jolt.

Both points are well illustrated by H. L. Mencken's anecdote of a World War I drill sergeant who was accustomed to interlard his speech so liberally with forms of one especially taboo word that when he ordered his men, "Go get your ——— rifles!" they knew it was a routine command and took their time about obeying. One day, though, he called out, "Go get your rifles!" and every startled G.I. in the platoon "lit out" for the barracks on the double.

Since response to a command affords the best possible pragmatic test of what meaning, if any, has been conveyed, this little story demonstrates also: (a) that emotive connotation is indeed part of meaning; (b) that, like the other components of meaning, it is not inherent in any given verbal symbol but is imputed by the users of the symbol; and (c) that the speaker's intention and the hearer's inference do not necessarily coincide.

WORKING WITH THE SELECTION

1. In another part of his book Salomon identifies the two components of the meaning of a word: (1) denotation ("the sum total of its referents") and (2) connotation ("the defining qualities of the category or class it names, and the emotive or affective responses it arouses in the minds of its users"). Thus the word *tree* "denotes every individual, unduplicatable object in the category"; it connotes the defining qualities of the class, such as "large woody stems, leaves, branches, greenness plus whatever emotional associations *tree* may have." Emotive meaning is therefore part of connotation. Distinguish between the emotive meanings of each of the following pairs of words, which are roughly synonymous in denotation:

intoxicated, drunk	continuous, incessant
fussy, fastidious	contempt, scorn
overweight, fat	saliva, spit
mediocre, average	pay, remuneration

2. Social pressures often push words into special, sometimes temporary, prominence; two examples are *ethnic* and *ecology*. How much of the effect of these words is emotional? Try to think of other currently popular words connected with social issues and consider their emotional meanings.

3. In his novel *The Sacred Giraffe,* Salvador Madariaga describes a society far in the future, in which some language habits differ from ours. For example, nobody would dare use in polite company any word connected with taking food into the body through the m——th, an activity practiced only in the strictest privacy. And small white squares of cloth thought to have been used in earlier civilizations in connection with nasal emissions are unmentionables. What tendency in language is Madariaga making fun of?

4. Fashions in taboo words change; words involving sex and other bodily functions, especially so-called four-letter words, have changed rapidly in recent years. The words listed below are some that have been unacceptable, at least in mixed company, in fairly recent times. How many of them would still cause raised eyebrows?

leg	bitch	butt
pants	crap	devil
lavatory	belly	drawers
john	bottom	water closet

5. Mention two current euphemisms for people who are poor, two for students who are stupid. Explain each of the following euphemisms as an example of one of the four types Salomon mentions.

expire	memorial park
Jeepers Creepers	halitosis
in the family way	mentally disturbed

3

Twenty-five Definition Routes

Hugh R. Walpole

One of the practical problems of any study of meaning is definition, finding ways of distinguishing among words so that users of the language can maintain enough agreement about them to communicate. Hugh R. Walpole extended the work in semantics of C. K. Ogden and I. A. Richards. The following selection is from Semantics *(1941).*

Logicians do not agree on the definition of "definition." Professor L. Susan Stebbing, in *A Modern Introduction to Logic,* will not accept exemplification, or definition by similarity ("a sonnet is a poem like Keats's poem on Chapman's *Homer,* or that poem of Wordsworth's on *Westminster Bridge*") as being definition at all. Nor does this scholar accept simple naming ("Mr. Robinson is that man I am pointing at") or definition by translation (*"Tapferkeit* means *courage"* is Miss Stebbing's example) as definitions in her sense of that term. Other logicians disagree on one or other of these points.

In this chapter, however, we are interested in all such processes of clarification or explanation, in the definitions of the scientist or the logician, but equally in definition as used by the man who has seldom even heard the word. ("What's all this about 'one man, one vote'?" asked the Nottingham miner. "Why, one bloody man, one bloody vote," Bill replied. "Well, why the 'ell can't they say so?") . . .

Throughout the discussion of the following list of definition routes—which covers all the different ways of expanding a symbol—to explain the way the author is using it gaps have been left for the reader to supply whatever word or words make the best sense to him. In doing this, the reader cannot help following the road which is being discussed. The proof of the road is in the journey. If any particular place gives trouble, this may be a sign that the reader's thinking is clogged a little along this line. (Though it is hard to make all examples equally lucid and the trouble may be the author's fault.)

This is the list of definition routes.

Route 1. This is it.

Direct Symbolization Many an argument has to be rooted to a concrete situation before it can branch out successfully. Conversation with foreigners proves this most dramatically; but all the time we do it more than we realize. "What I call my hand is . . ." and we touch it. "The window is . . ." and we point to it. In the last resort, we may have to take the stranger to his station, and point out the City Hall.

Route 2. It is similar to this.

Similarity You may draw the thing you are trying to describe, or you may express its similarity to something familiar to your hearer. "A bat is a quadruped ——— a mouse, with membranous wings."

Route 3. Its name may be translated by this word.

Translation A person who speaks a different dialect, or a foreign language, or has different interests, may know a lot about the referent, but may not recognize the symbol. "A stout fellow is a swell guy." "A mammal is an ———." "A gob-stopper is a marshmallow." "A concierge is ——— ———."

Route 4. It is contained in this.

Part and Whole "A foot is ——— ——— a leg." "A company is ——— ——— an infantry regiment."

Route 5. It contains this.

Whole and Part "A series is a number of ——— of one kind, following one another in order." "A committee is a ——— ——— ——— appointed or elected to perform some function."

Route 6. It is the opposite of this.

Opposition by Cut "Left is ——— ——— ——— right." "White is ——— ——— ——— black."

Route 7. It is at the opposite end of a scale from this.

Opposition by Scale Two opposition headings are necessary: one stands opposite one's mirror in a different sense of "opposite" from the way the top of a flagpole is opposite to its base. "Directly opposite" and "at the opposite end of" are two different relationships, just as opposite walls do not show the same kind of opposition as do the opposite ends of a carpet. The walls are cut apart by the intervening floor; while it is carpet, carpet, all the way, from one end to the other. "The top is ——— ——— ——— the bottom." "——— ——— of boiling water is ——— water."

Route 8. It resides in this place.

Place: Where "An occupant is a person —— —— a certain place." "A Siamese is a person —— —— —— the country of Siam."

Route 9. It comes from this place.

Place: Whence "Virginia tobacco —— —— Virginia, and Siamese cats from Siam." The distinction is clear enough, but it is not easy to find for nine examples which might not also apply to eight.

Route 10. It has this age.

Age "A centenarian is —— —— —— —— ——." "A parr is a —— salmon."

Route 11. It lived in this period.

Period "Medieval things belong to —— —— ——." "The Augustan period in Latin literature occurred —— —— —— of Augustus Caesar."

Route 12. It has this shape.

Form "A triangle is a rod of polished steel bent —— —— ——, which is sounded by being struck with a steel rod." "Siamese twins are twins who are —— —— each other." "A brachycephalic is a person with a —— ——, the breadth of whose skull is at least four fifths of its length."

Route 13. It has this size.

Size "A giant is a —— person." "A microbe is a —— living being."

Route 14. It has such and such a quality, characteristic or property to this extent.

Degree "A mule is an animal which is —— horse and —— donkey." "A saturated solution is one in which there is only just —— of the dissolving agent —— —— all of the substance." "A mulatto is a person whose ancestry is —— Negro, and —— white."

Route 15. It is made of this material.

Substance "A can is a —— vessel, in which fruit, fish, etc., are sealed up airtightly for preservation."

Route 16. Its material is in this condition.

State "A corpse is —— —— —— of a man." "A feudal society was based on the relation of lord and vassal arising out of the holding of lands in feud."

Route 17. It causes this emotional reaction in a human being.

Causation: Emotive "A darling is someone ——." "A cur is a —— dog." "A scoundrel is a person —— ——." "A friend is ——." Emotive definitions of this kind can be very tricky, as we saw in an earlier chapter. But though emotive language must not be used for referential purposes, it would be most unscientific to try to ignore its existence.

Route 18. It has this effect on the human mind.

Causation: Mental "A surprise is an event for which one —— —— ——." "A masterpiece is a piece of work —— —— ——." To what extent is it possible to distinguish between mental and emotive causation in actual communication? As was seen in Chapter Two, we can easily see the difference between extreme examples of the two types. But, especially in ethics, aesthetics, and philosophy, many definitions and utterances use Routes 17 and 18 together.

Route 19. It has this effect on the human senses.

Causation: Sensory The important thing to remember here is that a red curtain is a curtain which gives a "red" sensation to our eyes; a rough brick is a rough-sensation brick; bitter quinine is bitter-sensation quinine; and so on. No philosophy is involved here—I am not saying that bricks and curtains and quinine do not exist. The sole point here is that their characteristics of color, taste, smell, touch, and the like are specifically named *for* their effects on the senses. In general, when we want to be objective we leave out the human being, but obviously here that is just what we cannot do; it would be like emptying a flood from a deluge and expecting to find something left. This route could be subdivided and the sensations classified according to whether our muscles are affected or our skin, our taste buds, our olfactory cells, our auditory nerves, or the cells of our retinas. "A ruby is a —— precious stone." "Quinine is an alkaloid, —— in taste, which is found especially in cinchona bark." "A shout is a —— cry." "A file is a metal instrument with a —— face."

Route 20. It has this physical effect.

Causation: Physical We could split up all these causations, especially this last, according to whether the thing defined is cause or effect: assassin or victim, father or son. "——— ——— is a person who kills himself." "A parent is ——— ——— ———."

Route 21. It behaves in this way.

Behavior "An extrovert is a person who ——— ——— ———." "A puritan is someone who is, pretends to be, or is supposed to be ——— in religion or morals." "A dandy is a person who takes great pains to ——— ———."

Route 22. It is of this sex.

Sex "A boar is ——— ——— swine." "A hen is the ——— of the common domestic fowl."

Route 23. It serves this purpose.

Use "A hammer is ——— ——— ——— beating, breaking, driving nails, etc."

Route 24. He has this family connection with that person.

Family Relations "The brother of a person is the son of ——— ——— ——— as that person." "A household is a ——— establishment."

Route 25. He has this legal connection with that person.

Legal Relations "A plaintiff is a person who brings suit into ———." "The owner is the person who has ——— right to possession." "The person who is sued is called a ———."

These twenty-five routes are not the key to the riddle of the universe. They are a prescription for the more efficient use of words; and if the reader has the slightest qualm about any relationships he feels have been ignored, he should add them to this list, even though later they may be discarded as unnecessary. In fact, it would not be a bad idea to make the formal addition of *Route 26*, **Pragmatism:** *Any other kind of connection or connections, simple or complex, that you can think of.*

WORKING WITH THE SELECTION

1. A common description of a "logical" definition is that it places the item to be defined in a class (*A triangle is a plane figure*) and then distinguishes it from other members of the class (*with three sides*). Which aspect of this process is emphasized in Walpole's examples?

2. Select six examples used by Walpole and compare them with dictionary definitions. In which instances does the dictionary employ the same routes

Walpole follows? Do any of the examples you have selected seem inadequate in the light of the dictionary definitions, requiring additional distinction through another route?

3. Consider the following definitions in relation to Walpole's list of routes, indicating which route each seems to follow or whether it does not seem to follow any of those listed. Some, of course, may follow more than one route. Do some of the definitions seem inadequate?

> a. Osculation is kissing.
> b. A signature is part of a book.
> c. Evil is the opposite of good.
> d. An ostrich is a large bird.
> e. An oubliette is a dungeon having a trap door in the ceiling as its only opening.
> f. Religion is the opiate of the people.
> g. A shelf is a thin, flat length of wood or other material set horizontally at right angles to a wall and used for holding things.
> h. An example of a palindrome is *Able was I ere I saw Elba.*
> i. A hermit crab is a crab that lives in the shells of certain mollusks.
> j. A cruller is a doughnut without a hole.

4. Select a term that seems to have particular currency on campuses, or on your own campus, and write an extended definition of it, using several of the routes described by Walpole. Terms like *Panhellenic, big wheel, rap session, brain, jock* are possibilities, although some of them are dated and all of them have limited currency.

4

Connotation
in Dictionary Definition

David B. Guralnik

The problem of definition of meaning is a very practical one for the lexicographer. David B. Guralnik, editor of Webster's New World Dictionary, *2nd ed.* (1969), *discusses problems of presenting the full meaning of a word, including its emotive associations, in the following selection from an article that appeared in* College Composition and Communication, 9 (May, 1958).

In selecting and writing his definitions, the lexicographer is of course fully aware that he is not actually recording the "meaning" of a particular word, but that he is merely trying to suggest, within the available space, as many of the aspects of the thing defined as will recall it to the reader or will allow him to form an idea of it in his mind. That is to say, a dictionary definition such as "a tool or apparatus for boring holes in wood, metal, stone, etc." does not actually describe any single, particular device. It might suggest a hand drill or a power drill or a dentist's device for evoking exquisite pain, but it does in any case denote, or explicitly mark out, that class of objects to which English speakers have assigned the generic word *drill*. Of course, the more restricted the class, or the fewer the possible number of referents, the more precise the denotation. A proper name is the most restrictive of all. The term *William Shakespeare* will probably suggest the author of a number of enduring plays and poems. Or, if your interests incline in a somewhat different direction, it might recall a skillful member of the Yale backfield in the late thirties. But it will probably have no other "meaning" for most people.

The lexicographer is primarily concerned with pinpointing the possible denotations of a word, and there are those who believe that this is all he can or does do with the "meanings" of words. Such a notion is an erroneous one. The editor is also aware that what the word suggests, that is its connotation, can be fully as important as what it denotes, for he knows that words are not only grammatical tools and symbols, but that they embody as well an ensemble of notions, concepts, and psychological reactions. A politician and a statesman may both be concerned with carrying out the affairs of government, but unless the reader or user of these terms understands that the word *politician* is frequently used in a derogatory sense, with implications of seeking personal or partisan gain, scheming, opportunism, etc., and that *statesman* suggests able, farseeing, principled conduct of public affairs, he cannot have the full meanings of these words. The lexicographer knows clearly in such a case that his responsibility does not end with recording the denotation of these words. It occurs to me in passing that age must be the catalyst that invariably transforms the politician into a statesman. We seem to be burdened with an unconscionable number of elder statesmen, but I have yet to hear of an elder politician.

All words, with the possible exception of the particles, convey connotative notions of one sort or another. Very often these connotations are of a highly personal order. To the child who first becomes aware of polka dots as the embellishment of his mother's silk dress, the term *polka dot* may thereafter evoke the sensation of soft silkiness. Some words may have group, in addition to individual, suggestiveness; that is, their connotations may be sharply divided into opposing camps depending on whether the idea denoted is favorably or unfavorably received by the listener. Emotion-charged terms such as *integration, socialism,* and, on another level, *rock and roll* offer extreme examples of violently disparate connotation. It is clear that such individual or group reactions cannot be taken into account by dictionaries. The editor of a dictionary, and especially of a college desk dictionary, is constantly buffeted between the Scylla of excessive terseness and the Charybdis of an unwieldy, too expensive volume.

Other terms, however, may over a period of time acquire specific connotations that are sufficiently widespread to warrant recognition and recording by the lexicographer. The word *propaganda,* which until quite recently meant essentially "any systematic, widespread, deliberate indoctrination or plan for such indoctrination" today requires an annotation like the one in the *New World:* "now often used in a derogatory sense, connoting deception or distortion."

The line of demarcation between the denotative and connotative aspects of a word is not always clearly drawn. Frequently the elements blend and are merged into a single descriptive statement that serves as the dictionary definition. The lexicographer need not feel undue concern where this occurs naturally and easily. The problems of judgment and selection enter where the division is sharp and easily recognized. Here the editor must decide whether the exigencies of space will allow the extra connotative note that could round out the meaning of the term.

In addition to the explicit note, there are other devices used by dictionaries to suggest the connotative aspects of words. In a very large sense, the usage labels attached to many terms and senses constitute one such device. It is one thing to know that *haughty* can mean "lofty or noble," but unless one also knows that this sense is regarded as archaic, he may, if he uses it innocently in normal conversation, find himself misunderstood. In the same way it is only proper that a college dictionary record the word *hight,* meaning "named or called," but unless this too is labeled *Archaic,* the freshman who appropriates this term into his active vocabulary may find himself the victim of condescending smiles. The same situation would apply to words and meanings labeled "obsolete" or "colloquial" or "slang" or "British." Similarly, after some meanings, the dictionary may have a note stating that the word is used ironically (as *pretty,* meaning "fine or good" in a *pretty mess*) or familiarly or vulgarly or hyperbolically or as a counterword of wide application (e.g., *nice,* used as a generalized term of approval). Thus we can see that usage labels serve not only to nail down the period or level to which a term properly belongs, but also to suggest the flavor or odor which the term may emit in its context. This, too, is connotative. . . .

Sometimes the lexicographer must include some of the connotative affects of a word if only to illuminate its normal extensions in meaning. For example, the staff of our dictionary recently decided that although the word *jungle* denotes most simply "land covered with dense growth of trees, tall vegetation, vines, etc., typically in tropical regions," we shall be required to add the connotative information that jungles are generally inhabited by predatory beasts, so that the extended meaning of this word that has resulted in such Hollywoodisms as *asphalt jungle* and *blackboard jungle* might be properly understood.

Another word recently recorded by the *New World* is *exurbanite,* the coinage of A. C. Spectorsky. At its most elemental level, this word refers to "a person of the upper middle class who lives in the semirural areas beyond the suburbs but who works in the metropolis, especially in the communications fields, as in advertising, publishing, the theater, etc." That is essentially all the word "means." But unless we remark also that "exurbanites are regarded as conforming to social and cultural patterns as standardized as those of suburban life," Mr. Spectorsky's whole point in writing the book—and coining the word—is lost. And for *suburban,* too, we must have a note stating that this word variously connotes a combination of urban and rural features, middle-class conservatism, etc., since the word today is as frequently used for its connotative elements as for its explicit denotation.

A class of words that can and should receive explanatory notes in dictionaries concerning their suggestive tones are the terms of racial and ethnic opprobrium. The lexicographer, we feel, has the moral responsibility to inform the dictionary user that if he persists in using these terms he does so today, in the view of most cultivated people, only by jeopardizing his respectability and good taste.

Still another area in which the dictionary can convey connotation is in the little paragraph labeled "Synonymy" that follows most words of general vocabulary. These paragraphs serving to discriminate among various closely related words are as often concerned with the suggestive differences between these various terms as they are with the denotative differences. Take, for instance, the group *desire, wish, want,* and *crave.* All of these words, collectively, denote a strong longing or yearning, and within the definitions proper for these words it seems pertinent to employ the same or similar wording, often even using one or more of these terms as an approximate synonym for another. But within the synonymy it is possible to offer the extended nuances that make each of these more precisely appropriate in a particular context. The paragraph reads: "*desire,* generally interchangeable with the other words here in the sense of to long for, stresses intensity or ardor (to *desire* success); *wish* is not as strong a term as *desire* and has special application when an unrealizable longing is meant (he *wished* summer were here); *want,* specifically suggesting a longing for something lacking or needed, generally is a more informal equivalent of *wish* (she *wants,* or *wishes,* to go with us); *crave* suggests desire to gratify a physical appetite or an urgent need (to *crave* affection)."

Frequently where specific explanation must be forgone because of lack of space, connotation can be implied through the judicious use of illustrative examples. The discerning freshman soon learns that the phrases or sentences demonstrating the word in action serve not only to elaborate the definition, but often through context suggest the special nuances that the word has acquired in usage. For example, the word *ramble,* in one sense, might be defined: "to grow or spread in all directions." This clearly gives the proper denotation of one use of *ramble.* But if we add the illustrative "as, vines *rambled* over the fence," the graphic image conjured up by the example supplies suggestive tones that may help the dictionary user focus the true "meaning" of the word. Often the etymology will supply an interesting sidelight that can bring a flash of understanding to the student. To know that *supercilious* refers ultimately to raised eyebrows or that *sarcasm* derives from a Greek verb meaning "to tear flesh like dogs" is to have an additional insight into the subtle shades suggested by these words.

I have been speaking of the ways in which dictionaries can and frequently do supply the connotations that are essential to a proper grasp of meaning. But I do not mean to imply satisfaction with the extent to which these techniques have been carried out in existing dictionaries. It is the conviction of our staff that the use of these devices should be extended still further. The chief problem, of course, is one of space. But I believe that a way will be found, perhaps by a reapportionment of the space allotted to the various lexicographical elements and by securing the approval of the user of dictionaries to such a reapportionment. For in our opinion it is precisely the inclusion of connotation in dictionary definitions that can lend precision to the student's speech and art to his writing.

WORKING WITH THE SELECTION

1. Look up the following words in at least two desk dictionaries and record any information available on connotation. Consider especially lists of synonyms or references to lists of synonyms that follow regular definitions.

demand	dogma
collaborate	egghead
naughty	eliminate

2. Does Guralnik's definition of *propaganda* follow any of the routes to definition listed by Walpole? Does the part of the definition concerned with connotation follow any particular route?

3. Explain the sense in which, according to Guralnik, usage labels indicate part of the meaning of a word.

4. Would the kinds of connotations Guralnik is talking about be regarded by Salomon as part of meaning?

5. Try writing definitions of the following words, including any indications of connotation you feel are necessary. Then compare your results with a dictionary.

   nigger   languish   tycoon   Establishment

6. The words in each of the following groups are roughly similar in meaning but different in connotation, suggesting different attitudes toward the ideas they symbolize. For each group indicate which word seems to you most favorable in its connotation, which most nearly neutral, and which unfavorable.

antique, old, antiquated
plot, plan, strategy
think, meditate, daydream
conservative, stuffy, careful
grab, obtain, acquire
aromatic, stinking, odorous
obsequious, polite, gracious
indomitable, obstinate, firm
complimentary, laudatory, flattering
progressive, rash, enterprising

7. Read the following brief paragraph. Then for the words in italics, substitute in order the words following the paragraph. How does the tone of the new paragraph differ? In what ways are the words in the list fair or unfair substitutes for the original?

The *candidate* for the *position* is a *statesman* who has *earned* wide *fame* for his *zealous support* of *conservative plans* to *stabilize* the economy. He has *responded* to the *advice* of party *officials* and followed *loyally* the *rigid principles* of the *government*.

applicant, job, politician, acquired, notoriety, fanatic, defense, reactionary, schemes, immobilize, toadied, pressure, bosses, slavishly, narrow-minded, prejudices, Establishment

5

Meaning and Society

The following three selections, all from longer discussions, introduce some different sorts of speculations about how problems of meaning are related to the basic behavior of human beings. Biologist Grace de Laguna comments on words as reflections of the way human beings view their world in the selection from her article in Human Biology, *1 (December, 1929). Novelist Aldous Huxley (1894–1963), in* Words and Their Meanings (1940), *expands the idea that "words are magical in the way they affect the minds of those who use them." The selection by Thomas Hornsby Ferril, from his article "Western Half-Acre,"* Harper's Magazine, *193 (July, 1946), presents his observation of some effects of man's ability to think symbolically.*

Perception and Language

Grace de Laguna

It does not need argument to prove that without language we should none of us come to understand the sensible world about us. It is through the conceptual analysis effected by language that I may come to understand the construction of the automobile engine, and it has similarly been through the agency of language that we all acquired in childhood an understanding of the common objects of daily life. But the sights and sounds of everyday have not only acquired meaning in this way: they have also, through the analysis and synthesis effected by speech, become perceptually differentiated and organized as the objects and events we now see. Of course it is not language in isolation that has accomplished this transformation. But language does not exist in isolation from the culture of which it forms the chief vehicle. It is impossible to learn the language of an alien culture merely from grammar and dictionary. One really acquires a language only insofar as he acquires a culture. Otherwise, as Rousseau says, one may only speak French in six languages. It might well be argued that men of widely differing cultures and modes of speech perceive in correspondingly different terms. The Eskimo, for example, who discriminates by name a dozen varieties of snow surface and formation, each of which has for him its distinctive significance, must see a different landscape from that which meets the eye of the European traveler to the Arctic. But while this might be argued, the thesis here maintained is simpler: that man's ability to use language implies a perceptual experience fundamentally different in its content and organization from that possessed by any other animal.

Considered merely as a mode of discriminatory response, speech is unique. By speech it is possible to respond directly and specifically to an object as such, or even to a quality or relation as distinguished from what is qualified or related. Even the gesture of pointing cannot discriminate the object as such from its spatial location, while it is obviously impossible to point to a quality or a relation. But a word is not merely a vocal gesture which discriminates an object from its location or a quality from an object. By naming something a "tree," for example, I at once distinguish it as an object from its setting, and identify it as a member of a familiar system, in which "bark," "branches" and "leaves" each has its place, as well as "shade," or "ax" and "firewood," as the case may be. How much of this actually enters into perception at any one time depends on occasion and circumstance. But if I see it as a "tree," the content of my perception is so organized that every sensory detail of hue and brightness and contour is incorporated within it as qualifying just that whole. If I scrutinize it more closely, still regarding it as a "tree," fresh details emerge, each of which continues to have its place within the determining pattern. Thus I perceive more clearly the texture of the "bark," the color and form of the "leaves," etc. In such a case language serves to patternize perception, to determine the general framework into which sensory detail will fit.

But not all our perceptual experience is verbalized in so explicit a fashion. Human perception occurs on different levels. To look at something with a definite view to describing in language what one sees is to see with fresh eyes. What is seen takes on a noticeable transformation. Such explicitly verbalized perception is rare. I may indeed not see the tree as a "tree" at all, but only vaguely as an object to be avoided in my walk, and having no determinate color, shape or size. In such moments we doubtless approach more nearly an animal type of perception. Yet even here there is something distinctly human, in that later I may recall "that I met an obstacle in my path." The influence of language on perception is not limited to what may be termed "verbalization." What as men we see and hear and feel is already such that it *may become* verbalized. The specific organization that accompanies explicit verbalization is not an act of special creation *de novo*. It occurs as a natural development of what is already prepared.

Words and Their Meanings

Aldous Huxley

It is time now that I gave a few typical instances of the way in which words have power to modify men's thought, feeling and conduct. But before doing so, I must make a few more remarks of a general nature. For our present purposes, words may be divided into three main classes. The first class consists of words which designate definite and easily recognizable objects or qualities. Table, for example, is an easily recognizable object and brown an easily recognizable quality. Such words are unambiguous. No serious doubts as to their meaning exist. The second class contains words which designate entities and qualities less definite and less easily recognizable. Some of these are highly abstract words, generalizing certain features of many highly complex situations. Such words as "justice," "science," "society," are examples. In the same class we must place the numerous words which designate psychological states—words such as "beauty," "goodness," "spirit," "personality." I have already mentioned the apparently irresistible human tendency to objectify psychological states and project them, on the wings of their verbal vehicle, into the outer world. Words like those I have just mentioned are typical vehicles of objectification. They are the cause of endless intellectual confusion, endless emotional distress, endless misdirections of voluntary effort.

Our third class contains words which are supposed to refer to objects in the outer world or to psychological states, but which in fact, since observation fails to reveal the existence of such objects or states, refer only to figments of the imagination. Examples of such words are the "dragon" of the Chinese and the "death instinct" of Freudian psychologists.

The most effective, the most psychologically magical words are found in the second category. This is only to be expected. Words found in the second class are more ambiguous than any others and can therefore be used in an almost indefinite number of contexts. A recent American study has shown that the word "nature" has been used by the philosophers of the West in no less than thirty-nine distinct senses. The same philosopher will give it, all unconsciously of course, three or four different meanings in as many paragraphs. Given such ambiguity, any thesis can be defended, any course of action morally justified, by an appeal to nature.

Ambiguity is not the only characteristic which makes these words peculiarly effective in determining conduct. Those which stand for generalizations and those which designate psychological states lend themselves, as we have already seen, to objectification. They take verbal wings and fly from the realm of abstraction into the realm of the concrete, from the realm of psychology into the external universe.

The objectification and even the personification of abstractions is something with which every political speech and newspaper article has made us familiar. Nations are spoken of as though they were persons having thoughts, feelings, a will and even a sex, which, for some curious reason, is always female. This female, personal nation produces certain psychological effects on those who hear it (or rather her) being talked about—effects incomparably more violent than those that would be produced if politicians were to speak about nations as what in fact they are: organized communities inhabiting a certain geographical area and possessing the means to wage war. This last point is crucially important. California is an organized community; but since it does not possess an army and navy, it cannot qualify for a place in the League of Nations.

Another familiar entity in political speeches is the pseudo-person called "Society." Society has a will, thoughts and feelings, but, unlike the Nation, no sex. The most cursory observation suffices to show that there is no such thing as Society with a large S. There are only very large numbers of individual societies, organized in different ways for different purposes. The issue is greatly complicated by the fact that the people who talk about this nonexistent Society with a big S, tend to do so in terms of biological analogies which are, in many cases, wholly inapplicable. For example, the so-called philosophical historians insist on talking of a society as though it were an organism. In some aspects, perhaps, a society does resemble an organism. In others, however, it certainly does not. Organisms grow old and die and their component cells break down into inanimate substances. This does not happen to a society, though many historians and publicists loosely talk as though it did. The individuals who compose what is called a decadent or collapsed society do not break down into carbon and water. They remain alive; but the cells of a dead organism are dead and have ceased to be cells and become something else. If we want to talk about the decline and fall of societies in terms of scientific analogies, we had better choose our analogy from physics rather than biology. A given quantity of water, for example, will show least energy, more energy, most energy according to its temperature. It has most energy in the form of superheated steam, least in the form of ice. Similarly, a given society will exhibit much energy or little energy according to the way in which its individual members live their lives. The society of Roman Italy, for example, did not die; it passed from a high state of energy to a lower state of energy. It is for historians to determine the physiological, psychological, economic and religious conditions accompanying respectively a high and a low degree of social energy.

The tendency to objectify and personify abstractions is found not only among politicians and newspaper men, but also among those who belong to the, intellectually speaking, more respectable classes of the community. By way of example, I shall quote a paragraph from the address delivered by Clerk Maxwell to the British Association in 1873. Clerk Maxwell was one of the most brilliantly original workers in the whole history of physics. He was also what many scientists, alas, are not—a highly cultivated man capable of using his intelligence in fields outside his particular specialty. Here is what he could say before a learned society, when at the height of his powers.

"No theory of evolution," he wrote, "can be formed to account for the similarity of molecules." (Throughout this passage, Maxwell is using the word "molecule" in the sense in which we should now use the word "atom.")

> For evolution necessarily implies continuous change, and the molecule is incapable of growth or decay, of generation or destruction. None of the processes of Nature, from the time when Nature began, have produced the slightest difference in the properties of any molecule. We are therefore unable to ascribe either the existence of the molecules or the identity of their properties to any of the causes which we call natural. Thus we have been led along a strictly scientific path very near to the point at which Science must stop. . . . In tracing back the history of matter Science is arrested when she assures herself, on the one hand that the molecule has been made and, on the other, that it has not been made by any of the processes which we call natural.

The most interesting point that emerges from these lines is the fact that, like the Nation, but unlike Society, Science has a sex and is a female. Having recorded this item in our text books of natural history, we can go on to study the way in which even a mind of the caliber of Clerk Maxwell's can be led into absurdity by neglecting to analyze the words which it uses to express itself. The word "science" is current in our everyday vocabulary. It can be spelt with a capital S. Therefore it can be thought of as a person; for the names of persons are always spelt with capital letters. A person who is called Science must, *ex hypothesi,* be infallible. This being so, she can pronounce without risk of contradiction, that "none of the processes of Nature, since the time when Nature began" (Nature is also spelt with a capital letter and is of course also a female), "have produced the slightest difference in the properties of any molecule." Twenty-three years after the date of Maxwell's speech, Becquerel observed the radioactivity of uranium. Two years after that Mme. Curie discovered radium. At the turn of the new century Rutherford and Soddy demonstrated the fact that the radium atom was in a process of rapid disintegration and was itself derived from uranium whose atoms were disintegrating at a much slower rate.

This cautionary story shows how fatally easy it is for even the greatest men of science to take the particular ignorance of their own time and place, and raise it to the level of a universal truth of nature. Such errors are particularly easy when words are used in the entirely illegitimate way in which Maxwell employed the word "Science." What Maxwell should have said was something like this, "Most Western scientists in the year 1873 believe that no process has ever modified the internal structure of individual atoms. If this is so (and of course the beliefs of 1873 may have to be modified at any moment in the light of new discoveries), then perhaps it may be legitimate to draw certain inferences of a theological nature regarding the creation of matter."

How was it possible, we may ask ourselves, that a man of Clerk Maxwell's prodigious intellectual powers, should have committed a blunder so monstrously ridiculous, so obvious, when attention is called to it, to people of even the most ordinary mental capacities? The question demands a double answer—the first on the purely intellectual level, the second in terms of feeling and will. Let us deal with these in order. Maxwell made his mistake, first of all, out of a genuine intellectual confusion. He had accepted the English language without question or analysis, as a fish accepts the water it lives in. This may seem curious in the light of the fact that he had certainly not accepted the technical language of mathematics without question or analysis. We must remember, however, that nontechnical language is picked up in infancy, by imitation, by trial and error, much as the arts of walking and rudimentary cleanliness are acquired. Technical languages are learned at a later period in life, are applied only in special situations where analysis is regarded as creditable and the ordinary habits of daily living are in abeyance. Children and young people must be deliberately taught to analyze the nontechnical language of daily life. With very few exceptions, they will never undertake the task on their own initiative. In this respect, Maxwell was not exceptional. He turned his intensely original and powerful mind on to the problems of physics and mathematics, but never on those of everyday, untechnical language. This he took as he found it. And as he found in it such words as "Science" with a capital S and a female sex, he made use of them. The results, as we have seen, were disastrous.

The second reason for Maxwell's error was evidently of an emotional and voluntary nature. He had been piously brought up in the Protestant tradition. He was also, as the few letters to his wife which have been printed seem to indicate, a practising mystic. In announcing that "Science" with the capital S and the female sex had proved that atoms had not evolved, but had been created and kept unchangingly themselves by nonnatural forces, he had a specifically religious purpose in view. He wanted to show that the existence of a demiurge after the pattern of Jehovah, could be demonstrated scientifically. And he wanted also, I suspect, to prove to himself that the psychological states into which he entered during his moments of mystical experience could be objectified and personified in the form of the Hebraic deity, in whose existence he had been taught to believe during childhood.

Sensation and Cerebration

Thomas Hornsby Ferril

The other day I was looking at a spread of 10,000 sheep in a Colorado mountain valley way up high. Sheep are the most idiotic beautiful things that ever lived. I can't believe my senses when I look at them and I half envy people who don't have to make the effort. It occurred to me that the best place to find people who don't have to believe their senses about sheep or anything else would be New York, and I'd throw in Washington also. Ten thousand sheep wandering down Wall Street would be put up with as a temporary inconvenience but it wouldn't be remembered any longer than a Sioux war dance in Times Square. It would go down as just another stunt of some kind in the minds of people who believe their senses very resentfully because they have so little use for them.

The trouble is that these people's senses don't get enough exercise. Sensation is becoming vestigial among them, like the flabby muscles we still have for wiggling our ears like mules. About all their senses are used for is setting up reflexes that come in handy for getting around in traffic, eating, and mating.

The rest of what used to be called sensation has been taken over by cerebration, because these writhing seaboard masses are jammed together so tightly that they have to live for the most part by symbols instead of things real to the senses. They have no choice in the matter. There's nowhere near enough room for the people themselves to shove their bodies around in, while they work all day with all the biggest and bulkiest things in the world in the way of commerce: the vast herds and flocks of mountain and prairie, the food and fibre of millions of acres, the enormous tonnages of mines and mills. To be manageable at all, every bulky reality has to be pulled down into something it isn't—some tight little representation of itself, a symbol or cryptogram, such as converting 10,000 real sheep into a flicker of teletype. New York would be buried in half a day by the physical substance it handles symbolically in the same half day. (Be fun digging it up like Pompeii: way down deep, under the seventh layer of wheat or cotton, you'd find a mummified broker hugging a firkin of butter and his stenographer serenely clasping a pump handle.)

It follows that, in handling such volumes of physical material by spirit rather than sense, the mind feels a bit guilty. It feels that it ought to know more about the outside world, it ought to make some effort to connect up with the reality behind the symbol but, hang it all, there isn't time. You can't go high-tailing it off to Butte to learn about copper, or off to Kansas to learn about wheat. So you come to rely more and more on imagined concepts of what the outside world would be like if you could ever bring it into the field of sensation. These imagined concepts are fortified by no end of information services, respected because of their brevity. They presume to tell in one paragraph what Iowa is thinking or what California wants. But such summarization carries the mind, not closer to reality, but farther from it. The net effect has been to increase, rather than diminish, reliance on the symbol.

I never cease to marvel, and I shudder also, at what begins to happen when man, as a partially educated animal, becomes subject to mass congestion. Congestion and literacy, it seems to me, are heading seaboard people for the most skillful manipulation of unreality in history: they are well on their way to the mysticism of the lower Ganges Valley, but they lack the complacence that goes with the symbolic life. They are too well off, too healthy; they have been spared the fatalistic peace of mind that accompanies pestilence, famine, and high mortality. Thanks to literacy and prosperity, all they get out of this manipulation of unreality is the jitters. Their Karma is the sanitarium. Their capacity for fear thrives on having nothing real to be afraid of except each other.

The five senses in these congested areas are always at a loss to find anything to work on. The hardest-hitting seaboard realist, however close to Nature he may have started his life, owes his ultimate success to manipulating things he never sees or touches at all. His desk is clean save for one vacuum bottle of cold water. He no longer affects a telephone. He eschews all sensual pleasures: if he ever did any lusty helling around he has long since given it up. He is the top mystic, wearing his stomach ulcers like a hair-cloth shirt. In his air-conditioned retreat he is quietly attended by industrial nuns who whisper low rituals and occasionally give him some paper fetish to contemplate. This paper fetish is a ritualized art form—for example, the annual report of some corporation, representing symbolically the expenditures of life and energy of some whole countryside. The paper will show assets, say, of $26,109,612.04 and liabilities of precisely the same amount, $26,109,612.04. This has been got up by the accounting priesthood—artists highly trained in selection, emphasis, and understatement—assets and liabilities have to rhyme and chime as inexorably as the final couplet of an Elizabethan sonnet.

Somewhere along the line, far back in his youth, this top mystic qualified for this cloistered unreality by getting his hands into things that pushed back when he pushed them. He knew sensation: he worked in a steel mill or slaughter house. And he still has a Faust-like hankering for it. This protects his judgment; he still has some carry-over reference to Nature and, as long as he can keep it going, his wisdom is useful in mercantile abstraction. It isn't easy, for he is surrounded by small-fry mystics who have long since broken with Nature if they were ever integral to it at all. They flounder in the limbo of statistical cryptograms: the small virtues of interpolation become the fantastic vices of extrapolation. The statistical curve is so plausible to them that they think that all you have to do is push it just one mite farther to know all about tomorrow. These curves are as distinct a contribution to the history of mystical art as the Gothic arch was to substantial art.

Reliance on abstraction increases directly with density of population. Denver differs from New York only in degree. Our Seventeenth Street neophytes make devout pilgrimages to receive the blessings of the lamas of Wall Street. We are all on the road to congestion-abstraction but don't know what it is doing to us.

In small towns, with plenty of land around them, people are closer to original materials and farther apart from each other; consequently, they require fewer symbolic abstractions. Robinson Crusoe didn't need any. Go back to when nearly everybody lived in the country, a century or so ago, and note how slowly and begrudgingly people added new symbols to their traditional stock. Agricultural superstitions showed little variation from one generation to another. Established religions were constant and repetitive. Outrageous excursions such as Unitarianism or Mormonism shocked the whole country by their novelty; but symbolic innovations, for the most part, were quickly absorbed by cross-roads politics where such abstractions as "the tariff" or "nullification" could carry the venturing mind as far as it wanted to go. But nowadays less, I suppose, than one fourth of our people are farmers in the old-fashioned sense and our capacity for making new symbols is nourished by city congestion.

Everybody is hell-bent to live in the city and thinks that the biggest city is the best city. This means a wider chasm between men and original materials, more dependence on representation as a substitute for fact, and less dependence on sense for confirming truth. It's an odd contradiction that industrialization itself, which we think of as putting men very close to physical materials, carries with it, the farther it goes, the obligation to increase the number of representations of what the material once was and the kind of life it stood for. The extractions of the earth have to be pretty well fabricated into simpler forms before the city can tolerate them at all. The man who makes shoes out of leather has no sense of cattle. There's nothing about the garment worker's cloth to remind him of blue flax in bloom, fields of cotton, or sheep being clipped. Even a lamb chop—to go back to my 10,000 sheep again—gets all snarled up in symbolism blurring its original actuality.

To the Easterner who munches it down there's no hint of the ranges, grass, or water, because the lamb chop comes, if it comes at all, from the corner store: it stands for something wrong or right about the store, something wrong or right about the bureaucrats, wrong or right about the world food economy. The poor little lamb chop carries such a mystical burden that there's almost no fun eating it.

Being jammed into the symbolic life a good deal ahead of the rest of us, it is natural that seaboarders should be more adept at pure theory. Obviously, they have had more practice. It is easy to explain why they are more disposed to superstition, witchcraft, devil worship, and appeasement. This is characteristic of anybody who lives preponderantly in the world of the spirit. Their plant equipment for the vicarious life is superb. Nowhere else on earth does anybody have such access to all the representations of what life elsewhere *must* be like: here are the greatest libraries, the greatest museums of art and natural history, the greatest foundations to explore economic symbolism, and the greatest concentration of universities to make fullest use of every representation. Like anybody breaking new ground, these pioneers on the frontiers of abstraction naturally romanticize their activities. They are as blameless for parading their mental garments as the cowman for wearing a ten-gallon hat. It is inevitable that they should feel that they have superior intelligence, superior humanity, superior insight into world affairs.

What they actually have is, obviously, more mental activity with proportionate sacrifice of sense reference as to its accuracy. What they mistake for superior intelligence is no more than accelerated cerebration—quicker turnover of very volatile and interchangeable symbols. They work the mental squirrel cage harder simply because there are so many more squirrels queued up to get into it. Their claims to superior humanity and global love for their fellow man have a curious relationship to mass fear. With fear as a catalyst the seaboard masses churn themselves up to a crusading hysteria, but, in the absence of fear, these humanitarian impulses degenerate quickly, to the sad disillusionment of the intellectuals.

All these mental traits belong to the general phenomena of excess population that we don't understand very well and ought to try harder to understand because all our problems of war and peace are more concerned with them than anything else. What these masses want, but don't know how to say it, is some sort of integration with the land. They are bewildered when anybody tries to encroach on what little they have—witness the hue and cry about fundamental rights when the UN wanted to stake off a little acreage in Westchester County.

Clearly, seaboarders are doomed to a far greater variety of heavens and hells than we inlanders who have made slower progress on the road to abstraction. Quite apart from fear, which always thrives on congestion, emotional intensity of all kinds is part and parcel of the symbolic life. This is characteristic of all artists and prophets. A symbolist like Dorothy Thompson has as vivid a conviction of reality as the mad poet, William Blake. The eye surveys the whole world with stereopticon clairvoyance; international problems take on a four-cocktail clarity.

An Iowa farmer would have to get all hopped up on hard cider to have the faintest inkling of those burning awarenesses, even at their most sluggish Monday-morning level of intensity. As I look back on it, the only sin of the Corn Belt farmer in recent years was that he didn't stay plastered all day. It was metaphysical inagility rather than lack of patriotism that made him the arch-enemy of world peace. He was clumsy about swapping the abstractions of peace for the abstractions of war, for the simple reason that he'd never had much truck with abstraction of any kind in the first place. He couldn't transfer hysteria he didn't have to something somebody else was afraid of, nor did he have the stimulating disadvantage of being elbowed around by people who were afraid of each other. He was stigmatized for wanting to hide behind the haystack but, in my opinion, he was so well integrated with the land, and required so few abstractions to make what sense there was out of his life, that he had little feeling of either security or insecurity until people started calling him names.

I'd conclude these remarks by suggesting that people who live by symbols are forever fugitive from them. Somewhere behind the flicker of teletype that stands for 10,000 sheep there must be real sheep; somewhere behind the greatest library in the world there must be the kind of life that caused all those little black vowels and consonants to be put into all those millions of books. The real thing is worth going after. The horizon beckons. It becomes a consuming drive. But the first sally is merely the flight from the city itself, and the first destination is the pastoral illusion. Actually, it isn't a flight from the city: the city is more convenient than the country, more comfortable, healthier, the food is better. The real flight is from the symbolic life. You've got to make your senses go back to work, get your hands into materials that push when you push; you've got to get your nose into the smells of Nature and your eyes into the kind of distance that keeps on going. You've got to remodel some upstate barn or race off to Connecticut to fondle a real lamb.

The pastoral illusion, however, trips you up, because you are too experienced a symbolist to break whole-hog with the city you love best. All you are asking for is another adventure in symbolism. Unfortunately, rustic innocence is not retroactive. The only people who really have it are the ones who grew up with it and never found it out.

By the time you get to wanting it at all, it's too late to do more than increase the draft on your already over-developed talent for making the unreal stand for the real, plus a lot of fatigue in shuttling back and forth a good many miles from one illusion to the other. What I'm saying is as true of the city poor as the city rich, but the poor are spared the embarrassing privilege of running away only to traipse back home with their tails between their legs. And they thank no one for their good fortune, nor should they: every man to his own adventure!

WORKING WITH THE SELECTIONS

1. Describe the differences de Laguna mentions between ordinary perception and perception directed to verbalization.

2. Distinguish Huxley's three classes of words. On what basis does Huxley make his classification?

3. In the light of your other reading on meaning, would you agree with Huxley's comment that the words in his first class are unambiguous?

4. Explain what Huxley means by the tendency of abstract words to objectification.

5. Are Huxley and Ferril talking about the same thing when they discuss abstraction?

6. Ferril's article was published in 1946. Have there been changes in our society that make his observations seem out of date?

6

Sign and Symbol

Susanne K. Langer

Other readings in the book have spoken of meaning as symbolic. In the following selection from Philosophy in a New Key *(1942), Susanne K. Langer discusses more precisely the nature of symbolism and distinguishes between sign and symbol.*

There are, first of all, two distinct functions of terms, which have both a perfectly good right to the name "meaning": for a significant sound, gesture, thing, event (e.g. a flash, an image), may be either a *sign* or a *symbol*.

A sign indicates the existence—past, present, or future—of a thing, event, or condition. Wet streets are a sign that it has rained. A patter on the roof is a sign that it is raining. A fall of the barometer or a ring around the moon is a sign that it is going to rain. In an unirrigated place, abundant verdure is a sign that it often rains there. A smell of smoke signifies the presence of fire. A scar is a sign of a past accident. Dawn is a herald of sunrise. Sleekness is a sign of frequent and plentiful food.

All the examples here adduced are *natural signs*. A natural sign is a part of a greater event, or of a complex condition, and to an experienced observer it signifies the rest of that situation of which it is a notable feature. It is a *symptom* of a state of affairs.[1]

The logical relation between a sign and its object is a very simple one: they are associated, somehow, to form a *pair;* that is to say, they stand in a one-to-one correlation. To each sign there corresponds one definite item which is its object, the thing (or event, or condition) signified. All the rest of that important function, signification, involves the third term, the subject, which *uses* the pair of items; and the relation of the subject to the other two terms is much more interesting than their own bare logical coupling. The subject is related, essentially, to the other two terms *as a pair*. What characterizes them is the fact that they are paired. Thus, a white bump on a person's arm, as a mere sense-datum, would probably not be interesting, enough even to have a name, but such a datum *in its relation to the past* is noted and called a "scar." Note, however, that although the subject's relation is to the *pair* of other terms, he has also a relation to each one of them individually, which makes one of them the sign and the other the object. What is the difference between a sign and its object, by virtue of which they are not interchangeable? Two terms merely associated as a pair, like two socks, two balances of a scale, two ends of a stick, etc., could be interchanged without any harm.

The difference is, that the subject for which they constitute a pair must *find one more interesting than the other, and the latter more easily available than the former.* If we are interested in tomorrow's weather, the events now present, if coupled with tomorrow's weather-phenomena, are signs for us. A ring round the moon, or "mares' tails" in the sky, are not important in themselves; but as visible, present items coupled with something important but not yet present, they have "meaning." If it were not for the subject, or *interpretant,* sign and object would be interchangeable. Thunder may just as well be a sign that there has been lightning, as lightning may signify that there will be thunder. In themselves they are merely correlated. It is only where one is perceptible and the other (harder or impossible to perceive) is interesting, that we actually have a case of *signification belonging to a term*.[2]

Now, just as in nature certain events are correlated, so that the less important may be taken as signs of the more important, so we may also *produce* arbitrary events purposely correlated with important ones that are to be their meanings. A whistle means that the train is about to start. A gun-

---

[1] There is a fine distinction between sign and symptom, in that the object signified by a symptom is the *entire condition* of which the symptom is a proper part; e.g., red spots are a symptom of measles, and "measles" is the entire condition begetting and including the red spots. A sign, on the other hand, may be one part of a total condition, which we associate with another separate part. Thus a ring round the moon is part of a weather condition, but what it signifies is rain—another proper part—and not the entire state of "low-pressure" weather.

[2] Cf. Whitehead, *Symbolism* (New York: The Macmillan Co., 1927), pp. 9–13.

shot means that the sun is just setting. A crêpe on the door means someone has just died. These are artificial signs, for they are not part of a condition of which they naturally signify the remainder or something in the remainder. Their logical relation to their objects, however, is the same as that of natural signs—a one-to-one correspondence of sign and object, by virtue of which the interpretant, who is interested in the latter and perceives the former, may apprehend the existence of the term that interests him.

The interpretation of signs is the basis of animal intelligence. Animals presumably do not distinguish between natural signs and artificial or fortuitous signs; but they use both kinds to guide their practical activities. We do the same thing all day long. We answer bells, watch the clock, obey warning signals, follow arrows, take off the kettle when it whistles, come at the baby's cry, close the windows when we hear thunder. The logical basis of all these interpretations, the mere correlation of trivial events with important ones, is really very simple and common; so much so that there is no limit to what a sign may mean. This is even more obviously true of artificial signs than of natural ones. A shot may mean the beginning of a race, the rise of the sun, the sighting of danger, the commencement of a parade. As for bells, the world is mad with their messages. Somebody at the front door, the back door, the side door, the telephone—toast is ready—typewriter line is ended—school begins, work begins, church begins, church is over—street car starts—cashbox registers—knife grinder passes—time for dinner, time to get up—fire in town!

Because a sign may mean so many things, we are very apt to misinterpret it, especially when it is artificial. Bell signals, of course, may be either wrongly associated with their objects, or the sound of one bell may actually be confused with that of another. But natural signs, too, may be misunderstood. Wet streets are not a reliable sign of recent rain if the sprinkler wagon has passed by. The misinterpretation of signs is the simplest form of *mistake*. It is the most important form, for purposes of practical life, and the easiest to detect; for its normal manifestation is the experience called *disappointment*.

Where we find the simplest form of error, we may expect to find also, as its correlate, the simplest form of knowledge. This is, indeed, the interpretation of signs. It is the most elementary and most tangible sort of intellection; the kind of knowledge that we share with animals, that we acquire entirely by experience, that has obvious biological uses, and equally obvious criteria of truth and falsehood. Its mechanism may be conceived as an elaboration of the conditioned-reflex arc, with the brain doing switchboard duty, and getting the right or the wrong number for the sense organ that called up the musculature and expects an answer in terms of altered sensations. It has all those virtues of simplicity, componability, and intelligibility that recommend a concept for scientific purposes. So it is not surprising that students of genetic psychology have seized upon sign interpretation as the archetype of all knowledge, that they regard *signs* as the original bearers of meaning, and treat all other terms with semantic properties as subspecies—"substitute signs," which act as proxy for their objects and evoke conduct appropriate to the latter instead of to themselves.

But "substitute signs," though they may be classed with symbols, are of a very specialized sort, and play only a meagre and restricted part in the whole process of mental life. I shall return to them later, in discussing the relationship between symbols and signs, for they do stand with a foot in either domain. First, however, the characteristics of symbols in general, and their essential difference from signs, must go on record.

A term which is used symbolically and not signally does *not* evoke action appropriate to the presence of its object. If I say: "Napoleon," you do not bow to the conqueror of Europe as though I had introduced him, but merely think of him. If I mention a Mr. Smith of our common acquaintance, you may be led to tell me something about him "behind his back," which is just what you would *not* do in his presence. Thus the symbol for Mr. Smith —his name—may very well initiate an act appropriate peculiarly to his absence. Raised eyebrows and a look at the door, interpreted as a *sign* that he is coming, would stop you in the midst of your narrative; *that* action would be directed toward Mr. Smith in person.

Symbols are not proxy for their objects, but are *vehicles for the conception of objects*. To conceive a thing or a situation is not the same thing as to "react toward it" overtly, or to be aware of its presence. In talking *about* things we have conceptions of them, not the things themselves; and *it is the conceptions, not the things, that symbols directly "mean."* Behavior toward conceptions is what words normally evoke; this is the typical process of thinking.

Of course a word may be used as a sign, but that is not its primary role. Its signific character has to be indicated by some special modification—by a tone of voice, a gesture (such as pointing or staring), or the location of a placard bearing the word. In itself it is a symbol, associated with a conception,[3] not directly with a public object or event. The fundamental difference between signs and symbols is this difference of association, and consequently of their *use* by the third party to the meaning function, the subject; signs *announce* their objects to him, whereas symbols *lead him to conceive* their objects. The fact that the same item—say, the little mouthy noise we call a "word"—may serve in either capacity, does not obliterate the cardinal distinction between the two functions it may assume.

The simplest kind of symbolistic meaning is probably that which belongs to proper names. A personal name evokes a conception of something given as a unit in the subject's experience, something concrete and therefore easy

[3] Note that I have called the terms of our thinking conceptions, not concepts. Concepts are abstract forms embodied in conceptions; their bare presentation may be approximated by so-called "abstract thought," but in ordinary mental life they no more figure as naked factors than skeletons are seen walking the street. Concepts, like decent living skeletons, are always embodied—sometimes rather too much. I shall return to the topic of pure concepts later on, in discussing communication.

to recall in imagination. Because the name belongs to a notion so obviously and unequivocally derived from an individual object, it is often supposed to "mean" that object as a sign would "mean" it. This belief is reinforced by the fact that a name borne by a living person always is at once a symbol by which we think of the person, and a call-name by which we signal him. Through a confusion of these two functions, the proper name is often deemed the bridge from animal semantic, or sign-using, to human language, which is symbol-using. Dogs, we are told, understand names—not only their own, but their masters'. So they do, indeed; but they understand them *only in the capacity of call-names*. If you say "James" to a dog whose master bears that name, the dog will interpret the sound as a sign, and *look for* James. Say it to a person who knows someone called thus, and he will ask: "What about James?" That simple question is forever beyond the dog; signification is the only meaning a name can have for him—a meaning which the master's name shares with the master's smell, with his footfall, and his characteristic ring of the doorbell. In a human being, however, the name evokes the *conception* of a certain man so called, and prepares the mind for further conceptions in which the notion of that man figures; therefore the human being naturally asks: "What about James?" . . .

Since a name, the simplest type of symbol, is directly associated with a conception, and is employed by a subject to realize the conception, one is easily led to treat a name as a "conceptual sign," an artificial sign which announces the presence of a certain idea. In a sense this is quite justified; yet it strikes a strained and unnatural note, which is usually a fair warning that the attempted interpretation misses the most important feaure in its material. In the present case, it misses *the relation of conceptions to the concrete world,* which is so close and so important that it enters into the very structure of "names." A name, above all, *denotes* something. "James" may represent a conception, but *names* a certain person. In the case of proper nouns this relation of the symbol to what it denotes is so striking that denotation has been confused with the direct relation of sign and object, signification. As a matter of fact, "James" does not, without further ado, *signify* a person; it *denotes* him—it is associated with a conception which "fits" the actual person. The relation between a symbol and an object, usually expressed by "S denotes O," is not a simple two-termed relation which S has to O; it is a complex affair: S is coupled, for a certain subject, with a conception that fits O, i.e. with a notion which O satisfies.

In an ordinary sign-function, there are three essential terms: subject, sign, and object. In denotation, which is the simplest kind of symbol-function, there have to be four: subject, symbol, conception and object. The radical difference between sign-meaning and symbol-meaning can therefore be logically exhibited, for it rests on a difference of pattern, it is strictly a different function.[4]

---

[4] If a symbol could be said normally to "signify" anything, its object would be the occurrence of an act of conception. But such a function of a symbol is casual, and

Denotation is, then, the complex relationship which a name has to an object which bears it; but what shall the more direct relation of the name, or symbol, to its associated *conception* be called? It shall be called by its traditional name, *connotation*. The connotation of a word is the conception it conveys. Because the connotation remains with the symbol when the object of its denotation is neither present nor looked for, we are able to *think* about the object without reacting to it overtly at all.

Here, then, are the three most familiar meanings of the one word, "meaning": signification, denotation, and connotation. All three are equally and perfectly legitimate, but in no possible way interchangeable.

In every analysis of sign-using or symbol-using, we must be able to account not only for the genesis of knowledge, but also of that most human characteristic, error. How sign-interpretation can miscarry, has already been shown; but failures of denotation, or confusions of connotation, are unfortunately just as common, and have a claim to our attention, too.

WORKING WITH THE SELECTION

1. Explain in your own words Langer's distinction between sign and symbol, supplying an example or two of your own to illustrate.

2. In describing the fourth defining characteristic of language, Hill briefly comments on symbols. Does his view correspond with Langer's?

3. According to the evidence presented in Brown's report on the Gardners' experiment, would you say that the chimpanzee Washoe was behaving symbolically?

4. In a passage not included here, Langer quotes Helen Keller's account of learning the word *water*. Langer comments, "The passage is the best affidavit we could hope to find for the genuine difference between sign and symbol." How does Helen Keller's experience illustrate this difference?

---

crosses with its use as a *symbol*. In the latter function it is not the act of conception, but *what is conceived,* that enters into the meaning-pattern. We shall avoid much confusion and quibbling by recognizing that signification does not figure in symbolization at all.

7

Basic Principles of Semantics

Anatol Rapoport

The approach to meaning known as general semantics originated with the work of Alfred Korzybski (1899–1950), whose Science and Sanity *appeared in 1933. Anatol Rapoport, professor of mathematical biology at the University of Michigan, has long been active in the International Society for General Semantics and served as its president from 1953 to 1955. The following selection is from "What Is Semantics,"* American Scientist, 40 *(January, 1952).*

Perhaps the most important ideas in semantics (with which modern logic is intimately interlaced) are (1) the propositional function, (2) the operational definition, (3) predictive value as the criterion of truth, (4) the theory of types.

The first and last of these are largely the work of Bertrand Russell. The second and third have a long history. They emerged with the development of modern physics and are already recognizable in the work of Ernst Mach, the exponent of the "positivist" approach to physics, Rudolf Carnap (a philosopher-logician) and P. W. Bridgman (a physicist) have stated the principles of operational definition and the predictive criterion of truth in unambiguous terms.[1]

Like most great ideas, these four principles are relatively easy to grasp. One wonders how the great thinkers of past centuries missed them. But evidently it is the same with great ideas as with great inventions: they seem simple only after one has been shown how.

Let us take the propositional function first. Classical logic (whose founder was Aristotle) took it for granted that all judgments could be broken up into simple propositions, that is, statements in which something (a predicate) is asserted about something (a subject). Examples are *water is wet; grass is yellow; some Greeks are rich; no animal is rational*. It was also assumed that such propositions were either "true" or "false": *water is wet* is a true proposition; *grass is yellow* a false one. Logic was a set of rules for deriving propositions from other propositions. If *some Greeks are rich* is a true proposition, and *no Spartan is rich* is another true proposition, then *some Greeks are not Spartans* must also be a true proposition.

[1] See Carnap, *Philosophy and Logical Syntax* (London, 1935); Bridgman, *The Logic of Modern Physics* (New York, 1927).

From the days of Aristotle to the nineteenth century hardly any important innovations were made in logic. Logic was considered largely a closed system (like euclidean geometry) and was taught in Western universities in much the same way Aristotle had taught it about 350 B.C.

The notion of the propositional function, however, was an innovation. The central idea of that notion is that one can make an assertion which *grammatically* looks like a proposition (a predicate asserted about a subject) but which cannot be said to be either true or false. An example of such a function is the statement *x is green*. One cannot tell, without knowing what x stands for, whether the statement is true or false. If x is grass, it is true, but if x is milk, it is false. The idea of the propositional function is obviously rooted in mathematics, where statements like $x^2 - 5x + 6 = 0$ are commonplace. It is evident that this statement is true if x stands for 2 or 3, but is false otherwise.

The propositional function is important in the theoretical development of logic. Just as arithmetic became algebra with the introduction of symbols to stand for variables (unknown quantities), so classical logic became symbolic logic with the introduction of the propositional function and of symbols to stand for propositions. Rules were developed for operating on propositions (like the rules of algebra which operate on variables), and logic became a branch of mathematics (or, one might say, mathematics was shown to be a branch of logic). And just as mathematics found wide application in science and technology, so symbolic logic is beginning to bear fruit in the design of computing machines, for example, and some theories of the structure of the nervous system.

But the notion of propositional function has another consequence more pertinent for this discussion. It showed that practically all our judgments are made not in terms of propositions but in terms of propositional functions! Consider the statement *grass is yellow,* which looks like a proposition. If by "grass" is meant the stuff that grows in Vermont in May the statement is false, but if one means the similar thing in California in July, then it is true! But then again it is not true if by "yellow" one means the color of ripe pumpkins.

Potentially, then, the question "What do you mean?" is pertinent at all times even when the "simplest" things are talked about, because the truth of statements depends on the meaning one assigns to the terms involved. This brings us to the second notion of semantics, the operational definition.

Again we must go back to Aristotle, because he made the first rules about definitions. According to Aristotle, a definition does two things. It places the thing defined in a class and then it tells how the thing is to be distinguished from other members of its class.

"Man is a featherless biped" is an aristotelian definition. It places man in a class of two-legged animals (bipeds) and distinguishes him from other members of that class such as birds (by the qualification featherless). Aside from the fact that plucked chickens and kangaroos, are also featherless bipeds (as Norbert Wiener remarks), such definitions have even more serious pitfalls. Anything can be formally defined whether it exists or not. Furthermore, the class and the distinguishing characteristics, in terms of which aristotelian definitions are made, may be no clearer than the thing defined. If the purpose of definition is to make meaning clear, then many aristotelian definitions fail to do so. If a *xyphia* is defined as a three-legged bird, and if there are no three-legged birds, then *xyphia* is just as meaningless after having been defined as before. If *worry* is defined as a species of anxiety accompanied by hypertension, the definition is useless unless "anxiety" and "hypertension" are closer to our experience than "worry."

In contrast to the aristotelian definition by "class" and "characteristic," semanticists recommended the operational definition, which is widely used in science. An operational definition tells *what to do* to experience the thing defined. Asked to define the coefficient of friction, a physicist says something like this: "If a block of some material is dragged horizontally over a surface, the force necessary to drag it will, within limits, be proportional to the weight of the block. Thus the ratio of the dragging force to the weight is a constant quantity. This quantity is the coefficient of friction between the two surfaces." The physicist defines the term by telling *how to proceed* and *what to observe*. The operational definition of a particular dish, for example, is a recipe.

From the operational definition to the operational meaning of truth is only a step. Carnap and others distinguish two kinds of truth. One is the formal kind, based only on logical consistency within itself or with certain propositions *assumed* to be true. Carnap prefers to call propositions which are true in this sense "valid." For example, *If all x are y, and all y are z, then all x are z* is a valid proposition, because of its internal consistency independently of what *x, y,* and *z* stand for. The propositions of euclidean geometry are valid with respect to the postulates and axioms chosen for that geometry. One may also choose other postulates with respect to which some propositions of euclidean geometry will not be valid. Validity, then, has nothing to do with observation or experience.

A true proposition, on the other hand, must be related to some kind of experience. No amount of formal proof is sufficient to establish that grass is green. The decisive criterion is looking and experiencing greenness. In a way, the criterion involves a prediction of an experience: "Look and you will see that it is green." This is not to say, however, that "seeing is believing" is always a sound criterion. No amount of "seeing" will establish the roundness of the earth or the inverse square law of gravitation. The criteria for these "facts" are indirect. They consist of certain experiments, the results of which are *predictable* if the roundness of the earth or the law of gravity is assumed true. If we assume that the earth is round, we can predict that departing ships will seem to sink into the horizon, and that the shadow on the moon during an eclipse will have a round edge, and that one can circumnavigate the earth.

Now we come to the fourth idea in semantics, the theory of types. It was known in antiquity that formal logic can be driven into a blind alley by a number of paradoxes. A typical one is the following. Consider the statement within this square.

> Every
> statement
> in this
> square
> is
> false.

Suppose the statement is true. Then, since it is the only statement in the square, it must be false. On the other hand, suppose it is false. Then, there must be true statements in the square. But again it is the only one; so it must be true. The example is trivial, of course, but similar paradoxes arise in mathematics and make difficulties for mathematicians. Since progress in mathematics depends on its complete internal consistency, it was necessary to re-examine the logical foundations of mathematics. One of the results of this re-examination is the theory of types. The theory rests on the principle that "a class cannot be a member of itself." That is, if you make a statement about *all* statements of a certain class, the statement you have made cannot be itself considered to be in that class. This was the principle violated in the paradox just described.

Now let us look at Korzybski's basic principles (or the non-aristotelian postulates, as they are sometimes called), on which his "non-aristotelian system" is built: (1) the principle of non-identity, (2) the principle of non-allness, (3) the principle of self-reflexiveness.

As we shall see in a moment, logically the first principle is included in the second, so that it can be omitted. But we shall also see that, from the point of view of further development of Korzybski's system, there is a very good reason for not omitting it, and even for putting it first. However, we shall look first at the second principle. To use Korzybski's figure of speech, it says, "The map does not represent all of the territory"; that is, no matter how good a map you make, you cannot represent all of the territory in it. Translated in terms of language, it means that no matter how much you say about some "thing," "event," "quality," or what not, you cannot say *all* about it. The connection between this principle and the notion of propositional function is not hard to trace. According to the latter, *grass is green* is a propositional function, because both "grass" and "green" are variables. Grass can refer to vegetation in Vermont, Kentucky, or California. Green can range over the color of canaries, emeralds, or gall. Therefore, even such simple propositions as "grass is green," "the earth is round," etc., can be true only within limits.

Now let us go back to the first principle, which can be stated as "The map is not the territory"; that is, the word is not the thing it represents. Clearly, if the map does not even *represent* all of the territory, it cannot *be* the territory. So logically there is no need to state the principle of non-identity in addition to that of non-allness. However, the development of Korzybski's non-aristotelian postulates implies far more than relations between language and fact. His big point is that the structure of our language affects the *functioning of our nervous systems,* and this is where his work departs radically from that of the "classical" semanticists. To say "the word is not the thing it signifies" is not just to indicate the obvious. It is to draw attention to a fundamental inadequacy of human behavior and to trace this inadequacy to the interaction of nervous systems with language.

According to Korzybski (and his idea is corroborated by numerous psychological and psychiatric findings), people do behave *as if* they identified words with things. Identified does not mean "equated verbally." Practically everyone will agree that the *word* Negro is not the same as Mr. Smith, to whom the label Negro is applied. Nevertheless many people, in judging Mr. Smith, react to the label rather than to Mr. Smith. To take another example, a man may react to some situation, say a rejected application for a particular job, by labeling the situation "I am a failure." He may then react to the *label* in ways that are far removed from an effective remedy of the situation.

The orientation recommended by Korzybski to free the individual from the tyranny of words was called by him *extensional.* Roughly speaking, to be extensional is to be aware of things, facts, and operations in the way they are related in nature instead of in the way they are talked about. The extensionally oriented person differentiates better than the word-minded (intentionally oriented) one. He is aware of the basic uniqueness of "things," "events," etc., and so he is more aware of *change* than the intensionally oriented person, who mistakes the fluid, dynamic world around him for the static, rigid world of labels, "qualities," and "categories" in his head.

The extensional orientation of Korzybski is quite analogous to the "operationalism" of semantics. An operational definition is essentially an extensional definition, because it tells what to *do* (instead of what to say) to bring the thing defined within the range of experience. Likewise the criterion of predictive value in establishing truth is basically extensional. According to this criterion, statements, assertions, judgments, principles—in short, all kinds of talking—are rated much as checks are rated in our economy: they are accepted if one is reasonably sure they can be backed by currency. For an extensionally minded person, words that cannot be defined by operations, and statements that do not by implication contain predictions of experience, are like checks on nonexistent accounts.

This brings us to the third non-aristotelian postulate of self-reflexiveness. An ideal map of a territory, says Korzybski, would have to include a map of itself, if the map were part of the territory. But then it would have to include the map of the map of itself, etc., without end. This principle is illustrated on some packages, on which there is a picture of the package itself, which in turn contains another picture of itself, etc. To avoid this difficulty, the principle of non-identity is intended to the more general principle of multi-ordinality. The map is not the territory. Neither is map$_2$ of the map$_1$ itself a map$_1$. A map of map$_2$ would then be a map of the third order, etc., etc. In terms of language, this means that theoretically we may have a language$_1$ about things, a language$_2$ about language$_1$, etc. As Korzybski himself points out, this principle is an outgrowth of Russell's theory of types. It has "counterparts" in classical semantics, where logicians talk about languages of different order (metalanguages). In terms of human behavior, this suggests that one may react to the world, then react to his reaction, then to reactions of higher order, etc.

Thus, Korzybski's principles have a close relation to semantic principles. It follows that the whole Korzybskian system is an outgrowth of semantics. But the Korzybskian system goes much further. When its implications are worked out, it will be as far removed from semantics as semantics is from logic, and as logic is from grammar.

Grammar deals only with word-to-word relations. It teaches how to put words together into a sentence. It is not interested in how sentences are related to each other or how they are related to facts. Logic goes further. To a logician, sentences are assertions, and he is interested in relations between assertions (if this is true, then that is true). But for the logician words need not have any meaning except as defined by other words, and the assertions need not have any relation to the world of fact. The semanticist goes further than the logician. To him words and assertions have meaning only if they are related operationally to referents. The semanticist defines not only validity (as the logician does) but also truth. The general semanticist goes the furthest. He deals not only with words, assertions, and their referents in nature but also with their effects on human behavior. For a general semanticist, communication is not merely words in proper order properly inflected (as for the grammarian) or assertions in proper relation to each other (as for the logician) or assertions in proper relation to referents (as for the semanticist), but all these together, with the chain of "fact to nervous system to language to nervous system to action."

General semantics may indeed be considered of fundamental importance in the science of man. In Gestalt psychology, phenomenological psychology, psychiatry, and cultural anthropology, the "neurolinguistic" factors of human behavior are assuming an ever greater importance. Human experience (according to the views developed in those disciplines) consists of *selecting* certain ones out of innumerable stimuli in the environment: and human behavior consists of *organizing* experiences along certain patterns. There is strong evidence that both the selecting and the organizing patterns bear a definite relation to the structure of language and to linguistic habits.

WORKING WITH THE SELECTION

1. How do propositional functions differ from propositions?

2. How does operational definition as described by Rapoport compare with Walpole's definition procedure? Are any of Walpole's routes toward definition

operational? What are the advantages of operational definition? Do you see any disadvantages?

3. What is Rapoport's distinction between a valid proposition and a true proposition?

4. How does Rapoport explain his assertion that general semantics, when its implications are worked out, "will be as far removed from semantics as semantics is from logic, and as logic is from grammar"?

5. In the final section of his essay, not included here, Rapoport says that if Korzybski has not established an empirical science, he "has pointed a way toward the establishment of such a science. He was a precursor of an intellectual revolution which is just now beginning and which promises to match that of the Renaissance." What in Korzybski's thinking as described by Rapoport might justify this statement?

6. Write an essay considering some aspect of the significance of semantics for modern society, drawing on your study of the selection by Rapoport and other selections in Part 3. You might, for example, comment on Rapoport's judgment about the influence of Korzybski. Or you might develop your own opinions about the relations of semantics to various current phenomena—the importance of communication to race relations or civil liberties or the generation gap, the development of different media of communication, or problems of relations among nations.

part 4

From Use into Grammar

Grammar is the way language works, and the grammar of any given language is the way that language works, a way that is always unique, different from the way the grammars of all other languages work. A grammar is a device for making semantic units, often called words, do more and mean more than these same units would do and mean by themselves. Thus a grammar is an economical device, so useful that all known languages have one. Theoretically, we could have a language made up entirely of independent semantic units, but such a vocabulary, if it were to serve the complex needs of human intercourse, would be impossibly large and cumbersome—and needlessly so.

Since we have nothing that can be called a primitive grammar, we can only conjecture about how grammar developed, but some conjectures are probably reliable. During the times we know anything about, whatever way language has been employed extensively has become standardized, becoming part of a system, and thus it has become part of the grammar. Presumably language has always worked this way; that is, as soon as sounds became the basis for communication, ways of handling them became customary, and these customs were ordered into patterns and eventually into complex systems. For grammars are systems—systems that can eventually be codified into grammatical rules, which together reflect the working of the language.

These systems are therefore part of the growth of language—many-channeled, irregular, and erratic, like the evolution of man himself. Yet, in retrospect, we must think of this growth as a continuing process, from the irrecoverable past through the present and into the future. And we can distinguish different aspects of the development of the systems, or grammars.

In one sense, grammars may all be basically the same, as suggested by the term universal grammar, *since all grammars must reflect the human mind, and we can assume that minds, always and everywhere, have something in common. That is, we can think of grammar as expressing the ways in which human beings think, as what has sometimes been called universal grammar, deep grammar, or megalinguistics. Grammar in this sense has already been discussed, particularly in the selections by Liljeblad and Chomsky in Part I. But language is also a reflection of culture, of what men living together have done to basic communication over long stretches of time. Grammar can therefore be thought of as a codification of observable characteristics of a large body of speech. The grammar is the system through which users of a particular language can reveal relationships among semantic units.*

From any point of view, grammar needs to be distinguished from usage, which is a reflection of the linguistic fashions of a restricted time and place, although that is often popularly referred to as grammar. He done it like he should *is grammatical in English, in accord with the system and rules with which the language works. Questions about its propriety are questions of usage. Usage is the subject of the selections in Part 6. The readings in this part suggest what scholars are doing today to provide a reliable and revealing description of the grammatical system found in English. As will be apparent, these new attempts to provide adequate grammatical statements involve both fundamental concepts of the nature of language and the application of both new and old concepts to Modern English.*

1

Phonemes and Graphemes

Joseph H. Friend

Many people know the clarity of Friend's use of English, for he greatly influenced the definition-writing in Webster's New World Dictionary (*1951*). *He is professor of English at Southern Illinois University. The following selection is from* An Introduction to English Linguistics (*1967*).

Now let's turn to our second topic, the relations between the sound-system and the writing-system of Modern English. We may begin by asking the pertinent question, What is language?

Most of us, trained as we have been in literature and composition, think at once of the written or printed page—of books, journals, themes, typescript, and manuscript. But writing and printing, immensely important and valuable as they are, do not in themselves constitute language; they are merely ingenious ways of representing language visually. Language itself inheres in the flow of sound that comes out of the mouths of people talking. Language may be conveniently defined as *a system of arbitrary vocal sounds by which a group of people communicate with one another* and are thus enabled to carry on their various activities.

Examination of this system of vocal sounds, or rather, of the many hundreds of such systems used throughout the world, makes clear a number of things. One is that, although language can make use of any of the hundreds of distinctive sound signals that the human voice can produce, any given language makes use of only a limited number of such distinctive sound signals, called phonemes. And the selection of phonemes made by one language is virtually certain to be different from that made by any other language, though there may be some overlap.

Thus, the vowels of the French words *oeuvre* ("work"), *peu* ("little"), *lune* ("moon"), and *on* ("one") are not heard in American English, nor are the final consonants of German *ich* ("I") and *Sach* ("thing"). A second feature of language is that, though the individual phonemes do not of themselves carry any meaning, many sequences of these are meaningful. Thus the sounds indicated by the letters *p-a-t* in themselves are meaningless in English; but in that sequence they form an English word, *pat*. So too in reverse order these sounds form another English word, *tap;* and the sequence *apt* produces still another. But **atp* is meaningless; English does not allow such a sequence as **/tp/* (i.e., the phonemes /t/ and /p/) in final or initial position. [An asterisk can be used to indicate that a following locution is not in standard use.]

Table 1 Development of the alphabet.

Egyptian ca. 2000 B.C.		Sinitic ca. 1700 B.C.	West Semitic ca. 1200 B.C.	Ionic Greek ca. 500 B.C.	Early Roman
𓃾	head of ox			A	A
▭	house			B	ß B
⌐	corner of wall			Γ	‹ C
▱	door			Δ	D
𓀠	man with both arms raised			E	E ‖
𓆸	lotus (possibly man was model here too)			H	H
○	grain of sand			Υ Υ	F ‖'
👉	hand			I	I
𓃩	animal of Seth recumbent				
🤚	open hand			K	K
𓋂	sedge				

A third feature of language is that these meaningful sequences of phonemes are arbitrary; they bear no necessary relation to what they mean, in spite of such thinkers as Plato, who seems to have thought there was such a connection between a word and its referent. All this is merely a way of saying that, for instance, what we call a *dog* is called in French *chien,* in German *Hund,* in Latin *canis,* and so forth. Even the words by which various languages try to imitate the sounds in nature are by no means identical though they may show some similarities: roosters, we may say, don't crow alike, bees don't buzz alike, in English, Russian, and Turkish.

Table 1 *Continued.*

Egyptian ca. 2000 B.C.		Sinitic ca. 1700 B.C.	West Semitic ca. 1200 B.C.	Ionic Greek ca. 500 B.C.	Early Roman
	sandy tract, horizon (perhaps not origin of L)	ʔ—o	ᴌᴌ	Λ	ᴌᴌ
	ripples (suggested also for N and even L)	ᴍ	ᶯ	Μ	Μ
	cobra		Υ	Ν	ΝͰ
	ornament (often vertical) or weapon	=	ΙΖ	Ι	Ζ
	cobra				
	eye	⊘	ο	Ο	Ο
	mouth	δ∞	ᒣ	Γ	ΓP
	animal's belly with teats and tail	⊸o	φ		Q
	head	ᒍ ᵐ	ᐸ	P	R
	branch	ᴗ	w	⟨	ᶳᶘ
	sandy hills				
	unidentified cross or "ankh" the sandal strap	+ +	Τ×	Τ	Τ

Let's consider now the way in which we represent language by means of a graphic system, that is, a system of writing and printing. There are a number of different kinds of graphic systems; one of these is called *ideographic;* in it the symbols represent whole ideas. Our numerals, for example, are ideograms: for 5, the English speaker reads *five;* the Frenchman, *cinq;* the German, *fünf;* and so on. Another kind of system is the *logographic;* in this, a symbol stands for a whole word. The cumbersome ancient Chinese graphic system, with its thousands of characters, combines ideograms and logograms. Still other systems are called syllabaries; in these, one symbol stands for a single syllable, as in one way of writing Japanese and in the ancient cuneiform (wedge-shaped) writing of the Sumerians. But the most efficient graphic system ever devised, and now by far the most common, is the *alphabetic.* This, of course, is, the system we use. It has evolved over thousands of years from the ancient Egyptians' picture-writing, called hieroglyphics, by way of ingenious modifications made by ancient Phoenicians and Greeks. Most of the alphabetic systems now in use, including our own Roman alphabet, may be traced back to this common origin. Among these alphabets are the Cyrillic, used to write Russian and some other Slavic languages, the Greek, the Hebrew, and a number of others. Of this fact the very name of the system should remind us: the word *alphabet* combines Greek *alpha* and *beta,* the first two letters of the Greek alphabet, corresponding to Hebrew *alef* and *beth,* our *a* and *b.* If we study the form of ancient Egyptian hieroglyphics in comparison with their later descendants in such early alphabets as the Sinitic, the West Semitic, the Ionic Greek, and the early Roman, we can see the evolution of many of the characters we now use.

Thus our capital *A* still resembles the horned ox-head drawn by ancient Egyptian scribes; the chief difference is that the head now points downward and has been formalized as a triangle. So too we can see how our letter *B* evolved from the stylized picture of a simple house, how our *M* still suggests the hieroglyph for rippling water, how our *O* is a stylized version of the picture of a human eye, and how our *T* is not far removed from the ancient Egyptian cross, the *ankh,* or sandal-strap that presumably was its original.

The principle of the alphabetic system is that one character, or grapheme, represent one distinctive sound signal, or phoneme. Thus, ideally, the character *b* should always represent the phoneme /b/, as in *bet* or *rub;* the character *k* should always represent the phoneme /k/, as in *keg;* and so forth. (Note that we write phonemes between slant lines.) In some languages—for example, Finnish—this ideal state of affairs exists almost without exception In others, and notoriously in Modern English, the reality is at some distance from the ideal. No one who knows English needs to be told that though the letter *b* usually represents the phoneme /b/, it is sometimes "silent," as in *climb* and *debt;* or that *k* may also be silent, as in *knife;* or that the letter *c* may also represent the phoneme /k/, as in *cat,* though it may at times represent another phoneme, /s/, as in *receive.* And we are all painfully aware how many phonemes the letter *a* can represent, or the letter *o,* or *e,* or *u,* or *i*, or such combinations as *ou, ai, ei,* and so on. There is a correlation of sorts between English spelling and English pronunciation—between our *graphemic system* and our *phonemic system,* as the linguist puts it. If there were not, we could scarcely write or read English. But the correlation is imperfect and complex because of the divergence between our conservative spelling and our much less conservative pronunciation habits over the centuries. Today, as we have said, there is no single instance of a one-to-one correspondence in the English graphemic-phonemic systems. Nevertheless we manage.

Analysis of the phonemic system of Present-Day American English shows that it consists of 24 consonant phonemes and from 7 to 10 simple vowel phonemes; the variation in the number of vowel phonemes is the result of the fact that speakers in different parts of the country don't all make the same vowel sounds in the same words, as everyone knows.

Table 2   The phonemes of Present-Day American English (according to Trager and Smith).*

SEGMENTAL

Consonants

stops

/p/   *p*it, s*p*ot, ri*pp*le, ta*p*
/b/   *b*in, ho*bb*le, na*b*
/t/   *t*ip, bo*tt*le, po*t*
/d/   *d*o, lad*d*er, ha*d*
/k/   *k*ey, *c*ow, pi*c*nic, kno*ck*
/g/   *g*et, le*gg*ing, fin*g*er, bo*g*

continuants

fricatives	/f/	*f*an, *ph*enomenon, ta*ff*y, cou*gh,* wi*f*e
	/v/	*v*ine, ra*v*el, sa*vv*y, sal*v*e, li*v*e
	/θ/	*th*ick, e*th*er, brea*th*
	/ð/	*th*ey, ei*th*er, brea*the*
sibilants	/s/	*s*ay, *ps*yche, re*c*eive, mu*s*ter, ki*ss*
	/z/	*z*ip, hi*s,* schi*s*m, bu*zz*
	/š/	*sh*ine, na*t*ion, pa*ss*ion, ma*ch*ine, ca*ch*e, ca*sh*
	/ž/	bei*g*e, a*z*ure, inci*s*ion, rou*g*ed
affricates	/č/	*ch*ange, hi*tch,* situa*t*ion, cin*ch*
	/ǰ/	*j*u*dg*e, ima*g*ine, sa*g*e
nasals	/m/	*m*e, sli*m*y, ha*mm*y, so*m*e
	/n/	*n*o, fa*n*cy, ba*nn*ed, o*n*
	/ŋ/	sa*ng,* si*ng*er, dru*n*k
liquids	/l/	*l*eaf, te*ll*ing, *l*ow, c*l*ear, fu*ll,* handfu*l*
	/r/	*r*ib, su*rr*ogate, hea*r*ing, fa*r*

* A few symbols have been added to permit elimination of footnotes in the original.— *Eds.*

Vowels

front

high	/i/	*i*t, p*i*t, b*u*sy, pr*e*tty
mid	/e/	*e*ver, b*e*d, s*ai*d, tr*ea*d
low	/æ/	*a*cme, h*a*t, *a*sk

center

high	/ɨ/	ch*i*ldren, j*u*st, lesson
mid	/ə/	*u*p, *o*ther, m*u*d, comply, sof*a*, foc*u*s, fing*e*r
low	/a/	*o*tter, l*o*ck, f*a*r

back

high	/u/	l*oo*k, f*u*ll
mid	/o/	*o*pen, r*o*te, *oa*t
low	/ɔ/	*o*ff, *aw*ful, f*ou*ght, t*au*ght, t*au*t

Semivowels (glides)

/y/	*y*es, *y*ou		/ay/	l*i*ght, m*i*te
			/ɔy/	b*oy*, *oi*l
/w/	*w*ell, *w*on		/aw/	h*ow*, h*ou*se
/h/	*h*e, *wh*o, *h*oot		/æh/	*a*sk, *au*nt

SUPRASEGMENTAL*

Stresses

primary	/´/
secondary	/ˆ/
tertiary	/ˋ/
weak	/˜/

Pitch levels

low	/1/
	/2/
	/3/
high	/4/

Junctures (besides *internal close juncture*)

open (plus) /+/
terminals (3)

level (sustained) → ←	or	/|/
falling ↓	or	/#/
rising ↑	or	/‖/

There are also vocal sounds consisting of two vowel sounds spoken in rapid succession—the so-called "long vowels," which are more properly called diphthongs. The voice moves rapidly from the sound of *ah* to that of *ee* to give us the sound *ai*, and from the sound of *aw* to that of *ee* to give us the sound *oi*. Sometimes we hear triphthongs—three vowel-sounds uttered in rapid succession.

* Some linguists do not recognize suprasegmentals as phonemes.—*Eds*.

Now, the problem of learning and teaching spelling is in large part that of correlating the phoneme with the alphabetic character or characters that can represent it. This means, first of all, that we should understand such correlations; the better we understand them, the better job we can do.

We can't deal with all the phonemes of Modern English in detail here. But we can look at an example or two. Listen to the words *seat, sit, sate, set, sat, sot, suit, soot, sought,* or any similar sequence. You should notice that these words vary only with respect to one sound. Those sounds between the *s*-sound and the *t*-sound are the vowel phonemes of these words. We know they are phonemes because they are in contrast; that is, a change in the sound produces a change in the meaning of the sequence of sounds in which it occurs, and all these sequences are meaningful in English—are English words. Now look at the spelling of these words, and think of other words in which the same vowel phonemes could be differently spelled.

The vowel phoneme of *seat,* spelled *ea,* occurs with different spelling in *feet, machine, key, delete,* and so on. That of *set,* spelled with an *e,* is also found with different spelling in *said, dead,* etc. Obviously, the correlations aren't simple. We need to drill ourselves in the most frequent correlations first, and then go on to those that are found less frequently. And we need to understand that the matter is complicated even more by the fact that there are different ways of pronouncing English in different parts of the country, so that although we all spell our words alike, we may speak them with somewhat different phonemes.

Another interesting and complicated set of correlations exists between our sound-system and our writing-system. Consider how we know, when we listen to someone, that one sentence has ended and another begun; that one sequence of words is a statement, another a question, a third an exclamation; that there is a notable difference between two sequences of identical words in identical order: for example, between "What are we having for dinner tonight, Mother?" and "What are we having for dinner tonight—Mother?" Or between "a blue nose" and "a bluenose," "a French *teacher"* and a *"French* teacher," " a dancing *girl"* and "a *dancing* girl," and so on.

We know these things because we recognize differences in the way these sequences are spoken, differences in prosodic features. Analysis of these differences shows that they consist of three factors: stress, pitch, and juncture, or transition.

Let's consider each of these things. By *stress* is meant the *relative* loudness of a syllable (in comparison to that of other syllables in the same utterance). It's not a matter of special emphasis. Such normal stress differences are built into the structure of language though they are not indicated in our writing-system. Modern English has four such *significant degrees of stress*—four phonemes of stress, as many linguists would say (though other linguists prefer a different terminology). These are called primary, secondary, tertiary, and weak; they are conventionally marked with the acute accent, the circumflex accent, the grave accent, and the breve, respectively. In such a phrase as "wáshǐng mǎchǐne rĕpairmǎn" one can hear all four, as a little practice in listening will show.

The reason these degrees of stress are called phonemes by some linguists is that, like the distinctive sounds of the language, they signal differences of meaning; a dǎncǐng gìrl; a môvǐng ván is not a móvǐng vàn.

Significant differences of pitch also appear to be four. These are also relative; whether the speaker's voice is low-pitched or high-pitched, four levels, or degrees, of pitch are heard. They are also regarded by many linguists as phonemes (though again, others disagree), and are marked either with small superscript numerals, usually 1 for lowest and 4 for highest pitch level, or with contour lines, or by arranging the letters of a printed utterance in such a way as to show relative pitch levels. Thus, we may write

^{2} ^{3} ^{1}
"He's going to class," a simple declarative utterance, with superscript numerals as shown, indicating that the voice begins on 2—the usual pitch level at the start of an utterance—and remains on the same level until the beginning of the last word, where it rises to the next higher level, and then quickly drops to the lowest level, 1, as it fades into silence. This could also be written

"He's going to class." or "He's going to ^{cla}ss." (Probably either of the last

two ways is best for marking the pitch contours.)

To demonstrate the significance of these degrees of pitch, we may consider the difference in meaning between the declarative utterance as we have just

^{2} ^{2}
given it and the same sequence arranged as a question: "He's going to

^{3}
class?"↑ The fact that the voice goes to pitch level 3 on *class* and then rises slightly indicates that a question has been asked. Significant sequences of relative pitch levels and pauses are called intonation.

Closely related to pitch is what linguists call terminal juncture, or terminal transition, by which is meant the way in which the voice behaves between one linguistic phrase and another, or between a linguistic phrase and silence. This calls for an explanation of "linguistic phrase," a term that means a spoken sequence of words in which there occurs only one primary stress.

^{2} ^{3} ^{2} ^{2} ^{3} ^{2} ^{2}
Thus, in the sentence "Mỳ téachĕr→, ←Mìss Jónes→, ←ăssîgns tôo mùch

^{3} ^{1}
hómewòrk,"↓ there are three linguistic phrases: "mỳ téachĕr," "Mìss Jónes," and "ăssîgns too mùch hómewòrk." Clearly, the first syllable of *teacher,* the word *Jones,* and the first syllable of *homework* are all spoken with primary stress, and there is no primary stress on any other syllable in this sentence, in normal utterance. Between these linguistic phrases and after the last one there occur terminal junctures, or transitions—phenomena that have to do with the relative rise or fall of pitch in uttering the final syllable of a

phrase, and with the trailing off of the voice into silence, sometimes accompanied with a drawing out of the sound. Such terminal junctures, or terminal transitions, in Modern English, are generally regarded as three in number, a falling one, a rising one, and a level, or sustained, one, often symbolized by arrows, as in the example. A little observation will make clear that the falling terminal, as we may call it for convenience, is that which ends most declarative sentences, and many questions as well. It is also sometimes heard between phrases within a sentence. (There is another sort of juncture, or transition, which occurs between words or between syllables; this is usually termed open juncture. It may be observed in pronouncing *night rates* and *nitrates* or *see Nick* and *scenic,* and consists essentially in a slight pause, with slight prolongation of the final sound before the juncture. It is usually symbolized by a plus sign: *ni + trates, night + rates* and is hence sometimes called *plus juncture.*)

The pitch pattern 2–3–1 followed by a falling terminal is most frequent in

our language; it is illustrated in such utterances as: "Linguistics is a
²

science."↓ "He's a bright boy."↓ "We went to the movies."↓ "What's the
^{3 1 2} ... ^{3 1 2} ... ^{3 1 2}

trouble?"↓ The rising terminal also occurs at the end of many sentences and
^{3 1}

often after some questions and exclamations; it may be heard too between phrases within a sentence.

Thus, we often—though not necessarily—hear a rising terminal in counting; as, "one,↑ two,↑ three,↑ four,↑ five,"↓ (after *five,* the last word in this declarative utterance, we hear a falling terminal, of course, and it is possible to count aloud with falling terminals after every word). A rising terminal is also heard in many questions, notably those in which no interrogatory word is used. For example, if we choose to make a question of the sentence "He's a bright boy,"↓ all we need do is end with a rising instead of a falling terminal: "He's a bright boy?"↑ As for the level, or sustained, terminal juncture, it is never heard at the end of a sentence but is confined to use between linguistic phrases within the sentence. The level terminal signals that the utterance is not completed, that more is to come.

WORKING WITH THE SELECTION

1. You may well ask why we start the study of grammar with a study of sound. The question is a good one, worthy of being asked seriously. Do you recall the selection by Chomsky in Part 1? In considering grammar Chomsky assumed in man an innate sense for language. This assumption is characteristic of generative grammars and, as we shall see, of some others. This is probably not the assumption on which your teacher was relying when you were first introduced to grammar, nor is it likely to be the assumption on which your parents would rely if they were to discuss grammar. What are other possibilities for starting points if one is to think about grammar?

2. At some time you must have been introduced to what was probably called *phonics,* which as it is usually taught in elementary and secondary schools might be roughly, though not very precisely, defined as the study of English sounds and their use in recognizing, pronouncing, and spelling words. You may also have encountered the word *phonetics,* which refers to the objective study of sound. And you may have become aware of the International Phonetic Alphabet, a list of some hundreds of symbols with which, theoretically, one can represent all sounds in all known languages. Even if you have not heard of the IPA, you are already acquainted with some IPA symbols. Most modern dictionaries make some use of these symbols in their pronunciation systems, and some foreign-language teachers use phonetics, most often in this country in teaching French. Finally, Friend uses some IPA symbols when he comments on phonemes. So far as you can see, what are the major differences between the phonemic system described by Friend and the phonetic system, which you already know quite a bit about?

3. Those who work with phonemes define them somewhat variously, but for our purposes a phoneme might be defined as a working unit of sound at a given time and place. Since language as we use it is a sequence of sounds, at least from one point of view, these working units of sound could be put together into a working unit of language. Such a sequence is called a *morpheme.* For example, the three phonemes /g/, /e/, and /t/ can be combined to form the morpheme /get/. Thus /get/ in morphology is just what it is in spelling, *get,* although the word *head* contains the morpheme /hed/. Both /gets/ and /hedz/ contain two morphemes: /get/ is one morpheme and /s/ is another morpheme; together they form the word *gets.* What, apparently, are the principal differences between a word and a morpheme?

4. Understandably, Friend calls our system of spelling chaotic. Can anything be said for it? Suppose we had only a phonetic system and no graphemic system; would you be likely to find dictionaries harder or easier to use?

5. Clearly, there is some relationship between junctures and punctuation. Which system do you find the more precise? The more revealing? Why?

6. Using the phonemic system provided by Friend, transcribe the first sentence of his second paragraph. The sentence is printed in accordance with the graphemic system; you are asked to reproduce it in the phonemic system. Since phonemics records sound, you should have someone read the paragraph: you will probably be unable to make the sounds as you customarily do if you, yourself, are listening to them, and you are not likely to be able to hear your own sounds very accurately anyhow. There is no single, correct transcription, since every speaker will say the passage differently. For example, the word

literature might appear as /lítərətur/ if the word were sounded out as a single item by a Midwestern speaker, but few people would pronounce the word in this way in context. Among the many possible pronunciations are the

following: /lítrəčɔ̌r/, /lítəčɔ̌/, and lítu̇řɔ̌čyu̇r.

2

Where Our Grammar Came From

Karl W. Dykema

Karl W. Dykema, long a professor of English at Youngstown State University, has served as Dean of the College of Arts and Sciences there since 1963. He was educated both in this country, at Columbia University, and in Europe, and taught French, German, and music before he concentrated on his native language and literature. He has been active in both scholarship and pedagogy; the following selection is from a paper read before a convention of English teachers and published in College English, 22 *(April, 1961).*

The title of this paper is too brief to be quite accurate. Perhaps with the following subtitle it does not promise too much: A partial account of the origin and development of the attitudes which commonly pass for grammatical in Western culture and particularly in English-speaking societies.

The etymology of *grammar* shows rather sharp changes in meaning: It starts with Greek *gramma, letter* (of the alphabet), itself a development from *graphein, draw* or *write*. The plural *grammata* develops in meaning through *letters* to *alphabet* to the *rudiments of writing*, to the *rudiments of learning*. The adjective form *grammatike* with *techne* meant the art of knowing one's letters. From this form comes the Latin *grammaticus*. The medieval vernacular forms with *r* are something of a mystery, appearing first in Old Provençal as *gramaira* and developing in English with a variety of spellings, often with only one *m* and ending in *er*. One of the more amusing forms is that with the first *r* dissimilated to *l, glamour*.

In present usage at least four senses can be distinguished which have an application to language: (1) The complete structural pattern of a language learned unconsciously by the child as he acquires his native tongue; (2) an attempt to describe objectively and systematically this fundamental structure, usually called descriptive grammar; (3) a partial description of the language based on puristic or pedagogical objectives, usually called prescriptive grammar, (4) a conviction held by a good many people that somewhere there is an authoritative book called a grammar, the conscientious memorization of which will eliminate all difficulties from their use of language. This I call grammar as remedy. It is mainly with the last two of these notions of grammar that I shall concern myself, prescriptive grammar and grammar as remedy, and how the earlier conceptions of grammar were metamorphosed into them.

As the etymology of the word suggests, Western grammar begins with the ancient Greeks. As early as Plato we find in the *Sophist* the statement that a word describing action is a verb (rhema), one which performs the action is a noun (onoma). Aristotle adds conjunctions (syndesmoi), recognizes that sentences have predicates, and is aware of three genders and of inflection (*Rhetoric,* etc.). The Stoics attempted to separate linguistic study from philosophy and made important contributions to the discipline. In their writings we find terms which are approximately equivalent to *noun, verb, conjunction, article, number, gender, case, voice, mood,* and *tense.*[1] But the direct source of most of our widely used grammatical terms is Dionysius Thrax's little *Techne Grammatike,* which Gilbert Murray recollects his great-uncle still using at the Merchants Taylors' School in the nineteenth century to learn Greek from.[2]

A few quotations from this little work will illustrate how close many of our school grammars still are to their source of more than 2000 years ago:

> A sentence is a combination of words, either in prose or verse, making complete sense. . . . Of discourse there are eight parts: noun, verb, participle, article, pronoun, preposition, adverb, and conjunction. . . . A noun is a part of discourse having cases, indicating a body (as 'stone') or a thing (as 'education'), and is used in a common and a peculiar way (i.e., is common or proper). . . . A verb is a word without case, admitting tenses, persons, and numbers, and indicating action and passion (i.e., being-acted-upon). . . . A pronoun is a word indicative of definite persons and used in place of a noun. . . . The adverb is an uninflected part of discourse, used of a verb or subjoined to a verb . . . The conjunction is a word conjoining or connecting thought in some order and filling a gap in the expression.[3]

The few examples I have given emphasize analysis by meaning, because that is the aspect of classical grammar which our traditional grammar has dwelt upon. But the definitions of noun and verb, it should be observed, begin with formal distinctions—case and tense—and throughout the work there is clearly an awareness of the importance of structure in the functioning of the language. The contribution of the Greeks to linguistics was a great one, as Gilbert Murray and others have pointed out. But for twenty centuries their work was carried on by slavish and unimaginative imitators incapable of developing the work of their predecessors. Especially in the less highly inflected languages like English and French it did not occur to them that the inflectional devices of Latin and Greek must have some counterpart in the structure of the modern language.

[1] R. H. Robins, *Ancient and Medieval Grammatical Theory in Europe* (London, 1951), pp. 20–35.

[2] Gilbert Murray, *Greek Studies* (Oxford, 1946), p. 181.

[3] "The Grammar of Dionysius Thrax," translated . . . by Thos. Davidson, *Journal of Speculative Philosophy,* VIII (1874), 326–339.

Though today there are a few scholars in universities who assert that they pursue grammar for its own sake as an academic discipline, most people conceive of grammar only as a utilitarian thing, as a means of learning to use a language correctly. This notion was certainly completely absent from the thinking of Plato, Aristotle, and the Stoics, and probably from that of Dionysius Thrax. Grammar began as a philosophical inquiry into the nature of language. Now, for most people, it is merely a dogmatic means of achieving correctness. It is this transformation that I am mainly concerned with.

How the transformation took place is not easy to document. Perhaps the most plausible explanation lies in the familiar desire of younger teachers to regurgitate undigested fragments of what they have swallowed in the course of their higher education. All too often a high school teacher just out of college will use his college lecture notes as the foundation of his high school teaching, or a teacher of undergraduates tries to give them exactly what he got in his graduate seminar.

Then there is the fundamental difference between the prevailing purposes of elementary and advanced instruction. Primary education is severely utilitarian; and though it can hardly be denied that, especially in our society, graduate instruction is often infected by utilitarianism, the speculative approach does persist, and inquiry for its own sake plays a major role. The curriculum at all levels of education is and has been determined partly by tradition, partly by immediate utilitarian objectives, partly by a desire to perpetuate the best elements of the cultural heritage. The application of these criteria is of ascending difficulty. Easiest is to accept without question the practice of one's predecessors; not much harder is to accept a limited practical goal and provide instruction intended to achieve it. Most difficult is to select critically what is most valuable in the cultural heritage, and the Romans weren't up to it.

Because of Greek prestige in the ancient world, less developed cultures borrowed extensively from that of Greece. The influence of Greek art, philosophy, and literature on Rome is familiar, but Greek grammar was quite as influential and became the model not only for grammars of Latin but of Syriac, Armenian, Hebrew, and possibly Arabic as well.

It could not be a good model. The structure of every language is peculiar to itself—though there are, of course, similarities between members of the same linguistic family—and the best description of it derives from a careful examination of the language itself, not from an attempt to fit into the pattern of another. To be sure, both Greek and Latin are rich in inflections and the Latin of Varro was not much further away from the parent Indo-European than was the Greek of Dionysius Thrax; so the deformation imposed by the model was less distorting than when the same procedure was followed many centuries later and attempts were made to strait-jacket the modern vernaculars of Europe within the model of Latin grammar. For example, Greek had a definite article, Latin had none, though in Varro's *De Lingua Latina,* the term *articuli* is applied to the demonstrative *is* and *hic* (VIII, 45, 51). Latin has more cases but a different tense system and no dual. English has only two inflected active tenses against six for Latin, but many more periphrastic verbal constructions than had Latin.

The attention given to grammar by the ancients seems to have been considerable. Susemihl in his *History of Greek Literature in the Alexandrian Period* discusses over fifty grammarians. One of them, Aristophanes of Byzantium (ca. 257–ca. 180 B.C.), was librarian to Ptolomy Epiphanius, who imprisoned him to prevent the king of Pergamum from hiring him away.

Among the Romans, grammarians were also in demand. The slave Lutatius Daphnis, a grammarian, was bought for 700,000 sesterces, perhaps $35,000, which puts him about in the class of a lesser baseball player. Caesar put this Lutatius Daphnis in charge of the public libraries, though it was not until much later, according to Suetonius, that a regular salary of 100,000 sesterces was paid from the privy purse for Latin and Greek teachers of rhetoric (Suetonius, *Lives of the Caesars,* VIII, xviii). Caesar himself took part in one of the persisting grammatical quarrels of the time, that of the analogists and the anomalists, by producing a work called *De Analogia,* known to us only in fragments. Though he favored the analogists, who demanded complete inflectional consistency, it is significant that he wanted no radical departures from usage.[4] Suetonius also states that Claudius "invented three new letters and added them to the [Latin] alphabet, maintaining that they were greatly needed; he published a book on their theory when he was still in private life, and when he became emperor had no difficulty in bringing about their general use" (Suetonius, *Lives of the Caesars,* V, xli). Theodore Roosevelt was less successful when he tried to impose a few spelling reforms on the Government Printing Office; Congress refused to permit the changes.

Though Caesar favored the analogists, he was unwilling to depart from established usage. His position was that of many of his cultivated contemporaries, as it has been of many cultivated people ever since. The appeal of analogy is the appeal of logic, a creation of the Greeks and a tool that has been used with interesting and surprising effects in most areas of Western thought ever since. The foundation of Aristotelian logic is the syllogism. As the analogists applied the syllogism to language it worked like this: The form of the personal pronoun determines the form of the verb of which the pronoun is the subject. The form *you* is plural; therefore the form of the verb *be* which follows it must be plural; hence *you were,* not *you was.* So we have in cultivated English today only *you were.* But the cultivated dare not apply this syllogism to the intensive or reflective, where the eighteenth-century practice of agreement with the notional number of the pronoun still persists. The eighteenth century had both *you was there yourself* and *you were there yourselves;* while we have *you were there yourselves* when the notional number of *you* is plural, but *you were there yourself* when it is singular.

Language has its own logic, which it is the function of the descriptive

<hr />

[4] Jean Collart, *Varron, Grammairien Latin* (Paris, 1954), pp. 10, 19, 146; Robins, p. 58.

grammarian to discover if he can. Whatever it may be, it is not Aristotelian logic. But for two millennia our attitudes toward language have been colored by the assumption that the system of a language can be analyzed and prescribed by an intellectual tool that is inapplicable.

Conformity to a standard, or correctness if you like, is, of course, socially of the greatest importance. There is a long record of the penalties imposed on those who deviate from the standard, the earliest I know of being the account given in *Judges* (12, 4–6) of the forty and two thousand Ephraimites who were slain by the Gileadites because they pronounced *shibboleth sibboleth*. Later examples are less gory. Aristophanes in the *Lysistrata* (lines 81–206) ridicules the dialect of the Spartan women, though they are the allies of the Athenian women in their campaign of sexual frustration. Stephen Runciman in his *Byzantine Civilization* says "the Patriarch Nicetas in the Eleventh Century was laughed at for his Slavonic accent, and the statesman Margarites treated with disrespect in the Thirteenth because he spoke with a rough rustic voice." [5] And Chaucer's nun spoke the provincial French of the Benedictine nunnery of Stratford-Bow, the French of Paris—standard French—being to her unknown.

Conformity to the standard is what matters. But how is the standard to be determined? Quintilian, whom Professor T. W. Baldwin calls "The Supreme Authority" in his *Shakespeare's Small Latine and Lesse Greeke,* provides a most illuminating basis for discussion. In the *Institutes* Quintilian tells us that:

> Language is based on reason, antiquity, authority and usage. Reason finds its chief support in analogy and sometimes in etymology. As for antiquity, it is commended to us by the possession of a certain majesty, I might almost say sanctity. . . . Usage however is the surest pilot in speaking, and we should treat language as currency minted with the public stamp. But in all cases we have need of a critical judgment. . . . (I.vi.1–3)

This is fuller than Horace's neater statement: "Use is the judge, and law, and rule of speech" (*De Arte Poetica,* 72: *Quem [usus] penes arbitrium est et ius et norma loquendi.*) and shows more clearly why we have troubles. Usage "is the surest pilot" but "we have need of a critical judgment."

Quintilian has more to say on the matter:

> Usage remains to be discussed. For it would be almost laughable to prefer the language of the past to that of the present day, and what is ancient speech but ancient usage of speaking? But even here the critical faculty is necessary, and we must make up our minds what we mean by usage. If it be defined merely as the practice of the majority, we shall have a very dangerous rule affecting not merely style but life as

[5] Stephen Runciman, *Byzantine Civilization* (Meridian Books, New York, 1956), pp. 173, 176.

well, a far more serious matter. For where is so much good to be found that what is right should please the majority? The practices of depilation, of dressing the hair in tiers, or of drinking to excess at the baths, although they may have thrust their way into society, cannot claim the support of usage, since there is something to blame in all of them (although we have usage on our side when we bathe or have our hair cut or take our meals together). So too in speech we must not accept as a rule of language words and phrases that have become a vicious habit with a number of persons. To say nothing of the language of the uneducated, so we are all of us well aware that whole theatres and the entire crowd of spectators will often commit *barbarisms* in the cries which they utter as one man. I will therefore define usage in speech as the agreed practice of educated men, just as where our way of life is concerned I should define it as the agreed practice of all good men. (I.vi. 43–45)

. . . Greek grammar, is, then, a development of Greek philosophy, an attempt to treat systematically an important aspect of human behavior. It is a late development which in Alexandrian culture is given a practical application through its use in the editing, elucidation, and interpretation of texts, especially that of Homer; and in the correction of solecisms. Since there was little of the speculative in the Romans, Varro's encyclopedic treatment of Latin language and literature was the ultimate source of a host of school texts.

What has been presented so far is a partial account of the development of philology, though this ancient term has been an ambiguous one for almost as long as it has existed—naturally enough, since it derives from the Greek roots usually translated as *love* and *word.* Some people love words as the means of argument, others because they are the foundation of literature, others still for their forms and relations in discourse. All these senses have been designated by the word since it first appeared in Greek, and in nineteenth-century France and Germany it normally included literary history, textual and literary criticism, and linguistics. . . .

Increasingly in the Middle Ages the written heritage of Greece and Rome was accepted unquestioningly because literate men did not have a cultural background which would permit them to ask pertinent questions. We learn, for example, that one of the best sources for the text of Diogenes Laertius is a manuscript of about 1200 written by a scribe "who obviously knew no Greek." [6] To be sure, there were sometimes conflicts between the Christian heritage and the classical, usually resolved in favor of the Christian. In a medieval manuscript is this comment: "Concerning the words *scala* (step), and *scopa* (broom), we do not follow Donatus and the others who claim they are plural because we know that the Holy Ghost has ruled that they

[6] Diogenes Laertius, *Lives of Eminent Philosophers,* with an English translation by R. D. Hicks (Loeb Classical Library) (Cambridge & London, 1925), vol. 1, p. xxxv. (The quotations from Suetonius, Varro, Quintilian, and Aulus Gellius are from the translations in the Loeb Classical Library editions.)

are singular." And it was comforting when the traditions of classical grammar could be given divine corroboration. For example: "The verb has three persons. This I hold to be divinely inspired, for our belief in the Trinity is thereby manifested in words." Or this:

> Some maintain that there are more, some that there are fewer parts of speech. But the world-encircling church has only eight offices [Presumably Ostiariat, Lektorat, Exorzistat, Akolythat, Subdiakonat, Diakonat, Presbyterat, Episkopat]. I am convinced that this is through divine inspiration. Since it is through Latin that those who are chosen come most quickly to a knowledge of the Trinity and under its guidance find their way along the royal road into their heavenly home, it was necessary that the Latin language should be created with eight parts of speech.[7]

WORKING WITH THE SELECTION

Dykema defines four grammars. Do these account for universal grammar, as we observed Chomsky and Liljeblad discussing it? If you conclude that Dykema does not take account of universal grammar, how would you explain his oversight? Could one of his four grammars be so redefined that it would include universal grammar?

3

Grammar Before the Revolution

Goold Brown

Goold Brown (1791–1857), a highly successful teacher and administrator of boys' schools in the New York and Boston areas, is now largely forgotten, but in his day he was venerated as perhaps no other American grammarian has been, and he probably did more than any other to establish the fashion of parsing in the American school system. He prepared The Grammar of English Grammars *(1851), a monumental tome of more than one million words, loaded with learning and intended to be the greatest grammar book of all time—and of its sort, it was, running through many editions, growing bulkier if not more*

---

[7] J. J. Baebler, *Beiträge zu einer Geschichte der lateinischen Grammatik im Mittelalter*, (Halle a. S., 1885), p. 22/Hans Arens, *Sprachwissenschaft, der Gang ihrer Entwicklung von der Antike bis zur Gegenwart* (Munich, 1955), pp. 30, 31.

liberal with the years. For the book was authoritarian to the point of bigotry; it was based on eighteenth-century thinking, on an approach already obsolete among scholars even in Brown's time. Philology was revolutionizing thought as much in the nineteenth century as linguistics has been revolutionizing it in the twentieth, and Brown, instinct with neither scientific objectivity nor sweet reason, was no philologist.

His method was simple, and he was sure he was right, while doubting that anybody else was. He relied on rules. He recognized and defined ten parts of speech, and he insisted that students learn the definitions by rote and repeat the appropriate one every time they identified a part of speech. The first selection, from Part II, Praxis II, provides a sample of his method. He also believed in detecting errors. The second selection is the beginning of Lesson IV in this same "praxis." And he loved animadversions—his own, at any rate. The last selection is from his introduction to Chapter 9. In it he reviews the works of the great scholars from the dawn of grammatical writing on English to his own day and condemns them all. His Doctor Webster *is Noah Webster, his older contemporary, who was a lawyer, an essayist, and a grammarian before he became a lexicographer.*

EXAMPLE PARSED

The task of a schoolmaster laboriously prompting and urging an indolent class, is worse than his who drives lazy horses along a sandy road.
—G[oold]. Brown.

The is the definite article. 1. An article is the word *the, an,* or *a,* which we put before nouns to limit their signification. 2. The definite article is *the,* which denotes some particular thing or things.

Task is a noun. 1. A noun is the name of any person, place, or thing, that can be known or mentioned.

Of is a preposition. 1. A preposition is a word used to express some relation of different things or thoughts to each other, and is generally placed before a noun or pronoun.

A is the indefinite article. 1. An article is the word *the, an,* or *a,* which we put before nouns to limit their signification. 2. The indefinite article is *an* or *a,* which denotes one thing of a kind, but not any particular one.

Schoolmaster is a noun. 1. A noun is the name of any person, place, or thing, that can be known or mentioned.

Laboriously is an adverb. 1. An adverb is a word added to a verb, a particle, an adjective, or another adverb; and generally expresses time, place, degree, or manner.

Prompting is a participle. 1. A participle is a word derived from a verb, participating the properties of a verb, and of an adjective or a noun; and is generally formed by adding *ing, d,* or *ed,* to the verb.

And is a conjunction. 1. A conjunction is a word used to connect words or sentences in construction, and to show the dependence of the words so connected.

Urging is a participle. 1. A participle is a word derived from a verb, participating the properties of a verb, and of an adjective or a noun; and is generally formed by adding *ing, d,* or *ed,* to the verb.

An is the indefinite article. 1. An article is the word *the, an,* or *a,* which we put before nouns to limit their signification. 2. The indefinite article is *an* or *a,* which denotes one thing of a kind, but not any particular one.

Indolent is an adjective. 1. An adjective is a word added to a noun or a pronoun, and generally expresses quality.

Class is a noun. 1. A noun is the name of any person, place, or thing, that can be known or mentioned.

Is is a verb. 1. A verb is a word that signifies *to be, to act,* or *to be acted upon.*

Worse is an adjective. 1. An adjective is a word added to a noun or a pronoun, and generally expresses quality. . . .

Sandy is an adjective. 1. An adjective is a word added to a noun or a pronoun, and generally expresses quality.

Road is a noun. 1. A noun is the name of any person, place, or thing, that can be known or mentioned.

LESSON IV: CHANGE ARTICLES

To enable us to avoid the too frequent repetition of the same word.
—Bucke's Gr., p. 52.

FORMULE—Not proper, because the article *the* is used to limit the meaning of "repetition," or "too frequent repetition," where *a* would better suit the sense. But, according to a principle on page 225th, "The article can seldom be put one for the other, without gross impropriety; and either is of course to be preferred to the other, as it better suits the sense." Therefore, *the* should be *a,* which, in this instance, ought to be placed after the adjective; thus, "To enable us to avoid *too frequent a repetition* of the same word."

[There follow some twenty examples, mostly from the works of rival grammarians, which Brown apparently felt embodied "gross impropriety."]

BRIEF NOTICES OF THE SCHEMES
OF CERTAIN GRAMMARS

The history of *Dr. Webster,* as a grammarian, is singular. He is remarkable for his changeableness, yet always positive; for his inconsistency, yet very learned; for his zeal "to correct popular errors," yet often himself erroneous; for his fertility in resources, yet sometimes meagre; for his success as an author, yet never satisfied; for his boldness of innovation, yet fond of appealing to antiquity. His grammars are the least judicious, and at present the least popular, of his works. They consist of four or five different treatises, which for their mutual credit should never be compared: it is impossible to place any firm reliance upon the authority of a man who contradicts himself so much. Those who imagine that the last opinions of so learned a man must needs be right, will do well to wait, and see what will be his last: they cannot otherwise know to what his instructions will finally lead. Experience has already taught him the folly of many of his pretended improvements, and it is probable his last opinions of English grammar will be most conformable to that just authority with which he has ever been tampering. I do not say that he has not exhibited ingenuity as well as learning, or that he is always wrong when he contradicts a majority of the English grammarians; but I may venture to say, he was wrong when he undertook to disturb the common scheme of the parts of speech, as well as when he resolved to spell all words exactly as they are pronounced.

It is not commonly known with how rash a hand this celebrated author has sometimes touched the most settled usages of our language. In 1790, which was seven years after the appearance of his first grammar, he published an octavo volume of more than four hundred pages, consisting of Essays, moral, historical, political, and literary, which might have done him credit, had he not spoiled his book by a grammatical whim about the reformation of orthography. Not perceiving that English literature, multiplied as it had been within two or three centuries, had acquired a stability in some degree corresponding to its growth, he foolishly imagined it was still as susceptible of change and improvement as in the days of its infancy. Let the reader pardon the length of this digression, if for the sake of any future schemer who may chance to adopt a similar conceit, I cite from the preface to this volume a specimen of the author's practice and reasoning. The ingenious attorney had the good sense quickly to abandon this project, and content himself with less glaring innovations; else he had never stood as he now does, in the estimation of the public. But there is the more need to record the example, because in one of the southern states the experiment has recently been tried again. A still abler member of the same profession, has renewed it but lately; and it is said there are yet remaining some converts to this notion of improvement. I copy literally, leaving all my readers and his to guess for themselves why he spelled *"writers"* with a *w* and *"riting"* without.

> During the course of ten or twelv yeers, I hav been laboring to correct popular errors, and to assist my yung brethren in the road to truth and virtue; my publications for theze purposes hav been numerous; much time haz been spent, which I do not regret, and much censure incurred, which my hart tells me I do not dezerv. * * * The reeder wil obzerv that the *orthography* of the volum iz not uniform. The reezon iz, that many of the essays hav been published before, in the common orthography, and it would hav been a laborious task to copy the whole, for the sake of changing the spelling. In the essays ritten within the last

yeer, a considerable change of spelling iz introduced by way of experiment. This liberty waz taken by the writers before the age of queen Elizabeth, and to this we are indebted for the preference of modern spelling over that of Gower and Chaucer. The man who admits that the change of *housbonde, mynde, ygone, moneth* into *husband, mind, gone, month,* iz an improovement, must acknowledge also the riting of *helth, breth, rong, tung, munth,* to be an improovement. There is no alternativ. Every possible reezon that could ever be offered for altering the spelling of wurds, stil exists in ful force; and if a gradual reform should not be made in our language, it wil proov that we are less under the influence of reezon than our ancestors.—*Noah Webster's Essays, Pref.* p. xi.

But let us return, with our author, to the question of the parts of speech. I have shown that if we do not mean to adopt some less convenient scheme, we must count them *ten,* and preserve their ancient order as well as their ancient names. And, after all his vacillation in consequence of reading Horne Tooke, it would not be strange if Dr. Webster should come at last to the same conclusion. He was not very far from it in 1828, as may be shown by his own testimony, which he then took occasion to record. I will give his own words on the point:

> There is great difficulty in devising a correct classification of the several sorts of words; and probably no classification that shall be simple and at the same time philosophically correct, can be invented. There are some words that do not strictly fall under any description of any class yet devised. Many attempts have been made and are still making to remedy this evil; but such schemes as I have seen, do not, in my apprehension, correct the defects of the old schemes, nor simplify the subject. On the other hand, all that I have seen, serve only to obscure and embarrass the subject, by substituting new arrangements and new terms which are as incorrect as the old ones, and less intelligible. I have attentively viewed these subjects, in all the lights which my opportunities have afforded, and am convinced that the distribution of words, most generally received, *is the best that can be formed,* with some slight alterations adapted to the particular construction of the English language.

This passage is taken from the advertisement, or preface, to the Grammar which accompanies the author's edition of his great quarto Dictionary. Now the several schemes which bear his own name, were doubtless all of them among those which he had *"seen;"* so that he here condemns them all collectively, as he had previously condemned some of them at each reformation. Nor is the last exempted. For although he here plainly gives his vote for that common scheme which he first condemned, he does not adopt it without "some slight alterations;" and in contriving these alterations he is inconsistent with his own professions. He makes the parts of speech *eight,* thus: "1. The name or noun; 2. The pronoun or substitute; 3. The adjective, attribute, or attributive; 4. The verb; 5. The adverb; 6. The preposition; 7. The connective or conjunction; 8. The exclamation or interjection." In his Rudiments of English Grammar, published in 1811, "to unfold the *true principles* of the language," his parts of speech were *seven;* "viz. 1. Names or nouns; 2. Substitutes or pronouns; 3. Attributes or adjectives; 4. Verbs, with their participles; 5. Modifiers or adverbs; 6. Prepositions; 7. Connectives or conjunctions." In his Philosophical and Practical Grammar, published in 1807, a book which professes to teach "the *only legitimate principles,* and established usages," of the language, a twofold division of words is adopted; first, into two general classes, primary and secondary; then into "*seven species* or parts of speech," the first two belonging to the former class, the other five to the latter; thus: "1. Names or nouns; 2. Verbs; 3. Substitutes; 4. Attributes; 5. Modifiers; 6. Prepositions; 7. Connectives." In his "Improved Grammar of the English Language," published in 1831, the same scheme is retained, but the usual names are preferred.

How many different schemes of classification this author invented, I know not; but he might well have saved himself the trouble of inventing any; for, so far as appears, none of his last three grammars ever came to a second edition. In the sixth edition of his "Plain and Comprehensive Grammar, grounded on the *true principles* and idioms of the language," a work which his last grammatical preface affirms to have been originally fashioned "on the model of Lowth's," the parts of speech are reckoned "*six;* nouns, articles, pronouns, adjectives, verbs, and abbreviations or particles." This work, which he says "was extensively used in the schools of this country," and continued to be in demand, he voluntarily suppressed; because, after a profitable experiment of four and twenty years, he found it so far from being grounded on "true principles," that the whole scheme then appeared to him incorrigibly bad. And, judging from this sixth edition, printed in 1800, the only one which I have seen, I cannot but concur with him in the opinion. More than one half of the volume is a loose *Appendix* composed chiefly of notes taken from Lowth and Priestley; and there is a great want of method in what was meant for the body of the work. I imagine his several editions must have been different grammars with the same title; for such things are of no uncommon occurrence, and I cannot otherwise account for the assertion that this book was compiled "on *the model of Loweth's,* and on the same principles as [those on which] Murray has constructed his."— *Advertisement in Webster's quarto Dict.*

In a treatise on grammar, a bad scheme is necessarily attended with inconveniences for which no merit in the execution can possibly compensate. The first thing, therefore, which a skillful teacher will notice in a work of this kind, is the arrangement. If he find any difficulty in discovering, at sight, what it is, he will be sure it is bad; for a lucid order is what he has a right to expect from him who pretends to improve upon all the English grammarians. Dr. Webster is not the only reader of the EPEA PTEROENTA, who has been thereby prompted to meddle with the common scheme of grammar; nor is he the only one who has attempted to simplify the subject by reducing the parts of speech to *six*. John Dalton of Manchester, in 1801, in a small grammar which he dedicated to Horne Tooke, made them six, but not the same six. He would have them to be, nouns, pronouns, verbs, adverbs, conjunctions, and prepositions. This writer, like Brightland, Tooke, Fisher, and some others, insists on it that the articles are *adjectives*. Priestley, too, throwing them out of his classification, and leaving the learner to go almost through his book in ignorance of their rank, at length assigns them to the same class, in one of his notes. And so has Dr. Webster fixed them in his late valuable, but not faultless, dictionaries. But David Booth, an etymologist perhaps equally learned, in his "Introduction to an Analytical Dictionary of the English Language," declares them to be of the same species as the *pronouns;* from which he thinks it strange that they were ever separated! P. 21.

Now, what can be more idle, than for teachers to reject the common classification of words, and puzzle the heads of school-boys with speculations like these? It is easy to admit all that etymology can show to be true, and still justify the old arrangement of the elements of grammar. And if we depart from the common scheme, where shall we stop? Some have taught that the parts of speech are only *five;* as did the latter stoics, whose classes, according to Priscian and Harris, were these: articles, nouns appellative, nouns proper, verbs, and conjunctions. Others have made them *four;* as did Aristotle and the elder stoics, and, more recently, Milnes, Brightland, Harris, Ware, Fisher, and the author of a work on Universal Grammar, entitled Enclytica. Yet, in naming the four, each of these contrives to differ from *all the rest!* With Aristotle, they are, "nouns, verbs, articles, and conjunctions;" with Milnes, "nouns, adnouns, verbs, and particles;" with Brightland, "names, qualities, affirmations, and particles;" with Harris, "substantives, attributives, definitives, and connectives;" with Ware, "the name, the word, the assistant, the connective;" with Fisher, "names, qualities, verbs, and particles;" with the author of Enclytica, "names, verbs, modes, and connectives." But why make the classes so numerous as four? Many of the ancients, Greeks, Hebrews, and Arabians, according to Quintilian, made them *three;* and these three, according to Vossius, were nouns, verbs, and particles. "Veteres Arabes, Hebræi, et Græci, tres, non amplius, classes faciebant; 1. Nomen, 2. Verbum, 3. Particula seu Dictio." ["The ancient Arabs, the Hebrews, and the Greeks made the classes three, not more: noun, verb, and particle."]—*Voss. de Anal.* Lib. i, Cap. 1.

Nor is this number, *three,* quite destitute of modern supporters; though most of these come at it in another way. D. St. Quentin, in his Rudiments of General Grammar, published in 1812, divides words into the "three general classes" last mentioned; viz., "1. Nouns, 2. Verbs, 3. Particles."—P. 5. Booth, who published the second edition of his etymological work in 1814, examining severally the ten parts of speech, and finding what he supposed to be the true origin of all the words in some of the classes, was led to throw one into an other, till he had destroyed seven of them. Then, resolving that each word ought to be classed according to the meaning which its etymology fixes upon it, he refers the number of classes to *nature,* thus:

If, then, each [word] has a *meaning,* and is capable of raising an idea in the mind, that idea must have its prototype in nature. It must either denote an *exertion,* and is therefore a *verb;* or a *quality, and* is, in that case, an *adjective;* or it must express an *assemblage* of qualities, such as is observed to belong to some individual object, and is, on this supposition, the *name* of such object, or a *noun.* * * * We have thus given an account of the different divisions of words, and have found that the whole may be classed under three heads of Names, Qualities, and Actions; or Nouns, Adjectives, and Verbs.—*Introd. to Analyt. Dict.* p. 22.

This notion of the parts of speech, as the reader will presently see, found an advocate also in the author of the popular little story of Jack Halyard. It appears in his Philosophic Grammar published in Philadelphia in 1827. Whether the writer borrowed it from Booth, or was led into it by the light of "nature," I am unable to say: he does not appear to have derived it from the ancients. Now, if either he or the lexicographer has discovered in "nature" a prototype for this scheme of grammar, the discovery is only to be proved, and the schemes of all other grammarians, ancient or modern, must give place to it. For the reader will observe that this triad of parts is not that which is mentioned by Vossius and Quintilian. But authority may by found for reducing the number of the parts of speech yet lower. Plato, according to Harris, and the first inquirers into language, according to Horne Tooke, made them *two;* nouns and verbs: which Crombie, Dalton, McCulloch, and some others, say, are the only parts essentially necessary for the communication of our thoughts. Those who know nothing about grammar, regard all words as of *one* class. To them, a word is simply a word; and under what other name it may come, is no concern of theirs.

WORKING WITH THE SELECTION

1. Brown assured his readers that by parsing and only by parsing could a young person learn to use his native language correctly and elegantly. What does Brown seem to have ignored that you consider useful in the study of language?

2. Brown relies heavily on a classification scheme that recognizes ten parts of speech. Do you find sufficient evidence in his discussion to inspire confidence in his scheme? How does he know that he has the right number, that he has defined them correctly, and that repeating his rules will do any good?

3. Brown refers to etymology, which he says, "treats of the different parts of speech, with their classes and modifications." How does his use of the word differ from current use?

4. Recall what you have been told about prepositions. Now read the following definition of a preposition from Brown's discussion of syntax:

    The preposition (as its name implies) *precedes* the word which it governs. Yet there are some exceptions. In the familiar style, a preposition governing a relative or an interrogative pronoun is often separated from its object and connected with the other term of relation; as, "*Whom* did he speak to?" But it is more dignified and generally more graceful to place the preposition before the pronoun, as "*To whom* did he speak?"

Does such evidence in any way alter your estimate of Brown as you may have formed it on the basis of what he calls his "praxis"?

4

Revolution in Grammar: Structural Linguistics

The twentieth century has seen a revolution in grammar—a revolution in grammatical thinking and in attempts to describe grammar. This revolution—along with the rejuvenation that accompanied it—was manifested in at least two ways: (1) disillusionment over the inadequacy of previous grammatical statements, especially those that relied on "parts of speech," even when these were augmented and somewhat refined through a consideration of function, and (2) positive belief in a more scientific approach to grammar than had been possible with the undefinable parts of speech and vague concepts such as meaning and function. Various attempts were made to draft a more adequate grammatical statement; the first to gain a wide following became known as structural linguistics. *Its basic approach is embodied in the following two selections. The first is by W. Nelson Francis, professor of English and linguistics at Brown University, from his book* The Structure of American English (*1956*). *The second selection is by Sumner Ives, who was trained in linguistics at the University of Texas and is professor of English at Hunter College of the City University of New York. The selection is from* A New Handbook for Writers (*1960*).

Syntactic Structures

W. Nelson Francis

In the discussion that follows, a simple system of diagramming will be used to represent graphically the various structures which are encountered in English syntax. Most systems of diagramming in common use depend on rearranging the words and word groups of the structure being diagrammed in order to place them in a geometric pattern which reveals their logical relationship. There are two serious objections to this procedure. (1) Since it is based on a logical (meaning-based) understanding of what the structure means, it reveals the *logic,* rather than the *grammar,* of the structure. (2) By rearranging words, it obliterates the part played by word order, one of the basic syntactic devices of English. Systems of diagramming that depend on rearrangement thus conceal grammatical structure instead of revealing it.

In contrast, the system used here will leave the words in the order in which they appear. It is intended to be a graphic representation of structure based on two main principles: (1) English syntax is a many-layered organization of relatively few types of basic units; (2) every structure may be divided into its *immediate constituents* (often abbreviated IC's by linguists), almost always two, each of which may in turn be divided and subdivided until the *ultimate constituents* (in grammar, the words) are reached. This is graphically indicated by enclosing each ultimate constituent in a box and drawing larger and larger boxes around the immediate constituents of each of the increasingly complex structures into which they combine. The result is something like those famous "Chinese boxes" that fit one within another. The difference is that each of our syntactic boxes contains not one but usually two smaller boxes, thus:

Here the outer box incloses a syntactic structure whose immediate constituents are A and B. If this structure joins with another, whose immediate constituents are C and D, into a larger structure, we have

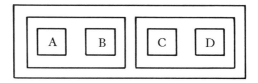

In this fashion, the immediate constituents on every layer of structure are made clearly apparent.

The four different structures are identified by placing simple symbols between the two immediate constituents. *Modification* is indicated by an arrow → pointing from the modifier toward the head:

Predication is indicated by a capital P with its back to the subject and its front facing the predicate. In the relatively few structures of predication where the subject follows the predicate, the P is reversed:

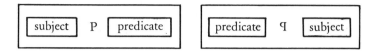

Complementation is similarly indicated by a capital C with its back to the verbal element:

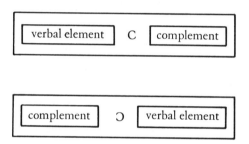

Coordination is indicated by parallel lines connecting the constituents. If a function word (*coordinator*) is present, it is written between these lines:

Prepositions, includers, and interrogators . . . are put into a smaller box, connected to the box containing the object, included clause, or question which they introduce:

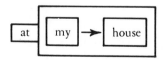

Within the complement, which is one of the two immediate constituents of a structure of complementation, the various kinds of complements are identified by labeling their boxes with initials: DO for direct object, IO for indirect object, SC for subjective complement, and OC for objective complement (these various elements will be discussed later):

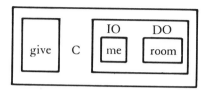

. . . As we have seen, the two components of a structure of modification are a *head* and a *modifier,* whose meaning serves to broaden, qualify, select, change, describe, or in some other way affect the meaning of the head. In the [following] examples—*hungry people, home town, easily superior*—both head and modifier are single words. But this is by no means always the case. Both the head and the modifier which are the immediate constituents of a structure of modification may themselves be structures of more or less complexity. Grammatical organization, as we have already observed, is a complex of many structural layers.

Each of the four parts of speech, and certain function words as well, may serve as the head of a structure of modification. Likewise, each of the four parts of speech, sometimes in special inflected forms, and certain function words may function as modifiers. Furthermore, though certain patterns are so frequent as to be considered in some sense "standard" or "regular," in actuality virtually all possible combinations of the four parts of speech are possible in structures of modification. The reader must clear his mind of the notion that it is somehow more "correct" for an adjective to modify a noun, for example, than it is for a noun to modify a noun, or for an adjective to modify a verb. These notions are derived from the grammar of other languages than English, and are not relevant to the grammar of present-day English. . . .

[Francis develops his analysis so that he is soon able to diagram relatively complex structures, as in the following:]

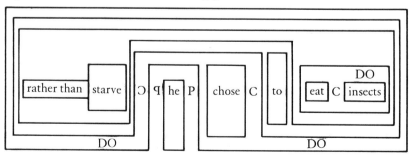

When the inversion is removed, this complicated pattern looks simpler:

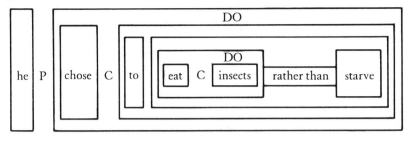

Sentence Formulas

Sumner Ives

When two English elements are joined together to make a larger element
—as the V and the second N are joined to make the predicate, and the subject and predicate are joined to make the sentence—they are IMMEDIATE
CONSTITUENTS within the element they make. An element so made of immediate constituents is a CONSTITUTE. This process of dividing elements into
constituent elements can be continued until the morphemes are revealed as
the ULTIMATE CONSTITUENTS. Similarly, the process of combining constituents
can be continued until the sentence (not the compound sentence) is revealed
as the ULTIMATE CONSTITUENT.

In discussing composition, the kind of sentence which is most important
is one that is grammatically independent and is a clause, with or without
dependent clauses. This kind includes "simple sentences" and "complex sentences," as these terms are used in traditional grammar. It is the basic unit in
CONNECTED DISCOURSE. Connected discourse includes college themes, letters to
Uncle Jim, the descriptive and narrative portions of novels, and any other
communication in which one person speaks or writes without specific dependence on something previously said or on something in the immediate
attention (like "Ouch!" in response to pain). . . .

The most efficient approach to sentence patterns is through the HIERARCHIES
of structure within them. The most common types of sentences in connected
discourse, statements and questions, have two main parts (constituents)—
subject and predicate. Each included clause likewise has a subject and predicate. In analysis, each sentence and, in turn, each included clause can be
divided into its subject and predicate. Subjects and predicates may be divisible into parts (constituents), and each part may be further divisible into
constituents, until the ultimate constituents, the morphemes, are reached.

Each stage in the analysis deals with a hierarchy in the total structure, and the sentence as a whole is a complex of interrelated and superimposed hierarchies, as shown in the following diagram, which does not, however, separate all the morphemes.

I				II				
Persons	who	throw	stones	should	live	in	strong	houses
A	B			A		B		
Persons	who	throw	stones	should	live	in	strong	houses
	1	2		1	2	1	2	
	who	throw	stones	should	live	in	strong	houses
		a	b				a	b
		throw	stones				strong	houses

First, the total sentence is divided into two parts—subject and predicate, represented by I and II. Each part is then further divided without regard to the other part. The subject (I) is divided into its head (IA) and a dependent clause (IB). The dependent clause is divided into its subject (IB1) and predicate (IB2). The predicate of the dependent clause is divided into verb (IB2a) and direct object (IB2b). Similarly, the predicate (II) is divided into verb phrase (IIA) and adverbial modifier (IIB). The verb phrase is divided into modal (IIA1) and head (IIA2). The modifier is divided into preposition (IIB1) and object (IIB2). The object is divided into adjectival modifier (IIB2a) and head (IIB2b). *Persons, stones,* and *houses* could be further divided, but this discussion of sentence patterns stops at the word level. Each stage of division represents a hierarchy in its own complex of related hierarchies. As the analysis is made by proper divisions, so the sentence was made by proper additions.

WORKING WITH THE SELECTIONS

1. Both selections stem from the tradition developed by such linguists as Saussure and Bloomfield. Clearly, Francis and Ives start from assumptions different from those of Goold Brown and they proceed by different methods. In what major ways do they differ from some of their predecessors?

2. The samples given here are too meager to permit much criticism of this approach to grammar. Working out a statement of any grammar, by whatever approach, requires a sizable book. You have probably concluded, however, that Francis and Ives rely mainly on structure for their analysis—such scholars are often called *structuralists* or *structural linguists.* The work of the two men is essentially similar even though they employ different sorts of diagrams. What might seem to be some advantages and some limitations of such an approach to grammar?

3. You will have noticed both Francis and Ives using a word that may have been strange to you in grammatical discussion, *head,* or *head word,* and Francis endeavors to define it. Does it have any counterpart in Goold Brown's terminology?

5

The Counterrevolution:
Generative Grammar

Robert P. Stockwell

Structural linguistics was only beginning to be known as "the new grammar" when other grammatical proposals appeared and gained such support that the particularizing article the was no longer appropriate in referring to any new grammar. At this writing the approaches attracting the most attention are the generative grammars, particularly what is called transformational or transform grammar, as it developed from the work of Noam Chomsky. This approach was formally presented in Chomsky's Syntactic Structures *(1957), but it had already been sketched by Chomsky and his followers at conferences, linguistic institutes, and the like. One of Chomsky's earliest and most eloquent exponents is Robert P. Stockwell, professor of linguistics at the University of California, Los Angeles, where he is department chairman. The following selection is Stockwell's contribution to* Linguistics Today *(1969), ed. Archibald A. Hill.*

The term "generative grammar" has come to refer to the research of a group of American linguists, and recently some others abroad, whose work depends on the theoretical advances made by Noam Chomsky. Chomsky teaches at the Massachusetts Institute of Technology, which remains the center of this activity even though several of the important scholars of this persuasion have been away from MIT for several years, and others never actually studied there at all but came into their generative convictions through Chomsky's published articles and books.

It is in fact a misnomer to refer to the work of this school of linguistics as "generative grammar," since the distinguishing claim of Chomsky's group is not that grammars should be generative but that a generative grammar should be of a certain form—namely, a type of rule known as a "transformational rule." Let us consider first what it means to speak of "generative grammar," in general.

The object of investigation of grammatical studies is sentencehood in natural languages. If it were possible to combine the words of a language in any way whatever in forming sentences—say, to select words from a dictionary list by some sort of random generating device—then grammatical studies would not be necessary, since there would be nothing to study except possibly the properties of random generating devices. But it is obvious that sentences are not formed by randomly stringing words together from a dictionary. There are exceedingly tight restrictions on what arrangements of words are possible in sentences. The grammatical study of a particular language is the attempt to characterize these restrictions in detail for that language. General linguistics is the theory of how such grammatical characterizations can best be achieved for all languages—that is, the study of the optimal form of grammars.

For the statement of such restrictions to be of scientific value, it must be absolutely explicit: it must make clear exactly what properties of the grammar of the language are covered by the descriptive account itself, as distinct from what information an intelligent human user of an *in*explicit description can infer about the language. To say that a descriptive account of the grammar of a language is "generative," therefore, is really to say no more about it than that it provides an explicit enumeration of its own claims about the structure of that language—such claims as what the sentences of the language are, what the internal structure of each sentence is, how each sentence is realized phonetically, how each sentence is interpreted semantically, which sentences are interpreted similarly, which ones are interpreted differently in spite of surface similarity, and so on—through a wide range of information about sentences that is clearly available to speakers and necessary for their understanding of the language.

"Generative" means, then, "explicit." But what is gained by such a term? What does the notion of generating sentences have to do with being explicit about grammatical structure? To answer this we must consider what possible answers there are to the challenge that the descriptive account must be explicit. We need consider only the absolutely minimal demand that can reasonably be placed on any grammatical study, namely that it should discriminate between those objects which are under study and those which are not—specifically, between strings of noises which are sentences of the language and any other object whatsoever, such as strings of noises which are ill-formed sentences of that language, strings of noises which don't belong to that language at all, and so on. It is immediately clear that the set of well-formed sentences of a particular language is a subset of the set of all sentences in all languages, and that both of these are subsets of the set of all strings of human communicative noises. It would be overwhelmingly difficult to define the set of well-formed sentences of a language by identifying all nonmembers of the set directly. What is necessary is the enumeration of the set of well-formed sentences for that language. One conceivable enumeration would be a list. A list is, at least, explicit. But there is no way to list all the members of a set which is indefinitely large (as is the case for the well-formed sentences of all natural languages). The only available alternative to a list is some rule or set of rules which has the mathematical property of *recursiveness*—the property of reapplicability indefinitely many times over, each successive application enumerating another member of the set. It is exactly in this sense that a simple rule for addition is said to generate, or enumerate, the infinite set of whole positive integers in mathematics.

To say, then, that a grammatical description is "generative" is only to say that it contains rules which formally enumerate the class of objects the description is about. This is equivalent to saying that the description is a testable one, since the objects it enumerates, along with their structural descriptions, can then be subjected to empirical verification with respect to such questions as the following: Are these hypothetically enumerated objects in fact sentences of the language, as claimed by the description? do they have the internal structure assigned by the description? are they interpreted in the way predicted by the description? do they have the phonological properties predicted by the description? It seems obvious that this property, the property of explicitness and therefore of potential empirical validation, is the least that can be asked of a scientific theory.

The use of the word "generative" by Chomsky and his group has been subject to deep misunderstanding among linguists all over the world, particularly among American "structuralists" but notably also in Great Britain and the Netherlands. The source of the misunderstanding seems to have been a confusion between the way a descriptive grammar generates a representation of the unconscious knowledge of the ideal speaker-hearer of the language, and the way an actual speaker-hearer produces his daily discourse (about which virtually nothing is known). That is, the grammatical description is an account of the intrinsic competence which must be assumed in principle to be available to the individual speaking the language if we are to explain how it is that he is able to do the subtle and intricate things he can in fact do with his language. This distinction of Chomsky's between *competence* and *performance* is a familiar distinction in general linguistics from quite early in the history of the science, one best known, perhaps, in the distinction made by the Swiss linguist Ferdinand de Saussure between *langue* ("competence") and *parole* ("performance").

Once it is clear that there is really no alternative to using recursive rules to characterize the structure of a natural language if the characterization is to be an explicit scientific account of the constraints on the formation of sentences in that language, the really interesting question arises: What is the form of the rules needed for this purpose? Prior to Chomsky's work, virtually no attention was given to this question in American linguistics. Chomsky's answers to this question have in effect revolutionized the discipline of linguistics, at least the discipline as practiced by the substantial segment of the academic community which has found itself persuaded by his arguments. Many assumptions and claims generally accepted before Chomsky's time have been challenged by the transformationalists, and as far as it is possible to judge in the almost total absence of serious replies to these challenges, have been successfully replaced by transformational views. The challenges strike deep into the basic concepts of earlier generations of structural linguistics—into such hallowed theoretical constructs as the phoneme, the regularity and independence of sound change, stratified levels within linguistic descriptions, and procedural requirements on description, and even into the sanctity of textual citation as supporting evidence for an analysis. The criteria that determine what constitutes adequate justification for an analysis are incomparably more complex after the transformational revolution, largely because a transformational grammar is interlocking and interdependent in its own structure to an extent hardly more than fractionally conceptualized before Chomsky's work. These developments of the past ten years are so extensive and range so totally through linguistic studies that here I shall only outline the aims of the rules in a transformational grammar and suggest the kinds of linguistic phenomena these rules are intended to account for explicitly.

In order to map a string of noises—represented as a string of phonetic symbols, or in any other representation appropriate to a basis for semantic interpretation—in order to understand an utterance of a language—a great many kinds of information must be available; and the converse of this mapping, namely taking a set of concepts and encoding them into a string of noises capable of receiving the intended interpretation, requires precisely the same information. This information may therefore be represented in a form which is independent of the manner or direction in which it is processed by the speaker-hearer. In this sense, then, a generative grammar, which is an abstraction of the information required for either of these operations as performed by people when they communicate by language, is totally neutral with respect to the manner in which the information is processed. In the following outline of the internal structure of the grammatical description, the sequence is a logical sequence only, though it is spoken of as a sequence of operations which follow each other as if through time. The grammatical description is an abstract characterization of the set of constraints under which the processing must be carried out; it is not a literal characterization of the way the constraints are processed in the act of speech, nor is there any assumption about the form the constraints take in the brain of the human being.

Let us consider, then, the kinds of information available in principle to the ideal speaker-hearer of a language, and the way in which the information is accounted for in a transformational generative grammar. First, in any sentence, words are grouped in two ways: by classes and by functions. Grouping by classes is a result of similarity in the way words combine with other words. For example, there is no sentence of the form * *he put it*, because one of the syntactic features of the verb *put* is that it must combine with a certain type of adverbial phrase, a *directional adverb*, as in *he put it into the garage*. To speak English one must know that there is such a class of verbs. In the grammar, these would be marked by having a certain syntactic feature, say [+ Directional Adverb], as a property assigned to them in the lexicon. This syntactic feature is then a part of the syntactic definition of the verb *put,* and the rules of sentence formation are devised in such a way that this verb can be inserted in a sentence only if a directional adverb is combined with it. The classes to which each word of the language belongs are, then, the various intersections of the syntactic features required for the description of the way words can combine in that language. The combinatory properties of the verb *put* would be accounted for by the set of features [+ Verb], [+ Transitive], [+ Directional Adverb], and so on. Any other verb with the same set of features would be identical in its combinatory behavior (total intersection of syntactic features), and other verbs would be similar to the extent that they shared any of these syntactic features (partial intersection).

But there must also be grouping by functions, since any single class can serve several functions. For example, a noun phrase may function as subject of the sentence or as object of the main verb. Function is a relational notion, each possible grammatical function being defined by a labeled branching-diagram which is generated by the first component of a transformational grammar, the base component, which contains what are referred to as the "branching rules," the "constituent structure rules," the "expansion rules," or the "phrase-structure rules." As these names suggest, these rules generate strings of words bracketed and labeled in such a way that the most closely related elements of the string are tied together as a unit, then the next most closely related elements, and so on, up to the final string of all items which are tied together under the label "Sentence." A function, such as "Subject of the Sentence," is assigned by virtue of the fact that the label "Sentence" appears directly above the topmost "Noun Phrase" in the usual diagrams.

The base component, then, generates the abstract structures which lie beneath the surface of sentences. These abstract structures, now commonly referred to as the "deep" or "underlying" structures of sentences, contain all the syntactic information required for the semantic interpretation of sentences (they also contain semantic information, perhaps in the form of atomized dictionary definitions attached to the atomic elements of the syntactic string). The deep structure specifies not only category information about words (the "syntactic features") and functional relations between words and phrases (by virtue of the labeled diagram), but also relations between the various simple sentences that may be combined to form a single more complex sentence. Thus a complex sentence like *The man who came to dinner ate the food that was on the table* is in some sense decomposable into a main sentence, *The man ate the food,* and two embedded sentences, one embedded in the subject—*The man came to dinner*—and the other embedded in the object—*The food was on the table.* The base rules for simple sentences in this case apply, recursively, three times. The intuition that the phrase *The man who came to dinner* somehow "contains" the simple sentence *The man came to dinner* is thus represented. There are infinitely many similar "containments." The great Danish linguist Otto Jespersen observed, for example, that an expression like *the furiously barking dog* somehow contained the sentence *The dog barked furiously;* similarly, *his shirt* somehow contains *He has a shirt,* and *his knowledge of her departure* contains both *He knows* and *She departed,* and so on. In these and all similar cases the deep structure would consist of a labeled branching-diagram where the simple sentences out of which the whole was composed would appear in their simple forms. . . .

A transformational grammar, then, may be said to enumerate the underlying structures of sentences of a language in its *base component.* The output of the base component is a labeled branching-diagram, of which the terminal nodes are formative elements contained in the dictionary. These formatives are simply the intersection of three sets of features: phonological features needed to map the sentence into a string of noises; syntactic features needed to map the deep structure into the surface syntactic structure; and semantic features needed to map the deep structure into the semantic interpretation. The *transformational component* of the grammar performs the mapping of deep to surface structure, and the surface structure in turn is the basis, along with the phonological features, for application of the rules of the *phonological component* which map the structure into the string of sounds that provide the basis for transmission of the message from one human being to others who speak the same language. The *semantic component,* about which very little is known yet, provides a mapping of the isolated minimal meaning-bearing elements into larger and larger units, related by virtue of the structure assigned to them in the base component, to, finally, the full sentence or larger unit of discourse.

What are some of the implications of transformational grammatical theory for the study of human behavior in a wider frame of reference? If Chomsky and his colleagues are right, ordinary, everyday communication in language—virtually every such act of communication—is a creative performance governed by rules of such abstractness and complexity that there is no reasonable likelihood that they could be acquired by a child unless he were born into the world with highly specific innate gifts for this particular kind of learning. Thus the notion that human beings acquire language merely as a set of conditioned responses—the notion that the use of language is habitual behavior in some meaningful sense of the term "habit"—is rendered quite improbable. On the contrary, the rationalist notion that this behavior is dictated by a set of prior, and uniquely human, mental capacities achieved by a million or more years of evolution is strongly supported.

The theory also provides intriguing speculations about linguistic change, and new insight into how it can come about that two people can readily communicate with each other even though they speak vastly different dialects—even though the surface structures of their utterances fail to correspond in any obvious way. Consider the second of these insights first, since linguistic change depends, in a rather direct way, on the existence of surface variation on underlying structures that are essentially identical. Suppose we consider a well-known dialect difference between British and American English, simplifying the details slightly. In American English, the normal answer to a question like *Have you lectured in Europe?* would be *Yes, I have,* or *No, I haven't.* That is, the answer would pick up the auxiliary element of the verb phrase in the question. Other examples, confining our answers to affirmatives:

> *Will you solve this problem for me?*   *Yes, I will.*
> *Could you have written this essay?*   *Yes, I could have.*

These same answers are possible also in British English, but very commonly one hears also the following ones:

> *Have you lectured in Europe?*   *Yes, I have done.*
> *Will you solve this problem for me?*   *Yes, I will do.*
> *Could you have written this essay?*   *Yes, I could have done.*

This usage is not yet well attested in literary documents (as far as I know), because it is a syntactic change of recent origin, or at least of recent prominence in British colloquial usage. What appears to be involved is that whereas the American rule that operates to generate such tag responses requires simply that the first auxiliary element of the main verb be echoed, all the rest being deleted (*Yes, I will* being a truncated version of *Yes, I will solve this problem for you*), the British rule allows an additional optional choice of a dummy verb (*do*) to stand in, so to speak, for the main verb phrase that has been deleted. Since *do* is the normal dummy verb in other grammatical situations—in, for example, *What were you doing last night?*, in which *doing* stands in for some specific action verb (*I was working late, I was watching my favorite television show, I was trying to get out of a traffic jam on the freeway*)—it is to be expected that *do* would drop naturally into this substitute function in the response to questions.[1]

Now this dialect difference—in this case a fairly trivial one which would never cause misunderstanding—is an instance of a difference which results from a very slight change (the addition of an optional replacement element in the rule that truncates the full-sentence response to a question) in the transformational rule which maps the deep structure into the surface structure. The deep structure is obviously the same for both dialects.

Consider now a more familiar kind of dialect difference: say, the British pronunciation and the Midwestern American pronunciation of the phrase *The panorama of the Far West.* A transformational theory would claim

---

[1] These descriptions are not intended to indicate actual historical developments. Consequently the reader is not to suppose that British English has at some time added a dummy verb to the American type. It should also be noted that other sentence types would be relevant to any historical discussion, namely, such forms as "Yes, I have done *so*" and "Yes, I have done *it*."

that these pronunciations have identical representations in the underlying phonological structure. In the case of British *far*, we must assume that an *r* is really present in order to explain the fact that in a phrase like *the Far East*, where a vowel follows the *r*, the *r* shows up in the surface phonetic form. In the case of *panorama*, we must assume that the penultimate vowel is really the same as the vowel of *cat* in order to explain the vowel in *panoramic*. Now it happens that historically the *r* in British but not in Midwestern American was dropped in all positions except where a vowel followed. And it happens that historically the æ vowel in British but not in Midwestern American was lengthened and change to *ah* in certain environments and left unchanged in others. In a generative grammar, exactly these historical facts would be incorporated as late rules (drop the *r* and change the vowel) which would operate in British, but not in American —that is, Midwestern American English would lack these late rules, but the underlying forms would be the same for both dialects. Thus there is a sense in which the ordering of certain kinds of rules within a generative grammar recapitulates historical change and provides a principled basis for saying under what conditions differences between languages or dialects are relatively trivial, and when they are spread pervasively to such a depth within the grammar that the two dialects must be differentiated as distinct languages. Linguistic change may be specified in terms of rules added to and deleted from the grammar, with subsequent restructuring of segments of the grammar brought about by inconsistencies and unneeded complications in the total grammar which such additions and deletions may have created.

In sum, I believe that a scientific revolution of major import is occuring in American linguistics under the impact of the fresh views of Chomsky and his followers, and, further, that the implications of his questions and formulations are only beginning to be spelled out in detail. In one of his recent books, *Aspects of the Theory of Syntax*, Chomsky suggests lines of investigation—in both the psycholinguistic area and the unexplored field of the relations between the general theory of grammar and the specific facts of natural languages—in such richness that experimental activity could be directed toward these formulations for at least a generation. I do not think that linguistics has ever shown greater interest in, or given so much hope of success at, explaining facts of such general import for the understanding of human behavior.

WORKING WITH THE SELECTION

1. At this point be sure you recall the selections by Chomsky and Liljeblad in part 1. You may have noticed that the terms *generative* and *transformational* are often used loosely, as though they were synonyms—perhaps because although neither Chomsky himself nor his best students ever make such blun-

ders, both concepts have been associated with Chomsky, and people who have understood neither idea very well have jumbled them together. Now, for your own use, try to write out a distinction between the two terms. Can there be a generative grammar that is not transformational? Can there be a transformational grammar that is not generative?

2. Compare and contrast generative grammar with structural linguistics. How are they similar? How do they differ?

3. Does generative grammar in any way represent a return to older grammatical approaches, a turning away from the directions in which structural linguistics seemed to be leading grammatical thinking?

6

The Revolution Spreads: Stratificational Grammar

John White

Stratificational grammar, one of the more recent theories of language, has been attracting increasing interest, notably in the United States, where it is associated especially with the work of Sydney M. Lamb, professor of linguistics at Yale University. The following article, "Stratificational Grammar: A New Theory of Language," College Composition and Communication, 20 (October, 1969), is by John White, professor of English at Quinnipiac College.

In the broadest sense, grammar is the study of how a language works. Traditional grammar provides our most familiar model of a language, but this century has seen a number of attempts by linguists to give descriptions of languages which are more accurate and objective than those provided by traditional grammar. Structural linguistics and transformational grammar are the best known. This article is concerned with still another attempt to describe how a language works.

Stratificational grammar is a theory of language being developed by Sydney Lamb of the Linguistics Department at Yale University. Lamb's earliest thoughts about a stratificational model of language go back to the mid-1950's, but he dates the modern form of this theory from 1965. Dissemination of it has so far been limited mostly to professional journals, a book by Lamb entitled *Outline of Stratificational Grammar* (Georgetown University Press, 1966) and graduate courses taught by him. At present, transformational theory seems to be the most widely-held view of language, but Lamb predicts that by the early 1970's stratificational theory will have superseded it.

Aiding the development of this theory are H. A. Gleason of University of Toronto and Peter A. Reich of Yale. Reich works as a chief assistant to Lamb on the Linguistic Automation Project, which was started by Lamb in 1966 to test and evaluate his theory. From a small office in downtown New Haven, tests are programmed by Project personnel to be run at the nearby Yale Computer Center. In England, M. A. K. Halliday at University of London is developing a related view of language called systemic grammar, and it is of sufficient importance to stratificational theory to be credited here.

According to Lamb, *a language is the system which its speakers use to speak to each other and understand each other*. Language is not to be understood in terms of words but rather in terms of mental systems. Speech and writing are not language; they are only *manifestations* of the system which is language, just as a lighted bulb is a manifestation of electricity. Every speaker of a language has a representation of that system in his brain, but his representation is only part of the total system. One speaker's representation approximates another's in varying degrees, depending upon cultural background, education, etc. The representation in the brain of an illiterate ghetto-dweller is noticeably different from that of a college professor. No single person, however, has within his brain the complete system because it includes both the representations just mentioned as well as those of all other speakers of that language. A language is always more diverse and complex than the representation in any speaker's brain.

Language, then, is a finite system (among many in the brain) which can be used for encoding (speaking or writing) and decoding (understanding) any of an infinite set of texts in that language. Through the definition of "text" we may attain historical perspective on stratificational grammar. According to Lamb, a text consists of both a message and an expression. The message of a text pertains to its content; the expression of a text pertains to sound.

In connection with this definition, Lamb distinguishes two major traditions in the history of linguistic theory: the Bloomfieldian tradition and the Hjelmslevian tradition. Leonard Bloomfield, of course, was the well-known American linguist who taught at Yale in the 1930's. Louis Hjelmslev was a lesser-known but equally great Danish linguist who taught at University of Copenhagen in the 1930-50's. The Bloomfieldian linguists, through structural linguistics, emphasized the study of the expressions of a language, while the Hjelmslevian linguists, through the system called glossematics, emphasized the study of the system which speakers use to produce the expressions. The two traditions may be outlined as follows:

Bloomfieldian Tradition
(emphasizes expressions)

Boas
Sapir
Bloomfield (1930–45)
Neo-Bloomfieldians (1940–60)
    Hockett
    Pike
    Bloch
    Trager
    et al.
Chomsky/Harris
    (Transformational grammar, 1955–70's)

Hjelmslevian Tradition
(emphasizes system)

de Saussure
  ↓
Hjelmslev (1935–55)
    ↓
Firth
    ↓
Halliday
    (Systemic grammar, 1960–?)
Lamb
    (Stratificational grammar, 1965–?)

Lamb, then, is attempting to formulate a theory of language which accounts for the system which relates meaning and expression, content and sound. He terms his theory "stratificational" because "one of its chief features is its treatment of linguistic structure as comprising several layers or strata. A language, by its nature, relates sounds (or writing) to meanings; the relationship turns out to be a very complex one, which can be analyzed in terms of a series of codelike systems, each of which has a structure analogous to that which earlier linguistic theories ascribed to language as a whole. . ." (*Outline,* p. 1). In making his analysis, it has appeared necessary to describe linguistic structures as consisting of levels or strata. Evidence to date suggests that "all natural languages have at least four [strata], and that at least some languages, including English, have six strata" (*Outline,* p. 1).

The six-stratum structure of English may be regarded as made of three major components—phonology, semology and grammar. Phonology is concerned with speech; semology is concerned with meaning; and grammar relates the two. Each major component includes two of the six levels in the structure. From lowest (the expression side of language) to highest (the meaning side), the levels are named as follows: hypophonemic, phonemic, morphemic, lexemic, sememic, hypersememic. The basic units of each level from lowest to highest are named hypophoneme, phoneme, morpheme, lexeme, sememe and hypersememe. The system of strata may be diagrammed as shown [below].

Speech sounds are produced by the articulatory mechanisms as signalled by the hypophonemic stratum. Hypophonemes, sometimes called distinctive features, are the components of phonemes. All the sounds of English can be produced by about fifteen hypophonemes (such as plosion, spirancy, nasality, labiality and voicing). For example, the Labial (Lb) hypophoneme closes or rounds the lips. In that position, nine phonemes can be produced, depending upon what other hypophonemes are used. If the oral passage is Closed (Cl), the phoneme /p/ is produced in the normal condition (no voicing). If the Voiced (Vd) component is present but all other features remain the same, the phoneme /b/ is produced. Therefore the phoneme /b/ differs from the phoneme /p/ by the addition of one hypophoneme:

$$/p/ = \text{Lb Cl}$$
$$/b/ = \text{Lb Cl Vd}$$

The concepts of phoneme and morpheme have been adequately discussed elsewhere, so here it will be sufficient to note only that the phonemic level deals with all possible combinations of sound in a language, while the morphemic level deals primarily with the structure of words in that language. The next higher stratum in the stratificational model, the lexemic, specifies the structure of clauses, while sentence structure and word meaning are dealt with at a still higher level, the sememic. Highest of all, the hypersememic stratum is concerned with the structure of narrative and units beyond the sentence from paragraphs to entire works.

This diagram is a graphic model of the system believed to be represented in

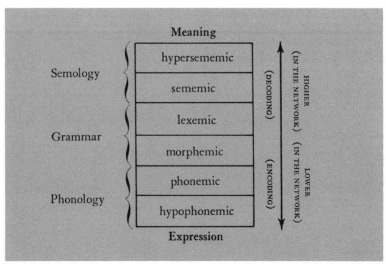

the brain. The linguistic system itself is not directly observable. Only the manifestations of language, such as speech or writing, are observable. Lamb cautions that it is still too early to attempt any correlation between such models and actual neurological structures in the brain. New evidence may demand considerable alteration of the theory's mechanical processes. However, it is hoped that eventually the theory will be confirmed by physiological evidence showing that we really *do* communicate like that.

A language has both *structure* and *process,* corresponding to neurological network and neural impulse. Structure provides the means whereby process may occur. In a language, the primary processes are encoding and decoding. Impulses move through the network, but the network itself does not normally change in the ordinary use of language. In stratificational grammar, this is shown in the diagram as moving downward to expression (encoding) and moving upward to meaning (decoding). Each level of the structure is discrete and self-contained. The structure does not change one form into another. Rather it allows impulses to move from one level to another, with linguistic forms being produced only at the lower end. In the production of a sentence (encoding), meaning always precedes expression, while the reverse is true for decoding. Therefore all the decisions necessary to produce any linguistic form are made *before* the expression is actualized. It is the decision-event, standing outside the linguistic structure at the higher end, which sends impulses through the network. Their emergence outside the lower end of the structure is expression, either as speech or writing.

In attempting to give a precise description of linguistic activity, stratificational grammar has moved from traditional description in ordinary words to description based largely on graphs depicting networks. In addition to graphic diagram, stratificational grammar uses algebraic notation as a mode of description. Thus one type of linguistic activity may be described in ordinary words like this: "An impulse moving downward along line *a* goes simultaneously down line *b* and line *c*. The same relationship may also be described algebraically like this:

$$a/b \cdot c$$

and it may be diagrammed like this:

The example of hypophonemes given above could be indicated like this:

p / Cl Lb   and

These can be translated as "An impulse moving downward along line *p* goes simultaneously down line Cl and line Lb." The triangular node in the center of the graphic diagram indicates a simultaneous "and" relationship. That is, both impulses are needed to make further transmission of impulse. If only one or the other is needed, this "either-or" relationship is indicated by a different node which looks like a bracket lying on its side.

This graphic diagram shows "an impulse moving downward along line *a* goes down either line *b* or line *c*."

If impulses have a fixed, rather than simultaneous, order of transmission or arrival, it is shown through the lines' connection to a node, with priority being given to the left line. In this diagram an impulse moving downward

along line *a* will move first downward along line *b*, or (if a complete connection cannot be made further below in the network) it will return to the node and then move downward along line *c*.

Likewise this diagram indicates that for an impulse to move upward along line *a*, there must arrive at the node, first, an impulse upward along line *b* and, second, an impulse upward along line *c*.

In brief, a triangular node indicates an "and" relationship while a bracket indicates an "either-or" relationship. The order of impulse arrival and transmission is indicated by the joining or separation of lines at a node, with priority in an ordered relationship given to the left-hand line on a non-joined multiple connection to a node.

For the sake of example, Figure 1 shows the network grammar of a highly simplified artificial language having only two partially developed strata of seven phonemes and nine morphemes. The diagram indicates that the phoneme /B/ [1] can move upward to either the morpheme /BON/ or

---

[1] Capital letters are used to indicate the difference between these phonemes of an artificial language and those of natural languages.

the morpheme /BOM/. If we follow the line upward to /BON/, we see the morpheme consists of three phonemes—/B/, /O/ and /N/—which have a definite ordering of first /B/, second /O/ and last /N/. Any other ordering to the arrival of impulses at the /BON/ morpheme node will result in no further transmission of impulse.

Figure 1

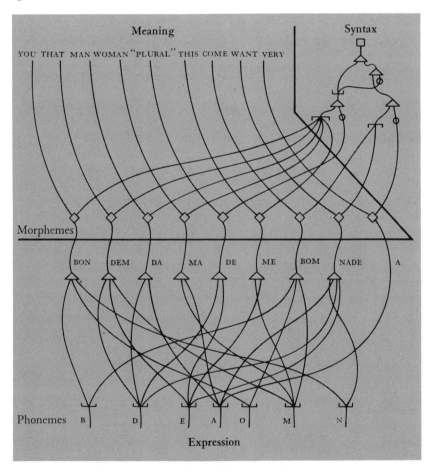

Suppose a speaker of this language received the message "Bon ma de bom." The ordered arrival of impulses through the phonemic section results in further transmission, indicating that each word is at least well-formed in that language, even if it is nonsensical.

Next the impulses are sent through the diamond node up the right-hand line to the syntax section, where their grammatical correctness is determined. Ungrammatical forms are not permitted to pass through the syntax section by virtue of the nodes and ordering of line connections.

The morpheme /BON/ sends an impulse up the right line from the diamond connection until it arrives at the bracket. Here, because the bracket indicates an "either-or" situation, the impulse is allowed to pass upward to the next node, the triangle indicating an "ordered and" situation. The circle on the right-hand line indicates a special situation in stratificational diagrams—an optional item—which is not absolutely necessary for transmission through an "ordered and" node. In this case, the line with a circle is connected to /DE/—which is a part of the message—and so a further transmission is made because both lines below the triangle have impulses arriving in the right order.

Passing upward from the triangle, the impulse goes through a bracket and then goes up the left-hand line because it would be blocked from further transmission if it took the right-hand line, since the "ordered and" node lacks the necessary prior impulse.

Thus the morpheme /BON/ has triggered a series of impulses which eventually arrive at the top of the syntax section, thereby proving its grammatical correctness in the message. The impulse will then return to the diamond connection along the path it chose and pass upward to meaning along the left-hand line. The same process will occur for all other items in the message. Each will have its syntactic correctness tested in the syntax section and, if not halted in transmission, eventually return to the diamond and then pass upward to meaning. By this process the message "Bon ma de bom" will be decoded and the hearer will understand it to mean "You women come."

This diagram (a simple one compared to stratificational descriptions of natural languages) lacks the necessary completeness to illustrate one of stratificational grammar's advantages over other linguistic models: the capability to predict new words and phrases. But it can be seen from the diagram that /BO/ and /NA/ are possible morphemes existing in the structure of this artificial language which simply have not been used. Likewise *fribble* is a possibility that exists in the sound combinations of English but phonetic ŋñtx is not, and this can be demonstrated in stratificational terms such as those above. In transformational terms, however, this can be done only in part while the formation of new idioms such as "uptight" and "brinkmanship" cannot be shown at all. Stratificational grammar handles the formation of new idioms quite easily.

Besides its predictive capability, stratificational theory offers a hypothesis of what happens in the brain. (Transformational theory does not, since its emphasis is on the competence of a speaker, not the system he actually uses for linguistic performance.) In stratificational theory, the decisions are all made before any linguistic forms are produced with those forms being actualized only at the lower end of the network. Lamb maintains this is a simpler and more economical description than transformational theory's rewrite rules, which suggest that one linguistic form is changed into another, and then another and another.

Last of all, stratificational theory offers a unified picture of language from the distinctive features of expression to the formal structure of texts beyond the sentence. Theoretically, even the *Encyclopaedia Britannica* could have a stratificational description of it made.

In summary, then, stratificational grammar is a new theory of language which may turn out to be the most precise, economical and complete of all existing models. It will become increasingly sophisticated as work on it proceeds at project headquarters and among other linguists. By the early 1970's stratificational theory may well replace transformational theory as a description of language.

WORKING WITH THE SELECTION

1. You need not assume that you have lost your mind because you found this essay puzzling. It takes more than an introduction to feel comfortable with any idea so radically different from what you already know. And in this instance, the machinery, too, is strange. Nor has the approach been much worked out; too few scholars understand stratification, and they have had but little time to work with it. Lamb himself says that his conclusions are "extremely tentative." But perhaps you can appreciate the approach as revolution, if not as language study. If stratification can ever be refined so that it is readily understandable and readily learnable, what might be some of its advantages?

2. You have read about several sorts of grammars. How would you categorize stratification? It is not mainly a part-of-speech grammar. Can you discover relationships it has with any of the other grammars you have encountered?

3. Lamb predicts that by the early 1970's stratification will have replaced generative grammar relying on the transforms as the most widely practiced of the recent grammatical statements. Can you think of any reasons why this estimate may prove to be optimistic? As a shift in basic philosophy which is the more removed from its predecessors? Which requires more fundamentally different diagraming?

7

More Revolution: Tagmemics

Kenneth L. Pike

A linear sequence of units may be called a string. All strings contain units arranged sequentially, but they differ according to the sequence, kind, and number of units they contain. Here are some examples of strings:

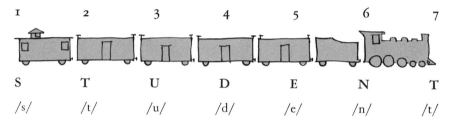

1	2	3	4	5	6	7
S	T	U	D	E	N	T
/s/	/t/	/u/	/d/	/e/	/n/	/t/

Each of these strings is significantly altered if the units it contains are rearranged. For example, the units 1, 2, 3, 4, 5, 6, 7 can be rearranged to form a new string, 4,567,321, which has a different use and a different meaning. The sequence of units in these two strings is rigid: 4,567,321 differs from all other possible combinations of these symbols, and in the sequence 1 through 7 the symbol 4 must appear between 3 and 5. The concept of 4 in a natural sequence of numerical ideas must appear there and nowhere else. The sequence of other strings is not so rigid; either the caboose or the locomotive could appear anywhere in the string, but neither could occur at right angles to it without causing a wreck.

Many sorts of strings involving language are possible. A string can be made up of linguistic units ranging from letters—or even parts of a sound wave—through extended pieces of writing.

w	o	r	d
the	wicked	old	wolf
in	the	best	manner
He	hates	new	grammars
topic sentence	paragraph development	further development	conclusion
Volume I	Volume II	Volume III	Volume IV

One of the most useful modern approaches to grammar is string grammar. A grammatical string might be thought of as a sequence of containers, or slots, each of which can receive one sort of filler:

subject	verb	modifier	complement
He	displayed	bad	manners
She	had to ask	specific	directions
Washington	was to become	our very first	president

*In the preceding example, the second slot can contain a verb; it can accommo-*date displayed, had to ask, *or* was to become, *but not* bad *or* specific. *This kind of string grammar can be called a* slot and filler grammar.

Probably the most unusual of the slot and filler grammars proposed recently is tagmemics, *a system and theory developed by Kenneth L. Pike, professor of linguistics at the University of Michigan, and his students. To date it has been used mainly as a means of dealing with unwritten languages. It is growing rapidly, and by the end of 1970 at least, tagmemicists had not agreed on a description that could be accepted as standard. You might, therefore, regard the following selection by Pike as a partial and provisional formulation of tagmemic thinking rather than as a definitive statement. The selection is taken from a manuscript Pike wrote during the summer of 1968, which is tentatively entitled* Linguistic Concepts: An Introduction to Tagmemics.

Since the basic theory of tagmemics may be rather different from the grammatical statements you have previously encountered, you may wish to keep these points in mind as you read: (1) tagmemicists have a very broad concept of how grammar fits into language and life; (2) tagmemics is in part a slot and filler grammar, but tagmemicists have an unconventional concept of what the filler should be; and (3) tagmemicists believe that any adequate statement about language requires that we look at every linguistic phenomenon from more than one point of view.

Whatever man studies, man contaminates. Even the moon may not be immune. When man becomes part of its environment, the moon itself is different: it weighs more, it has biological bits on its surface, and the man *of* the moon thinks *for* the moon *about* the moon. Man becomes part of the moon when he is on its surface, as we are part of the world.

When man studies "things" he injects part of himself into their definition. What is a chair, with no man to sit in it? a flute, with no player? a concert, with no listeners? a saw, with no carpenter? The intended use of a thing *is* part of its nature—a component added to it by its designer, or user, or observer.

One approach to studying language has been called tagmemics. This approach emphasizes that man as a user of language affects the nature of the units of his language. His reactions to language become part of the data for the study of language, because his reactions are part of the structure of language.

If some men—called linguists—try to study the way they talk, they either find or create units with which they are inextricably mixed up. One cannot say that they *merely create* the units; they are trying to describe something that was *already there* before they came along. And—more surprisingly— it turns out that they cannot say that they *merely find* units of sound, grammar, or dictionary in a language; the list and kind of things they "find" will vary radically if they adopt different theories as tools with which to search for these units. The theory is part of the observer, not of the data; a different theory makes a different observer; a different observer sees different things, or sees the same things differently.

Tagmemic theory is, in this respect, a theory of theories which tells how the observer affects the data or in some sense becomes part of the data. No wonder, therefore, that tagmemic theory cannot stop with confining its interest to mere language—but must view language in a broader context of ordinary lay behavior, as well as in the context of the behavior of that special observer, the linguist. . . .

In treating language as behavior tagmemicists first make the point that language elements are *combinations of form and meaning*. We try very hard to avoid studying form by itself or meaning by itself. We deal with them both together. We believe that we can never discuss either of them usefully unless somewhere, lurking in the background, is the other. Even when a person tries to talk about isolated forms, it turns out that somehow or other he knows that they are meaningful—or he knows that somebody knows that they are meaningful—or he is not handling language. Similarly, if a person tries to make a classification of all possible meanings, he is likely to end up without helpful results unless somehow these meanings are tied into words which in turn are tied into some system of behavior (including scientific behavior and its classificatory devices). . . .

HIERARCHIES OF ELEMENTS

In language there are three kinds of hierarchies, which partly are independent but partly interlock. On the one hand is a hierarchy of meaningful or purposeful chunks—simple words like *boy,* which one can find in the dictionary, and suffixes like the plural *-s;* then larger words like *boys* and *boyishness;* word groups revolving around a noun, such as *for the boys;* and still larger items, such as *The boys saw the dog.* These items may in turn come in very long sentences, or conversations, or in short stories, novels, and so on.

On the other hand, units of pronunciation may also be arranged in the form of wheels within wheels—smaller items within larger and larger and larger ones. *Cat* is a one-syllable word in which the three sounds spelled *c, a, t* occur. In the long word *prestidigitator,* there are several syllables, but just one accented, or *stressed,* syllable, so that the whole word forms a single larger pronunciation unit, one stress group. Stress groups become important in the meter of some poems; a line of verse sometimes forms a still larger pronunciation unit; and an entire poem, when read aloud, may be pronounced in such a way that a person can tell that the reader is "going to stop"—evidence that it, too, is just one pronunciation unit of some kind.

In addition to the hierachy that contains words, suffixes, and so on (the *lexical* hierarchy) and the one that involves sounds (the *phonological* hierarchy), there is a third hierarchy, one that involves the way in which parts of sentences (or of words, or of stories, etc.) are put together and are related. This is the *grammatical* hierarchy. In many English words there is the stem part followed by the suffix part. The stem-plus-suffix, seen as a *pattern* of such elements, is a grammatical *construction.* The words *boys, girls, trees,* are different instances of a single pattern. A prepositional phrase is another, larger, construction, which can be "manifested" by different instances of that phrase pattern (*for the boys, to the house, under a floor*). Still larger patterns occur, until one gets up to the structure of a conversation.

Figure 1 *Hierarchies* include larger and larger lexical items (i.e., dictionary elements) (A); pronunciation units (e.g., the phonetically spelled sounds, syllables, and stress group of *the cat* (B); and construction units of grammar (e.g., the noun-phrase construction and the clause construction of C, as well as the various tagmemes labeled subject, object, transitive predicate, modification, and head of the personal-noun phrase). The hierarchies are related in intricate ways.

A The boys saw the cat   B [ðə kæt]
    for the boys   [kæt]
      boys   [æ]
      boy

C + Subject: Noun Phrase + Trans. Predicate + Object: Noun Phrase
      + Modif.: Adj. + Head: Person Noun

Within a construction, parts can be recognized. Each part of the pattern can have a variety of manifestations, a set of units that can come in that place (i.e., can fill that slot). This place may have a meaning different from a dictionary meaning, but important to the construction: *Bill hit Johnny on the nose* is not the same as *Johnny hit Bill on the nose* because the subject part of the sentence (the subject tagmeme) has a different *function* from the object part.

Figure 2 A *clause pattern* like this one has a significant difference in the meaning of its subject (A) and object (B) tagmemes. Each includes a functional relation to the clause and a set of lexical elements filling that functional slot.

A		B	
Bill	hit	Johnny	on the nose
Big Joe		Bill	
Susie		Big Joe	

The combination of significant function in a construction, plus a set of forms coming in that place in the construction, is called a *tagmeme*. A tagmeme, then, is a function-set, and gives the name to the theory as a whole. . . .

PARTICLES

Human beings see the world—sometimes—as made up of *particles,* i.e., as "things." Houses, trees, and people seem to be obvious physical objects. But often experiences or concepts that obviously are not objects are talked about as if they were, and perhaps even counted, weighed, or measured. Such a concept is the term *movement,* which implies that something is going on; but movements can be counted like houses: *I saw two houses/I saw two movements.*

An abstraction like *beauty* or *force* can be thought of as an object: *Food is desirable/Beauty is desirable; The bomb moved us/Some force moved us.* A *class* of items can be treated as if it were a unit: *the class of Americans.* Or a sample of a class can somehow be treated as representing the whole class: *He is the average American.* A symphony may be heard as a unit, even though it may take an hour to play.

Man's mental computer seems to be able to operate only if the whole world is processed into bits, each of which is treated as a particle, punched onto a mental IBM card.

Most of the time people think of the world as if it were made of particles. Perhaps this is one reason why many people think that a language is just a collection of words one after the other. Translation to them appears merely to require the translator to look up a word in a bilingual dictionary and replace it by the proper equivalent.

In the word *kit* there is a sequence of three units of sound. The first is the pronunciation of [k]. This is the same unit as found at the beginning of *cat* (in spite of the change in spelling) and *character.*

Speech sounds are made by moving parts of the mouth, throat, and lungs. If one takes an X-ray moving picture of these motions, a single frame of the movie taken at the central part of the sound gives a static "picture" of it. Some sounds are very complicated. In certain African languages, for example, a combination of [p] and [k] together, with the tongue moving backward to make a little suction in the mouth, gives a very peculiar popping noise. Yet in spite of its complexity, the sound is but one, just as would be the [k] of *kit* in English.

Words are particles. They often include within them small particles. The central (nuclear) part of a word is the stem, which carries the principal meaning of the word. Smaller parts (affixes) affect the way in which the principal meaning is to be interpreted. In Candoshi of inland Peru, for example, the word *tayanchshatana* is made up of parts: ta-ya-nch-sha-t-a-na. This means 'be-recent-complete-next-individually-I-emphatically,' or 'I was recently and completely just then individually emphatically there,' or 'I've stayed there then.' [1]

Some particles are larger than words. For example, the whole clause *The ugly dog bit the mail carrier* is one unit or particle. The particle *The ugly dog* is a smaller unit, a phrase, which serves as the subject of that clause. Other phrases, however, could have taken its place. One could have said *A small terrier bit the mail carrier,* or *Something bit the mail carrier,* and so on. The whole range of possible actors in this relationship to the verb *bit* and to the object *mail carrier* makes up a set of forms. The set plus this functional relationship to the rest of the clause can be treated as a particle called subject-as-actor. This unit would be one kind of tagmeme, *the mail carrier* would be an instance of another tagmeme, an object tagmeme, as *bit* would be an instance of the transitive-predicate tagmeme. A formula of the type noun-verb-noun (N V N) is not enough to represent the full tagmemic content of this clause.

Nouns themselves enter classes that may also be viewed as particles of a kind different from construction, tagmeme, or separate words.

Often one has expectations of a form that is to come long before the form is fully visible. This may be true, for example, of a limerick.

> There was a young lady from Clyde
> Who ate some green apples and died.
>   The apples fermented
>   Inside the lamented
> And made cider inside her insides.

A limerick is not a random sequence of sentences, but a unit, a particle. Intimate interlocking of quasi-independent lexicon, phonology, and grammar all contribute to the expectation of form that is early elicited from the

[1] Doris Cox, "Candoshi Verb Inflection," *International Journal of American Linguistics,* 23, (1957) 129–40.

listener. The first line, *There was a young lady from Clyde,* with the stresses on *was, lady,* and *Clyde,* starts a phonological pattern that may alert the listener to something coming. The choice of the words *there* and *young* contributes to the beginning expectation. The grammatical structure of *was* after *there* adds a further clue, as does the choice of *lady.* By the time one has heard the second line, *Who ate some green apples and died,* he is probably quite certain that he is headed into a limerick. The rhyming of *Clyde* with *died,* the rhythm, and the lugubrious flavor encourage this guess.

The expectation of limerick form leads one to hope for some kind of difficulty that is solved only in the last line by a surprise verbal twist. In this limerick, the pleasure is heightened by the pun of *cider* with *(in)side 'er.* No such expectation of form, and delight in finding it, could occur unless the limerick *as a whole* were some kind of particle, a unity.

WAVE

When one tries to read a paragraph as if it were made up of completely separate particles of sound an astonishing result is heard. The material is very jerky and practically unintelligible. It is worth trying in order to hear the effect. If each sound of the following rhyme is artificially separated by a pause, speech becomes jerky and unintelligible.

O — l — d — M — o — th — e — r — H — u — bb — a — r — d

w — e — n — t — t — o — th — e — c — u — p — b — o — a — r — d

Natural speech *never* sounds like that. Why not, if speech is made up of "particles" of sound? Surely the analysis of speech into separate chunks is in *some* manner false—a model useful for some purposes, awkward for others.

The same material will sound very different if instead of putting spaces between the sounds one reads the lines very, very slowly indeed—as if a phonograph record were slowed down to half speed—and lets one's mouth movements glide slowly from one sound into another. . . .

The clearest or steadiest part of a sound during slow pronunciation can be called the *nucleus* of a *wave.* The borders or transitions from one sound to another can be called the *margins.* In wave types that interest him, a person often looks for the nuclei and margins. If his attention is almost exclusively on the nucleus, however, he may be thinking in terms of particles. When a person's attention is on the whole flowing movement from margin to nucleus to margin he is thinking in terms of the unit as a wave.

Human nature requires that people *focus* attention in certain directions—on certain elements or concepts or views. Language reflects this capacity for directing focus. Stressed pronunciation can be used to emphasize or high-light parts of a sentence. So can grammar, as in *It is indeed the cat that swallowed the rat;* the phrase *It is indeed* forces focus on *cat.* If the two kinds of attention crisscross, one may be called emphasis (*the RAT*) and the other focus (*It is indeed the cat*). When whole paragraphs are involved, the focused nuclear element may be called a topic sentence.

Even when no special attention is called for, the dynamics of behavior organizes speech and action into wave units with nuclei and margins.

A *grammar wave* is one in which there is a central, crucial part of a con-struction preceded or followed by less important elements that in some way modify it. When such a wave is made up of just one word, the nucleus is traditionally called a *stem,* and the margin a *prefix* or a *suffix,* as in *inactive* and *singing.* A two-word phrase, smaller than a clause, may be said to have a head and a modifier, as in *my* (margin) *alligator* (nucleus). When two clauses are in a sentence, one may be independent, nuclear, and the other dependent, as in *The doctor treated the boy* (nucleus) *after he broke his leg on a skate board* (margin). Similarly, a question-answer re-lation gives a higher level of nucleus and margin: *Will you come? Perhaps.*

A phonological wave can be as short as a single sound or as large as a lecture. Each may have nucleus and margins. The entire sentence *I don't want to* is a single phonological wave. The *I don't* is premargin, *to* is post-margin, and *want* is the stressed syllable making up the nucleus of the stress-group wave. The smearing of words in English is often the result of pronouncing the premarginal section very fast. The nucleus is usually pro-nounced more slowly and is less likely to be lost or changed. Even a story (considered here as a large lexical unit) can be viewed as a wave. A pre-margin sets the stage; the plot warms up; the climax (the nucleus) occurs; the hero gets out of trouble and lives happily ever after (postmargin). . . .

The use of waves in analysis does not eliminate need for the use of particles. Even a wave, when it is viewed as a unit, may itself be considered a particle, just as the particle, when viewed in its physical smearing aspects, can be viewed as a wave. Even a part of a wave can be abstracted to be viewed as a particle. The transition periods between steadier states of scien-tific research, for example, can be treated as particles themselves—as "revolu-tions" to be described or counted.

FIELD

We have discussed the way in which elements can be viewed by them-selves as particles, or as waves smearing into some kind of continuum whose prominent parts make up nuclei. Now we turn to sets of relationships that occur when units are linked to one another by some larger context. A total context of relationships and of units in these relationships is called a *field.*

No item by itself has significance. A unit becomes relevant only in relation to a context. Outside of such a context the item will necessarily be uninterpretable by the observer. A simple circle, for example, may be interpreted by an observer as a numeral if it is in the context of the number 1,000. On the other hand, a circle may be interpreted as a letter of the alphabet in the context *pop* or as eyes, nose, or teeth, or buttons, in a picture. When, therefore, one asks what *is* the circle in one of these circumstances, it seems clear that its "factness" is relative to the observer.

To the theist the theory suggests that "things-in-themselves" apart from human observers find definition or relevance only in relation to God as absolute observer. Otherwise, the theory is silent about "things-in-themselves." It does not deny their existence. Rather it finds no structured way of talking about them.

The observer interprets data relative to a context—within a field. In this sense a datum of sensation "becomes" a "fact" of human significance when seen relative to its distribution in an environment, relative to a field as structured in the perception of some observer. . . .

Certain consonants can be organized into rows, each of which has at least one feature (or component, property, characteristic) common to each unit of the row. Units in the columns are similarly related. If the symbols for the sounds are removed but the presence of features is shown by arrows, a circle around the place formerly occupied by a consonant symbol contains a point of intersection of two of the arrows. The field in the first case is defined graphically as units related by shared properties; in the second as an array of intersecting features. The unit can be treated either as merely a "point" at the intersection of features of a field which is assumed to be "already" there; or the presence of the units can be treated as setting up the field by the relations between them.

Figure 3 *Field* seen from several viewpoints: as a structured array of units (A); as a pattern of features that intersect (B); and as a set of points at the intersection of features (C).

A   p   t   k

    b   d   g

    m   n   ŋ

B	With lips closed	With tongue tip closing the mouth	With mouth closed at the soft palate
Stopped air stream without vocal cord vibration			
With vocal cord vibration			
Air escaping from the nose			

C

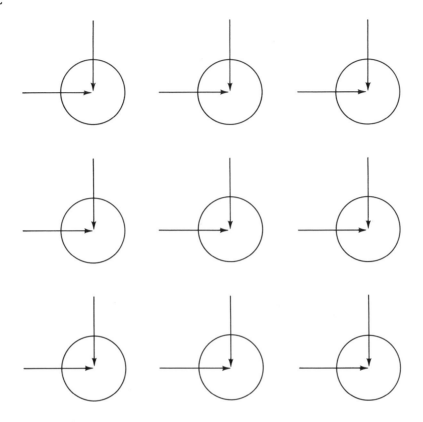

This kind of display shows that several (intersecting) characteristics are *simultaneously* present. In Figure 3B the labels of the rows and columns specify these features. The field display shows that a behavior particle is not an unstructured "chunk" but something with internal pattern, with components related to the properties of the field containing it. . . . In tagmemic theory charts are used to show the field structure of clauses just as charts have been used for centuries for phonology. . . . It is intriguing, also, to study much larger units than the sentence in reference to field structure. Suppose, for example, that we take Robert Browning's poem "Memorabilia."

> Ah, did you once see Shelley plain,
>   And did he stop and speak to you,
> And did you speak to him again?
>   How strange it seems and new!
>
> But you were living before that,
>   And also you are living after;
> And the memory I started at—
>   My starting moves your laughter!

I crossed a moor, with a name of its own
And a certain use in the world no doubt,
Yet a hand's-breadth of it shines alone
'Mid the blank miles round about:

For there I picked up on the heather,
And there I put inside my breast
A moulted feather, an eagle-feather!
Well, I forget the rest.

One could choose to interpret the poem as representing a kind of storage of miscellaneous particles within the memory. The memory in this sense can be viewed as a special field.

Figure 4 Large units may show field structure. The Roman numerals in the cells represent the stanzas of the poem by Browning. As particles (I, IV) the events seem isolated and unchanging, therefore strange and new. As waves (II, III) the events are known to have been tied in to a before and an after, with movement and integration into the real world as a whole.

Field = Memory

	Particle	Wave
Event I Meeting a man who had met Shelley	I	II
Event II Finding a feather	IV	III

Within this field two happenings are described. The first deals with Browning's meeting a man who met Shelley. The shock of this meeting caused Browning to pale, since even such an indirect contact with the great Shelley was staggering. The second event deals with his finding a feather. In some sense each event seems to be perceived as abstracted from experience, as if without relationship to time before or after. Therefore they seem strange, because unchanging, and so somehow eternally new, like some carved figure frozen on a Grecian urn. Art and emotion share these characteristics. I well remember, myself, when a friend took his three-month-old baby to the hospital for emergency brain surgery. "As the elevator door closed behind the cot with my child on it, time stood still." The picture congealed.

Under appropriate circumstances, the same event can be viewed as particle, or as wave, or as field. A person's emotional state, or his immediate or remote experience, affects his conscious or unconscious choice of priorities to be given to one (or to two) of the three.

1. Work through the following exercise prepared by Kenneth and Evelyn Pike. See if it clarifies your notions of what is meant by *tagmeme, particle, wave,* and *field.*

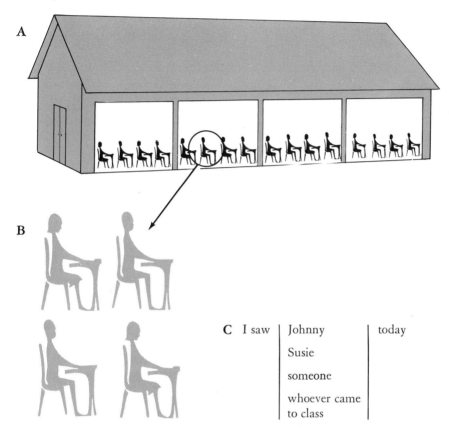

C I saw | Johnny | today

Susie

someone

whoever came
to class

Distribution in a slot determines membership in a distribution class filling the slot. Joe is in a classroom slot (A) distributed as a specific member of that class (B). This fact is part of the definition of Joe himself. If we do not know what roles he fills, we do not know Joe well. In language, tagmemic slots like object (C) serve a similar role for classification of units. Class plus slot make up a tagmeme.

2. The Pikes devised the following exercise from a suggestion by Donald Stark. Add circles to the illustrations, and observe how these circles, viewed as particles, are influenced by the "fields" into which they are inserted. For example, put two circles on the face, rather high up and somewhat separated. The field makes the circles into eyes. Now see what other circles you can put into the sketches to illustrate how the field affects the particle. Can you add any

circles that will affect the field as well as being affected by it? You may add other symbols besides circles if you wish.

O   I,000   pop!

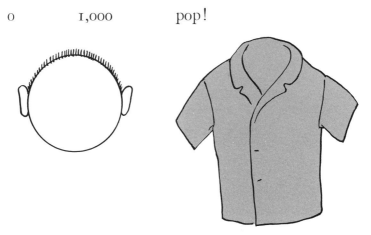

3. Scrutinize the following as a possible definition of tagmemics.

> Tagmemics is at once a theory and a practice which treats language as a string of slots, each of which can be filled with an appropriate kind of unit. A tagmeme is a combination that might result from the fusion of slot and filler class. A tagmeme will inevitably be complex; for example, what is commonly called a subject-as-actor tagmeme will ultimately involve the pronunciation of its filler elements, its meaning, social usage, grammatical relationships, artistic potentialities, and much more. If we are to understand any linguistic phenomenon, we must observe it in three ways: as a particle, as a wave or as something involved in wavelike movements, and as part of a field.

Is this an accurate and adequate definition insofar as tagmemics seems to have been delineated by 1970? Refer to Pike's notes in checking your answers, reminding yourself that Pike's thinking may have transcended these notes somewhat.

4. The description of the various ways of looking at language as particle, wave, and field has lately come into question. Pike himself, who borrowed the terms from physics, has been considering whether the idea or the elucidation of it should not be revised. He recognizes, of course, that it is at best an analogy—although language is clearly composed of what may be called particles, the comparison of what happens in language with waves and fields in physics introduces some distortion. Did you find the analogy helpful? Analogies can never be competely accurate, of course, but they may help in understanding and in teaching. How would you define wave? Field? Can you think of any better general statement than the particle-wave-field analogy? You might recall that tagmemicists feel sure that language must be viewed at once in more than one way, but that three may not be the only possible number. And surely waves and fields do not provide the only possible analogies.

5. Once you believe you know what tagmemics is and how it works, compare it with other approaches you have encountered. How is it like stratification? How is it different? Does either have unique advantages? Similarly,
how does tagmemics compare and contrast with transformational grammar?
With structural linguistics? With the older conventional statement based on
Latin grammar?

8

Sanity, Even in Revolution

David DeCamp

*David DeCamp has been involved in several areas of linguistics in this country
and abroad, perhaps notably dialectology. He has also been concerned with
teaching and with the teaching of teachers, and his fresh and acerbic wit has
made him an unusually welcome public speaker. The following piece was
originally an address: "Sequence of Tenses, or Was James Thurber the First
Transformational Grammarian?" It is taken from* College Composition and
Communication, *18 (February, 1967). DeCamp teaches English and linguistics
at the University of Texas at Austin.*

I'm getting pretty tired of that old canard about the permissiveness of
linguists. Very few linguists ever really wanted to leave your language
alone anyway. Maybe they wanted you to leave their language alone, but
they didn't want to leave your language alone. I think that most linguists,
especially recently, are like James Thurber and me: Calvinist to the core,
confident that the world is doomed to grammatical perdition, gnawed by
agenbite of inwit; and inwardly doubtful of our own state of grace, we
whistle and parse in the dark, and try to act like members of the grammatically elect.

The trouble is that during the recent structural unpleasantness we got
ourselves boxed in by an inadequate theory of language which had very
little place for grammatical rules. Structural linguistics, which grew out of
attempts to describe the structure of Middle High Swadesh, was—and is—a
remarkable technique of analysis. In the competent hands of Kenneth Pike's
linguistic missionaries from the Summer Institute of Linguistics, for ex-

ample, it has opened windows to the minds of primitive peoples all over the world. It has been the glass through which we can see our brothers, not darkly but clearly.

Central to classical structural theory, however, was the analysis of a text into atomic entities. Though the valences of these elements were among the properties described, few of us then were very comfortable in the presence of processes, especially those which operate across a whole span, for example, grammatical concord. Back when we were all true-blue structuralists, we were not a bit dismayed by the strangest of clicks and grunts, belches and whistles. We could isolate an ergative infix or an agentive postposition without even raising sweat, but we had an awful time explaining how a singular verb must go with a singular subject, and we just gave up on sequence of tenses. Way back in 1960 a linguist named Leslie A. Hill published an admirably honest article on sequence of tenses in "if"-clauses.[1] You know the old sequence-of-tenses rule: If the verb in the main clause is in a past tense, the verb in a subordinate clause must also be in a past tense. Mr. Hill informs us, "Twice before, such utterances as 'If you wouldn't mind waiting here a moment, I'll tell the manager you've arrived' and 'If you'll pardon my saying so, you've made a big mistake in taking this house' prompted me to begin an investigation into the sequence of tenses. . . . However, each time the results were so alarming that I stopped my research." Mr. Hill had good reason to be alarmed. He took eighteen different English "tenses" and tried which would go with which if he put one of them in the "if"-clause and another in the main clause. "I discovered that every combination was possible, i.e., that I was able to produce 324 (18 x 18) combinations." At this point, Mr. Hill quite prudently retreats from further discussion and merely presents all of his 324 sentences without further comment, beginning with his No. I/1, "If you go, I go too," and ending with his No. XVIII/18, "If he used to be a thief, he used, at least, to be able to avoid being found out." The effect is indescribable: Only an ardent devotee of bellringing could properly appreciate this flawless ringing of the changes on *if*.

Our problem with structural theory was not just the fact that we analyzed texts. After all, we didn't analyze just any old texts which happened to be lying around the attic, and we indeed worried about what could go with what in those texts. We wanted good English just as much as we wanted good Swahili, though we were often misquoted or deliberately misunderstood on this point. Contrary to what you might have heard from some journalists, we never said "If it's audible, emicize it." All this "anything goes" stuff came only from amateurs. Good professional linguists like Thurber, Trager, and Chomsky never said any of this nonsense like "Let's be descriptive, not prescriptive."

No, our problem as structuralists was not just that we analyzed texts

---

[1] Leslie A. Hill, "The Sequence of Tenses with 'If'-Clauses," *Language Learning,* X (1960), 165–78.

but that we analyzed them into things rather than into operations. If we deviated and talked about items in process rather than items in arrangement, the still small voices would come from places like Ithaca, New Haven, and Buffalo to warn us back to the right path. Some, like Zellig Harris,[2] went all the way and proposed the only rigorously consistent treatment of concord which was possible as long as we insisted on dealing only in terms of entities and their arrangements. He suggested that the elements of concord agreement (e.g., the masculinity of the pronoun *he* and the masculinity of its antecedent) might be two parts of a single grammatical unit, one element of grammatical masculinity broken in half, sort of like tearing a dollar bill in half so that the spy can recognize his contact man. This idea of a discontinuous morpheme with a fragment in each part of the sentence that had to agree with some other part was theoretically possible but awfully complicated. It especially messed up our diagrams. Nelson Francis, for example, already had enough trouble with discontinuous constituents messing up his Chinese boxes without trying to get all the past tenses of a complex sentence into the same box. Fortunately for us, he preferred inconsistency to obscurity, and gave us his *Structure of American English* rather than a contorted maze which only a topological mathematician would have been able to explore. It is to his credit that he went ahead and gave us some honest-to-gosh, old-fashioned concord rules, even though it was pretty hard to explain theoretically how an element in one of his boxes could "govern" the form of another element way off in a different box at the other end of the sentence.

Generative grammar did not automatically solve all of these problems just by being generative. Context-free phrase-structure rules, the kind that generated what they used to call "kernel sentences" in the early generative grammars, could not by themselves handle problems of concord without including some grammatical long element (e.g., plurality) which extended throughout the sentence; in other words, Zellig Harris's old discontinuous morpheme again. That is, the only way to get the subject and verb to agree within the phrase structure was to decide at the very beginning of the rules that this was to be not just any old sentence, but a *plural* sentence, then to state that this plural sentence consisted of a plural subject and a plural predicate, and so on, carrying the element of plurality down through all the rules until it finally made both *men* out of *man* and *are* out of *be*.

It was the transformations, not just the generative nature of modern grammar, that provided the two keys to concord. First, a transformation can change around the order of parts in a sentence and so make continuous elements discontinuous. For example, the phrase *those ravenous little mongooses* can be shown to have an underlying phrase structure in which the demonstrative and the noun are adjacent, *those mongooses,* making it easy to get them into plural number agreement. Then and only then, after

[2] Zellig S. Harris, *Structural Linguistics,* Chicago: The University of Chicago Press, 1951, pp. 167, 304–5n.

this concord business has been cleared up, is the phrase *those mongooses* split apart by a transformation which inserts the intervening words *ravenous* and *little*. So now Nelson Francis can keep his Chinese boxes simple and tidy and rely on transformations to bridge the gap between the simple underlying structure and the tangled complexity of the sentence as we finally speak or write it.

The other advantage of transformations is that we can specify the environment in which they will operate. We say they are "context sensitive," or "context restricted." We can write an obligatory rule, for instance, that when in the austere and awful presence of a plural subject, the word *be* must take the form *are*, not *is*. Sound familiar? At last! A grammatical theory which allows us to do what we've wanted all along: to go back to writing the same kind of grammatical rules that our grandfathers wrote. What a glorious day for freedom it was when we could once again say things like "Always use a plural verb with a plural subject"—and right out loud in public too!

In the old days, when there were wolves in Wales and kernels in grammar, we used to account for a complex sentence by generating two or more simple or "kernel" sentences and then hitching them together by means of "generalized" transformations, sometimes also called "two-string" or "double-base" transformations. (No pun was intended in the term "double-base"; everyone knows that a double bass has four strings, not two.) Of course this process of generating the separate kernel sentences was stopped short of actually pronouncing them or writing them out, and the kernels were combined while they were still pretty much in a state of abstraction. Not even linguists go around muttering "This is my mongoose. I dearly love my mongoose" before coming out loud with "This is my mongoose, whom I dearly love." At least I never heard a linguist do this, and I think I would have noticed. Nevertheless, a certain pedagogical technique has gained some vogue, of having the student rewrite a complex sentence as a series of short simples ones, or, conversely, having him combine a series of simple sentences into one long complex one. This is altogether harmless and commendable. It can improve a student's writing by expanding his repertoire of sentence-connecting devices, just as the carpenter's apprentice presumably learns that there are ways to fasten two boards together other than pounding a nail through them.

The kernel technique can also be the basis of an amusing parlor game called "Let's Dissect Literature," sometimes also called "Literary Criticism." Did you know that if you take a Henry James sentence apart and then put it back together the wrong way (additive instead of embedded) it comes out sounding like Faulkner? Of course you must be careful not to stop midway in the process, or you will get Hemingway. James Thurber was aware of this long before Noam Chomsky. In fact, he might have been the one who suggested transformations to Chomsky. I don't know. I've never asked either gentleman. In 1929, in his *Ladies' and Gentlemen's Guide to*

Modern English Usage,[3] warning against reckless use of the relative pronoun *which,* Thurber wrote,

> The safest way to avoid such things is to follow in the path of the American author, Ernest Hemingway. In his youth he was trapped in a which-clause one time and barely escaped with his mind. He was going along on solid ground until he got into this: "It was the one thing of which, being very much afraid—for whom has not been warned to fear such things—he. . . ." Being a young and powerfully built man, Hemingway was able to fight his way back to where he had started, and begin again. This time he skirted the treacherous morass in this way: "He was afraid of one thing. This was the one thing. He had been warned to fear such things. Everybody has been warned to fear such things." Today Hemingway is alive and well, and many happy writers are following along the trail he blazed.

The kernel technique can even be helpful, in a practical, simple-minded classroom sort of way, with some kinds of sequence of tenses. In case your student ever produces a flagrantly intolerable sequence of tenses like *He arrived twenty minutes after I will milk the mongoose,* you can "transform" his sentence into the following two separate sentences: *I will milk the mongoose. Twenty minutes later he arrived.* Point out that these two sentences, although each impeccably grammatical when considered in isolation, have very little coherent connection. Hemingway's sentences almost always have coherent connection. Of course this is really just turning an absurdity around, in hope that the student will see it better from the other side, but very often, surprisingly, it works. Incidentally, it is quite possible to take apart each of those 324 complex "if"-sentences of Leslie Hill's, and each pair of halves is indeed sort of logically compatible. Of course this doubles the total number of sentences to 648 and makes Mr. Hill's contribution even more breathtaking.

Of course you must be careful, when using this technique, to make all the adjustments necessary to split one complex sentence into two simple ones. Changing a word here and there may not be enough. Thurber warns us that silly little things like end punctuation and capitalization can really mess up the results when we apply a "kernel" test to a sentence. He writes (p. 101):

> A common rule for determining whether "who" or "whom" is right is to substitute "she" for "who," and "her" for "whom," and see which

[3] James Thurber, *Ladies' and Gentlemen's Guide to Modern English Usage,* pp. 105–6. Originally published as separate pieces in *The New Yorker,* this remarkable work was later assembled by Thurber and printed in his *The Owl in the Attic and Other Perplexities,* New York: Harper and Brothers, 1931. It has since been reprinted in paperback in the Grosset's Universal Library series, $1.25. Unfortunately neglected by grammarians, this work is now known only to Thurberphiles, who may or may not outnumber grammarians in our society today.

sounds the better. Take the sentence, "He met a woman who they said was an actress." Now if "who" is correct then "she" can be used in its place. Let us try it. "He met a woman she they said was an actress." That instantly rings false. It can't be right. Hence the proper usage is "whom."

The toughest problem of all in the sequence of tenses will, unfortunately, not yield to this explication by kernels. This is the so-called "attracted sequence in indirect discourse." There are many pairs of clauses which are quite compatible in direct discourse or as simple sentences, but which must bow to the rule in indirect discourse that a past tense in the main clause requires a past tense in the dependent "that"-clause. For example, using direct discourse it is quite proper to say, *"Your mongoose is killing every chicken in downtown Boston," he warned.* But indirect discourse requires *He warned me that my mongoose was killing every chicken in downtown Boston.* Whether my mongoose is now still continuing his raids on the Boylston Street henhouses is not an issue. It is a rule of grammar, not the appetite of my mongoose or the intolerant attitude of the downtown poultry breeders, which requires the past tense.

It's not a complicated rule, not if you are a traditional grammarian or a transformationist, but if you are a structuralist, you face a very nasty choice. You *could* say, if you wanted to describe the sequence of tenses in a very complex sentence such as the one I am now writing, one in which the past tense of the verb *could* in the main clause requires that the verb *contained* in the dependent clause also be past tense, even though the two verbs are separated by a long intervening element of 68 words, that the sentence *contained* one of Zellig Harris's long broken morphemes. See? It did come out right! But the parts of this discontinuous morpheme are so widely separated as to make intelligible diagramming impossible. Or, your other unhappy choice, you could temporarily step outside your theory and throw in a concord rule anyway, even though you have provided no way for that rule to operate.

In modern transformational theory, the concept of the kernel no longer exists. You can continue to use kernels, of course, whenever you think they will do more good than harm, but you can no longer claim to have the power and glory of MIT behind you. The old idea that you found in Paul Roberts' *English Syntax* of a group of kernel sentences stapled together by means of double-base transformations was replaced several years ago by a new conception of the sentence as a single structure which can be expanded by putting another entire sentence inside it. This embedded sentence can in turn be expanded by building still another sentence inside it, and so on ad infinitum—meaning that the longest and most complex sentence possible in English never has been written and never will be. That is, we can generate something like *I know (the fact that) S,* and then expand S to another complete sentence: e.g., *I know that he loves mongooses.* But we can repeat this process: *I know that he knows (the fact that) S.* Thus we can get things like *I know that he knows that they know that she knows that . . .* Sooner or later we get tired of this and simply omit that optional final *S* rather than keep on snapping at the bait, not because the addition of further *that*-clauses would be ungrammatical, but because our audience has got tired of the silly thing and gone home. Even "The House that Jack Built" has to end sometime, though not for grammatical reasons. This process is called *recursiveness* and is the same thing that happens on a Morton's salt box, which bears a picture of a little girl in the rain carrying a Morton's salt box, which bears a picture of a little girl in the rain carrying a Morton's salt box, which bears a . . . . Did you ever use a magnifying glass and try to follow this endless progression of little girls and salt boxes down into the picture? If so, you should have no trouble with the new grammar.

Don't be unhappy that they've taken your kernels away from you. The revised theory is actually much easier to get across to beginners than the old one, because it more nearly mirrors the psychological processes by which we make our sentences. When I start out on a sentence, I usually don't know in advance just how complex it's going to be, and I keep building in more clauses and phrases as I go along. That's the way the new grammar describes a sentence. Very seldom, on the other hand, do I first plan out the structures of two separate sentences and then, as a sort of afterthought, decide to combine them. Furthermore, as I pointed out, though the kernel technique may be useful on some problems of grammatical concord, such as pronoun agreement, it only misleads the student on sequence of tenses.

There are additional advantages in the new grammar. For one thing (glory be!) semantics is definitely back in. No more of this pretending that meaning is irrelevant to the structure of a sentence. The grammaticalness of sentences like *The purple mongoose is immolating my typewriter* no longer messes up the syntax. It now is treated as a matter of semantic incompatibility. You may remember that Nelson Francis was doing something like this back in 1956, though he then called it "lexical probability." The idea was pretty far out then, but now it's right in style. No grammatical analysis of a sentence is now considered adequate unless it accounts for the meaning as well as the form. In fact, transformations are now used only when they preserve the meaning of the original sentence. If you've ever taught transformational grammar, haven't you had trouble convincing little Johnny that *I like mongooses* and *I dislike mongooses* are supposed to be two separate, independent sentences, but that *I don't like mongooses* isn't supposed to be really independent from *I like mongooses*, just a derivation from it? In the new grammar, these two pairs of sentences now have the same kind of relationship to each other.

Perhaps most important, the revised theory emphasizes a distinction between the *deep structure* and the *surface structure*. A sentence is generated in the deep structure: i.e., the words and their meanings and their syntactic relationships are all put together into an underlying structure which may be either simple or complex. Then the transformations tidy up the mess, perhaps changing around the order of elements, perhaps deleting unwanted or unnecessary items; e.g., the understood *you,* which has now regained its rightful place as the subject of an imperative sentence. The result of these transformations is the surface structure, something which we can write or pronounce. A structural ambiguity like the sentence *He made his wife a hamburger* is merely a surface structure which might have been derived from either of two deep structures.

A sentence can't get out of the deep structure and into the surface structure where it can be spoken or written unless the transformations work on it. And these transformations are very choosy. They won't even touch a deep structure unless it meets certain specifications. They're sort of like a doorman who examines your NCTE [National Council of Teachers of English] membership card before letting you into the meeting. When this doorman sees a sentence beginning with the words *We were certain that,* he checks to be sure that the verb of the subordinate clause is in past tense. Otherwise he won't let it through the door. When we set a stupid computer to generating sentences randomly, it generates a high proportion of unacceptable junk back in the deep structure, and the doorman turns away far more than he allows through. The human mind, however, has better sense than the computer and doesn't work at random. Presumably it anticipates the doorman's requirements and doesn't try to send out very many candidates unless they have a fairly good chance of getting through. Nevertheless, the doorman is still there. He is the grammatical conscience, our inhibitions against uttering ungrammatical structures.

Yes, they are inhibitions. I think we are coming back to the healthy old attitude that grammar is basically a negative operation. We all want to communicate, and the grammar is a filter which ensures that only the permissible forms of communication will get through. Grammar is primarily a series of thou-shalt-nots. I began this paper by insisting that the alleged permissiveness of linguists is a red herring. In fact, the biggest challenge before us now is to build variability into the theory, to account for the way the doorman changes his requirements when we shift styles. Do several different doormen work in shifts? Or does one doorman deal with the whole spectrum of phenomena which Martin Joos has shown us in *The Five Clocks* and now in his new book *The English Verb?* If we can't solve this, I fear that the generative model of the future might accidentally come up with an e. e. cummings poem—after all, there are a lot of monkeys pounding away at the typewriters back in there—but that the doorman will reject it and consign it to deep-structure oblivion with a cold and metallic "That does not compute."

Thurber, of course, knew all about this. In his *Ladies' and Gentlemen's Guide* (pp. 142–5), a gentleman and his wife, calling on friends, find them not at home. The gentleman decides to leave a note of regret, and there follows a scene of pure torment of soul. He struggles with such unpleasant alternatives as "We would have liked to have found you in" and "We had hoped to have been able to have found you in." A dull pain takes him behind the ears. He considers but rejects the kernel approach: "Called. You were out. Sorry." Thurber's own solution is correct as always: a concord rule for sequence of tenses. He warns, "Avoid the perfect infinitive after the past conditional as you would a cobra." Unfortunately Thurber didn't have quite all the answers. He never thought of putting arrows in his rules, thereby making Chomsky and MIT unnecessary. Therefore he was only the *first* transformational grammarian, and *Aspects of the Theory of Syntax* is now the grammatical best seller instead of the *Ladies' and Gentlemen's Guide to Modern English Usage*. Still, credit must be given where credit is due, and Thurber did come first.

WORKING WITH THE SELECTION

1. After the two previous selections, you may have found this one a pleasant change. But it is not quite so light as it purports to be. The title suggests that it deals with the sequence of tenses and the first transformationalist. But transformationalists were not, on the whole, much concerned with problems of usage as reflected in the sequence of tenses or anything else. What is the paper actually about?

2. DeCamp is of course being satirical. To what extent might his paper fittingly be entitled "A Plague on Both Your Houses"? On the other hand, DeCamp has himself used modern linguistic techniques; which does he praise, either specifically or by inference? Does he ignore any? If so, can you guess why?

part 5

Dialect and Dialects

Few concepts in modern language study have been more fruitful than that of dialect, for dialect theory has both linguistic and social implications. And dialects themselves are phenomena, natural phenomena in the sense that they grow inevitably as indispensable stages in language. Recently, scholars have developed a better understanding of dialect, and as a result a better understanding of the importance of dialects. Today the new body of knowledge is being applied to one of our most baffling educational problems, that of teaching children, particularly children from minority groups, who speak nonstandard English.

The word dialect *itself requires some explanation. Like most common words, it can be used in various senses. The* Century Dictionary, *published at the end of the nineteenth century, offers this definition: "The idiom of a locality or class, as distinguished from the generally accepted literary language, or speech of educated people." This was no doubt the commonest use of the word in the United States at the time the* Century *was edited, and it still may be; certainly it is the only use known to many people. Furthermore, as the word was used it was almost always uncomplimentary. It implied ignorance, even stupidity, or at best the funny way foreigners and immigrants could be expected to speak. One is reminded of the tale of the Chinese man who, on a crowded streetcar, sat down beside a matronly-looking woman. "Velly cold," he said politely. "If you'd tuck your shirt in," the woman snapped, "your belly wouldn't be so cold." Clearly, the Chinese was behaving more considerately than the offish lady, but no doubt she felt self-righteous about the encounter. Her racial prejudice no doubt made her consider the Chinese an inferior person; and her racial prejudice was reinforced by her linguistic prejudice, for she certainly considered* belly *a vulgar word and any dialect a degraded form of speech.*

This is not, of course, what a student of language means when he uses the word dialect, *but what he does mean can perhaps best be made clear by the readings that follow.*

1

"Rapping" in the Black Ghetto

Thomas Kochman

A dialect may have special richness and precision, but it may also cause its users social problems. The following selection and the two in the next section concern language in the black ghetto; the first provides some examples of what ghetto speech is like, the second and third discuss teaching problems related to it.

Thomas Kochman is a student of black speech, particularly vocabulary. Professor of linguistics at Northeastern Illinois State College, he divides his time between the Northside Chicago campus and the Southside Center for Inner City Studies. The selection is from his article in Transaction, 6 *(February, 1969).*

"Rapping," "shucking," "jiving," "running it down," "gripping," "copping a plea," "signifying" and "sounding" are all part of the black ghetto idiom and describe different kinds of talking. Each has its own distinguishing features of form, style, and function; each is influenced by, and influences, the speaker, setting, and audience; and each sheds light on the black perspective and the black condition—on those orienting values and attitudes that will cause a speaker to speak or perform in his own way within the social context of the black community. . . .

While often used to mean ordinary conversation, rapping is distinctively a fluent and a lively way of talking, always characterized by a high degree of personal style. To one's own group, rapping may be descriptive of an interesting narration, a colorful rundown of some past event. An example of this kind of rap is the answer from a Chicago gang member to a youth worker who asked how his group became organized:

> Now I'm goin tell you how the jive really started. I'm goin to tell you how the club got this big. 'Bout 1956 there used to be a time when the Jackson Park show was open and the Stony show was open. Sixty-six street, Jeff, Gene, all of 'em, little bitty dudes, little bitty . . . Gene wasn't with 'em then. Gene was cribbin (living) over here. Jeff, all of 'em, real little bitty dudes, you dig? All of us were little.
>
> Sixty-six (the gang on sixty-sixth street), they wouldn't allow us in the Jackson Park show. That was when the parky (?) was headin it. Everybody say, If we want to go to the show, we go! One day, who was it? Carl Robinson. He went up to the show . . . and Jeff fired on him. He came back and all this was swelled up 'bout yay big, you

know. He come back over to the hood (neighborhood). He told (name unclear) and them dudes went up there. That was when mostly all the main sixty-six boys was over here like Bett Riley. All of 'em was over here. People that quit gang-bangin (fighting, especially as a group), Marvell Gates, people like that.

They went on up there, John, Roy and Skeeter went in there. And they start humbuggin (fighting) in there. That's how it all started. Sixty-six found out they couldn't beat us, at *that* time. They couldn't *whup* seven-o. Am I right Leroy? You was cribbin over here then. Am I right? We were dynamite! Used to be a time, you ain't have a passport, Man, you couldn't walk through here. And if didn't nobody know you it was worse than that. . . .

Rapping to a woman is a colorful way of "asking for some pussy." "One needs to throw a lively rap when he is 'putting the make' on a broad." (John Horton, "Time and Cool People," *Trans*-action, April, 1967.)

According to one informant the woman is usually someone he has just seen or met, looks good, and might be willing to have sexual intercourse with him. My informant says the term would not be descriptive of talk between a couple "who have had a relationship over any length of time." Rapping then, is used at the beginning of a relationship to create a favorable impression and be persuasive at the same time. The man who has the reputation for excelling at this is the pimp, or mack man. Both terms describe a person of considerable status in the street hierarchy, who, by his lively and persuasive rapping ("macking" is also used in this context) has acquired a stable of girls to hustle for him and give him money. For most street men and many teenagers he is the model whom they try to emulate. Thus, within the community you have a pimp walk, pimp style boots and clothes, and perhaps most of all "pimp talk." [The following] is a colorful literary example of a telephone rap. One of my informants regards it as extreme, but agrees that it illustrates the language, style and technique of rapping. "Blood" is rapping to an ex-whore named Christine in an effort to trap her into his stable:

> Now try to control yourself baby. I'm the tall stud with the dreamy bedroom eyes across the hall in four-twenty. I'm the guy with the pretty towel wrapped around his sexy hips. I got the same hips on now that you X-rayed. Remember that hump of sugar your peepers feasted on?
> She said, "Maybe, but you shouldn't call me. I don't want an incident. What do you want? A lady doesn't accept phone calls from strangers."
> I said, "A million dollars and a trip to the moon with a bored, trapped, beautiful bitch, you dig? I'm no stranger. I've been popping the elastic on your panties ever since you saw me in the hall. . . ."

When "whupping the game" on a "trick" or "lame" (trying to get goods or services from someone who looks like he can be swindled), rapping is often descriptive of the highly stylized verbal part of the maneuver. In well established "con games" the rap is carefully prepared and used with great skill in directing the course of the transaction. An excellent illustration came from an adept hustler who was playing the "murphy" game on a white trick. The "murphy" game is designed to get the *trick* to give his money to the hustler, who in this instance poses as a "steerer" (one who directs or steers customers to a brothel), to keep the whore from stealing it. The hustler then skips with the money.

> "Look Buddy, I know a fabulous house not more than two blocks away. Brother you ain't never seen more beautiful, freakier broads than are in that house. One of them, the prettiest one, can do more with a swipe than a monkey can with a banana. She's like a rubber doll; she can take a hundred positions."
> At this point the sucker is wild to get to this place of pure joy. He entreats the con player to take him there, not just direct him to it.
> The "murphy" player will prat him (pretend rejection) to enhance his desire. He will say, "Man, don't be offended, but Aunt Kate, that runs the house don't have nothing but highclass white men coming to her place. . . . You know, doctors, lawyers, big-shot politicians. You look like a clean-cut white man, but you ain't in that league are you?" (Iceberg Slim, *Pimp: The Story of My Life*)

After a few more exchanges of the "murphy" dialogue, "the mark is separated from his scratch."

An analysis of rapping indicates a number of things. For instance, it is revealing that one raps *to* rather than *with* a person supporting the impression that rapping is to be regarded more as a performance than verbal exchange. As with other performances, rapping projects the personality, physical appearance and style of the performer. In each of the examples given, the intrusive "I" of the speaker was instrumental in contributing to the total impression of the rap. . . .

[In a passage not reprinted here Kochman delineates other specialties of ghetto speech, such as "shucking" and "jiving."]

A summary analysis of the different forms of language behavior which have been discussed above permit the following generalizations:

The prestige norms which influence black speech behavior are those which have been successful in manipulating and controlling people and situations. The function of all of the forms of language behavior discussed above, with the exception of "running it down," was to project personality, assert oneself, or arouse emotion, frequently with the additional purpose of getting the person to give up or do something which will be of some benefit to the speaker. Only running it down has as its primary function to communicate information and often here too, the personality and style of the speaker in the form of rapping is projected along with the information.

The purpose for which language is used suggests that the speaker views the social situations into which he moves as consisting of a series of transactions which require that he be continually ready to take advantage of a person or situation or defend himself against being victimized. He has absorbed what Horton has called "street rationality." As one of Horton's respondents put it:

"The good hustler . . . conditions his mind and must never put his guard too far down, to relax, or he'll be taken."

I have carefully avoided limiting the group within the black community of whom the language behavior and perspective of their environment are characteristic. While I have no doubt that it is true of those who are generally called "street people" I am uncertain of the extent to which it is true of a much larger portion of the black community, especially the male segment. My informants consisted of street people, high school students, and blacks, who by their occupation as community and youth workers, possess what has been described as a "sharp sense of the streets." Yet it is difficult to find a black male in the community who has *not* witnessed or participated in the dozens or heard of signifying, or rapping, or shucking and jiving at some time during his growing up. It would be equally difficult to imagine a high school student in a Chicago inner city school not being touched by what is generally regarded as "street culture."

In conclusion, by blending style and verbal power, through rapping, sounding and running it down, the black in the ghetto establishes his personality; through shucking, gripping and copping a plea, he shows his respect for power; through jiving and signifying he stirs up excitement. With all of the above, he hopes to manipulate and control people and situations to give himself a winning edge.

WORKING WITH THE SELECTION

1. Eskimos have many words for snow. Similarly, some South American Indians who live mainly on potatoes are said to have some two hundred specialized terms for various sizes, shapes, and varieties of potatoes. If the inferences derived from such evidence are valid, what can you plausibly conclude from the large number of specialized terms for talking in some black communities?

2. Are there specialized terms for talking on your campus, terms for different ways of asking for a date or for bluffing in class, for example, that do not appear in regular dictionaries or in the dialectal speech of other groups? If you find such locutions, use methods like those employed by Kochman to attempt definitions of the terms. For example, you might listen closely to speech on the campus and record it, ask students what they mean by the terms they use, and analyze the purposes and effects of local terms.

3. In *The Dictionary of American Slang* (1960), editors Harold Wentworth and Stuart Berg Flexner define *rap to* as 'to speak to.' Under the date 1932, they cite the following from underworld slang: "I wish Moosh a hello, and he never raps to me but only bows, and takes my hat." *The Dictionary of American Underworld Lingo* (1950), edited by Hyman E. Goldin, Frank O'Leary, and Morris Lipsius, provides this example: "Don't rap to that rat; he's a fink for the cops." What does evidence allow you to infer about the contribution of blacks to the use and meaning of the term *rapping*?

4. Several of Kochman's black informants used the word *dig* to mean 'under-stand.' Most of us have probably assumed that the word was first used in this way by bohemians on the West Coast during the 1950's. Wentworth and Flexner define the word as 'to comprehend fully' and quote "Dig me?" from *Life*, December 15, 1941. In a passage not reprinted here Kochman implies that black speakers have done something to the phrase *cop a plea*. *The Dictionary of American Underworld Lingo* defines it as 'to apologize; to ask mercy,' and quotes the following: "That crumb went around shooting his mouth off about me. When I carved my initials in him, you shoulda heard him cop a plea." The same dictionary lists *cop a breeze* 'to slip quietly away,' *cop a drag* 'to smoke a cigarette,' *cop a gander* 'to look furtively,' *cop a mope* or *a figary* 'to leave suddenly,' and several others, including *cop a heel* with six listed meanings. On the basis of this evidence, comment on the role of blacks in inventing or developing slang.

5. Wentworth and Flexner associate *jive* with music but include as one defi-nition 'to talk idly or confusedly, in a jazzy rhythm and up-to-date slang.' *The Dictionary of American Underworld Lingo* does not include the term, but *The American Thesaurus of Slang* (1943), edited by Lester V. Berrey and Melvin Van den Bark, includes it as a word meaning 'suave talk'—though not as a verb 'to talk suavely'—and as meaning both 'deception' and 'to deceive or cheat.' What would you infer from this evidence?

6. Try to make an objective appraisal of ghetto speech so far as you have en-countered it. Obviously, it has its limitations. For many purposes, "rapping" is of little use, and it may do its users positive damage: a bank teller who "raps" with the patrons of the bank may not have his job very long. On the other hand, can something be said for it? What are the uses of language; are any of them served passably well or even superlatively by "rapping"?

2

Ghetto Dialects
and Language Teaching

In some areas dialects pose both linguistic and social problems, since they be-come involved in racial prejudice, along with economic, political, and cultural imbalance. Many minority groups in America—including most blacks, Indians, Mexicans, and Puerto Ricans—have remained more or less socially ostracized. Dialects that have developed among such groups have helped to intensify feel-ings of unity and pride within the groups. For people outside the groups, how-

ever, they have served also to exaggerate differences. Speakers of a standard dialect often consider a minority dialect inferior and use their sense of superiority as a basis for discrimination. Whether justly or unjustly, speakers fluent only in a minority dialect may be almost totally excluded from many opportunities— jobs, education, economic advancement. Minority dialects are not inferior to standard dialects as language—although they are characteristically used by people of meager education and limited experience and thus may seem inadequate— but social attitudes judge them unacceptable in many of the world's activities.

Appropriately, educators have been concerned with these problems; in fact, according to one earlier view, the major business of language teaching was to drill children in the use of an accepted dialect. Such drill has never been very successful and is no longer widely accepted, but alternatives are still subjects for debate. Should children with minority dialects be taught a new dialect as an aid in helping them out of the ghettos, of overcoming some of the handicaps promoted by ignorance and prejudice? And if so, what should be the teacher's attitudes or approaches toward the minority dialects? Or should educators direct their efforts toward eradicating the prejudices that create condescension toward minority dialects, rather than trying to alter well-formed speech habits or super-impose additional ones? The following two selections consider such questions.

The first selection is by James Sledd, a member of the department of linguistics at the University of Texas. Sledd has written widely on various aspects of language from Old English to modern pedagogy, perhaps especially on grammar and lexicography, and although these are popularly supposed to be dull subjects, Sledd's remarks are never dull. The selection below, originally an address, appeared in the English Journal, *58 (December, 1969). The second selection, by Robert H. Bentley, is a reaction to Sledd's address, in part a rejoinder to it and an assessment of it. It also serves to suggest academic and professional concern for today's problems. Bentley teaches at The Creighton University. His statement, which explains his involvement in ghetto speech, was written in December, 1969, and is printed here for the first time.*

Bi-Dialectalism: The Linguistics of White Supremacy

James Sledd

Because people who rarely talk together will talk differently, differences in speech tell what groups a man belongs to. He uses them to claim and proclaim his identity, and society uses them to keep him under control. The person who talks right, as we do, is one of us. The person who talks wrong is an outsider, strange and suspicious, and we must make him feel inferior if we can. That is one purpose of education. In a school system run like ours by white businessmen, instruction in the mother tongue includes formal initiation into the linguistic prejudices of the middle class.

Making children who talk wrong get right with the world has traditionally been the work of English teachers, and more recently of teachers of that strange conglomerate subject which we call speech. The English teacher in the role of linguistic censor was once a kind of folk heroine (or anti-heroine), the Miss Fidditch of the linguists' diatribes. Miss Fidditch believed in taking a strong stand. It never occurred to her that her main job was making the lower classes feel so low that they would try to climb higher. Instead, Miss Fidditch taught generations of schoolchildren, including future linguists, to avoid *ain't* and double negatives and *used to could* and *hadn't ought,* not because *ain't* would keep them from getting ahead in the world, but because *ain't* was wrong, no matter who used it, and deserved no encouragement from decent people who valued the English language. She did her job all the better for thinking that she was doing something else.

Miss Fidditch is not popular any longer among educators. Though the world at large is still inclined to agree with her, the vulgarizers of linguistics drove her out of the academic fashion years ago, when they replaced her misguided idealism with open-eyed hypocrisy. To the popular linguists, one kind of English is as good as another, and judgments to the contrary are only folklore; but since the object of life in the U.S.A. is for everybody to get ahead of everybody else, and since linguistic prejudice can keep a man from moving up to Schlitz, the linguists still teach that people who want to be decision-makers had better talk and write like the people who make decisions. The schools must therefore continue to cultivate the linguistic insecurity which is already a national characteristic but must teach the youngsters to manipulate that as they manipulate everything else; for neither Miss Fidditch's dream of a language intrinsically good, nor a humbler ideal of realizing the various potentialities of the existing language in its responsible use, can get in the way of the citizenry in its upward anguish through the pecking order. The linguists think that people who do knowingly what Miss Fidditch did in her innocence, will do it more efficiently, as if eating the apple made a skilled worker out of Eve.

As long as most people agreed that up is toward Schlitz and another TV set, and as long as they could pretend that every American eaglet can soar to those great heights, Fidditch McFidditch the dialectologist could enforce the speech-taboos of the great white middle class without complaint: either the child learned the taboos and observed them, or he was systematically penalized. But the damage done to the Wasps' nest by World War II made difficulties. People who talked all wrong, and especially black people, began to ask for their share of the loot in a world that had given them an argument by calling itself free, while a minority of the people who talked right began to bad-mouth respectability and joined the blacks in arguing that it was time for a real change. Some black people burned up the black parts of town, and some students made study impossible at the universities, and in general there was a Crisis. Optimists even talked of a revolution.

The predictable response of the frightened white businessman's society was to go right on doing what it had done before—which had caused the crisis—but to do it harder and to spend more money at it. Education was no exception. Government and the foundations began to spray money over the academic landscape like liquid fertilizer, and the professional societies began to bray and paw at the rich new grass. In that proud hour, any teacher who could dream up an expensive scheme for keeping things as they were while pretending to make a change was sure of becoming the director of a project or a center and of flying first-class to Washington twice a month. The white businessman strengthened his control of the educational system while giving the impression of vast humanitarian activity.

Black English provided the most lucrative new industry for white linguists, who found the mother lode when they discovered the interesting locutions which the less protected employ to the detriment of their chances for upward mobility. In the annals of free enterprise, the early sixties will be memorable for the invention of functional bi-dialectalism, a scheme best described by an elderly and unregenerate Southern dame as "turning black trash into white trash." Despite some signs of wear, this cloak for white supremacy has kept its shape for almost a decade now, and it is best described in the inimitable words of those who made it. Otherwise the description might be dismissed as a malicious caricature.

The basic assumption of bi-dialectalism is that the prejudices of middle-class whites cannot be changed but must be accepted and indeed enforced on lesser breeds. Upward mobility, it is assumed, is the end of education, but white power will deny upward mobility to speakers of black English, who must therefore be made to talk white English in their contacts with the white world.

An adequate florilegium may be assembled from a volume entitled *Social Dialects and Language Learning* (NCTE, 1964), the proceedings of a conference of bi-dialectalists which was held in 1964. William A. Stewart of the Center for Applied Linguistics begins the chorus (p. 13) by observing among our educators "a commendable desire to emphasize the potential of the Negro to be identical to white Americans"—a desire which is apparently not overwhelming, however, among the Black Muslims or among the young men who have enjoyed pot-shooting policemen for the past few summers. Editor Roger W. Shuy next speaks up (p. 53) for social climbing by our American Indians, who have been notably reluctant, throughout their unfortunate association with their conquerors, to adopt our conquering ways. Our linguistic studies, Shuy remarks in the purest accents of fidditchery, "should reveal those elements, both in speech and writing, which prevent Indians from attaining the social status which, with socially acceptable language, they might otherwise attain." A similar desire to be at peace with status-holders is suggested (p. 66) by Ruth I. Golden, who opines that "a human being wants most of all to be recognized as an individual, to be accepted, and to be approved." Since Southern speech brings "negative reactions when heard by employers in Detroit," where Dr. Golden labors in the schools, she devotes herself to stamping out /i/ for /e/ in *penny* and to restoring /l/ in *help* (pp. 63 f.).

An admirable scholar from New York, William Labov, then agrees (p. 88) that "recognition of an external standard of correctness is an inevitable accompaniment of upward social aspirations and upward social mobility," and advises that people who (like Jesus) prefer not to take excessive thought for the morrow can probably be made to. In Labov's own words, "since the homes of many lower class and working people do not provide the pressures toward upward social mobility that middle-class homes provide," and since adults in those lower reaches are sometimes resistant to middle-class values, we must "build into the community a tolerance for style shifting which is helpful in educational and occupational advancement," and we must build into the children, "starting from a level not much above the nursery school and going on through high school, a tolerance for practice in second role playing" (pp. 94–97, 104).

Presumably Labov sees nothing wrong in thus initiating children into the world of hypercorrection, insecurity, and "linguistic self-hatred" which marks, as he has said elsewhere, "the average New Yorker" (*The Social Stratification of English in New York City,* Center for Applied Linguistics, 1966, Chapter XIII); and Charles Ferguson, the eminent ex-director of the Center for Applied Linguistics, is equally confident of *his* right and duty to remake his fellow men in his directorial image. Talking about the Negroes in our Northern cities, Ferguson says that "we have to face a rather difficult decision as to whether we want to make these people bi-dialectal . . . [please to remark Ferguson's choice of verbs] or whether we want . . . to impose some kind of standard English on these people and to eradicate the kind of substandard English they speak" (p. 116). To cite another NCTE volume (*Language Programs for the Disadvantaged* [NCTE, 1965], p. 222), if the black children of the ghetto "do not learn a second kind of dialect, they will be forever prevented from access to economic opportunity and social acceptance." Middle-class white prejudice will rule eternally.

The bi-dialectalists, of course, would not be so popular with government and the foundations if they spoke openly of the supremacy of white prejudice; but they make it perfectly clear that what they are dealing with deserves no better name. No dialect, they keep repeating, is better than any other—yet poor and ignorant children must change theirs unless they want to stay poor and ignorant. When an NCTE "Task Force" set out to devise *Language Programs for the Disadvantaged* (NCTE, 1965), it laid down a perfect smoke screen of such hypocrisy, as one would expect from persons who felt called upon to inform the world that "without the experience of literature, the individual is denied the very dignity that makes him human" (p. v) but that not "all disadvantaged children are apathetic or dull" (pp. 24 f.).

"In this report" (p. 117), "teachers are asked to begin by accepting the dialect of their students for what it is, one form of oral communication. . . ." Teachers are warned particularly that they "need to accept the language which Negro children bring to school, to recognize that it is a perfectly appropriate vehicle for communicating ideas in the Negro home and subculture" (p. 215), that it is "essentially respectable and good" (p. 227). But though teachers must not attack "the dialect which children associate with their homes and their identity as Negroes" (p. 215), they must still use all the adult authority of the school to "teach standard informal English as a second dialect" (p. 137), because the youngster who cannot speak standard informal English "will not be able to get certain kinds of jobs" (p. 228).

The most common result of such teaching will be that white middle-class Midwestern speech will be imposed as mandatory for all those situations which middle-class white businessmen think it worth their while to regulate. In the words of Chicago's Professors Austin and McDavid (p. 245), "future educational programs should be developed in terms of substituting for the grammatical system of lower-class Southern speech [read: black Chicago speech] that of middle-class Chicago white speech—at least for those economic and social situations where grammatical norms are important." Labov goes so far as to ask (*Social Dialects and Language Learning*, p. 102) whether Northern schools should tolerate Southern speech at all— whether they should not also correct the "cultivated Southern speech" of privileged children who move North.

The description of compulsory bi-dialectalism may be completed by examining the methods which its proponents advocate for perpetuating the supremacy of white prejudice. Essentially, those methods are derived by analogy from structuralist methods of teaching foreign languages—methods whose superiority has been claimed but never demonstrated and whose intellectual foundations vanished with the demise of structuralist ideas. As an eminent grammarian privately observed after a recent conference, "The achievements of the operators will continue to lie in the field of getting and spending government money. . . . They seem to have an unerring instinct for finding ways of spending it unprofitably—on conferences at which they listen to each other, for example. Now they're out to teach standard English as a second dialect through techniques that have served very poorly in teaching second languages."

High on the list of those techniques is incessant drill on inessentials. In theory, the drills are the end-product of a long process of systematic comparison of the children's nonstandard dialects with the standard dialect which they are to be taught; but since the systematic comparisons have never been made, the bi-dialectalists fall back on a simple enumeration of a few dozen "features of pronunciation, grammar, and vocabulary which can be considered indices of social stratification" (Roger Shuy, "Detroit Speech," in A. L. Davis, ed., *On the Dialects of Children*, p. 13). Professor Rudolph Troike of the University of Texas was thus simply platitudinizing piously when he told the TESOL convention in 1968 that "any instructional program . . . must begin with as full an *objective* knowledge as possible" of both or all the dialects involved. The escape hatch in Troike's statement is the phrase *as full as possible*. What is usually possible is an unsystematic list of shibboleths—the simplification of consonant clusters, the Southern pronunciations of *walk* and *right*, *ax* for *ask*, the dropping of post-vocalic /r/, *ain't* and *fixin' to*, *bofe* and *mouf* for *both* and *mouth*, and the like. These innocent usages, which are as familiar as the sun in the late Confederacy, are apparently the terror of Northern employers, who the bi-dialectalists assume are almost suicidally unconcerned with such details as character, intelligence, and training for the job. The fact is, of course, that Northern employers and labor leaders dislike black faces but use black English as an excuse.

Having established, however, that a child of darkness under her tutelage says *mouf*, the pretty white lady sets out to rescue his soul. First she plays tapes of Southern speech to convince her victims, who understand Southern speech far better than they understand hers, that Southern speech often makes "complete understanding of content . . . difficult," "not readily comprehensible"—as is demonstrated by the fact that the pretty white lady would never have detected her victim's four-letter word just by listening and without watching his lips (New York Board of Education, *Nonstandard Dialect*, pp. 1, 14, 17). The difficulty of detecting him is all the more reason for fearing the iniquitous *mouf*-sayer: it proves he is a cunning devil who probably says *dentissoffice* too and who perpetrates such subversive "malapropisms" as "The food in the lunch room is not fitting to eat" (*On the Dialects of Children*, p. 23). How else *would* he spell *fitten*? But for such a hardened rogue, a good many "motivational activities" are likely to be necessary before the pretty white lady can really start twisting the thumbscrew with her drills.

Yet the drills are available, and the pretty white lady will use them when she sees her time. She has drills of all kinds—repetition drills, substitution drills, replacement drills, conversion drills, cued answer drills, the reading in unison of long lists of words like *teeth/reef, toothbrush/waffle, bathtub/alphabet, weather/weaver*. To get rid of *dentissoffice*, she may have students debate such propositions as "Ghosts do exist" or "Formal school tests should be eliminated"; and before a really "culminating activity" like playing "Pack the Trunk" she may "divide the class into consonant-cluster committees to seek out words containing" clusters like *sks, sps*, or *kt* (*Nonstandard Dialect, passim*). At this point the class might be invited to suggest a context for a replacement drill—maybe something like "Teacher! teacher! Billy Joe say that Tommy —— Bessy!" This last suggestion, it must be confessed, has not yet been made in the literature, but it seems considerably more stimulating than choral recitation of Poe's "Bells" (*ibid.*, p. 35).

Perhaps it need not be added that existing tests and evaluations of such "instructional materials" are something of a farce. If bi-dialectalism is really harder to acquire than bilingualism (Einar Haugen in *Social Dialects and Language Learning*, p. 125), teachers and texts ought surely to be superb, and judgments on them ought to be severe; but New York City's curriculum developers can give "highest priority" to making the children change *a* to *an* before nouns beginning with a vowel (*Nonstandard Dialect,* p. 14), and Texas' Professor Troike can argue the success of his methods by showing that after six months of drills a little black girl could repeat *his hat* after her teacher, instead of translating automatically to *he hat.* Unfortunately, tapes do not record psychological damage, or compare the effectiveness of other ways of teaching, or show what might better have been learned in the same time instead of learning to repeat *his hat.*

So much for a description of mandatory bi-dialectalism, a bit enlivened (since the subject is dreary) by irreverent comment, but not distorted in any essential way. In the U.S.A., we are being told, everybody wants approval—not approval for doing anything worth approving, but approval for doing whatever happens to be approved. Because approval goes to upward mobility, everybody should be upwardly mobile; and because upward mobility is impossible for underdogs who have not learned middle-dog barking, we must teach it to them for use in their excursions into the middle-dog world. There is no possibility either that the present middle class can be brought to tolerate lower-class English or that upward mobility, as a national aspiration, will be questioned. Those are the pillars on which the state is built, and the compassionate teacher, knowing the ways of his society, will change the color of his students' vowels although he cannot change the color of their skins.

It is not at all certain that the bi-dialectalists, for all their absurdities, can be dislodged from their well-carpeted offices. They are supported by the National Council of Teachers of English, the Modern Language Association of America, the Center for Applied Linguistics, the federal government, the foundations, the governments of a number of major cities, and by black people who have made it into the middle class and so despise their origins and their less efficient fellows. In the best of times our top dogs are pleased by docility, if not mobility, among the beasts below; and in 1969 a new ice age is beginning. Newspaper headlines tell us that the Department of Health, Education, and Welfare has been urged to relax its requirements for desegregation of schools immediately but quietly, and President Nixon loses his Miami tan at the thought that militant students will "politicize" our universities—as if government grants to upwardly mobile faculty had not politicized them long ago. In Lyndon Johnson's Texas the citizens of Austin vote down an open housing law, their board of education then justifies segregated schooling by the established pattern of segregated housing, and the governor of the state praises the state university as the source of brain-power to assist the businessman in the lucrative exploitation of what the governor proudly calls the "insatiable appetite" of Texans. The only revolution we are likely to see is the continued subversion, by the dominant white businessman, of the political and religious principles on which the nation was founded.

Yet though the times are bad, they are not hopeless, at least not in the small, undramatic world of English education; and the bi-dialectalists are so gorgeously absurd that the breath of laughter may collapse their card-house if only enough people can be brought to see it as it is. It is not simply quixotic, then, to add to a laughing description of imposed bi-dialectalism a more serious statement of reasons why it cannot succeed and should not be tolerated even if it could—a statement which can lead, in conclusion, to the proposing of an alternative policy.

The argument that bi-dialectalism cannot be forced is easy to make out, even, in part, from the reluctant admissions of some of its proponents. Two principal reasons have already been suggested, the ignorance and unproved methods of the bi-dialectalists. The term *ignorance* is used literally, and in all fairness. Whatever one thinks of teaching standard English by methods like those for teaching foreign languages, contrastive analyses of our differ-ent dialects are a prerequisite—but a prerequisite which has not yet been supplied. Until very recently, the principal sources of information were the collections for the *Linguistic Atlas;* but they are unsystematic, partially out-of-date, and in some respects inaccurate and superficial. Where, for example, should one go for descriptions of intonation and its dialectal variants, for accurate accounts of the system or systems of verbal auxiliaries, for analyses of the speech of ghetto children instead of rustic ancients? Such minimal essentials are simply lacking. In fact, it might be said that for all the talk about revolutionary advances in linguistics, neither the structural nor the generative grammarians have yet produced a satisfactory basic description of even standard English.

The best descriptions of all our kinds of English would still not be enough to make coercive bi-dialectalism a success. The English teacher's forty-five minutes a day for five days in the week will never counteract the influence, and sometimes the hostility, of playmates and friends and family during much the larger part of the student's time. Formal education could produce real bi-dialectals only in a vast system of state nurseries and boarding schools to which the children of the poor and ignorant would be consigned at an early age; but such establishments would be prohibitively expensive, intol-erable to the people, and still not absolutely certain of success, because the most essential of all conditions might not be met—namely, the desire of the children to talk like the white middle class.

When one thinks about it in these realistic terms, the whole argument about bi-dialectalism begins to look schizophrenic, as out-of-this-world as an argument whether Lee should surrender at Appomattox or fight back. There is no evidence that the bi-dialectalists, if they actually had good text-books, better teachers, and as much money as the country is spending to devastate Vietnam, would really know what to do with those fictional re-sources. Instead of clear ideas, they offer clichés, like the familiar attacks on "traditional methods and approaches" or the protected pedagogue's arrogant assurance that illiterates can have no human dignity. They fly off quickly into high-sounding vaguenesses, talking (for example) about "differences in social dialect and associated versions of reality" (*Social Dialects and Lan-guage Learning,* p. 68), as if metaphysics rested on a preconsonantal /r/.

At their most precise, they suggest the prudential avoidance of Southern pronunciations of *walk* and *cough* in Washington because Negroes there look down on new arrivals from Georgia and the Carolinas. They happily assume what they should prove—that intensive training in "standard informal English as a second dialect" has produced or can produce large numbers of psychologically undamaged bi-dialectals, whose new accomplishment has won them or will win them jobs that otherwise would have been impossible for them to get. When their guard is down, the bi-dialectalists actually confess that they *have* no concrete program, since "no one program at any level yet seems applicable to a significant number of other classes at the respective level" (*Language Programs for the Disadvantaged*, pp. 30 ff.).

Some awareness of their difficulties, and some uncertainty about priorities, seem indeed to be spreading among the bi-dialectalists (though it would be too much to hope that if their present bandwagon falls apart they will consider themselves discredited and resign their membership in the Society of Mandarin). For one thing, they have become aware of the significance of reading, which William A. Stewart, as late as 1964, could reduce to the level of "socially desirable embellishments" (*Social Dialects and Language Learning*, p. 10). In his latest book, however, *Teaching Black Children to Read*, Editor Shuy announces "the simple truth that speaking standard English, however desirable it may be, is not as important as learning to read" (p. 118). His colleagues Walter A. Wolfram and Ralph W. Fasold are even closer to enlightenment. In the same new volume (p. 143), they hesitantly admit that "there is some question about the degree to which Standard English can be taught to the ghetto child in the classroom at all"; and Fasold meant what he said, for he had said it before at the Milwaukee convention of the NCTE. Though that august body was still congratulating itself on its concern with "a language component for the so-called culturally divergent," it had to bear with Fasold's embarrassing confession: "Because of the operation of social forces in the use of language," he said, "forces which are only poorly understood, it may not be possible to teach Standard English as a second language to Black English speaking children unless they are interacting with Standard English speakers in a meaningful way outside the classroom" (*Convention Concerns—1968*, p. 10). The Center's linguistician came as close as standard English would allow to saying that it is segregation which makes black people talk different and that there would be no slum children if there were no slums.

No doubt the most important of Fasold's poorly understood social forces is one which everybody but white linguists has understood for a long time: black people may just not want to talk white English. Several years ago, Labov observed that some of his more rebellious New York subjects were deliberately turning away from social-climbing New York speech toward a black Southern model (*Social Dialects and Language Learning*, pp. 96 f.), and today comment on "the new feeling of racial pride among black Americans" (*Teaching Black Children To Read*, p. 142) is a platitude. Wolfram and Fasold go on to the quite unsurprising speculation that that pride may even extend to the Negro's speech. "If a realization develops that this dialect, an important part of black culture, is as distinctively Afro-American as anything in the culture, the result may well be a new respect for Black English within the community" (p. 143). More plainly, condescending middle-class white charity is not wanted any more, if it ever was, in language-teaching or anywhere else. We should learn from the example of the British: the social cataclysm of the Second World War, and the achievement of political power by labor, did more to give the "disadvantaged" English youngster an equal chance than charitable bi-dialectalism ever did. We are past the stage when white teachers, whether Africans or Caucasians, can think well of themselves for trying to turn black people into uneasy imitations of the whites.

The immorality of that effort is the chief reason why enforced bi-dialectalism should not be tolerated even if it were possible. Predators can and do use dialect differences to exploit and oppress, because ordinary people can be made to doubt their own value and to accept subservience if they can be made to despise the speech of their fathers. Obligatory bi-dialectalism for minorities is only another mode of exploitation, another way of making blacks behave as whites would like them to. It is unnecessary for communication, since the ability to understand other dialects is easily attained, as the black child shows when she translates her teacher's prissy white model "*his* hat" into "*he* hat." Its psychological consequences are likely to be nervous affectation, self-distrust, dislike for everyone not equally afflicted with the itch to get ahead, and eventual frustration by the discovery that the reward for so much suffering is intolerably small. At best the altered student will get a somewhat better job and will move up a few places in the rat-race of the underlings. At worst he will be cut off from other blacks, still not accepted among whites, and economically no better off than he was before.

White teachers should hope, then, that their black students will be recalcitrant, so that bi-dialectalism as a unilateral condition for employment can be forgotten. It would make better sense, if pedagogues insist on living in a fantasy world, to require whites to speak black English in their dealings with blacks, since the whites have more advantages than the blacks and consider themselves more intelligent; or perhaps we should be hard-headedly consistent in our brutalities and try to eradicate the vices which really do enrage employers—like intellectual questioning, or the suspicion that ours is not the best of possible worlds.

Indeed, the educationists' faith in education would be touching if it were not their way of keeping up their wages. Nothing the schools can do about black English or white English either will do much for racial peace and social justice as long as the black and white worlds are separate and hostile. The measure of our educational absurdity is the necessity of saying once again that regimented bi-dialectalism is no substitute for sweeping social change—*necessity* being defined by the alternative of dropping out and waiting quietly for destruction if the white businessman continues to have his way.

The reply that the educational system should not be politicized is impossible for bi-dialectalists, since bi-dialectalism is itself a political instrument. They may purge themselves of inconsistency, and do what little good is possible for English teachers as politicial reformers, if instead of teaching Standard English as a second dialect they teach getting out of Vietnam, getting out of the missile race, and stopping the deadly pollution of the one world we have, as horribly exemplified by the current vandalism in Alaska.

One use for a small fraction of the resources that would thus be saved would be to improve the teaching of the English language. Bi-dialectalism would never have been invented if our society were not divided into the dominant white majority and the exploited minorities. Children should be taught that. They should be taught the relations between group differences and speech differences, and the good and bad uses of speech differences by groups and by individuals. The teaching would require a more serious study of grammar, lexicography, dialectology, and linguistic history than our educational system now provides—require it at least of prospective English teachers.

In the immediate present, the time and money now wasted on bi-dialectalism should be spent on teaching the children of the minorities to read. Already some of the universal experts among the linguists have boarded this new bandwagon, and the next round of government grants may very well be for programs in reading and writing in black English. That might be a good thing, particularly if we could somehow get rid of the tired little clique of operators who have run the professional societies of English teachers for so long. Anyway, the direct attack on minority language, the attempt to compel bi-dialectalism, should be abandoned for an attempt to open the minds and enhance the lives of the poor and ignorant. At the same time, every attempt should be made to teach the majority to understand the life and language of the oppressed. Linguistic change is the effect and not the cause of social change. If the majority can rid itself of its prejudices, and if the minorities can get or be given an education, differences between dialects are unlikely to hurt anybody much.

(The phoniest objections to this proposal will be those that talk about social realism, about the necessity for doing something even—or should one say particularly?—if it's wrong. That kind of talk makes real change impossible, but makes money for bi-dialectalists.)

On Black Dialects, White Linguists, and the Teaching of English

Robert H. Bentley

In the weeks since the convention, I have given much thought to Sledd's remarks. To some extent, he has attacked virtually every English teacher in the country, and I feel I have been insulted. I have also thought about Kochman's response. He was certainly insulted: he is perhaps the most knowledgeable of the white linguists I have read on the subject of black idiom. Perhaps what Blake said is true: opposites *are* equally true.

Let me explain why I feel insulted: I feel our position has been misrepresented by Professor Sledd. By "our" I mean this NCTE-Center for Applied Linguistics-foundation-English teachers in general "conspiracy" to teach standard English. I am white, an English teacher with training in linguistics. With a black man who is a reading specialist, I team-teach a course for teachers who work in the "inner-city" schools. The course is double-listed in both the English and education departments. In the English department it bears the title "The Afro-American Dialects of English"; translated into Educationese, the class is entitled "Dialectology and Developmental Reading for Disadvantaged Youth."

I feel insulted because, since class number one, I have insisted that the way people speak, especially the young black children that my students teach, is as legitimate as anyone's speech. I have insisted that we, as teachers, must convince the upcoming generation that *all* dialects of English are legitimate or, as one of my students puts it, "full-blown, legal" dialects. I have also contended that our present society demands "standard" English of those who are to be successful. I stress that I don't like this state of affairs, but I tell my students that we must continue to teach the dialect of the marketplace. For the part of the course that I teach, I assign articles on the subject of black dialect and bidialectal instruction. These are reported back to the class and discussed. By the end of the course, the students will be familiar with the entire Stewart-Shuy-Labov-Malmstrom-Johnson-Kochman-*et al.* canon. Our textbook is the *Florida FL Reporter,* anthology issue (1969), which is devoted, in part, to the above topic.

I think I have told my teachers the truth. I think the people who hire them, and ultimately the society at large, expect them to teach "correct" English— the dialect of the marketplace. I would also contend that there are black dialects of English. These social dialects are, of course, influenced by geographical dialects, by parents, and by teachers. The mass media are no doubt having an effect on all dialects as well. But anyone who reads the "canon" must see *systematic* differences at work. One who teaches the dialect of the marketplace, therefore, appears to have a choice. He may tamper with the speech (and/or writing) of a student, or he may try to understand the system underlying the speech (and/or writing) act and compare and contrast that system to the dialect of the marketplace for his student. I said above that the teacher "appears to have a choice": it seems to me that this is no choice at all. For the time being, if we are to call ourselves teachers in the truest sense of the word, we must teach bidialectalism to some of our students.

But what of Sledd? He is, in Blakian terms, "equally true." We in the profession have for years been insisting on tolerance, but it seems to me that our message has not gotten through. We must call upon all college English teachers to observe and propagate priorities long recognized by the leadership of the profession.

Our number one priority must be to spread the word to educated society that dialects, both geographical *and social,* are real, legitimate, "legal", deserving of respect, and a fact of language. We must become militant on this point. We must tell Super-Grammar (long skirt and tennis shoes; Max Rafferty scrapbook) once and for all, loud and clear, that "correct English" is a myth. In our tell-it-like-it-is climate we can be successful. We should forget our widespread aversion of "popularizers" and start writing articles for popular magazines.

Further, we must make sure that the generation coming up gets educated; we must teach them some facts about language. All teachers of Freshman English should include a unit on social dialects and differentiate rhetoric and grammar; the knowledge is available—all that is necessary is that the teacher do some reading. The aforementioned "Anthology" issue is a good place to start. All teachers of courses in language (History of, Modern Grammar, Intro. to, and so on) should do likewise. The animosity that has existed between education and English departments has been dying out; we can and should insist that education courses in methods of teaching English, if taught by the linguistically naive, be supplemented by guest lecturers who are linguistically sophisticated. I am, in short, convinced by Sledd: our number one priority must be the education of society. We can no longer tolerate intolerance of dialect and idiolect—particularly on the part of English teachers who teach black children.

Our number two priority must become eyes-open bidialectal teaching. (In many areas of the country, we must include bilingual teaching.) We must admit, finally, that some speakers (and writers) differ from the dialect of the marketplace in systematic ways. We must make ourselves knowledgeable of the system(s) and address ourselves to it (them). Our alternatives are (1) to ignore those differences (when society pays us to eliminate them), and (2) to tamper with surface manifestations of the differences—long recognized as a negative and reductive process (Shuy's "Bonnie-and-Clyde eradication" metaphor).

We must also recognize sub-priorities. As we teach "standard" English, we must separate at least phonology from grammar, and grammar from lexicon. We cannot live with the old right-wrong categories as we deal with the problems of bidialectal instruction.

Let us not tamper with phonology. I explained to my "Dialects class" (actually, only half mine) the difficulty many black speakers have with the word *ask*. One student, herself black and a teacher, responded that she couldn't say the word and that it always came out /ækst/. She related to the class how she had been humiliated, threatened, and ridiculed by her teachers to the point that she no longer used the word at all; she added that she was relieved to find out, after all these years, that it wasn't her stupidity that caused this. How many other inferiority complexes have we caused over the years? If we must drill, let it be in areas that matter (to white society) like the verb *to be* and participial endings. As we consider rhetorical matters, such as word choice, we must teach that some words are taboo and some not in the lexicon of uptight white society. If we separate out the "levels" of language we have a better chance of success.

But let's get our priorities straight. Let's teach all our students, with Sledd, that the way a man talks is special, legitimate, "legal" and—finally—"holy" and "sacred." We might then start to answer some of those questions "Related to the Teaching of Language"—those questions we discussion leaders felt were important enough to vote ourselves out of a job for.

WORKING WITH THE SELECTIONS

1. Many people believe that college professors, perhaps particularly teachers of language and literature, dwell in ivory towers, ignoring other human beings and human problems, incapable of doing anything practical even if they want to. Would this seem to be a just estimate, at least of teachers concerned with ghetto speech?

2. You have probably inferred that Sledd believes in the virtues of controversy and that at least in part he was trying to promote it. In addition, he points out that he is attempting to discredit compulsory bidialectalism by showing it to be ridiculous. This intent somewhat obscures the main lines of his argument; to be sure you know what his position is, you might work through his article again and jot down his main ideas.

3. Which of Sledd's main charges does Bentley largely ignore? Which does he attempt to answer? Does he add anything that Sledd did not include?

4. Sledd uses the phrase *compulsory bidialectalism* more often than some linguists and educators do. Does the word *compulsory* have anything to do with the apparent differences among the disputants?

3
Everybody Speaks a Dialect

Speaking a dialect is no more disgraceful than having hands and feet. Every-
body speaks at least one dialect, and most people speak several; dialects are
among the ways languages live and grow. But dialects are not one thing, nor
do they work in only one way, although they all have this in common: they
are all encouraged by isolation, which may be geographical, social, racial, oc-
cupational, or some other kind.

This section contains samples of various sorts of language that have resulted
from dialectal variation. The first is from a pamphlet entitled The Fraternitye
of Vacabondes both rusling and beggarly, Men and women, Boyes and Gyrles,
with their proper names and qualities, *published in 1565 by one John Awdeley,*
a journalist working in London in Shakespeare's time; it was reprinted in 1869
by the Early English Text Society, Extra Series 9, edited by Edward Viles and
F. J. Furnivall. It represents two dialects: a regional and social dialect, what a
cultured person living in London in Shakespeare's time would have expected
to read in the morning paper if there had been any morning papers in that
day, and from our point of view, a temporal dialect, since it represents English
of four hundred years ago. It also represents a third dialect, that of a different
social stratum, since the terms defined are apparently those common among
thieves and beggars.

The second piece reflects the same dialects as the first; it is from Thomas
Harman's Caueat or Warening, for Commen Cvrsetors Vulgarely Called Vaga-
bones (1567). *One might notice that* u *and* v, *historically the same letter, had*
not yet become standardized. The letters i *and* j *also were often interchangeable;*
whipiacke *is presumably* whipjack. *Like Awdeley, Harman was a journalist;*
the conversation he reports is imaginative but probably relatively reliable. He
gives a version in what was called canting speech, that is, the language of thieves
and other rogues, which was deliberately made obscure to keep law-abiding
folk from understanding it, and a translation (printed here in italics) into his
own dialect, the educated London English of the day.

When two or more languages compete over long periods they may all break
down more or less, resulting in what is called creolizing. This has happened
but little in the Americas, where usually English, French, Spanish, or Portuguese
has triumphed rather quickly, but in some areas new languages have appeared,
made up of remnants of various African, American, and European bodies of
speech. In the United States, Goose Creek Gullah is an example, and in Canada,
Chinook Jargon. In some areas an interim kind of speech has appeared, called a
pidgin, *a limited means of communication—not really a language, although it*

may grow into one—which is a growth from native speech and one or more languages that are used for trade. In practice these have been most frequently English, Chinese, *and* Dutch. *The third selection provides examples of a New Guinea pidgin, sometimes called Talk-talk, from* Pidgin English: Dictionary of Common Nouns and Phrases Used in Conversation with Natives (*1937*).

Immigrants always become dialect speakers, especially if they do not know the mother tongue of their new country. Usually, unless the immigrants live isolated in a ghetto, their dialects disappear in a generation. Sometimes, however, immigrants contribute to the language of their new motherland, especially if they bring with them a rich cultural heritage. The Dutch on Manhattan provided cruller *and probably* Yankee; *the French trappers introduced* prairie *and* portage; *the Germans,* turnverein *and* hasenpfeffer; *the Mexicans,* rodeo *and* calaboose. *Currently, among the liveliest imports are Yiddish words, including* kibitzer, mazuma, *and* shmo. *The fourth selection is from* The Joys of Yiddish (*1968*) *by Leo Rosten, a former college professor, a columnist, and the author of many books, including the ever-delightful* Education of H*Y*M*A*N K*A*P*L*A*N (*1937*).

All trades and professions develop dialectal speech. Among masons, mortar *is called* mud, *and among plumbers a* snake *is not the sort of thing studied by a herpetologist.* Clean *means something to car salesmen that it does not mean to most drivers. The fifth selection is from Norman D. Hinton, "The Language of Jazz Musicians,"* Publications of the American Dialect Society, *No. 30 (November, 1958*).

Many dialects are regional, reflecting the speech characteristic of a particular geographical area. In recent years linguists have made revealing studies of regional dialects through the use of a technique known as linguistic *or* dialect geography. *This technique is described in the selection by Harvard University professor Dwight Bolinger from his book* Aspects of Language (*1968*). *The book is notable among introductory books on language for the reliance Bolinger places on reports of original research and for its comprehensiveness. The last two selections rely on linguistic geography: in the first, from* The English Language in the School Program (*1966*), *edited by Robert F. Hogan, Hans Kurath describes pronunciations on the East Coast of the United States; in the second, from* Dialects of American English (*1967*), *Carroll E. Reed provides lists that suggest to what extent words characteristic of dialects in the Northeast, the East Midlands, and the South have found their way to the West Coast. Kurath is the dean of American linguistic geographers; he directed the pioneer study in the United States, which led to the monumental* Linguistic Atlas of New England (*1939–43*), *then went on to compile* A Word Geography of the Eastern United States (*1949*) *and to write many other books, including his authoritative* Phonology and Prosody of Modern English (*1964*). *A scholar with a special interest in Pennsylvania German, Reed is professor of Germanic languages and literature at the University of Massachusetts.*

Language of the Underworld

John Awdeley

An Abraham man. An Abraham man is he that walketh bare armed, and bare legged, and fayneth hym selfe mad, and caryeth a packe of wool, or a stycke with baken on it, or such lyke toy, and nameth himselfe poore Tom.

A Russeler. A Russeler goeth wyth a weapon to seeke seruice, saying he hath bene a Seruitor in the wars, and beggeth for his reliefe. But his chiefest trade is to robbe poore wayfaring men and market women.

A Prygman. A Prygman goeth with a stycke in hys hand like an idle person. His propertye is to steale cloathes of the hedge, which they call storing of the Rogeman: or els filtch Poultry, carying them to the Alehouse, whych they call the Bowsyng In, & ther syt playing at cardes and dice, tyl that is spent which they haue so fylched.

A Whipiacke. A whypiacke is one, that by couler of a counterfaite Lisence, (which they call a Gybe, and the seales they cal Iarckes) doth vse to beg lyke a Maryner, But hys chiefest trade is to rob Bowthes in a Faire, or to pilfer ware from staules, which they cal heauing of the Bowth.

A Frater. A Frater goeth wyth a like Lisence to beg for some Spittlehouse or Hospital. Their pray is commonly vpon poore women as they go and come to the Markets.

A Quire bird. A Quire bird is one that came lately out of prison, & goeth to seeke seruice. He is commonly a stealer of Horses, which they terme a Priggar of Paulfreys.

An Vpright man. An Vpright man is one that goeth wyth the trunchion of a staffe, which staffe they cal a Filtchman. This man is of so much authority, that meeting with any of his profession, he may cal them to accompt, & commaund a share or snap vnto him selfe, of al that they haue gained by their trade in one moneth. And if he doo them wrong, they haue no remedy agaynst hym, no though he beate them, as he vseth commonly to do. He may also commaund any of their women, which they cal Doxies, to serue his turne. He hath ye chiefe place at any market walke, & other assembles, & is not of any to be controled.

A Curtall. A Curtall is much like to the Vpright man, but hys authority is not fully so great. He vseth commonly to go with a short cloke, like to grey Friers, & his woman with him in like liuery, which he calleth his Altham if she be hys wyfe, & if she be his harlot, she is called hys Doxy.

A Palliard. A Palliard is he that goeth in a patched cloke, and hys Doxy goeth in like apparell.

An Irishe toyle. An Irishe toyle is he that carieth his ware in hys wallet, as laces, pins, poyntes, and such like. He vseth to shew no wares vntill he haue his almes. And if the good man and wyfe be not in the way, he procureth of the ch[i]lldre*n* or seruants a fleece of wool, or the worth of xij.d of some other thing, for a peniworth of his wares.

A Iackman. A Iackeman is he that can write and reade, and somtime speake latin. He vseth to make counterfaite licences which they call Gybes, and sets to Seales, in their language called Iarkes.

A Swygman. A Swygman goeth with a Pedlers pack.

A Washman. A Washman is called a Palliard, but not of the right making. He vseth to lye in the hye way with lame or sore legs or armes to beg. These men y*e* right Pilliards wil often times spoile, but they dare not co*m*playn. They be bitten with Spickworts, & somtime with rats bane.

A Tinkard. A Tinkard leaueth his bag a sweating at the Alehouse, which they terme their Bowsing In, and in the meane season goeth abrode a begging.

A wylde Roge. A wilde Roge is he that hath no abiding place but by his coulour of going abrode to beg, is commonly to seeke some kinsman of his, and all that be of hys corporation be properly called Roges.

A Kitchen Co. A Kitchin Co is called an ydle runagate Boy.

A Kitchen Mortes. A Kitchin Mortes is a Gyrle, she is brought at her full age to the Vpryght man to be broken, and so she is called a Doxy, vntil she come to y*e* honor of an Altham.

Doxies. Note especially all which go abroade working laces and shirt stringes, they name them Doxies.

A Patriarke Co. A Patriarke Co doth make mariages, & that is vntill death depart the maried folke, which is after this sort: When they come to a dead Horse or any dead Catell, then they shake hands and so depart euery one of them a seurall way.

A Caueat or Warening

Thomas Harman

> The vpright Cofe canteth to the Roge.
> *The vpright man speaketh to the Roge.*

Vprightman. Bene Lightmans to thy quarromes, in what lipken has thou lypped in this darkemans, whether in a lybbege or in the strummell?

   God morrowe to thy body, in what house hast thou lyne in all night, whether in a bed, or in the strawe?

Roge. I couched a hogshead in a Skypper this darkemans.

   I layd me downe to sléep in a barne this night.

Vprightman. I towre the strummel trine vpon thy nabchet *and* Togman.

   I sée the strawe hang vpon thy cap and coate.

Roge. I saye by the Salomon I will lage it of with a gage of benebouse; then cut to my nose watch.

I sweare by the masse, I wull washe it of with a quart of good drynke; then saye to me what thou wylt.

Man. Why, hast thou any lowre in thy bonge to bouse?

Why, hast thou any money in thy purse to drinke?

Roge. But a flagge, a wyn, and a make.

But a grot, a penny, and a halfe penny.

Man. Why, where is the kene that hath the bene bouse?

Where is the house that hath good drinke?

Roge. A bene mort hereby at the signe of the prauncer.

A good wyfe here by at the signe of the hors.

Man. I cutt it is quyer bouse, I boused a flagge the laste dark mans.

I saye it is small and naughtye drynke. I dranke a groate there the last night.

Roge. But bouse there a bord, *and* thou shalt haue beneship.

But drinke there a shyllinge, and thou shalt haue very good.

Tower ye yander is the kene, dup the gygger, and maund that is bene shyp.

Se you, yonder is the house, open the doore, and aske for the best.

Man. This bouse is as benshyp as rome bouse.

This drinke is as good as wyne.

Now I tower that bene bouse makes nase nabes.

Now I se that good drinke makes a dronken heade.

Maunde of this morte what bene pecke is in her ken.

Aske of this wyfe what good meate shee hath in her house.

Roge. She hath a Cacling chete, a grunting chete, ruff Pecke, cassan, and popplarr of yarum.

She hath a hen, a pyg, baken, chese and mylke porrage.

Man. That is beneshyp to our watche.

That is very good for vs.

Now we haue well bousd, let vs strike some chete.

Nowe we haue well dronke, let us steale some thinge.

Yonder dwelleth a quyere cuffen, it were beneship to myll him.

Yonder dwelleth a hoggeshe and choyrlyshe man, it were very well donne to robbe him.

Roge. Nowe bynge we a waste to the hygh pad, the ruffmanes is by.

Naye, let vs go hence to the hygh waye, the wodes is at hand.

Man. So may we happen on the Harmanes, and cly the Iarke, or to the quyerken and skower quyaer cramprings, and so to tryning on the chates.

So we maye chaunce to set in the stockes, eyther be whypped, eyther had to prison house, and there be shackled with bolttes and fetters, and then to hange on the gallowes.

Gerry gan, the ruffian clye thee.

A torde in thy mouth, the deuyll take thee.

Man. What, stowe your bene, cofe, and cut benat whydds, and byng we to rome vyle, to nyp a bong; so shall we haue lowre for the bousing ken, and when we byng back to the deuseauyel, we wyll fylche some duddes of the Ruffemans, or myll the ken for a lagge of dudes.

What, holde your peace, good fellowe, and speake better wordes, and go we to London, to cut a purse; then shal we haue money for the ale house, and when wee come backe agayne into the country, wee wyll steale some lynnen clothes of one [off'n?] hedges, or robbe some house for a bucke of clothes.

Pidgin English Phrases

I want the boy here.
Bringim boy 'e come.

Take the boy away.
Talkim 'e go.

Lift together.
O! Sarlo!

Go and change your loincloth, we are going for a walk.
Go puttim clean fella lap lap, now me two fella walkabout.

Make the house tidy.
Straightim alla something, long 'ouse.

I am going out, should a master call, tell him I have gone to the Club.
Behind me go long house play belong me fella. Suppose one fella master im 'e like lookim me, talkim where sat me stop.

Give me an envelope.
Bringim skin belong pass.

Was the master that called bald, or old?
Master 'e like lookim me, im 'e lapun? Now grass belong im a kaylah finis?

Why don't you listen to what I have to tell you?
Ear belong you 'e fas long harim talk.

You say your leg is swollen up, have you a boil?
Talk belong you, leg belong you 'e sellup, sellup along whatname? Buk?

Have you a cold, or a pain in the chest?
'e got kus? Brest belong you 'e pain?

I think your brain is defective.
Kru belong you 'e stink finis.

Lock up the store.
Fasim store.

How long is it before your contract expires?
Callim how much Xmas long paper 'e finis.

Have you only to work a few months? or have you to work a year and some months?
You got moon thas all long finis time? Thas all you got One Xmas now moon one time?

Who did you work with before?
You work long what name masta before?

Do you want to go to gaol?	You likeim calaboose?
Do you want to make trouble?	You likeim trouble?
I want you to go to the market.	Behind you go along bung.
I notice there is blood on your skin, what's the matter?	Bluud 'e stop along sekim belong what name? You got sore?
I am sick in the stomach.	Bel belong me 'e cry.
Is this true or did you dream it?	Talk belong you 'e straight? True you no can tream long this fella talk you givim me.
	'E got sick? now cranky lic lic? alla same whatname something?
What is the matter with you? Are you ill?	
Are you married?	You married finis? or, you yan married finis?
Where is your wife?	Mary belong you 'e stop where?
You go from me.	You rouse! or Rause!
Clear out of the house and grounds.	Rause! altogether along banis belong me fella.
I do not wish you to do this.	Me no like.
I am very angry with you.	Me cross too much along you.
I am very angry.	Bell belong me 'e ot.
We shall forget the matter.	Scrubim talk.
Have you washed your hands?	You washim hand finis?
How long is it since you had a bath?	Skin belong you 'e stink. Callim ow much time 'e loose, long you you wash wash?
I want to shave, bring some hot water.	Me like cuttim grass, lineim water 'e ot.
I am sorry for you.	O! Kalipa long you.
Why do you tell me a lie?	You like gammon long what name something?
I understand.	Me savvi finis.
Don't answer me back.	Fassim talk belong you.
Make the bed.	Workim bed.
Set the table.	Workim table.
Serve the dinner.	Shootim kai-kai.
Sweep the house.	Broomim house.
Why are you so lazy?	You laze belong whatname?

The Joys of Yiddish

Leo Rosten

chutzpa (noun)
chutspa
chutzpadik (adjective)

> Pronounced KHOOTS-*pah;* rattle that *kh* around with fervor; rhymes with "Foot spa." Do *not* pronounce the *ch* as in "choo-choo" or "Chippewa," but as the German *ch* in *Ach!* or the Scottish in *loch.* Hebrew: "insolence," "audacity."

> Gall, brazen nerve, effrontery, incredible "guts"; presumption-plus-arrogance such as no other word, and no other language, can do justice to.

The classic definition of *chutzpa* is, of course, this:

Chutzpa is that quality enshrined in a man who, having killed his mother and father, throws himself on the mercy of the court because he is an orphan.

A *chutzpanik* may be defined as the man who shouts "Help! Help!" while beating you up.

In Paris, a plump Brooklyn *touristeh* entered a fine linen shop and, fingering a lace tablecloth, asked the proprietress the price thusly: "*Combien pour cette tishtoch* (tablecloth)?"

"*Cinquante francs, madame.*"

"*Cinquante francs?*" echoed the American. "*Mais, c'est une shmatte* (rag)!"

The *baleboosteh* drew herself up in high dudgeon. "*Une shmatte, madame? Quelle chutzpa!*"

A woman, feeling sorry for a beggar who had come to her door, invited him in and offered him food. On the table was a pile of dark bread—and a few slices of *challa.* The *shnorrer* (beggar) promptly fell upon the *challa.*

"There's black bread, too," the woman hinted.

"I prefer *challa.*"

"But *challa* is much more expensive!"

"Lady," said the beggar, "it's worth it."

That, I think, is *chutzpa.*

And if you need one more example, *regardez* this:

A *chutzpanik,* having dined well in a restaurant, summoned the proprietor, to whom he said as follows, "My friend, I enjoyed your food, but to tell you the truth, I haven't a penny to my name. Wait: Don't be angry! Hear me out. I am, by profession, a beggar. I happen to be an extremely talented *shnorrer.* I can go out and within an hour *shnorr* the entire amount I owe you. But naturally, you can't trust me to come back. I understand. You'll be well-advised to come with me and not let me out of your sight for a minute, right? But can a man like you, a well-known restaurateur, be seen in the company of a man who is *shnorring?* Certainly not! So, I have the perfect solution. I'll wait here—and you go out and *shnorr* until you have the cost of this dinner!"

That, certainly, is *chutzpa.*

"The bashful go to Paradise," said Judah ha-Nasi, twenty centuries ago, "and the brazen go to Purgatory."

A friend of mine swears that in a Jewish restaurant he once asked a passing waiter: "What time is it?"

Icily, the waiter said, "You aren't my table."

The Language of Jazz Musicians

Norman D. Hinton

This glossary makes no pretensions to completeness. It is simply a list of words used by jazz musicians in their everyday speech with equals. Some of the etymologies may seem fanciful; these men do not worry themselves about the origins of their words. I believe, however, that the etymologies are correct, and I can vouch for the use of the words.

Apple, the, *n.* New York City. Derivation obscure, but dates from the late '30's, when New York was the center of jazz in America. Occ. [occasional], o.f. [old-fashioned]

ax, *n.* Any of the solo reed or (less commonly) brass instruments. Orig. a saxophone. Fr. fancied resemblance in shape plus the abbr. *sax.* Occ.

bad, *adj.* & *adv.* Good. However, at times, it may mean "bad," and the listener must determine meaning fr. context, tone of voice, facial expression, etc. Occ., older.

beat, *n.* & *v.* (*p.p.*) (1) As *n.,* musical rhythm, "the beat" (fr. *beat time*). (2) As *v.,* tired, exhausted (preservation of old p.p.; comm. [common] usage particularly adopted by jazzmen. *OED* citations from 1830 on). Both comm. (Actually 1 & 2 *altogether* separate terms.)

blow, *v.* Orig. to play a wind instrument. Generalized to performing upon any instrument (thus, one can "blow guitar"). Probably fr. fact that all solo instruments in traditional jazz are wind instr. Comm.

box, *n.* A piano (undoubtedly fr. shape of upright piano and spinet, usually found in jazz night clubs). Comm., rec. [recent]

bread, *n.* Money. A double pun—(1) "dough," (2) bread, the necessity. Occ., rec. (Invented by Dizzy Gillespie.)

bring down, *v.* To make one feel low. See *put down.* Occ., rec. in this sense. (Obs.—to make one feel good—out of use since the '30's.)

bug, *v.* To bother, especially to get one in such a state that he cannot play well. Extended to mean getting annoyed at anything.

cat, *n.* Orig., one who was "hep." Obs. in this sense; now, any person. (Thus, a musician can now speak of a "square cat"—a contradiction in terms in the '30's.) Comm.

changes, *n.* The chords for whatever melody is being used as a basis for improvisation. Comm., older.

chase, *n.* A 32-bar chorus divided so that two men (usually) take alternate four- or eight-bar sections. Occ.

chick, *n.* A girl. Not specifically a jazzman's term, but very common.

clinker, *n.* A missed note, or other error in playing. Largely replaced by *goof* (q.v.). Occ., o.f.

combo, *n.* A small band, a "combination" of from three to ten pieces. Basic, comm.

come on, *v.* Strictly, to begin a chorus, but almost always used with an approving or disparaging phrase—"Man, you came on like the end." Older (one of the oldest words still in use), comm.

cool, *n. & adj.* Agreeing with the generally received aesthetic standards of the modern jazzman. Basic, comm.

corny, *adj.* Non-jazz, extremely commercial music. Origin doubtful, but since it is often expanded to "corn-fed" and "corn-ball" (or may actually have been a clipped form of one of these words), I think it once meant "country" music: polkas, square dance music, etc. Comm., basic, older.

crazy, *adj.* Like *cool* and almost interchangeable with it. Fr. description of bop as "crazy music." Has to do most basically with harmonies used in playing, but generalized like *cool.* Comm., basic.

cut, *v.i. & t.* (1) (intr.) To leave. Usually to "cut out" (cut = leave out, leave). "Man, nothin's happening, let's cut out!" Occ., rec. (2) (tr.) To play an instrument better than another musician, or to produce better jazz than another. Also said of whole orchestras. The winner in a musical contest is said to have "cut" the other. Comm., older (even pre-'30's).

cute, *adv.* (Playing) in an ingenious, intriguing manner. Occ., in an amusing manner. Occ., rec.

dig, *v.* To understand and agree with: not limited to music alone. (Perhaps fr. a sense of "getting to the bottom" of things.) Comm., older, basic.

end, the, *n.* The best, the most pleasing. Like *most* (q.v.), but better. *Absolute end, n.,* intensified form. Comm., basic.

eyes, *n.* An expression denoting approval. "I've got eyes for that" means "I like it." Extreme approval is expressed by the qualifying words "big" or "bulging." Invented by Lester Young. Comm.

fake, *v.* To imrovise. Sometimes also means to pretend to know a tune, but usually has meaning above. Comm., older.

flip, *v.* To approve wildly. Orig. to "flip one's wig" (akin to "blow one's top," but never denotes anger for jazzmen). Usually indicates response to another's solo. Comm.

funky, *n.* An old word, orig. meaning earthy or odorous. Now, a piece or player imbued with the basic spirit of the blues, although in a modern idiom. Occ. (The *original* meaning is obs.; the newer meaning is rec.)

gas, *v.* & *n.* To please, or, as noun, spoken of a situation which pleases—"It's a gas!" gasser, *n.* Something which pleases extremely. Origin unknown, at least to me. Occ.

go, *expl.* Really a fan's word, to express excitement at a particularly "swingin' " solo. Often used derisively, sometimes approvingly, by musicians. (The fan's full phrase is "Go, man, go!") Occ.

gone, *adj.* In the ultimate state of happiness, usually inspired by music. *Real gone, adj.,* intensified form. (Perhaps from dope addiction, but it is equally possible that the borrowing went the other way.) Occ., older. the gonest, *n.* *The most, etc.*

goof, *n.* & *v.* A mistake in playing, and to make that mistake. Extended to all errors. Comm., basic.

greatest, *n.* See *most, end.* Comm.

head arrangement. A musical arrangement which is not written down and never has been, but is known by all the members of the ensemble. Usually the product of group effort. Comm.

hep, *v.* See *hip.* O.f.

hip, *v.* "In the know," or one of the elite. Occ. means simply to understand. Comm., basic.

horn, *n.* Any musical instrument, but especially (and originally *only*) the wind instruments. (See *blow* for a similar extension.) Comm.

jazz, *n.* Nonsense, completely worthless information or attitude. "Don't hand me that jazz" = "quit kidding." Comm., rec.

jive, *n.* Same as *jazz.* Occ., o.f.

lead, *n.* The top, or melody part in an arrangement: therefore, the melodic line. lead man, *n.* One who plays the "lead" in his section of the ensemble. Comm., basic.

least, the, *n.* Opposite of *the most.* Occ.

like, *interj.* Means little or nothing. Used to fill up gaps in the sentence. Comm., rec.

Man, *interj.* Used in direct address. Comm., basic.

Mickey, *adj.* "Corny," old-fashioned, "ricky-tick" music. Short for "Mickey Mouse music," but usually abbreviated. Originally referred to the sort of pseudo-jazz that accompanied animated cartoons. Sometimes referred to as "businessman's bounce." Occ., o.f.

moldy fig. One who likes or plays "traditional" jazz exclusively. Comm. (Refers mostly to fans, not musicians.) Often abbr. *fig.*

most, *n.* The best, the most in line with jazzmen's aesthetic standards; see *cool, crazy.* Comm.

number, *n.* A tune. Perhaps from the fact that bands give their arrangements numbers rather than names, to make filing easier. Comm., basic.

pad, *n.* A bed. Extended to mean bedroom, or even apartment. Occ.

put down, *v.* To belittle, criticize adversely, another man's playing. Perhaps related to *bring down* (q.v.). Occ., rec.

ride-out, *n.* The final chorus of an arrangement. (In dixieland, the clarinet "rides" above the ensemble.) Occ., o.f.

riff, *n.* & *v.* A short musical phrase (usually 4 or 8 bars), whose chords, repeated the length of a chorus, become the basis for improvisation. To play a riff. Origin doubtful. Comm., older, basic.

see, *v.* To read music. Occ., rec.

session, *n.* Shortened form of obs. *jam session;* an informal gathering of musicians playing for their own amusement. Occ., older.

square, *n.* Not in accordance with the jazzman's aesthetic standards. Probably comes from steady 1-2-3-4 rhythm without variation. Many musicians, while saying the word, will make a motion similar to the band director's indication for 4/4 time—the hand moves in a square for the four beats. Comm., older, basic.

swing, *v.* To play well in all senses, technically and otherwise, but especially to have the basic feel for jazz rhythms. A man can play well harmonically and rhythmically, but he will not swing without a feel for "the beat." Comm., older, basic.

swingin', *adj.* Actually, the participle of *swing,* but used for many non-musical things. The highest term of approval. May be applied to anything a jazzman likes, or any person. (Although the verb is of long standing, the use of the participle is relatively recent.) Comm., basic.

too much, *adj.* Same as *the most, the greatest.* Comm.

way out, *adj.* Departing greatly from the norm; especially said of unusual (or unusually good) treatment of melody or harmony; now of anything that seems especially good—though still used in the original sense too. Occ., older (found on records in the '30's).

wig, *v.* To think; to play extremely intellectual music. Occ., rec.

wild, *adj.* Same as *crazy, cool.* Occ.

worst, the, *n.* Opposite of *most, end,* etc. See *least.* Occ.

write, *v.* To make an arrangement. writer, *n.* Arranger. Comm.

you know, *inter. phr.* Means nothing (see *like*), but used as a question at the end of a statement.

Linguistic Geography

Dwight Bolinger

Serious investigation of geographical dialects began in the latter part of the nineteenth century. The first comprehensive study was made in North and Central Germany by Georg Wenker. A smaller study followed in Denmark, and between 1902 and 1908 Jules Gilliéron published his *Atlas Linguistique de la France*, the most influential work of its kind. Since the turn of the century materials have been collected for similar atlases all over the world. In the United States the model has been the *Linguistic Atlas of New England*, directed by Hans Kurath and published between 1939 and 1943. Other regional atlases covering most of the country have been drawn up as part of a comprehensive *Linguistic Atlas of the United States and Canada*, still in preparation.

As the name implies, a linguistic atlas is a collection of maps showing the prevalence of particular speech forms in particular areas. What the dialect geographer most often selects to mark off a dialect area is simply its preference for certain words. Differences in pronunciation or syntax yield a more reliable measure, but words are easier to work with; information can even be gathered by mail through a questionnaire that asks what words a speaker uses for particular meanings: is a field enclosure made of stone called a *stone wall*, a *stone fence*, a *rock wall*, or a *rock fence?* Are drains that take rainwater off a roof called *eaves troughs, water spouting, gutters,* or *rain spouts?* For greater accuracy, detailed phonetic information is needed. Trained interviewers must be sent to the scene and may spend hours with a single informant. Does he pronounce *soot* to rime with *boot* or with *put?* Is his final consonant in *with* like that of *bath* or that of *bathe?* Does his pronunciation of *tomato* end with the same vowel sound as *panda* or is it like *grotto?* The Swiss German atlas, published in 1962, was based on a questionnaire containing 2,600 items, which took from four to eight days to administer. Its phonetic discriminations were exquisite—as many as twenty-one different tongue heights, for example, in front unrounded vowels.[1] The items chosen for a questionnaire to test differences in vocabulary, pronunciation, and syntax are the ones most likely to reveal the peculiarities of everyday speech: names of household objects, foods, parts of the body, weather phenomena, numbers, and so on.

---

[1] William Moulton, review in *Journal of English and German Philology* 62.831 (1963).

AMERICAN DIALECT GEOGRAPHY

Unless he is combining his interest as a linguist with an extracurricular one as a folklorist or sociologist, the dialect geographer is less concerned with the items in a questionnaire for their own sake than as indicators of where to draw the boundary lines and how to trace the routes of speakers as they migrated from one area to another. The latter—the fanning out of dialects from their original centers and their crisscrossing and blending as the wave moves outward—is of special significance in a country like the United States, with its extraordinarily mobile population.

Boundaries are set by mapping the farthest points to which a given form has penetrated. When a line—termed an *isogloss* if it has to do with words, an *isophone* if with sounds—is drawn connecting these points, it is usually found to lie close to the lines drawn for other forms—for instance, the same speakers who say *snake feeder* for 'dragonfly' are also apt to pronounce the word greasy as greazy. The interlocking lines form a bundle of isoglosses (or isophones) and represent the frontier of the dialect in question.

American English divides rather clearly into three grand dialect areas in the eastern part of the country. They reflect the settlement of these areas by early migrants from England who brought their dialects with them. One such dialectal transplant from England is the vowel in words like *half, bath, aunt, glass,* and *laugh.* We easily recognize one way of pronouncing these words as a feature of cultivated speech in the East and of over-cultivated speech elsewhere. It is by no means uniform (in Eastern Virginia, for example, it will be heard in *master* and *aunt* but not in many other words), and represents one side of a split that took place in the eastern counties of England before the American Revolution. The /a/ was transplanted from those counties as folk speech by immigrants to New England, but it also took root in London and so became established as fashionable speech in the parts of the country that maintained the closest ties with England.[2] The map shows the three areas (plus subdialectal sections) known, from their geographical position, as Northern, Midland, and Southern.

As the population spread westward the boundaries became more and more blurred. The earlier, more gradual movement extended them fairly evenly as far as the Mississippi. . . . By the time the migrants had flowed up against the Rocky Mountains, the three tides had broken into a series of rivulets and eddies. Where a given area was settled mainly by speakers of a given dialect, that dialect of course prevailed. The area around Hayden, Colorado, was turned into a kind of Northern island by a group of women schoolteachers who came out from Ann Arbor, Michigan, and married ranchers there. Later, as younger speakers grew up and intermarried, Northern and Midland traits were blended. . . .

---

[2] Hans Kurath, "Some Aspects of Atlantic Seaboard English Considered in Their Connections with British English," in *Communications et Rapports du Premier Congrès International de Dialectologie Générale* (Louvain, Belgium, 1965), pp. 239-40.

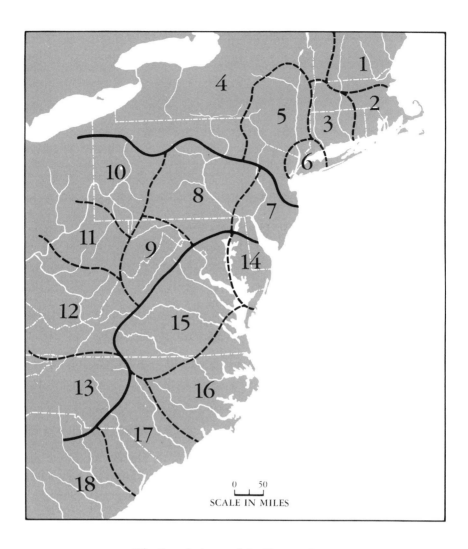

The Speech Areas of the Eastern States

The North	The Midland	The South
1. N.E. New England	7. Delaware Valley	14. Delamarvia (E. shore of Maryland and Virginia, and S. Delaware)
2. S.E. New England	8. Susquehanna Valley	
3. S.W. New England	9. Upper Potomac and Shenandoah Valleys	
4. Upstate New York and W. Vermont	10. Upper Ohio Valley	15. Virginia Piedmont
5. Hudson Valley	11. N. West Virginia	16. N.E. No. Carolina (Albemarle Sound and Neuse Valley)
6. Metropolitan New York	12. S. West Virginia	
	13. W. No. and W. So. Carolina	17. Cape Fear and Peedee Valleys
		18. So. Carolina

Dialect blending is not confined to the West but goes on wherever the streams of communication, which seem to grow swifter every day, overflow the earlier lines. In northern Illinois, for example, which [is divided into] a Northern and a Midland dialect area, the lines again are growing dim. The following list—of interest also as a sample of the kind of vocabulary used—enumerates words that are receding in the predominantly Midland area of Illinois, even though half of them were Midland to begin with:

1. window blind 'shade for a window, on a spring roller' (Midland)
2. woodshed
3. pigpen
4. pulley bone 'breastbone of a chicken, wishbone' (Southern, South Midland)
5. light bread 'bread made with yeast' (Southern, South Midland)
6. hay doodle 'small pile of hay' (Midland)
7. trestle 'saw horse with an X-frame'
8. poo-wee!, a call to hogs
9. poison vine 'poison ivy'
10. cement road 'concrete road'
11. to favor 'to resemble,' as in *John favors his father*
12. baby cab 'baby carriage' (Midland)
13. belling 'shivaree' (Midland)
14. belly buster 'dive in coasting prone on a sled, belly flop' (Midland)[3]

Two metaphors describe the extremes of diffusion. One is the relay race, the other the cross-country. In the first, a speaker picks up something from his neighbor to the east and runs with it as far as his neighbor to the west, always staying between them. In the second, a speaker breaks loose from the paternal neighborhood and travels to all points of the compass, picking up pieces at each stop and dropping them all along the way. The latter is the kind of diffusion that makes dialectology a hazardous business. As Robert Louis Stevenson wrote in *The Amateur Emigrant,*

> I knew I liked Mr. Jones from the moment I saw him. I thought him by his face to be Scottish; nor could his accent undeceive me. For as there is a *lingua franca* of many tongues on the moles and in the feluccas of the Mediterranean, so there is a free or common accent among English-speaking men who follow the sea. They catch a twang of a New England port, from a cockney skipper, even a Scotsman sometimes learns to drop an *h;* a word of a dialect is picked up from another hand in the forecastle; until often the result is undecipherable, and you have to ask for a man's place of birth.[4]

[3] Roger W. Shuy, "The Northern-Midland Dialect Boundary in Illinois," *Publications of the American Dialect Society* No. 38, November, 1962, p. 59. Professor Shuy was kind enough to provide definitions.
[4] South Seas Edition (New York: Charles Scribner's Sons, Inc., 1925), p. 9.

The compilers of the new *Dictionary of American Regional English* are at present engaged in one of the largest word-gathering projects in history—a five-year (1965–70) survey of the dialects of the United States from Florida to Alaska in an effort "to collect the greater part . . . of the words and phrases, pronunciations, spellings, and meanings used . . . up to the present time." [5] Besides bringing to light the quantities of unregistered written forms in obscure places, this project will rescue uncounted expressions that would otherwise be lost as their users died away because the forms existed only in the spoken language. The estimated five million entries will be processed by computers. (The compilers of the vast *Oxford Dictionary* assembled three and a half million entries by hand.)

But geography is not all. The fading of differences is accelerated by social pressures. Where a normalized, cultivated speech gains in favor—and this, we should remember, was until recently the largest single result of formal schooling—everything with a pronounced local or, especially, rustic flavor tends to be rooted out. Thus, in the area of northern Illinois already discussed, the cultivated forms *I ran home yesterday, He did it, I'm going to lie down* are replacing the uncultivated—whether Northern or Midland—*I run home yesterday, He done it, I'm going to lay down*.[6]

DIALECT GEOGRAPHY IN EUROPE

In Europe, dialect geography lacks much of the here-and-now flavor that it has in the United States. With a more stable population and with more radical linguistic as well as geographical and political barriers to surmount, European dialects are bound more tightly to their localities and have more to tell us about events long ago than about recent ones.

The most thoroughly investigated dialects anywhere in the world are those of the Romance languages, which are themselves, of course, just dialects of Latin that drifted apart in the early years of the Christian era. Since more is known about Latin—thanks partly to the very dialectal facts that it helps to illuminate—than about any other ancient language, dialectology in the Romance area has closer ties to historical linguistics than it has anywhere else.

As an illustration of these ties, take the conflict of homonyms, which was one of the main interests of those who worked on the French atlas. A perennial linguistic question is why words disappear. The most famous example is the French word for *cock*. In southern France, the normal development of the expected Latin word, *gallus*, would have been *gat*. But in the same area the word *cattus* had an equal right to give *gat*, and it actually did produce

[5] Frederic G. Cassidy, "American Regionalism and the Harmless Drudge," *Publications of the Modern Language Association* 82:3.14 (1967).
[6] Shuy, *op. cit.*, p. 64.

that form. Had *gallus* been retained, the result would have been two meanings, 'cat' and 'cock,' both carried by the same form; and, unlike *so* and *sew* or *be* and *bee,* these two were the same part of speech and were apt to occur in similar contexts where they would have caused confusion. As with English *queen* and *quean,* one of them had to go, so speakers substituted other words for *gallus:* one meaning 'chicken,' one meaning 'pheasant,' and a third meaning, literally, 'priest.' In this case, knowing the dialectal facts helped to interpret the historical ones.

The dialectologist who looked most consistently to geography as a key to the history of dialects was the Italian Matteo Bàrtoli. It should be possible, he thought, to correlate the past evolution of dialects with their positions relative to one another, and he expressed the correlation in a set of four "areal norms":

1. Norm of the isolated area. An area that is cut off and shielded from communication tends to retain older forms.
2. Norm of the lateral area. Where a central area is wedged into the middle of a zone that presumably was once homogeneous, the edges tend to retain older forms.
3. Norm of the principal area. If the zone is split into two segments, the larger one tends to have the older forms. (This is in partial conflict with 1 and 2.)
4. Norm of the later area. An area that has been overrun—as by conquest— at a more recent date tends to have older forms.

Spain	France	Italy	Rumania
hermoso	beau	bello	frumos
mesa	table	tavola	masa
hervir	bouillir	bollire	a fierbe
entonces	alors	allora	atunci
día	jour	giorno	zi
más	plus	più	mai

FROM Eugenio Coseriu, *La Geografía Lingüística* (Montevideo: Instituto de Filología, 1956), p. 38.

The norm of the lateral area is the most picturesque, with its suggestion of an adventurous dialect driving across the territory of a sedentary one and overspreading it everywhere except at the edges. Using the Romance languages in their present state as evidence of what probably happened while the speakers of Vulgar Latin were still more or less in touch with Rome, we can see in the table above the effect of continued contact in France and Italy as against interrupted contact, and hence the retention of older forms, in Spain and Rumania.

The norm of the lateral area explains how it can happen that countries as far apart as Rumania and Spain share forms and meanings that are missing in the areas that lie between.

Regionalism in American English

Hans Kurath

I'll describe the regional dissemination of some variant pronunciation on the Atlantic Seaboard, where about 1500 speakers have been interviewed in their homes by the field workers of the Linguistic Atlas of the United States. . . .

1. door, care, here [Page references to Hans Kurath and Raven I. McDavid, Jr., *The Pronunciation of English in the Atlantic States* (1961), following these and other key words have been omitted.] Four geographically separate areas in the Atlantic States lack final and preconsonantal /r/: Eastern New England (as far west as the Connecticut River); Metropolitan New York and surroundings; Virginia east of the Blue Ridge with adjoining sections of Maryland and north central North Carolina; and South Carolina and Georgia. The last of these "*r*-less" areas extends westward along the Gulf of Mexico to south central Texas and is roughly coextensive with the cotton belt, the old plantation country. On the periphery of these four areas, the "*r*-less" type carries social prestige and is being adopted by the better educated. This feature of pronunciation is current in well defined subareas and follows clear rules. It is characteristic of the speech of about one third of the population of the United States. I see no reason whatever why our dictionaries should not convey this information, either once for all in the Introduction or by printing the *r* in italics in the body of the dictionary, when it is not sounded as such in the four areas mentioned above. They might even point out that these areas agree with Standard British English in this respect.

2. glass, pasture, afternoon, bath Most Americans have the vowel of *hat* also before friction sounds, as in *after, bath, rather, glass*. But some New Englanders use the low-front or low-central vowel of *father* in such words. This usage is especially common in eastern Massachusetts (the Boston area) and in Maine. Elsewhere in New England this sound is used rather sporadically by better educated urbanites, and, curiously enough, by old fashioned rustics. This social dissemination points to conflicting trends in usage within New England. Outside of New England, this sound is used to some extent in Metropolitan New York and in Virginia, where it is a mark of distinction among persons of social pretensions. Not very long ago some Midwesterners, especially those of New England descent, were inclined to adopt it; but the waning prestige of New England has discouraged this effort. One might say that the Midwest has grown up.

What should the dictionaries do in this case? They should certainly state in the Introduction that the low vowel in such words is chiefly a New Englandism, but has some currency elsewhere; and that is rather often used by actors in the serious classical drama in conformity with British English usage. However, owing to its inconsistent use even in Eastern New England, this regional variant must be given for each word in which it occurs in the body of the dictionary. The *Pronouncing Dictionary of American English* by J. S. Kenyon and T. A. Knott (1944) will serve them well for New England, and the collections of the Linguistic Atlas of the Eastern States provide at least some information on Metropolitan New York and Virginia.

3. new Words like *new, tube, student, due,* usually have no consonant /y/ before the vowel in Pennsylvania and to the north of it. Here *news* begins like *noose, tube* like *tool, student* like *stool,* and *due* is homophonous with *do.* From Virginia southward, on the other hand, the consonant /y/ is always there, however faintly articulated. The regional dissemination of these two types of pronunciation is so clear in the Eastern States that every dictionary should provide this information. As far as the Midwest is concerned, it is fairly safe to predict that it agrees with the North Atlantic States; and the Lower South from Georgia westward may be expected to fall in line with Virginia and the Carolinas. But we will not really know this until the findings of field surveys of these areas have been completed and published. Usage in the wide Midland belt, including the valleys of the Ohio River and its southern tributaries, is hard to forecast. Only a systematic survey will give us the answer. Does Iowa fall in with the North or with the Midland?

In passing, I should perhaps say that after labial and velar consonants, as in *pure, beauty, accuse, argue,* all varieties of cultivated American English have the consonant /y/ before the vowel.

4. coop Before lip consonants, as in *coop, hoop, hoof, roof, room, broom,* and also before /t/ as in *root, soot,* some areas have the vowel of *too,* others that of *book.* In *coop* the regional dissemination of the variants is clear-cut. North of a line running along the southern boundary of Pennsylvania *coop* has the same vowel as *too,* south of it that of *book.* This fact should of course be recorded in any good dictionary of American English. Unfortunately, the incidence of these two different vowels is apt to vary from word to word. Thus, for instance, *room* usually has the vowel of *book* in Eastern New England and in Eastern Virginia, but rarely elsewhere. For this variant feature we must have a regional record of each word in which it occurs. Failing that, the dictionary can only report the existence of the variation without indicating the habitat of the variants.

5. creek North of a line passing from west to east in West Virginia and Virginia, *creek* generally rhymes with *sick,* to the south of it with *seek.* In New England and especially in New York City, some cultured speakers deviate from the regional "norm," prompted by the spelling. In this case the dictionaries should report not only the existence of the variants, but also where each predominates. Of course, we do not yet have the relevant information for large sections of the country.

6. tomato As a curiosity, I will describe the choice of the stressed vowel in *tomato* on the part of 150 cultured speakers in the Eastern States. In New England, Metropolitan New York, Philadelphia, and Virginia, the vowel of *father* predominates in this word, elsewhere that of *fate*. Middle class speakers predominantly rhyme the word with *Plato* in the entire area, and some of the "folk" with *matter*. The social distribution of these three pronunciations makes it a convenient social shibboleth in parts of the Atlantic States. Whether this "gadget" works in other parts of the country, I do not know.

7. four, forty *Four* and *forty, hoarse* and *horse, mourning* and *morning* have different (contrasting) vowels in the greater part of the Eastern States, but in a belt extending westward from Metropolitan New York through New Jersey and Pennsylvania such pairs have the same vowel, so that *hoarse* and *horse* are homophonous.

8. stairs, care In words like *stairs, care*, the vowel varies regionally in a striking manner. The greater part of the South has here the vowel of *bat*, Pennsylvania the vowel of *bet*, coastal South Carolina the vowel of *bait*. New England exhibits all three variants, their frequency varying regionally.

9. Mary When we turn to words like *Mary* and *fairy* we find yet another dissemination pattern. Here the vowel of *bait* predominates in all of the southern coastal plain and in all of New England.

Dialects of American English

Carroll E. Reed

Figures given for each item in each of the states listed represent percentages of total responses for the item described. Data from California are incomplete, because the questionnaire was augmented after the appearance of David Reed's article on California variants and before the survey of the Pacific Northwest was started. Especially significant differences in percentages among the Pacific Coast states are highlighted here by the italicized figures.

	Washington	Idaho	Oregon	California
1. Words of general distribution throughout the Atlantic Coast states.				
haystack	98	100	100	94
mantel	98	100	98	
(*clothes*) *closet*	97	97	96	98
(*front*) *porch*	97	96	87	
(*just*) *a* (*little*) *way*(*s*)	88	96	95	92
shafts, shavs, shays	98	95	100	
wishbone	82	82	81	81

	Washington	Idaho	Oregon	California
(*saw*) *horse* (for wood)	77	85	86	
moo	61	58	62	59
privy	25	24	24	
backhouse	24	12	26	
faucet	91	68	97	96
corn bread	88	77	95	92
cottage cheese	71	62	77	79
dragonfly	66	49	66	61
(*back*) *porch*	61	41	60	
corn on the cob	67	66	49	
frying pan	69	61	59	72
seesaw	14	5	21	45
sick at the stomach	44	41	68	41
pancake	44	54	45	43

2. Words occurring in parts of the North, Midlands, and South (almost general)

	Washington	Idaho	Oregon	California
gutters	28	29	26	46
string beans	75	80	67	80
hay/barn loft	61	84	48	81
a bite (to eat)	12	16	7	16
snack	49	40	66	63
(*window*) *shades*	61	42	48	86
burlap bag/sack	2	6	8	26

3. Words occurring throughout the North and Midlands.

	Washington	Idaho	Oregon	California
sheaf	32	38	31	

4. Words occurring in parts of the North and Midlands.

4.1 Throughout the North and North Midlands.

	Washington	Idaho	Oregon	California
skunk	95	93	89	93
quarter of	12	13	18	27
(*hay*) *mow*	39	16	43	2
whinny	68	52	46	43
(*hay*) *cock*	0	17	3	18
whinner	3	4	0	

4.2 Parts of the North and Midlands.

	Washington	Idaho	Oregon	California
sled ("stoneboat")	37	16	51	
fish worm	14	4	31	21
sawbuck (for wood)	21	15	8	
drag ("stoneboat")	7	22	12	
stone drag ("stoneboat")	4	3	2	

	Wash-ington	Idaho	Oregon	Cali-fornia
5. Words occurring throughout the North and South.				
quarter to	81	54	*37*	66
baby carriage	13	13	13	23
6. Words occurring in parts of the North and South.				
6.1 Throughout the North and part of the South.				
kerosene	57	60	58	64
curtains ("shades")	2	*11*	2	5
6.2 Parts of New England and the South.				
low (of a cow)	15	*26*	13	11
serenade	3	4	2	11
whicker	2	0	0	0
7. Words occurring throughout the Midlands and the South.				
coal oil	42	38	41	*53*
skillet	24	36	*40*	34
spicket	2	2	1	2
pulley bone	0	0	3	4
corn pone	1	2	1	2
8. Words occurring in parts of the Midlands and the South.				
8.1 Everywhere south of the Mason-Dixon Line.				
singletree	91	97	94	
mush	86	82	80	
second crop	51	58	53	
bundle (of wheat)	50	37	62	
clabber(ed) (milk)	35	40	45	57
roasting ears	19	22	*40*	
dog irons	4	0	7	2
polecat	4	7	3	
barn lot	1	0	9	2
8.2 Virginia and West Midland.				
nicker	16	23	*37*	26
snake doctor ("dragonfly")	1	2	*10*	9
fishing worm	3	4	4	4
lamp oil	0	0	1	2
8.3 Restricted parts of the Midlands and the South.				
second cutting	48	38	45	
quarter till	5	10	*27*	4

	Wash-ington	Idaho	Oregon	Cali-fornia
smearcase	7	0	9	12
a (little) piece ("way")	4	2	3	4
fish bait	3	2	7	
(hay) rick	2	0	1	2
pile of hay	0	0	0	8

9. Words occurring throughout the North.

come/co/here boss(ie)	90	91	75	
eaves troughs	38	22	*48*	18
(devil's)darning needle ("dragonfly")	23	*45*	9	13
johnny cake	11	*21*	4	7
spider ("frying pan")	5	3	1	4

10. Words occurring in part of the North.

10.1 Throughout New England and in some other Northern areas.

outhouse	**34**	*44*	37	
Dutch cheese	17	*24*	9	6
teeter(ing) board	3	2	4	*26*

10.2 Restricted parts of the North.

stoneboat/-bolt	51	44	35	
hay-tumble	10	0	0	0
stoop	10	10	6	
bellow, beller (of a cow)	8	6	2	
whippletree	6	3	5	
minnies ("minnows")	4	7	5	

11. Words occurring throughout the Midlands.

(window) blinds	37	46	*50*	27
soo(k)(ie) boss(ie)	11	9	25	
snake feeder ("dragonfly")	8	2	*11*	6
spouts, spouting	2	4	1	1
spigot	1	0	0	1

12. Words occurring in part of the Midlands.

green beans	25	20	31	17
bawl (of a cow)	13	4	20	
piece ("snack")	12	14	10	6
curdled milk	1	2	3	
cruddled milk	0	0	2	3
thick milk	0	0	2	2

	Wash-ington	Idaho	Oregon	Cali-fornia
13. Words occurring throughout the South.				
snap beans	0	0	2	4
14. Words occurring in part of the South.				
mosquito hawk	1	2	3	9
earthworm	1	0	5	8
shelf ("mantel")	1	0	1	
hand irons	0	0	0	2
15. Words of "unexpected frequency."				
15.1 Primarily Northern.				
angleworm	63	73	37	53
sick to the stomach	49	53	29	46
15.2 North and Midland.				
shivaree	97	96	98	78
gunny bag/sack	86	86	82	66
teeter-totter	83	93	78	43
baby buggy	80	74	81	85
15.3 Primarily Midland.				
hot cakes	49	40	53	65
(hay) shocks	30	41	72	55
15.4 Western.				
grate	18	25	20	20
corral	8	40	22	51
flapjacks	3	4	1	7
barley sack	0	0	0	6
15.5 Ohio Valley.				
rack ("sawhorse")	2	0	0	
15.6 Due to urban unfamiliarity with the item.				
sour(ed) milk	64	58	54	46
breast bone ("wishbone")	18	18	16	19
worm ("angleworm")	16	19	13	19
drainpipes	15	26	15	26
eaves	10	19	6	21
hay stack (for "shock")	3	2	2	12

	Wash-ington	Idaho	Oregon	Cali-fornia
15.7 Others.				
tap ("faucet")	6	*36*	2	
veranda ("back porch")	3	4	*13*	
slip ("stoneboat")	0	*3*	0	

WORKING WITH THE SELECTIONS

1. Do not be surprised if you find some of the details of the rogue's cant puzzling—it was meant to be, and some of it is still obscure. An *vpright man* was anything but what would now be called an upright man, but he may have been named that because he need not bow to any man, at least not among the rogues. Nor do we know why a rogue's trollope was called a *doxy,* perhaps from an old word for buttock, perhaps from a Dutch word for a doll, perhaps from some source not as yet thought of. Some you should be able to figure out; *pecke* would seem to be food and *chete* a generic term. What is probably the modern form of *bouse?* What is the relationship between *bene, benebouse,* and *beneship?* Try a few more.

2. Both the vocabulary and the grammar of this sample of a pidgin are interesting—*pidgin* is presumably only the pidgin word for *business;* that is, *pidgin* is the English used for business, but it seems to be used also for any conversation with a native in New Guinea who has not learned English. Most of the words are English, *boy,* for example,—although *boy* is obviously not used as it is in English—or are made up of English words, *walkabout, whosat, allasame,* however corrupted. Some look as though they are native. Some are apparently borrowed from other languages; one wonders how *calaboose* got to New Guinea. Through some American sailor? It is presumably Mexican Spanish borrowed into American English. If you have studied German, you can probably guess why *rausim* means what it seems to. What, apparently, does *finis* do in a sentence? Try to find out what *belong* means. Does it mean the same as *long?* What does *Xmas* mean? Try to figure out some of the grammar. The pronominal system is interesting; how does this pidgin handle what we would call the genitive or possessive? In this connection, also, you may want to consider a grammatical device common in many languages, although not much used in English, called incorporation, in which either the subject or the complement or both can be built into the verb, just as though *He spoke to her* could be *hespoketo her* or *he spoketoher* or even *hespoketoher.* Can you find examples of incorporation in this pidgin?

3. You will recall that in Part 1 you read a description of how a chimpanzee, Washoe, learned a little English by sign language. In some ways Washoe's experience must have paralleled that of the New Guineans developing a pidgin, except that Washoe had no native language to start with. In the light of this pidgin, reexamine some of Washoe's language. Can you find her doing any things to English that the speakers of pidgin did?

4. One can appreciate *chutzpa* better after reading Rosten's exposition, but few of us who do not have an intimate knowledge of Yiddish are ever likely to grasp either its connotation or its denotation entirely. If you are familiar with any other language, you must be aware of words that cannot be adequately rendered into English. Try providing examples.

5. Hinton published his collection of jazz musicians' terms in 1958. What musical terms have appeared since then? How can you determine what they mean? You might try making up a list, defining the terms, indicating their currency, their origin, their recency, and the like. Try the same thing for another pursuit with which you are familiar—perhaps skiing, selling cosmetics, or working in a service station.

6. Bolinger is endeavoring to describe a complex subject in a simple way. He identifies two main dialect areas in the United States: (1) the eastern part of the country, which contains three dialect areas itself, and (2) areas to the west. Describe for yourself briefly what he claims are the main characteristics of each. Then pick an area you know—presumably a place where you have lived for some time—and see if you can describe the dialect there as a result of the influences Bolinger analyzes.

7. Using Kurath's key words, try to describe your own dialect. Do you speak a typical dialect, apparently characteristic of one area? Perhaps you live in one of those areas—much of the country, as a matter of fact—for which we have no very good evidence. Kurath was relying for evidence mainly on the Atlantic seaboard. If you live outside this area, can you see any relationship between your speech and the pronunciations Kurath describes? Do you find that Kurath identifies correct pronunciation, or the best English?

Later in the address from which the selection is taken, Kurath says that the statements about pronunciation in dictionaries are "a mess." He points out that general dictionaries are not well situated to reflect the multiplicity of dialects, but he seems to feel, also, that most dictionaries have handled pronunciation badly. Some dictionaries have improved their statements about pronunciation since Kurath read his paper. Does your dictionary reflect the multiplicity of American pronunciation, or does it seem to suggest that there is one right pronunciation and only one?

8. To have any fun with the lists Reed provides you will have to work backward and forward. For example, notice the various synonyms for *dragonfly* and for *angleworm*. If you are like most young Americans you have never seen a *stoneboat*—or is it a *slip*? The words and the synonyms that Reed lists are among those that have notable regional distribution in the United States. By observing which dialectal words you use and do not use, you may be able to make some inferences about your own speech.

4

Slang and College Slang

The two best reference works on American slang are The Dictionary of American Slang *(1960), edited by Harold Wentworth and Stuart Berg Flexner, and* The American Thesaurus of Slang *(1943), edited by Lester V. Berrey and Melvin Van den Bark. The first two selections below are taken from these works. The third selection, by Henry Kratz from* American Speech, *39 (October, 1964), broaches a more linguistic problem, "What Is College Slang?" Kratz, a professor of German at the University of Tennessee, was involved in the preparation of* Webster's Third New International Dictionary *(1961).*

Lovers

Lester V. Berrey and Melvin Van den Bark

Lovers; pair of lovers. 1. Arm-clutchers, arm-in-armers, bill-and-cooers, canoodlers, cuddle birds *or* doves, heart team, Jack and Jill, love birds *or* doves, playmates, twosome. *Spec.* sandwich, *a man between two women;* rose between two thorns, *a woman between two men;* the long and short of it, *a tall and short person together.*

2. LOVER. Adhesive plaster, arm-clutcher, arm-in-armer, bosom fly, chaser, crusher, cuddler, cuddler and cooer, dove, eye-gazer, fan, hanger-on, heart bandit, heart breaker *or* breaker-upper, heart palpitator *or* pumper, heaver, hot, hottotot, in-lover, love bird *or* dove, spoon, spooner, torch carrier, turtle-dove. *Spec.* Billy noodle, spoon, spooney, spoony, *a sentimental or silly lover;* thriller, *an exciting lover;* far-goner, gone case, *one seriously in love;* love pirate, spare, spare tire, *a rival lover;* cradle robber *or* snatcher, *one who makes love to a person much younger than himself;* loverly, *blend of "lover" and "lovely";* blind boy, *Cupid.*

3. LOVED ONE; SWEETHEART. Apple of the eye, captive, case, cream in one's coffee, crush, crushee, darl', darlink, date, dearie, dollink, enthusiasm, flame, flare, friend, headache, heart, heart beat, –flutter –interest, –rave, –throb &c., hon, honey, honey-bunch, honey-bunny, hun (*variant of "hon"*), idol, insomnia, jewel, light-of-his (*or* her) eyes *or* life, light o' love, love, lovee, love interest, lovey, lovey-dovey, mash, one's weakness, pash, pashtime, passion, pet, playmate, precious, precious heart, –lamb &c., prospect, pulse accelerator *or* upperer, purple passion, soft spot, sweetheart-darlin', sweetie, sweety, that

certain party, tootsy-wootsy, voom-voom, yoo-hoo. *Spec.* current, current excitement, latest enthusiasm, *the sweetheart of the moment;* the ex, ex-heart, His *or* Her Ex, old *or* extinguished flame, *a former sweetheart;* spare, spare tire, *a sweetheart in reserve;* hot and heavy, sweet-hot, *a passionate sweetheart;* secret sorrow, *a loved one who is unaware of one's affections.*

4. INAMORATA; "GIRL-FRIEND." Babe, baby, baby doll, bay-bee, bébé, broad, bunny, cherub, chick, chicky, cooky, cupid, cutems, cutie-pie, doll, dolling (*darling doll*), dolly, fair, fancy frail, femme fatale, friend-girl, gal, G.F. (*"girl-friend"*), Gill, girl, girl-friend, goody, goody-goody, goo-goo, honey child, jane, Jill, ladybird, lady friend, ladylove, little one *or* 'un, lovely, mamma, me goil *or* skoit, the missis, –missiz *or* missus, my *or* one's broad, –curve, –dame, –evie, –femme, –frail, –girl, –hotsy, –jane, –moll, –skirt, –twist, –wench, –woman &c., patootie, peach, plaything, pretty, pretty-pretty, puss, pussy, queen, queenie, sheba, sugar, sweet, sweetalums, sweet baby, –mama, –kid, –stuff, –thing, –woman &c., sweetie-pie, sweetkins, sweetness, sweet patootie, sweets, sweetums, toy, the young lady, the Y.L. (*Include also above,* 443.3.) *Spec.* moll, *esp. a gangster's sweetheart;* black *or* dark meat, sweet chocolate, brown sugar, sugar-brown, *a Negress sweetheart;* spare, sparerib, *a "girl friend" who is not one's steady sweetheart;* Her Ex, X.Y.L., *the "ex-young lady" or former sweetheart;* chased woman, drag, dragout, rushee, *one being "rushed" or courted;* college widow, *a noncollege girl who goes with students.*

5. BEAU. Ace of hearts, angler, answer to a maiden's prayer, bachelor of hearts, bagdaddy, B.F. (*"boy-friend"*), bosom buddy *or* pal, boy, boy-friend, buddy, cake, Casanova, courteer, crusher, daddy, ding-dong daddy, Don Juan, fellow, feminine heart pumper, flame, follower, friend-boy, goof, guy, handy man, honey-boy, Jack, Jack of hearts, John, Johnnie, knave of hearts, Lothario, man, man on the make, papa, promoter, pursuer, queener, Romeo, rusher, spark, sparker, squire, stud, Sunday man, swain, sweet man, sweet papa *or* daddy, young man. (*Include also above,* 443.2,3.) *Spec.* Billy Noodle, *one who is foolish over girls;* high-pressure papa, hotcha papa, (red-) hot papa *or* daddy, hot flame, *a passionate lover;* cooler-offer, *the lover of a "hot mamma";* billy goat, bull, turkey gobbler, (old) rooster, *a lover of advanced years;* money-honey &c. (*see* "Sugar daddy," 445.5), *a wealthy lover, esp. of a "gold digger";* uncalcimined daddy, *an unpolished lover;* apache, caveman, *a violent, tempestuous lover;* old *or* extinguished flame, His Ex, *a former beau;* cineman on the make, Hollywooer, screen *or* shadow lover, *a motion-picture lover;* fancy man, freeholder, *a prostitute's lover;* court plaster, *an unwanted lover;* no Casanova, –Lothario &c., *said of one who is not the lover type;* stag line, *one's corps of beaux.*

6. STEADY SWEETHEART. The Big *or* Biggest Enthusiasm, –Excitement *or* Moment, favorite *or* main dish, the Grandest Passion, grand passion, the Great Weakness, heavy, hot and heavy, main enthusiasm, the One and Only, O.A.O. (*the "one and only," humorously the "off-and-on" sweetheart*), one's habit *or* everything, onliest, onliest one, the Only and Only, preferred stock, principal rave, regular, soulmate, steady, steady goer. *Spec.* ball-and-chain,

best girl, Guinea, heavy girl, HER, the Right Girl, the wife, *a steady "girl-friend"*; best boy, boke-regular, HIM, leading man, scriviss, heavy cake, –cookie *or* muffin, *a steady lover;* monog, *one who courts but one person at the time.*

Smooching

Harold Wentworth and Stuart Berg Flexner

smooch, smooge, smouge *v.i., v.t.* 1 To smudge, smear, or make dirty. *c1825–c1875.* 2 To cheat on an examination, esp. by copying another student's answers or by using a pony. *Some student use c1900.* → 3 To take; to borrow, esp. to borrow an item too insignificant to return; to mooch; to steal. 1941: "Then she went over to the cash box [and] smooched four $10 bills." Cain, *M. Pierce,* 152. 4 To kiss and caress; to pet or neck. 1937: "Once upon a time you 'spooned,' then you 'petted,' after that you 'necked'—still the most widely used term—but now you may 'smooch' or 'perch' or, reaching the heights of college argot, you may 'pitch and fling woo.'" E. Eldridge in *SEP,* Feb. 20, 89/2. 1951: "College kids are still smooching. . . ." M. Shulman, *Dobie Gillis,* 33 f. 1955: "After a few minutes of *torrid* hugging and smooching. . . ." C. Willingham, *To Eat A Peach,* 229. *n.* A kiss; kissing and caressing; necking. 1945: "'I'd rather have hooch/And a bit of a smooch.' When I asked [an Australian girl] what 'smooch' meant, she replied: 'Don't you know your own American slang?'" H. Boyle, AP, Oct. 27. **—er** *n.* 1 A habitual borrower; one who borrows or takes things without returning them; one who mooches. 2 A man or woman, usu. of student age, who will or likes to kiss and caress; one who indulges in smooching or necking. **—ing** *n.* Kissing; necking. 1949: "Good luck with the smooching!" Fibber McGee, radio, Oct. 18.

What Is College Slang?

Henry Kratz

This failure to distinguish clearly between college slang and general American slang is a common one in the college slang lists, and I have culled a few items from a number of these lists by way of example. I have not tried to be exhaustive, and many more could be pointed out for each article. In R. Bolwell, "College Slang Words and Phrases from Western Reserve University,"[1] I find *beef* "complain(t)," *buttonhole* (*v.*), *two bits;* in H. J. Savage, "College Slang Words and Phrases from Bryn Mawr College,"[2] *jazz, moron, snooty;* in William R. Morse, "Stanford Expressions,"[3] *fag* "cigarette," *corked* "intoxicated," *fall guy, rodeo* "a wild west show," *straight shooter;* in Carl Pingry and Vance Randolph, "Kansas University Slang,"[4] *bag* "a girl —usually a rather unattractive girl," *bitch* "something difficult or formidable," *frig* "to trick, to take advantage of," *shin-dig;* in Jason Almus Russell, "Colgate University Slang,"[5] *break* "good luck" (my definition), *big-shot, shut-eye;* in Virginia Carter, "University of Missouri Slang,"[6] *ask me another, big shot, cute as a bug's ear, I'll bite;* in J. Louis Kuethe, "Johns Hopkins Jargon,"[7] *knockout, to know one's onions, nuts, scram;* in John Ashton Shidler, "More Stanford Expressions,"[8] *Yarborough* "a worthless hand at bridge" (my definition), *suds* "beer"; in William White, "Whitman College Slang,"[9] *canned* "intoxicated," *make up my mind, time's a-wasting;* in Fred Eikel, Jr., "An Aggie Vocabulary of Slang,"[10] *bitch* "to gripe, complain," *shoot the bull, spuds* "potatoes"; in Lalia Phipps Boone, "Gator (University of Florida) Slang,"[11] *on cloud 88, the greatest, the most.*

Some of the lists present more specialized versions of the same problem. Many of the expressions in R. I. McDavid, Jr., "A Citadel Glossary,"[12] and in Eikel's "An Aggie Vocabulary . . . ," cited above, are surely general military slang. I suspect, also, that many of the expressions in Hugh Sebastian's interesting "Negro Slang in Lincoln University"[13] are general Negro slang, although he claims they are not.

Occasionally investigators have been aware of the problem. As early as 1905, E. H. Babbitt wrote:

> Of course the college student uses, in general, the same language as his brother who does not go to college, including probably a good many colloquialisms which may be classed as slang; that is, figurative expressions, which are not recognized as part of the literary language. Now the student is likely to have in circulation most of the slang current among all persons of his age, and he may have some which is current

---

[1] *Dialect Notes,* IV, Part 3 (1915), 231–38.

[2] *Ibid.,* V, Part 2 (1922), 139–48.

[3] *American Speech,* II (1927), 275–79.

[4] *Ibid.,* III (1928), 218–21.

[5] *Ibid.,* V (1930), 238–39.

[6] *American Speech,* VI (1931), 203–6.

[7] *Ibid.,* VII (1932), 327–38.

[8] *Ibid.,* pp. 434–37.

[9] *Ibid.,* XVIII (1943), 153–55.

[10] *Ibid.,* XXI (1946), 29–36.

[11] *Ibid.,* XXXIV (1959), 153–57.

[12] *Ibid.,* XIV (1939), 23–32.

[13] *Ibid.,* IX (1934), 287–90.

only among students or even only at particular institutions. The latter naturally belongs to our collection, while the former does not unless it presents distinctive features.[14]

In spite of the fact that he made a big point of eliminating general slang terms, we find in his list such general terms as *fluke, foxy, fresh, fudge* "a kind of candy," *hot tamale, josh, peach, sponge,* and *woozy.*

Sebastian[15] made the effort to leave out terms of general slang and **was** successful, so far as I can determine, except possibly for the general Negro terms I mentioned above. Kuethe felt that "a great deal of the slang in use" at Johns Hopkins was "adapted from outside sources,"[16] but then included many such expressions anyway. William White in "Whitman College Slang"[17] included only such terms as were not in the *American Thesaurus of Slang*[18] (although in "Wayne University Slang"[19] he gave many items that he felt were from other spheres, even though he believed most of the students at Wayne University were not even familiar with them).

The failure to consider the basic problem of specialized versus general slang often leads to the semantic inexactness to which I have alluded above. For instance, *fuzz* is given by Dundes and Schonhorn as meaning "the university police force," but it is, as I suppose everybody knows, a general slang term for "police." I cannot believe that the University of Kansas students interrogated really use it to mean specifically "the university police force," rather than "the police" in general. This is as if the interrogator had pointed to a piece of *filet mignon*, had received the response *meat*, and had reported *meat* as meaning "filet mignon" in the speech of the informant. In the same vein (although it is doubtful whether some of the following expressions given by Dundes and Schonhorn should be called slang at all), *bore* does not really mean specifically "an extremely poor and dull lecturer," but rather "a dull person"; *be called on the carpet* does not mean specifically "to be called to the Dean's office," but rather "to be reprimanded"; *clod, loser, dope,* and *dumb shit* do not mean specifically "a rather stupid student," but rather "a stupid person." The expressions garnered for "wasting time" (which is not a peculiarly collegiate pastime, and thus does not belong to the authors' group of academic terms) are also clearly general slang: *goofing off* (probably of military provenience), *screwing around, killing time, messing around, shooting the breeze.* The terms *odd ball, queer, fink, squirrel,* and *weird-o* mean not "an unusually odd student," but "an odd person"; *fink, queer, squirrel,* and *twink* mean not "a male student who never engages in social activities," but "an odd person"; *clod, slob, farmer, fink,* and *hick* mean not "an ill-

---

[14] "College Words and Phrases," *Dialect Notes*, II, Part 1 (1905), 11.

[15] See n. 13.

[16] Kuethe, "Johns Hopkins Jargon," *American Speech*, VII (1932), 327.

[17] See n. 9.

[18] Lester V. Berrey and Melvin Van den Bark, *American Thesaurus of Slang* (New York, 1942).

[19] *American Speech*, XXX (1955), 301–5.

mannered student with poor, unpolished manners," but "an ill-mannered person"; *tightwad, cheapskate, penny pincher, miser,* and *skin flint* mean not "a noticeably cheap date," but rather "a stingy person"; *whore, slut, bitch, easy mark,* and *punch* mean not "a female dated because of lax sexual habits," but simply "a female of lax sexual habits"; *slop, chow,* and *crap* mean not "college meals," but (for *chow*) "food," and (for *slop* and *crap*) "poor food."

While this kind of misdefining appears sporadically in the other college slang lists, it is especially prevalent in Dundes and Schonhorn's article because of the nature of their questionnaire: not wishing to be suggestive, they listed definitions, and it was their informants who supplied the words. Most of the other lists begin from the slang words themselves, at least in large measure. To avoid this type of misunderstanding, a possible corrective could be to submit the list of words garnered to an equal number of different students and to ask for definitions.

From a strictly descriptive point of view, the question of the provenience of a word is irrelevant, so that if a word is general slang there is no point in calling it college slang, even though it originated there, unless it has in college slang a meaning not present in general slang. If one wishes to include words of general slang because of their academic provenience, he must face the difficulty of determining whether they really are of academic provenience —something that frequently can be accomplished only by long individual investigations. Some cases are confused both semantically and historically. The word *brain* for "an intellectual" (or "a highly intelligent person"—my definition) is certainly general slang, as is *egghead.* However, the first citation for the former in the *DAS,* dated 1941, seems to indicate campus provenience, so perhaps it is not amiss here. I wonder whether *brain* and *bookworm* for "a studious classmate" are not further instances of too specific defining. The *DAS* inclines to the view that the odious term *brown nose* originated in the colleges and was transferred from there to the armed forces. The *DAS* claims student use c.1940 but gives no citations. I think that nevertheless it means "to curry favor," not specifically "to curry favor with a professor," as Dundes and Schonhorn would have it, so that its only justification in this list is its possible campus provenience. I myself rather suspect that its route is from the armed forces to academe. How prim and innocent our old term *apple-polish* sounds beside it!

Some of the terms that appear in college slang word lists are really technical terms of academic life. This was especially true on older lists, where one can find such terms as *fraternity, sophomore, undergraduate,* and so on. This is no longer the case; today our lists often include terms which, though originally perhaps slang, are now so old and well established as to be almost, if not entirely, out of the slang category. I am thinking of such words, included by Dundes and Schonhorn, as *cram* "to study extremely diligently for an examination," *cut* "to miss class," *crib* "to cheat during an examination," *flunk* "to fail to pass an examination," and *campus him* "to deprive a student . . . of campus privileges." It is interesting to note that the third edition of Webster's *New International Dictionary* lists all of these words in their academic meanings without any distinctive usage labels. Of course, this edition has been much assailed for its lack of such labels, but even the "stodgy" second edition, published twenty-seven years earlier, labeled *cram, cut,* and the verb *flunk* "colloq.," whereas *crib* is called "school slang," the noun *flunk* is labeled "sl. U.S.," and the verb *campus* is simply labeled "U.S."

The net effect of the publications on college slang has been to encourage the image of perky Joe College, who has only reluctantly discarded his raccoon coat and roadster in favor of a leather jacket and a motorcycle and who now plays a stereo set instead of a ukulele. Our impression is that his conversation combines all the more *outré* elements of jive talk, beatnik lingo, armed forces slang, and prison argot with a number of mysterious terms purely his own. We somehow feel that he is the luminous center of the slang universe, the creative force from which the rest of humanity draws its strength and inspiration.

To anyone who has spent much time among college students, this can come only as a tremendous surprise. The average college student is as creative in the area of slang as he is in the classroom. He is not unaffected by the various streams of slang that are constantly flowing, but not only is he not their main source of supply, he is, for the most part, not even directly in their path.

As a matter of fact it is the members of the younger set, the group in junior and senior high school, who are probably most directly responsible for the spread of slang. They are much more susceptible to the world of television comedians and commercials, to comic strips and disk jockeys, and are much more receptive to the tasteless and synthetic ephemera which these media do so much to promote.

But how *do* college students talk? Do they possess a really distinctive class dialect? I think so, but it does not consist simply of a number of outrageous slang expressions with which they interlard their speech. It consists, for one thing, of a number of technical terms pertaining to the curriculum, the grading system, dormitory living, and so on. It is full of all sorts of designations for buildings, parts of the campus, fraternities and sororities, and so on. It contains a great number of designations for the social affairs that are a major concern for most students, such as the various dances (the *Icebreaker, Junior Prom, Sophomore Soirée*), parties, games, homecoming weekends, and pledge and rush weeks. Such terms vary considerably from campus to campus, but there is a hard core that is the same everywhere; a lot of others are regional rather than local. Many of the terms are slang.

WORKING WITH THE SELECTIONS

1. Both the book by Berrey and Van den Bark and that by Wentworth and Flexner are wordbooks, but the editors have given them different generic terms. What is the difference between such books?

2. In their Introduction Berrey and Van den Bark refer to the contents of the

book sometimes as "slang," sometimes as "slang and colloquial expressions," but they do not define slang. How do they know that all these words are either slang or colloquialisms? How would you know? Do you find any terms in the passage quoted above that you would say are neither slang nor colloquial expressions?

3. The Berrey-Van den Bark book is dated 1943, but older scholars will recall receiving questionnaires for this volume in the 1930's. Thus most of what is in the book—particularly since editing and printing a book like this one take some time—must be more than thirty years old. If you were now re-editing the book, what new expressions would you insert in this entry? Which would you label college slang?

4. Flexner, in a signed introduction, defines the contents of the Wentworth-Flexner dictionary as follows: "American slang, as used in the title of this dictionary, is the body of words and expressions frequently used by or intelligible to a rather large portion of the general American public, but not accepted as good, formal usage by the majority." This makes "acceptance by the majority" the basis of the usage label *slang*. Can you think of any other possible basis?

5. Kratz suggests that there is such a thing as college speech, but that if there is such a category as college slang, it is much more restricted than has been assumed. Make a list of the first twenty-five words that occur to you that you would consider slang and would expect to hear on the campus. How many of them would you defend as college slang by Kratz's definition? What other words can you think of or discover by asking your colleagues that you could defend as college slang?

6. Although Berrey and Van den Bark provide subheadings for what they call special slang—that is, the slang of special groups, such as the underworld, trades and occupations, sports, entertainment, and so on—they have no sub-heading for college slang. Thus they would seem to agree with Kratz that there is relatively little distinctive college slang. If you were preparing a dictionary of college slang, what would be the main categories? Using the Wentworth-Flexner book as a model, try to edit part of such a dictionary.

5

Slang to Standard English /
Standard English to Slang

The following two selections recount the history of two words, one a respectable old English word that has had lively developments in the New World, the other an Americanism. The first piece, from Word Study, 45 *(October, 1969), was written by Edward Hanford Kelly, professor of English at the State University of New York at Oneonta. The second selection is from* The American Language *(1963), Raven I. McDavid's revision of the monumental study of American English made by H. L. Mencken (1880–1956). Mencken more than anyone else popularized the study of American English, and he himself made one of the greatest contributions to our knowledge of it. McDavid, professor of English and linguistics at the University of Chicago and a leader in the field of dialect geography, updated Mencken's rather rambling volumes and condensed them into one. Most of the selection printed below was written by McDavid, and we have therefore removed the brackets that served to distinguish McDavid's sentences from Mencken's; Allen Walker Read's final results, which are discussed in this selection, were published after Mencken's death.*

A "Bitch" by Any Other Name
Is Less Poetic

Edward Hanford Kelly

" 'I'll light a piece of fat pine,' shouted the boy. . . . 'Where's your bitch?' asked Dillon"; and, a modern reader of Elizabeth E. Robins' *Magnetic North* (1904) might very well ask, what a *bitch* has to do with lighting a fire. But this bitch was essential to the frontiersman of the northwest on long winter nights when, without the luxury of an oil lamp or candle, he had to depend on it alone for a source of light. The bitch, a tin cup filled with bacon grease and with a twisted rag wick,[1] was only used when circumstances prohibited

[1] Mitford M. Mathews, "Bitch," *A Dictionary of Americanisms on Historical Principles,* (Chicago, 1951).

a more civilized means of obtaining fire. Similarly when the need arises to-day, one often resorts to the term "bitch" for lack of a more civilized means of expression; however, this newer usage exemplifies a shift in meaning by metaphoric association as the word emerges etymologically in English. Yet it would be incorrect to think that the many modifications evident in the history of "bitch" point toward linguistic degeneration ending in mere vulgarism.

A native English word, "bitch" derives from the OE *bicce* (akin to ON *bikkja*) [2] and has a long literary history as a substantive, an adjective (attributive in combination forms), and as a transitive and intransitive verb. Its original Anglo-Saxon meaning, the female of the dog, wolf, fox,[3] or others of the genus *Canis,* is still the first listed in dictionaries today; but because words mean what particular cultures make them mean the first listed is not always the popular choice. Few twentieth-century American city dwellers would think it polite to refer to a female dog as a bitch, although they might use the word on other occasions. Yet a person raised in a rural area would probably think the word appropriate. Because the English-speaking population is largely urban, the second and third entries would be in more general usage today. The second entry defines bitch as a "bad, lewd, sensual woman," and warns of the slang term's indecency; the third reference cites the word as a slang verb "to complain," and some dictionaries do not bother to list its adjectival usages. Even the *OED* fails to discuss the word in full despite its lengthy native pedigree, but the concrete definition must have developed into the figurative in the Anglo-Saxon period. Although female animals of the canine variety behave similarly when in heat, man's early companionship with the dog allowed him to observe at first hand the male's reaction to the female in estrus. *The Maistre of Game* (c. 1410), a treatise on hunting, describes this propensity in simile, "As houndes 'folowyn after a bicche or a brach" (1. 14) and "As houndes do after a byches, when she is Joly" (1. 31). It was a simple analogy to compare two-legged promiscuity with that which went on four.

From the ME period to the present, English literature records both the denotative and connotative meaning of bitch side-by-side. Chaucer's Pardoner laments the fruit that comes from the "bicched bones two" (1. 656), or from shooting dice. Bones, for dice, has fallen into the category of slang too. In the Renaissance period all-embracing Shakespeare used both the original sense of the word and its metaphoric associations in four plays. For example, in *The Merry Wives of Windsor* Falstaff complains of being tossed in the river "as they would have drowned a blind bitch's puppies" (III, v, 15); and in *Lear* Kent curses Oswald as "the son and heir of a mongrel bitch" (II, ii,

---

[2] The *OED* lists other older English forms: *bicge, bicche, bycche, bytch,* etc.; and cites Aelfric's use of the word (1000). OE *bicce* ME *bicche* Mod. E. *bitch.*

[3] In OE *bicce* might occasionally refer to the female of other animals too, as *dēor* meant "animal" before denoting specifically "deer." See also *An Anglo-Saxon Dictionary,* J. Bosworth and T. N. Toller (London, 1964).

24); later in the play, when Regan and Goneril are "in heat," Shakespeare
depends on the audience to fulfill the metaphor of the two sisters as bitches.
Milton, partial to aureate poetic diction, never uses bitch; he puts the words
"execrable son" into Adam's mouth (PL, XII, 64), and once uses "son of
despite," which terms may be appropriate and accurate but less emotionally
satisfying to the caller. In Thomas Hobbes' translation of the *Odyssey* (1675)
Odysseus calls the unfaithful maids "bitches" (XVIII, 310); but of the
modern translators only T. E. Lawrence uses the same term on the same
occasion. E. V. Rieu leans toward euphemism, calling them "brazen hussies,"
while Robert Fitzgerald renders the fairly effective "sluts," another term for
female dogs. In *Tom Jones* (1749) Squire Western's technical metaphor on
seizing Tom at the inn, "we have got the dog fox, I warrant the bitch is not
far off" (X, vii), contrasts with his later inexact but purposefully opprobrious
description of the male landlord as a "vast, comical bitch" (XV, iii). The
term "bitch" applied to a man becomes humorous, even ironical, and casts
doubts on the landlord's masculinity, for a man cannot logically be a bitch;
and in the modern homosexual's parlance the appellation "bitch" is a testy
compliment.

About the same time *Tom Jones* was published another noun form of the
word was coming into being. Miners used what they called a "bitch" for
boring and drawing up sunken rods. To hold this iron bitch while unscrew-
ing it, they used two other instruments called "dogs," capable of recovering
broken rods from a borehole. The lewd connotation is obvious, and in today's shop jargon machinists employ bitches to clamp work to a lathe. In
these instances the term reinforces the function of the tool so named; and,
as in the case of the frontiersmen, it is interesting to note that the word is
applied to devices expected to perform necessary duties for rough men living in isolation or working outside the immediate association of women.

As a verb, "to bitch" originally meant to frequent the company of "bad"
women. In his burlesque of the *Aeneid* (1675), Charles Cotton writes "Jove,
thou now art going a-bitching." The more exact "to whore" seems to have
replaced "to bitch" in our society, the infinitive form having shifted again in
connotation to complaining. But "to bitch" in the sense of "to complain" was
in use both early and late in the eighteenth century. Edmund Burke's correspondence (1777) shows "bitch" in still another shade of meaning, "to
hang back or hedge": "Norton bitched a little at last; but though he would
recede, Fox stuck to his motion." [4] And to "bitch up," meaning to spoil or
bungle, some etymologists find thinning in polite usage to "botch" or "botch
up"; but botch, according to Skeat might have always been a separate word.[5]

Victorian writers avoided the slang use of bitch and stuck to its denotative
meaning if they used it at all. They had to fulfill the demands of editors
who catered to family readers with impressionable daughters, so "bitch"
was unquestionably taboo to the Grundian guardians of moral, social, and

[4] *OED*, for examples from Cotton, Burke.
[5] Skeat, *Principles of English Etymology*.

literary conventions of the period. Mencken saw similar conventions prevailing in America. He points out that from 1820–1880 in England and America sow, stallion, buck, bitch, and even mare were thought of as "racy" in refined circles. Nice swearers in those days often reached for a blend like "bastrich," a combination of bastard and bitch, but considered to be more respectable.[6] Imagine having to consider an oath before spontaneously uttering it! But twentieth-century vernacular has moved to a pole opposite to any antipathy toward the use of "bitch" and other stronger words.

Eric Partridge lists many common expressions using bitch in various contexts. At Cambridge and Oxford hostesses "stand bitch," or preside at tea. They even "bitch the pot" (pour) at their "bitch gatherings," a more pointed label than our nice "hen parties." He notes that since 1840 the queen in playing cards has been called a bitch[7]—and what poker player has not taken the stakes at one time or another with three bitches? And like Barney's bull, men too become "bitched, b***red, and bewildered"—a catch phrase not far removed from the recurrently popular song of *Pal Joey* (1940), "Bewitched" (bothered, and bewildered), which certainly recalls the older rural alliterative expression.

Perhaps the sense of opprobriousness attached to the word early in its history accounts for the current lexicographical stigma still associated with it, but the fact remains that one gets a perverse satisfaction from merely uttering "bitch," especially in its combination and attributive forms. Robert Burns says "I've been bitchfou 'mang godly priests" (1786), or literally "drunk as a bitch." One might be sick as a dog, but he generally has a bitch of a cold or hangover, as the case may be. One might be plastered or bitchified; he might "sound off" or "bitch-off," and whether one is using slang or being vulgar would depend on the tone and context of such utterances. A laborer working on a hot summer day could sincerely complain of a "bitch of a sun," while simple chiasmus of sound in this expression gives the English language one of its most offensive and provoking appellations, while at the same time, paradoxically, one of the most satisfying to say.

The glorious release of emotion one experiences in mouthing "son of a bitch"[8] is almost poetical in the light of Pope's statement that "the sound must seem an echo to the sense." And if Korzybski, Stuart Chase, Carnap, *et al.* had ruled that overuse had wrung dry the meaning of the term, its effect on human emotion would still be therapeutic. Son of a bitch! To say it meaningfully one must set his teeth firmly, bare them to the gums, and let the air hiss lingua-dentally through taut lips as he vehemently stresses the first word. The unaccented "of a" is uttered with no unclenching of teeth, and the speaker is then ready to explode BITCH! with all the residual air he can muster: teeth, gums, lips, facial expression keeping the same fe-

---

[6] H. L. Mencken, *The American Language.*

[7] Eric Partridge, "Bitch," *A Dictionary of Slang and Unconventional English* (London, 1963).

[8] First reference to "son of a bitch" *per se* seems to occur in *Arthur and Merlin* (1330): "Bice sone! thou drawest amiss," (8487), *OED.*

rocious attitude held at beginning the sibilant as the air exhausts itself in [tʃ]. Even in isolation, bitch, if uttered with sincerity, remains a word of great force in releasing pent-up feelings. The voiced stop-plosive [b] can be uttered at any volume, the vowel continuant [i] can be held at length, while the unvoiced affricate [tʃ] moves away from the plosive in a whisper—and all without ever thinking of a lewd woman or even directing the expression at an animate object. Although our society generally thinks a sow dirtier than a female dog, and a rat or snake certainly more odious than man's best friend, the balanced assonance of "son of a sow" does not offer the cathartic benefits of the older term. Although all meaning has been wrung from the word in its present poetic usage, the biological gestures, coupled with sound and movement, provide it with a satisfying sublinguistic, almost symbolical meaning.

O.K. Becomes O.K.

H. L. Mencken and Raven I. McDavid, Jr.

The most successful of these innovations—indeed, the most successful of all Americanisms—is *O.K.* Its long-disputed etymology has been practically settled by Allen Walker Read.[1] It arose from a vogue for acronyms which developed in Boston in the summer of 1838. In the Boston *Morning Post* for June 12 appeared the following announcement:

> *Melancholy.*—We understand that J. Eliot Brown, Esq., Secretary of the Boston Young Men's Society for Meliorating the Condition of the Indians, F.A.H. (fell at Hoboken, N.J.) on Saturday last at 4 o'clock, p.m. in a duel W.O.O.O.F.C. (with one of our first citizens). What measures will be taken by the Society R.T.B.S. (remains to be seen).

The most popular of the acronyms, according to Read, was *O.F.M.*, for "Our First Men," a semi-satirical phrase. In the *Morning Post* for June 20 appeared the query: "Does he [a turtle] *rare up* when you suggest to him that soup is called for by O.F.M. (our firstmen), and he is 'wanted'?" A clear forerunner of *O.K.* is the frequent and still surviving *n.g.* for *no go* (or *no good*), as in the comment on a lawsuit in the *Morning Post* for June 25: "They then went to the plaintiff's to try to settle, but it was *n.g.*"

---

[1] The First Stage in the History of *O.K.*, *AS*, Vol. XXXVIII, Feb. 1963, pp. 5–27; The Second Stage in the History of *O.K.*, *ibid.*, May 1963; The Evidence on *O.K.*, *Saturday Review of Literature*, July 19, 1941, pp. 3–11. See also Postscripts to The American Language: The Life and Times of *O.K.*, by H. L. Mencken, *The New Yorker*, Oct. 1, 1949, pp. 56–61.

Drink names were often abbreviated, such as *G.C.* for *gin cocktail* and *m.j.* for *mint julep*. The use of abbreviations was so prevalent that it was denounced on June 19:

> Mr. Greene.—The present age is one pregnant with experiments. . . . There is yet one other sect, whose efforts carry them back to still remoter ages—disciples, it may be, of the illustrious Noah [Webster]—who, in their fondness for a brevity in writing, would discard every letter in a word, but that with which it commences.
>
> They extend this principle to speech too—they glory in hyroglyphics—they rejoice in *steno*graphics—but it is to this very class that I would send forth my denunciations—let it be understood that they are a dangerous sect—men whom Caesar would have regarded with a suspicious eye—for they do not "sleep o' nights"—they may be men of high standing in the community—for they speak of our "leading citizens" with a familiar air, and seem conversant with "our first people," and they claim to be literary, and aver that the efforts of their Society will be truly beneficial to the cause of *Letters*. But sir, I mistrust them—let them come out freely and openly, and show us that their cabalistic signs are not omens of evil. . . . Above all, let them give us the lengthy English signification of their W.B.'s—G.C.'s—B.C.'s and last, though not least, their P.W.S. Garee's that we may rest in the assurance that they are not incantations unholy, to call up spirits withal!
>
> Yours,
>
> I. C.

"The background for *O.K.*," Read goes on to say, "was so thoroughly set by the summer of 1838 that it is surprising that it was not yet found. Probably it was delayed by a close forerunner, *O.W.*, standing for 'All Right,' as if spelled *Oll Wright*. See the Boston *Morning Post*, June 18, 1838, in a reporter's account of taking a hack in Newport, R.I.: 'We jumped in, and were not disappointed either with the carriage, distance, or price. It was O.W.—(all right).'"

Next Read presents "the very matrix out of which the first known instance of *O.K.* was parturiated":

> An organization called the Anti-Bell-Ringing Society (usually referred to as the A.B.R.S.) was founded on October 26, 1838, to combat an ordinance of the Boston Common Council prohibiting the ringing of dinner bells. In December it instituted a suit in the police court to show the ridiculousness of the law; and throughout the next year they had high-spirited meetings. Concerning a visit of members of the A.B.R.S. to New York by way of Providence, the following appeared in the Boston *Morning Post*, March 23, 1839: "The 'Chairman of the Committee on Charity Lecture Bells' [Thomas B. Fearing] is one of the deputation, and perhaps if he should return to Boston, via Providence, he of the [Providence] Journal, and his *train*-band, would have the 'contribution box,' et ceteras, *o.k.*—all correct—and cause the corks

to fly, like *sparks,* upward." Ah! This contains the first instance of *O.K.* so far known. Inasmuch as it appears in repartee between editors, it can be pinpointed to the writing of Charles Gordon Greene, nationally famous for his wit.

Later in 1839, Read shows, the interest in initials was transferred to New York. "On July 8th two of the leading literary figures, Park Benjamin and Rufus W. Griswold, founded the New York *Evening Tatler,* and they were so waggish as to use *K.G.,* standing for 'No Go,' as if spelled *Know Go,* and *K.Y.,* standing for 'No Use,' as if spelled *Know Yuse.*" Both appeared in the first month of the *Evening Tatler's* existence. On September 2 *O.K.* appeared, glossed as "all correct," in commenting on a proposed lecture tour by Thomas Carlyle. The vogue of acronyms in New York was attested in the New York *Evening Signal* for November 14:

> Wall Street Phraseology.—The editor of the Philadelphia Gazette, who appears to have flitted through our city a day or two since, writes as follows to his "round table":
> They have a curious, short-handed phraseology in Wall-street which it is amusing to hear. A man offers another a note with the endorsement of a third—and saying of it—"You see it's A 1, the man is decidedly O.F.M."
> "Yes—that's good—O.K.—I.S.B.D."
> "Will you make that contract we spoke of yesterday?" says a fourth person to a fifth. "I have brought my friend as witness."
> "Yes; we'll close it to-morrow."
> "A.R., N.S.M.J.," is the reply; and the parties bow and separate. O.K., all correct; I.S.B.D., it shall be done; A.R., N.S.M.J., all right, 'nough said 'mong gentlemen—and so forth. This tongue-relieving process is quite in vogue here—it saves the common enemy, and is considered extremely useful.[2]

However, *O.K.* owes its vogue to the political campaigns of 1840, when it took a second, independent start as a symbol of the Democrats to counteract the "log cabin" and "hard cider" of the Whigs. In this new sense it made its first appearance in print in the New York *New Era* on March 23, 1840, as part of the name of the Democratic *O.K. Club,* an organization of sup-

[2] The original of this, in the Philadelphia *Gazette,* Nov. 12, 1839, was discovered by Woodford A. Heflin, and was presented by him in *O.K.* and Its Incorrect Etymology, *AS,* Vol. XXXVII, Dec. 1962, pp. 243–8. It was reprinted not only in the New York *Evening Signal* but also in the Baltimore *Patriot and Commercial Gazette* (country ed., tri-weekly), Nov. 13, 1839. The knowledge of *O.K.* lingered on in Baltimore, as we find in the Baltimore *Sun,* Feb. 24, 1840, concerning the gift of a mint julep: "We hope this will satisfy him, and that he will give us an acknowledgment that it is *o.ķ.* (all correct)." This was found by Robert G. Gunderson and referred to in his book *The Log-Cabin Campaign* (Lexington, Ky., 1957), p. 235, *n.* 7, and the significance of it admirably presented by Ralph T. Eubanks, The Basic Derivation of *O.K., AS,* Vol. XXXV, Oct. 1960, pp. 188–92.

porters of Martin Van Buren for a second presidential term, and was an abbreviation of *Old Kinderhook,* the Hudson Valley village in which he had been born in 1782. Van Buren had been known to his political enemies since the early days of the Albany Regency as the *Kinderhook Fox,* and to his followers as the *Sage, Magician* or *Wizard of Kinderhook,* and it was natural for the name to extend to one of the rowdy clubs which supported him. Reducing the name to *O.K.* was in accord with the liking for mystification that then marked politics. The Democratic *O.K. Club* held its first recorded meeting in the house of Jacob Colvin, at 245 Grand Street, on March 24, 1840, and the new name caught on at once. It was brief, it had a bellicose ring, and it was mysterious enough to suggest the sinister. By the next day *O.K.* had become a slogan among the other Locofocos of the city, the lower orders of whom had been masquerading under similar dark and puzzling names, *e.g., Butt Enders, Huge Paws* and *Ball Rollers.* On March 27, when the New York Whigs held a meeting in Masonic Hall, a gang of Locofocos, using *O.K.* as their war cry, tried to break it up. "About 500 stout, strapping men," said the New York *Herald* the next morning, "marched three and three, noiselessly and orderly. The word *O.K.* was passed from mouth to mouth, a cheer was given, and they rushed into the hall upstairs like a torrent." Naturally *O.K.* provoked speculation, and at once the anti-Locofoco newspapers began to print derisory interpretations. A categorical statement of the *New Era,* that the term was "significant of the birthplace of Martin Van Buren, *Old Kinderhook,*" did not shut off the rising flood of rival etymologies. One of these, appearing in the *Herald* on March 30, was accepted gravely, in one form or another, for a full century:

> A few years ago some person accused Amos Kendall to General Jackson of being no better than he should be. "Let me examine the papers," said the old hero. "I'll soon tell you whether Mr. Kendall is right or wrong." The general did so and found everything right. "Tie up them papers," said the general. They were tied up. "Mark on them *O.K.,*" continued the general. *O.K.* was marked on them. "By the eternal," said the good old general, taking his pipe from his mouth, "Amos is *Oll Kurrect* and no mistake." [3]

Various other jocose etymologies for *O.K.* were suggested during the years following its appearance in the New York *New Era,* for the term seized the fancy of the country, and was soon in wide use. So early as December 18, 1840, a Philadelphia music publisher named George Willig was copyrighting "The *O.K.* Quick Step," "composed and arranged for the piano-forte and especially dedicated to the citizens of Richmond, Va., by Jos K. Opl." Willig's son, George, Jr., operated a music publishing business in Baltimore, and before the end of 1840 he brought out an "*O.K.* Gallopade," "dedicated to

[3] Kendall (1789–1869) was perhaps the most influential of Jackson's Kitchen Cabinet. He was made Postmaster General in 1835, and founded the tradition that the holder of that office should be a practical politician.

the Whig ladies of the United States by John H. Hewitt."[4] Thus by the end of 1840 *O.K.* had already lost its exclusively Democratic significance. On April 2 the New York *Daily Express,* referring to the fact that the *O.K.* raid on the Whigs was repulsed, said that it was an Arabic word which, read backward, came to *kicked out.* After the Whigs had carried Connecticut over the Democrats, the *Express* reported that *O.K.* meant *Old Konnecticut.* Says Read:

> Another Whig version, soon current, was *Out of Kash, Out of Kredit, Out of Karacter* and *Out of Klothes.* Some months later a congressman from Illinois, on the floor of the House of Representatives, offered the interpretation *Orful Kalamity.*

Read's reports, of course, have not abated the efforts of amateur etymologists to account for *O.K.,* and new guesses are being added all the time. A few of the more picturesque or preposterous:

1. That *O.K.* comes from *aux quais,* used "in the American War of Independence by French sailors who made appointments with American girls."[5]
2. That it may be derived from *oikea,* a Finnish word signifying correct.[6]
3. That it arose during the Civil War, when "the War Department bought large quantities of crackers from the Orrins-Kendall Company. This company always put their initials on their boxes and as the crackers were of a high quality the initials gradually came to be used as a synonym for *all right.*"[7]
4. "Certain bills in the House of Lords must be read and approved by the Lord Chairman of Committees, Lord Onslow, and by his counsel, Lord Killbracken, and then initialed by them. They are then *O.K.*"[8]
5. "*O.K.* had its origin several hundred years ago in an expression common among Norwegian and Danish sailors: *H.G.* (pronounced *hah gay*), meaning shipshape, ready for action. *H.G.* was short for the Anglo-Saxon *hofgor,* meaning ready for the sea."[9]
6. "Liddell and Scott have an entry, ὠχ, ὠχ, a magical incantation against fleas. The authority is a work called 'Geoponìca,' the date of which is given with a query, as 920 A.D."[10]
7. "The Prussian general Schliessen, who fought for the American colonies,

---

[4] See *O.K.,* 1840, by H. L. Mencken, *AS,* Vol. XVII, Apr. 1942, p. 126.
[5] *Aux Quais,* by Beachcomber, London *Daily Express,* June 28, 1940.
[6] *Main Library News Notes,* Cleveland Public Library, July 1940.
[7] *O.K.,* by Robert Greenburger, *Linguist* (Horace Mann School for Boys, New York), Vol. IV, 1939, p. 15.
[8] *O.K.,* by John Godley, London *Times,* Nov. 2, 1939.
[9] Reported but by no means certified by Frank Colby in his newspaper column Take My Word for It, Mar. 21, 1943.
[10] *O.K.,* by W. Snow, London *Times,* Oct. 26, 1935. The first edition of the Greek Lexicon of Henry G. Liddell and Robert Scott was published in 1843.

in the War of Independence, endorsed his letters and orders *O.K.* (*Oberst Kommandant*). Consequently the letters *O.K.* came to be applied to anything having the meaning of official assent."[11]

8. That *O.K.* may have some sort of connection with the Scotch *och aye*.[12]

9. "*O.K.* is an abbreviation of *orl korrec,* all correct. It is English, I think Cockney—not an Americanism. I was born in the 60s and remember it when I was a boy."[13]

10. That *O.K.* may come from *O qu-oui,* an emphatic French form of *yes,* to be found in Sterne's "A Sentimental Journey" (1768).[14]

Of all Americanisms *O.K.* has been the greatest success. It was in use by English telegraphers, as a signal that a message had been clearly received, so early as 1873, and first appeared in an English slang dictionary a year earlier.[15] Before 1888 it was already familiar enough to the patrons of London music halls to enter into the refrain of a popular song.[16] But it remained for the American movies to make *O.K.* familiar to all Englishmen, low or high. When it began to displace the English *righto,* there were the usual vain protests from patriots and pedants. An especially violent war upon it in 1935 was supported by the Anglomaniac Mrs. Nicholas Murray Butler, who was then in London, but before the end of the year the London *Times* heaved a bomb into the patriot ranks by giving its awful *O.K.* to *O.K.* H. W. Horwill did not think it necessary to explain *O.K.* or even to list it in his "Dictionary of Modern American Usage."[17] During this same *annus mirabilis* the Judicial Committee of the Privy Council decided formally that inscribing *O.K.* upon a legal document "meant that the details contained . . . were currently given."[18]

In 1937 the Edinburgh *Evening News* described *O.K.* as "now universal" in Great Britain,[19] and in 1940 a provincial journalist was reporting that "almost everybody says *O.K.* now instead of *all right.*"[20] Finally Lord

---

[11] *O.K.,* by Sir Anthony Palmer, London *Times,* Oct. 28, 1939. *Oberst Kommandant* is German for colonel in command. In *AS* for Oct. 1938 Gretchen Hochdoerfer Rogers published a translation of an article in the Omaha (Neb.) *Tribune,* a German daily, of Jan. 23, 1938, in which the German officer was changed to Baron F. W. von Steuben, inspector general of the Continental Army, and *Oberst Kommandant* to *Ober-Kommando,* meaning high command.

[12] The Cry of the English: Words That Bless and Burn, Nottingham *Journal,* Apr. 30, 1943.

[13] *O.K.,* by Charles A. Christie, London *Times,* Oct. 24, 1939.

[14] I am indebted here to William McDevitt, of San Francisco.

[15] Sir William Power, *O.K.,* London *Times,* Oct. 21, 1939.

[16] *O.K.*—The Victorians Used It, by J. W. Lee, *John o' London's Weekly,* Aug. 29, 1936. See also *O.K.* in History, by M. E. Durham, London *Spectator,* Jan. 14, 1938, p. 57.

[17] Oxford, 1935.

[18] *Chemical Trade Journal* (London), quoted in *The New Yorker,* Oct. 19, 1935, p. 70.

[19] The Mystery of *O.K.,* June 4.

[20] How the Tank Got Its Name, by Sam Bate, *Northern Daily Telegraph* (Blackburn), Aug. 19, 1940.

Beaverbrook made *O.K.* impeccable by using it at the Moscow Conference in a formal pledge as official representative of the British Commonwealth of Nations.[21]

O.K. is sometimes spelled *okeh, okay* or *okey,* and about 1930 an abbreviation *oke* appeared, quickly followed by *oke-doke* (more often *oky-doke*), *oky-doky* and *oky-dory.* The forms terminating in *-y* were perhaps suggested by the current *all-righty,* and maybe *oky-dory* was also influenced by *hunky-dory.* Woodrow Wilson used *okeh* in *O.K.-ing* documents, and seems to have subscribed to the theory that the term came from a Choctaw word, *oke, hoke,* signifying "yes, it is."

During their far-flung operations in World War II, American troops rarely encountered a people to whom *O.K.* was unknown. Lieutenant Colonel W. E. Dyess recorded that it was known to and used by every Japanese guard in Davao prison camp.[22] It was equally familiar to the Moslem allies of the Allies in North Africa,[23] and even earlier the American volunteers in the Spanish Civil War found that it had displaced *salud* as a greeting among the village children of Spain.[24] In several places *O.K.* encountered congeners which coalesced with it, *e.g., ola kala* in Greece, *o-ke* in the Djabo dialect of Liberia and *hoak-keh* (literally "is so") in Burmese.

WORKING WITH THE SELECTIONS

1. Kelly points out that rural dwellers are more likely to use *bitch* than are urbanites. He might have added that dog fanciers use *bitch* with no more hesitation than a farmer uses the word *cow* to designate a female of the genus *bos.* Thus being slang or vulgar or colloquial or what-not may be associated with a particular use of a word, but not with the word in all uses. Can you think of any other words of which this is true?

2. Probably most of the four-letter words that one is not supposed to print in a textbook have ancestries as respectable as has *bitch.* Most of these words can now be printed in novels, and they have for decades been permitted in scholarly research works and in some reference books. Can you think of any words frowned on by older people, or by a previous generation, that can now be printed anywhere?

3. Slang that becomes standard English is rarer than many users of slang assume. You probably do not know *new issue* as a slang term for a black man, but it was once common for a former slave who was thought to take his freedom too bumptiously. You may not know *diving hook* as a device for picking pockets, common American slang of about 1800. Most slang never becomes standard. But some locutions have; what besides *OK* are some of the most important?

[21] The Moscow Conference, by Lord Beaverbrook, *Listener* (London), Oct. 16, 1941, p. 320.

[22] Installment published in the newspapers of Feb. 18, 1944.

[23] Amen, *The New Yorker,* Aug. 28, 1943.

[24] Associated Press dispatch from Madrid, June 24, 1937.

4. When *bitch,* a word once as reputable as *cow* or *mare,* became a word thought to be unfit for delicate ears, a practice in language known as taboo was at work. A term to replace a taboo word is sometimes called a noa word, *stock beast* for *bull,* for example. Can you think of more examples of each?

6

Dialect and Language

Dwight Bolinger

This selection by Bolinger is also from his Aspects of Language *(1968).*

Linguistic history records sweeping changes that affect vast bodies of speakers over long periods—some abrupt, even cataclysmic, so that everyone is conscious of what is happening, others so gradual that speakers may be unaware of them during their lifetimes. Dialectology looks upon the differences that set one community apart from another, that characterize the individual speaker even when they do not necessarily interfere with communication, that give society its flavor and no small amount of its mirth. Linguistic history is dialectology writ large, and dialectology is the idiosyncracies of particular speakers writ medium. There is no clear separation of what one speaker does that others of his community do not do; nor is there any between what communities do that makes them different from one another or what it is that distinguishes one language from another. Techniques of discovery may differ—historical linguistics has elaborate strategies to hypothesize what cannot be observed because the evidence has long since vanished, whereas dialectology may be contemporary, capturing many of its facts almost as they happen. The facts in both fields are the same; the size of the bite is what distinguishes them.

But size makes a difference in our appreciation, for dialect differences are cut to the measure of our comprehension, while differences between languages may overwhelm us. Comparatively few individuals are bilingual. Every speaker is multilingual in the sense of understanding more than one dialect. And most speakers command different styles of speech which, if they are not to be called different dialects, are denied the name only because we want to reserve it for contrasts that are more pronounced. Whenever we speak in a more "reserved" or "decorous" manner, whenever we strive to avoid "grammatical mistakes," we pass from one dialect to another.

KINDS OF DIALECT

Every speaker speaks as many dialects as there are groups among which he moves that have different modes of speech. Some groups are biologically determined. Others are formed by more or less voluntary association. Here are some important ones:

Profession

The speech of the minister differs from the speech of the merchant. Each occupation has its own things to talk about. But the difference goes beyond merely having different words for different things. It often embodies a variety of names for the same thing: the soothsayer has his *augury*, the weather man his *forecast*, the doctor his *prognosis*, and the scientist his *prediction*.

Sex

Men's talk differs from women's talk. This line is somewhat blurred in our society, but it remains legible. Adjectives like *dreadful, precious, darling* are more apt to be encountered in women's speech than in men's—in fact, women are more liberal with adjectives in general. In some levels of society men are less inhibited in their choice of words than women. Women are less inhibited in their intonational range.

Age

The infant differs from the child, the child from the adolescent, the adolescent from the adult. The most extreme case is baby talk, which, in the sense that its speakers are physically unable to speak otherwise, is not really a dialect, but it becomes one when its forms are imitated—and sometimes fabricated—by adults and used by them with young children. As with all dialects, forms from this one may be picked up and broadcast; a recent instance is *bye-bye,* which is heard more and more as an ordinary friendly farewell, not necessarily an intimate one. At the other extreme is the dialect that time imposes on us all: older speakers do not always adopt newer ways of speaking, and the older they grow the more quaint their speech becomes. Nor is the process always purely automatic—a transition between age levels may be made consciously. Among the Ainu of Japan, "there is a kind of speech that is characteristic of older people which persists in its own right and is adopted by younger people as they gradually mature"—an "old speech" which does not itself grow old and die out.[1]

[1] Shiro Hattori, "A Special Language of the Older Generations Among the Ainu," *General Linguistics* 6.43–58 (1964).

Occasion

Even the most careful speakers permit themselves a style of speech at home that is different from the one they use in public. Many societies set up—not by legislation but by tacit consent—a standard dialect that is used on formal occasions and that serves as a kind of inter-lingua, available to any speaker when he wants to identify himself with speakers at large rather than with speakers at home. The standard dialect takes on the local color of the speaker but is nevertheless different from the relaxed style used with friends, family, and neighbors. It is more neutral and as a rule is more generally understood, but intelligibility is not essential to its authority.[2] In some countries, any relaxation of the formal standard in occasions that call for it is resented even if, as happens sometimes, speakers have difficulty understanding it (this may be likened to the reactions of some people in our own culture to attempts to make the Bible more intelligible by modernizing the English).[3] In India, formal Hindi is stiffened by generous doses of Sanskrit.[4] In Chinese, a formal lecture and a conversation may even differ syntactically: the idea that one group of officials (A) is more numerous than another group (B) is expressed in the lecture as

A	dwō	yú	B
A	numerous	than	B

and in the conversation as

A	bǐ	B	dwō
A	compared to	B	numerous[5]

The standard in English is not clear-cut (it is never entirely so anywhere), but certain tendencies mark it off. The obvious ones are in the choice of words. Where a university press, announcing a competition, reserves to itself the "*first refusal* of manuscripts," the intent is not to be candidly pessimistic but to avoid the more accurate but too colloquial *first chance at*.[6] At a graduation one hears *All seniors will please rise* (or possibly *stand*); a relaxed occasion would call for *get up* or *stand up*. Certain contractions are avoided on formal occasions: the easygoing *show* harmonizes with *'em* in *Let's show 'em* but would hardly be used with the stiff verb *reveal*: *Let's*

---

[2] Experiments have shown that "speakers of high status are more comprehensible for speakers of all statuses." See L. S. Harms, "Status Cues in Speech: Extra-race and Extra-region Identification," *Lingua* 12.300–06 (1963).

[3] Charles A. Ferguson, "Diglossia," *Word* 15.330 (1959).

[4] Paul W. Friedrich, *Language* 37.168 (1961).

[5] John de Francis in *Georgetown University Monograph Series on Languages and Linguistics,* September, 1951, p. 50.

[6] MLA-Oxford Award, 1952–53: "Under the terms of the competition, Oxford will have first refusal of all manuscripts submitted," *Hispania* 36.116 (1953).

reveal them. In the supremely formal atmosphere of the church, even *let's* may be avoided: *Let's pray* would sound secular, if not sporting. And there are syntactic differences here and there. Take the use of adverbs. There is a variety of English, regarded as substandard, in which most adverbs are distinguished from adjectives not by the suffix *-ly* but by position after the verb or verb phrase: in *He wrote the letter real careful, careful* is an adverb; in *He wrote a careful letter* it is an adjective. (All dialects of English do this part of the time: *He made the trip fast, He made a fast trip*.) Standard English adds the *-ly* and uses the resulting adverbs rather freely as to position: *They left rapidly, They rapidly left*. But very informal—not necessarily substandard—English does not favor *-ly* adverbs before the verb or verb phrase. It prefers the other position or some adverb not ending in *-ly:* instead of *He grew steadily worse, I promptly told him*, and *She's constantly complaining* it will say *He grew worse and worse, I told him right there*, and *She's all the time complaining*.

There is practically no limit to the number of social affinities revealed in differences of language. To age, sex, occupation, and occasion it would be necessary to add religion, politics, lodge affiliation, preference as to sports or amusements, and any other circumstances under which people meet and speak. But overshadowing them all are two coordinates laid on every society that determine far wider differences than any thus far mentioned. One is horizontal, as on a map: Bostonese, for example, differs from the speech of the rest of New England, and the speech of New England differs from that of the Coastal South; geographical dialects are inevitable, because people do more talking to their neighbors than to those who are farther away, and where more is shared, differences are fewer. The other is vertical, as with layers: in stratified societies people are born to a social class; nothing stigmatizes a class more indelibly than its language, and differences in speech are often cultivated for this very purpose.

Probably because they touch us in a tender spot, the vertical and horizontal differences are the ones that come first to mind when dialects are mentioned. Geographical differences have ties with our loyalties to home, town, and state. Social differences are nourished on feelings of superiority and inferiority, and to some extent color all other differences. In a society where women and farmers are regarded as inferior, sex differences and occupational differences become class differences. As for differences due to occasion, inability to handle the standard dialect when the occasion calls for it is especially likely to be taken as a class difference, for the dominant social class is the one whose traits of speech are most fully embodied in the standard.

The linguist and the sociologist are selective in different ways in their attitudes toward dialect. The linguist focuses mainly on the horizontal coordinate. Differences from region to region are the specimens that attract him most, probably because they are the same, though on a smaller scale, as the ones already familiar to him from language to language. When he speaks of dialectology it is almost always in this sense, more specifically referred to as "linguistic geography," "areal linguistics," or "dialect geography." The sociologist focuses mainly on the vertical coordinate. He is interested in how social groups interact within a single speech community, in how language influences our opportunities and our behavior. He views language as a series of codes by which the individual acts out his roles in society.

LINGUISTIC CODES

The language of a profession, say that of law, is social distinction in its crudest form. It is part of an economic order in which everyone's way of earning a living somehow influences his speech because of the need to manipulate a certain set of objects and concepts that are the tools of the profession. But ordinarily it goes no deeper than the choice of terms to match the objects. What really counts for the sociologist is how the lawyer interacts with his banker and his grocer, and how the banker's son and the grocer's son are able, through having certain models to emulate in their parents, teachers, and others, to define themselves and by so doing to open or close the doors to growth and change of status.

The sociologist Basil Bernstein distinguishes two types of code that are socially significant: restricted and elaborated.[7] A restricted code allows one to interact with one's fellows in a highly predictable way. It is associated with a certain social set or activity where only a limited number of things can be done. They are not necessarily prescribed in a particular order, as they would be in a game, but the choices are few. An example is the cocktail party, where the nature of the language used and the nature of the things talked about is known in advance and what one learns about new-made acquaintances is transmitted not so much by language as by look and gesture. The conventionality of the language enables speakers to relax in one another's company and communicate in other ways, much as the set movements of a dance remove the necessity of deciding what to do next. In a restricted code, individuality is submerged. The speaker and listener are in a well-defined relationship with each other, with verbal routines laid out in advance. There is not much choice of what to say simply because there is no need to say much, and the little that is said carries a heavy load of implicit meaning. The speaker is acting a role with speeches perhaps not fully written for him as they would be on the stage, but well supplied with stock items by the small department within the social structure where he happens to be moving at the moment. There is room for a bit of ad-libbing but little more.

In an elaborated code, the speaker and listener are acting parts in which they must improvise. Their standing with each other is such that neither can take much for granted about the other. Intentions and purposes have to be

[7] "A Socio-linguistic Approach to Social Learning," in *Survey of the Social Sciences, 1965,* ed. Julius Gould (Baltimore, Md.: Penguin Books, Inc., 1965), pp. 144–68.

brought into the open and defined. What the speaker will say is hard to predict, because it is not about commonplaces but about something more or less unique, related less to some foreseeable role and more to him as an individual. He is wearing not a comic nor a tragic mask but his own face, and that is harder to put into words. An example would be that of a man told to do something by his boss and having to explain why it is impossible for him to comply.

All speakers communicate with both restricted and elaborated codes, but not all are able to switch codes with the ease that is needed to interact to their advantage with other members of their society. Some speakers have little practice except with restricted codes, and unfortunately some of the roles in the social structure that are carried by those codes—implanted in the child by his exposure to them—are looked down upon. A speaker who is forced to operate with a certain code because he has never had any other models to imitate will find that his only communication will be with other speakers who use the same code—it becomes self-enforcing and self-perpetuating. One of the tasks of education is to lead to an awareness of the limitations of one's code and to a large amount of practice with elaborated codes, where the speaker is forced to become conscious of his language, to "orient towards the verbal channel." [8] This is the individual's road of escape from the confinement of his every act by restricted codes laid on him by the social structure without regard for his individuality, capacities, or intelligence.

WORKING WITH THE SELECTION

1. Bolinger mentions "intonational range" as an ingredient of dialect. You may have been thinking of dialect as involving mainly vocabulary, usage, and grammar, but clearly it includes pitch and variety of pitch. You may be able to distinguish a Texan from a Bostonian more readily by the tone of the voice than by anything else, although you may have difficulty describing this difference. Do you know any other body of speakers who have characteristic pitch and rhythm? Are tonal differences more characteristic of regional or social dialects?

2. Identify a campus situation that would encourage use of a restricted code; one that would require an elaborated code. Can you define college education as preparation for the skillful use of elaborated codes? If one adopted such a definition of education, how would it change existing courses and curricula, if at all?

---

[8] Bernstein, *op. cit.,* p. 161.

part **6**

Usage

Both grammar and dialect relate to another aspect of language, usage. *Popularly,* they are often confused with usage. The self-appointed policers of language tend to refer to anything they disapprove as "bad grammar." Obviously, they are not using the word grammar *as it has been used in this book. They are usually not referring to grammar at all but to usage, which concerns the status a locution has acquired from the circumstances in which it customarily occurs, the degree of respectability it enjoys at any time and place.*

Any expression communicates in at least three ways: through meaning by its denotation and connotation, through grammar by its relationship with other words in the sentence, and through usage by its customary status, its reputation. Thus, the word contact *may mean 'to get in touch with,' but to a small group of people this use is annoying; to them it implies some inadequacy in the speaker's education or intellectual status. This is not a question of whether the word in this use is right or wrong. Nevertheless, anyone who uses the word in this way risks communicating more than he intends if he is dealing with one of the few on whom it has an undesirable effect. This may be a minor fact about the word, but it is still a fact to be reckoned with. With* contact *most people today take the risk, knowingly or not.*

With ain't I? *most people today do not take the risk, at least in writing or in any kind of formal speech.* Ain't I *is grammatical; it follows the standard grammatical patterns of the language and uses a familiar form of the verb* be. *It is understood by all native speakers, and it is useful; no other equally efficient way of expressing the idea exists—compare* am I not, amn't I, *or* aren't I. *But since the eighteenth century, when the word was quite respectable,* ain't *has been so extensively labeled uneducated that it has lost caste.*

In one sense, then, usage is little more than linguistic etiquette, using the words that fit a particular set of language customs, like picking the appropriate fork at a dinner party. In another sense, usage is a serious part of communication, because part of an expression's total effect, total meaning, is the listener's opinion of its status. And usage problems are complicated because the status of a word may change quite rapidly and because observations about usage tend to be negative, defining what one should not do rather than what one should do.

In still another sense, usage is a part of dialect study, since it depends heavily on the tendency of people to regard their own dialect as right and any variation as wrong or at least peculiar. The helpful facts of usage are usually those that identify a locution with a geographical, social, or educational dialect or with a particular functional variety of language—that is, language customarily used for one purpose but not another; it can be used for speech, for example, but not for formal writing.

Usage is not the most profound subject in language study; arguments about whether one should say It is me *or* It is I *generally reveal more ignorance than understanding of how language works. But questions of usage usually are of greater popular concern than any other aspect of language study. People make snap judgments about a person's intellect or his moral character on the basis of his ability to distinguish* lay *and* lie, *and even intelligent people can work their emotions to high moral indignation at the sound of* drug *for* dragged *or* throwed *for* threw. *Of course usage is not a legitimate index of morality or intelligence, but questions of usage do have practical importance. Social and economic status, for example, are often strongly affected by a person's awareness of usage problems and by his ability to make appropriate choices among alternate expressions. The selections in Part 6 begin with some looks at specific usage questions and then go on to broader discussions of the whole problem.*

1

Using "Unique"

Unique *is only one of many expressions whose usage today is frequently described as "divided." The variation in the attitudes expressed in the following excerpts from books on usage illustrates some of the hazards of being very positive about what is "right" or "wrong" or "good" English.* Unique, *from the Latin* unicus *'single,' was used in English by the early seventeenth century to mean 'sole' or 'having no equal.' It appeared as both adjective and noun, spelled either* unic *or* unicke. *The* Oxford English Dictionary *cites* He hath lost . . . his unic son, *1645; and* A coin, which I have reason to think is a Unic, *1774. The word is no longer used as a noun, but it has gained popularity as an adjective, with some generalization of its meaning.*

A Dictionary of Modern
English Usage

H. W. Fowler

Oxford, 1926

unique. A watertight definition or paraphrase of the word, securing it against confusion with all synonyms that might be suggested, is difficult to frame. In the first place, it is applicable only to what is in some respect the sole existing specimen, the precise like of which may be sought in vain. That gives a clean line of division between it & the many adjectives for which the illiterate tend to substitute it—*remarkable, exceptional, rare, marvellous,* & the like. In the qualities represented by these epithets there are degrees; but uniqueness is a matter of yes or no only; no unique thing is more or less unique than another unique thing, as it may be rarer or less rare; the adverbs that *u.* can tolerate are e.g. *quite, almost, nearly, really, surely, perhaps, absolutely,* or *in some respects;* and it is nonsense to call anything *more, most, very, somewhat, rather,* or *comparatively u.* Such nonsense, however, is often written:—*M. Georges Buisson, in recognition of his valuable services as short-hand writer to the Chamber of Deputies, has been made an Officer of the Legion of Honour; this is a* rather unique *distinction./I have just come* *across the production of a boy aged seven which is, in my experience,* some-what unique.*/Sir, I venture to send you a copy of a* rather unique *inscription on a tombstone./A* very unique *child, thought I.*

But, secondly, there is another set of synonyms—*sole, single, peculiar to,* &c.—from which *u.* is divided not by a clear difference of meaning, but by an idiomatic limitation of the contexts to which it is suited. It will be admitted that we improve the two following sentences if we change *u.* in the first into *sole,* and in the second into *peculiar:—In the always delicate and difficult domain of diplomatic relations the Foreign Minister must be the* unique medium *of communication with foreign Powers./He relates Christianity to other religions, and notes what is* unique to the former *and what is common to all of them.* The emendations are easy to make or accept; to explain the need of them is more difficult; but the reason why *u.* is unsuitable is perhaps that it belongs to the class of epithets discussed in POSITIVE WORDS.

A Dictionary of Contemporary American Usage

Bergen Evans and Cornelia Evans

New York, 1957

unique once meant "only," as in *his unique son.* It can no longer be used in this sense. Today *unique* may mean "in a class by itself," but it more often means "unparalleled" or simply "remarkable." In this, it is following the pattern of *singular.* In all its current senses *unique* may be used with words that imply degrees, such as *more unique* and *quite unique.* Some people believe that there is something about the meaning of *unique* that makes expressions of this kind "illogical" or improper, but these expressions are used freely by outstanding writers and educators today. One grammarian, commenting on the much condemned *quite unique* points out that the word here means "unparalleled" and that we certainly do say *quite unparalleled.* He then says of the word *unique* itself: "I don't see anything quite unique in it."

Current American Usage

Margaret M. Bryant

New York, 1962

COMPARISON, ILLOGICAL . . . Adjectives like *perfect, unique, round, straight, dead, final, black, impossible, complete* are compared freely even though some textbooks contend that these adjectives should not be compared since their meaning is absolute; i.e., they name qualities that do not vary in degree. Yet a famous example comes from the Constitution: "We the people of the United States, in order to form a *more perfect* union. . . ."

In formal usage, one finds *more nearly perfect, more nearly round, more nearly complete* as in "The day we went to Belmont was the *most nearly perfect* in the history of the New York Weather Bureau . . ." (*The New Yorker*, July 26, 1958, 15).

Headlines and Deadlines:
A Manual for Copy Editors

Robert E. Garst and Theodore M. Bernstein

New York, 3rd ed., 1961

UNIQUE—NOVEL *The art of Benvenuto Cellini is unique. The hostess devised a novel way of entertaining her guests. Most unique* is never correct.

Writer's Guide
and Index to English

Porter G. Perrin

Chicago, 4th ed., 1965

unique. In strict Formal usage *unique* means "single, sole, unequaled," and consequently is not compared. In General usage, like so many other words of absolute meaning, it has become somewhat extended, and as an emphatic *rare,* it is sometimes found compared with *more* or *most:*

> . . . the more unique his nature, the more peculiarly his own will be the colouring of his language.—OTTO JESPERSEN, *Mankind, Nation and Individual from a Linguistic Point of View,* p. 204.

The American Heritage
Dictionary of the English
Language

Boston, 1969

Usage: Unique, in careful usage, is not preceded by adverbs that qualify it with respect to degree. Examples such as *rather unique,* with reference to a book, and *the most unique,* referring to the most unusual of a rare species of animals, are termed unacceptable by 94 per cent of the Usage Panel, on the ground that the quality described by *unique* cannot be said to vary in degree or intensity and is therefore not capable of comparison. The same objection is raised about examples in which *unique* is preceded by *more, somewhat,* and *very.* In such examples an appropriate substitute for *unique* can usually be found from among *unusual, remarkable, rare, exceptional,* or the like, which are weaker and can be qualified freely. However, *unique* can be modified by terms that do not imply degree in the sense noted: *almost* (or *nearly*) *unique; really* (or *quite,* meaning *truly*) *unique; more* (or *most*) *nearly unique.*

1. Do the authorities agree in their comments on the use of *unique*? Summarize the attitudes expressed in the selections. How can you account for differences in the statements?

2. The Evanses mention the word *singular* but provide no entry discussing it. *The American Heritage Dictionary* also has no entry treating usage for *singular*. By the kind of logic used in the *Heritage* discussion of *unique*, should it also have a discussion of *singular*?

3. Consider other words with what is sometimes called an absolute meaning—*perfect, opposite, complete, waterproof, outstanding.* Would you use *more* to modify any of them? Look them up in a usage dictionary.

2

Facts About Usage

Albert H. Marckwardt and Fred G. Walcott

In the late 1920's Professor Sterling A. Leonard surveyed the opinions of a panel of 229 "judges" about the appropriateness of 230 expressions "of whose standing there might be some question." The judges, who included linguistic specialists, editors, authors, businessmen, and teachers, were asked to classify the expressions —according to their observation of what usage was, not what it ought to be— as formally correct, acceptable for informal conversation, or illiterate. Some years later, Albert H. Marckwardt, professor of English and linguistics at Princeton University, and Fred G. Walcott, professor of education and English at the University of Michigan, reconsidered Leonard's findings, partly to ascertain their relation to recorded facts of usage found in extensive dictionaries such as The Oxford English Dictionary. *The opinions of the judges on Leonard's panel did not always agree with the recorded data. For example, Leonard's judges did not agree about 121 items; Marckwardt and Walcott found sixty-three of these recorded as belonging to literary usage. Marckwardt and Walcott reprinted the Leonard study along with their own in* Facts About Current English Usage *(1938). The following selection brings together comments from both studies. To avoid confusion, abbreviations have been expanded.*

They invited my friends and *myself*.   (91: established)

One linguist says: "It occurs to me that I am willing to make an exception of Omar's 'Myself when young,' because of its sheer charm. But I would shut it out everywhere else save for emphasis."

The editors rated this highest, linguists second, business men last. 62 per cent of all the judges approved it, thus placing it low among established usages. This would suggest that, while perhaps people who are especially careful of their speech would avoid this expression, nevertheless it would hardly be safe to condemn it as incorrect.

New English Dictionary, third usage, 1205–1856, "in an enumeration, when not occupying first place . . . commonly preferred to me."

It is me.   (73: established)

This is a construction which has been made the subject of newspaper editorials beyond counting; and every purist who has felt the sanctity of grammatical English threatened has gone forth to do battle against those who would permit the verb *to be* thus to be followed by an objective pronoun. The fact seems to be that schematic grammar has little to do with usage.

Many of the comments recorded were flatly contradictory. Here are some of them:

"Unpardonable grammar."

"Incorrect—*bad*—but used often by discriminating people who rebel against the formalism of 'it is I.' I prefer 'it is I.' "

"Many purists approve it, but it seems not to have gained respectability."

"This expression is used so commonly that, among certain classes of people, it is considered quite correct. Others, however, never use it."

"Emerging into [literary English]."

"*I* sounds quite mad in certain cases: e.g., point to a photo: 'Which is I?' ! ! ! 'Oh, I see, that's I' ! ! ! Absolutely non-English, hang all the grammarians on earth."

This expression is listed here among the established usages on the basis of the way the linguists voted—only three of twenty-eight condemning it as illiterate. If all the judges' estimates had been taken into consideration, without weighting on the basis of the greater expertness of one group as against another, this sentence would have been placed among the disputable usages —only the business men, of whom eighteen condemned and five approved, would place it among expressions clearly illiterate. One hundred thirty judges altogether approved this; ninety-one condemned. This can hardly constitute sufficient reason for taking time to teach "it is I" in school. As a matter of fact, both forms are at present avoided by careful speakers.

New English Dictionary, sixth usage, 1591–1758, Shakespeare and Goldsmith cited. *New International Dictionary* (1934), "colloquial and dialect."

> I am older than *him*.   (181: disputable)

Linguists say:

"Personally I generally say 'I am older than *he is*.' But never 'older than *he*.' Sometimes, no doubt, 'older than him.' "

"We all know that these expressions are taboo. Also that most people (educated or otherwise) use them to the exclusion of the alternate form." . . .

Speech teachers and business men place this expression at the bottom of the list of expressions on the first ballot; the other groups of judges place it higher, but there is a decided majority against its inclusion among allowable expressions.

New English Dictionary, third usage, 1759–1764, but the predicative *him* citations range from 1381–1840. "Common in colloquial language from the end of the sixteenth century."

> If John *had of* come, I needn't have.   (224: illiterate)

This expression has no standing in current usage.

> Do it *like* he tells you.   (186: disputable)

A British linguist says: "I rate this as good colloquial English—good literary English where clause-verb is suppressed; e.g. 'Roared like a bull.' Where *like* means definitely 'in the very manner' I should rather say, 'Do it the way he tells you,' or even 'Do it how he tells you,' though I feel the latter (not the former) to be doubtful—children's English.

"When I use *like* it is rather, so to speak, apposition. 'I ran away of course, like you did' (the same thing which you did).

"When the clause-verb is omitted, everyone uses *like* (even the blithering purists—not realizing, with their usual ignorance, what they are doing). 'He drank like a fish.' ('He drank as a fish' would mean, of course, when he was a fish.) So that one is forced, of course, to say, 'He danced like a child' since 'as a child' would mean 'when he was.' Meredith says, 'threading it with color, like yewberries the yew.' " . . .

The various groups of judges agreed rather closely on this expression. Their vote gives little support to those who consider use of *like* permissible.

New English Dictionary, 1530–1886, "Now generally condemned as vulgar or slovenly, though examples may be found in many recent writers of standing." Citations include Shakespeare, Southey, and William Morris.

WORKING WITH THE SELECTION

1. A more recent survey of opinions on usage was conducted in the late 1960's by the editors preparing *The American Heritage Dictionary* (1969). They

consulted one hundred judges, fewer than Leonard, but discovered equal disagreement among the experts. Compare the following statements from the dictionary with the observations by Marckwardt and Walcott. Are there any differences in the attitudes expressed? Is there any indication of a change in usage during the time between the two surveys? Do the comments suggest any differences in the kinds of opinions solicited by the two surveys?

> **myself** . . . *Usage:* The use of *myself* (for *me*) in compound objects, as in *He asked John and myself* is condemned by 95 per cent of the Usage Panel (Gilbert Highet: "a prissy evasion of *me*"; Walter "Red" Smith: "the refuge of idiots taught early that *me* is a dirty word"). Also strongly condemned is the use of *myself* (for *I*) in subjects, as in *Mr. Jones and myself are undecided.*

> **me** . . . *Usage: I,* rather than *me,* is the grammatically prescribed first person pronoun for use after the verb *be: It is I.* In formal writing, *it is I* is the construction specified by 78 per cent of the Usage Panel. The variant *it is me* (or *it's me*) is felt by many persons to be much more natural in speech, and this form is termed acceptable in speech on all levels by 60 per cent of the Panel.

> **Like** . . . *Usage: Like,* as a conjunction, is not appropriate to formal usage, especially written usage, except in certain constructions noted below. On other levels it occurs frequently, especially in casual speech and in writing representing speech. In formal usage the conjunctive *like* is most acceptable when it introduces an elliptical clause in which a verb is not expressed: *He took to politics like a fish to water. The dress looked like new.* Both examples, which are acceptable on a formal level to 76 per cent of the Usage Panel, employ such elliptical, or shortened, expressions following *like.* If they were recast to include full clauses containing verbs, *like* would preferably be replaced, in formal usage, by *as, as if,* or *as though: took to politics as a fish takes to water; dress looked as if it were new.* The examples that follow illustrate the difference. All employ *like* to introduce full clauses containing verbs; all are termed unacceptable by more than 75 per cent of the Usage Panel, and in every case a more desirable construction is indicated: *He manipulates an audience like* (preferably *as*) *a virtuoso commands a musical instrument. The engine responds now like* (preferably *as*) *good machinery should. It looks like* (preferably *as if*) *they will be finished earlier than usual. He had no authority, but he always acted like* (preferably *as if*) *he did.* . . .

2. Try a survey of your own on some "disputed" usages, selecting a panel from among your friends or teachers. You might ask their opinions about the usages discussed in the selection. Or you might use others: for example, *Who do you want to see? Everybody knew their jobs. They wanted Mary and I to go. The books were laying on the table.* Compare your results with the views in a usage dictionary.

3. Can you think of any inadequacies of surveys like those described above as devices for collecting facts about usage? Can you think of another way to go about getting data on usage?

A Teacher Declines to Turn the Other Cheek

Ellsworth Barnard

Ellsworth Barnard, who has taught English at a number of American colleges and universities, was a visiting lecturer at Bowdoin College, on leave from the University of Chicago, when the following exchange appeared in two issues of The Reporter, *15 (December 27, 1956); 16 (January 24, 1957). The first comment is from a regular column entitled "*The Reporter's *Notes"; the second part is the teacher's reply.*

FOR WHO THE BELL TOLLS

It is sad enough when standards slip; it is horrifying when they are officially encouraged to slip. We refer to some remarks made by an English Professor at Bowdoin College, who said among other things that "People should not worry so much about their grammar," and that it made no difference whether a person used "who" when he should have said "whom," or "will" when "shall" was correct. "Any large group of people sets its own standards," he said.

If ever there were incitement to mob rule, this is it.

LETTER TO THE EDITOR

I am the "English professor at Bowdoin College" (actually "Visiting Lecturer") so vehemently reprehended in *"The Reporter's* Notes" in your December 27 issue, and I hope you will let me be heard in my own defense. This kind of comment one expects, and can laugh at, in the Chicago *Tribune.* But in *The Reporter,* which I have been praising for years as the best magazine of news and opinions, it is not funny.

In the first place, your quarrel is only partly with me. It ought to be mainly with the ethical standards of newspaper editors. The original story was based on a telephone interview between me and a United Press reporter following a talk that I gave to a group of English teachers; and although I never saw it, I judge that, though oversimplified and misleading in some passages, it was an honest story. But the editors of the country's newspapers evidently had no scruples about cutting and revising it to suit their own notions of what is "news." In particular, I have heard of but one version (I believe in the Providence *Journal*) that included the two most important paragraphs, which read as follows:

"Dr. Barnard said teachers should teach Johnny a few fundamental grammar rules—that is all. This will leave all concerned more time for more important matters.

"He said four points should be hammered into students in high schools. They are: sentences ('knowing the difference between a complete and an incomplete sentence'); making sure that subjects and verbs agree; direct, straightforward language instead of flowery poetic words; and organization of material."

You will agree that the omission of these paragraphs totally falsifies the point that I was trying to make. Perhaps you will also forgive me, as a mere English teacher who tries to teach his freshmen not to quote inaccurately or out of context, and to have respect for facts, for not anticipating that the nation's news editors and editorial writers would be quite so contemptuous of the truth.

There *is* a quarrel between us, however, even on the basis of the mangled versions of the story whose authenticity you did not bother to check. You seem not to have heard of certain principles accepted by all competent students of linguistic science. The first is that a living language is organic and ever-changing, that therefore usage is the only ultimate determinant of correctness, and that lexicographers and grammarians record and do not legislate. The second is that there are "levels of usage," generally held to be three: formal written English; the informal spoken English of educated people ("colloquial" English); and the normal spoken English of nonprofessional people (called, with no implied disparagement, "vulgate"). Language is like dress: The question is one of manners and not morals, of what is appropriate and not what is legal. "Ain't," for instance, has a long and honorable etymological pedigree, and it is a useful word, which I envy ordinary folk the right to use with propriety, as I cannot—simply because professional people do not use it.

But, further, many of the textbook "rules" bear no relation to actual practice, even on the level of formal English. The multifarious textbook distinctions between "shall" and "will" are cheerfully ignored by practically everybody—as any honest observer will have to agree—and no harm is done to anyone or to the language. As for "who" and "whom," even educated people get hopelessly confused. And so on through a lengthy list.

My appeal is simply to honesty and common sense—is simply that we do not force students to join us in the pretense that certain verbal expressions are taboo, although they and we meet these expressions every day of our lives in the most respectable newspapers and magazines and in the most highbrow radio and television programs. We can then concentrate on the *real* problems of communication—some of which I mentioned in the paragraph that most editors did not see fit to print.

1. Is *The Reporter* columnist using the term *grammar* in the way it is used in this book?

2. What is your estimate of the two arguments? Is Barnard's attitude an "incitement to mob rule"? Barnard asserts that there is some quarrel between him and the journalist; what, apparently, is it?

4

A Word to End a Sentence With

Hugh Sykes Davies

Hugh Sykes Davies, Fellow of St. Johns College, Cambridge University, writes mainly on novels and novelists. The following discussion of an old schoolroom "rule" is a chapter of his Grammar Without Tears *(1953).*

It is not surprising to find that the fuss about prepositions at the end of sentences was started by Dryden. Brought up on the grammatical principles of Mulcaster, Greaves, and Hewes, which based English usage on Latin, and himself addicted to the method of translating English into Latin when he wanted to find out what he was saying, it was natural enough that he should have made at least one outstanding contribution to the confusion of real English grammar.

Dryden had already spent some twelve years in the energetic pursuit of letters when he suddenly announced that the preposition at the end of a sentence was a 'fault': one which 'he had but lately observed in his own writings,' and which was very common in Ben Jonson. He might well have added that it was very common in the great masters of English contemporary with Ben Jonson. Shakespeare, for example, in *As You Like It*, feels no qualm in making a very courtly and polished gentleman say: 'I would have told you of good wrestling, which you have lost the sight of.' And Macbeth thus addresses Banquo's Ghost: 'Thou hast no speculation in those eyes Which thou dost glare with.' The Authorised Version, generally (and perhaps wrongly) thought to be a very good example of English, has at Genesis 28: 'for I will not leave thee, until I have done that which I have spoken to thee of.' And Lord Bacon has: 'Houses are built to live in, and not to look on.'

So far as 'Custom, the most certain Mistresse of language,' is concerned, there can be no doubt that the placing of the preposition at the end of a sentence was fully authorised. Dryden himself, in the earlier part of his career, had given it further authorisation of the same kind, by writing freely such phrases as 'the age I live in.' But having come to his great decision, he resolutely changed his own custom for the future, and when he got the chance of re-editing his older writings, he amended them, so that the phrase just quoted became 'the age in which I live.'

Unfortunately, he never explicitly stated the principle which thus led him to interfere with the custom of the best English writers, and with his own earlier practice. But it is not difficult to see how he arrived at it. Whenever he wrote Latin to stabilise his English grammar, he would find the prepositions always removed from the end of the sentence. He could not conceivably have written 'aetas qua vivo in'; the Latin order was always 'aetas in qua vivo.' But to follow the example of Latin here was to ignore a great difference between Latin and English in their manner of connecting verbs and prepositions. In Latin, following the generally synthetic method of grammar, the prepositions tended to become prefixes, and to be fused with the verbs. For example, the preposition *in* was fused with the verbal root *pos* to make the word which we have in English as *impose,* meaning literally 'to put upon.' But when the English version is used, the preposition remains a separate word, and it follows the verb. The same is true of the nouns derived from these two verbs; the Latin noun is the synthetic 'imposter,' the English is the analytic phrase 'a person you are put upon by.'

It follows naturally from this difference in the handling and placing of the preposition that in English it very often comes after the verb, and may well work its way to the end of the sentence. The attempt to place it somewhere else can produce effects of great awkwardness, such as Dr. Johnson's 'wonders of which he proposed to solace himself with the contemplation.'

On the other hand, it must be admitted that sometimes the end preposition may produce, if not quite the same awkwardness, an impression of untidiness and weakness, as it does in these examples from Fielding:

> *Many stories of the lady, which he swore to the truth of.*
> *His Sophia, whom he now resolved never more to abandon the pursuit of.*
> *He expressed so much devotion to serve me, which at least I was not certain of the falsehood of.*

It would seem, therefore, that any simple grammatical rule for the placing of the preposition is liable to lead to trouble. It is wrong to say that it never ought to appear at the end of a sentence; but it would be just as wrong to say that it ought always to be placed there.

It may well be that no rule at all is needed, that the common linguistic instinct of the English is well able to look after placing prepositions, now, as it did before Dryden set the unhappy example of meddling with them in the Latin manner. But if a rule should be needed, it must be sought by means of a consideration of English grammar, and its special, non-Latin use of meaning and word-order. A rule of this kind might perhaps be derived from the fact that in the average English sentence, one of the positions of greatest emphasis is the ending. The reasons for this are not quite clear; perhaps the ending remains especially clear in the reader's mind because he has heard it more recently than the rest of the sentence; or it may be that the usual intonation of English speech, which affects the 'inner voice' of the reader, gives a kind of climax at the end of the sentence. But whatever the reason may be, the fact itself is clear enough. And it would suggest this much guidance for the placing of prepositions: when the meaning of the sentence demands that weight and emphasis should fall upon them, they are well placed at the end, but when the meaning demands no such weight, they are best placed elsewhere, in a less conspicuous position that befits their less emphatic role.

On this principle, all the examples just quoted from Fielding would be bad, because the prepositions are doing merely grammatical hack-work, and no important stress of meaning is intended to fall on them. On the other hand, the sentence quoted from Bacon is good: 'Houses are built to live in, and not to look on.' It is entirely in harmony with the meaning, and adds greatly to the force of the expression, to give the greatest emphasis to 'in' and 'on.' To a lesser extent, the same might be said of this sentence from Pope: 'In the most regular gardens, art can only reduce the beauties of nature to more regularity, and such a figure, which the common eye may better take in, and is therefore more entertained with.'

This principle, which no doubt has many limitations, would at any rate be superior to the dismal little piece of pedantry so unhappily introduced by Dryden. It would avoid latinisation and formalism, and it would serve the purpose of directing attention to what is really important in the use of English: to the attainment of an effective harmony between the meaning and the natural properties of emphasis in the different parts of the sentence.

WORKING WITH THE SELECTION

1. What does Davies mean by suggesting that the "rule" on final prepositions was based on Latin grammar and that any new principle should be based on English grammar? How do the grammars differ? If you need to refresh your memory, review the selection by Dykema in Part 4.

2. Try changing some of Davies' examples with final prepositions so that these particles do not occur at the end. Do any of them seem to you to be improved by the change? Collect twenty examples from your reading or from speech that you hear of prepositions at the ends of sentences. Then try moving the prepositions and survey the results.

5

Usage and Society

Robert A. Hall, Jr.

Robert A. Hall, Jr., professor of linguistics at Cornell University, is a specialist in Italian and Romance philology as well as an expert on pidgin and creole languages. The following survey of some social influences on usage is from Introductory Linguistics (*1964*).

Language is . . . both an individual and a social phenomenon. It is individual because it manifests itself only in the habits—potential or actualized —of each individual speaker. Since these habits are controlled in the brain— though it is not yet known for certain in which part of the brain, or even if there is a specific part of the brain which controls language habits—we may speak of linguistic activity as having its *locus existendi* in the individual brain. At the same time, language is intimately connected with society through its function, which is primarily that of communicating messages from any given individual to one or more others; nor could human society exist without language. These two aspects of language, the individual and the social, are therefore extremely closely interconnected. Language forms the major link between the individual and society, and makes it possible for him to live at the same time as an individual personality complete in himself, and as a fully functioning member of his social group.

By the age of twelve or thirteen, the normal individual has a fully developed and functioning linguistic system, and may be referred to as a linguistic adult. (We are referring here to the *structure*, not to the *vocabulary*, involved in the linguistic system; one's stock of vocabulary items can of course undergo even considerable expansion after the age of twelve or thirteen.) Each person's total set of language habits is termed his *idiolect*, and is peculiar to him as an individual. This does not mean that the individual invents his idiolect out of thin air. On the contrary, the individual "creates" nothing in his idiolect, except in the sense that he has been building it up, in his behavior patterns, since his earliest childhood; but every idiolect is developed through imitation of other idiolects. The individual normally imitates very closely those models with whom he has been in continual and intensive contact, especially in his early years (parents, playmates, teachers), and less closely those with whom his contacts have been less intimate. Yet, since each individual has different experiences from those of every other individual, in language as in other matters, each idiolect is different, at least in slight details, from every other. No two idiolects are absolutely identical in every respect, any more than any two sets of fingerprints.

Yet of course, humans are able to communicate with each other, by virtue of the similarity of idiolects. Whenever two or more individuals are able to talk together and understand each other, the resultant group is termed a *speech-community*. The degree of closeness of similarity between two or more idiolects—and hence the degree of mutual comprehension, and of cohesiveness of the speech-community—is relative. In small, closely-knit groups, all of whose members are in continual contact with each other, the cohesiveness of the speech-community is correspondingly great, and the differences between idiolects are minor. This is the case in small families, tribes, or communities which live isolated from other groups while having intense contacts within their own group (e.g., the Amish in eastern Pennsylvania, or many mountain tribes in Central and South America). At the opposite extreme is the type of large, even immense modern speech-community like those of English, French, or Chinese, with hundreds of millions of speakers and numerous sub-divisions. In such large groups, the speakers within each major sub-division (say, North America, Great Britain, Australia, etc., within the English-speaking world) have little difficulty in understanding each other, and even speakers from neighboring sub-divisions (e.g., Australia and New Zealand). At the extremes of linguistic divergence, however, even those who belong to the same over-all speech-community (say, a Georgia "cracker" and a Scottish Highlander, or a North Chinese and a Cantonese) have considerable difficulty in achieving mutual comprehension.

It follows that all the terms which refer to linguistic groupings (*language, dialect, sub-dialect*) larger than the individual idiolect are likewise all relative. (Here we must avoid a widespread confusion of terms: linguistic analysts use the term *dialect,* not in its popular pejorative sense of "vulgar, uneducated, foreign, or rustic speech," but to refer to any sub-division of a language, even the most prestigious literary variety.) Usually, the term *language* is reserved for the largest linguistic grouping within any speech-community (e.g., English, French, German, Italian, Spanish). The term *dialect* refers to any sub-division thereof, such as Tuscan, Lombard, Piedmontese, etc., in Italian; and *sub-dialect* refers to a lesser division within a dialect, such as Milanese, Bergamasque, and so on among the varieties of Lombard. At the other extreme of size, larger groups of related languages which have developed by differentiation out of a common source are called *families,* and a group of related families is a *stock.* Thus, Spanish, Italian, French, and the other Romance languages, which are developed out of Latin, form the Romance family; and the Latin, Celtic, Germanic, Balto-Slavic, Indo-Iranian, and several other families make up the Indo-European stock. However, since these terms too are relative, considerable variation exists in their use, and some scholars will even refer to the language families which make up the Indo-European stock as "the Indo-European dialects" because, at one time, they undoubtedly were simply varieties of one language.

Within any given speech-community, there are lines of greater or lesser *density of communication*—in other words, any given individual talks more to some people than to others. In theory, those individuals who talk most to each other—between whom the density of communication is greatest— should influence each other most and should therefore show the greatest similarity in their speech. Actually, however, other factors enter into play as well, especially that of prestige, so that any given speaker may be influenced more (say, in following a given pronunciation, grammatical feature, or item of vocabulary) by one or more prestige-bearing persons who are relatively removed from him socially, than by a much larger number of close everyday associates. The interplay of social contact and prestige groups, in influencing any given idiolect, is often very complicated, especially in modern times, when prestige figures are beginning to exert considerable influence through newspapers, radio, and television.

In analyzing the reflection of social structure in the differentiation of a speech-community, we must distinguish two planes: that of dialectal divisions, and that of functional levels of usage. Leonard Bloomfield's statement of the relation between dialects is classical (*Language*, p. 52):

> The main types of speech in a complex speech community can be roughly classified as follows:
>
> (1) *Literary standard*, used in the most formal discussion and writing (example: *I have none*);
>
> (2) *Colloquial standard*, the speech of the privileged class (example: *I haven't any* or *I haven't got any*—in England only if spoken with the southern "public school" sounds and intonation);
>
> (3) *Provincial standard*, in the United States probably not to be differentiated from 2, spoken by the "middle class," very close to 2, but differing slightly from province to province (example: *I haven't any* or *I haven't got any*, spoken, in England, with sounds or intonations that deviate from the "public school" standard);
>
> (4) *Substandard*, clearly different from 1, 2, and 3, spoken in European countries by the "lower middle" class, in the United States by almost all but the speakers of types 2 and 3, and differing topographically, without intense local difference (example: *I ain't got none*);
>
> (5) *Local dialect*, spoken by the least privileged class; only slightly developed in the United States; in Switzerland used also, as a domestic language, by the other classes; differs almost from village to village; the varieties so great as often to be incomprehensible to each other and to speakers of 2, 3, and 4 (example: *a hae nane*).

Intersecting with these lines of dialectal division, and especially with that between standard and nonstandard, is the difference in functional level, between formal and informal, first formulated by the late John S. Kenyon, one of the ablest observers of American English speech. Kenyon established a four-way distinction, between:

(a) *Formal standard:* Normally used only in very "correct" situations and elegant writing, oratory, and what used to be termed "elocution" (e.g., *it is I*).

(b) *Informal standard:* Used by socially acceptable people in their ordinary everyday contacts (e.g., *it's me; he went away; that's yours*).

(c) *Informal nonstandard:* Essentially equivalent to Bloomfield's "substandard" (e.g., *he beat it; he took it on the lam; that's yourn; you and me better go home*).

(d) *Formal nonstandard:* A variety which arises when those whose native speech is informal nonstandard try to achieve the formal level, and often create forms or combinations which no standard speaker would ever use on any level (e.g. *between you and I*).

The boundaries between dialectal divisions and between functional levels are, of course, subject to many gradations and are constantly shifting in space, time, and social level. Features of usage are constantly passing from one status to another, either rising or falling in prestige. Thus, *leisure* used to be pronounced with the vowel of *beat* in the first syllable throughout the English-speaking world, as it still is in the United States; in British standard usage, this pronunciation has been replaced by one rhyming with *measure,* and the earlier pronunciation has been relegated to the status of a rather archaic provincialism. To pronounce the names of the days of the week (*Sunday, Monday,* etc.) with the full vowel of the word *day* in the second part of the compound (e.g., *Sún-dày* instead of *Súndy*) used to be an outstanding example of formal nonstandard usage; Kenyon cites the instance of a broadcaster who announced "Sún-dày will be Móther's Dày," which many of his hearers interpreted as "Some day will be Mother's Day." Similarly, the use of *presently* in the sense of "at present" instead of "soon" used to be formal nonstandard, with a connotation of rather vulgar, pretentious journalese. Both of these usages, however, and many others like them, have by now become so widespread that they have passed from the status of formal nonstandard to that of informal standard, even though many members of the speech-community (the present writer included!) still dislike them.

In a geographical sense, too, the boundaries of speech-communities or of their subdivisions are almost never absolutely sharp or fixed. Even in the case of different languages (e.g., French and Flemish in Belgium, French and German in France and Switzerland, or French and English in Canada), there are often tiny islands or enclaves of one language within the territory along the frontier. In a city like Brussels, which lies athwart the boundary between French and Flemish, the interpenetration of the different speech-communities becomes extremely complicated. Furthermore, there are continual shifts taking place from day to day and from hour to hour, not only with the casual movements of individuals along the frontier and beyond it, but also with changes of residence on a more or less permanent basis. Many individuals, both in and out of border zones, are bilingual or multilingual, and hence can be said to have two or more idiolects and to belong to more than one speech-community. The same considerations hold true, with even greater force, for the boundaries between dialects within a single speech-community; here, social mobility is a further factor tending to blur the divisions even more. Consequently, any lines which we may draw between one dialect and another, or even one language and another, can never be more than an approximation. However, in this as in many other aspects of mass phenomena, we must use approximations, *faute de mieux,* simply because a complete and detailed description would be beyond any possibility of achievement.

Linguistic features serve both centripetal and centrifugal purposes in social structure. Without the cement of communication through language, humans could never have achieved anything like the complicated methods of cooperation on which even the simplest society depends. On the other hand, most social divisions, although not caused by language, are accentuated by the existence of linguistic differences and the use which many persons make of these latter for enhancing their social position, a process of linguistic snobbery. Both positively and negatively, our use of language is inextricably interwoven with our existence both as individuals and as members of human society.

WORKING WITH THE SELECTION

1. What is the difference between dialectal divisions and functional levels of usage? In the article referred to by Hall, Kenyon objects to the use of the word *level* to refer to different styles of language. He says he prefers *varieties* to distinguish differences in the language suitable for different uses. Can you see any reason for his preference?

2. One of Kenyon's objections to the use of *level* is that it perpetuates the notion that colloquial English is somehow inferior. What is the meaning of *colloquial?*

3. Recalling discussions on dialect in Part 5, describe the different sorts of dialectal considerations in Bloomfield's classification presented by Hall.

6

Doctrines of English Usage

Charles V. Hartung

Charles V. Hartung is professor of English at the University of California, Los Angeles. His article describing four different approaches to problems of usage appeared in the English Journal, *45 (December, 1956).*

Generally speaking, the four main doctrines current among those concerned with judging the propriety of language usage are: (1) the doctrine of rules; (2) the doctrine of general usage; (3) the doctrine of appropriate usage; (4) the doctrine of the linguistic norm. Rarely do those interested in language adhere consistently to any one of those doctrines. Instead there is the usual divergence between theory and practice; some linguists profess one doctrine and practice another. Also there is the usual eclectic compromise. Nevertheless, it is possible to make roughly approximate groupings of schools of opinion according to the degrees of emphasis given to these various doctrines.

THE DOCTRINE OF RULES

From the point of view of the modern school of linguistics the doctrine of rules is, or at least should be, moribund. But even a cursory glance at handbooks and grammars of recent date reveals what a tenacious hold it has on life. And even when the doctrine is disclaimed in theory, we find grammarians following it in spirit and practice. For example, in the preface to R. W. Pence's *A Grammar of Present-Day English,* we find the following statement: "Grammar is not a set of rules thought up by and imposed by some invisible godlike creature." [1] Yet the text itself consists of a set of prescriptions in the spirit of the eighteenth century grammarians and having the effect if not the form of the old rules. Here is an example:

> . . . inasmuch as an interrogative pronoun normally introduces a clause and so may not have the position that a noun of like function would have, the function of an interrogative pronoun may be easily mistaken. Care needs to be exercised to meet the demands of subjective complements of finite verbs and of infinitives. But especial care needs to be

[1] New York: The Macmillan Co., 1947, p. v.

taken that the proper objective form is used when an interrogative pronoun coming first functions as the object of a preposition that is delayed.

1. Subjective complement
   Whom do you mean? (*Whom* is the object of *do mean*.)
2. Object of a preposition
   Whom were you with last night? (*Whom* is the object of the preposition *with*. *Not:* Who were you with last night?)[2]

In a note some concession is made to the demands of spoken discourse: "Who are you looking for? (Accepted by some in spoken discourse.)" But in the same note we find this comment: "This use of the nominative in informal spoken discourse is regarded by a few as acceptable, although the fastidious person will probably look upon it as sloppy speech." It is noteworthy that the text in which this judgment is to be found reached its seventh printing in 1953. Yet the sentence *Who are you looking for* is listed as *Accepted* in the Leonard survey printed in 1932.

It would be possible, of course, to multiply examples of the continuing hold that the doctrine of rules still has on a large proportion of present day students of language, but it is more to the point to examine the reasons for this hold. Probably the most important reason is that the doctrine has behind it the weight of over a century and a half of almost undisputed dominance. This is the result of two main sources of authority: the assumed correspondence of the rules of grammar with basic principles of reason and the supposed correspondence of the rules with the usage of the best writers. Some grammarians have assumed that reason has the prior claim and determines usage: others have placed usage first and have claimed that rules are inductively derived from the best usage. The eighteenth century grammarian William Ward gives typical expression to the view of the first group:

> Use and Custom are considered as the only Rules by which to judge of what is right or wrong in Process. But is the Custom which is observed in the Application of any Language the Effect of Chance? Is not such a Custom a consistent Plan of communicating the Conceptions and rational discursive Operations of one Man to another? And who will maintain, that this is, or can be, the Effect of unmeaning Accident? If then it be not so, it must be the Effect of the Reason of Man, adjusting certain means to a certain End: And it is the Business of Speculative or Rational Grammar to explain the Nature of the Means, and to show how they are applied to accomplish the End proposed. If this can be done with sufficient Evidence, the most simple of the Elements of Logic will become familiar to those who engage in a Course of Grammar, and Reason will go Hand in Hand with Practice.[3]

[2] *Ibid.,* pp. 204–205.
[3] William Ward, *English Grammar* (1765). Quoted by C. C. Fries, *The Teaching of English* (Ann Arbor: The George Wahr Publishing Co., 1949), p. 13.

Ward's linking of grammar and logic was a common eighteenth century practice and carried over into the nineteenth century, receiving the approval of even such a great philosopher as John Stuart Mill. Mill says that "the principles and rules of grammar are the means by which forms of language are made to correspond with the universal forms of thought." [4] The weakness of this thesis was, of course, evident to the language experts of Mill's own time. Henry Sweet and A. H. Sayce brought to bear their great knowledge of comparative philology to show how little actual correspondence there is between logic and grammar, and modern linguists and semanticists have agreed with them. Probably the most judicious summation of the problem is that of Otto Jespersen:

> Most linguists are against any attempt to apply a logical standard to language. Language, they say, is psychology, not logic; or "language is neither logical nor illogical, but alogical." That is to say, language has nothing to do with logic. To many philologists the very word, logic, is like a red rag to a bull. . . . It would be surprising however if language which serves to express thoughts should be quite independent of the laws of correct thinking.[5]

As Jespersen demonstrates, however, what often has pretended to be logic is no more than Latin grammar disguised, and arguments declaring the correspondence of grammar with logic have often been little more than the forcing of English into Latin syntactical patterns. For example, the rule that the predicative must stand in the same case as the subject is not, as has been claimed, an incontrovertible law of thought but merely a rule of Latin grammar. Many languages of different types violate this so-called incontrovertible law.

The authority that the rules have derived from deductive logic has never been equal to the support given them by the belief that rules are inductively derived from examination of the best usage. George Campbell's dictum that reputable, national, and present usage determines correctness has been cited with approval from the days of Lindley Murray, probably the most popular of eighteenth century grammarians, to the present day. Many writers on language have, in fact, cited Campbell's doctrine as liberalizing in effect, but it is difficult to see how such a belief can be accepted. Campbell so restricted the field of acceptable usage that the doctrine of rules lost little of the force it had held in the writings of such prescriptive grammarians as Bishop Lowth and William Ward. Lowth had, of course, declared the independence of grammar from the usage of even the best writers, whereas Campbell paid lip service to the doctrine of usage. But in practice Campbell, as S. A. Leonard has shown, repudiated the very theory he had set up as a guide. We

[4] See I. A. Richards, *Interpretation in Teaching* (London: Routledge & Kegan Paul, 1938), p. 280.
[5] *Mankind, Nation and the Individual* (London: Geo. Allen, 1946), p. 114.

can see what the doctrine of usage actually became when we examine the following statement from a latter day follower of Campbell:

> By good usage is meant the usage generally observed in the writings of the best English authors and in the speech of well-educated people. Dictionaries, grammars, and books on rhetoric and composition record this usage, on the basis of wide observation and study.[6]

This definition follows a pattern dating from the eighteenth century and repeated in scores of nineteenth century handbooks and grammars. The doctrine of usage in the hands of the grammarians has been practically identical with the doctrine of rules.

THE DOCTRINE OF GENERAL USAGE

Joseph Priestley, the eighteenth century scientist and grammarian, was probably the first writer in English to show a consistent regard for the doctrine of general usage. But his views were neglected, and it was not until the rise of scientific linguistics in the late nineteenth century that the doctrine began to make headway against the doctrine of rules. Among the pioneers were W. D. Whitney, Fitzedward Hall, and Alexander Bain. The first full-fledged popular exposition and exemplification of the doctrine, J. Lesslie Hall's *English Usage* (1917), was not published until well into the twentieth century. In contrast with most of his predecessors, who only paid lip service to the doctrine of usage, Hall is consistent and documents his opinion with particular examples. In his article, "Who for Whom," for instance, Hall cites the opinions of contemporary liberal grammarians in favor of *who* as the objective form in questions, and he gives a number of examples from usage, citing Shakespeare, Marlowe, Defoe, Kingsley, and Froude, as well as less well-known writers.

Comprehensive as it is, Hall's work is limited primarily to an examination of written documents, and it was not until Leonard's *Current English Usage* that there was a systematic survey of spoken usage to support Hall's findings. Strictly speaking, the Leonard report is not a survey of the facts of English usage but of opinion about the relative standing of various debatable items. The guiding principle of the survey is indicated succinctly in the statement that "allowable usage is based on the actual practice of cultivated people rather than on rules of syntax or logic."[7] In keeping with this principle, Leonard submitted a number of items of debatable usage to a jury consisting of linguistic specialists, editors, authors, business men, and teachers of English and speech. These judges were to decide the standing of the items

---

[6] Edwin C. Woolley, *Handbook of Composition*, Revised Edition (Boston: D. C. Heath, 1920), p. 1.

[7] Sterling Andrus Leonard, *Current English Usage* (Chicago: The National Council of Teachers of English, 1932), p. 95.

according to what they thought the actual usage to be. Four levels of acceptability were indicated: "literary English," "standard, cultivated, colloquial English," "trade or technical English," and "naif, popular, or uncultivated English." The findings of the report provided evidence to demonstrate the discrepancy between actual usage and the rules of common school grammar. Among the items indicated as *established,* or acceptable on the cultivated colloquial level by more than seventy-five percent of the judges, were *it is me, who are you looking for, I feel badly,* and many other locutions that had long been proscribed by the handbooks and grammars.

The Leonard report was not a survey of "general" usage but of "cultivated" usage. It is not until the research studies of C. C. Fries that we find a truly inclusive and adequately documented study of general usage. Eschewing the guidance of the grammars and even of polls of "educated" usage, Fries stated that "it is probably much more sound to decide that the spontaneous usage of that large group who are carrying on the affairs of English speaking people is the usage to be observed and to set the standard."[8] To provide evidence of actual usage, Fries has used letters and transcripts of telephone conversations. Like other modern advocates of the doctrine of usage, Fries has not held to the theory that the standard of general usage should apply in all language situations. In concession to the demands of effective communication and to the practical problems of the teacher in the classroom he has given assent to the doctrine of appropriateness. The problem of the teacher, according to Fries, is to develop in the student the habits that will enable him to use freely the language appropriate to his ideas, the occasion of their expression, and the needs of his hearers. To bring about this end, the teacher needs to become sensitive to the different levels and functional varieties of usage and to develop a program of study designed to meet the particular needs of each class. Although the teacher must take into account the prevailing demand that he equip his pupils with the language habits that have attained the most social acceptability, he needs to develop also an intelligently liberal attitude toward the particular language habits of any group of students.

THE DOCTRINE OF APPROPRIATENESS

In its essentials the doctrine of appropriateness has not changed since the full exposition by George Philip Krapp in his *Modern English* (1909). Krapp introduces his exposition by making a distinction between "good" English and "conventional" or "standard" English. Good English, according to Krapp, is any language which "hits the mark." Since the purpose of language is the satisfactory communication of thought and feeling, any language which satisfactorily performs this function is good English. Standard English is that usage which is recognized and accepted as customary in any particular community. Such locutions as *he don't* or *these kind of people* or

---

[8] *The Teaching of English,* p. 35.

I will may be standard in one community and not standard in another. Custom is the only relevant determinant of the standard. Krapp's relativism is evident in the following statement:

> What is defended as customary use by a community, or even by a single speaker, to carry the matter to its final analysis, is standard, or conventional, or "right," or "correct," in that community or for that speaker.[9]

In analyzing the concept of "good" English, Krapp arrives at the doctrine of appropriateness. He describes three tendencies in English speech—"popular English," "colloquial English," and "formal or literary English"—and declares that each of these has its appropriate uses. They are three kinds of arrows by which the speaker attempts to hit the mark of good English. Whether the speaker hits the mark or not depends upon his skill and upon his acumen in sizing up the particular speech situation:

> . . . the degree of colloquialism which one permits, in one's self or in others depends on the subject of conversation, on the intimacy of the acquaintanceship of the persons speaking, and in general on all the attendant circumstances . . . language which may be adequately expressive, and therefore good, under one set of circumstances, under a different set of circumstances becomes inadequately expressive, because it says more or less than the speaker intended, and so becomes bad English. One learns thus the lesson of complete relativity of the value of language, that there is no such thing as an absolute English, but that language is valuable only as it effects the purpose one wishes to attain, that what is good at one time may be bad at another, and what is bad at one time may be good at another.[10]

This doctrine has been somewhat qualified by some of its recent exponents, particularly by Pooley and Perrin, but it has not been changed in its essentials. And it is still subject to the same sort of objection that J. Lesslie Hall made to Krapp's statement of it. Hall pointed out that Krapp's conception of "good" English was unprecedented and varied from the commonly accepted meaning of the term. He also deprecated Krapp's advocacy of "a sort of isolated, neighborhood English" and declared that the consistent carrying out of Krapp's ideas would mean the decline of a *general* and reputable usage for which students of language had been struggling. Consistent application of the doctrine of appropriateness would mean that every newcomer to a community would need to learn a new set of speech habits and that every traveler would need to be sensitive to innumerable local dialects and to cater to the personal language habits of his listeners. This would finally result in the decline of a general standard of cultivated speech understood

[9] New York: Charles Scribner's Sons, 1909, p. 332.
[10] *Ibid.,* pp. 327, 329–330.

everywhere and acceptable everywhere. In answer to Hall's objections Krapp might very well have repeated what he had said in *Modern English:* that the completely consistent adherence to the idea of general usage would mean finally a fixed language inadmissive of improvement and that the interplay of standard English and good English makes for a language constantly improving in expressiveness and effectiveness of communication.

THE DOCTRINE OF THE LINGUISTIC NORM

Under the heading of the linguistic norm may be grouped those concepts which emphasize that language is above all responsible to an expressive ideal. Some advocates of the normative approach hold that language should not be subservient to usage and should be judged by consciously derived criteria. I. A. Richards, for instance, has characterized the doctrine of usage as "the most pernicious influence in current English teaching." [11] In attacking the doctrine of usage, Richards does not recommend a return to the doctrine of rules and of what he calls the illegitimate application of logic and philosophy to language. Instead he recommends a self-critical reflection about the conduct of thought in language. Richards' evaluation of modern linguistic theories and his own program are explicitly stated in his latest book:

> There are vast areas of so-called "purely descriptive" linguistics which are a grim danger at present to the conduct of language, to education, to standards of intelligence, to the reserves in theory and in sensibility of the mental tester. . . . The appeal to mere *usage:* "If it's widely in use, it's O.K.," is a case in point. Every useful feature of language was *not in use* once upon a time. Every degradation of language too starts somewhere. Behind usage is the question of efficiency. Inefficient language features are not O.K., however widespread their use. Of course, to the linguistic botanist it is important to preserve all varieties until they have been collected and described. But that is not the point of view of the over-all study of language, its services and its powers. That over-all view is, I am insisting, inescapably NORMATIVE. It is concerned (as every speaker and every listener is always concerned) with the maintenance and improvement of the use of language.[12]

As instances of degradation in language Richards cites the current practice of using *uninterested* and *disinterested* and *imply* and *infer* as synonyms. In each instance the confusion has brought about a loss in precision without a corresponding gain.

Not all adherents to the concept of a linguistic norm have held as strongly as Richards to the principle of consciously critical evaluation of language. Instead such linguistic scholars as Otto Jespersen and Edward Sapir have

[11] *Op. cit.,* p. 174.
[12] *Speculative Instruments* (Chicago: University of Chicago Press, 1955), pp. 123–124.

held that linguistic efficiency is often the result of the spontaneous and intuitive expression of the folk. Probably the best known statement of the belief that language tends constantly toward a norm of maximum expressiveness with least effort is Otto Jespersen's theory of energetics, most recently restated in his *Efficiency in Linguistic Change* (1941).[13] According to Jespersen's theory, linguistic changes involve a constant interplay of opposing demands, one by the individual seeking ease of expression and the other of a social character calling for distinctness of communication. The first tendency is subversive of traditional forms of expression; the second is conservative and tends to keep alive the traditional norm. The interaction between these two demands brings about language changes designed to conserve the energy of the speaker and at the same time to retain power of exact communication.

Edward Sapir's *Language* contains a discussion of the expression *Who did you see* that may serve to illustrate Jespersen's theory.[14] Sapir declares that the syntax of "whom" in *whom did you see* is logically and historically sound but psychologically shaky. The construction is kept alive by social snobbery but will eventually succumb to the pressure put on it by the uncontrolled speech of the folk. Meanwhile, users of *whom* are torn between an unconscious desire to say *who* and a fear of social penalty. The correctness of *whom* is fundamentally false and within a couple of hundred years the "whom" will probably be as delightfully archaic as the Elizabethan "his" [f]or "its." In his analysis, Sapir cites four reasons for the linguistic shakiness of *whom*. First, *who* is becoming invariable because of its linguistic similarity to such invariable forms as the interrogative and relative pronouns, *which, what,* and *that* and the interrogative adverbs *where, when* and *how.* Second, interrogative pronouns normally play an emphatic part in the sentence, and emphatic elements are typically invariable. The third powerful reason for the interrogative use of *who* rather than *whom* is its position in the sentence. Normal word order in English places the subject at the beginning of the sentence, before the verb. And the word in the subject position normally takes the subjective form. A fourth difficulty in *whom did you see* is that the *m* sound slows down the movement of the sentence and calls for a deliberate mental and physical effort at odds with the spontaneous speech situations in which the expression is normally used. For these reasons then *whom* is on psychologically shaky grounds and will eventually be replaced by the more natural and expressive *who.* As another instance of the prevalence of psychology over logic in language usage we may cite the rule about the placement of adverbial modifiers. The latest version of Woolley's handbook still carries the following precept and example: "Place such adverbs as *only, merely, just, almost, ever, hardly, scarcely, quite, nearly* next to the words they modify. COLLOQUIAL: *I only want three.* BETTER: *I want only three;* (or)

[13] Copenhaven: Ejnar Munksgaard, 1941, pp. 15–16.
[14] New York: Harcourt, Brace, 1921, pp. 156–162.

I want three only." [15] It may be that the constructions labeled BETTER are more logically sound, but rhetorically and psychologically they may not be as effective as the COLLOQUIAL version. The intention of the speaker may be to emphasize the reasonableness of his request, not the request itself or the exact amount being requested. If such is his intention, the sooner he introduces the idea of reasonableness into his expression the truer he is to his actual meaning and the more likely he is to get a favorable response. The placement of a modifier depends therefore not on an invariable rule of logic or grammar but on the speaker's full meaning. It is this insistence on precision and fullness of meaning which gives force to the doctrine of the linguistic norm. In its expressive aims it is similar to the doctrine of appropriateness, but whereas the doctrine of appropriateness emphasizes the social situation, particularly the effect on an audience, the doctrine of the linguistic norm holds in balance the intention of the speaker, the nature of the language itself, and the probable effect on the audience.

Because of its over-all point of view the doctrine of the linguistic norm is probably the best vantage ground for the teacher. It provides criteria by which to evaluate both the conservative and the liberalizing forces in language. It does not, to be sure, provide the sense of psychological security and social approval so long associated with the doctrine of rules. But submission to dogmatic authority merely out of a desire to gain security hardly seems a constructive attitude. Nor does it seem desirable to compromise personal conviction in the way so often demanded by consistent adherence to either the doctrine of general usage or the doctrine of appropriateness. The most suitable philosophy of language for the teacher would seem to be one calling for a maximum expression. And this is the point of view of the doctrine of the linguistic norm.

WORKING WITH THE SELECTION

1. Hartung says that the "doctrine of rules is, or at least should be, moribund." Examine a handbook or rhetoric you know that is used in composition courses. Which of the doctrines does it seem to follow?

2. Do you find any expressions of the doctrine of rules in the selections from usage manuals at the beginning of this part? Was either Barnard or his journalistic opponent relying on the doctrine of rules?

3. In the discussion of the doctrine of general usage, Hartung comments on the Leonard survey. Would the comments apply also to the survey by the editors of *The American Heritage Dictionary?*

4. Which of the doctrines does Fowler seem to hold? Explain your answer.

5. Write a paper discussing what seems to you a sensible attitude toward usage. Take advantage of the evidence in the selections to provide support for any position you take or any doctrine you espouse.

[15] *College Handbook of Composition* (Boston: D. C. Heath, 1951), p. 89.

part 7

A Changing Language

We know little about where language came from and can only project where it is going, but we know much about where it has been. This knowledge reveals what it is, and correspondingly, how it can be used. Three great discoveries have helped order this knowledge: (1) language always changes, or at least all known languages always have, and we assume that they always will and that change is healthy, or at the least natural, for language; (2) language grows to a great extent through dialects, both regional and social; and (3) extant languages have come from earlier languages, and can thus be understood in part through knowledge of their ancestors and their sister and cousin languages. The selections in Part 7 illustrate the third principle, that languages develop in relation to other languages, particularly that they stem from ancestor languages. In the light of this principle the past, present, and probable future of English become clearer.

We are still ignorant of much that must be knowable about language; nevertheless, we now believe, on the basis of language history, that our ancestors of even a few centuries ago were very wrong about human speech and that we are essentially right. Scholars formerly trusted that language could be fixed so that it would not change, and that it ought to be made unchangeable; presumably, if the Lord gave language, he gave it as he wanted it. Man's job was to preserve it, not to analyze it. Furthermore, scholars assumed that preserving language meant preserving all its details. They seem not to have considered that if a supreme being established language, he probably established its fundamental principles, and that if one of those principles was that of change, attempting to preserve the details of language worked against divine will. In any event, so long as students were concerned with an impossible attempt to stop language, not to study it, they were not very likely to learn much about it.

The breakthrough came with the discovery that languages exist in families, families that reflect the descent of language, but we were not able to understand this growth very well until we had recognized also the importance of dialects. Languages tend to standardize, to build together into systems, but they also tend to pull apart. They pull apart by dialects, that is, they break up into segments of speech habits. People isolated geographically from other people develop their own regional dialect; this change is so inevitable in language that the smallest bodies of speech we have ever discovered, used by only a few hundred speakers, are somewhat fractured into regional dialects. Similarly, the social and occupa-

tional groups within a geographical community develop dialects. When dialects operate long enough without much disturbance, they standardize into languages. Thus every language we know of, throughout language history, reflects its descents from earlier languages. We can understand languages, their growth and their relationships—and to a degree their natures—only if we study them from the points of view of dialect and language families. Fortunately, for students, historical investigation of this sort can be fascinating as well as revealing.

1

The Backgrounds of English

Thomas Pyles

The following selection by Thomas Pyles is from The Origins and Development of the English Language, *2nd ed. (1971). The asterisks before Indo-European roots and words indicate that these forms have been reconstructed; Indo-European was an unwritten language.*

LANGUAGE FAMILIES

In the discussion of so-called linguistic families which follows, we must bear in mind that a language is not born, nor does it put out branches like a tree —nor, for that matter, does it die except when every single one of its speakers dies, as has happened to Etruscan, Gothic, Cornish, and a good many other languages. When we speak of Latin as a dead language, we are referring to a highly artificial literary language; but spoken Latin still lives in various developments in Italian, French, Spanish, and the other Romance languages.

Hence the terms *family, ancestor, parent,* and other genealogical expressions when applied to languages must be regarded as no more than metaphors. Languages are developments of older languages rather than descendants in the sense in which people are descendants of their forefathers. Thus, Italian and Spanish are different developments of an earlier, more unified language, Latin. Latin in turn is one of a number of developments, which include Oscan and Umbrian, of a still earlier language called Italic. Italic in its turn is a development of Indo-European. Whether or not Indo-European has affinities with other languages spoken in prehistoric times and is hence a development of an even earlier language, no one is prepared to say with certainty; for, as we have seen, we are quite in the dark about how it all began.

Older scholars—and they were to some extent theorists—classified languages as monosyllabic, agglutinative, incorporative, and inflective, these being exemplified respectively by Chinese, Turkish, Eskimo, and Latin. The monosyllabic languages were supposed to represent the most primitive type —a notion which doubtless grew out of investigations into languages of our own Indo-European group, with their large number of monosyllabic roots. But even the earliest (middle of second millennium B.C.) records of Chinese, a monosyllabic language in its modern form, represent not a primitive but actually a late stage in linguistic development. It obviously cannot be inferred from such evidence as this that our prehistoric ancestors prattled in words of one syllable each.

The older scholars also observed, quite correctly, that in certain languages, such as Turkish and Hungarian, words were made up of parts "stuck together," as it were; hence the term *agglutinative*. In such languages the suffixal elements are usually whole syllables having very definite meanings. The inflectional suffixes of the Indo-European languages were supposed likewise once to have been independent words; hence, some believed that the inflective languages had grown out of the agglutinative. Little was known of what were called incorporative languages, in which all sentence elements are combined into a single word; the elements have no independent existence, but can appear only as infixes.

The trouble with such a classification is that, though apparently objective, it is not really so, but is instead based on the out-of-date theory that early man spoke in monosyllables. Furthermore, the difference between agglutinative and inflective was not well defined, and there was considerable overlapping. Nevertheless, the terms are useful and widely used in the description of specific languages or even groups of languages. Modern objective and well-informed typological classifications have been especially useful in showing language similarities and differences from a particular point of view.

From our point of view, however, a much more satisfactory and more objective classification of languages is the so-called genetic one, made on the basis of such correspondences of sound and structure as indicate relationship through common origin. Perhaps the greatest contribution of nineteenth-century linguistic scholars was the painstaking investigation of these correspondences, many of which had been noted long before.

Such investigation indicated unmistakably that practically all of the languages of Europe (and hence of the Americas and other parts of the world colonized by Europeans) and some of Asia have in common certain characteristics of sound and structure and to some extent a stock of words which make it perfectly obvious that they have all developed out of a single language spoken in prehistoric times. This earlier language is usually called Indo-European.[1] What it was called by those who spoke it we have no way of knowing, nor do we know what they called themselves. We shall here follow the usual practice of referring to them as the Indo-Europeans, but it must always be borne in mind that the term has no racial connotations; it refers only to a group of people who lived in a relatively small area in early times and who spoke a more or less unified language out of which many

---

[1] *Indo-Germanic* is not now much used except by German scholars. Its coinage was not due to German patriotism; it was intended to do no more than indicate what were thought to be the easternmost and westernmost limits of the geographical distribution of the languages recognized as belonging to the group. Another term, *Aryan*, has been used synonymously. Originally this term referred only to the Asiatic languages of the group. This is still the reference which it has in learned use, where its occurrence is now somewhat rare, *Indo-Iranian* and *Indo-Persian* being the preferred terms.

languages have developed in the course of thousands of years. These languages are spoken today by approximately half of the world's population.

THE NON-INDO-EUROPEAN LANGUAGES

Before proceeding to a more detailed discussion of the Indo-European group, we may perhaps best delimit it by briefly noting those languages and groups of languages which are *not* Indo-European. Two important groups have names which reflect the Biblical attempt to derive all the races of men from the three sons of Noah: the Semitic (from the Latin form of the name of the eldest son, more correctly called Shem in English) and the Hamitic. The term *Japhetic,* once used for Indo-European, has happily long been obsolete. On the basis of many phonological and morphological features which they share, Semitic and Hamitic are thought by many scholars to be related through a hypothetical common ancestor, Hamito-Semitic; there are also those who believe in an ultimate relationship, impossible to prove, between Semitic and Indo-European.

The Semitic group includes the following languages: (Eastern) Akkadian, called Assyrian in the periods of the oldest texts, and later Babylonian; (Western) Hebrew, Aramaic[2] (the native speech of Jesus Christ), Phoenician, and Moabitic; (Southern) Arabic and Ethiopic. Of these, only Arabic is spoken by large numbers of people over a widespread area. Hebrew has comparatively recently been revived in Israel, to some extent for nationalistic reasons.[3] Ethiopic survives mainly in Geez, a Christian liturgical and learned language of Ethiopia, and in Amharic, which is used in state documents in that country. It is interesting to note that two of the world's most important religious documents are written in Semitic languages—the Old Testament in Hebrew (with large portions of the books of Ezra and Daniel in Aramaic) and the Koran in Arabic.

To the Hamitic group belong Egyptian (called Coptic after the close of the third century of the Christian Era), the Berber dialects of North Africa, and various Cushitic[4] dialects spoken along the upper Nile. Coptic is used in the liturgy of the Coptic Christian Church in Egypt, much as Geez is used

---

[2] Formerly—and incorrectly—called Chaldean, Chaldaic, or Chaldee. Though he should have known better, the foundations of modern linguistic science having already been laid in his day, Noah Webster thought that "Chaldee," which he believed to be the language of pre-polyglot Babel, was the ancestor of all languages. In his *American Dictionary of the English Language* (1828) he proposed a good many "Chaldee" etymologies which later and better-informed editors have quietly consigned to the wastepaper basket.

[3] Hebrew is not of course to be confused with Yiddish (that is, Jüdisch), a German dialect to be further defined later. It has become a sort of international language of the Jews, with a literature of high quality. American newspapers printed in Yiddish use Hebrew characters.

[4] Cush was a son of Ham.

in the Ethiopian Church and Latin in the Roman Catholic Church, but is not spoken elsewhere. Arabic became the national language of Egypt in the course of the sixteenth century.

Semitic is thus essentially Asiatic, and Hamitic North African. Hamitic is in no way related to any of the languages spoken by blacks in central and southern Africa, the vast region south of the Sahara. These languages are usually classified into three main groups: Sudanese, extending to the equator, a large and highly diversified group of languages whose relationships to one another are difficult and in some cases impossible to establish; Bantu, extending from the equator to the extreme south, a large and well-defined group of related languages; and Hottentot and Bushman, remotely related languages spoken by small groups of people in the extreme southwestern part of Africa. Hottentot and Bushman have no relationship to the other black groups, nor is it demonstrable that the Sudanese and the Bantu groups are in any way connected with each other.

Languages belonging to the Dravidian group were once spoken throughout India, where the earlier linguistic situation was radically affected by the Aryan invasion. These are the aboriginal languages of India. They are now spoken mainly in southern India.

The Indo-Chinese group includes Chinese proper and the languages of Tibet and Indochina. Japanese is totally unrelated, though it has borrowed the Chinese written characters and many Chinese words. Attempts to relate Korean to either Chinese or Japanese have not been successful. Ainu, the language of the aborigines of Japan, is totally unrelated to any other language of which we have any knowledge; it is now spoken by no more than a handful of people.

A striking characteristic of the Malay-Polynesian languages is their wide geographical distribution in the islands of the Indian and the Pacific oceans, stretching from Madagascar to Easter Island. The more or less moribund Australian native languages, spoken by only a few Australian aborigines nowadays, have no connection at all with Malay-Polynesian, nor have the more than a hundred Papuan languages spoken in New Guinea and neighboring islands.

The American Indian languages constitute a geographic rather than a linguistic grouping, comprising many languages showing very little relationship, if any, to one another. It has been estimated [5] that at the time of Columbus's discovery only about a million and a half Indians occupied the huge area north of Mexico, with about forty million more in Mexico and Central America, the Antilles, and South America. A very important and widespread group of American Indian languages is known as the Uto-Aztecan, which includes Nahuatl, the language spoken by the Aztecs, and various closely related dialects. Aleut and Eskimo, which are very similar to each other, are spoken in the Aleutians and all along the extreme northern coast

[5] By P. Rivet, cited by Willem L. Graff, *Language and Languages* (New York, 1932), p. 427.

of America and north to Greenland. The isolation of the various groups, small in number to begin with and spread over so large a territory, may to some extent account for the great diversity of American Indian tongues.

Basque, a very intricate language spoken in many dialects by no more than half a million people living in the region of the Pyrenees, has always been something of a popular linguistic mystery. It now seems fairly certain, on the basis of coins and scanty inscriptions of the ancient Iberians, that Basque is related to the almost completely lost language of those people who once inhabited the Iberian peninsula and in Neolithic times were spread over an even larger part of Europe. Efforts to relate it to Etruscan, a language of which we know very little, to the non-Indo-European languages spoken in the Caucasus Mountains (not mentioned elsewhere here), and to the Hamitic languages have not been successful.

An important group of non-Indo-European languages spoken in Europe, as well as in parts of Asia, is the Ural-Altaic, which falls into two subgroups: the Ural, or Finno-Ugric, which includes Finnish, Estonian, Livonian, Lappish, and Hungarian, among others of less importance; and the very remotely related Altaic—though there are those who deny any such connection. Altaic includes several varieties of Turkish, such as Ottoman Turkish (Osmanli) and that spoken in Turkestan and in the Azerbaijan Soviet Socialist Republic, as well as Mongolian and Manchu.

The foregoing is by no means a complete survey of non-Indo-European languages. We have merely mentioned some of the most important groups and individual languages, along with some which are of little significance as far as the numbers or the present importance of their speakers are concerned, but which are nevertheless interesting for one reason or another. Louis H. Gray lists twenty-six linguistic groups and two isolated languages (spoken respectively in China and India by small groups of people), and comes up with a total of 2796 languages, of which 132 are Indo-European.[6] His figure coincides with that arrived at by the French Academy. But Gray rightly had no faith in such a count, for, as he points out, it is often impossible to reach agreement as to what constitutes a language: the line demarcating dialect and language is difficult to draw, and linguists do not always agree on where it should be drawn. Furthermore, depending largely upon one's point of view, Old English, Middle English, and Modern English might be regarded as one, two (on the basis that the transition from Middle English to Modern English is somewhat less well defined than that from Old English to Middle English), or three. And there are yet further difficulties pointed out by Gray, who concludes that between 2500 and 3500 might be given as an estimate, but admits that such an estimate is "so rough as to be practically worthless." . . .

[6] *Foundations of Language* (New York, 1939), p. 418.

COGNATE WORDS
IN THE INDO-EUROPEAN LANGUAGES

Words of similar structure and similar, related, and in many instances identical meanings in the various languages of the Indo-European group may be recognized, once one knows what to expect in the way of sound-shifting, as cognate—that is, of common origin (Lat. *co* plus *gnātus* 'born together'). Thus all the roots just cited (*bhar-, pher-, fer-, bair-, ber-*) are of common origin, all being developments of Indo-European **bher-*; so, for that matter, are the thematic vowels and the personal endings, though the untrained observer may sometimes find it difficult to recognize the relationship. For cognates, as we have seen, do not necessarily look much alike: sound shifts have occurred in the various languages of the Indo-European group (these languages may also be referred to as cognate) which may make related words as unlike in sound as *father,* Sanskrit *pitā,* and Irish Gaelic *athir*[7]— all developments of Indo-European **pətēr.* Sometimes, however, there is sufficient similarity—for example between *maharaja,* ultimately Sanskrit, and Latin *māius rēx* 'great king'—to be apparent even to the untrained observer.

The most frequently cited cognate words are those which have been preserved in a large number of Indo-European languages; some have in fact been preserved in all. These common related words include the numerals from one to ten; the word meaning the sum of ten tens (*cent-, sat-, hund-*) in various quite dissimilar-looking but nonetheless quite regular developments; words for certain bodily parts (related, for example, to *heart, lung, head, foot*); words for certain natural phenomena (related, for example, to *air, night, star, snow, sun, moon, wind*); certain plant and animal names (related, for example, to *beech, corn, wolf, bear*); and certain cultural terms (related, for example, to *yoke, mead, weave, sew*). It is interesting to note in passing that cognates of practically all of our taboo words—those monosyllables that pertain to sex and excretion and which seem to cause great pain to many people—are to be found in other Indo-European languages. Historically, if not socially, these ancient words are just as legitimate as any other words.

One needs no special training to perceive that our *one, two, three* are akin to Latin *ūnus, duo, trēs;* to Greek *oinē* 'one-spot on a die,' *dyo, treis;* to Welsh *un, dau, tri;* to Gothic *ains, twai, *þreis;* and to Dutch *een, twee, drie.* Comparison of the forms designating the second digit indicates that non-Germanic (as in the Latin, Welsh, and Greek forms) *d* corresponds to Germanic (English, Gothic, Dutch) *t.* A similar comparison of the forms for the third digit indicates that non-Germanic *t* corresponds to Germanic *þ,* the initial sound of *three* and *þrír* in English and Icelandic. Allowing for later changes, as in the case of *þ,* which became *d* in German (*drei* 'three'),[8] as also in Dutch, and *t* in Danish, Norwegian, and Swedish (*tre*), these same

---

[7] Indo-European *p,* which corresponds to Germanic *f,* was lost completely in Celtic.

[8] German has *t* from earlier *þ* in a very few words, for instance, *tausend* 'thousand.'

correspondences come to light perfectly regularly in other cognates in which the consonants in question appear. We may safely assume, for reasons unnecessary to go into here, that the non-Germanic consonants are older than the Germanic ones. Hence we may accept with the greatest confidence (assuming a similar comparison of the vowel systems) the reconstructions *oinos, *dwo, *treies as accurately representing the Indo-European forms from which the existing forms have developed. The comparative linguists have of course used all the Indo-European languages as a basis for their conclusions regarding correspondences, not just a few such as are cited here.

INDO-EUROPEAN CULTURE

On the basis of these cognates, which must not be confused with loan-words, we can infer a good deal about the state of culture attained by the Indo-Europeans before the various migrations began, probably during the third millennium B.C. or even somewhat earlier.[9] This culture was not contemptible; it was in fact considerably more advanced than that of some groups of people living today. As we have seen, they had a clear sense of family relationship and hence of the family organization, and they could count. They made use of gold and perhaps silver as well; copper and iron were not to come until later. They drank a honey-flavored alcoholic beverage whose name has come down to us as *mead*. Words corresponding to *wheel, axle,* and *yoke* make it perfectly clear that they used wheeled vehicles. They were small farmers, not nomads, who worked their fields with plows, and they had domesticated animals and fowls. They had religious feeling of a sort, with a conception, not of God, but of gods. This much we can say on the basis of forms which were not actually recorded until long after Indo-European had ceased to be a more or less unified language.

THE INDO-EUROPEAN HOMELAND

Conjectures differ as to the original Indo-European homeland—or at least the earliest for which we have any evidence. Plant and animal names are the principal clues, and the flora and fauna which these denote are northern European. The existence of cognates denoting trees which grow in northern Europe (*oak, birch, willow*), though they may grow elsewhere as well, coupled with the absence of such related words for Mediterranean or Asiatic trees (*olive, cypress, palm*); the similar occurrence of cognates of *wolf, bear, lax* (Old English *leax* 'salmon'), and of a word signifying 'turtle,' but none for creatures indigenous to Asia—all this points to northern Europe as the

---

[9] See Calvert Watkins, "Indo-European and the Indo-Europeans," particularly the subsection "Lexicon and Culture," in the Appendix to *The American Heritage Dictionary* (Boston, 1969). In an appendix to this Appendix ("Guide to the Appendix"), Watkins lists the Indo-European stems that occur in items listed in the dictionary proper. It all makes for fascinating, and at the same time rewarding, browsing.

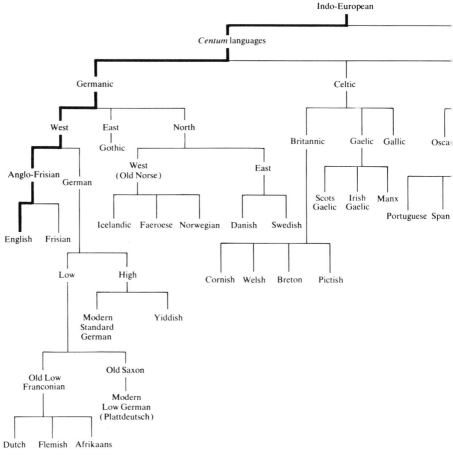

predispersion home, just as the absence of a common word for *ocean* indicates, though it does not in itself prove, that this homeland was inland. Paul Thieme in his cogently reasoned *Die Heimat der indogermanischen Gemeinsprache* (Wiesbaden, 1954) . . . localizes the Indo-European homeland in the northern part of Central Europe, between the Vistula and the Elbe, on the basis of evidence adduced from the prehistoric geographical distribution of the beech, the turtle, and the salmon. Other Indo-Europeanists have argued from similar evidence for southern Russia, the Carpathians, Scandinavia, and southwestern Asia. The preponderance of scholarly opinion nowadays is in favor of a European center of dispersion—an opinion which implies that the earliest migrations were in a southeasterly direction.

THE MAIN DIVISIONS
OF THE INDO-EUROPEAN GROUP

Of some Indo-European languages—for example Phrygian, Scythian, Macedonian, and Illyrian—we possess only the scantiest remains. We may be

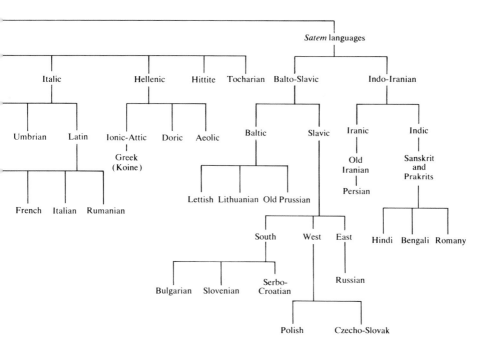

Indo-European and the more important languages developed from it.

certain that others have disappeared without leaving a trace. Members of the following subgroups survive as living tongues: Indo-Iranian, Balto-Slavic, Hellenic, Italic, Celtic, and Germanic. Albanian and Armenian are also Indo-European, but do not fit into any of these subgroups.

The Indo-European languages have been conveniently classified into *satem* languages and *centum* languages, *satem* and *centum* being respectively the Avestan (a form of Old Persian) and Latin words corresponding to *hundred*. The classification is based on the development, in very ancient times, of Indo-European palatal *ķ*. In the *satem* languages—Indo-Iranian, Balto-Slavic, Armenian, and Albanian—this *ķ* sound became some sort of sibilant: for example Sanskrit (Indic) *śatam,* Lithuanian (Baltic) *śiṁtas,* Old Slavic *sŭto.*[10] In the other Indo-European languages the earlier *ķ* of

[10] Linguistic history often repeats itself: the prehistoric treatment of palatal *ķ* in the *satem* languages resulting ultimately in its becoming a sibilant was precisely the same thing which took place much later—perhaps about the third century of the Christian Era—in Latin *centum* (and in all other words in which the sound [k] spelled with *c* in Latin, occurred before the palatal, or front, vowels *e* and *i*). This change is responsible for the occurrence of a sibilant in all the languages

Indo-European *ḱmtóm either remained or, in the Germanic group, shifted to *h* in the First Consonant Shift (Grimm's Law), as in Greek (Hellenic) (*he*)*ḱaton,* Welsh (Celtic) *cant,* and Old English (Germanic) *hund.*[11]

The discovery of Tocharian, a *centum* language, early in our century was somewhat disturbing to the general supposition that this division according to the development of Indo-European palatal *ḱ* represented a dialectal split in Indo-European, with those who migrated eastward coming to assibilate the sound. But the assumption of an earlier migration of Tocharians and Hittites, who also spoke a *centum* language, from Central Europe would account for the presence of *centum* languages in what was thought of as *satem* territory. It must be remembered, however, that this is only an inference.

WORKING WITH THE SELECTION

1. In Part 2 a distinction was drawn between what we called native words in English—words that have descended directly from Indo-European—and borrowed words (Pyles uses the term *loan-word*), and we drew some conclusions about the difference between native and borrowed words. Most words in Old English, we saw, are native. If we now observe that a few words were borrowed into Old English and that among these were *port* and *street* from Latin, does this evidence call into question the conclusions drawn earlier?

2. Many people think of any change in language as corruption. This was perhaps natural before it was understood how modern languages have grown out of earlier languages, when scholars still believed that the similarity between Latin and Greek resulted from the fact that Latin was corrupted Greek. In light of what we now know about groups of languages like those that stem from Indo-European, what must we assume about the importance of growth in language?

3. Many people believe that language survives only because it is kept pure in written form, that it would decay were it not at least partly protected by being enshrined in dictionaries and grammar and usage books. Are such beliefs still tenable?

4. What do some people you know seem to mean by *pure* and *purity* in connection with language? Taking into consideration both borrowing and descent within a language, can you justify the concept of purity in language? Which would be the purest language—provided an absolute word like *pure* can be compared?

---

derived from Latin; for example the [č] in Italian *cento* and the [s] in French *cent,* Portuguese *cento,* and non-Castilian Spanish *ciento.*

[11] Modern English *hundred* is a compound, first occurring late in the Old English period. The *-red* is a development of what was once an independent word meaning 'number.'

2

From Indo-European to Modern English: Etymological Entries

Most good dictionaries provide some information about the origin and growth of at least the commoner words. Some ar e veritable mines of etymological riches The following selections from some of the best of these reveal the origin and relationship of much *and* master, *both of which grew from the Indo-European root* *meg-.

Webster's New World Dictionary

Cleveland, 2nd college ed., 1970

mas·ter (mas'tər, mäs'-). *n.* [ME. *maistre* < OE. *mægester,* magister & OFr. *maistre,* both < L. *magister,* a master, chief, leader, orig., double comparative < base of L. *magnus,* great < IE. base **meĝ-,* great, whence Gr. *megas,* large]

much (much) *adj.* more, most [ME. *muche* < *muchel,* large, much < OE. *mycel,* large in size or quantity < IE. base **meĝ(h)-,* large, whence Gr. *megas,* L. *magnus*]

The Oxford Dictionary of English Etymology

Oxford, 1966

master mà·stəɹ A. man having control or authority; B. teacher OE. (one who has received an academic degree orig. conveying authority to teach xiv); C. title of rank or compliment xiii; title of presiding officer, etc. xiv. OE. *mægister, magister* (corr. to OFris. *māster* (and OS.) *mēster,* (O)HG.

meister, ON. *meistari*), a CGerm. adoption from L.; reinforced by OF. *maistre* (mod. *maître*) = Pr. *ma(g)estre-s,* Sp., It. *maestro,* etc.—L. *magistru-m,* nom. *magister* (OL. *-ester*), usu. referred to *magis* adv. more, as *minister* to *minus* adv. less (but Etruscan forms with *macstr-* are cited, which may be the scource). Cf MISTER[1]. Hence **ma·ster-FUL**[1]. XIV. **ma·ster-**PIECE XVII; after Du. *meesterstuk* (adopted in Sc. as *meisterstik* XVI) or G. *meisterstück* piece of work qualifying a craftsman. **ma·stery**[3]. ME. *meistrie* (XIII, AncrR.)—OF. *maistrie* (superseded by *maistrise,* mod. *maîtrise,* which was repr. in ME. by *maistris, -ice, -yse*).

much mʌtʃ †great (surviving in place-names, as *M. Wenlock*); great amount of XIII; adv. greatly; sb. great deal XIV. ME. *muche, moche* (with vars. *miche, meche*), shortening of *muchel, mochel,* repr. late OE. *mycel,* var. of *micel;* for the development of ü to ʌ cf. *blush, crutch, cudgel, rush, such, thrush;* the loss of *l* may have been furthered by the relation of *lut* to *lutel* LIT-TLE, but for the loss of *l* after *ch* cf. *wenchel* WENCH. OE. *micel* = OS. *mikil,* OHG. *michil,* ON. *mikill* (cf. MICKLE), Goth. *mikils;* CGerm. deriv. of IE. **meg-,* repr. by L. *magnus* (cf. MAGISTRATE, MAGNATE, MAGNITUDE, MAJOR, MAS-TER), Gr. *mégas* (see MEGA-, MEGALO-), Skr. *mahā-* great (see MAHARAJAH, MAHATMA), *majmán* greatness, Toch. *māka-, māk-;* cf. ON. *mjǫk* much, very (:—**meku-*). Hence **mu·chLY**[2]. XVII (in XIX a new joc. formation). **mu·ch-**NESS. XIV (*m. of a muchness* XVIII).

Origins:
A Short Etymological Dictionary
of Modern English

Eric Partridge

New York, 2nd ed., 1959

master, n, whence **masterful** and **masterly;** hence also adj, whence **masterpiece,** and v (cf the MF-F *maîtriser*); **mastery** (cf pal*mistry* at PALM); **mister,** a thinned form, influenced by **mistress,** whence the coll **missus** and, by contr, **miss,** whence **missy;** F *maître* (OF *maistre*), as in *maître d'hotel,* a major-domo, a hotel-manager, and It *maestro,* both partly adopted by E.—L **magister,** E **magistral** (cf **mistral**) and **magisterial**—**magistrand** and **magistrate** (whence **magistracy**); **Magna** Carta—**mag-nanimous, magnanimity,** sep at ANIMAL, para 6—**magnate**—**magnific, Magnificat, magnification** (whence, anl, **magnificative**), **magnificence, magnificent, magnifico, magnify, magnitude**—**magnum;** **majesty,**

whence **majestic; major** (cf **majuscule), majority**—cf **mayor, mayoralty**—**Majorca,** see MAJOLICA; **marino; May** (month) and **may; maxim**—cf **maximum** (whence **maximal).**—maha, maharaja, maharani, mahatma.—Cf the element *magni-,* where, e.g., *magniloquence.*—For the derivatives from Gr *megas,* great, see *mega-* in Elements.—Gmc: **mickle,** var **muckle; much,** whence **muchness.**

I. Indo-European

1. All these words derive from one or other of the Skt, Gr, L, L-via-R, Gmc derivatives from the IE r **mag-,* var **meg-,* with extnn **magh-* and **megh-* (L *magn-* exhibiting a different radical suffix): even **mag-, *meg-,* are *-g-* extnn of the still more fundamental **ma-* or **me-,* with varr **mi-, *mo-, *mu-,* big: cf OE *micel, mycel,* great, from Gmc r **mik-;* L *magnus,* great—*maior,* greater—*maximus* (? for **magsimus*), greatest; Gr *mega,* much, *megas* (f *megale*), great; Skt *mah-, mahat-, máhi,* great, *máhas, majmán-,* greatness, cf *mahēyān,* greater, and *mahiṣṭhas,* greatest; Hit *mah,* strong, *makkess-,* to become great, *mekkis,* great, numerous, pl *meggaes,* and *mekki,* very, much: cf Tokh A *mak,* Tokh B *makī-,* great, much, Alb *math* and Arm *mec,* great (instr *mecaw*): cf also MIr *mag,* great, and *māl* (from extn **magl-*), nobleman, prince, *mass* (from **magsos*), important, OC r **mag-,* var **mac-,* great, perh akin to **mac-, mag-,* to nourish,—with the C var **magal-,* cf the *megal-* of Gr *megalē.*

II. Sanskrit

2. Skt *mah-,* great, occurs in the Singhalese *maha,* a species of monkey, a species of deer. *Maharaja* is Skt *maharaja,* great king (*raja,* cf L *rex*); *maharani,* Hi *maharānī,* great queen (cf L *regīna*); *mahatma,* a (Hindu) sage, Skt *mahātman,* (lit) great soul (*ātman*).

III. Greek

3. See Elements at *mega-* (where also *megalo-*): e.g., *megaphone* and *megalomania.*

IV. Latin *magnus*

4. L *magnus,* great, retained in the names of ancient and medieval kings and medieval alchemists and others, has f *magna,* as in *Magna Carta* (or *Charta*). The Great Charter, cf *chart* at the 1st CARD; the neu *magnum* is, in E, used as n for a 2-quart bottle.

5. *Magnus* has two simple derivatives affecting E:

LL *magnātes,* leading people, and LL *magnātus,* a leading man, a nobleman, (Oriental ML) a prince; hence, by b/f, the F *magnat* (Rousseau, 1772), a (Polish) grandee; whence E *magnate* (Burke, 1790);

L *magnitūdō,* greatness, whence E *magnitude.*

6. For cpds, see *magnanimus* at ANIMAL, para 6; cf *magni-* in Elements; but note esp:

magnificus (adj), great-making or -rendering, whence, perh via MF-F *magnifique*, the obsol E *magnific;* whence also the It title *Magnifico*, whence E *magnifico*, a grandee;

derivative *magnificāre*, to enlarge, whence, perh via OF-F *magnifier*, the E *magnify; magnificat*, it enlarges, hence glorifies, occurs in Christian European literature as *Magnificat*, My soul doth magnify the Lord (*Luke*, i, 46–55); on the pp *magnificāt*us arises the LL *magnificātiō*, praise, o/s *magnificātiōn-*, whence, as to form only, the E *magnification;*

likewise derivative from *magnificus* is the syn LL *magnificens*, o/s *magnificent-*, whence both MF-EF and E *magnificent;* subsidiary LL *magnificentia* becomes MF-F and E *magnificence.*

V. Latin *māior* (neu *māius*), greater

7. L *māior* is for OL *maiior*, itself from *magyōs (r *mag-*+suffix element *yō-*+nom ending *-s*); it becomes ML *major*, whence OF-F *majeur* and EF-F and E *major*, with derivative F *majorité* (ML *majoritās*) yielding E *majority*, the attainment of 21 years, *majority* in the other senses coming straight from E *major*. ML *major domūs*, the head of the household, becomes It *maggiordomo*, which joins with the syn Sp *mayordomo* to produce F *major-dome* and E *majordomo*. Based on the neu *māius* is the L dim derivative *māiusculus*, a little greater, whence, via (*litera*) *māiuscula*, the EF-F *majuscule*, adopted by E.

8. In OF, L *māior*—already in LL used as n—becomes *maire*, adopted by ME, whence *mayor*, whence *mayoress* (cf LL *māiōrissa*, the chief slave-woman); derivative MF *mairalté* yields *mayoralty*.

9. From ML *mājōrīnus*, of a larger kind, hence, as n, an overseer, via the ML contr *mērīnus*, overseer of pastures, comes the syn Sp *merino*, whence (OED, EW, Webster) a special breed of sheep reared in Estremadura; perh, however (B & W), Sp *merino* derives from *merīnī*, the adj of Bani-*Merīn*, the great Ar dynasty of late medieval Morocco and members of an important Berber tribe that specialized in sheep-raising.

10. From the ancient Italic goddess *Māia* (for *Maiia;* ancient var *Māiesta*) —? for (*dea*) *māia*, the greater goddess, f of *māius, prob akin to *magnus* and perh an ancient var of *māior*—comes *Māius mensis*, Maia's month, whence, by ellipsis, *Māius*, OF-F *mai*, E *May*, whence the Spring-blooming, spiny shrub *may*, applied esp to the hawthorn and its bloom.

11. *Māiesta*, that ancient var of *Māia*, suggests that rather from some ancient var of *māior*, greater, than direct from *māior* itself, derives L *māiestas*, greatness, esp grandeur, ML *mājestas*, whence, via OF-F *majesté*, the ME *majestee*, whence E *majesty*, whence, anl, *majestic*.

VI. L *māximus, greatest*

12. L *māximus* (var *māxumus*), for *magsomos (r *mag-*+formative element *-som-*+declensional *-o-*, later *-u-*+case-ending *-s*), has neu *māximum*, which, used as n, is adopted by E for 'the greatest value, size, quantity, speed, etc.' The elliptical L *māxima* (? for *m. sententia*), the greatest sentence, hence thought or axiom, becomes MF-F *maxime*, whence E *maxim*.

VII. L *magis,* more, rather

13. Closely akin to—and perh, as a contr of *magnis,* with great (things), hence greatly, deriving from—*magnus* is the adv *magis,* whence L *magister,* lit a greater (person), hence a superior, chief, master, much as L *minister* derives from *minus,* less (*minor,* lesser) : partly adopted by E. The derivative L adj *magistrālis,* masterly, becomes F and E *magistral;* its LL mdfn *magisterius* has neu *magisterium,* which, used as LL n for 'body of teachers', etc., yields *magistery;* either imm from *magisterium* or as as extn of *magisterius* is the LL adj *magisteriālis,* of teaching, ML of command, whence *magisterial.*

14. L *magistrālis,* masterly, dominant, becomes OProv *maistral,* whence Prov *mistral,* esp as n, 'dominant wind', adopted by E; B & W, however, derive *maistral* from OProv (and OF) *maistre,* master (cf para 16).

15. L *magister* has LL derivative *magistrāre,* to master, hence to rule, to teach, whence ML *magistrandus,* lit one to be trained, hence a university student in his final year, hence Sc *magistrand. Magister* has the further derivative *magistrātus,* lit control of the people, hence a magistrate's function and the magistrate himself: *magistrātus* (gen *-ūs*) produces EF-F *magistrat* and E *magistrate;* derivative EF-F *magistrature,* adopted by E, is rare for *magistracy* (*magistrate+cy;* cf *accuracy* from *accurate*).

VIII. OF *maistre*

16. L *magister* becomes OF-MF *maistre* (F *maître*), adopted by ME, whence E *master;* sem, OE-from-L *magister* has contributed. Derivative OF-MF *maistrie* leads to *mastery.*

17. OF *maistre* has MF f *maistresse* (F *maîtresse*), adopted by ME, which partly anglicizes it as *maistress,* whence, by thinning (cf *mister* from *master*), the E *mistress.*

IX. Germanic

18. *Much* (adj, hence adv and n), great, esp in size or degree, derives from ME *muche,* var *moche,* from earlier *muchel,* var *mochel,* from OE *mycel,* var *micel;* ME *muchel* has the thinned var *mikel,* whence *mickle,* now Sc (*meikle*) and dial. OE *mycel* (*micel*) is akin to OS *mikil,* OFris *mikili,* OHG *mykill: mihhil, mihil,* MHG *michel,* Go *mikels, mikils,* ON *mikell, mikill, mykill:* Gmc r, **mikil-.* The parallel E *muckle* is a var—influenced by *much* —of *mickle.*

The American Heritage Dictionary of the English Language

Boston, 1969

meg-. Great. **1.** Germanic suffixed form **miǩ-ila-* in: **a.** Old English *micel, mycel,* great: MUCH; **b.** Old Norse *miǩill,* great: MICKLE. **2.** Suffixed form **mag-no-* in Latin *magnus,* great: MAGNANIMOUS, MAGNATE, MAGNIFIC, (MAGNIFICENT), (MAGNIFICO), (MAGNIFY), MAGNILOQUENT, MAGNITUDE, MAGNUM. **3.** Suffixed (comparative) form **mag-yos-* in: **a.** Latin *mājor,* greater: MAJOR, MAJOR-DOMO, MAJORITY, MAJUSCULE, MAYOR; **b.** Latin *mājestās,* greatness, authority: MAESTOSO, MAJESTY; **c.** Latin *magister,* master, high official (< "he who is greater"): MAESTRO, MAGISTERIAL, MAGISTERY, MAGISTRAL, MAGISTRATE, MASTER, (MISTRAL), (MISTER), (MISTRESS). **4.** Suffixed (superlative) form **mag-samo-* in Latin *maximus,* greatest: MAXIM, MAXIMUM. **5.** Suffixed form **mag-to-,* "made great," in Latin *mactus,* worshiped, blessed, sacred: MATADOR. **6.** Suffixed (feminine) form **mag-ya-,* "she who is great," in Latin *Maia,* name of a goddess: MAIA[3], MAY[1]. **7.** Suffixed form **meg-al-* in Greek *megas* (stem *megal-*), great: MEGA-, MEGALO-; ACROMEGALY, ALMAGEST, OMEGA. **8.** Variant form **megh-* in Sanskrit *mahā,* great: MAHABHARATA, MAHARAJAH, MAHARANI, MAHATMA, MAHAYANA, MAHOUT. [Pok. *meg(h)-* 708.]

WORKING WITH THE SELECTIONS

1. The first selection means that Latin *magister* 'master' or 'leader,' a double comparative from the Latin *magnus* 'great,' was borrowed into both Old English as *mægester* and into Old French as *maistre.* These two words, both the Old English and the Old French, influenced the Middle English form, *maistre,* from which we get *master.* The word came into Latin from the Indo-European base or root **meg-,* which descended also into Greek, producing the word *megas.* Now interpret the statement of the etymology of *much.*

2. The entry for *master* in *The Oxford Dictionary of English Etymology* does not differ essentially from that in *Webster's New World Dictionary,* since the etymology of the word does not present unusual problems, and both books have made use of modern etymological study. The *ODEE* adds some details. It roughly dates some uses; for example, although *master* was borrowed into Old English in the sense of 'teacher,' it did not acquire the meaning 'one authorized to teach' until the fourteenth century. The *ODEE* also provides a second spelling of the word in Old English and notes that the two Old English forms correspond with *māster* in Old Frisian, *mēster* in Old Saxon, *meister* in both High German and Old High German, and Old Norse *meistari,* since the word was a common Germanic adoption from

Latin. The *ODEE* also points out that the Old French word, which gave Modern French *maître*, corresponds to words in other Romance languages, to Spanish and Italian *maestro* and to Portuguese *magestre* (also spelled *maestre*). Although the Latin form in the nominative was *magister*, from Old Latin *magester*, the words in more recent languages seem to have come from an oblique case, *magistrum*. This noun is believed to derive from the adverb *magis* 'more,' as the noun *minister* is presumably related to the adverb *minus* 'less.' The word may, however, come from an Etruscan form like *maestr-*. More on the etymology will be found under the entry for the first use of *mister*. *Masterful* has developed from *master*. *Masterpiece*, on the other hand, meaning 'a work worthy of a master,' presumably derives from Dutch *meesterstuk*, which was adopted into Scottish as *meisterstik* in the sixteenth century, or from German *meisterstück*. *Mastery*, in its third use, derives from Middle English *maistre*, which has been first recorded in the thirteenth century in a work of religious instruction called the *Ancrean Riwle*. Old French *maistrie* was superseded by *maistrise*, which became Modern French *maîtrise* and which was represented in Middle English by *maistris*, with alternate spellings *maistrice* and *maistryse*.

Now see what you can do with the etymology for *much*. In addition to the abbreviations mentioned above, you will need to know that Toch. stands for Tocharian (or Tokarian), Goth. for Gothic, and Skr. for Sanskrit.

3. If you understood the basic problem in exercise 2, above (that of distinguishing native words like *much* from the cognates in other languages, some of which have been borrowed into English), you should not have too much trouble with this exercise. Partridge is saying essentially what the others are, but he brings all cognates into one treatment and supplies much more detail. Partridge's discussion approaches completeness, but he does not treat phrases, of which there are many. He starts with a survey of *master* and related words in English; then he sketches the Indo-European foundation of the words, noticing what must have been dialectal variations on the root **meg-*, and then traces each of the five streams by which words arrived in English, borrowing from Sanskrit, Latin, and Greek, and from Latin through a Romance language, in this case French. He does little with Greek here, since he has treated the *mega-* words elsewhere. He includes English under the Germanic tradition, that is, the tradition in which the words survive by direct descent, not by borrowing from any other linguistic stream.

Here is some miscellaneous information you may find useful: Alb is Albanian, MIr is Middle Irish, LL is Late Latin, which Partridge defines as Latin of A.D. 180–600, ML is Medieval Latin, MF is Medieval French, EF is Early Modern French, OProv is Old Provencal, OED is the *Oxford English Dictionary*, EW is etymologist Ernest Weekley, Webster is the second edition of the *New International Dictionary*. The symbol o/s is Partridge's indication for an oblique stem; words that passed from Latin into a Romance language usually developed from an oblique form of the word, especially from the dative-instrumental, since these forms were more common than the nominative.

Work through the entry, checking to be sure you understand it.

4. *The American Heritage Dictionary* entry should contain little that is new

to you except the analysis of various suffixed forms that account for variations in the cognates that have descended from them. Now you can put all this material together into a sketch of *much* and its relatives in other languages, especially those that have been borrowed into English.

3

The Growth of English

What English was like before about A.D. 700 we can know only by a learned sort of guessing. Working from known languages, living and dead, we can reconstruct Indo-European and stages of the language between Indo-European and English, such as Proto-Germanic. By working from Indo-European through Proto-Germanic to existing English, we can establish the line of growth for the language. Of course, the line is not straight, but we know enough about its twists and turns to postulate what our native tongue was like at any time during the last five thousand years.

But for the last thirteen hundred years we need not guess—or at any rate we need not guess so much. We have documents, written records, some from as early as the late seventh century—not so many as we should like and not of every sort we should like, but more than most languages have for early dates and enough so that we can speak from evidence.

The following selections summarize some of what these documents tell us about the growth of English. The first is from a sort of editorial that Charles Dickens (1812–70) printed in his periodical Household Words, *18 (1858). Dickens is known today mainly as a novelist, but he was known in his own day as traveler, editor, and social critic as well. He wrote little about language, but he liked to use it. The second selection is by Paul Roberts (1917–67), from his* Understanding English *(1958). One of America's most skillful textbook writers, Roberts adapted new linguistic ideas for language textbooks used from kindergarten through college.*

The Growth of English Words

Charles Dickens

During the last twenty or thirty years great attention has been paid by scholars, both in England and in Germany, to the youth of our language; its mother, its nurses, and its schools, have been looked up, and we know more than we did about its origin. We are beginning, in fact, to understand the History of the Language: and it may be worth while to take a rapid view of the facts now most commonly received.

Although we often speak of the Saxons or Anglo-Saxons as the invaders of Britain in the fifth century, yet it must not be forgotten that other tribes, such as the Jutes and Frieslanders, came over, too. Foremost, however, were the Angles and the Saxons, and these two names appear side by side in various ways; the Angles gave their name to the country, Engla-land; and the Saxon version of the gospels is headed, 'That Godspell on Englisc.' But, on the other hand, to this day the Welsh call the English language Saeson-aeg, or the Saxon speech; and the Scotch Highlanders call an Englishman, Sassenach. Some have maintained that a few of the tribes, and particularly the Jutes, were Scandinavians; but it is admitted that the greater part of the invaders were men of Teutonic (or Dutch) race, who came over from the North of Germany, or the South of Denmark. In the widest sense, we may look on the terms German, Teutonic, and Dutch, as all meaning the same thing: and we may say that the same Teutonic race inhabits Europe from the Alps to the North Sea, between the Rhine upon the west, and the Elbe, or even the Vistula, upon the east. This race includes Austrians, Tyrolese, Northern Swiss, Bavarians, Prussians, Hanoverians, Hollanders, Flemings, and others: but when speaking without reference to politics, they are to be divided into High and Low Dutch; Dutch of the highlands of Southern Germany, and the Dutch of the low lands of Northern Germany. High Dutch happens to have become the polite dialect, the language of German literature; and Low Dutch, fallen into disrepute, is cultivated now in Holland only. But to Low Dutch belongs honour, as the parent of our modern English. Our very sailors who trade to Rotterdam or Hamburgh, cannot help being struck with the likeness of the two languages, and their conclusion is, that 'after all, Dutch is only a sort of broken English.' English, in truth, is a sort of broken Dutch. The Dutch skippers (that is, shippers) who trade to Liverpool or Whitehaven, have no great difficulty in understanding our own northern dialects. A Lancashire boy, who was sent to school at Hamburgh, happening to land on a very hot day, went up to some maid-servants who were drawing water at a fountain, and said, 'Will you give me a drink?' 'Wat sagt-en?' was the reply. 'Will you—give me—a drink?' he repeated. 'Ja, ja, du kanst drinken,' (Yea, yea, thou canst drink), was the ready answer. The broad Lancashire and the broad Dutch were soon at home together.

The Angles, the Saxons, and other Teutonic tribes, made sundry descents on the kingdom of Britain for about one hundred years, and at last conquered a large part of the country, driving the native Britons (whom they called the Welsh, or foreigners), to the fastnesses of Wales, to Cumberland, and the Strathclyde.

They held possession till the year one thousand and sixty-six; and as they adopted few Welsh words, it follows that a pure Teutonic was spoken in

England for six hundred years. It is true that divers dialects of the same language were current in divers parts; and it seems that the Angles, who were settled in the north and east, spoke in a broader dialect than Saxons who lived in the south and south-west. To this day, therefore, the pronunciation common in the North of England remains broader and more open than that of the South. But probably the tribes could understand one another, as well as in our day a Yorkshireman can understand a Somersetshire peasant.

This language, commonly called the Anglo-Saxon, was cultivated with great diligence, especially from the time of King Alfred, who laboured hard to promote the cause of native literature. The laws were written in that language; and useful books were translated, in order that a love of learning might be fostered among the people. Some few Latin words were adopted; but in most cases the foreign terms were translated into the mother tongue; the Evangelium was the God-spell, that is, good-spell, or good-tiding; the Saviour was the Haelend, or Healer. In speaking of God, they called him not only the Ael-mihtig, or all-mighty, but likewise the All-walda, or all-wielder, and the Ael-craeftig, or all-skilful. For infinite, they said Un-ge-end-ed, that is, un-ended or unbounded; and consciousness was the in-witness.

We may thus see, that in Anglo-Saxon there was not only a power of making compound words, but a habit of translating Latin or Greek compounds into the corresponding Saxon; and the same principle was carried out in all the sciences, as far as the learning of the time extended. Astronomy was Star-craft; literature was Book-craft, and a literary man was a Book-man; botany was Herb-craft; magic was Witch-craft; and even yet, the labour of the hands is said to be used in a Hands-craft.

This Teutonic, or Anglo-Saxon language, prevailed for about six hundred years; but, when the Normans came over and subdued the country, they made great changes. Thenceforward, while Saxon was the language of the common people, French was spoken by their lords and masters. This French, which is a sort of corrupt Latin, was taught in the schools, spoken in the courts of justice, and used in the drawing up Acts of Parliament. And so, from the Conquest till the time of Henry the Third, there were two distinct languages in the country, both undergoing change in their own way; the Saxon losing the purity which it had in Alfred's days; the French of London failing to keep pace with the French of Paris. But the common people did not give up their own language; and they have retained for us some very pure fragments of it in our county dialects.

Thus, for about three hundred years, the two languages went side by side, though both were changing,—drawing closer to each other. The changes undergone by Saxon, are seen in the later portions of the Saxon Chronicle, which was a note-book kept through a long series of years, until the reign of Henry the Second, and also in poems of a later time. As for the French, Chaucer tells us that the French spoken in the neighbourhood of Stratfordle-Bow was no longer recognised at Paris: for, when describing the Prioress, in his Canterbury Tales, he says:—

> And French she spake ful fayre and fetisly
> After the schole of Stratford-atté-Bowe;
> The French of Paris was to hir unknowne.

Victors and vanquished were to speak one tongue; the groundwork of it and the grammar remained Saxon; but a large number of words, particularly of compound words, were French; for the custom of translating Latin into Saxon ceased. And thus, towards the end of these three hundred years, a language was formed, which was intelligible both to the gentry and the common people.

Dean Trench, in his valuable work on the Study of Words, has considered the relations of the Saxon and Norman occupants; and thinks, that from an intelligent study of the contributions which they have severally made to the English language, we might almost get at the main story of the country, even though we had lost our written records. He observes, that at one period there would exist duplicate terms for many things; but that when a word was often upon the lips of one race, while its equivalent was seldom employed by the other, the word frequently used would very probably be handed down, and its equivalent would be forgotten. In other cases, only one word may have existed; inasmuch as the thing which it represented was confined to one half of the nation, and remained strange to the other.

He also remarks that our words which denote dignity, state, or honour, are mostly derived from the Norman-French. Such words are, sovereign, sceptre, realm, chancellor, palace, &c., whence we may infer that the Normans were the ruling race. For the word king, which is an exception, he gives an ingenious explanation. On the other hand, the objects of nature, the affairs of daily life, the ties of domestic life, are denoted by Saxon terms. 'The palace and the castle may have come to us from the Norman, but to the Saxon we owe far dearer names,—the house, the roof, the home, the hearth. The instruments used in cultivating the earth, the flail, the plough, the sickle, the spade, are Saxon; so, too, the main products of the earth, as wheat, rye, oats, &c. And observe, that the names of almost all animals, so long as they are alive, are Saxon, but, when dressed and prepared for food, become Norman; a fact which we might have expected beforehand; for the Saxon hind had the labour of tending and feeding them, but only that they might appear at the table of his Norman lord. Thus ox, steer, cow, are Saxon, but beef, Norman; calf is Saxon, but veal, Norman; sheep is Saxon, but mutton, Norman; so it is severally with swine and pork, deer and venison, fowl and pullet. Bacon, the only flesh, which, perhaps, ever came within his reach, is the single exception.'

We may remember also the anecdote told about the order of the Garter, and the remark ascribed to King Edward the Third, 'Honi soit qui mal y pense,' a motto which still remains upon our coat of arms, and which, like Dieu et mon droit, is a daily memento that the ruling race formerly spoke in the French language. But we hear a different speech in the mouths of the commons under Wat Tyler and John Ball, with their popular outcry:—

> When Adam dalf and Eva span,
> Where was then the gentleman?

or as the Germans still have it in almost the same words:—

> Als Adam grub und Eva spann,
> Wo war da der Edelmann?

The best and most agreeable way of learning the state of the English language, as it existed during the latter part of the fourteenth century, is to read John Wycliffe's version of the New Testament, and Geoffrey Chaucer's Canterbury Tales. In these works the two streams combine, though perhaps not in equal proportions; for the writings of Wycliffe, being designed for the people, contain a larger proportion of Saxon words; and those of Chaucer, composed for readers who were not unacquainted with the French metrical romances, include a number of terms used in romance and chivalry; and, as we have seen, most of these terms were Norman. It is to be regretted that more attention is not paid by English readers to Wycliffe and Chaucer.

It unfortunately happens that Chaucer's English is just old enough to require the aid of a glossary, and yet not difficult enough to confer upon those who master it, credit as linguists. Many a person would not refuse to spend several hours upon a hundred lines of Ariosto or Tasso, who would grudge equal labour to a tale of Chaucer's; for, after all, Chaucer is only an Englishman, and we feel that we have a birth-right to consider ourselves English scholars. As reader of Italian, one can make some pretence of the accomplishments. But if any one caring to work at English, should desire to render his course of study easy, he would find it worth while to study with care Wycliffe's version of St. John's Gospel; he would then be prepared, in some measure, to go on with Chaucer's Canterbury Tales; and, after reading two or three thousand lines, he would be surprised to find himself almost as much at home with the father of English poetry, as he can be with Shakespeare or with Milton. At the same time he may find it good suggestive work to compare the original of the Knight's Tale, or the Wife of Bath's Tale, with modernised versions of the same by Dryden and Pope.

In examining the words of Wycliffe and Chaucer, we find that most of them are either Saxon or French, and that a few are derived directly from Latin. Sometimes Wycliffe employs a Latin word, as Resurrection, at other times he translates it, the Agen-rysynge (or again-rising); so also the word Except appears as Out-taken, thus, Out-taken women and children, for Except women and children.

From the fourteenth century until the Reformation, the language received constant accessions of Latin words, particularly in works which treated of art or science, law or religion. For as the authors had all studied in Latin, they were apt to introduce school phrases whenever they attempted to convey their thoughts in English. And when, after the fall of Constantinople, and the consequent dispersion of the Greeks, old Greek literature released from the ban first set on it, began to attract notice in Western Europe, it became the fashion to imitate the languages of classical antiquity, and to regard Teutonic literature as barbarous. This influence was very strongly felt between the reigns of Queen Elizabeth and Charles the First.

The Reformation worked both ways: on the one hand it aroused a desire of translating the Bible into English, and the translators had a direct object in using words which the common people could understand; but, on the other hand, the religious disputes which ensued, caused many theological and scholastic terms, such as justification, sanctification, transubstantiation, consubstantiation, and others, to become part of our ordinary language.

Hence it is, that we find Latimer, Bishop Hall, and Bunyan, addressing themselves to the plain intelligence of the people; while Hooker and Jeremy Taylor, adopting a much more ambitious style, wrote for the educated classes in society.

Roger Ascham has, however, well observed, that a good writer must speak as the common people do, and think as wise men do; for so shall every man understand him, and the judgment of wise men approve him.

The Growth of Sounds
and Grammar

Paul Roberts

We may now have an example of Old English. The favorite illustration is the Lord's Prayer, since it needs no translation. This has come to us in several different versions. Here is one:

> Fæder ure þu ðe eart on heofonum si þin nama gehalgod. Tobecume þin rice. Gewurðe þin willa on eorðan swa swa on heofonum. Urne gedæghwamlican hlaf syle us to dæg. And forgyf us ure gyltas swa swa we forgyfaþ urum gyltendum. And ne gelæd þu us on costnunge ac alys us of yfele. Soðlice.

Some of the differences between this and Modern English are merely differences in orthography. For instance, the sign *æ* is what Old English writers used for a vowel sound like that in modern *hat* or *and*. The *th* sounds of modern *thin* or *then* are represented in Old English by þ or ð. But of course there are many differences in sound too. *Ure* is the ancestor of modern *our,* but the first vowel was like that in *too* or *ooze*. *Hlaf* is modern *loaf;* we have dropped the *h* sound and changed the vowel, which in *hlaf* was pronounced something like the vowel in *father*. Old English had some sounds which we do not have. The sound represented by *y* does not occur in Modern English. If you pronounce the vowel in *bit* with your lips rounded, you may approach it.

In grammar, Old English was much more highly inflected than Modern English is. That is, there were more case endings for nouns, more person and number endings for verbs, a more complicated pronoun system, various endings for adjectives, and so on. Old English nouns had four cases—nominative, genitive, dative, accusative. Adjectives had five—all these and an instrumental case besides. Present-day English has only two cases for nouns —common case and possessive case. Adjectives now have no case system at all. On the other hand, we now use a more rigid word order and more structure words (prepositions, auxiliaries, and the like) to express relationships than Old English did.

Some of this grammar we can see in the Lord's Prayer. *Heofonum,* for instance, is a dative plural; the nominative singular was *heofon*. *Urne* is an accusative singular; the nominative is *ure*. In *urum gyltendum* both words are dative plural. *Forgyfaþ* is the third person plural form of the verb. Word order is different: "urne gedæghwamlican hlaf syle us" in place of "Give us our daily bread." And so on. . . .

Sometime between the years 1000 and 1200 various important changes took place in the structure of English, and Old English became Middle English. The political event which facilitated these changes was the Norman Conquest. The Normans, as the name shows, came originally from Scandinavia. In the early tenth century they established themselves in northern France, adopted the French language, and developed a vigorous kingdom and a very passable civilization. In the year 1066, led by Duke William, they crossed the Channel and made themselves masters of England. For the next several hundred years, England was ruled by kings whose first language was French.

One might wonder why, after the Norman Conquest, French did not become the national language, replacing English entirely. The reason is that the Conquest was not a national migration, as the earlier Anglo-Saxon invasion had been. Great numbers of Normans came to England, but they came as rulers and landlords. French became the language of the court, the language of the nobility, the language of polite society, the language of literature. But it did not replace English as the language of the people. There must always have been hundreds of towns and villages in which French was never heard except when visitors of high station passed through.

But English, though it survived as the national language, was profoundly changed after the Norman Conquest. Some of the changes—in sound structure and grammar—would no doubt have taken place whether there had been a Conquest or not. Even before 1066 the case system of English nouns and adjectives was becoming simplified; people came to rely more on word order and prepositions than on inflectional endings to communicate their meanings. The process was speeded up by sound changes which caused many of the endings to sound alike. But no doubt the Conquest facilitated the change. German, which didn't experience a Norman Conquest, is today rather highly inflected compared to its cousin English. . . .

Middle English, then, was still a Germanic language, but it differed from Old English in many ways. The sound system and the grammar changed a good deal. Speakers made less use of case systems and other inflectional devices and relied more on word order and structure words to express their meanings. This is often said to be a simplification, but it isn't really. Languages don't become simpler; they merely exchange one kind of complexity for another. Modern English is not a simple language, as any foreign speaker who tries to learn it will hasten to tell you.

For us Middle English is simpler than Old English just because it is closer to Modern English. It takes three or four months at least to learn to read Old English prose and more than that for poetry. But a week of good study should put one in touch with the Middle English poet Chaucer. Indeed, you may be able to make some sense of Chaucer straight off, though you would need instruction in pronunciation to make it sound like poetry. . . .

Sometime between 1400 and 1600 English underwent a couple of sound changes which made the language of Shakespeare quite different from that of Chaucer. Incidentally, these changes contributed much to the chaos in which English spelling now finds itself.

One change was the elimination of a vowel sound in certain unstressed positions at the end of words. For instance, the words *name, stone, wine, dance,* were pronounced as two syllables by Chaucer but as just one by Shakespeare. The *e* in these words became, as we say, "silent." But it wasn't silent for Chaucer; it represented a vowel sound. So also the words *laughed, seemed, stored,* would have been pronounced by Chaucer as two-syllable words. The change was an important one because it affected thousands of words and gave a different aspect to the whole language.

The other change is what is called the Great Vowel Shift. This was a systematic shifting of half a dozen vowels and diphthongs in stressed syllables. For instance, the word *name* had in Middle English a vowel something like that in the modern word *father; wine* had the vowel of modern *mean; he* was pronounced something like modern *hey; mouse* sounded like *moose; moon* had the vowel of *moan.* Again the shift was thoroughgoing and affected all the words in which these vowel sounds occurred. Since we still keep the Middle English system of spelling these words, the differences between Modern English and Middle English are often more real than apparent.

The vowel shift has meant also that we have come to use an entirely different set of symbols for representing vowel sounds than is used by writers of such languages as French, Italian, or Spanish, in which no such vowel shift occurred. If you come across a strange word—say, *bine*—in an English book, you will pronounce it according to the English system, with the vowel of *wine* or *dine*. But if you read *bine* in a French, Italian, or Spanish book, you will pronounce it with the vowel of *mean* or *seen*.

These two changes, then, produced the basic differences between Middle English and Modern English. But there were several other developments that had an effect upon the language. One was the invention of printing, an invention introduced into England by William Caxton in the year 1475. Where before books had been rare and costly, they suddenly became cheap and common. More and more people learned to read and write. This was the first of many advances in communication which have worked to unify languages and to arrest the development of dialect differences, though of course printing affects writing principally rather than speech. Among other things it hastened the standardization of spelling.

WORKING WITH THE SELECTIONS

1. Dickens provides a good, orderly statement, and considering how ignorant the eighteenth century was about language, we may well marvel that a nineteenth-century person who was no specialist understood the sources of English vocabulary as well as Dickens did. Although he seems to think he is sketching "The History of the Language," he misses some important aspects of language. What are they?

2. You probably concluded that Dickens ignored almost everything except vocabulary. In his defense one should say that he apparently wanted to advise people about word selection, but within limits he was thinking of writing as the selection of words; his topic sentence reads, "When a man has anything of his own to say, and is really in earnest that it should be understood, he does not usually make cavalry regiments of his sentences, and seek abroad for sesquidelian words." In view of Dickens' essay and in light of what you have encountered in earlier sections of this book, what can you say about the average man's awareness of language? Is he more conscious of some aspects of language than of others?

3. Roberts is guilty of no such oversights as you probably found in Dickens (his discussions of vocabulary were omitted). Dickens found that much of our vocabulary has been borrowed; does Roberts find that this is true of many sounds or much grammar? What would you conclude about the relative ease with which various linguistic means can be borrowed?

4

Old and Middle English

Early English is commonly divided into Old English, or Anglo-Saxon, which was used from the earliest times to about A.D. 1100, and Middle English, which began about 1100 or a little earlier and was common until 1500. Some samples of Old English appear in the first reading below, a selection from Remaines, Concerning Britaine, *3rd ed. (1623), a translation of the Latin* Britannia, *written by William Camden (1551–1623). About 1200 one Orm, perhaps the dullest monk who ever supposed he was writing English seriously, compiled a digest of biblical and ecclesiastical lore, which he called the* Ormulum. *He apparently invented his own system of spelling, which he considered the only right one. The second selection is reprinted from the unique manuscript, perhaps his own copy; only the punctuation has been modernized. The verbatim equivalent that follows preserves the word order of the original. The third piece purports to be an account by one Sir John Mandeville, Gentleman, of his travels in the Orient, especially the Holy Land. It probably is not, but whoever wrote or translated it must have done so about 1400. The selection is reprinted from* Mandeville's Travels, *edited by P. Hamelius for the Early English Text Society, Original Series 153 (1909). The modernized version preserves the word order of the original. Mandeville's contemporary, Geoffrey Chaucer (d. 1400), scarcely requires introduction. The first of the two selections by Chaucer is the description of the Clerk, or graduate student, from* The Text of the Canterbury Tales *(1940), edited by John M. Manly and Edith Rickert. The second is the Introduction to a textbook that Chaucer apparently wrote for his young son; for older students such a book would have been written in Latin. It is reprinted from* The Works of Geoffrey Chaucer, *2nd ed. (1957), edited by F. N. Robinson. The punctuation is modern. The final selection is by William Caxton (1422?–91), recognized as England's first printer and publisher. The passage is from his Introduction to his translation of the* Aeneid, *published in 1490. The text is diplomatic, reproducing Caxton's printing as found in Nellie Slayton Aurner,* Caxton, Mirror of Fifteenth Century Letters *(1926).*

Remains of Early English

William Camden

I dare not yet here affirme for the antiquity of our Language, that our great-great-great-Grandsires tongue came out of *Persia*, albeit the wonderfull Linguist *Iosoph Scaliger* hath obserued, *Fader, Moder, Bruder, band, &c.* in the Persian tongue in the very sence as we now vse them.

It will not be vnproper I hope to this purpose, if I note out of the Epistles of that learned Ambassour *Busbequius,* how the inhabitants of *Taurica Chersonessus,* in the vttermost part of *Europe* Eastward, haue these words, *Wind, Siluer, Korne, Salt, Fish, Son, Apple, Waggen, Singen, Ilanda, Beard,* with many other in the very same sence and signification, as they now are in vse with vs, whereat I maruelled not a little when I first read it. But nothing can be gathered thereby, but that the *Saxons* our progenitours, which planted themselues here in the West, did also to their glory place Colonies likewise there in the East.

As in the Latine tongue, the learned make in respect of time, foure *Idioms,* the *Ancient,* the *Latine,* the *Romane,* the *Mixt:* so we in ours may make the *Ancient English-Saxon,* and the *Mixt.* But that you may see how powerable *Time* is in altering tongues as all things else, I will set downe the Lords Prayer as it was translated in sundry ages, that you may see by what degrees our tongue is risen, and thereby coniecture how in time it may altar and fall againe.

If we could set it downe in the ancient *Saxen,* I meane in the tongue which the Enlish vsed at their first arriuall here, about 440. yeeres after Christs birth, it would seeme most strange and harsh Dutch or Gebrish, as women call it; or when they first embraced Christianity, about the yeere of Christ 600. But the ancientst that I can find, was about 900. yeere since, about the yeere of Christ 700. found in ancient *Saxon* glossed *Euangelists,* in the hands of my good friend Master *Robert Bowyer,* written by *Eadfride* the eight Bishop of *Lindisfarne,* (which after was translated to *Durham*) and diuided according to the ancient *Canon of Eusebius,* not into Chapters: for *Stephen Langton,* Archbishop of *Canterbury,* first diuided the holy Scripture into Chapters, as *Robert Stephan* did lately into Verse, and thus it is.

> *Our Father which art in heauen*
> Vren Fader thic arth in heofnas,
>
> *be hallowed thine name. come*
> Sic[1] gehalgud thin noma. to cymeth
>
> *thy Kingdome. Be thy will so as in*
> thin ric. Sic[1] thin willa sue is[2] in
>
> *Heauen and in earth. Oure lofe*
> heofnas, and in eortho. Vren hlaf
>
> *Super-substantiall giue vs to day, and*
> ofer wirtlic[3] sel vs to dæg, and

[1 Probably a transcriptural error for *sie*.]

[2 The misprint here must be in the Anglo-Saxon, which should read something like *sue*, since *sue sue* means *even as*.]

[3 Presumably a misprint for *oferwistlic*. Since *wist* can mean *reality*, this translation

forgiue vs debts ours so we for-
forgef vs scylda urna, sue we for-

giue debts ours and do not leade
gefan scyldgum vrum, and do inlead [4]

vs into temptation. But deliuer euery one
vsith[5] in custnung. Ah gefrig vrich[5]

from euill.
from ifle. Amen.

Some two hundred yeeres after, I find this somewhat varied in two translations.

<table>
<tr><td></td><td>Thu vre fader the eait on heofenum</td></tr>
<tr><td></td><td>Si thin nama gehalgod. Cum thin ric.</td></tr>
<tr><td>* Gewurth thin willa.</td><td>* Si thin willa on eorthan, swa on heofe-</td></tr>
<tr><td></td><td align="center">*dayly*</td></tr>
<tr><td></td><td>num. Syle vs to dæg vrn dægthanlican[6] hlaf.</td></tr>
<tr><td></td><td align="center">*trespasses*</td></tr>
<tr><td></td><td>And forgif vs vre glytas swa, swa we for-</td></tr>
<tr><td></td><td align="center">*against vs haue trespassed*</td></tr>
<tr><td>* Vrum Gyltendum.</td><td>gifath* tham the with vs agyltath. And ne</td></tr>
<tr><td></td><td>led the vs on costnung, Ac alys vs from</td></tr>
<tr><td></td><td align="center">*Be it so.*</td></tr>
<tr><td>* Sothlice.</td><td>yfle. * Si it swa.</td></tr>
</table>

About an hundred and threescore yeares after, in the time of King *Henry*
the second, I finde this rime sent from *Rome* by Pope *Adrian* the Englishman, to be taught to the people.

Vre fadyr in heauen rich,
Thy name be halyedeuer lich,
Thou bring vs thy michell blisse,
Als hit in heauen y-doe,
Evar in yearth beene it also:
That holy bread that lasteth ay,
Thou send it ous this ilke day.
Forgiue ous all that we haue don,
As wee forgivet vch other mon:
Ne let ous fall into no founding,
Ac shield ous fro the fowle thing. Amen.

---

is possible, but *wist* can also mean a *feast, plenty,* giving the more probable translation *plentiful, abundant.*]
[4 *Inlead* means *lead into,* not *not lead; do* may be an error for *no* or *ne.*]
[5 *Vsith* and *vrich* should probably read *vsich,* meaning *us.*]
[6 Presumably an error for *dægwhamlican,* which means *daily.*]

. . . In the time of King *Richard* the second about a hundred and odde yeares after, it was so mollified, that it came to be thus, as it is in the Translation of *Wickeliffe,* with some Latine words now inserted, whereas there was not one before.

> Our *fadyr, that art in heauen, halloed be thy name,*
> *thy kingdom comto, be thy will done, so in heauen,*
> *and in erth: gif to vs this day our bread ouer other*
> *substance: and forgif to vs our* dettis, *as we forge-*
> *uen to our* detters, *and leed vs not into* temptation,
> *but* deliuer *vs fro euill. Amen.*

Hitherto will our sparkefull Youth laugh at their great grandfather *English,* who had more care to do wel, than to speak minion-like, and left more glory to vs by their exployting of great actes, than we shall do by our forging a new words, and vncuth phrases.

Great verily was the glory of our tongue before the *Norman* Conquest, in this, that the old *English* could expresse most aptly, all the conceipts of the minde in their owne tongue, without borrowing from any. As for example:

The holy seruice of God, which the *Latines* called *Religion,* because it knitted the mindes of men together, and most people of *Europe* haue borrowed the same from them they called most significantly *Ean-fastnes,* as the one and onely assurance and fast anker-hold of our soules health.

The gladsome tidings of our saluation, which the *Greekes* called *Euangelion,* and other Nations in the same word, they called *Godspell,* that is *Gods speech.*

For our *Sauiour,* which we borrowed from the *French,* and they from the *Latine Saluator,* they called in their owne word, *Hae-lend* from *Hael,* that is, *Salus,* safety, which we retaine still in *Al-hael,* and *Was-hael,* that is *Aue, Salue, Sis, saluus.*

They could call the disciples of Christ, *Leorning Cnihtas* that is, *Learning Seruitours.* For *Cniht* which is now a name of worship, signified with them an *Attendant,* or seruitour.

Ormulum

Orm

Forr itt maȝȝ hellpenn alle þa   Þatt bliþelike itt herenn
Annd lufenn itt annd follȝhen itt   Wiþþ þohht, wiþþ word, wiþþ dede,
Annd whase wilenn shall þiss boc   Efft oþerrsiþe writtenn,
Himm bidde icc þatt het write rihht   Swasumm þiss boc himm taecheþþ,
All þwerrtut affterr þatt itt iss   Uppo þiss firrste bisne,

Wiþþ all swillc rime alls her iss sett   Wiþþ allse fele wordess;
Annd tatt he loke wel þatt he   An bocstaff write twiȝȝess
Eȝȝewhaer þaer itt uppo þiss boc   Iss writenn o þatt wise.
Loke he well þatt het write swa;   Forr he ne maȝȝe nohht elless
Onn ennglissh writenn rihht te word,   þatt wite he wel to soþe.

For it [the *Ormulum*] may help all those   that gladly it hear
And love it and follow it   with thought, with word, with deed,
And whoso wish shall this book   Again anothertime write,
Him bid I that it write right   As this book him teaches,
All throughout after that it is   Upon this first example
With all such rhyme as here is set   With as many words;
And that he look well that he   One letter write twice
Everywhere there it upon this book   Is written in that wise.
Look he well that he write so;   For he may not else
In English write right the word,   That knows he well for truth.

Travels

Sir John Mandeville

In Ethiope all the Ryueres & all the watres ben trouble & þei ben somdell salte for the gret hete þat is þere. And the folk of þat contree ben lyghtly dronken & han but litill appetyt to mete And þei han comounly the flux of the wombe & þei lyuen not longe. In Ethiope ben many dyuerse folk And Ethiope is clept Cusis. In þat contree ben folk þat han but o foot & þei gon so blyue þat it is meruaylle And the foot is so large þat it schadeweth all the body aȝen the sonne Whanne þei wole lye & reste hem. In Ethiope whan the children ben ȝonge & lytill þei ben all ȝalowe And whan þat þei wexen of age þat ȝalowness turneth to ben all blak. In Ethiope is the cytee of Saba & the lond of the whiche on of the .iij. kynges þat presented oure lord in Bethleem was kyng offe. Fro Ethiope men gon into ynde be manye dyuerse contreyes And men clepen the high ynde Emlak. And ynde is devyded in .iij. princypall parties þat is [ynde] the more þat is a full hoot contree & ynde the less þat is a full atempree contrey þat streccheth to the londe of Mede. And the .iij. part toward the Septentrion is full cold so þat for pure cold & contynuell frost the water becometh Cristall. And vpon the roches of cristall growen the gode dyamandes þat ben of trouble colour; ȝalow Cristall draweth colour lyke oylle And þei ben so harde þat noman may pollysch hem & men clepen hem dyamandes in þat contree & Hamese in anoþer contree. Othere dyamandes men fynden in Arabye þat ben not so gode & þei ben more broun & more tendre. And oþer dyamandes also men fynden in the Ile of Cipre þat ben ȝit more tendre & hem men may wel pollischen; And in the lond of

Macedoyne men fynden dyamaundes also, But the beste & the moste *pre*cyiouse ben in ynde. And men fynden many tyme harde dyamaund*es* in a masse þat cometh ut of gold when men pure*n* it & fyne*n* it out of the myne whan men breken þat mass in smale peces. And sum tyme it happeneth þat men fynden sum*me* as grete as a pese & sum*me* lasse & þei ben als harde as þo of y*n*de. And all be it þat men fynden gode dyamand*es* in ynde, ȝit natheles men fynden hem more comou*n*ly vpon the roches in the see & vpon hilles where the myne of gold is; And þei growen many to gedre on lytill another gret And þer ben sum*me* of the gretness of a bene & sum*me* als grete as an hasell note & þei ben square & poynted of here owne kynde boþe aboue*n* & benethen wit*h*oute*n* worchinge of ma*n*nes hond & þei growe*n* togedre male & female And þei ben norysscht wit*h* the dew of heuene And þei engendre*n* comouly & bryngen forth smale children þat m*u*ltiplyen & growen all the ȝeer. I have ofte*n* tymes assayed þat ȝif a man kepe he*m* wit*h* a lityll of the roche, & wete he*m* wit*h* may dew ofte sithes þei schull growe eu*er*yche ȝeer, & the smale wole wex*es* grete. For right as the fyn perl congeleth and wexeth gret of the dew of heuen right so doth the v*er*ray dyamand, And right as the perl of his owne kynde taketh roundness right so the dyamand be v*er*tu of god taketh squareness. And men schall ber*e* the dyamaund on his left syde for it is of grettere v*er*tue þa*n*ne þan on the right syde; For the strengthe of her*e* growynge is toward the north þat is the left side of the world, & the left p*ar*tie of ma*n* is whan he turneth his face toward the est.

In Ethiope [northeast Africa] all the rivers and all the waters are troubled, and they are somewhat salt for the great heat that is there. And the people of that country are lightly drunk [easily become drunk] and have but little appetite for food and they have commonly the flux of the belly and they live not long. In Ethiopia are many diverse people, and Ethiopia is called Cusis. In that country are people that have but one foot, and they go so rapidly that it is a marvel, and the foot is so large that it shadows all the body from the sun when they wish to lie and rest them. In Ethiopia when the children are young and little they are all yellow, and when that they grow of age that yellowness turns to be all black. In Ethiopia is the city of Saba [a supposed city, probably not in Ethiopia, but across the Red Sea in southwest Arabia], and the land of which one of the three kings that presented our Lord in Bethlehem was king of. From Ethiopia people go into India by many diverse countries, and men call the high India *Emlack*. And India is divided in three principal parts, that is [India] the Greater, that is a very hot country, and India the Less that is a very temperate country that stretches to the land of Media [a country between the Caspian Sea to the north and the ancient city of Ecbatan to the south]. And the third part toward the Septentrion [the north, since the Great Bear was called the Seven Plow Oxen] is very cold so that for pure cold and continual frost the water becomes crystal. And upon the rocks of crystal grow the good diamonds that are of cloudy color; yellow crystal draws color like oil, and they are so hard that no man may polish them, and people call them diamonds in that contree and *hamese* in another country. Other diamonds people find in Arabia that are not so good and they are browner and more tender. And other diamonds, also, people find in the Isle of Cyprus that are yet more tender, and them people can easily pollish. And in the land of Macedonia people find diamonds, also, but the best and the most precious are in India. And people find many times hard diamonds in a mass that come out of gold when they purify it and refine it out of the mine when they break that mass into small pieces. And sometimes it happens that people find some as large as peas and some less, and they are as hard as those of India. And although people find good diamonds in India, yet nevertheless people find them more commonly upon the rocks in the sea and upon hills where the mine of gold is; and they grow many together, one little, another large. And there are some of the size of a bean, and some as great as a hazelnut, and they are square pointed of their own nature, both above and beneath, without working of man's hand, and they grow together, male and female, and they are nourished with the dew of heaven, and they engender together and bring forth small children that multiply and grow all the year. I have often proposed that if a man keep them with a little of the rock, and wet them with May dew often times they would grow every year, and the small would grow great. For just as the fine pearl congeals and grows great from the dew of heaven, just so does the true diamond, and just as the pearl of its own nature takes roundness, just so the diamond by virtue of God takes squareness. And people should wear the diamond on the left side, for it is of greater virtue then than on the right side, for the strength of their growing is toward the north, that is the left side of the world, and the left part of man is when he turns his face toward the east.

The Language of One Who Would Gladly Learn and Gladly Teach

Geoffrey Chaucer

THE CLERK

A CLERK ther was of Oxenford also
That vn to logyk hadde longe ygo
   As leene was his hors as is a rake
And he nas nat right fat I vndertake
But looked holwe and ther to sobrely
Ful thredbare was his ouereste courtepy

For he hadde geten hym yet no benefice
Ne was so worldly for to haue office
For hym was leuere haue at his beddes heed
Twenty bookes clad in blak or reed
Of Aristotle and his philosophie
Than robes riche or fithele or gay sautrie
　　But al be that he was a philosophre
Yet hadde he but litel gold in cofre
But al that he myghte of his frendes hente
On bookes and on lernynge he it spente
And bisily gan for the soules preye
Of hem that yaf hym wher with to scoleye
　　Of studie took he moost cure and moost heede
Noght oo word spak he moore than was neede
And that was seid in forme and reuerence
And short and quyk and ful of heigh sentence
Sownynge in moral vertu was his speche
And gladly wolde he lerne and gladly teche.

There was also a student from Oxford, who had devoted himself long since to logic. His horse was as lean as is a rake, and I will bet you [vndertake] that he was not very fat, but he looked hollow and also somewhat solemn [sobrely]. His jacket [ouereste courtepy] was quite threadbare, for he had as yet got himself no benefice [an ecclesiastical appointment], and he was not worldly enough to accept a job [office; that is, employment outside the church]. For to him it was preferable [leuere] to have at his bed's head twenty books, bound in black or red, of Aristotle and his philosophy, than rich clothes, or a fiddle, or gay music [sautrie]. But although he was a philosopher, yet he had but little gold in his coffer. [Chaucer is joking about the tradition that the "philosopher's stone," sought by alchemists, could change base metals into gold.] But all that he could borrow [myghte . . . hente], he spent it on books and learning, and busily went about [gan] praying for the souls of those that gave him the wherewithall to go to school [to scoleye]. Of learning he took the most concern [cure] and most care [heede]. He spoke not one word more than necessary [neede], and that was said in form [probably rhetorical form] and with due respect [reuerence] and brief and lively and full of lofty meaning; his speech tended to [was sownynge (sounding) in] moral virtue, and gladly would he learn and gladly teach.

A TREATISE ON THE ASTROLABE

Lyte Lowys my sone, I aperceyve wel by certeyne evydences thyn abilite to lerne sciences touching nombres and proporciouns; and as wel considre I thy besy praier in special to lerne the tretys of the Astrelabie. Than for as mochel as a philosofre saith, "he wrappith him in his frend, that condescendith to the rightfulle praiers of his frend," therfore have I yeven the a suffisant Astrolabie as for oure orizonte, compowned after the latitude of Oxenforde; upon which, by mediacioun of this litel tretys, I purpose to teche the a certein nombre of conclusions aperteynyng to the same instrument. I seie a certein of conclusions, for thre causes. The first cause is this: truste wel that alle the conclusions that han be founde, or ellys possibly might be founde in so noble an instrument as is an Astrelabie ben unknowe parfitly to eny mortal man in this regioun, as I suppose. Another cause is this, that sothly in any tretis of the Astrelabie that I have seyn there be somme conclusions that wol not in alle thinges parformen her bihestes; and somme of hem ben to harde to thy tendir age of ten yeer to conceyve.

This tretis, divided in 5 parties, wol I shewe the under full light reules and naked wordes in Englissh, for Latyn ne canst thou yit but small, my litel sone. But natheles suffise to the these trewe conclusions in Englissh as wel as sufficith to these noble clerkes Grekes these same conclusions in Grek; and to Arabiens in Arabik, and to Jewes in Ebrew, and to the Latyn folk in Latyn; whiche Latyn folk had hem first out of othere dyverse langages, and writen hem in her owne tunge, that is to seyn, in Latyn. And God woot that in alle these langages and in many moo han these conclusions ben suffisantly lerned and taught, and yit by diverse reules; right as diverse pathes leden diverse folk the righte way to Rome. Now wol I preie mekely every discret persone that redith or herith this litel tretys to have my rude endityng for excusid, and my superfluite of wordes, for two causes. The first cause is for that curious endityng and hard sentence is ful hevy at onys for such a child to lerne. And the secunde cause is this, that sothly me semith better to writen unto a child twyes a god sentence, than he forgete it onys.

And Lowys, yf so be that I shewe the in my light Englissh as trewe conclusions touching this mater, and not oonly as trewe but as many and as subtile conclusiouns, as ben shewid in Latyn in eny commune tretys of the Astrelabie, konne me the more thank. And preie God save the king, that is lord of this langage, and alle that him feith berith and obeieth, everich in his degre, the more and the lasse. But considre wel that I ne usurpe not to have founden this werk of my labour or of myn engyn. I n'am but a lewd compilator of the labour of olde astrologiens, and have it translatid in myn Englissh oonly for thy doctrine. And with this swerd shal I sleen envie.

Little Lewis, my son, I perceive well by certain evidences your ability to learn sciences involving numbers and proportions, and also I consider your busy prayer to study an exposition of the astrolabe. In as much as a philosopher says, "He wraps himself in his friend who condescends to the reasonable prayers of his friend," I have given you a sufficient astrolabe for our horizon, calculated according to the latitude of Oxford; by means of this little treatise I intend to teach you certain conclusions pertaining to this same instrument. I say certain conclusions for three causes. The first cause is this: you may well believe that all the conclusions that have been found, or else possibly might be found in so noble an instrument as is an astrolabe, are not perfectly known to any mortal in this region, as I suppose. Another cause is this, that truly in any treatise of the astrolabe that I have seen there are some conclusions that will not live up to their promises in all things; and some of them are too hard for your tender age of ten years to conceive.

This treatise, divided into five parts, I shall show you with very easy rules and simple words in English, for of Latin you as yet know but little, my young son. Nonetheless, these true conclusions suffice in English as well as they sufficed the noble learned Greeks in Greek, and the Arabians in Arabic, and the Jews in Hebrew, and the Latin people in Latin, which Latin people had them first out of other various languages, and wrote them in their own tongue, that is to say, in Latin. And God knows that in all these languages and in many more these conclusions have been sufficiently taught and by diverse rules, just as various paths lead various people the right way to Rome. Now I shall pray every understanding person who reads or hears this little treatise that for two reasons he will excuse my crude composition and my superfluity of words. The first cause is that elaborate constructions and difficult meaning are very hard for such a little child to comprehend at once. And the second is this, that truly it seems to me better to write a good idea to a child twice than that he forget it once.

And Lewis, if I am able to show you in my easy English as true conclusions in this subject, and not only as true but as many and sharply reasoned conclusions, as have been shown in Latin in any common treatise of the astrolabe, you may thank me the more. And pray God save the King, who is lord of this language, and all that bear faith to him and obey him, each in his social station, greater or less. But remember that I do not pretend to have discovered this learning by my own labor or by my ingenuity. I am but an ignorant compiler of the work of old astrologers, and have translated it into English only for your education. And with this sword shall I slay envy.

Eggys or Eyren

William Caxton

I delybered and concluded to translate it [the *Aeneid*] in to englysshe And forthwyth toke a penne & ynke and wrote a leef or tweyne/which I ouer-sawe agayne to correcte it/And whan I sawe the fayr & straunge termes therin/I doubted that it sholde not please some gentylmen whiche late blamed me sayeng y^t [that] in my translacyons I had ouer curyous termes whiche coude not be vnderstande of comyn peple/and desired me to vse olde and homely termes in my translacyons. and fayn wolde I satysfye euery man/and so to doo toke an olde boke and redde therin/and certaynly the englysshe was so rude and brood that I coude not wele vnderstande it. And also my lord abbot of westmynster [Westminster] ded do shewe to me later certayn euydences wryton in olde englysshe for to reduce it in to our englysshe now vsid/And certaynly it was wreton in such wyse that it was more like to dutche than englysshe   I coude not reduce ny brynge it to be vnderstonden/Ande certaynly our langage now vsed varyeth ferre from that. whiche was vsed and spoken whan I was borne/For we englysshe men ben/born vnder the domynacyon of the mone. whiche is neuer stedfaste/but euer wauerynge/wexynge one season/and waneth & dyscreaseth another season/And that comyn englysshe that is spoken in one shyre varyeth from another. In so much that in my dayes happened that certayn marchauntes were in a shippe in tamyse [Thames] for to haue sayled ouer the see into zelande [Holland]/and for lacke of wynde thei taryed atte forlond [at the foreland]. and wente to lande for to refreshe them And one of theym named sheffelde a mercer [Sheffield, a clothier] came into a hows and axed for mete. and specyally he axyd after eggys And the good wyfe answerde. that she coude speke no frenshe. And the merchaunt was angry. for he also coude speke no frenshe. but wolde haue hadde egges/and she vnderstode hym not/And thenne at last a nother sayd that he wold haue eyren/[cf. modern German *Eier*, eggs] then the good wyf sayd that she vnderstod hym wel/Loo what sholde a man in thyse dayes now wryte. egges or eyren/certaynly it is harde to playse euery man/by cause of dyuersite & chaunge of langage. For in these dayes euery man that is in ony reputacyon in his country. wyll vtter his comynycacyon and maters in suche maners & termes/ that fewe men shall vnderstonde theym/And som honest and grete clerkes haue ben wyth me and desired me to wryte the moste curyous termes that I coude fynde/And thus betwene playn rude/& curyous I stande abasshed. but in my Iudgement/the comyn terms that be dayli vsed ben lyghter to be vnderstonde than the olde and auncyent englysshe/And for as moche as this present booke is not for a rude vplondysshe man to laboure therin/ne rede it/but onely for a clerke & a noble gentylman that feleth and vnderstondeth in faytes of armes in loue & noble chyualrye/Therfor in a meane bytwene bothe I haue reduced & translated this sayd booke in to our englysshe not ouer rude ne curyous but in such termes as shall be vnderstanden by goddys grace accordynge to my copye. and yf ony man wyll intermete in redyng of hit and fyndeth suche termes that he can not vnderstande late hym goo rede and lerne vyrgyll/or the pystles of ouyde [*Epistles* of Ovid] and ther he shall see and vnderstonde lyghtly all/

WORKING WITH THE SELECTIONS

1. First check the version of the Lord's Prayer given by Roberts and note his discussion of it. You will recall that until much after the Middle Ages *u* and *v,* historically the same letter, were used interchangeably, as either vowel or consonant. Now compare the various versions given by Camden; the last

two we would call Middle English. Camden notes that there are no French or Latin loan-words until late. Notice some other details. Are there many articles? (The word *þe* is not *the*, but a relative meaning 'who.') What about the pronouns? *Þu* and *þin* are obviously *thou* and *thine*. Do you find more forms of *we* than are now used? Roberts calls attention to some endings; do there seem to be any others? Does the same ending always appear on the same word in apparently the same grammatical situation?

2. In the passages from Old English—but not in the Middle English—the sound that we would write with a *v* is spelled with an *f*, as in *heofonum* and *heofnas*. What may this fact suggest about *f* as a letter and /f/ as a phoneme? You may want to consider the phonetic relationship between /f/ and /v/.

3. What about word order in Old English? *Fæder ure* seems to be the same as *Vren Fader*. Do you find any other examples in which the word order seems to be less fixed than in Modern English?

4. Nobody has figured out for sure what Orm's spelling system was, but in part he was marking short vowels by doubling following consonants. What would this suggest about the vowels in inflectional endings? What, apparently, could the ending *-enn* be used for? You probably found no articles in Old English; do you find any here? Do the endings seem to be more or less common in this early Middle English than in late Old English? The symbol ȝ, called *yogh*, was sometimes used for /g/, sometimes for /j/, and for various stops and fricatives between them.

5. Notice that Mandeville frequently uses verbs like *happenneth*. Where, apparently, did this ending come from? Mandeville also frequently uses a word he spells *ben*, our word *been*. What does he seem to use it for? Work through the selection by Mandeville, noticing interesting constructions, such as the sentence ending *kyng offe*. Does Mandeville use any articles? How do you account for his using the sequence *a pese*? Does he use the word *tendre* 'tender' as we would? Incidentally, the letters printed here in italics are represented by special abbreviations in the manuscript.

6. Compare the pieces by Chaucer with that by Mandeville. You probably cannot do much with pronunciation or with mechanics, such as spelling and punctuation; these two matters were usually determined by individual scribes and are often modernized in present-day editions. But compare the pieces on other important bases: word choice, sentence structure, grammar, organization, and the like. You should consider both the authors and their audiences.

7. Many infinitives in Middle English preserved the *-n* of Old English. What is Chaucer's practice with infinitives? What is Mandeville's? In Chaucer's time two sets of third-person plurals were in use; forms that were spelled something like *hie, her,* and *hem,* which had survived from Old English, and the ancestors of our pronouns *they, their, them,* which had presumably come from Old Norse. Do Chaucer and Mandeville use either of these pronominal systems consistently?

8. Clearly, the problem of usage had arisen in the fifteenth century. What was Caxton's solution?

9. Caxton must have had some system of punctuation—and we have clear evidence for it—since he was after all a publisher as well as an author. Can you work out his system? Punctuate a portion of the passage and compare your punctuation with Caxton's.

10. Does Caxton have a spelling system? If not, does he have some spelling practices that differ from earlier writers you have seen? What about the consistency of his spelling?

5

Early Modern English

By the sixteenth century, English had passed through its period of most rapid change. Analytic devices like word order had largely replaced synthetic devices like inflection—even the final e's that remained were mostly evidence of spelling conventions, not of pronunciation. The vocabulary, mainly Germanic in Old English, was now heavily larded with loan-words, mostly from French and Latin. Meanwhile, printing had become much more common, and the whole economy had advanced sufficiently so that many more people could read and write and could afford reading and writing materials. Consequently, we have more examples of language and can more readily study language as dialect. Part 5 contains examples of two dialects: the dialect of the journalists Awdeley and Harman, and the dialect of the thieves. A third sort of dialect, the dialect of learned discourse, can be observed in the translation of Camden's work. Examples of three more follow: a Scots dialect of about 1500, the dialect of some workmen in about 1600, and the dialect of the court at the same time. The first selection, by Robert Henryson (1430?–1506), one of the so-called Scottish Chaucerians, is from The Poems of Robert Henryson, edited by G. Gregory Smith (2 vols., 1906). It is part of Henryson's modernization, in imitation of Chaucer's Nun's Priest's Tale, of the fable of the town mouse and the country mouse. When the selection opens, the Country Mouse has been frightened by a "spenser," a sort of butler, and has fallen in a faint. The second selection presents facsimiles of scenes from two plays by William Shakespeare (1564-1616), A Midsummer Night's Dream, III, 1, and Hamlet, II, 2. In the first, a group of "rude mechanicals," tradesmen from Athens, are rehearsing a play in a forest. In the second, Hamlet talks with Polonius, a minister of state and the father of his intended, Ophelia. Hamlet is either insane or pretending to be so.

The Town Mouse and the Country Mouse

Robert Henryson

'Quhy ly ȝe thus? ryse vp my sister deir,
Cum to ȝour meit, this perrell is ouerpast.'
The vther answerit hir *with* heuie cheir,
'I may not eit, sa sair I am agast;
I had leuer thir fourtie dayis fast,
With watter caill and to gnaw benis and peis,
Than all ȝour feist in this dreid and diseis.'

With fair tretie ȝit scho gart hir vpryse,
And to the burde thay went and togidder sat;
And scantlie had thay drunkin anis or twyse,
Quhen in come Gid hunter, our Iolie Cat,
And bad God speid: the Burges vp with that,
And till the hole scho went as fyre on flint:
Bawdronis the vther be the bak hes hint.

Fra fute to fute he kest hir to and fra,
Quhylis vp, quhylis doun, als cant as ony kid;
Quhylis wald he lat hir rin vnder the stra,
Quhylis wald he wink, and play *with* hir buk heid.
Thus to the selie Mous greit pane he did,
Quhill at the last, throw fortune and gude hap,
Betuix ane burde and the wall scho crap.

"Why lie you thus? Rise up my dear sister, come to your meat; this peril is past." The other answered her with heavy cheer; "I can not eat, so sorely I am frightened; I had rather fast these forty days, with cold water and gnaw beans and peas, than all your feast with this dread and trouble."

With fair entreaty she got her up, and they went and sat together to the board, but they had only drunk once or twice when in came Gid the Hunter, our jolly cat, and bade them Godspeed; the Town Mouse jumped up with that, and to her hole she went like fire on flint; Bawdronis [the cat] grabbed the other by the back.

From foot to foot he cast her to and frow, sometimes up, sometimes down, as gay as any kid; sometimes he would let her run under the straw, sometimes he would pretend to sleep, and play cutting off hedge thorns with her. Thus he did the poor mouse great pain, until at last, through fortune or good luck, she crept in between a board and the wall.

Two Scenes from the First Folio

William Shakespeare

A MIDSUMMER NIGHT'S DREAM

Enter the Clownes.

Bot. Are we all met?

Quin. Pat, pat, and here's a maruailous conuenient place for our rehearsall. This greene plot shall be our stage, this hauthorne brake our tyring house, and we will do it in action, as we will do it before the Duke.

Bot. Peter quince?

Peter. What saist thou, bully *Bottome*?

Bot. There are things in this Comedy of *Piramus* and *Thisby*, that will neuer please. First, *Piramus* must draw a sword to kill himselfe; which the Ladies cannot abide. How answere you that?

Snout. Berlaken, a parlous feare.

Star. I beleeue we must leaue the killing out, when all is done.

Bot. Not a whit, I haue a deuice to make all well. Write me a Prologue, and let the Prologue seeme to say, we will do no harme with our swords, and that *Pyramus* is not kill'd indeede : and for the more better assurance, tell them, that I *Piramus* am not *Piramus*, but *Bottome* the Weauer; this will put them out of feare.

Quin. Well, we will haue such a Prologue, and it shall be written in eight and sixe.

Bot. No, make it two more, let it be written in eight and eight.

Snout. Will not the Ladies be afear'd of the Lyon?

Star. I feare it, I promise you.

Bot. Masters, you ought to consider with your selues, to bring in (God shield vs) a Lyon among Ladies, is a most dreadfull thing. For there is not a more fearefull wilde foule then your Lyon liuing : and wee ought to looke to it.

Snout. Therefore another Prologue must tell he is not Lyon.

Bot. Nay, you must name his name, and halfe his face must be seene through the Lyons necke, and he himselfe must speake through, saying thus, or to the same defect; Ladies, or faire Ladies, I would wish you, or I would request you, or I would entreat you, not to feare, not to tremble: my life for yours. If you thinke I come hither as a Lyon, it were pitty of my life No, I am no such thing, I am a man as other men are ; and there indeed let him name his name, and tell him plainly hee is *Snug* the ioyner.

Quin. Well, it shall be so; but there is two hard things, that is, to bring the Moone-light into a chamber: for you know, *Piramus* and *Thisby* meete by Moone-light.

Sn. Doth the Moone shine that night wee play our play?

Bot. A Calender; a Calender, looke in the Almanack, finde out Moone-shine, finde out Moone-shine.

Enter Pucke.

Quin. Yes, it doth shine that night.

Bot. Why then may you leaue a casement of the great chamber window (where we play) open, and the Moone may shine in at the casement.

Quin. I, or else one must come in with a bush of thornes and a lanthorne, and say he comes to disfigure, or to present the person of Moone-shine. Then there is another thing, we must haue a wall in the great Chamber; for *Piramus* and *Thisby* (saies the story) did talke through the chinke of a wall.

Sn. You can neuer bring in a wall. What say you *Bottome*?

Bot. Some man or other must present wall, and let him haue some Plaster, or some Lome, or some rough cast about him, to signifie wall ; or let him hold his fingers thus ; and through that cranny, shall *Piramus* and *Thisby* whisper.

Quin. If that may be, then all is well. Come, sit downe euery mothers sonne, and rehearse your parts. *Piramus*, you begin; when you haue spoken your speech, enter into that Brake, and so euery one according to his cue.

Enter Hamlet reading on a Booke.

Qu. But looke where sadly the poore wretch
Comes reading.
Pol. Away I do beseech you, both away,
Ile boord him presently.   *Exit King & Queen.*
Oh giue me leaue. How does my good Lord *Hamlet* ?
   Ham. Well, God-a-mercy.
   Pol. Do you know me, my Lord ?
   Ham. Excellent, excellent well : y'are a Fishmonger.
   Pol. Not I my Lord.
   Ham. Then I would you were so honest a man.
   Pol. Honest, my Lord ?
   Ham. I sir, to be honest as this world goes, is to bee
one man pick'd out of two thousand.
   Pol. That's very true, my Lord.
   Ham. For if the Sun breed Magots in a dead dogge,
being a good kissing Carrion————
Haue you a daughter ?
   Pol. I haue my Lord.
   Ham. Let her not walke i'th'Sunne : Conception is a
blessing, but not as your daughter may conceiue. Friend
looke too't.
   Pol. How say you by that? Still harping on my daugh-
ter: yet he knew me not at first; he said I was a Fishmon-
ger: he is farre gone, farre gone : and truly in my youth,
I suffred much extreamity for loue : very neere this. I
speake to him againe. What do you read my Lord?
   Ham. Words, words, words.
   Pol. What is the matter, my Lord ?
   Ham. Betweene who ?

   Pol. I meane the matter you meane, my Lord.
   Ham. Slanders Sir : for the Satyricall slaue saies here,
that old men haue gray Beards; that their faces are wrinkled ; their eyes purging thicke Amber, or Plum-Tree
Gumme : and that they haue a plentifull locke of Wit,
together with weake Hammes. All which Sir, though I
most powerfully, and potently beleeue ; yet I holde it
not Honestie to haue it thus set downe : For you your
selfe Sir, should be old as I am, if like a Crab you could
go backward.
   Pol, Though this be madnesse,
Yet there is Method in't : will you walke
Out of the ayre my Lord?
   Ham. Into my Graue?
   Pol. Indeed that is out o'th'Ayre :
How pregnant (sometimes) his Replies are?
A happinesse,
That often Madnesse hits on,
Which Reason and Sanitie could not
So prosperously be deliuer'd of.
I will leaue him,
And sodainely contriue the meanes of meeting
Betweene him, and my daughter.
My Honourable Lord, I will most humbly
Take my leaue of you.
   Ham. You cannot Sir take from me any thing, that I
will more willingly part withall, except my life, my
life.
   Polon. Fare you well my Lord.
   Ham. These tedious old fooles.
   Polon. You goe to seeke my Lord *Hamlet* ; there
hee is.

WORKING WITH THE SELECTIONS

1. Northern English preserved an Old English sound that you may approximate
by trying to say *k̠-k̠-h-w;* or if you know German, use the pronunciation of
ch known as the hackle. Do you find any apparent attempts to represent this
sound? The Old English feminine pronoun was often spelled *heo,* but this
h-spelling often represented the hackle. This sound proved to be very unstable, and thus our word *she* takes many forms dialectally; in the poem by
Henryson it is spelled *scho,* perhaps pronounced like something between our
word *show* and the first syllable of *Schofield.* Northern scribes often used an
extra *i* to indicate that a preceding vowel was long; thus our words *dear* and
cheer were *deir* and *cheir,* pronounced something like *dare* and *chair,* but
with trilled *r*'s. *Drunkin* is a past participle, preserving the Old English form
of /n/, preceded by a vowel. The past participle in the Old English versions
of the Lord's Prayer, however, is *gehalgod* or *gehalgud,* but that was a new
verb, made up from *halig* 'holy'—perhaps the old Germanic warriors were
not much interested in making things holy. At any rate, all verbs from Indo-
European had a vowel plus /n/ for the past participle; all verbs made up in
English—what are sometimes called weak verbs—had past tenses and past

participles with /d/ or /t/. The /d/ and /t/ past participles and past tenses began to increase during the late sixteenth century, and as English kept developing more verbs, these newer forms became so numerous, that even the old verbs took on the new endings. A good example is *crept*, which appears in Henryson's poem as *crap*. *Crap* preserves the Old English *crep* or *creap* with slight change in the vowel.

2. You have examples of various contemporary dialects in the selections by Harman, Awdeley, Henryson, Camden, and Shakespeare. Notice the verbs. Observe, for example, the speech by Bottom beginning, "Not a whit." He says, "I have a device to make all well." The words *have* and *to make* are surely verbal, but they are combined in a rigid sequence with other words that apparently are not verbs. *Device* and *all well* seem to be two parts of a complex complement; Bottom could not have said, *I* (as subject) *have to make* (as verb) *device all well* (as complement). We have something similar in "let the prologue seem to say," with the complex verb *let . . . seeme to say,* and in "this will put them out of fear," in which *out of fear* can be thought of as an adverbial modifier, or one can think of *will put . . . out of* as the verb and of *them* and *fear* as a sort of complex dispersed complement. These constructions, however one analyzes them, are common in Modern English but almost nonexistent in Old English. What can you say about the spread of such constructions in the samples you have in this book?

3. We have seen that Old English had a third-person verb ending -*aþ*, which was represented in Middle English by something like -*eth*. Modern English uses /s/ or /z/, *wraps* not *wrappith, forgives* not *forgiveth*. This is believed to be a Northern dialectal form that developed, perhaps with influence from Old Norse. On the basis of the passages you have examined, what can you say about the replacement of Old English forms by the forms that eventually triumphed in /s/ and /z/?

4. Notice the spelling and punctuation in the selections from Shakespeare's plays. We should remind ourselves that these passages are from what is called the First Folio, a very carefully printed book. Accordingly, these selections represent the best usage of the day. Was the spelling consistent? The ending -*e* was very common in Middle English because there had been *e*-endings in Old English, and endings like -*en* and -*um* as they became weaker were written with an *e*, however they were pronounced. Presumably Shakespeare did not pronounce these final *e*'s. Perhaps, if you know something about the requirements of printing, you can account for them. Today *ea* is likely to carry the same sound as *ee*, but in Shakespeare's time these combinations apparently represented separate sounds; *ea* was pronounced rather like the vowel in modern *hat* or *mat*, though somewhat higher. From what you can tell by looking at the facsimiles, was the printer consistent in his use of *ee* and *ea*?

With the development of printing, punctuation became much more consistent. The punctuation in the First Folio is not, however, just like modern punctuation. Can you work out the theory of punctuation in the First Folio? What are capital letters used for? Italics?

5. Do you notice any rather obvious ways in which Shakespeare is suggesting that the "rude mechanicals" speak a dialect? What dialect might Shakespeare

have had in mind if he was thinking of tradesmen he might have known in London?

6. Roberts surveys changes in sound. You will probably have difficulty applying his principles to the samples you have of Old, Middle, and Early Modern English, but you should be able to notice whether vowels or consonants have changed more. Why?

7. Drawing evidence from the selections in Old and Middle English and in Early Modern English, write a paper on some aspect of the history of English spelling—or punctuation or other mechanical devices.

6

Early Dictionaries: The Growth of Language and Language Concepts

Dictionaries are relatively modern inventions. Earlier scholars would sometimes gloss strange words; they might write into a manuscript a synonym for a word in another language or add an explanation of a strange term. Some of these glosses were brought together into collections, but nothing we would call a dictionary appeared until the sixteenth century. The first in English was presumably Robert Cawdrey's A Table Alphabetical *(1604), which lists "hard words" and "difficult terms," but it is so inadequate that it is worth mentioning only as the earliest exemplar of what was to become one of the most important sorts of books. The following selections are taken from five dictionaries published in the late seventeenth and eighteenth centuries. The excerpts include parts of Martin's and Sheridan's Introductions to their dictionaries and all the entries Coles, Bailey, Martin, and Sheridan give under* horse. *The selection from the dictionary edited by Samuel Johnson (1709–84) is a partial listing of the entries he provides that involve the word* horse. *These passages can be studied for both the history of English and the growth of our understanding of how to study language.*

An English Dictionary
Explaining Difficult Terms

Elisha Coles

London, 1685 (1st ed., 1676)

Horse, a rope fasten'd to the fore-mast shrouds, to keep the sprit-sail sheats clear of the anchor-flooks.
Horse-habet, a horse-danse.
Horsham, a town in *Sussex.*
Horse-heal, Elicampane.
Horse-tail, an herb good for inward wounds or ulcers.

An Universal Etymological
Dictionary

Nathaniel Bailey

London, 4th ed., 1728 (1st ed., 1721)

HOR'SA, a famous Saxon Commander, brother to *Hengist,* so called from the Figure of an Horse, which he and his Brother had upon their Coats of Arms.
HORSE [Horsa, *Sax.*] a Beast well known, the generical Name of it's kind, taking in both Male and Female. [The abbreviation *Sax.* stands for Saxon, that is, Old English.—*Eds.*]
HORSE [in a *Ship*] is a Rope made fast to one of the Fore-mast Shrouds, having a dead Man's Eye at it's End, through which the Pendant of the Sprit-sail Sheet is reeved.

> *It is a good horse that never stumbles.*

This Proverb intimates to us, that there is no Creature that ever went upon four *Legs,* but has made some false Step or other; and that every Mother's Son of us, who goes upon two, hath his *Slips,* and his *Imperfections;* that there is no Person in the World without his *weak Side;* and therefore pleads a Pardon for Mistakes, either in *Conversation,* or *Action,* and puts a Check upon intemperate *Mockery,* or uncharitable *Censure.* And so the *French* say,

Il n'y a bon cheval, qui ne bronche; and *Quandoque bonus dormitat Homerus,* says *Horace.* [The French is the equivalent of the English; the Latin means 'Even Homer may sleep,' that is, fail to be sufficiently alert.— *Eds.*]

HORS'HAM [*q.d.* Horsa and Ham, or *Horsa's* Town] in *Sussex,* so called from *Horsa,* a famous *Saxon* General, Brother of *Hengist.* [The abbreviation *q.d.* stands for *quasi dicat,* which means roughly 'that is.'—*Eds.*]

HORSE-*Knobs,* Heads of Knapweed.

HORSE-*Leechery,* the Art of curing Horses of Diseases.

HORSEMANSHIP, the Art of riding or managing Horses.

HORSE-*Measure,* a Measuring Rod, divided into Hands and Inches, for measuring the Height of Horses.

HORSE-*Shoe* [in *Fortification*] is a Work either of a round or oval Figure, raised in the Ditch or a marshy Place, and bordered with a Parapet, either to secure a Gate, or to lodge Soldiers in, to Prevent a Surprize.

HORSE-*Twitchers,* a Tool used by Farriers to hold unruly Horses by the nostrils.

HORSTED [of Horsa Steð, *Sax. q.d. Horsa's* Place; so called from being the Place where *Horsa's* Corpse was buried] a Village in *Kent.*

Lingua Brittanica Reformata
[The British Language Reformed]

London, 1765

Orthoepy teaches the true Method of spelling and pronouncing Words; and is therefore a principal Requisite in a Dictionary. And since Speech is much more common and public, than our Writing, it greatly behoves us to be as just and correct as possible, in that Particular. For what can reflect more on a Man's Reputation for Learning, than to find him unable to pronounce or spell many Words in common Use? Yet how often do we hear the grating Sounds of *A'n-ti-podes,* for *An-ti''po-des; Ho''-ri-zon,* for *Ho-ri'-zon; Cy-cloi'd,* for *Cy'-clo-id; Di'-a-stole,* for *Di-a''-sto-le;* and many others in like Manner. But whom shall we blame for such false Pronunciation? Not those, surely, who make the Mistake, but more justly those who occasion them; that is, those who, as Dictionary Writers, are no others than blind Leaders of the Blind. For by what Dictionary extant can a Man regulate his Pronunciation, or correct his Errors in this Respect? Certainly, by no one at all. No Man that has not the Happiness of a learned Education or Conversation, can possibly guard against this Imperfection of Speech. To remedy which, I have been more than ordinarily anxious, and hope I have in a great measure succeeded by the following Expedient. For, (I.) where I have observed the Number of Syllables in a Word to be any ways doubtful or uncertain to the Unlearned, I have shewn the Number by a Figure at the End of the Word. Thus in the Word *Antipodes*[4], the Figure (4) shews there are *four* Syllables; in the Word *Cycloid*[3], the Figure (3) shews there are *three* Syllables; and so in others throughout the Book. Again, (2dly,) In order that no Mistake, or even Doubt, about the true Emphasis may arise, I have taken Care to set that Affair right by single and double Accents placed over the proper Syllables in every Word, where they could be supposed in the least necessary; some very few Words excepted, in which I could arrive at no Certainty myself. The single Accent shews the Syllable on which the Emphasis or Stress of the Voice lies, and the double one shews the same Thing if alone. But the Use of the double Accent is everywhere to denote that the Letter which begins the Syllable to which it is prefix'd has a double Sound, one of which belongs to the preceding Syllable. Thus the Word *A``nimal* is sounded with a double *n, as An-nimal.* So *Mi``croscope* is sounded *Mic-croscope;* *Centri``fugal* is sounded *Centrif-fugal;* and the like of others. I imagine this Matter is hereby rendered so very easy, that if a Person gives but the least Attention to it, it must be rarely possible for him to be at any Loss about an accurate Pronunciation.

HORSE, 1 a beast well known. 2 horsemen, or cavalry. 3 a stand to put barrels of beer or wine upon. 4 an utensil used by women to air linen on. 5 a place for school-boys to be whipped upon. 6 an instrument used by labourers to saw wood upon.

HORSE-*leech,* 1 a sort of insect that lives in the water, which, if it sticks to the flesh, will not let go till he is full of blood. 2 a farrier, or horse-doctor.

HORSE-*shoe* (in Fortification) is a work of a round, and sometimes oval figure, raised in the ditch of a marshy place, or in low ground, and bordered with a parapet. It is made to secure a gate, or to serve as a lodgment for soldiers to prevent surprizes, or to relieve over-tedious defence.

HO'RSEMANSHIP, 1 the art of breaking, disciplining, and managing horses. 2 the art of riding, or of directing a horse to advantage.

Dictionary of the English Language

Samuel Johnson

London, 3rd ed., 1765 (1st ed., 1755)

HORSE. *n. s.* [hors, Saxon.]
1. A neighing quadruped, used in war, and draught and carriage.

Duncan's *horses,* the minions of the race,
Turn'd wild in nature, broke their stalls.   *Shakespeare.*

A *horse!* a *horse!* my kingdom for a *horse!*   *Shakespeare.*

I would sell my *horse,* and buy ten more
Better than he.   *Shakespeare.*

Thy face, bright centaur, Autumn's heats retain,
The softer season suiting to the man;
Whilst Winter's shivering goat afflicts the *horse*
With frost, and makes him an uneasy course.   *Creech.*

We call a little horse such a one as comes not up to the size of that idea
which we have in our minds to belong ordinarily to *horses.   Locke.*

I took *horse* to the lake of Constance, which is formed by the entry of
the Rhine.   *Addison.*

2. It is used in the plural sense, but with a singular termination, for horses,
   horsemen, or cavalry.

> I did hear
> The galloping of *horse:* who was't came by?   *Shakespeare.*

> The armies were appointed, consisting of twenty-five thousand *horse*
> and foot, for the repulsing of the enemy at their landing.   *Bacon.*

> If they had known that all the king's *horse* were quartered behind them,
> their foot might very well have marched away with their *horse.   Claren-*
> *don.*

> Th' Arcadian *horse*
> With ill success engage the Latin force.   *Dryden.*

3. Something on which any thing is supported: as, a *horse* to dry linen on.
4. A wooden machine which soldiers ride by way of punishment. It is sometimes called a timber-mare.
5. Joined to another substantive, it signifies something large or coarse; as, a
   horseface, a face of which the features are large and indelicate.

To HORSE. *v. a.* [from the noun.]
1. To mount upon a horse.

> He came out with all his clowns, *horsed* upon such cartjades, and so
> furnished, as in good faith I thought with myself, if that were thrift, I
> wisht none of my friends or subjects ever to thrive.   *Sidney.*

After a great fight there came to the camp of Gonsalvo, the great captain, a gentleman proudly *horsed* and armed: Diego de Mendoza asked the great captain, Who's this? Who answered, It is St. Ermin, who never appears but after the storm. *Bacon.*

2. To carry one on the back.
3. To ride any thing.

> Stalls, bulks, windows
> Are smother'd, leads fill'd, and ridges *hors'd*
> With variable complexions; all agreeing
> In earnestness to see him. *Shakespeare.*

4. To cover a mare.

> If you let him out to *horse* more mares than your own, you must feed him well. *Mortimer.*

HO'RSEBACK. *n. s.* [*horse* and *back.*] The feat of the rider; the state of being on a horse.

> I've seen the French,
> And they can well on *horseback.* *Shakespeare.*

> I saw them salute on *horseback,*
> Beheld them when they lighted. *Shakespeare.*

> He fought but one remarkable battle wherein there were any elephants, and that was with Porus, king of India; in which notwithstanding he was on *horseback.* *Brown's Vulg. Err.*

> When mannish Mevia, that two-handed whore,
> Astride on *horseback* hunts the Tuscan boar. *Dryden.*

> If your ramble was on *horseback,* I am glad of it, on account of your health.

HORSEBEA'N. *n. s.* [*horse* and *bean.*] A small bean usually given to horses.

> Only the small *horsebean* is propagated by the plough. *Mort.*

HO'RSEBLOCK. *n. s.* [*horse* and *block.*] A block on which they climb to a horse.
HORSEBOA'T. *n. s.* [*horse* and *boat.*] A boat used in ferrying horses.
HORSEBO'Y. *n. s.* [*horse* and *boy.*] A boy employed in dressing horses; a stable-boy.

> Some *horseboys,* being awake, discovered them by the fire in their matches. *Knolles.*

HO′RSEBREAKER. *n. s.* [*horse* and *break*.] One whose employment it is to tame horses to the saddle.

> Under Sagittarius are born chariot-racers, *horsebreakers,* and tamers of wild beasts. *Creech.*

HORSECHE′SNUT. *n. s.* [*horse* and *chesnut.*] A plant.

> It hath digitated or fingered leaves: the flowers, which consist of five leaves, are of an anomalous figure, opening with two lips; there are male and female upon the same spike: the female flowers are succeeded by nuts, which grow in green prickly husks. Their whole year's shoot is commonly performed in three weeks time, after which it does no more than increase in bulk, and become more firm; and all the latter part of the Summer is occupied in forming and strengthening the buds for the next year's shoots. *Miller.*

> I may bring in the *horsechesnut,* which grows into a goodly standard. *Mortimer.*

HO′RSECOURSER. *n. s.* [*horse* and *courser. Junius* derives it from *horse* and *cose,* an old Scotch word, which signifies to change; and it should therefore, he thinks, be writ *horsecoser.* The word now used in Scotland is *horsecouper,* to denote a jockey, seller, or rather changer of horses. It may well be derived from *course,* as he that sells horses may be supposed to *course* or exercise them.]
1. One that runs horses, or keeps horses for the race.
2. A dealer in horses.

> A servant to a *horsecourser* was thrown off his horse. *Wiseman.*

> A Florentine bought a horse for so many crowns, upon condition to pay half down: the *horsecourser* comes to him next morning for the remainder. *L'Estrange.*

HO′RSECRAB. *n. s.*

> A kind of fish. *Ainsworth.*

HORSECU′CUMBER. *n. s.* [*horse* and *cucumber.*] A plant.

> The *horsecucumber* is the large green cucumber, and the best for the table, green out of the garden. *Mortimer.*

HO′RSEDUNG. *n. s.* [*horse* and *dung.*] The excrements of horses.

> Put it into an ox's horn, and covered close, let it rot in hot *horsedung. Peachum.*

HORSEE'MMET. *n. s.* [*horse* and *emmet.*] Ant of a a large kind.

HO'RSEFLESH. *n. s.* [*horse* and *flesh.*] The flesh of horses.

> The Chinese eat *horseflesh* at this day, and some gluttons have colts-flesh baked. *Bacon.*

> An old hungry lion would fain have been dealing with a good piece of *horseflesh* that he had in his eye; but the nag he thought would be too fleet for him. *L'Estrange.*

HO'RSEFLY. *n. s.* [*horse* and *fly.*] A fly that stings horses, and sucks their blood.

HO'RSEFOOT. *n. s.*

> An herb. The same with coltsfoot. *Ains.*

HO'RSEHAIR. *n. s.* [*horse* and *hair.*] The hair of horses.

> His glitt'ring helm, which terribly was grac'd
> With waving *horsehair*. *Dryden.*

HO'RSEHEEL. *n. s.*

> An herb. *Ainsworth.*

HO'RSELAUGH. *n. s.* [*horse* and *laugh.*] A loud violent rude laugh.

> A *horselaugh*, if you please, at honesty;
> A joke on Jekyl. *Pope.*

[For brevity fourteen entries for compounds are omitted.]

HORSESTEA'LER. *n. s.* [*horse* and *steal.*] A thief who takes away horses.

> He is not a pickpurse, nor a *horsestealer;* but for his verity in love, I do think him as concave as a covered goblet, or a worm-eaten nut. *Shakespeare.*

HO'RSETAIL. *n. s.* A plant.

HO'RSETONGUE. *n. s.*

> An herb. *Ainsworth.*

HO'RSEWAY. *n. s.* [*horse* and *way.*] A broad way by which horses may travel.

> Know'st thou the way to Dover?
> —Both stile and gate, *horseway* and footpath. *Shakespeare.*

A General Dictionary
of the English Language

Thomas Sheridan

Dublin, 1784 (1st ed., 1780)

It must be obvious, that in order to spread abroad the English language as a living tongue, and to facilitate the attainment of its speech, it is necessary in the first place that a standard of pronunciation should be established, and a method of acquiring a just one should be laid open. That the present state of the written language is not at all calculated to answer that end, is evident from this; that not only the natives of Ireland, Scotland, and Wales, who speak English, and are taught to read it, pronounce it differently, but each county in England has its peculiar dialect, which infects not only their speech, but their reading also. All attempts to reform this by any alteration in our written language would be utterly impracticable: And the only plan which could possibly be followed with any prospect of success, is what the Author has pursued in his Rhetorical Grammar and Dictionary. . . .

In his Dictionary he has reduced the pronunciation of each word to a certainty by fixed and visible marks; the only way by which uniformity of sound could be propagated to any distance. This we find effectually done in the art of music by notes; for in whatever part of the globe music is so taught, the adepts in it read it exactly the same way. A similar uniformity of pronunciation, by means of this Grammar and Dictionary, may be spread through all parts of the globe, wherever English shall be taught by their aid. . . .

There was a time, and that at no very distant period, which may be called the Augustan age of England, I mean during the reign of Queen Anne, when English was the language spoken at court; and when the same attention was paid to propriety of pronunciation, as that of French at the Court of Versailles. This produced a uniformity in that article in all the polite circles; and a gentleman or lady would have been as much ashamed of a wrong pronunciation then, as persons of a liberal education would now be of misspelling words. But on the accession of a foreign family to the throne amid the many blessings conferred by that happy event, the English language suffered much by being banished the court, to make room for the French. From that time the regard formerly paid to pronunciation has been gradually declining; so that now the greatest improprieties in that point are to be found among people of fashion; many pronunciations, which thirty or forty years ago were confined to the vulgar, are gradually gaining ground; and if something be not done to stop this growing evil, and fix a general standard at present, the English is likely to become a mere jargon, which every one may pronounce as he pleases.

HORSE, hor′se. s. A neighing quadruped, used in war, and draught and carriage; it is used in the plural sense, but with a singular termination, for horses, horsemen, or cavalry; something on which any thing is supported; a wooden machine which soldiers ride by way of punishment; joined to another substantive, it signifies something large or coarse, as a horse-face, a face of which the features are large and indelicate. . . .

HORSEMATCH, hor′s-matsh. s. A bird.

HORSEMEAT, hor′s-met. s. Provender.

HORSEMINT, hor′s-mint. s. A large coarse mint.

HORSEMUSCLE, hor′s-musl. s. A large muscle.

HORSEPLAY, hor′s-pla. s. Coarse, rough, rugged play.

HORSEPOND, hor′s-pond. s. A pond for horses.

HORSERACE, hor′s-ras. s. A match of horses in running.

HORSERADISH, hor′s-rad′-ish. s. A root acrid and biting, a species of scurvy-grass.

HORSESHOE, hor′s-sho. s. A plate of iron nailed to the feet of horses; an herb.

HORSESTEALER, hor′r-stel-ur. s. A thief who takes away horses.

HORSETAIL, hor′s-tal. s. A plant.

HORSETONGUE, hor′s-tung. s. An herb.

HORSEWAY, hor′s-wa. s. A broad way by which horses may travel.

WORKING WITH THE SELECTIONS

1. Do you find any evidence that Coles did, indeed, restrict his book to "difficult terms"?

2. Martin was much concerned with reform, particularly with reforming pronunciation. Can you, on the basis of his system, be sure how a word is pronounced? What does he need to add to his system?

3. When Johnson started his dictionary, Bailey's was the best available. Johnson had a copy of Bailey's dictionary cut up and interleaved to use as the basis of his first edition. Obviously, Johnson produced a much better book. What did Johnson seem to know that Bailey did not know? Johnson's dictionary earned him the title "the father of English lexicography." Can you discover any reasons why the title might better apply to Bailey?

4. Both Bailey and Johnson rely on citations; can you see any difference in the way they use them?

5. When the first edition of Johnson's dictionary came out in 1755, it was universally recognized as being superior to all previous dictionaries in English; some Englishmen even said it was better than the great Italian and French dictionaries, which were considerably larger. Johnson's friend, the actor David Garrick, quipped that Johnson "beat sixty Frenchmen and could beat sixty more," referring to the fact that sixty scholars had contributed to the volumes edited by the French Academy. What specific evidence can you adduce that Johnson did, indeed, produce a better book than did his English competitors?

6. From what you know of language, would you be inclined to accept Sheridan's explanation of what he believed to be the corruption of pronunciation? Is it likely that he did succeed in reforming pronunciation? How adequate is his system for indicating sound?

7

The Modern Dictionary:
A Reflector of Language

The broad lines of lexicography were well worked out for English during the eighteenth century, but neither Johnson's great work nor Noah Webster's An American Dictionary of the English Language (2 vols., 1828), *in some ways a great improvement over Johnson, adequately exemplifies dictionary-making as we know it today. Some of what lexicographers have subsequently learned appears in the following selections from four dictionaries. The first is from a multivolume work published between 1888 and 1928. Variously bound, often in ten volumes, it is called both* The Oxford English Dictionary *and* A New English Dictionary on Historical Principles *and is frequently referred to as either the* OED *or the* NED. *No comparable dictionary exists for any other language; it was started soon after 1850, and eighty years later C. T. Onions was preparing a supplement. Hundreds of scholars throughout the English-speaking world contributed to it, amassing more than six million citations, which were edited into 15,487 double-column pages. The second selection is from* The Century Dictionary and Cyclopedia (1889–97), *edited under the direction of William Dwight Whitney. The* Century, *variously bound in ten to fourteen volumes, is the result of what was probably the greatest single lexicographical effort in this country.*

The Oxford English Dictionary

Oxford, 1888–1928

Horse (hǭ.ɹs), *sb.* Forms: *sing.* 1–6 hors, (3 *Orm.* horrs, 4 horce, ors, 5 orse, 6 horsse), 4- horse; *pl.* 1–6 hors, 4- horse, 3- horses. [Com. Teut.: OE *hors* = OFris. *hors, hars, hers* (Fris. *hoars*), OS. *hros* (MLG. *ros, ors*, MDu. *ors*, LG. and Du. *ros*), OHG. *hros, ros*, MHG. *ros, ors*, G. *rosz*, all neuter, ON. *hross* masc.; not recorded in Goth. The affinities of the word outside Teutonic are uncertain: the conjecture that OTeut. **horso-*, pre-Teut. **ḳurso-* was from the root **ḳurs-* of *L. currere* 'to run' is favoured by many; but other derivations have also been suggested. Like several other names of animals (*sheep, swine, neat, deer*), this was originally neuter, applicable to the male and female alike; and like these words and other neuters in a long syllable, the nom. plural was the same as the singular. The plural *horses,* and the tendency to restrict the name to the male came in later: see 1 b, c.]

I. The animal, and senses immediately related.

   1. A solid-hoofed perissodactyl quadruped (*Equus caballus*), having a flowing mane and tail, whose voice is a neigh. It is well known in the domestic state as a beast of burden and draught, and esp. as used for riding upon.

     c 825 *Vesp. Psalter* xxi[i]. 9 Nyllað bion swe swe hors & mul in ðaem nis ondȝet. *c* 1205 LAY. 21354 þe king . . his hors he gon spurie. *c* 1290 Beḳet 1151 in *S. Eng. Leg.* I. 139 Hors ne hadde he non. *c* 1300 *Haveloḳ* 126 Mi douhter . . Yif scho couþe on horse ride. *c* 1380 WYCLIF *Sel. Wḳs.* III. 231 A horce . . þat haves a sore back, wynses when he is oght touched. *c* 1400 MAUNDEV. (1839) xxii. 237 [Thei] presenten the white Hors to the Emperour. 1567 *Gude & Godlie B.* (S. T. S.) 9 Nor wis His hors, his oxe, his maide nor page. 1584 POWEL *Lloyd's Cambria* 288 Falling off his horsse. 1594 SHAKS. *Rich. III,* v. iv. 7 A Horse, a Horse, my Kingdome for a Horse! 1654 WHITLOCK *Zootomia* 143, I believe Banks his Horse was taught in better language, then some would have Christians taught. 1782 COWPER *Gilpin* 45 John Gilpin at his horse's side Seized fast the flowing mane. 1848 W. H. BARTLETT *Egypt to Pal.* v. (1879) 116 Not a horse appears on the monuments prior to Thothmes III, who clearly in his conquests brought them from Asia.

   b. *Plural.*

   The plural was in OE. the same as the sing.; *horse* plural was in general use down to 17th c., and is still frequent dialectally; but *horses* appears as early as Layamon (*c* 1205), and its use increased till in 17th c. it became the usual plural in the literary language; sometimes *horse* appears as the collective and *horses* as the individual plural, which explains the retention of *horse* in military language as in 'a troop of horse.' The OE. dat. pl. *horsum* appears in early ME. as *horsen, horse.*

   a. a 900 in *O. E. Texts* 177 Fiow(er) wildo hors. *Ibid.* 178 Ða cwom Godes engel . . and ȝestillde ðaem horssum. *c* 1200 *Trin. Coll. Hom.* 179 Hundes and hauekes, and hors and wepnes. *c* 1205 Lay. 1025 He sculde beon . . mid horsen [*c* 1275 horse] to-drawen. 1375 Barbour *Bruce* viii. 446 Syne thame lay Apon their horss. 1387 Trevisa *Higden* (Rolls) VII. 121 Two gentil hors. 1422 tr. *Secreta Secret., Priv. Priv.* (E. E. T. S.) 219 We seen that knyghtis knowyth the goodnys of horsyn. 1480 Caxton *Chron. Eng.* clxxxix. 167 Oftymes the poure peple . . ete also the houndes . . and eke hors and cattes. *a* 1533 Ld. Berners *Huon* lxii. 215 Gerames . . bought horse and mules to ryde on. 1588 Shaks. *Tit. A.* ii. ii. 18 Come on then, horse and Chariots let vs haue. 1702 *Lond. Gaz.* No. 3783/3 We brought away . . above 500 Horse belonging to their Cavalry and Artillery. 1818 Byron *Mazeppa* xvii, A thousand horse—and none to ride! 1832 Lander *Adv. Niger* I. iv. 177 A few rough, ragged-looking ponies are the only 'horse' of which he has the superintendence.

β. *c* 1205 Lay. 3561 Hundes & hauekes & durewurðe horses [*c* 1275 hors]. 1297 R. Glouc. (1724) 50 Here folc heo loren . . & heore horses [*MS. A* hors] ney echon. 1382 Wyclif *Rev.* xix. 14 The hoostes . . sueden him in whijte horsis [*v.r.* hors]. 1434 *Priv. Purse Exp. Eliz. of York* (1830) 262/2 Three of her best horses. *c.* 1511 *1st Eng. Bk. Amer.* (Arb.) Introd. 33/2 They haue horseys as great as a great dogge. 1584 Powel *Lloyd's Cambria* 41 They were driuen to eat their own horsses. 1697 Dryden *Virg. Georg.* iii. 178 Bold Ericthonius was the first, who join'd Four Horses for the rapid Race design'd. 1735 Somerville *Chase* iii. 322 Intrepid Bands, Safe in their Horses Speed. 1859 F. A. Griffiths *Artil. Man.* (1862) 156 The ride and spare horses will be on the left when picketed, the gun horses on the right.

c. *spec.* The adult male of the horse kind, as distinguished from a mare or colt: a stallion or gelding. *To take the horse:* (of the mare) to conceive.

c 1485 *Digby Myst.* (1882) ii. 119. He was nother horse ne mare, nor yet yokyd sow. 1549 *Compl. Scot.* vi. 39 Baytht horse & meyris did fast nee, & the folis nechyr. 1577 B. Googe *Heresbach's Husb.* iii. (1586) 117 What age doe you thinke best for the Mare to go to the horse? *Ibid.* 117 b, To put the Mare to the Horse. 1606 Shaks. *Ant. & Cl.* iii. vii. 7. 1617 Moryson *Itin.* iii. 56 They have goodly Mares to draw these Waggons, using Horses for the troops in their Army. 1697 Dryden *Virg. Georg.* iii. 223. 1854 Owen *Skel. & Teeth* in *Circ. Sc., Organ. Nat.* I. 285 Upon the rising of the third permanent incisor, or 'corner nipper' . . the 'colt' becomes a 'horse', and the 'filly', a 'mare'. 1870 Blaine *Encycl. Rur. Sports* § 1013 Having taken the horse, i.e. being fecundated, is therefore a matter of uncertainty usually for three or four months, particularly in pastured mares.

d. In *Zool.* sometimes extended to all species of the genus *Equus,* or even of the family *Equidae,*

e. With qualifications denoting origin, variety, or use, as *Arabian, Barbary, Flemish, wild horse.* Cf. also Cart-, Dray-, Saddle-, War-horse, etc.

c 1000 Ælfric *Gloss.* in Wr.-Wülcker 119/33 Equifer, wilde cynnes hors. *a* 1400–50 *Alexander* 1250 þe multitude was sa mekill . . Of wees & of wild horsis [*v.r.* horse]. 1577 B. Googe *Heresbach's Husb.* i. (1586) 13, I have another stable . . for my Horses of service and Hackneyes. 1607 Top-sell

Fouf-f. Beasts (1658) 252 Single horses, which therefore they called Coursers, and now a days a Horse for Saddle. 1889 *Spectator* 21 Sept., As good, if not better, than the shire or cart-horse. 1890 BESANT *Demoniac* xv. 179 To have his flesh wrenched off with red-hot pincers and to be torn to pieces by wild horses.

[Uses of *horse* and entries for related words continue for some thirty columns more; that is, the passage quoted here constitutes less than five percent of the space given to this word and to compounds and phrases involving it.]

The Century Dictionary and Cyclopedia

New York, 1889–97

horse[1] (hors), *n.* [< ME. *hors* (pl. *hors* and *horses*), < AS. *hors* (pl. *hors*) = OS. *hors, hros* (*hross-*) = OFries. *hors, hars* = D. *ros* = OHG. *hros, ros,* MHG. *ros* (*ross-*), G. *ross* (> It. *rozza* = Pr *rossa* = F. *rosse,* a jade) = Icel. *hross, hors* = Sw. Dan. dial. *hors,* a horse. Root uncertain; some connect the word with AS. *horsc* = MHG. *rosch,* swift, referring both to a root shown in L. *currere* (for **cursere?*), run: see *current*[1]. The Indo-Eur. word for 'horse' is that represented by Skt. *açva* = Gr. ἵπποζ = L. *equus* = AS. *eoh,* etc.: see *Equus.* The ordinary Teut. terms outside of E. are D. *paard,* G. *pferd* (see *palfrey*); Sw. *häst,* Dan. *hest* (see *henchman*); the Rom. words are F. *cheval,* Sp. *caballo,* etc. (see *cheval, caple*[1], *cavalry,* etc.).] 1. A solidungulate perissodactyl mammal of the family *Equidae* and genus *Equus; E. caballus.* It has a flowing mane and tail, comparatively small erect ears, comparatively large rounded hoofs, shapely head, arched neck, a callosity on the inner side of the hind leg below the hock, in addition to one on the fore leg above the so-called "knee," and a peculiar voice called a "neigh." These are the principal distinctive characters of the existing horses, of whatever variety, in comparison with the asses and zebras, which are commonly placed in the same genus (*Equus*). The horse has no distinctive coloration, but is never conspicuously striped in any regular pattern, and seldom shows even the dorsal and shoulder stripe characteristic of the ass, though there is often an indication of this marking in horses which have reverted to a feral state and tend to assume a dun color. The horse is now known only as a domesticated and artificially bred animal, though in both North and South America, in Australia, and in some parts of Asia the descendants of domesticated ancestors run wild in troops. The native country of the horse and the period of its subjection to man are unknown. Animals congeneric with the present horse, if not conspecific, have left their remains with those of the mammoth and other extinct animals in the bonecaves of both the old and new worlds, but the genus *Equus* appears not to have been fully established before the close of the Pliocene. The evolution of the modern forms has been traced back through the whole Tertiary period, by the discovery of such genera as *Hipparion* and *Pliohippus* of the Pliocene, *Anchitherium, Miohippus,* and *Mesohippus* of the Miocene, and *Orohippus* and *Eohippus* of the Eocene. In the course of this evolutionary series is observed a very gradual and un-broken geologic pedigree, going back to a small animal, not larger than a fox, with several separate toes on each foot. The size has steadily increased, and other progressive modifications, especially of the limbs, have resulted in the existing horse in all its numberless artificial breeds, races, and strains, combining in various degrees the qualities of size, strength, speed, and bottom. Two breeds—namely, the large, powerful, black breed of Flanders, and the Arabian—have contributed more than all others to develop the present varieties. The former laid the foundation of size, strength, and vigor for draft-horses and for those formerly used in war; while, when mailed armor was laid aside, and the horse began to be used for the chase, the latter conferred the speed and endurance which distinguish the hunter. The ladies' palfrey is largely derived from the Spanish genet, a small, beautiful, fleet variety of the Moorish barb. The race-horse has less of Flemish and more of Arabian blood. Other leading varieties are the Suffolk Punch and Clydesdale, both chiefly of Flemish blood, and best for draft and agriculture; and several varieties of ponies, as Galloway, Shetland, etc. Carriage, riding, and other horses combine the above breeds in varying degrees, as speed, endurance, strength, or size, etc., may be required. Horses are said to have "blood" or "breeding" in proportion as they have a greater or less strain of Arab blood. The wild horse of Tatary is called a *tarpan,* that of northern Africa a *koomrah,* and that of America a *mustang,* the last being descended from imported Spanish parents. The male of the horse is a *stallion;* when gelded, a *gelding;* the female is a *mare;* the young, a *foal*—if a male, a *colt,* if a female, a *filly.* The colt and filly become "of age" when the "corner-nippers" (outer incisors) attain functional development. The age of the horse may be determined by the marks on the front teeth, which change with the wearing down of the crowns by use. When the mark disappears, as it generally does in the eighth or ninth year, the horse is "aged." The period of gestation is eleven months, and foals are generally dropped in the spring. Horses vary greatly in size, some standing more than twice as high as others. Very small horses are called *ponies,* as those bred in Shetland.

> A-noon he made tweyne of his sones for to make hem redy and sette hem on two swifte *horse.* *Merlin* (E. E. T. S.), iii. 525.

> Hast thou given the *horse* strength? hast thou clothed his neck with thunder? Job xxxix. 19.

> The *horse* that guide the golden eye of heaven,
> And blow the morning from their nostrils. *Marlowe.*

In the earliest period, the *Horse* seems to have been the favourite animal for sacrifice; there is no doubt that before the introduction of Christianity its flesh was universally eaten. *Grimm*, Teut. Mythol. (trans.), I. 47.

2. *pl.* In *zoöl.*, the horse family, or *Equidae;* the species of the genus *Equus* and related genera. These include all the existing asses of the restricted genus *Asinus,* and the quagga, dauw, and zebra, of the restricted genus *Hippotigris,* together with all the extinct forms of the Tertiary period which, however different from the modern horse, are connected closely by intermediate links. See *Equidae.*

3. The male of the horse kind, in distinction from the female or mare; a stallion or gelding.

> Lo, the unback'd breeder, full of fear,
> Jealous of catching, swiftly doth forsake him,
> With her the *horse,* and left Adonis there.
> > *Shak.,* Venus and Adonis, l. 322.

> No cow-boy ever rides anything but *horses,* because mares give great trouble where all the animals have to be herded together. *T. Roosevelt,* The Century, XXXV. 656.

4. A body of troops serving on horseback; cavalry; in this sense a collective noun, used also as a plural: as, a regiment of *horse.*

> Our nineteen legions thou shalt hold by land,
> And our twelve thousand *horse.*
> > *Shak.,* A. and C., iii. 7.

> The *horse* was the first that marched o'er,
> The foot soon followed a'ter.
> > *The Boyne Water* (Child's Ballads, VII. 254).

> Back fly the scenes, and enter foot and *horse;*
> Pageants on pageants in long order drawn.
> > *Pope,* Imit. of Horace, II. i. 315.

5. A frame, block, board, or the like, on which something is mounted or supported, or the use of which is in any way analogous to that of a horse. Compare etymology of *easel.*[1]

> A kind of *horse,* as it is called with you, with two poles like those of chairmen, was the vehicle; on which is secured a sort of elbow-chair in which the traveller sits. *Richardson,* Sir Charles Grandison, IV, 299.

Specifically—(*a*) A vaulting-block in a gymnasium. (*b*) A wooden frame on which soldiers are made to ride as a punishment: sometimes called a *timber mare.* (*c*) A saw-horse. (*d*) A clothes-horse. (*e*) A curriers' board, used in dressing hides. (*f*) In *printing,* a sloping board, with its support, placed on the bank close to the tympan of a hand-press, on which is laid the paper to be printed. (*g*) A support for the cables of a suspension-bridge. (*h*) A board on which the workman sits in grinding the bevels and edges of tools in their manufacture. Also *horsing.*

6. In *mining,* a mass of rock inclosed within a lode or vein, usually of the same material as the "country," or rock adjacent to the lode on each side.

> The miner takes his chance of luck. He is generally content if he manages to pay his way along while the ores are poor; to lay by a little for the day when a *horse* or cut makes its appearance in the vein, confident that sooner or later he may strike a rich stretch of ore.
> Quoted in *Mowry's* Arizona and Sonora, p. 128.

[The entry totals fifteen long columns; the following will suggest the variety of compounds and phrases.]

horse-godmother (hôrs'god"muᴛʜ-ėr), *n.* A large masculine woman, coarsely fat. [Prov. Eng.]

> In woman, angel sweetness let me see;
> No galloping *horse-godmothers* for me.
> > *Wolcot,* Peter Pindar's Ode upon Ode (In Continuation).

> How do, my dear? Come to see the old man, hay? 'Gad—you've a pretty face, too. You ain't like that old *horse-godmother,* your mother.
> *Thackeray,* Vanity Fair, xxxix.

horse-gogs (hôrs'gogz), *n.* A kind of wild plum, a variety of *Prunus domestica.*

horse-gowan (hôrs'gou"an), *n.* One of several plants, as *Chrysanthemum Leucanthemum, Matricaria Chamomilla,* and *Taraxacum officinalis.*

horse-gram (hôrs'gram), *n.* A leguminous plant, *Dolichos biflorus,* a native of tropical and subtropical Africa and Asia, extensively cultivated in southern India as a food-plant.

horse-guards (hôrs'gärdz), *n. pl.* 1. A body of cavalry for guards. See *guard.*—2. [*cap.*] The public office in Whitehall, London, appropriated to the departments under the commander-in-chief of the British army: so called from the two horsemen standing sentry at the gates.—3. [*cap.*] The military authorities in charge of the war department of Great Britain, in distinction from the civil chief, the Secretary for War.

A Dictionary of Americanisms
on Historical Principles

Mitford M. Mathews

Chicago, 2 vols., 1951

[The following entry is one use of *horse* taken from more than ten broad columns.]

3. b. In less frequent, often obs. or rare, combs.: (1) **horse ail,** some unidentifiable ailment or distemper of horses; (2) **bone limestone,** (see quot.); (3) **book,** a book of information about horses and their diseases; (4) **card,** a currycomb; (5) ***chestnut,** a color like that of a horse chestnut; (6) **dam,** (see quot.); (7) **dance,** an Indian dance in which, app., horses were imitated; (8) **duty,** ?signals or calls blown on a trumpet for a cavalry company; (9) **hunting,** (see quot.); (10) **jog,** designating something slow or old-fashioned; (11) **lawyer,** a lawyer without ability or standing; (12) **piano,** a calliope; (13) ***piece,** a horse drama; (14) **rail,** a horse rack; (15) **rattle,** prob. a bull-roarer; (16) **round-up,** *W.* the bringing together of horses on a ranch; (17) **shedder,** (see quot.), cf. 8. b. (2) below, and see **horse shedding** as a main entry; (18) **smoke,** (see quot.); (19) **trumpet,** ?a very large trumpet.

(1) 1872 HOLMES *poet* iii. 75 Something like horse-ail, very likely—horses get it, you know, when they are brought to city stables.—(2) 1870 *Rep. Comm. Agric.* 551. By leaching and concretion it sometimes forms a singularly irregular, perforated rock, known in Alabama as the 'bored,' and in Mississippi, where it also occurs, as the 'horse-bone,' limestone.—(3) 1643 *Essex Prob. Rec.* I. 30, I give to him my horse booke alsoe a pitchforke.—(4) 1832 *Louisville Pub. Advt.* 3 March, Whittemore's cotton and horse cards.

(5) 1897 MARK TWAIN *Following Equator* 622 (R.), There is every shade of complexion: ebony, old mahogany, horse-chestnut, sorrel.—(6) 1905 *Foresty Bureau Bul.* 61 B. Horse dam. A temporary dam made by placing large logs across a stream, in order to raise the water behind it, so as to float the rear. (N.F.)—(7) 1899 H. B. CUSHMAN Hist. Indians 499 Then followed the fun-making dances, such as chicken dance, horse dance.—(8) 1777 *N.J. Archives* 2 Ser. I. 327 A man well acquainted with blowing the trumpet, and capable of teaching the horse duty on that instrument.—(9) 1708 OLDMIXON *Brit. Empire in Amer.* I. (1708) 293 [The Virginians] also have other sorts of Hunting, as Vermine-hunting, and Horse-hunting; the latter is much delighted in by young People, who pursue wild Horses with Dogs, and sometimes without them.

(10) 1853 FOWLER *Home for All* 53, I leave you to either proceed in the

old horse-jog mode of building, or adopt this new railroad style.—(11) 1890 *Cong. Rec.* 1 July 6900/2 If you speak of John McSweeney as a horse lawyer, God knows what will become of Missouri.—(12) 1920 C. R. Cooper *Under Big Top* 202 The calliope player takes him along on parade and tells him the story of steam, to the accompaniment of the screaming notes of the howling, screeching 'horse piano.'—(13) 1856 *Chi. Democrat* 22 Oct., The stage is so constructed that it can be used to the best advantage for the exhibition of what are termed 'horse pieces.'—(14) 1861 Tallack *Friendly Sk.* 41 On arriving at the meeting-house, the horses are not usually taken out from their vehicles, but merely 'hitched up' to a tree, or 'horse-rail.'

(15) 1858 *Harper's Mag.* June 133/1 A 'horse-rattle' which he was whirling round and round to the disturbance of the town.—(16) 1927 Siringo *Riata & Spurs* 15, I had to attend the horse round-up . . . to brand up the W. G. B. colts.—(17) 1846 Cooper *Redskins* xiv, Your regular 'horse-shedder' is employed to frequent taverns where jurors stay, and drop hints before them touching the merits of causes known to be on the calendars.—(18) 1807 in Pike *Sources Miss.* ii. App. 22 The chief . . . filled a calumet, which several different Indians took from him, and handed the Osages to smoke. This was called the *horse-smoke,* as each person who took the pipe from the chief intended presenting the Osages a horse.—(19) 1850 H. C. Watson *Camp-Fires Revol.* 254 Bill Hurley had also brought with him an old horse-trumpet.

Dictionary of American Slang

Harold Wentworth and Stuart Berg Flexner

New York, 1960

horse *n.* 1 A joke, esp. a joke played on a person; a practical joke. *Some c1890 use. Obs. except in the stand. "horseplay."* 2 A literal translation or list of answers used while taking an examination; a pony. *Some c1900 student use.* →3 A diligent, able student; a grind. *Some c1900 student use; still some dial. use. Prob. from the expression "to work as hard as a horse" plus "pony" or "horse"* (def. 2). 4 Meat, specif. corned beef. *Sometimes modified as "young horse," "red horse," "salt horse," etc. Some student, USN, and Army use, mainly c1900–c1935.* 5 A thousand dollars; the sum of $1,000. *Some circus use. Perhaps from "G" and "gee-gee."* 6 Heroin. 1951: "Then he started on heroin, or 'horse.' " Kinkead, 16. 1952: "So Diane became a junkie, hooked by horse." P. Prescott in N. Y. *Times,* Apr. 29, 25. *Wide addict use.*

Fairly well known to the general public. See H. 7 A stupid, rude, stubborn, or contemptible person. *Dial*. 8 A truck; a tractor. *Some farm and truck-driver use*. Cf. iron horse.

WORKING WITH THE SELECTIONS

1. The passage from the *OED* warrants careful study. Unless you are in a position to look up the many abbreviations in the table in the dictionary itself, you will have to let some things go unexplained, but there is still much to observe. To appreciate the first paragraph, you will want to recall some of what you have learned about etymology; you might find it particularly useful to review the etymological entries given earlier. The various uses of the word *horse* are given with the date of the first occurrence in English discovered by the editors of the *OED;* other dated occurrences follow. Full forms of a few abbreviated titles are *Vespasian Psalter,* Layaman's *Brut, South English Legendary, Havelok the Dane,* and *Selected Works* of John Wyclif. According to the *OED,* the first appearance of the word *horse* in English was in the *Vespasian Psalter,* which can be dated about 825. This does not mean that the word was never used before; it came down at least from Proto-Germanic (here called Old Teutonic) and thus has been in the language for thousands of years, but few manuscripts survive until after about Alfred's time. The first occurrence of the plural was about 900, but that means only that plural was then recorded, not that it was then developed (the two passages from the *Oldest English Texts* mean 'four wild horses' and 'Then came God's angel . . . and quieted the horses'). Notice that the use of *horse* to distinguish the male from the female was not recorded until 1485 in the *Digby Mysteries.*

   After you have worked through the passage, try to decide what is meant by "on historical principles" in the alternate title, *A New English Dictionary on Historical Principles.* What would seem to be the peculiar virtue of a dictionary like the *OED?*

2. Like the *OED,* the *Century* uses citations, but the *Century* uses them differently. Can you describe this difference? The *Century* was edited under the direction of William Dwight Whitney, one of the greatest Sanskrit scholars of his day. Obviously, he could have included more from Sanskrit if he had wished. Whitney caused great quantities of material to be assembled that had never before been brought together and printed in a dictionary. Imagine that you are Whitney, and try to make a statement that will tell your editors what they should include and exclude.

3. Ambrose Bierce wrote in *The Devil's Dictionary* that a dictionary is "a malevolent literary device for cramping the growth of a language and making it hard and inelastic." Bierce is, of course, having fun, but many commentators would have taken him seriously and agreed with him; some of the lexicographers quoted above might have agreed in essence—some at least seem to deserve the charge. Could the charge be brought against either the *OED* or the *Century?* Could it properly be leveled at your own dictionary? What is the philosophy of a modern dictionary?

4. Before Mathews could edit a dictionary of Americanisms, he had to define an Americanism. Otherwise he would not have known what to put in and what to leave out. Can you infer from the sample above how he defined an Americanism?

5. Wentworth and Flexner faced the same sort of problem in editing a dictionary of slang. Perhaps, by now, you can see further reasons for their having given no very precise definition of a slang term.

part **8**

Language, Literature, and Style

Literature is the art that uses language as its medium. The medium matters; we have only to remind ourselves how different are music, dance, and painting to see that the medium does much to determine the nature of art, the excellence of artistic expression, and the amount of artistic production.

Some of what the medium does is clear enough. The possibilities for expression available to a composer in the fifteenth century were not what they are today. The composer's medium has been enriched by such developments as the discovery of musical relationships like counterpoint and harmony and the invention of varied and complex musical instruments, to name a few. If Beethoven had lived a few centuries earlier, he would not have become the Beethoven we know.

The possibilities for literary expression have changed greatly too. Few men have been more revered than Homer, but most of his contemporaries never heard him or heard of him, and if there was a comparable poet in the Americas during the first millennium B.C. we would not know it. Oral language was in many ways an inadequate medium; it could not travel far nor survive well. During subsequent centuries language became a written medium, then a printed medium. Today it is one component of what we call the mass media. These changes have subtly altered the literature for which language is the vehicle. And literature will grow and change more as films, television, and the stored content of computers are used in new ways, and as the mass media develop in directions we cannot as yet imagine.

Writing has been studied for centuries and so has literature; critics have asked how language has been used to create literature and how writers best use language. We are getting better answers to these questions than critics have in the past because we know much more about language, and we are learning more every day. We now have some clear understanding of how language is made, what it is, what it can do for minds, and what it does to minds.

Not only are we getting better answers; we are learning to ask more searching questions. What has language done to literature, and literature to language? What has the printing press done to literature, to the nature of the literature composed? What is television now doing to literature? What does it mean for literature that the author writes in Arabic or Chinese or Swedish, or that although the artist produces literature in standard English, he grew up speaking a subdialect of the black ghetto or of the rural Midwest? For a long time such questions were not often asked, and when they were they were not usually answered well. But now much has changed; critics are coming to realize that they cannot think clearly about literature without thinking also about the medium of literature: if style is the man, it is also the language. The selections in Part 8 are examples of some of the new questions being asked about the relationships among man, language, and literature.

1

"Isaiah" and the Computer

Just as language itself is subtle and varied, so is its impact, perhaps especially in literature. In the study of literature even the most routine details about the use of language may have artistic implications. The following selection, from Time, 95 *(April 13, 1970), suggests what careful analysis of language can reveal.*

As early as the 12th century, Hebrew scholars began to question whether the entire *Book of Isaiah* was written by the same author. Liberal Scripture scholars have long agreed that there are at least two distinct collections in *Isaiah,* one comprising the first 39 chapters, the other the remaining 27. Now modern technology has ratified that thesis.

Using an Elliott 503 computer, Yehuda Radday, a lecturer in biblical studies and Hebrew in Haifa, produced a 175-page statistical linguistics analysis of *Isaiah.* He applied 18 standard tests to measure such features as word length and vocabulary eccentricity. An additional test, devised by Radday, measured *Isaiah*'s war idioms and metaphors. In the first 39 chapters such terms accounted for 8.65% of all nouns, *v.* only 5.72% in the next 27 chapters—which supports the theory that the first author or group of authors lived during the violent period of the Assyrians, the second during the peaceful reign of the Persians, 200 to 250 years later. All 19 tests turned up significant differences between the two parts. Radday's conclusion: the probability that one prophet wrote the book is one in 100,000.

WORKING WITH THE SELECTION

First, you might notice that the computer cannot think. Biblical scholars had to discover that what passes as "Isaiah" must contain the writing of more than one man, probably two. Once this thesis had been propounded, however, it could be checked to a degree of certainty that would have been impossible—or at least impractical—for the unaided scholar. Can you think of any other literary problems that data-processing machines might solve? Would there be any dangers in such methods?

2

The Language of "The Catcher in the Rye"

Donald P. Costello

Donald P. Costello, professor of English at the University of Notre Dame, is interested in both linguistics and literature. The following selection is from American Speech, *39 (October, 1959).*

Most critics who looked at *The Catcher in the Rye* at the time of its publication thought that its language was a true and authentic rendering of teenage colloquial speech. Reviewers in the Chicago *Sunday Tribune*, the London *Times Literary Supplement*, the *New Republic*, the New York *Herald Tribune Book Review*, the New York *Times*, the *New Yorker*, and the *Saturday Review of Literature* all specifically mentioned the authenticity of the book's language. Various aspects of its language were also discussed in the reviews published in *America*, the *Atlantic*, the *Catholic World*, the *Christian Science Monitor*, the *Library Journal*, the Manchester *Guardian*, the *Nation*, the *New Statesman and Nation*, the New York *Times Book Review*, *Newsweek*, the *Spectator*, and *Time*.[1] Of these many reviews, only the writers for the *Catholic World* and the *Christian Science Monitor* denied the authenticity of the book's language, but both of these are religious journals which refused to believe that the 'obscenity' was realistic. An examination of the reviews of *The Catcher in the Rye* proves that the language of Holden Caulfield, the book's sixteen-year-old narrator, struck the

[1] See reviews in *America*, LXXV (August 11, 1951), 463, 464; *Atlantic*, CLXXXVIII (1951), 82; *Catholic World*, CLXXIV (1951), 154; Chicago *Sunday Tribune*, July 15, 1951, Part 4, p. 3; *Christian Science Monitor*, July 19, 1951, p. 9; *Library Journal*, LXXVI (1951), 1125; *Times* [London] *Literary Supplement*, September 7, 1951, p. 561; Manchester *Guardian*, August 10, 1951, p. 4; *Nation*, CLXXIII (September 1, 1951), 176; *New Republic*, CXXV (July 16, 1951), 20, 21; *New Statesman and Nation*, XLII (August 18, 1951), 185; New York *Herald Tribune Book Review*, July 15, 1951, p. 3; New York *Times Book Review*, July 15, 1951, p. 5; New York *Times*, July 16, 1951, p. 19; *New Yorker*, XXVII (August 11, 1951), 71–76; *Newsweek*, XXXVIII (July 16, 1951), 89, 90; *Saturday Review of Literature*, XXXIV (July 14, 1951), 12, 13; *Spectator*, CLXXXVII (August 17, 1951), 224; *Time*, LVIII (July 16, 1951), 96, 97.

ear of the contemporary reader as an accurate rendering of the informal speech of an intelligent, educated, Northeastern American adolescent.[2]

In addition to commenting on its authenticity, critics have often remarked —uneasily—the 'daring,' 'obscene,' 'blasphemous' features of Holden's language. Another commonly noted feature of the book's language has been its comic effect. And yet there has never been an extensive investigation of the language itself. That is what this paper proposes to do.

Even though Holden's language is authentic teenage speech, recording it was certainly not the major intention of Salinger. He was faced with the artistic task of creating an individual character, not with the linguistic task of reproducing the exact speech of teenagers in general. Yet Holden had to speak a recognizable teenage language, and at the same time had to be identifiable as an individual. This difficult task Salinger achieved by giving Holden an extremely trite and typical teenage speech, overlaid with strong personal idiosyncracies. There are two major speech habits which are Holden's own, which are endlessly repeated throughout the book, and which are, nevertheless, typical enough of teenage speech so that Holden can be both typical and individual in his use of them. It is certainly common for teenagers to end thoughts with a loosely dangling 'and all,' just as it is common for them to add an insistent 'I really did,' 'It really was.' But Holden uses these phrases to such an overpowering degree that they become a clear part of the flavor of the book; they become, more, a part of Holden himself, and actually help to characterize him.

Holden's 'and all' and its twins, 'or something,' 'or anything,' serve no real, consistent linguistic function. They simply give a sense of looseness of expression and looseness of thought. Often they signify that Holden knows there is more that could be said about the issue at hand, but he is not going to bother going into it:

. . . how my parents were occupied and all before they had me (5.)[3]

---

[2] If additional evidence of the authenticity of the book's language is required, one need only look at the phenomenal regard with which *The Catcher in the Rye* is held by today's college students, who were about Holden's age at the time the book was written. In its March 9, 1957, issue, the *Nation* published a symposium which attempted to discover the major influences upon the college students of today. Many teachers pointed out the impact of Salinger. Carlos Baker, of Princeton, stated: "There is still, as there has been for years, a cult of Thomas Wolfe. They have all read J. D. Salinger, Wolfe's closest competitor.' Stanley Kunitz, of Queens College, wrote: 'The only novelist I have heard praised vociferously is J. D. Salinger.' Harvey Curtis Webster, of the University of Louisville, listed Salinger as one of the 'stimulators.' R. J. Kaufman, of the University of Rochester, called *The Catcher in the Rye* 'a book which has complexly aroused nearly all of them.' See 'The Careful Young Men,' *Nation*, CLXXXIV (March 9, 1957), 199–214. I have never heard any Salinger partisan among college students doubt the authenticity of the language of their compatriot, Holden.

[3] Whenever *The Catcher in the Rye* is substantially quoted in this paper, a page number will be included in the text immediately after the quotation. The edition to which the page numbers refer is the Signet paperback reprint.

. . . they're *nice* and all (5.)

I'm not going to tell you my whole goddam autobiography or anything (5.)

. . . splendid and clear-thinking and all (6.)

But just as often the use of such expressions is purely arbitrary, with no discernible meaning:

. . . he's my *brother* and all (5.)

. . . was in the Revolutionary War and all (6.)

It was December and all (7.)

. . . no gloves or anything (7.)

. . . right in the pocket and all (7.)

Donald Barr, writing in the *Commonweal*, finds this habit indicative of Holden's tendency to generalize, to find the all in the one:

> Salinger has an ear not only for idiosyncrasies of diction and syntax, but for mental processes. Holden Caulfield's phrase is 'and all'—'She looked so damn *nice*, the way she kept going around and around in her blue coat and all'—as if each experience wore a halo. His fallacy is *ab uno disce omnes;* he abstracts and generalizes wildly.[4]

Heiserman and Miller, in the *Western Humanities Review,* comment specifically upon Holden's second most obvious idiosyncrasy: 'In a phony world Holden feels compelled to reenforce his sincerity and truthfulness constantly with, "It really is" or "It really did." '[5] S. N. Behrman, in the *New Yorker,* finds a double function of these 'perpetual insistences of Holden's.' Behrman thinks they 'reveal his age, even when he is thinking much older,' and, more important, 'he is so aware of the danger of slipping into phoniness himself that he has to repeat over and over "I really mean it," "It really does." '[6] Holden uses this idiosyncrasy of insistence almost every time that he makes an affirmation.

Allied to Holden's habit of insistence is his 'if you want to know the truth.' Heiserman and Miller are able to find characterization in this habit too:

> The skepticism inherent in that casual phrase, 'if you want to know the truth,' suggesting that as a matter of fact in the world of Holden Caul-

[4] Donald Barr, 'Saints, Pilgrims, and Artists,' *Commonweal,* LXVII (October 25, 1957), 90.

[5] Arthur Heiserman and James E. Miller, Jr., 'J. D. Salinger: Some Crazy Cliff,' *Western Humanities Review,* X (1956), 136.

[6] S. N. Behrman, 'The Vision of the Innocent,' *New Yorker,* XXVII (August 11, 1951), 72.

field very few people do, characterizes this sixteen-year-old 'crazy mixed up kid' more sharply and vividly than pages of character 'analysis' possibly could.[7]

Holden uses this phrase only after affirmations, just as he uses 'It really does,' but usually after the personal ones, where he is consciously being frank:

> I have no wind, if you want to know the truth. (8.)
>
> I don't even think that bastard had a handkerchief, if you want to know the truth. (34.)
>
> I'm a pacifist, if you want to know the truth. (44.)
>
> She had quite a lot of sex appeal, too, if you really want to know. (53.)
>
> I was damn near bawling, I felt so damn happy, if you want to know the truth. (191.)

These personal idiosyncrasies of Holden's speech are in keeping with general teenage language. Yet they are so much a part of Holden and of the flavor of the book that they are much of what makes Holden to be Holden. They are the most memorable feature of the book's language. Although always in character, the rest of Holden's speech is more typical than individual. The special quality of this language comes from its triteness, its lack of distinctive qualities.

Holden's informal, schoolboy vernacular is particularly typical in its 'vulgarity' and 'obscenity.' No one familiar with prep-school speech could seriously contend that Salinger overplayed his hand in this respect. On the contrary, Holden's restraints help to characterize him as a sensitive youth who avoids the most strongly forbidden terms, and who never uses vulgarity in a self-conscious or phony way to help him be 'one of the boys.' *Fuck,* for example, is never used as a part of Holden's speech. The word appears in the novel four times, but only when Holden disapprovingly discusses its wide appearance on walls. The Divine name is used habitually by Holden only in the comparatively weak *for God's sake, God,* and *goddam.* The stronger and usually more offensive *for Chrissake* or *Jesus* or *Jesus Christ* are used habitually by Ackley and Stradlater; but Holden uses them only when he feels the need for a strong expression. He almost never uses *for Chrissake* in an unemotional situation. *Goddam* is Holden's favorite adjective. This word is used with no relationship to its original meaning, or to Holden's attitude toward the word to which it is attached. It simply expresses an emotional feeling toward the object: either favorable, as in 'goddam hunting cap'; or unfavorable, as in 'ya goddam moron'; or indifferent, as in 'coming in the goddam windows.' *Damn* is used interchangeably with *goddam;* no differentiation in its meaning is detectable.

Other crude words are also often used in Holden's vocabulary. *Ass* keeps

---

[7] Heiserman and Miller, *op. cit.,* p. 135.

a fairly restricted meaning as a part of the human anatomy, but it is used in a variety of ways. It can refer simply to that specific part of the body ('I moved my ass a little'), or be a part of a trite expression ('freezing my ass off'; 'in a half-assed way'), or be an expletive ('Game, my ass.'). *Hell* is perhaps the most versatile word in Holden's entire vocabulary; it serves most of the meanings and constructions which Mencken lists in his *American Speech* article on 'American Profanity.'[8] So far is Holden's use of *hell* from its original meaning that he can use the sentence 'We had a helluva time' to mean that he and Phoebe had a decidedly pleasant time downtown shopping for shoes. The most common function of *hell* is as the second part of a simile, in which a thing can be either 'hot as hell' or, strangely, 'cold as hell'; 'sad as hell' or 'playful as hell'; 'old as hell' or 'pretty as hell.' Like all of these words, *hell* has no close relationship to its original meaning.

Both *bastard* and *sonuvabitch* have also drastically changed in meaning. They no longer, of course, in Holden's vocabulary, have any connection with the accidents of birth. Unless used in a trite simile, *bastard* is a strong word, reserved for things and people Holden particularly dislikes, especially 'phonies.' *Sonuvabitch* has an even stronger meaning to Holden; he uses it only in the deepest anger. When, for example, Holden is furious with Stradlater over his treatment of Jane Gallagher, Holden repeats again and again that he 'kept calling him a moron sonuvabitch' (43).

The use of crude language in *The Catcher in the Rye* increases, as we should expect, when Holden is reporting schoolboy dialogue. When he is directly addressing the reader, Holden's use of such language drops off almost entirely. There is also an increase in this language when any of the characters are excited or angry. Thus, when Holden is apprehensive over Stradlater's treatment of Jane, his *goddams* increase suddenly to seven on a single page (p. 39).

Holden's speech is also typical in his use of slang. I have catalogued over a hundred slang terms used by Holden, and every one of these is in widespread use. Although Holden's slang is rich and colorful, it, of course, being slang, often fails at precise communication. Thus, Holden's *crap* is used in seven different ways. It can mean foolishness, as 'all that David Copperfield kind of crap,' or messy matter, as 'I spilled some crap all over my gray flannel,' or merely miscellaneous matter, as 'I was putting on my galoshes and crap.' It can also carry its basic meaning, animal excreta, as 'there didn't look like there was anything in the park except dog crap,' and it can be used as an adjective meaning anything generally unfavorable, as 'The show was on the crappy side.' Holden uses the phrases *to be a lot of crap* and *to shoot the crap* and *to chuck the crap* all to mean 'to be untrue,' but he can also use *to shoot the crap* to mean simply 'to chat,' with no connotation of untruth, as in 'I certainly wouldn't have minded shooting the crap with old Phoebe for a while.'

Similarly Holden's slang use of *crazy* is both trite and imprecise. 'That

---

[8] See H. L. Mencken, 'American Profanity,' *American Speech*, XIX (1944), 242.

drives me crazy' means that he violently dislikes something; yet 'to be crazy about' something means just the opposite. In the same way, to be 'killed' by something can mean that he was emotionally affected either favorably ('That story just about killed me.') or unfavorably ('Then she turned her back on me again. It nearly killed me.'). This use of *killed* is one of Holden's favorite slang expressions. Heiserman and Miller are, incidentally, certainly incorrect when they conclude: 'Holden always lets us know when he has insight into the absurdity of the endlessly absurd situations which make up the life of a sixteen-year-old by exclaiming, "It killed me." '[9] Holden often uses this expression with no connection to the absurd; he even uses it for his beloved Phoebe. The expression simply indicates a high degree of emotion— any kind. It is hazardous to conclude that any of Holden's slang has a precise and consistent meaning or function. These same critics fall into the same error when they conclude that Holden's use of the adjective *old* serves as 'a term of endearment.'[10] Holden appends this word to almost every character, real or fictional, mentioned in the novel, from the hated 'old Maurice' to 'old Peter Lorre,' to 'old Phoebe,' and even 'old Jesus.' The only pattern that can be discovered in Holden's use of this term is that he usually uses it only after he has previously mentioned the character; he then feels free to append the familiar *old*. All we can conclude from Holden's slang is that it is typical teenage slang: versatile yet narrow, expressive yet unimaginative, imprecise, often crude, and always trite.

Holden has many favorite slang expressions which he overuses. In one place, he admits:

> 'Boy!' I said. I also say 'Boy!' quite a lot. Partly because I have a lousy vocabulary and partly because I act quite young for my age sometimes. (12.)

But if Holden's slang shows the typically 'lousy vocabulary' of even the educated American teenager, this failing becomes even more obvious when we narrow our view to Holden's choice of adjectives and adverbs. The choice is indeed narrow, with a constant repetition of a few favorite words: *lousy, pretty, crumby, terrific, quite, old, stupid*—all used, as is the habit of teenage vernacular, with little regard to specific meaning. Thus, most of the nouns which are called 'stupid' could not in any logical framework be called 'ignorant,' and, as we have seen, *old* before a proper noun has nothing to do with age.

Another respect in which Holden was correct in accusing himself of having a 'lousy vocabulary' is discovered in the ease with which he falls into trite figures of speech. We have already seen that Holden's most common simile is the worn and meaningless 'as hell'; but his often-repeated 'like a madman' and 'like a bastard' are just about as unrelated to a literal meaning

[9] Heiserman and Miller, *op. cit.*, p. 136.
[10] *Ibid.*

and are easily as unimaginative. Even Holden's nonhabitual figures of speech are usually trite: 'sharp as a tack'; 'hot as a firecracker'; 'laughed like a hyena'; 'I know old Jane like a book'; 'drove off like a bat out of hell'; 'I began to feel like a horse's ass'; 'blind as a bat'; 'I know Central Park like the back of my hand.'

Repetitious and trite as Holden's vocabulary may be, it can, nevertheless, become highly effective. For example, when Holden piles one trite adjective upon another, a strong power of invective is often the result:

> He was a goddam stupid moron. (42.)
>
> Get your dirty stinking moron knees off my chest. (43.)
>
> You're a dirty stupid sonuvabitch of a moron. (43.)

And his limited vocabulary can also be used for good comic effect. Holden's constant repetition of identical expressions in countless widely different situations is often hilariously funny.

But all of the humor in Holden's vocabulary does not come from its unimaginative quality. Quite the contrary, some of his figures of speech are entirely original; and these are inspired, dramatically effective, and terribly funny. As always, Salinger's Holden is basically typical, with a strong overlay of the individual:

> He started handling my exam paper like it was a turd or something. (13.)
>
> He put my goddam paper down then and looked at me like he'd just beaten the hell out of me in ping-pong or something. (14.)
>
> That guy Morrow was about as sensitive as a goddam toilet seat. (52.)
>
> Old Marty was like dragging the Statue of Liberty around the floor. (69.)

Another aspect in which Holden's language is typical is that it shows the general American characteristic of adaptability—apparently strengthened by his teenage lack of restraint. It is very easy for Holden to turn nouns into adjectives, with the simple addition of a -y: 'perverty,' 'Christmasy,' 'vomity-looking,' 'whory-looking,' 'hoodlumy-looking,' 'show-offy,' 'flitty-looking,' 'dumpy-looking,' 'pimpy,' 'snobby,' 'fisty.' Like all of English, Holden's language shows a versatile combining ability: 'They gave Sally this little blue butt-twitcher of a dress to wear' (117) and 'That magazine was some little cheerer upper' (176). Perhaps the most interesting aspect of the adaptability of Holden's language is his ability to use nouns as adverbs: 'She sings it very Dixieland and whorehouse, and it doesn't sound at all mushy' (105).

As we have seen, Holden shares, in general, the trite repetitive vocabulary which is the typical lot of his age group. But as there are exceptions in his figures of speech, so are there exceptions in his vocabulary itself, in his word stock. An intelligent, well-read ('I'm quite illiterate, but I read a lot'), and educated boy, Holden possesses, and can use when he wants to, many words which are many a cut above Basic English, including 'ostracized,' 'exhibitionist,' 'unscrupulous,' 'conversationalist,' 'psychic,' 'bourgeois.' Often Holden seems to choose his words consciously, in an effort to communicate to his adult reader clearly and properly, as in such terms as 'lose my virginity,' 'relieve himself,' 'an alcoholic'; for upon occasion, he also uses the more vulgar terms 'to give someone the time,' 'to take a leak,' 'booze hound.' Much of the humor arises, in fact, from Holden's habit of writing on more than one level at the same time. Thus, we have such phrases as 'They give guys the ax quite frequently at Pency' and 'It has a very good academic rating, Pency' (7). Both sentences show a colloquial idiom with an overlay of consciously selected words.

Such a conscious choice of words seems to indicate that Salinger, in his attempt to create a realistic character in Holden, wanted to make him aware of his speech, as, indeed, a real teenager would be when communicating to the outside world. Another piece of evidence that Holden is conscious of his speech and, more, realizes a difficulty in communication, is found in his habit of direct repetition: 'She likes me a lot. I mean she's quite fond of me.' (141), and 'She can be very snotty sometimes. She can be quite snotty.' (150). Sometimes the repetition is exact: 'He was a very nervous guy—I mean he was a very nervous guy.' (165), and 'I sort of missed them. I mean I sort of missed them.' (169). Sometimes Holden stops specifically to interpret slang terms, as when he wants to communicate the fact that Allie liked Phoebe: 'She killed Allie, too. I mean he liked her, too' (64).

There is still more direct evidence that Holden was conscious of his speech. Many of his comments to the reader are concerned with language. He was aware, for example, of the 'phony' quality of many words and phrases, such as 'grand,' 'prince,' 'traveling incognito,' 'little girls' room,' 'licorice stick,' and 'angels.' Holden is also conscious, of course, of the existence of 'taboo words.' He makes a point of mentioning that the girl from Seattle repeatedly asked him to 'watch your language, if you don't mind' (67), and that his mother told Phoebe not to say 'lousy' (160). When the prostitute says 'Like fun you are.' Holden comments:

> It was a funny thing to say. It sounded like a real kid. You'd think a prostitute and all would say 'Like hell you are' or 'Cut the crap' instead of 'Like fun you are.' (87.)

In grammar, too, as in vocabulary, Holden possesses a certain self-consciousness. (It is, of course, impossible to imagine a student getting through today's schools without a self-consciousness with regard to grammar rules.) Holden is, in fact, not only aware of the existence of 'grammatical errors,' but knows the social taboos that accompany them. He is disturbed by a schoolmate who is ashamed of his parents' grammar, and he reports that his former teacher, Mr. Antolini, warned him about picking up 'just enough education to hate people who say, "It's a secret between he and I" ' (168).

Holden is a typical enough teenager to violate the grammar rules, even though he knows of their social importance. His most common rule violation is the misuse of *lie* and *lay,* but he also is careless about relative pronouns ('about a traffic cop that falls in love'), the double negative ('I hardly didn't even know I was doing it'), the perfect tenses ('I'd woke him up'), extra words ('like as if all you ever did at Pency was play polo all the time'), pronoun number ('it's pretty disgusting to watch somebody picking their nose'), and pronoun position ('I and this friend of mine, Mal Brossard'). More remarkable, however, than the instances of grammar rule violations is Holden's relative 'correctness.' Holden is always intelligible, and is even 'correct' in many usually difficult constructions. Grammatically speaking, Holden's language seems to point up the fact that English was the only subject in which he was not failing. It is interesting to note how much more 'correct' Holden's speech is than that of Huck Finn. But then Holden is educated, and since the time of Huck there had been sixty-seven years of authoritarian schoolmarms working on the likes of Holden. He has, in fact, been overtaught, so that he uses many 'hyper' forms:

> I used to play tennis with he and Mrs. Antolini quite frequently. (163.)
>
> She'd give Allie or I a push. (64.)
>
> I and Allie used to take her to the park with us. (64.)
>
> I think I probably woke he and his wife up. (157.)

Now that we have examined several aspects of Holden's vocabulary and grammar, it would be well to look at a few examples of how he puts these elements together into sentences. The structure of Holden's sentences indicates that Salinger thinks of the book more in terms of spoken speech than written speech. Holden's faulty structure is quite common and typical in vocal expression; I doubt if a student who is 'good in English' would ever create such sentence structure in writing. A student who showed the self-consciousness of Holden would not *write* so many fragments, such afterthoughts (e.g., 'It has a very good academic rating, Pency' [7]), or such repetitions (e.g., 'Where I lived at Pency, I lived in the Ossenburger Memorial Wing of the new dorms' [18]).

There are other indications that Holden's speech is vocal. In many places Salinger mildly imitates spoken speech. Sentences such as 'You could tell old Spencer'd got a big bang out of buying it' (10) and 'I'd've killed him' (42) are repeated throughout the book. Yet it is impossible to imagine Holden taking pen in hand and actually writing 'Spencer'd' or 'I'd've.' Sometimes, too, emphasized words, or even parts of words, are italicized, as in 'Now *shut up,* Holden. God damn it—I'm *warn*ing ya' (42). This is often done with good effect, imitating quite perfectly the rhythms of speech, as in the typical:

I practically sat down on her *lap,* as a matter of fact. Then she *really* started to cry, and the next thing I knew, I was kissing her all over— *any*where—her eyes, her *nose,* her forehead, her eyebrows and all, her *ears*—her whole face except her mouth and all. (73.)

The language of *The Catcher in the Rye* is, as we have seen, an authentic artistic rendering of a type of informal, colloquial, teenage American spoken speech. It is strongly typical and trite, yet often somewhat individual; it is crude and slangy and imprecise, imitative yet occasionally imaginative, and affected toward standardization by the strong efforts of schools. But authentic and interesting as this language may be, it must be remembered that it exists, in *The Catcher in the Rye,* as only one part of an artistic achievement. The language was not written for itself, but as a part of a greater whole. Like the great Twain work with which it is often compared, a study of *The Catcher in the Rye* repays both the linguist and the literary critic; for as one critic has said, 'In them, 1884 and 1951 speak to us in the idiom and accent of two youthful travelers who have earned their passports to literary immortality.'[11]

[11] Charles Kaplan, 'Holden and Huck: the Odysseys of Youth,' *College English,* XVIII (1956), 80.

WORKING WITH THE SELECTION

1. Like the writers represented in Part 6, Costello is concerned with usage, but his approach differs from that of Hartung and the editors of usage books. What is the main difference between his approach and theirs?

2. In *The Catcher in the Rye* Salinger captures the slang used by teenagers in 1951. Is teenage slang as you know it markedly different? Costello is interested in the manner in which Holden Caulfield as an individual used the slang of his day; can you detect differences in the ways in which your contemporaries use slang? Is the slang used on your campus different from that used in the secondary school you attended?

3. Try to think of a contemporary writer who has employed slang as a literary device. What might you gain from making a critical analysis of his use of slang?

4. Select a short story written in the first person, preferably one in which the writer is supposedly illustrating some special dialect, and make an analysis of the narrator's dialect, using procedures like those of Costello. Stories by Ring Lardner, Dorothy Parker, Sherwood Anderson, Damon Runyan, and John Updike are possibilities.

Backlogs, Bottlenecks, and the Choice of Words

Sir Ernest Gowers

Sir Ernest Gowers, who has been honored frequently for his long and distinguished career as a public servant, is best known in this country for Plain Words: Their ABC *(1955), from which the following selection is taken.* Plain Words *is a combination of two books published in England, which Gowers says "were written at the invitation of the Treasury as a contribution to what they were doing to improve official English." The books were addressed to his fellow civil servants, striking at what he called* pudder.

OVERWORKED METAPHORS

backlog   The new use of *backlog* to mean an accumulation of arrears is common in the United States. For example, the list that our Telephone Department calls "List of waiting applicants" is called by the American Telephone Company "Backlog of held orders". This use is spreading here, and a Government department already finds it natural to write:

> The most important step is to eliminate a very heavy backlog of orders on the manufacturers' books.

The metaphor seems to be from a log fire in which the backlog is the large log at the back that is never burned. Like *stockpile* the word is likely to establish itself here and to be regarded eventually as an enrichment of the language.

blueprint   This word has caught on as a picturesque substitute for *scheme* or *plan* and the shine is wearing off it. It is not reasonable to ask that metaphors should be anchored at their points of origin, but it would make for accuracy of language if writers who use this one remembered that in the engineering industries, where it comes from, the blueprint marks the final stage of paper design.

bottleneck   *Bottleneck* is a useful and picturesque metaphor to denote the point of constriction of something that ought to be flowing freely:

Even if the manufacturers could obtain ample raw material, the short-age of skilled labour would constitute a bottleneck in production.

The metaphor is not new, but it has had a sharp rise in popularity, perhaps because our economy has been so full of bottlenecks. It needs to be handled carefully in order to avoid absurdity, as Mr. Henry Strauss pointed out in this letter to *The Times*:

> In order to illustrate the progress (or whatever it is) of our language I am compiling a brochure on bottlenecks. I shall accordingly be grateful for any significant additions to these examples from recent journalism:
>
> (1) "The biggest bottleneck in housing", meaning the worst, most constricting and presumably narrowest bottleneck.
> (2) "Bottlenecks must be ironed out" (leading article in the daily press).
> (3) "Bottlenecks ahead" and "Bottleneck in bottles" (recent headlines).
> (4) "The economy of the Ruhr is bound to move within a vicious circle of interdependent bottlenecks."
> (5) "What is planned is actually a series of bottlenecks. The most drastic bottleneck is that of machine tools."
> (6) "One bottleneck . . . which is particularly far-reaching and de-cisive."

Mr. Strauss has recently made some additions to his collection:

> Finally, before leaving my Hon. Friend, I must thank him for adding his delightful "overriding bottleneck" to my celebrated collection of bottlenecks. Hitherto, my favourites were the "drastic bottleneck", the "vicious circle of interdependent bottlenecks" and, perhaps the best of the whole collection, the "worldwide bottleneck".* . . .

THE ABSTRACT APPENDAGE

This brings us to what has been called the *abstract appendage*, for *position*, *situation* and *conditions* find themselves in that role more commonly than any other words. I take the term from a letter in *The Times* from Mr. John Bux-ton:

> Sir,—How long are we to suffer from "weather conditions"? There was a time when the Englishman's favourite topic of conversation was the weather. . . . Now it is no longer recognised as a substantial and elemental thing, but is reduced, by the addition of this abstract ap-pendage, to the status of a symptom or an excuse, and no one knows what to do about it. Prime Minister, back bencher and Civil servant all irritate us with the phrase in print; it is left to the B.B.C. to go even

* *Hansard*, 10th July 1953.

further and, omitting the word "weather", to refer to "cold, wintry, snowy (etc.) conditions".

> This is the weather the shepherd shuns
> And so do I,

wrote Thomas Hardy, not "The present weather conditions are causing considerable inconvenience to the sheep-farmer". We cannot shun (or like) "weather conditions", and the sooner the sloppy phrase is destroyed the sooner our rulers will realise its powers for good or ill.

This may be thought over-critical. What exactly is the writer's objection to *weather conditions?* It cannot be the objection of a grammarian to using the word *weather* adjectivally; it is a common and useful English idiom to make nouns serve this purpose, and few words can claim a better right to be so employed than that which has given us *weather forecast, weather prophet, weather eye, weather quarter* and *weather tiles.* The objection must then be to the use of two words where one would do, a sound objection if it can be sustained. But can it here? *Weather conditions* imports a larger idea than *weather* does, at least in time of snow and frost. It embraces the conditions created by yesterday's weather and the likelihood of to-morrow's weather changing them. But the attack, even if badly aimed, was directed against a real fault in official English. If the writer had waited until the next day and attacked, as he might have done, the announcement that *blizzard conditions* had returned to the Midlands, he could not have met with any such plea. It was not blizzard conditions that had returned; it was a blizzard. Similarly it is both unnecessary and quaint to say that temperatures will return to normal values instead of merely that they will return to normal. *Level* has also been greatly in demand of late as an abstract appendage. A correspondent has kindly presented me with a collection of hundreds of specimens, ranging from *pub-and-street-corner-level* to *world-level* through every conceivable intermediate level. This passion for picturing all our relations with one another as stratifications is an odd phenomenon at a time when we are supposed to be developing into a classless State. . . .

TROUBLES IN ARRANGEMENT

The simplest type of faulty arrangement, and the easiest to fall into, is illustrated by the following examples. Their offence is that they obscure the writer's meaning, if only momentarily, and usually make him appear to be guilty of an absurdity.

> There was a discussion yesterday on the worrying of sheep by dogs in the Minister's room.

> The official statement on the marriage of German prisoners with girls made in the House of Commons. . . .

It is doubtful whether this small gas company would wish to accept responsibility for supplying this large area with all its difficulties.

Whatever her thoughts, they were interrupted as the hotel lobby door opened and a young woman carrying a baby and her husband entered. (Quoted by *The New Yorker* from a novel.)

Faulty arrangement of this sort is not unknown even in model regulations issued by Government departments to show local authorities how things ought to be done:

No child shall be employed on any weekday when the school is not open for a longer period than four hours.

"For a longer period than four hours" qualifies *employed*, not *open*, and should come immediately after *employed*.

And in departmental regulations themselves:

Every woman by whom . . . a claim for maternity benefit is made shall furnish evidence that she has been, or that it is to be expected that she will be, confined by means of a certificate given in accordance with the rules. . . .

It is not surprising that a Department which sets this example should receive letters like this:

In accordance with your instructions I have given birth to twins in the enclosed envelope.

WORKING WITH THE SELECTION

1. On the basis of examples in the selection, how would you define *pudder?* Are there any American synonyms?

2. The selection of words is perhaps the most obvious feature of the style of any written work. Although Gowers is not addressing himself to literary artists, do his comments apply to their work? Do you know of any modern writers with literary pretensions who might read Gowers with profit? Does Gowers say anything applicable to your own prose?

3. The first three items Gowers discusses concern metaphoric uses of words. Which of the metaphors seem to work and which do not?

4

Bottom's Dream: The Likeness of Poems and Jokes

Howard Nemerov

If jokes have something in common with poems, Howard Nemerov should understand the interrelationship. He is perhaps best known as a poet; his work has been published in many periodicals and collected in several volumes, among them The Image and the Law *(1947) and* New and Selected Poems *(1960). He has also written many satirical short stories and several satirical novels, such as* Federigo, or The Power of Love *(1954) and* The Homecoming Game *(1957). Awarded the 1971 fellowship of the Academy of American Poets, he promises to continue as one of America's productive creative writers. In addition to being a poet, short story writer, and novelist, Nemerov is a professor of English at Washington University in St. Louis. The following selection is from an article in* The Virginia Quarterly Review, 42 *(Autumn, 1966).*

The poetic attempt to say the world, to name it rightly, is perhaps a matter altogether too mysterious to be talked about. When someone, behaving "poetically," looks into the landscape and tries to speak it, this mystery turns inward and takes the form of an anxious searching and striving, until (sometimes) the mind by some wild reach having an evident relation with insanity produces a phrase, and this phrase—somehow—*expresses* . . . whereupon some quiet click of accurate conjunction tells us that what has happened is somehow reasonable.

Yet this moment of expressiveness itself occurs at a crossing point, and tells us that something in language is not linguistic, that something in reason is not reasonable. It speaks of a relation between inside and outside, an identity between inside and outside, but this relation, this identity, is itself unspeakable:

Suddenly, I saw the cold and rook-delighting heaven. . . .

That has no meaning, strictly, that can be expressed otherwise, or translated. How, then, to someone who for a long time entertains the phrase as a sort of empty and objectless talisman, a piece of jade turned over in the hand, does it—suddenly, as the poet says—come to identify one alone sort of weather, one alone sort of poetry, that quality the poet wanted, he said elsewhere, of "cold light and tumbling clouds"?

Echo answers. Which is not to say that nothing answers, for it may be by a species of radar that intelligence moves through the world. We might say of expressiveness itself, of the irreducible phrase, that first it is, and then it finds a meaning in the world. Or else: Whatever the mind invents, it also discovers. Or again: Whatever is revealed, in poetry, plays at being revealed.

It is that element of play that I wish to talk about as an essentially poetic quality. This quality, I think, somehow exists in all language, in language considered as an unstable fusion of practicality and dream, in language which is in so large part an instrument for repeating, but in some small part an instrument for inventing and discovering what is invented—which is only to say, perhaps, that epic poems and systems of theology are all written by people who, whatever their talents, could not have been the first to say "cat," because it had already been said for them.

Though this poetic quality exists in all language, it will most often and most easily be visible in expressions which time or custom has set free from the urgencies of exhortation and the immediate claims of life: inscriptions on tombs, the proud dominations of antiquity, Ozymandias in his desert—surely the superfluity I mean has its relations equally with the ideal and the idea of death. Yet it may as certainly be identified in the most trivial examples. If you remove, say, the headline from an advertisement and let it dry in the sun until it shrivels out of context, it will grow other and rather surprising relations:—

. . . new shades of youth. . . .

Its valency, standing thus alone, is other than what it is when you put it back in its intentional place as an incitement to buy something called Ogilvie Creme Hair Color Foam. The tonality of *shades,* for instance, is more Stygian.

So in seeking to identify, if possible, something of the quality of expressiveness called "poetic" you might start, not with the sublime, but down at the humble end of the scale, with such things as that, with appearances of this quality in misprints, newspaper items, jokes . . . working your way up in Horatio Alger style to see how far your descriptions will take you (whether in the end you will marry Sophia, holy wisdom, the boss's daughter). In doing this we shall rely on the help of Freud—in some particulars on his fine joke book, "Wit and Its Relation to the Unconscious," and in general on his attempt to demonstrate systematically how mental life is continuous with itself in all its manifestations, from slips of the tongue to systems of philosophy and the visions of religion.

Also of Shakespeare, who in giving a title to these remarks gives also an instance of the quality we are trying to say something about. When Nick Bottom wakes in the forest from the true dream in which he wore an ass's head and was adored by Titania, he speaks of what has happened in language whose comic effect has much to do with its tone of reverence, its being so full of garbles from scripture, and so on; and he says:

> It shall be called Bottom's Dream, because it hath no bottom.

Probably there can be no better definition of poetry—no better definition, I am tempted to say, of anything that matters to us—, though all the same it is clearly better for Bottom than for the rest of us.

Something of the quality I mean may be discovered in misprints. The mathematical probability must be quite large that any misprint, such as the omission or addition or substitution of a single letter, will produce merely a moment of nonsense in the result, and indeed that happens often enough. But given this preponderant possibility it is surprising to notice how often misprints make a curious other sense, and surprising, too, how economically such transformations may be effected. Here are a few examples:

a. The Russians are dredging what will be "the largest man-maid lake in the world." Nearly nonsense, and not quite; though not quite witty, either. Between man and lake the idea of mixed bathing has intervened to pervert the spelling by the nicest economy so that it gives another sense which hovers between the appropriate and the absurd; perhaps this secondary sense is not quite strong enough, and that may have to do with the fact that we cannot hear the difference but have to see it or spell it.

b. A reviewer of one of Kinsey's reports was made to say, "The sexual urge in females in demonstarted by" . . . . Who would bother reading the rest of the sentence? Not only does "demonstarted" make sense instead of nonsense; it makes a sense which is as it were subversively appropriate to the serious discussion which was supposed to be going on.

c. A girl escaping from East Berlin "swam the icy river to be with her finance in the West." One imagines a Communist reading this with deepest satisfaction, since it confirms what he has always believed about love and money in the West. And the compositor was so taken with his invention that he used it again in the next sentence, while giving the finance's name. One observes, too, that the pertness of the criticism is enhanced by the somewhat ballad-like romance of the subject.

The effect common to all three examples is that one reality gives place to another, and a tension is revealed between them: the world of information and, we might say, the symbolic world, reflect one another in this tension. Moreover, the reality revealed by inadvertence is in each instance subversive of the reality intended; this is not so surprising in the first example, since we generally expect the sexual to be the hidden reality in statements, as it is in the second and third, where sexual and marital concerns themselves give way to themes of deeper mystery and deeper obsession still, theology of sorts, and money.

As to the relation of all this with the quality of the poetic, which many have called "vision," it is the first effect of Freud's demonstrations, on errors, dreams, jokes, to show that vision begins with a fault in this world's smooth façade.

The examination now of a few rather more complicated and elaborated examples will perhaps enable us to go further in our description of this quality and its mechanisms.

In "A Handbook of Arms and Armor," by Bashford Dean, I read that Japanese feudal warfare was especially rough on horses because they were not armored; there followed this sentence: "Not until the Tokugawa period, when warfare disappeared, was the horse given adequate armor."

This statement takes the mind away from arms and armor, but not entirely away. It combines with the subject another subject, of symbolic reflexions and resonances, in which the sentence bears a sadly ironic truth (everything is always too late) without in any way losing its pleasant and somehow Oriental flavor of bland paradox calmly mastered (as in the report of an English-language Japanese newspaper, that "the entire aircrew climbed out on the wing of the burning plane and parachuted safely to their death"). It would be possible, no doubt, to appreciate intellectually the wit of the proposition alone, dismissing all that was not abstract as irrelevant; but that would be to lose the nice particularity of "the Tokugawa period," the elegant coup de grâce given in "adequate," and the fine intricate play of sounds (r and w especially) and internal rimes (like that between "period" and "disappeared") which stitches the words together and gives decisive character to the entire statement.

The second example is an AP dispatch reporting that a former lawyer of Al Capone's is convicted of income tax evasion. "I have in mind that you've suffered enough," said the judge, who also said, "Ten years ago . . . you were a well-to-do man. Now you're a man without means because of the debts you incurred in paying off the taxes. You've lost your law practice. This is a strong reminder that the power to tax is the power to destroy."

Something here, maybe the biblical austerity of the last sentence especially, strikes me as bearing the quality of expressiveness I am after; something both tragic and funny, featured by the judge's deadpan style—is he aware, right there, of the comparison implied between gangsters and governments? —and the whole rather complicated situation of the feelings wants only a touch of arrangement, a little bit of pointing, to be brought out. I imagine the former lawyer brooding on what has been said to him:

> Ten years ago, I was a well-to-do man,
> Now I am a man without means.
> I have received
> The strong reminder.
> The power to tax is the power to destroy.
>
> The lesson of the State's Do What You Can,
> That is what the law means

Though we are deceived,
O strong reminder
Of Alcatraz, my master, my joy.

Out here beyond the average life span
The end no longer means
What it did. Reprieved
By the strong reminder,
I get up the ante and go to destroy.

. . . Our next step will be to see if the mechanism of a joke in any way illuminates that of a lyric poem; we shall limit ourselves to brief examples.

One critical resemblance between the two will be clear to anyone who has ever tried to make up either—(by the way, how do jokes get made? I do not know that anyone has seriously studied this question)—and this is the problem of the ending. Anyone can begin a poem, anyone can begin a joke (the pointlessness of doing that is very clear, it seems, but many people begin poems). As Plato says in the Laws, "The beginning is like a god, who while he lives among men redeems all." There is a grand feeling of liberty about beginning anything, for it looks as though any gesture in the whole world will do. But, in the difficult world of forms, the gesture you elect will entail consequences good and bad, seen and unseen. Sooner or later, you have to ask yourself how to stop, what it means to stop, what it is that has finished. This is the question we will now examine, first with reference to a few jokes.

a. A riddle. How do you catch the lions in the desert? Answer: you strain off the sand, and the remainder will be lions.
b. From Shipley, "Dictionary of Word Origins," s.v. Strategy. A Chinese general sent his advance guard up to the edge of a forest. To find out if the enemy were in ambush there, he ordered each man to throw a stone into the forest, and if birds flew up there were no men there, so that it would be safe to advance. All this was done, birds flew, the army marched forward—and was captured. For the opposing general, also as it happened Chinese, had said to *his* soldiers: Men, I want each of you to grab a bird, and let it go when they throw those stones.

These instances are perhaps directed against the intellect's characteristic wish to simplify situations so as reductively to bring out logical structure at the expense of everything else in experience, the wit being that this same essentializing structure is employed to bring out the absurdity of logic in this world. Both jokes make use of the same almost absolute economy, using as much as possible in the response what was given in the stimulus, merely revising the elements of the relation in an "impossible" way.

The pleasure we get must come from the fulfillment of an expectation that the resolution in both instances will make use very purely, indeed exclusively, of the given materials, plus our surprise at the use made, which as straight men for the occasion we should not have thought of. But note that although we should not have thought of the reply, the very fact of its employing *only* terms already used gave us a not quite explicit sense that we might have thought of it in another instant; that though we did not in fact think of it, our minds were playing with the possibilities of lions-deserts, stones-birds, so that the answer, as a matter of timing, seemed "right" or "inevitable," responsive to a wish on our part for symmetry and economy together with a certain shock, the compounded fulfillment of fairly definite formal expectations with a material surprise. We might compare what happens with what happens in music, eighteenth-century music, say, where to a strict and relatively narrow canon of harmonic possibility, including certain clichés of cadence, is added the composer's originality at handling his materials within the convention.

c. From Freud, "Thoughts for the Times on War and Death" (1915). A husband to his wife, "If one of us should die, I would go and live in Paris."

Here we observe, as with so many jokes, and especially those bearing on sex and marriage, that the sentiment itself is about as unfunny as it could be, setting the death of one partner against the pleasure of the other and leaving no doubt of the choice that would be made. The wit, we suppose, the element which allows us to laugh, comes from two circumstances: first, that the wish expressed is one very widely entertained but usually concealed; second, that it breaks from its concealment so economically, using as its means a very slight grammatical displacement of the solemn, "objective" statement, with its air of entertaining the worst contingencies, which the husband must have consciously intended.

Thus, like our misprints earlier, this remark makes a revelation of sorts. A revelation can be only of that which is hidden, what is hidden is secret, what is secret is so because it is, or is thought to be, evil, shameful, taboo (sacred); finally, this evil represents something we believe to be true. So that the revelation is subversive of the usual order of appearances, beneath which it shows another order, one that gains its reality from the comparison of the two. . . .

We may suspect that makers of jokes and smart remarks resemble poets at least in this, that they too would be excluded from Plato's Republic; for it is of the nature of Utopia and the Crystal Palace, as Dostoevsky said, that you can't stick your tongue out at it. A joke expresses tension, which it releases in laughter; it is a sort of permissible rebellion against things as they are—permissible, perhaps, because this rebellion is at the same time stoically resigned, it acknowledges that things are as they are, and that they will, after the moment of laughter, continue to be that way. That is why jokes concentrate on the most sensitive areas of human concern: sex, death, religion, and the most powerful institutions of society; and poems do the same. We might consider in this connection how grave a business civilization must be, to require professional comedians. Or, as Mr. Empson said (in a poem), "The safety valve alone knows the worst truth about the engine."

In general, to succeed at joking or at poetry, you have to be serious; the least hint that you think you are being funny will cancel the effect, and there is probably no lower human enterprise than "humorous writing." Still, there are poems which clearly also are jokes, though yet by no means light verse, and one of these may serve for a bridge between the two realms; the inscription on the collar of a dog which Alexander Pope gave the Prince of Wales:

> I am His Highness' dog at Kew.
> Pray tell me, sir, whose dog are you?

This couplet possesses fully the characteristics we have distinguished in jokes: the sentiment itself is tendentious, might even come near to being savage were it not spoken by a dog with an air of doggy innocence; by cleverness it gets away with the sort of revelation of how societies exist which might at various times and in various realms cost a man his life or liberty; it works economically, by transformation of the given material. Probably, to be pedantic, the wit consists in getting us to accept the literal meaning of "dog" in the first line, so that we receive the metaphorical "dog" of the second line with surprise, but a surprise conditioned by expectation, for it is after all the same word.

The example raises another point, that one mechanism of economy in joking is the pun, either in the use of one word in two senses, as here, or in the use of two words of similar sound which mean different things but still somehow establish a resemblance beyond that of the sound. Notice that in the archaic economy of poetry it frequently happens that a resemblance in sound is, though cryptically, a resemblance in sense, as in the kind of logical connection hinted by a rime, or in these examples:

> For ruin hath taught me thus to ruminate   (Shakespeare)

> O Attic shape! Fair attitude!   (Keats)

We may add this as well. The "purely formal" arrangements of poetry, such as measure, rime, stanza, which it appears not at all to share with the joke, are in fact intensifications of a characteristic we have already noticed in jokes: the compound of expectation with a fulfillment which is simultaneously exact and surprising, giving to the result that quality sometimes thought of as inevitability, or rightness. Observe, too, that many jokes show a rudimentary form of stanzaic progression, by being arranged in a series of three, with similar grammatical structure, so that the hearer correctly anticipates the punch-line as coming the third time a character says something, does something, and so forth.

Here is an example in which the humor is overtly savage, and any responsive smile might be accompanied by some gnashing of teeth; it is from Swift's "Satirical Elegy on the Death of a Late Famous General"; he means the Duke of Marlborough:

> Behold his funeral appears,
> Nor widow's sighs, nor orphan's tears,
> Wont at such times each heart to pierce,
> Attend the progress of his herse.
> But what of that, his friends may say,
> He had those honours in his day.
> True to his profit and his pride,
> He made them weep before he dy'd. . . .

What is possibly the oldest joke in the world says, With friends like that you don't need enemies. Its present form seems to be Jewish, but I have found it in Tacitus, who remarks on the persecutions under Nero, Those who had no enemies were betrayed by their friends. . . .

But by now you may have the serious objection that I am being unduly free with the idea of a joke. Engrossed in my pedantries, I seem to have forgotten that the first thing to see about a joke is that it makes us laugh; whatever doesn't do that cannot really be likened to a joke.

I should reply as follows. There is a great range of jokes whose intent is indeed to make us laugh. But can you really distinguish these as absolutely separate from and in no way resembling the range, at least as great, of such artifacts of speech as: riddles, proverbs, aphorisms, epigrams, gnomic sayings, anecdotes, parables . . . ? Jokes, it is reasonable to claim, have often been the instruments of moral teaching, and even religious revelation. Their humor may be far indeed from laughter (consider the other meaning of "funny": strange, wrong), or may be close to it without invoking it, as in the riddles of the Zen Koan or those Tales of the Hasidim collected by Martin Buber. To take one example only, with what sort of laughter does one respond to this joke by Nietzsche: The last Christian died on the Cross? . . .

The real resemblance, the illuminating one, is that poems and jokes to succeed must do something decisive; which may seem to mean that their endings are somehow contained in their beginnings. This of course is precisely the magical, illusionist, or religious character of art, which has customarily rested on the assumption that God in creating the world did something coherent although mysterious, and that therefore history, at the last great day, would be seen as "like" a drama. So that poetic art has concerned itself characteristically with doubleness, and with what oneness can possibly or impossibly be made out of doubleness: with freedom and necessity, with changelings, with going out and coming back, with echo, mirror, radar, with serious parody; here we approach Aristotle's notions of recognition and reversal, and may see them operant not only in the major forms of tragic poetry, but also and equally in the minute particulars of the poet's art, e.g.,

> With eager feeding food doth choke the feeder,

or,

> Property was thus appalled,
> That the self was not the same;
> Single nature's double name
> Neither two nor one was called.

We see also that the mechanism we have attempted to describe is like that of the plot in a story, also a magical device for dealing with time as though it were eternity, a way of doing two things—at least two!—at once, a way of handling appearance and reality as mirror images of one another. As Rebecca West says, "I am never sure of the reality of a thing until I have seen it twice." The mechanism we mean is what gives us this power of seeing a thing twice: it is like those striking moves in chess, called generally double attack—the pin, the fork, double check, disclosed check—, which show the contrapuntal effect of getting two moves for one and thus, as it were, making time stand still.

Our examples thus far have been chiefly epigrammatic in nature anyhow, and so the resemblance to jokes has been clear enough. But a poem is, for one thing, more ambitious than a joke; literally, it takes more world into its ambit. . . .

> Glory be to God for dappled things,
> For skies of couple-colour as a brindled cow;
> For rose-moles all in stipple upon trout that swim;
> Fresh firecoal chestnut-falls; finches' wings;
> Landscape plotted and pieced—fold, fallow and plough;
> And all trades, their gear and tackle and trim.
>
> All things counter, original, spare, strange;
> Whatever is fickle, freckled (who knows how?)
> With swift, slow; sweet, sour; adazzle, dim;
> He fathers forth whose beauty is past change:
>   Praise Him.

This poem of Hopkins' seems not only to illustrate the relation we have been discussing, but also to take this relation for its subject: it gives a religious guarantee, which is perhaps the only guarantee available, for the real resemblance between particular and generality, between detail and meaning; it so relates the unique with the universal as to show them the same and not the same; its transaction seems to define metaphor for us as: the exception caught becoming the rule. . . .

By the romance of the beginning we are drawn into one sort of world, a belief in one sort of world; of which the decisive emblem at the end offers a sudden and absolute vision. The change could not be more abrupt, but neither could the harmony be more convincing, and one is a function of the other, and both are mysterious. As though to say once more, "It shall be called Bottom's Dream, because it hath no bottom." But now the leaves begin to fall.

WORKING WITH THE SELECTION

1. Nemerov may well have convinced you early on that there is more similarity between jokes and poems than you had supposed. But he saves "the real resemblance, the illuminating one," until the end. What does he say it is?

2. Toward the end of his essay Nemerov suggests that some poetry, and some very good poetry, can be compared only inadequately to a joke. Read the following sonnet by John Keats:

> When I have fears that I may cease to be
>   Before my pen has gleaned my teeming brain,
> Before high-pilèd books, in charact'ry,
>   Hold like rich garners the full ripened grain;
> When I behold, upon the night's starred face,
>   Huge cloudy symbols of a high romance,
> And think that I may never live to trace
>   Their shadows, with the magic hand of chance;
> And when I feel, fair creature of an hour,
>   That I shall never look upon thee more,
> Never have relish in the faery power
>   Of unreflecting love;—then on the shore
> Of the wide world I stand alone, and think
> Till love and fame to nothingness do sink.

To the author this poem was no joke. At about the time he started it he was nursing his brother, fatally ill with tuberculosis, a disease of which he, also, was to become a victim; and whether or not the "fair creature of an hour" was the Fannie Brawne to whom he soon became engaged, Keats, when writing the poem, was deeply involved with life, love, and death. Even so, does the poem give some evidence of supporting Nemerov's thesis?

3. Granted that jokes do, in some particulars, resemble poems, would it be true to say that the better the poem the less it resembles a joke?

5

Literature as Sentences

Richard Ohmann

Richard Ohmann, professor of English at Wesleyan University and editor of
College English, *a journal published by the National Council of Teachers of*
English, *is another of the scholars working to illuminate the interrelationships
of linguistics, literature, rhetoric, and criticism. The following selection appeared
in* College English, *27 (January, 1966).*

Critics permit themselves, for this or that purpose, to identify literature
with great books, with imaginative writing, with expressiveness in writing,
with the non-referential and non-pragmatic, with beauty in language, with
order, with myth, with structured and formed discourse—the list of definitions is nearly endless—with verbal play, with uses of language that stress
the medium itself, with the expression of an age, with dogma, with the *cri
de coeur,* with neurosis. Now of course literature is itself and not another
thing, to paraphrase Bishop Butler; yet analogies and classifications have
merit. For a short space let us think of literature as sentences.

To do so will not tax the imagination, because the work of literature in-
dubitably *is* composed of sentences, most of them well-ordered, many of
them deviant (no pejorative meant), some of them incomplete. But since
much the same holds for dust-jacket copy, the Congressional Record, and
transcripts of board meetings, the small effort required to think of literature
as sentences may be repaid by a correspondingly small insight into literature
as such. Although I do not believe this to be so, for the moment I shall hold
the question in abeyance, and stay mainly within the territory held in common by all forms of discourse. In other words, I am not asking what is special
about the sentences of *literature,* but what is special about *sentences* that
they should interest the student of literature. Although I employ the framework of generative grammar and scraps of its terminology,[1] what I have to
say should not ring in the traditionally educated grammatical ear with out-
landish discord.

First, then, the sentence is the primary unit of understanding. Linguists
have so trenchantly discredited the old definition—"a sentence is a complete
thought"—that the truth therein has fallen into neglect. To be sure, we de-

---

[1] I draw especially on Noam Chomsky, *Aspects of the Theory of Syntax* (Cambridge,
Mass., 1965) and Jerrold J. Katz and Paul Postal, *An Integrated Theory of Linguistic
Descriptions* (Cambridge, Mass., 1964).

limit the class of sentences by formal criteria, but each of the structures that qualifies will express a semantic unity not characteristic of greater or lesser structures. The meanings borne by morphemes, phrases, and clauses hook together to express a meaning that can stand more or less by itself. This point, far from denying the structuralist's definition of a sentence as a single free utterance, or *form,* seems the inevitable corollary of such definitions: forms carry meanings, and it is natural that an independent form should carry an independent meaning. Or, to come at the thing another way, consider that one task of a grammar is to supply structural descriptions, and that the sentence is the unit so described. A structural description specifies the way each part of a sentence is tied to each other part, and the semantic rules of a grammar use the structural description as starting point in interpreting the whole. A reader or hearer does something analogous when he resolves the structures and meanings of sentences, and thereby understands them. Still another way to approach the primacy of the sentence is to notice that the initial symbol for all derivations in a generative grammar is "S" for sentence: the sentence is the domain of grammatical structure— rather like the equation in algebra—and hence the domain of meaning.

These remarks, which will seem truisms to some and heresy to others, cannot be elaborated here. Instead, I want to register an obvious comment on their relevance to literary theory and literary criticism. Criticism, whatever else it does, must interpret works of literature. Theory concerns itself in part with the question, "what things legitimately bear on critical interpretation?" But beyond a doubt, interpretation begins with sentences. Whatever complex apprehension the critic develops of the whole work, that understanding arrives mundanely, sentence by sentence. For this reason, and because the form of a sentence dictates a rudimentary mode of understanding, sentences have a good deal to do with the sublimal meaning (and form) of a literary work. They prepare and direct the reader's attention in particular ways.

My second point about sentences should dispel some of the abstractness of the first. Most sentences directly and obliquely put more linguistic apparatus into operation than is readily apparent, and call on more of the reader's linguistic competence. Typically, a surface structure overlays a deep structure which it may resemble but little, and which determines the "content" of the sentence. For concreteness, take this rather ordinary example, an independent clause from Joyce's "Araby": "Gazing up into the darkness I saw myself as a creature driven and derided by vanity." The surface structure may be represented as follows, using the convention of labeled brackets:[2] $^S[^{Adv}[V + \text{Part} \ ^{PP}[P \ ^{NP}[D + N]]] \ ^{Nuc}[N$

---

[2] Each set of brackets encloses the constituent indicated by its superscript label. The notation is equivalent to a tree diagram. Symbols: S = Sentence, Adv = Adverbial, V = Verb, Part = Particle, PP = Prepositional Phrase, P = Preposition, NP = Noun Phrase, D = Determiner, N = Noun, Nuc = Nucleus, VP = Verb Phrase, Adj = Adjectival.

$^{VP}[V + N\ ^{PP}[P\ ^{NP}[D + N\ ^{Adj}[V + and + V\ ^{PP}[P + N]]]]]]]$ The nucleus has a transitive verb with a direct object. In the deep structure, by contrast, the matrix sentence is of the form $^{S}[NP\ ^{VP}[V + Complement + NP]]$: "I + saw + as a creature + me." It has embedded in it one sentence with an intransitive verb and an adverb of location—"I gazed up into the darkness"—and two additional sentences with transitive verbs and direct objects—"Vanity drove the creature," and "Vanity derided the creature." Since "darkness" and "vanity" are derived nouns, the embedded sentences must in turn contain embeddings, of, say "(Something) is dark" and "(Someone) is vain." Thus the word "vanity," object of a preposition in the surface structure, is subject of two verbs in the deep, and its root is a predicate adjective. The word "creature," object of a preposition in the surface structure, also has a triple function in the deep structure: verbal complement, direct object of "drive," and direct object of "deride." Several transformations (including the passive) deform the six basic sentences, and several others relate them to each other. The complexity goes much farther, but this is enough to suggest that a number of grammatical processes are required to generate the initial sentence and that its structure is moderately involved. Moreover, a reader will not understand the sentence unless he grasps the relations marked in the deep structure. As it draws on a variety of syntactic resources, the sentence also activates a variety of semantic processes and modes of comprehension, yet in brief compass and in a surface *form* that radically permutes *content*.

I choose these terms wilfully: that there are interesting grounds here for a form-content division seems to me quite certain. Joyce might have written, "I gazed up into the darkness. I saw myself as a creature. The creature was driven by vanity. The creature was derided by vanity." Or, "Vanity drove and derided the creature I saw myself as, gazer up, gazer into the darkness." Content remains roughly the same, for the basic sentences are unchanged. But the style is different. And each revision structures and screens the content differently. The original sentence acquires part of its meaning and part of its unique character by resonating against these unwritten alternatives. It is at the level of sentences, I would argue, that the distinction between form and content comes clear, and that the intuition of style has its formal equivalent.[3]

Sentences play on structure in still another way, more shadowy, but of considerable interest for criticism. It is a commonplace that not every noun can serve as object of every verb, that a given noun can be modified only by adjectives of certain classes, and so on. For instance, a well-defined group of verbs, including "exasperate," "delight," "please," and "astound," require animate objects; another group, including "exert," "behave," and "pride," need reflexive objects. Such interdependencies abound in a gram-

---

[3] I have argued the point at length in "Generative Grammars and the Concept of Literary Style," *Word*, 20 (Dec. 1964), 423–439.

mar, which must account for them by subcategorizing nouns, adjectives, and the other major classes.[4] The importance of categorical restrictions is clearest in sentences that disregard them—deviant sentences. It happens that the example from Joyce is slightly deviant in this way: in one of the underlying sentences—"Vanity derided the creature"—a verb that requires a human subject in fact has as its subject the abstract noun "vanity." The dislocation forces the reader to use a supplementary method of interpretation: here, presumably he aligns "vanity" (the word) with the class of human nouns and sees vanity (the thing) as a distinct, active power in the narrator's psyche. Such deviance is so common in metaphor and elsewhere that one scarcely notices it, yet it helps to specify the way things happen in the writer's special world, and the modes of thought appropriate to that world.

I have meant to suggest that sentences normally comprise intricacies of form and meaning whose effects are not the less substantial for their sublety. From this point, what sorts of critical description follow? Perhaps I can direct attention toward a few tentative answers, out of the many that warrant study, and come finally to a word on critical theory. Two samples must carry the discussion; one is the final sentence of "The Secret Sharer":

> Walking to the taffrail, I was in time to make out, on the very edge of a darkness thrown by a towering black mass like the very gateway of Erebus—yes, I was in time to catch an evanescent glimpse of my white hat left behind to mark the spot where the secret sharer of my cabin and of my thoughts, as though he were my second self, had lowered himself into the water to take his punishment: a free man, a proud swimmer striking out for a new destiny.

I hope others will agree that the sentence justly represents its author: that it portrays a mind energetically stretching to subdue a dazzling experience *outside* the self, in a way that has innumerable counterparts elsewhere in Conrad. How does scrutiny of the deep structure support this intuition? First, notice a matter of emphasis, of rhetoric. The matrix sentence, which lends a surface form to the whole, is "# S # I was in time # S #" (repeated twice). The embedded sentences that complete it are "I walked to the taffrail," "I made out + NP," and "I caught + NP." The point of departure, then, is the narrator himself: where he was, what he did, what he saw. But a glance at the deep structure will explain why one feels a quite different emphasis in the sentence as a whole: seven of the embedded sentences have "sharer" as grammatical subject; in another three the subject is a noun linked to "sharer" by the copula; in two "sharer" is direct object; and in two more "share" is the verb. Thus thirteen sentences go to the semantic development of "sharer," as follows:

[4] Chomsky discusses ways of doing this in *Aspects of the Theory of Syntax*, Chapter 2.

1) The secret sharer had lowered the secret sharer into the water.
2) The secret sharer took his punishment.
3) The secret sharer swam.
4) The secret sharer was a swimmer.
5) The swimmer was proud.
6) The swimmer struck out for a new destiny.
7) The secret sharer was a man.
8) The man was free.
9) The secret sharer was my second self.
10) The secret sharer had (it).
11) (Someone) punished the secret sharer.
12) (Someone) shared my cabin.
13) (Someone) shared my thoughts.

In a fundamental way, the sentence is mainly *about* Leggatt, although the surface structure indicates otherwise.

Yet the surface structure does not simply throw a false scent, and the way the sentence comes to focus on the secret sharer is also instructive. It begins with the narrator, as we have seen, and "I" is the subject of five basic sentences early on. Then "hat" takes over as the syntactic focus, receiving development in seven base sentences. Finally, the sentence arrives at "sharer." This progression in the deep structure rather precisely mirrors both the rhetorical movement of the sentence from the narrator to Leggatt via the hat that links them, and the thematic effect of the sentence, which is to tranfer Leggatt's experience to the narrator via the narrator's vicarious and actual participation in it. Here I shall leave this abbreviated rhetorical analysis, with a cautionary word: I do not mean to suggest that only an examination of deep structure reveals Conrad's skillful emphasis—on the contrary, such an examination supports and in a sense explains what any careful reader of the story notices.

A second critical point adjoins the first. The morpheme "share" appears once in the sentence, but it performs at least twelve separate functions, as the deep structure shows. "I," "hat," and "mass" also play complex roles. Thus at certain points the sentence has extraordinary "density," as I shall call it. Since a reader must register these multiple functions in order to understand the sentence, it is reasonable to suppose that the very process of understanding concentrates his attention on centers of density. Syntactic density, I am suggesting, exercises an important influence on literary comprehension.

Third, by tuning in on deep structures, the critic may often apprehend more fully the build of a literary work. I have already mentioned how the syntax of Conrad's final sentence develops his theme. Consider two related points. First, "The Secret Sharer" is an initiation story in which the hero, through moral and mental effort, locates himself vis á vis society and the natural world, and thus passes into full manhood. The syntax of the last sentence schematizes the relationships he has achieved, in identifying with

Leggatt's heroic defection, and in fixing on a point of reference—the hat—that connects him to the darker powers of nature. Second, the syntax and meaning of the last sentence bring to completion the pattern initiated by the syntax and meaning of the first few sentences, which present human beings and natural objects in thought-bewildering disarray. I can do no more than mention these structural connections here, but I am convinced that they supplement and help explain an ordinary critical reading of the story.

Another kind of critical point concerns habits of meaning revealed by sentence structure. One example must suffice. We have already marked how the sentence shifts its focus from "I" to "hat" to "sharer." A similar process goes on in the first part of the sentence: "I" is the initial subject, with "hat" as object. "Hat" is subject of another base sentence that ends with "edge," the object of a preposition in a locative phrase. "Edge" in turn becomes object of a sentence that has "darkness" as subject. "Darkness" is object in one with "mass" as subject, and in much the same way the emphasis passes to "gateway" and "Erebus." The syntax executes a chaining effect here which cuts across various kinds of construction. Chaining is far from the only type of syntactic expansion, but it is one Conrad favors. I would suggest this hypothesis: that syntactically and in other ways Conrad draws heavily on operations that link one thing with another associatively. This may be untrue, or if true it may be unrevealing; certainly it needs clearer expression. But I think it comes close to something that we all notice in Conrad, and in any case the general critical point exemplified here deserves exploration: that each writer tends to exploit deep linguistic resources in characteristic ways—that his style, in other words, rests on syntactic options within sentences (see fn. 3)—and that these syntactic preferences correlate with habits of meaning that tell us something about his mode of conceiving experience.

My other sample passage is the first sentence of Dylan Thomas' "A Winter's Tale":

> It is a winter's tale
> That the snow blind twilight ferries over the lakes
> And floating fields from the farm in the cup of the vales,
> Gliding windless through the hand folded flakes,
> The pale breath of cattle at the stealthy sail,
>
> And the stars falling cold,
> And the smell of hay in the snow, and the far owl
> Warning among the folds, and the frozen hold
> Flocked with the sheep white smoke of the farm house cowl
> In the river wended vales where the tale was told.

Some of the language here raises a large and familiar critical question, that of unorthodox grammar in modern poetry, which has traditionally received a somewhat facile answer. We say that loss of confidence in order and reason leads to dislocation of syntax, as if errant grammar were an appeal to the irrational. A cursory examination of deep structure in verse like Thomas', or even in wildly deviant verse like some of Cummings', will show the matter to be more complex than that.

How can deviance be most penetratingly analyzed? Normally, I think, in terms of the base sentences that lie beneath ungrammatical constructions. Surface structure alone does not show "the river wended vales" (line 10) to be deviant, since we have many well-formed constructions of the same word-class sequence: "machine made toys," "sun dried earth," and so on. The particular deviance of "the river wended vales" becomes apparent when we try to refer it to an appropriate underlying structure. A natural one to consider is "the river wends the vales" (cf. "the sun dries the earth"), but of course this makes "wend" a transitive verb, which it is not, except in the idiomatic "wend its way." So does another possibility, "NP + wends the vales with rivers" (cf. "NP + makes the toys by machine"). This reading adds still other kinds of deviance, in that the Noun Phrase will have to be animate, and in that rivers are too cumbersome to be used instrumentally in the way implied. Let us assume that the reader rejects the more flagrant deviance in favor of the less, and we are back to "the river wends the vales." Suppose now that "the vales" is not after all a direct object, but a locative construction, as in "the wolf prowls the forest"; this preserves the intransitivity of "wend," and thereby avoids a serious form of deviance. But notice that there is *no* transformation in English that converts "the wolf prowls the forest" into "the wolf prowled forest," and so this path is blocked as well. Assume, finally, that given a choice between shifting a word like "wend" from one subclass to another and adding a transformational rule to the grammar, a reader will choose the former course; hence he selects the first interpretation mentioned: "the river wends the vales."

If so, how does he understand the anomalous transitive use of "wend"? Perhaps by assimilating the verb to a certain class that may be either transitive or intransitive: "paint," "rub," and the like. Then he will take "wend" to mean something like "make a mark on the surface of, by traversing"; in fact, this is roughly how I read Thomas' phrase. But I may be wrong, and in any case my goal is not to solve the riddle. Rather, I have been leading up to the point that every syntactically deviant construction has more than one possible interpretation, and that readers resolve the conflict by a process that involves deep and intricately motivated decisions and thus puts to work considerable linguistic knowledge, syntactic as well as semantic.[5] The decisions nearly always go on implicitly, but aside from that I see no reason

[5] See Jerrold J. Katz, "Semi-sentences," in Jerry A. Fodor and Jerrold J. Katz, eds., *The Structure of Language* (1964), pp. 400–416. The same volume includes two other relevant papers, Chomsky, "Degrees of Grammaticalness," pp. 384–389, and Paul Ziff, "On Understanding 'Understanding Utterances,'" pp. 390–399. Samuel R. Levin has briefly discussed ungrammatical poetry within a similar framework in *Linguistic Structures in Poetry* (The Hague, 1962), Chapters 2 and 3.

to think that deviance of this sort is an appeal to, or an expression of, irrationality.

Moreover, when a poet deviates from normal syntax he is not doing what comes most habitually, but is making a special sort of choice. And since there are innumerable kinds of deviance, we should expect that the ones elected by a poem or poet spring from particular semantic impulses, particular ways of looking at experience. For instance, I think such a tendency displays itself in Thomas' lines. The construction just noted conceives the passing of rivers through vales as an agent acting upon an object. Likewise, "flocked" in line 9 becomes a transitive verb, and the spatial connection Thomas refers to—flocks in a hold—is reshaped into an action—flocking —performed by an unnamed agent upon the hold. There are many other examples in the poem of deviance that projects unaccustomed activity and process upon nature. Next, notice that beneath line 2 is the sentence "the twilight is blind," in which an inanimate noun takes an animate adjective, and that in line 5 "sail" takes the animate adjective "stealthy." This type of deviance also runs throughout the poem: Thomas sees nature as personal. Again, "twilight" is subject of "ferries," and should thus be a concrete noun, as should the object, "tale." Here and elsewhere in the poem the division between substance and abstraction tends to disappear. Again and again syntactic deviance breaks down categorical boundaries and converts juxtaposition into action, inanimate into human, abstract into physical, static into active. Now, much of Thomas' poetry displays the world as process, as interacting forces and repeating cycles, in which human beings and human thought are indifferently caught up.[6] I suggest that Thomas' syntactical irregularities often serve this vision of things. To say so, of course, is only to extend the natural critical premise that a good poet sets linguistic forms to work for him in the cause of artistic and thematic form. And if he strays from grammatical patterns he does not thereby leave language or reason behind: if anything, he draws the more deeply on linguistic structure and on the processes of human understanding that are implicit in our use of well-formed sentences.

Most of what I have said falls short of adequate precision, and much of the detail rests on conjecture about English grammar, which at this point is by no means fully understood. But I hope that in loosely stringing together several hypotheses about the fundamental role of the sentence I have indicated some areas where a rich exchange between linguistics and critical theory might eventually take place. To wit, the elusive intuition we have of *form* and *content* may turn out to be anchored in a distinction between the surface structures and the deep structures of sentences. If so, syntactic theory will also feed into the theory of *style*. Still more evidently, the proper *analysis* of styles waits on a satisfactory analysis of sentences. Matters of *rhetoric,* such as emphasis and order, also promise to come clearer as we

---

[6] Ralph Maud's fine study, *Entrances to Dylan Thomas' Poetry* (Pittsburgh, 1963), describes the phenomenon well in a chapter called "Process Poems."

better understand internal relations in sentences. More generally, we may be able to enlarge and deepen our concept of literary *structure* as we are increasingly able to make it subsume linguistic structure—including especially the structure of deviant sentences. And most important, since critical understanding follows and builds on understanding of sentences, generative grammar should eventually be a reliable assistant in the effort of seeing just how a given literary work sifts through a reader's mind, what cognitive and emotional processes it sets in motion, and what organization of experience it encourages. In so far as critical theory concerns itself with meaning, it cannot afford to bypass the complex and elegant structures that lie at the inception of all verbal meaning.

WORKING WITH THE SELECTION

1. Costello, Gowers, and to a degree Nemerov were all concerned with the use of words in literature; Ohmann is interested in the use of sentences. What insights does Ohmann say can be gained by examining sentences that cannot be gained by examining words?

2. Ohmann analyzes style within the framework of the transformational generative grammar elucidated by Chomsky and his followers. Would his method and his conclusions be altered if he had used Lamb's stratificational grammar or Pike's tagmemics?

3. Reconsider Ohmann's final paragraph. What does he conclude? Now recall that this article was published in *College English*, the official publication of the College Section of the National Council of Teachers of English. Ohmann probably felt that he was addressing his fellow English teachers. How might he have altered his conclusion if he had been addressing you?

4. You are familiar with such concepts as universal grammar and deep and surface structure. What sort of grammar does Ohmann think will reveal much about style?

6

Tough Talk and How to Detect It

Walker Gibson

*Walker Gibson, professor of English at the University of Massachusetts, combines the perceptivity of a poet (*The Reckless Spenders, *1954;* Come as You Are, *1958) with the good sense of a master teacher and the wit and patience of a serious student of rhetoric. In* Tough, Sweet & Stuffy: An Essay on Modern American Prose Styles *(1966), Gibson shows how the study of language and rhetoric can contribute to our understanding of literature and criticism. The first part of the following selection from the book illustrates what Gibson means by Tough Talk. The second part of the selection is taken from Appendix A, in which he describes his method of analyzing style and elaborates some of his results. Included are all Gibson's questions about grammatical-rhetorical qualities but only a few of his detailed discussions of the questions.*

TOUGH TALK: THE RHETORIC OF FREDERIC HENRY

I did not say anything. I was always embarrassed by the words. . . .

When a new style swims into our ken, as Hemingway's did in the 1920s, it is new, or was new, in respect to a historical situation. People brought to their reading, just as they still do of course, a set of assumptions about how books ought to be written. No novelist would be interested in a reader who had never read a novel, or who had never experienced, as *he* has experienced, the going literature of the recent past. So Hemingway's assumed reader of the 1920s had an ear tuned to nineteenth-century rhythms and attitudes; it was in their light that Hemingway's style appeared so fresh and exciting. It is still exciting, if not exactly fresh, a generation later, which is testimony enough to the power of a great writer.

But in order to remind ourselves of some of the stylistic expectations against which Hemingway was first read, and to some extent must still be read, it will be useful to contrast the opening of *A Farewell to Arms* (1929) with the opening of a standard sort of American novel of forty years earlier. The opening I have chosen, from W. D. Howells' *A Modern Instance* (1888), has some superficial resemblance in stage setting to Hemingway's opening that may make the contrast in style the more striking. In each case a narrator is introducing us to a scene as well as to himself, and both scenes include a *village* on a *plain*, in the *summer*, with a view of *mountains* and a *river*.

The village stood on a wide plain, and around it rose the mountains. They were green to their tops in summer, and in the winter white through their serried pines and drifting mists, but at every season serious and beautiful, furrowed with hollow shadows, and taking the light on masses and stretches of iron-grey crag. The river swam through the plain in long curves, and slipped away at last through an unseen pass to the southward, tracing a score of miles in its course over a space that measured but three or four. The plain was very fertile, and its features, if few and of purely utilitarian beauty, had a rich luxuriance, and there was a tropical riot of vegetation when the sun of July beat on those northern fields. They waved with corn and oats to the feet of the mountains, and the potatoes covered a vast acreage with the lines of their intense, coarse green; the meadows were deep with English grass to the banks of the river, that, doubling and returning upon itself, still marked its way with a dense fringe of alders and white birches.

In the late summer of that year we lived in a house in a village that looked across the river and the plain to the mountains. In the bed of the river there were pebbles and boulders, dry and white in the sun, and the water was clear and swiftly moving and blue in the channels. Troops went by the house and down the road and the dust they raised powdered the leaves of the trees. The trunks of the trees too were dusty and the leaves fell early that year and we saw the troops marching along the road and the dust rising and leaves, stirred by the breeze, falling and the soldiers marching and afterward the road bare and white except for the leaves.

The plain was rich with crops; there were many orchards of fruit trees and beyond the plains the mountains were brown and bare. There was fighting in the mountains and at night we could see the flashes from the artillery. In the dark it was like summer lightning, but the nights were cool and there was not the feeling of a storm coming.

Who are these two people talking to us?

The narrator in Passage A (Howells) is concerned with making us see and know the landscape surrounding the village, and he can do this because he can occupy a position where *he* sees and knows this landscape intimately. Let us begin by locating this position, which is expressible in respect to both space and time. Physically, the narrator can speak as from a cloud, a balloon, floating wide-eyed over the plain. He sees large features of the scene—the mountains, the course of the winding river, the fields with their crops. It is a bird's-eye view. He also occupies a favorable position in time. He has been here before, he *knows*. He knows, for example, how the mountains look not only in summer (the *then* of the opening scene), but in winter as well. (Sentence A-2.) He knows (A-3), even though it is not at present visible, that the river slips away "through an unseen pass" to the southward. This is a speaker whose particular rhetorical personality, which would look very strange in a novel of the second half of the twentieth century, serves to inspire our confidence, partly from its very antiquity. Note that as assumed readers we date the speaker immediately, however vaguely, and date ourselves as well, by ruling out some twentieth-century suspicions and expectations. We are introduced to a familiar kind of traditional gentlemanly voice whose tones we associate with Standard Literature, and whose word we accept absolutely. This man knows what there is to know about this scene. We are in good hands.

The man talking in Passage B speaks to us from an utterly different position. As he thinks back on his experience in the village—and note that it is *his* experience that he thinks back on—the positions he occupies are drastically more limited than those of our airborne observer in A. Everything described in B can be seen (or almost seen) from one place, the house where *he* lived. The language keeps reminding us of this limitation by returning to the speaker and his companions (*we*) and their vantage point for seeing and feeling. The house "looked across the river"; "we saw the troops"; "we could see the flashes"; "there was not the feeling of a storm coming." The speaker's range is similarly limited in time; all he tells us about is the way things looked during one particular late summer as it became autumn. The other seasons, before he came to live in the village, or after he left, he presumably doesn't know about. We hear the familiar "flatness" of the voice addressing us, the speaker's refusal to say more than he knows from ordinary human experience. He is close-lipped. The simplicity of his style, the apparent simplicity of it, is of course notorious. You would not call this man genial. He behaves rather as if he had known us, the reader, a long time and therefore doesn't have to pay us very much attention. He is more tense, more intense, than A. And after all, we should observe, he is dealing with images of war, and not with a peaceful New England landscape.

So much for one reader's quick first impression of the two personalities addressing us and the positions from which they speak. But I propose a longer look at some grammatical and rhetorical peculiarities of these two speakers, returning often to their personalities and positions to ask how these have been created, and how we may refine our first impressions. How are these impressions justified by the language, if they are? How do details of wording force us to certain conclusions about the man we're being introduced to? If some of what follows seems alarmingly statistical and detailed,

I would argue that only by such devices can we begin to understand the effort that went into these two creative acts.

Words, Their Size

Everybody knows that Hemingway's diction is characterized by short, simple, largely Anglo-Saxon words. Howells' vocabulary is more conventionally extensive. Actually, in the Howells passage, almost three-quarters of the words are monosyllables, while only one word out of twenty is longer than two syllables. It is hardly an elaborate or affected diction. Yet we recognize in Howells that there are particular words, especially the longer words, which for various reasons would be unthinkable in Hemingway. Among them are *beautiful, utilitarian, luxuriance*—and I shall have more to say about them below. For the present, we note that in passage B, the Hemingway passage, over four-fifths of the words (82 per cent) are of one syllable only, an extremely high proportion. What is more remarkable only two words, or about one in a hundred, are more than two syllables in length. (These two are *afterward* and *artillery,* neither of them very formidable.) The rigorous selection, or limitation, in vocabulary that these figures imply is drastic, and certainly contributes largely to our sense of a laconic, hard-bitten, close-talking fellow. He is literally *curt.*

Modifiers

An important distinction in the way the two speakers choose words has to do with the frequency of their modifiers. What would we expect of a man who knows, who is magically airborne over the landscape, as against a speaker who is laconically reporting the facts of his own limited experience? We would expect that the former would be more free with his modifiers, would be, that is, willing to name the qualities and virtues of things, not just the things themselves. Actually there are about twice as many modifiers in the Howells as in the Hemingway. Some of Howells' adjectives, in particular, have obvious implications of value: *serious, beautiful, rich, utilitarian*. While many others are simply descriptive (if that is possible), such as *green, deep, dense,* every one of the modifiers in B is of the type that purports to avoid value and simply state facts, especially physical facts: *dry, white, blue, dusty, swiftly,* and so on.

Nouns and Repetition

A count of nouns in the two passages results in almost identical figures. But because of a great difference in repetition of nouns, there is a difference in the actual repertoire the two writers use. There are 47 appearances of nouns in A, and because repetition is negligible there are 43 different nouns used. In Hemingway I count 46 noun appearances with a remarkable refrain of repetition. Fourteen nouns appear twice or three times; only 32 different nouns are to be found in the passage. The effect of this rather astonishing contrast is worth speculating on. It helps us, again, to understand why we could call the B narrator "close-lipped." He simply doesn't use many words! There is a critical suggestion to the speaker's personality, as if he were saying, I'm not one of your fancy writers, always scrabbling around for elegant variation. I say what I mean. If I mean the same thing twice, I *say* the same thing twice, and I don't care if it offends the so-called rules of so-called graceful prose.

Imagery, Abstract and Concrete

It is a commonplace about modern writers, and it may seem to be borne out by our analysis up to this point, that the more recent writers are concerned hardheadedly with things-as-they-are, with precise description rather than with the evaluative blur that we like to think characterizes the older literature. Everybody's passion nowadays for being "concrete" rather than "abstract" represents a fashionable general attitude. But, judging from the present evidence, the commonplace may not be true. Nobody knows, I suspect, how to distinguish concrete words from abstract in any very satisfactory way, but suppose we apply in all innocence this rule of thumb: which of our two speakers tells us more about the scene, supposing we wanted to paint a picture of it? There is no doubt that it is Howells. It is not simply Hemingway's paucity of nouns and modifiers that handicaps him as a scene-painter. It is his very choice of the nouns and modifiers that he does use. Where Hemingway writes *trees*, Howells names them—*alders, birches*. Where Hemingway refers to *crops* and *orchards*, Howells gives us *corn, oats*, and *potatoes*. It is true that Howells includes some words normally thought of as "abstract" (*features, beauty, luxuriance*), while Hemingway gives us plenty of "concrete" nouns, *pebbles* and *boulders, mountains, orchards, soldiers*. But the result is what matters, and in this case the result is that the language creates, in A, a narrator who *cares* about telling us what the landscape looked like, and in B we sense a narrator who cares about something else.

What else does he care about? Why does he, in spite of his superficial and apparent concreteness, tell us so little specifically about the scene? Because the scene, from his position, is not important except as it contributes to his own feelings, his remembered feelings. His recurrences to the act of personal viewing mentioned earlier (*We saw, we could see*) are reminders of the highly personal interest of this speaker. He is not concerned with having us see the landscape, but in having us understand *how he felt*. This is a very different aim; all his devices of grammar and rhetoric are chosen to achieve this aim.

Sentences, Their Size and Structure

Again the short sentence in Hemingway is a commonplace observation, and it no doubt contributes to the curtness we have been noticing. Actually, in these two passages, the difference is only between an average length of 38 words and of 28 words—nothing very spectacular. Much more interesting is the grammatical structure of the sentences of each passage. In A we have both compound and compound-complex sentences, with considerable subordination of clauses. In B we have largely compound sentences made up of coordinate clauses strung together with *and*. (Sentence B-4 is a good example.) When we count up subordinate clauses in the two passages, we discover that in B there are only two, and they are informal and inconspicuous. "The dust they raised," for instance, gives us a modifying clause without the signal *that,* an omission common in oral speech. We are reminded that the narrator knows us, speaks familiarly, doesn't in fact go out of his way for us much. Modifying clauses in A, on the other hand, are crucially different. Here their formal qualities are directed not toward maintaining a pose of familiarity with a reader, but instead toward seriously clarifying for the reader, whom the speaker has only just met, what the landscape looked like. The second half of Sentence A-5, for example, offers us a subordinate clause of some elegance and considerable skill.

> . . . the meadows were deep with English grass to the banks of the river, that, doubling and returning upon itself, still marked its way with a dense fringe of alders and white birches.

One may not wish to go so far as to say that the very phrasing here, in its leisurely meandering, doubles and returns upon itself like the river, but one would have to say, at least, that a subordinate clause of this kind, punctuated in this way, would look very odd in Hemingway. You do not talk this way to someone you know easily and intimately.

More spectacular in the Hemingway style, of course, are the successions of coordinate clauses linked by *and*. It is a highly significant grammatical expression, and its significance can be grasped if one tries irreverently to rewrite a coordinate Hemingway sentence in more traditional patterns of subordination. Here is the original sentence B-4, for instance:

> The trunks of the trees too were dusty and the leaves fell early that year and we saw the troops marching along the road and the dust rising and leaves, stirred by the breeze, falling and the soldiers marching and afterward the road bare and white except for the leaves.

Now here is a version attempting to subordinate some of the clauses:

> The leaves fell early that year, which revealed the dusty trunks of the trees and the marching troops on the road; when the troops went by, we saw the dust rise, while the leaves fell, stirred by the breeze, but

after the soldiers had gone the road was bare and white except for the leaves.

The original B-6 reads this way:

> There was fighting in the mountains and at night we could see the flashes from the artillery.

If we subordinate one of these clauses, we must state a relation between them—for example the relation of logical cause:

> We knew there was fighting in the mountains, for at night we could see the flashes from the artillery.

Now the damage done to the original, in both cases, is of course catastrophic. In the original B-6, the speaker doesn't say how he knew there was fighting in the mountains. It was just there, ominous, baldly stated. The awareness of the fighting and the seeing of the flashes are all part of a huge complex of personal feeling, and the connections between the various sensations are left (deliberately of course) ambiguous. This is a highly refined example of the leave-it-up-to-the-reader teachnique that I found so irritating in "Private World" of the preceding chapter.

> This is why so many people do not know how to read. They have been taught to turn books into abstractions.

There, as in Hemingway, the logical connection between the two unconnected independent structures was unstated. But there is a difference. In "Private World," the intended connection is plain. What in Hemingway was a suggestive technique for implying several possible connections while stating none, becomes merely a rhetorical gimmick for forcing the reader to supply an obvious meaning. This is what we mean by the Misuse of a Style.

The Definite Article

I have mentioned a difference in relation with their assumed readers that the two speakers suggest. Whereas the speaker in A keeps his distance, using what we think of as fairly formal discourse, the speaker in B seems to have known the reader before and doesn't trouble himself to explain things as one must for an acquaintance one has just met. A possible cause of this difference between the two speakers can be found in the different ways they use a simple three-letter word—the word *the*. To be statistical again, the incidence of the definite article in the Howells paragraph comes to about 8 per cent; in the Hemingway passage it is about 18 per cent, or almost one word out of every five. It is clearly the Hemingway passage that is unconventional, labeling every other noun with *the*.

What is the effect of such an extraordinary preoccupation?

> In the late summer of that year we lived in a house in a village that looked across the river and the plain to the mountains.

One's first naive response to that sentence might be some perfectly pardonable questions. "What year? What river, what plain, what mountains? I don't know what you're talking about." Precisely: the *real* reader doesn't know what the speaker is talking about, but the assumed reader doesn't bother about that. *He* has been placed in a situation where he is expected to assume that he does know what the speaker is talking about. It is as if, for the assumed reader, a conversation had been going on before he opened the book, a conversation that laid the groundwork for all this assumed intimacy. Or it is as if—another analogy—we were suddenly plopped down in a chair listening to a man who has begun telling a story to another man who has just left the room. Curiously the storyteller confuses us with the friend who has just departed, and we find ourselves taking the place of this friend, yoked to the teller as he was. And of course, as always, we can't talk back.

The difference can be realized if again we try an irreverent revision, excising most of the definite articles:

> Late in 1915, when I was an officer in the Italian army, my unit lived in a house in a northern Italian village that looked across a river toward some mountains.

In this version, the speaker makes no such assumptions about the common knowledge shared by himself and his assumed reader. Now he names the year and the locale, he defines who "we" are, and his consistent indefinite articles maintain a more distant posture with his reader.

My revision again, naturally, is disastrous. It does more than create distance between reader and speaker. Reading it, one has the impression that the narrator doesn't care much about what he's saying. It starts off like any old war reminiscence. But in Hemingway's version, for many more reasons than I've been able to express here, we feel already the excitement, or what I have to call the intensity, of the narrator. He is deeply involved in his feelings about what he is going to tell us, and perhaps one reason he can give that impression is that he can pretend not to have to worry very much about us, about cueing us in in the conventional way.

The first word of the Howells passage is *The,* but the quickest reading reveals the difference. Here the narrator is describing a scene as if we had never seen it before—as indeed we have not. We need not assume the same kind of intimate relation with the narrator; he keeps us relatively at a distance, and he does not use (as Hemingway does) the first person pronoun.

Yet even the Howells narrator launches us somewhat *in medias res,* assuming we will not ask, of his first two words, "What village?" Again the removal of the definite article will show how a speaker can back off even further from his reader, beginning a wholly new relationship with new information: A village stood on a wide plain, and around it rose mountains. One feels, of that sentence, that it should be prefaced by "Once upon a time," and it may be that in telling a fairy story, part of the trick is to assume very little from your reader. Nor is there any effort, in the fairy story, to make the narrator or his tale sound "real." In fact the effort must be just the other way. In the Hemingway kind of story, quite a lot is implied, through intensity of tone, about how seriously, how real, we are to take all this. There is a scale of pretension we could trace, something like this:

Fairy story: Here's a little tale of something that (let's pretend) might have happened a long, long time ago in the Land of Nod.

Howells: Here is a story about people behaving much as people in life do behave; I hope you enjoy it.

Hemingway: This is how it really felt to me when it all happened. (Oh yes, if you insist, it's a *story.*)

My passages can't possibly justify all that. But if there is anything to such a scale, then the Hemingway rhetoric has the effect of including, as part of its fiction, the fiction that all this really happened to a narrator who felt intensely about it, and the reader is maneuvered into a position of sympathy with a person whose principal concern is not with the reader, not with the scene he is describing, but with himself and his own feelings. There is a consequent lift of the voice, a tension in the vocal chords. That is no armchair, relaxed and comfortable, that the Tough Talker occupies.

It will be useful now to summarize the Tough Talker's manner by means of a tentative definition of his personality and rhetoric. In doing so, we remember that our source is only the first 189 words of one Hemingway novel. Nor should we assume that the character described here is absolutely new to literature. What we do have here is an identifiable speaker (Frederic Henry by name), defined in an identifiable rhetoric, some of whose qualities we will be able to recognize in later prose.

A Description of a Tough Talker

Frederic Henry is a hard man who has been around in a violent world, and who partially conceals his strong feelings behind a curt manner. He is in fact more concerned with those feelings than he is with the outward scenes he presents, or with cultivating the good wishes of the reader to whom he is introducing himself. He can ignore these traditional services to the reader because he assumes in advance much intimacy and common knowledge. (We are beyond explanations, beyond politenesses.) He presents himself as a believable human character, without omniscience: he knows only what he knows, and is aware of his limitations.

His rhetoric, like his personality, shows its limitations openly: short sentences, "crude" repetitions of words, simple grammatical structures with little subordinating. (I have no use for elegant variation, for the worn-out gentilities of traditional prose.) His tense intimacy with his assumed reader, another man who has been around, is implied by colloquial patterns from oral speech and by a high frequency of the definite article. He lets his reader make logical and other connections between elements. (You know what I mean; I don't have to spell it all out for *you*.) He prefers naming things to describing them, and avoids modification, especially when suggestive of value. All these habits of behavior suggest that he is self-conscious about his language—even about language generally. He is close-lipped, he watches his words.

This suspiciousness about language, only implied in our passage, deserves amplification particularly because it will concern us again later, in other writers. Part of the violent world that the Tough Talker has been around in is the violent verbal world, where words have been so abused that they have lost their lives. In a famous passage later on in *Farewell to Arms* Frederic Henry makes the point explicitly:

> I did not say anything. I was always embarrassed by the words sacred, glorious, and sacrifice, and the expression in vain. We had heard them, sometimes standing in the rain almost out of earshot, so that only the shouted words came through, and had read them, on proclamations, now for a long time, and I had seen nothing sacred, and the things that were glorious had no glory and the sacrifices were like the stockyards at Chicago if nothing was done with the meat except to bury it. There were many words that you could not stand to hear and finally only the names of places had dignity. Certain numbers were the same way and certain dates and these with the names of the places were all you could say and have them mean anything. Abstract words such as glory, honor, courage, or hallow were obscene beside the concrete names of villages, and the numbers of roads, the names of rivers, the numbers of regiments and the dates.

Such a negative attitude toward language, however understandable and right in this novel, becomes deadly in later and less skillful hands. For some members of the Beat Generation all language became meaningless—a conviction peculiarly difficult for a writer to live with. The conviction may have had something to do with the poverty of beat style, and with the early demise of that movement. In any event, a self-conscious anxiety about the very reliability of words has become one of the crosses the modern writer has to bear. Fortunately it can be borne in many ways, from comedy to despair. . . .

STYLES AND STATISTICS: A MODEL T STYLE MACHINE

Out of the various observations we have made about our three styles, is it possible—is it even proper—to construct a systematic grammar and rhetoric for each? No, possibly not. Nevertheless what follows is an effort to make a beginning in that direction. I offer here a kind of Style Machine, of a pre-Model T order, designed to measure the tone of a prose passage. It considers only a tiny fraction of the possibilities, it will not discriminate between good and bad writing, it is full of bugs. Much of its terminology is hopelessly square, derived from traditional grammar at least as much as from modern linguistics. But it will serve at least to summarize some of the distinctions setting Tough Talk apart from Sweet Talk and from Stuffy Talk, and it may furthermore suggest to somebody else a way of improving on this primitive beginning. . . .

The classification of these passages [those Gibson has analyzed] into the three categories was made, in the first place impressionistically. That is, it was a question simply as to whether our reading experience brought us into contact with a speaker or voice of the indicated type. The types of individuals we were looking for, to repeat, were defined briefly like this: (1) a hard fellow who has been around in a violent world and who pays us very little mind; (2) an affable fellow who is explicitly familiar with us and who knows just who we are; (3) a bloodless fellow who often speaks for an organization and not for himself, and who keeps his distance from us.

How are these impressions of personalities to be explained in terms of grammar and rhetoric—if they are?

Out of dozens of possibilities, I propose sixteen grammatical-rhetorical qualities as ways of isolating styles, of accounting for distinctions that we feel in the voices addressing us. Several of them we have already considered at some length. I put them in the form of questions.

Questions About Word-Size

1. What is the proportion of monosyllables in the passage?
2. What is the proportion of words of more than two syllables?

Questions About Substantives

3. How many first- and second-person pronouns does the passage contain? How many imperatives are there ("*you* understood")?
4. Are the subjects of the finite verbs mostly neuter nouns, or do they refer to people?

Questions About Verbs

5. What is the proportion of finite verbs to total words?
6. What proportion of these finite verbs are forms of *to be?*
7. What proportion of these verbs are in the passive voice?

Modifiers

8. What proportion of the total words are true adjectives?
9. How many of these adjectives are themselves modified by adverbs?
10. What proportion of the total words are noun adjuncts?

Subordination

11. What is the average length of the subordinate ("included") clauses?
12. What proportion of the total passage is inside such clauses?
13. How frequently are subject and main verb separated by intervening subordinate structures? How long are these interruptions?

Other Effects of Tone

14. How frequent is the determiner *the?*
15. Are there any sentences without subjects, or without verbs, or both? Are there any contractions?
16. How many occurrences are there of these marks of punctuation: parentheses, italics, dashes, question marks, exclamation points?

I now consider each of these questions in detail, with some statistics from my samples. . . .

4. Are the subjects of the finite verbs mostly neuter nouns, or are they nouns referring to people?

The distinctions here depend to some extent, of course, on what the speaker is talking about: it is predictable that a first-person-singular narrator in a novel should talk about people while the Internal Revenue Service should be concerned with facts and figures. But style matters too, as we can appreciate by returning once more to those first three passages of Chapter 2. There we encountered three voices, each talking more or less about the same "thing," but each using a different style. (I ignore, for a moment, the fourth passage, Mr. Eliot's.) In those three passages two-thirds of the grammatical subjects in "Teaching Literature" (Stuffy) were neuter, two-thirds of the subjects in "Unrequired Reading" (Sweet) were human beings, and "Private World" (Tough) divided its subjects exactly evenly between neuter nouns and people. It simply makes a difference how you say what you say— for example, how you state a conclusion. You can say "I believe . . . ," or you can say "You will understand . . . ," or you can say "The facts demonstrate. . . ." By such choices you create your voice.

The totals in all my samples are as follows: Tough Talk, 52 neuter subjects of finite verbs, 72 people; Sweet Talk, 45 neuters and 70 people; Stuffy Talk, 52 neuters and only 12 people. Two Tough Talkers and two ads (Henry, Earl Horter, Ads 7 and 8) are exceptional in using more neuter subjects than human beings. All Stuffy Talkers use at least two-thirds neuter nouns as their subjects. This concentration on the nonhuman in Stuffy Talk, as the doer of the action, contributes largely to the general air of no-personal-responsibility that I advanced in Chapter 7. . . .

5. What is the proportion of finitive verbs to total words?

The distinction here is remarkably consistent through my samples. The Stuffy Talker uses far fewer finite verbs (6 per cent of total words) than do the Sweet and the Tough Talker (both 11 per cent). This is part of the general distinction that pervades these figures, between formal-written language and informal-conversational language. We mentioned in Chapter 3 the classic Tough Talker's unwillingness to subordinate, an unwillingness that makes for simple sentence structures and a high proportion of finite verbs. The Stuffy Talker, on the other hand, qualifies his remarks with much subordination and modification, so that in officialese we find the verb followed by a whole series of constructions added to prevent misunderstanding. "Advice *has been requested* concerning the deductibility for Federal income tax purposes of research expenses, including traveling expenses, incurred by college and university professors in their capacity as educators." (One verb in a 29-word sentence.)

My figures are too tiny, but a word can be said in passing about base verbs —that is, uninflected verb forms used without any auxiliary. These are far more common in Sweet Talk than in either of the other two styles, partly because of Sweet Talk's fondness for the second person, including imperatives. "Wait till you taste these new dinners." Two base verbs in a 7-word sentence.

A note may also be added about the modal auxiliaries—may, might, can, could, would, should, must, and ought. These words express some kind of attitude (it has been called "emotional") toward the action that the verb names. Again Sweet Talk is well in the lead, though the figures are minute. In Tough Talk the characteristic verb form seems to be a simple inflection: this happened and that happened. Stuffy Talk, fond of elaborate qualification, takes more advantage of the subtleties offered by auxiliaries. But all this is guesswork needing to be tested.

6. What proportion of the finitive verbs are forms of to be?

Here I am not considering *to be* as an auxiliary. The Tough Talker in my samples is fonder of this verb than the others are; the figures are 36 per cent against 25 per cent for Sweet Talk and 17 per cent for Stuffy Talk. I submit that this is part of the urge for naming mentioned in Chapters 3 and 4, a liking for a particular sentence pattern of the "this-is-that" construction. In some of its appearances, it can come close to omniscience, as in *Time*'s "The scenes in Birmingham were unforgettable." The six Tough Talkers are not very consistent about this, but I include the point for what it may be worth.

7. What proportion of the finitive verbs are in the passive voice?

There is no problem here. Stuffy Talkers use the passive voice, others do not. It is a sure-fire technique for avoiding personal responsibility for one's statements, and when the Revenue Service winds up for a decision, it does not say "we conclude . . ." but "it is held that. . . ." By whom?

Slightly over one-quarter (26 per cent) of the finite verbs in my samples of Stuffy Talk are in the passive. The figure for Tough Talk is 4 per cent and for Sweet Talk 2 per cent. In all Stuffy Talkers except the marginal "Teaching Literature" the writers use a passive at least once in every six verbs. . . .

10. What proportion of the total words are noun adjuncts?

The particular inventiveness which characterizes many noun adjuncts in advertising was discussed in Chapter 6. Made-up phrases like *Foodarama living* and *stretch-out interior room* are characteristic of Sweet Talk. Every example in our Sweet Talk collection (except Ad #3) contains at least two noun adjunct constructions, and many of them are of the nonce sort I have illustrated. But the frequency (not the inventiveness) of noun adjuncts in Stuffy Talk is even higher—there are 55 such constructions, over 5 per cent of the total words. The Revenue passage is illustrative: *income tax purposes, research expenses, traveling expenses, college and university professors.* The Tough Talkers, on the other hand, employ only ten noun adjuncts throughout, three of them in *Time*'s journalism. The others are conventional expressions like *fruit trees, dirt shoulder, world brotherhood.*

The explanation here is complex. In Sweet Talk, I have argued, the passion for noun adjuncts is part of the passion for naming, and a substitute for Tough Talk's abundance of *to be* and the "this-is-that" sentence pattern. In Stuffy Talk, the multiple names have already been coined, and they roll off the stuffy tongue in great official bundles, like *the College Entrance Examination Board's Scholastic Aptitude and Achievement Test* ("Admissions"). But Tough Talk, often, aspires to speech patterns like those of Fries' Vulgar English samples in his famous study. More than once Fries has occasion to point out the relative conservatism, linguistically, of his Vulgar writers; they cling to old forms when others have given them up. Similarly they fail to leap on to current linguistic bandwagons, notably the noun-adjunct bandwagon. Fries found noun adjuncts in his so-called Standard writers four times as frequent as in his Vulgar. This is almost exactly the relation between my Sweet and Stuffy Talkers as against my Tough Talkers.

One would at first surmise that the adman's language aspires to Vulgarity too, but this is only partly true. Unlike Vulgar English and unlike the conversation of most people, Sweet Talk can be daring and resourceful in inventing new forms of expression. This daring is most conspicuous, I think, in the use of the noun adjunct.

Associated with noun adjuncts is the question of the inflected genitive, though my figures are too tiny for more than speculation. The substitution of the inflected genitive for the phrase with *of* is another of *Time*'s contributions to modern journalistic style, exemplified in our materials by the expression *Birmingham's Negroes* in place of the more orthodox *the Negroes of Birmingham*. But that is the only example of an inflected genitive in all of Tough Talk, while the only one in Stuffy Talk is *the College Board's . . . Tests* ("Admissions"). In Sweet Talk, with its desire to give things names, perhaps also to add that crisp authority conveyed by the mannerisms of Timestyle, there are nine instances of the inflected genitive. *Chase Manhattan's dish of tea. The world's best-selling scotch. Foodarama's supermarket selection.* (Inflected genitive and noun adjunct all in one phrase.) All examples are not from adwriters, either; there are three in "Unrequired Reading," though they lack the commercial touch of the ones I mentioned. . . .

And now the style machine. I summarize below the answers to my fifteen questions, as they are worked out in averages for the thousand words of each style. Then I propose criteria for each question, by means of which any passage of prose might be tested to see whether it qualifies, in that particular category, as Tough, Sweet, or Stuffy. After that I try the machine at measuring individually the various passages we have been examining in this study. Finally, in a Style Sampler (Appendix B), I try measuring other prose passages, to see whether the machine can provide a numerical score that might be taken as a reasonable translation of our impression of a voice.

Facts About The Passages

	Tough	Sweet	Stuffy
1. What is the proportion of monosyllables in the passage?	78%	68%	56%
2. What is the proportion of words of more than 2 syllables?	5%	12%	24%
3. How many first-person and second-person pronouns does the passage contain?	13 1st	12 1st	2 1st
	21 2nd	42 2nd	0 2nd
4. Are the subjects of finite verbs neuter nouns, or nouns referring to people?	52 N	45 N	51 N
	72 P	70 P	14 P
5. What is the proportion of finite verbs to total words?	11%	11%	6%
6. What proportion of finite verbs are forms of *to be*?	36%	25%	17%
7. What proportion of verbs are in the passive voice?	4%	2%	26%

8. What proportion of words are true adjectives?	6%	11%	8%
9. How many adjectives are modified by adverbs?	4	13	5
10. What proportion of words are noun adjuncts?	1%	4%	5%
11. What is the average length of included clauses?	8 wds	7 wds	18 wds
12. What proportion of total passage is inside such clauses?	24%	23%	32%
13. How many words separate subject and verb?	24 wds	36 wds	182 wds
14. How frequent is the determiner *the?*	97	39	65
15. How many fragments? How many contractions?	2 fr / 16 cn	20 fr / 24 cn	0 fr / 0 cn
16. How many parentheses, italics, dashes, question marks, exclamation points?	0 P / 0 I / 2 D / 1 Q / 0 E	4 P / 7 I / 9 D / 8 Q / 5 E	2 P / 0 I / 0 D / 0 Q / 0 E

Criteria For Measuring Style

	Tough	*Sweet*	*Stuffy*
1. Monosyllables	over 70%	61–70%	60% or less
2. Words of 3 syllables and more	under 10%	10–19%	20% or more
3. 1st and 2nd person pronouns	1 *I* or *we* per 100 words	2 *you* per 100 words	no 1st or 2nd person pronouns
4. Subjects: neuters vs. people	½ or more people	½ or more people	⅔ or more neuters
5. Finite verbs	over 10%	over 10%	under 10%
6. *To be* forms as finite verbs	over ⅓ of verbs	under ¼	under ¼
7. Passives	less than 1 in 20 verbs	none	more than 1 in 5 verbs
8. True adjectives	under 10%	over 10%	over 8%
9. Adjectives modified	fewer than 1 per 100 words	1 or more	fewer than 1
10. Noun adjuncts	under 2%	2% or more	4% or more
11. Average length of clauses	10 words or less	10 words or less	more than 10 words
12. Clauses, proportion of total words	¼ or less	⅓ or less	over 40%
13. "Embedded" words	less than ½ S/V combinations	less than half	more than twice
14. *The*	8% or more	under 6%	6–7%
15. Contractions and fragments	1 or more per 100 words	2 or more	none
16. Parentheses & other punctuation	none	2 or more per 100 words	none

WORKING WITH THE SELECTION

1. Gibson offers the Hemingway passage as an example of Tough Talk; the Howells passage presumably illustrates Sweet Talk. The following passage is a sample of Stuffy Talk.

> The community in question is typical of many mountain valley population centers, resting upon an agricultural base with some light industry related to the available local flora. The valley itself is mainly a rich alluvial plain, penetrated by a river geologically sufficiently mature to have developed meanders, irregularly elongate, about fifteen miles in length and some four miles in width at its greatest extent. It is mainly under cultivation, devoted to botanical species suitable for short-season agriculture, since frosts can be expected as late as June and as early as September, notably to oats, potatoes, and short-season root crops like sugar beets and rutabagas, to leguminous forage, timothy and clover, and, increasingly, alfalfa. Surrounding mountains rise to something less than two thousand feet above the valley floor (Mount General Winchester, 4592 feet) and are heavily wooded with coniferous forests. Winchester Center, formerly Winchester Corners, situated near the lower end of the valley, numbered a population of 6842 according to the 1970 census. It has one high school, three junior high schools, eight elementary schools, two hotels, a number of small motels, seven churches, two highways, and one railroad. Population is distributed in four relatively distinct areas, as follows: the business district, roughly three blocks by seven blocks; Winchester Heights, a fashionable district, including a country club and golf course, along the river bluffs to the west of the town; two new housing developments, north and east of the business district; and the old French Flats area to the south, formerly occupied mainly by French-Canadian immigrants, but now inhabited by their descendants, some recently migrated Negroes, and what are locally called "mountain people," who formerly were employed in lumbering in the adjacent mountains, but who have now been replaced by modern logging equipment. This last district merges into a belt of older residential areas about the business section, now variously declining into slums. Four small factories process local products: a paper mill that has absorbed buildings centered upon a log pond, structures formerly devoted to a box factory and a sash-and-door mill; a plant converting dessicated potatoes into a product sold nationally as Winchester Potato Flowers; a manufactory processing alfalfa, oats, and some other agricultural products for a composition intended as chicken feed; and a processing establishment preparing sugar beets, the *Beta vulgaris*, for shipment.

Consider Gibson's description of a Tough Talker and the discussion that leads to it. Then, on the basis of the passage above, attempt a similar description of a Stuffy Talker.

2. Gibson's Style Machine should provide you with a more nearly objective method for describing a piece of writing. Review Gibson's techniques for isolating styles; then apply them to the sample of Stuffy writing given above

and add to your previous observations. You will probably not want to attempt a complete statistical analysis, but do work out at least three or four percentages. Pick a few percentages from Gibson's list under criteria for measuring style and see how the Stuffy passage above would compare.

3. Gibson's book also includes what he calls A Style Sample, in which he gives passages that he considers "mostly Tough, mostly Sweet, mostly Stuffy," along with some that he characterizes as "mixtures," those in which no one style dominates. Gibson recognizes, of course, that no piece of writing can be all Tough or all anything else. One of his selections is part of a poem by Andrew Marvell, "To His Coy Mistress," printed as though it were prose:

> Had we but world enough, and time this coyness, Lady were no crime. We would sit down and think which way to walk and pass our long love's day. Thou by the Indian Ganges' side should rubies find; I by the tide of Humber would complain. I would love you ten years before the Flood, and you should, if you please, refuse till the conversion of the Jews. My vegetable love should grow faster than empires, and more slow; an hundred years should go to praise thine eyes and on thy forehead gaze; two hundred to adore each breast, and thirty-thousand to the rest; an age at least to every part, and the last age should show your heart.

Gibson catalogues this sample as "mostly" one style; under which would you expect him to include it, and why?

4. You may be curious enough to try Gibson's Style Machine on your own prose, whether or not you report the results.

7

Linguistics, Stylistics; Criticism?

Roger Fowler

Roger Fowler teaches in England at the University of East Anglia and has edited Essays on Style and Language *(1966). The following selection is from an essay by Fowler published in* Lingua, 16 *(1966).*

I shall elaborate on two aspects of linguistic criticism: the potentiality of its methods and approaches in the service of literary studies, and the adjustment in the linguists' views of their own contribution necessary before the contribution can become really worthwhile.

However inadequate the analyses of Chatman and Hill may seem as an approach to poetry, however suspect in their assumptions about the oral performance of poems, their technical merit as (partial) descriptions cannot be doubted. They are founded on a powerful and productive theory of language, and by reference to this (as documented in Trager and Smith and the tradition behind them) their terms and concepts can be understood and their statements utilised. The Trager-Smith analysis of English is now viewed as outmoded (but still, I think, often useful).[1] Now we have a range of techniques for description. The precision of the early fifties can still be achieved or bettered, and the repertoire of statements we can make about the language of literature is much wider. Two chief modes of analysis are now available, and not necessarily in opposition. The *transformational-generative* mode, propounded by Noam Chomsky and all-powerful in America, has already produced some very interesting discussion of poetry.[2] Admittedly, there is a strong suspicion that those transformationalists who have interested themselves in poetry have been using poetic utterances merely to test the efficiency of their grammatical concepts. But in their writings there has been a steady focus on utterances of a type highly likely to appear in poetry: *colourless green ideas sleep furiously, seven oceans answer from their dream, argumentative windows cook with their destinies, he danced his did, a grief ago,* utterances on the borderlines of poetry and nonsense, grammar and non-grammar, lexical decorum and anarchy of diction. Here is a conscientious attempt to make a grammar of English adequate to describe language outside normal (colloquial, casual, common, etc.) usage, and adequate to explain the place of *any* utterance within the corpus of possible English sentences: to state not just that an utterance is "grammatical" or "ungrammatical" but that it has an understandable place on the scale of grammaticalness.

The second popular mode of analysis is the *levels-and-categories* method, based on the thought of J. R. Firth and developed by M. A. K. Halliday and others.[3] The [method] operates on the basis of a model of language which postulates the existence of the relevant levels *substance, form* and *context.*

[1] An interesting use of the Trager-Smith methods is John Thompson, *The Founding of English Metre*, London, 1961.

[2] The classic book is N. Chomsky, *Syntactic structures*, The Hague, 1957, and an elementary account of the method is E. Bach, *An introduction to transformational grammars*, New York, 1964. S. R. Levin proposed the application of T. G. to poetry in *Linguistic structures in poetry*, The Hague, 1962. See also his "Poetry and grammaticalness", in H. G. Lunt (ed.) *Proceedings of the ninth international congress of linguists*, The Hague, 1964, pp. 308–314; J. P Thorne, "Stylistics and generative grammars", *Journal of Linguistics* i (1965) pp. 49–59; Richard Ohmann, "Generative grammars and the concept of literary style", *Word* xx (1964) pp. 423–439.

[3] See J. R. Firth, *Papers in linguistics*, London, 1957; M. A. K. Halliday, "Categories of the theory of grammar", *Word* xvii (1961) pp. 241–292; Halliday, Angus McIntosh and Peter Strevens, *The linguistic sciences and language teaching*, London, 1964. John Spencer and Michael J. Gregory describe the Hallidayan position and its application to stylistics in "An approach to the study of style", *Linguistics and style*, London, 1964, pp. 59–105. Among literary descriptions on this basis are:

Substance is the physical matter of speech or writing, a "surface" or a "medium" without meaning. Form (linked to substance by phonology, sound-patterning) is the level at which meaningful patterns are found. It is the primary level for analysis, and has two sub-levels, grammar and lexis. Here patterns are discovered and described. Context comprises all relevant things outside language. The connexion between context and particular linguistic forms ("contextual meaning") may be said to constitute the field for semantic analysis. One positive assertion of the theory, however, is that there is formal, as well as contextual, meaning. Language functions, and its manner of functioning is significant. The implications of this theory for the study of literary language are obvious. Linguists, when describing grammatical, lexical or metrical patterns, believe themselves to be making statements of meaning. Also important is the habit of separate recognition and description of the categories of literary language: the ability to say, for example, "this is a grammatical and not a lexical feature". Needless to say, sets of terms are available to aid analysis of features within these categories (although lexical analysis is still at a relatively primitive stage).

We must add to these two versions of linguistic analysis the older *structural* analysis associated with Bloomfield and his pupils and followers, only recently displaced by transformational grammar. As shown above, it first manifested itself in linguistic criticism in the form of phonological metrics, but its range is wider than that. It can still supply many useful and very precise analytic techniques.[4, 5]

All I have wanted to show in the brief survey above is that a range of very exact techniques for linguistic analysis is available. If one is interested in the grammar, metre, sound-structure, or vocabulary of a literary text, one has a wide choice of means to the understanding and discussion of the selected feature. Much space has been wasted by linguists justifying their methods: a necessary public-relations job that has now been done often enough. Nor is the applicability of linguistic analysis to literature a really fundamental issue worthy of discussion. Literature is (among other things,

---

Halliday, "The linguistic study of literary texts" in *Proceedings of the ninth international congress of linguists* pp. 302–307; Geoffrey Leech, "Language and interpretation", *A Review of English Literature* vi (April, 1965) pp. 66–75; J. M. Sinclair, "Taking a poem to pieces", in Roger Fowler (ed.) *Essays on Style and Language* (London, 1966) pp. 68–81.

[4] 'Structural' linguistics is massively documented between 1930 and 1960. The important works (apart from those cited [earlier]) are: L. Bloomfield, *Language,* New York, 1933; Bloch and Trager, *Outline of linguistic analysis,* Baltimore, 1942; Z. S. Harris, *Methods in structural linguistics,* Chicago, 1951; M. Joos, *Readings in linguistics,* New York, 1958; the journal *Language*; and a number of books by K. L. Pike and E. A. Nida.

[5] Other linguistic writings relevant to literary study include the books of Stephen Ullman on semantics and stylistics; Halliday, "The tones of English", *Archivum Linguisticum* xv (1963) pp. 1–28; A. McIntosh, "Patterns and ranges", *Language* xxxvii (1961) pp. 327–337; D. Abercrombie, "A phonetician's view of verse structure", *Linguistics* vi (June, 1964) pp. 1–13, "Syllable-quantity and enclitics in English", *In honour of Daniel Jones,* London, 1964, pp. 216–222.

perhaps) language and evidently analysable: this is a presupposition of much modern criticism, and need not be set up as an assumption peculiar to linguistic criticism. We can say that modern descriptive linguistics is a natural companion to modern criticism because both are text-centred: both involve analysis, close reading, and both set a premium on accuracy and usefulness of description. It is arguable that explicit linguistics alone can provide a real basis for descriptive criticism, and that if descriptive criticism had succeeded in developing intelligent modes of analysis of its own, this whole problem would not exist: linguistic analysis would be detectable as a natural part of criticism.

I have affirmed the usefulness of linguistic methods as part of the critic's equipment. But is the contribution merely technical, just part of conscious method? In a publication which came into my hands during the writing of this article, Professor Jeffares asks (and I hope he knows the answer) "How much more, in fact, does [the linguist] offer beyond a new vocabulary, a jargon which gives him that sense of exclusiveness often beloved by new groups in academic society, a new system of analysis, a new set of categories, to set against those of his rival colleagues?" [6] In fact, the linguist offers something perhaps more important than technique and terminology: a set of attitudes which are reinforcement of, not substitutes for, those of descriptive criticism. He is practised in that essential of much modern criticism, close reading; in the recognition of what is language and what is not; in seeing what are the separately analysable parts of a text; in spotting patterns and meanings. These faculties—comprising a kind of mood for analysis—are summed up in an ideal honoured by linguists since the early years of this century, "the descriptive attitude". The linguist focuses automatically on what is the first concern of descriptive criticism: "what is "there" in the poem". That phrase is from the first sentence of a book whose method demonstrates the point I am making here: that criticism can benefit from the linguistic frame of mind as well as from the techniques and jargon of the linguist.[7] "Linguistic" criticism, as here, is often brilliant through the fact that its linguistics comes so naturally that it hardly appears at all. There are no morphemes, tagmemes, sememes within sight, but just a steady focus on the form of the text. The two extremes of linguistic explicitness are well illustrated by two essays by J. M. Sinclair. In "Taking a poem to pieces" (see fn. 3) he demonstrates an almost complete and very technical analysis of a poem; in "When is a poem like a sunset?" [8] his linguistics is simply a controlled and rational handling of language: there is an implication of analysis which carries respect.

For students, the techniques of linguistics should probably be kept largely out of sight. One of my duties as a linguist teaching literature and criticism is to teach, and direct practice in, Practical Criticism. In this context I can

[6] *A Review of English Literature* vi (April, 1965) p. 7.
[7] The book is Winifred M. T. Nowottny, *The language poets use,* London, 1962.
[8] *A Review of English Literature* vi (April, 1965) pp. 76–91.

use a linguistic approach entirely compatible with a critic's "close reading". The aim is to stimulate reading habits and opinions which achieve a nice balance between response and analysis—which can allow rationalisation of response without its inhibition. This is met by concentration on form and by creating a mood which makes detailed linguistic analysis always possible but hardly ever practised. If I use terms like "sentence", "phoneme", "lexical item" occasionally, my students will not be shocked: their class-discussion provides a sympathetic environment for formal statements, which can arise naturally and be understood easily, without the students knowing that anything as "difficult" or "scientific" or "inhuman" as linguistics is in the air.

The "public" critic ought to operate in such a state of mind; but he will also need to have explicit linguistics (of whatever sort) at his fingertips. The good Practical Critic needs to be a very good linguistician. But even the most excellent linguisticians have failed to gain respect as critics, for technical virtuosity is not a guarantee of critical success. It is not, as I think linguists have tended to believe, that critics have failed to acknowledge the efficiency of linguistic techniques. Nor, except superficially, is it a question of interdisciplinary hostility, though we linguists have given enough cause for hostility. The fault is with the linguists: to be critics, we must be competent linguists and then become less of linguists. The development of precise techniques, and theorising in linguistic terms,[9] though essential, carry us only a short distance. A programme for linguistic criticism cannot be proposed in terms of a theory of language only. After the refinement of methods, and some thought on elementary questions (literature is basically a use of language, a literature is a part of a particular language, etc.), all remaining issues are critical problems. We should not ask "how can linguistic criticism be established as a branch of linguistics?" More proper and rewarding is "what is the place of objective formal description in literary studies?"

At this point there is a need for some scrutiny of our terminology. I have argued that there is an important part of criticism—and a prominent part in twentieth century criticism—which consists of the close examination of the language of literature *qua* language before statements are made about it as literature. Differences of method of analysis are more superficial than may appear. One method is *linguistic analysis,* described in the earlier part of this article. Another is *explication de texte,* defined by H. A. Hatzfeld as

> a close analysis of . . . lexicological and syntactic features, including the so-called figures of speech and rhythmical elements.[10]

[9] Æsthetic and other theory, put in terms of general linguistics, is very adequately represented in the literature of what has come to be called "linguistic stylistics". While much of it is essential to the adjustment of the linguists' and critics' attitudes to their disciplines, it has hardly penetrated into profitable critical theory and practice. For some discussion see T. A. Sebeok, *Style in language,* New York, 1960; Fowler, "Linguistic theory and the study of literature", *Essays on style and language* pp. 1–28.

[10] *A critical bibliography of the new stylistics applied to the Romance literatures, 1900–1952,* Chapel Hill, 1953, p. 1.

Then we have "Practical Criticism" in the Cambridge sense—not a method, but an approach which "*involves* a minute scrutiny of the verbal detail of works of literature".[11] The "New Criticism" is another powerful approach which demands critical analysis or close reading.[12] At least these four historically definable phenomena—two methods and two approaches involving similar methods—can be identified. What needs to be named is the common element, focus on the text and analysis, for whatever critical uses or dependent on whatever aesthetic presuppositions. "Critical analysis", "practical criticism", "close reading" are best used for whole approaches, in which verbal study is only a part; "linguistic analysis" and "explication de texte" have too specific connotations. I propose "verbal analysis" as a term for the process of describing the language of literature: the analysis itself, not the criticism founded on it. I shall now consider the process of utilising verbal analysis, and specifically that form based on linguistics, in criticism.

The aims and assumptions of criticism will determine the most important aspects of verbal analysis, irrespective of particular techniques used. There are, in a sense, two "hows" of analysis: the "technical", with criteria such as objectivity, precision and flexibility of method, criteria which may select methods derived from general linguistics; the "critical", wholly determined by questions of a critical nature, problems largely concerned with what to select for analysis and how to select it. A further question is involved in the transition from verbal analysis to critical statement: what to add to the verbal analysis to make complete statements about the work being discussed.

Here I would like to suggest three "levels of achievement": description, stylistics and criticism. This tripartite division of the field incorporates—I believe most significantly for the confrontation between linguists and critics—a value scale, with criticism (including "evaluation", "interpretation", etc.) at the top. Linguists have already shown themselves to be most adroit at "mere description". A linguistic description of any text (literary or not) is, ideally, absolutely revealing: it can lay bare the formal structure of the language in more detail than any critic would want. We can find out about all aspects of grammatical structure from that of words to that of sentences; about lexical distribution, history and etymology; about phonological shape. The description is, in a technical sense, "meaningful": it reveals formal meaning, the meaning of information theory seen in patterns, contrasts, choices.[13] Completeness and revealingness (with simplicity and consistency) are ideals for linguistic description, and so one can understand why linguists seem to re-

---

[11] A. C. Spearing, *Criticism and medieval poetry*, London, 1964, p. 1 (my italics). At this point one would cite (as Spearing quotes) the writings of Empson, Leavis and Brooks. For a clear exposition of the tenets of the Practical Criticism of today, see Cox and Dyson, [*Modern Poetry, Studies in Practical Criticism*, London, 1963].

[12] See J. C. Ransom, *The new criticism*, Norfolk, Conn., 1941; Robert Wooster Stallman, *Critiques and essays in criticism*, 1920-1948, New York, 1949.

[13] For linguistics as the revelation of meaning by analysis, see the items by Firth and Halliday cited in fn. 3, especially Firth pp. 190-215 ("Modes of meaning"); Leech, *A Review of English Literature* vi (April, 1965) pp. 66-7.

verse the "scale" with which I began this paragraph. There has been an understandable defensive tendency to stay at the lower end of my scale, or to urge the ideals of description passionately. So Halliday:

> In talking of "the linguistic study" of literary texts we mean, of course, not "the study of the language" but "the study (of the language) by the theories and methods of linguistics". There is a crucial difference between the *ad hoc*, personal and arbitrarily selective statements offered, frequently in support of a preformulated literary thesis, as "textual" or "linguistic" statements about literature, and an analysis founded on general linguistic theory and descriptive linguistics. It is the latter that may reasonably be called "linguistic stylistics".[14]

In fact, however linguistically wholesome these sentiments may be, and however much apparently in accord with the views of modern criticism insofar as they are anti-impressionistic and anti-prejudice in spirit, the stubborn adoption of this position will be the very thing which disqualifies linguistic description from contributing significantly to literary criticism. Of course, any form of verbal analysis must take pains to ensure the validity and meaningfulness of its description. But verbal analysts, to become critics, must then renounce some part of their position. To pass on to stylistics, we must point to patterns which are meaningful not simply because they are efficient carriers of information, but because they are significant in a comparative context ("Browne's style is different from Burton's in these ways . . ."). To go farther up the scale still, we must acknowledge that the meaning of a poem is more than the sum of its cognitive and formal meanings, and that perhaps some of the causes of this meaning and value are inaccessible to verbal analysis. In both cases progress involves losing some of the description, or making it "impure" by invoking non-linguistic matters, or postulating the existence of an aesthetic area beyond the linguist's power to explore.

Mere description—whether linguistic, of literary or nonliterary texts, or any kind of verbal analysis conducted for its own sake—is of no great use, except possibly as an exercise to promote awareness of language or of method. And for a linguist to say that he will do the description, or show the critic how to do it, and leave the *using* of the description to the critic, is not constructive. It implies that description is nine-tenths of the critical task, and that interpretation has to, and can, follow directly on. No: the description itself must be purposeful. The crucial point is that linguistic study (in the sense given by Halliday) is essentially unselective. It describes everything, and all data are of equal significance. To analyse usefully (could one say "critically"?) one must know (or have some at least marginally positive clue) *why* one is undertaking verbal analysis: and this knowledge will inevitably direct the manner of the analysis. A "preformulated literary thesis" is essential in a very real way; to have this thesis, or hunch, or feeling, is the property of the sensi-

---

[14] "The linguistic study of literary texts", *Proceedings of the ninth international congress of linguists*, p. 302.

tive critic or reader, and to have it is not to cheat.[15] Whether one is proceeding only to stylistics, or beyond the language to interpretative or evaluatory criticism, one must, and can without falsifying, select for description certain features which one feels to be significant.

The most obvious first use of verbal analysis is in stylistics. This is a tortured subject. The definition of "style" is of course a sitting target for the linguist, and too often he progresses no further.[16] However one defines style, pure verbal analysis is not the same thing as stylistic description. One is concerned to *characterise* a style, not simply list all the features of the language of a text. One seeks to provide objective evidence for feelings about the distinctive linguistic character of an author or a text. A feature, or group of features, is usually isolated as a result of asking not "what linguistic choices are made here?" but "what *sorts of* linguistic choices are made here?" These features are characteristic—they identify a text (or author) against a norm, a norm defined by reference to the language as a whole (a difficult concept) or that of some other text or author. Stylistics is comparative, for a stylistic feature has meaning or force only against a background of usage. Granted a hunch to make him select the significant feature(s), and the patience to describe the normative background, the linguist may be an extremely revealing stylistician. He still needs an educated reader's sensitivity, of course: but there are signs that, if he has this, his equipment for handling significant variation (*deviation* in his terms[17]) can be rewardingly productive.

The linguist's "formal meaning" perhaps provides a clue to the limits of stylistics as a branch of criticism. Stylistics examines the cause of only a narrow range of responses in the reading of literature: one's response to form and pattern. It may be a characteristic of literary expression that it draws attention to itself, is a significant artefact as well as a signifying medium: in any event, stylistics is concerned with the cause of this attention only. And for a handful of motives which are often connected with literary history rather than criticism.

To date, linguistics has tended to press no further than stylistics. A survey of the titles listed in the footnotes to this article reveals a limitation in labelling, if not in aim. Even the recent issue of *A Review of English Literature* (vi, April, 1965) calls itself "New Attitudes to Style", although the contents are manifestly of wider critical interest than just stylistics. There is probably a feeling in both camps that the contribution of linguistics to literary studies is too limited to go beyond stylistic description. The linguist is too politicly

---

[15] Spencer and Gregory speak of "a response to a work of literature which is a kind of hypothesis, a basis for further observation and testing" (p. 61).

[16] Notable tormentors are several of the contributors to Sebeok's *Style in Language*; M. Riffaterre, "Criteria for style analysis", *Word* xv (1959) pp. 154–174; N. E. Enkvist, "On defining style", in Spencer and Gregory, *Linguistics and style,* pp. 3–56; M. Joos, "The five clocks", *IJAL* xxviii (April, 1962).

[17] Discussion of "deviation" is to be found in Sebeok, op. cit., especially pp. 91–2, 420–22; in the article by Leech cited in fn. 3, and in his "Linguistics and the figures of rhetoric" in *Essays on style and language*.

cautious to claim too much, and the critic too jealous to admit too much. Of course, there is a limitation; but not that linguistic analysis has no part to play in higher criticism. Once linguistic description has become verbal analysis (in the sense I have proposed) by being selective and purposeful, its place in criticism beyond stylistics can be challenged only by arguments which will also throw out Practical Criticism and all similar and highly-respected modern critical approaches. The limitation is that verbal analysis, though vital, is only a part of criticism: and a smaller part than of stylistics. In evaluatory and interpretative criticism verbal analysis has a basic role, because language is at once the medium and the central focus. However, criticism, acknowledging that the total meaning of a text is more than the sum of its formal and referential meanings, and probably ultimately unanalysable by objective means, must exploit all the aids it knows: verbal analysis is only the chief among many.

WORKING WITH THE SELECTION

1. Addressing himself to British critics, perhaps especially British academic critics, Fowler suggests that they should know more about language and linguistics than they do. The importance of modern linguistics was recognized somewhat later in England than in the United States and has been less embraced outside a restricted circle. In this country most, but not all, academic critics are aware that there has been a revolution in language study and that it concerns them. Many professional critics, however—mainly magazine and newspaper reviewers who are not also scholars—seem still ignorant of modern language study. Have you encountered any? You undoubtedly have if you have read reviews critically, which generally is a good idea.

2. Fowler makes a distinction between the terms *linguistic description* and *verbal analysis*. Can you explain the distinction? How important does it seem to you? By Fowler's definition, would the discussions by Ohmann and Gibson be linguistic description or verbal analysis?

3. You might consider Fowler's essay a summary view of language, literature, and style. That is what he intended, and certainly within limits he succeeded. Fowler, an Englishman, quotes both influential British scholars, such as Firth and Halliday, and prominent American linguists, such as Sebeok, Nida, Pike, Bloch, Trager, Ullman, and Chomsky. Clearly, he has kept himself informed about developments in linguistics on both sides of the Atlantic. Has he evaluated them judiciously? Has he missed anything important? In order to judge the adequacy of Fowler's essay as a summary, you will need to take dates into account, for scholars are venturing new thoughts about language more and more frequently these days. Are you aware of any developments, perhaps some reported in this book, that Fowler did not have an opportunity to evaluate when he wrote his essay?

Index of Authors

Awdeley, John, 280

Bailey, Nathaniel, 407
Barnard, Ellsworth, 341
Beattie, James, 5
Bentley, Robert H., 275
Bernstein, Theodore M., 335
Berry, Lester V., 305
Bloomfield, Leonard, 16
Bolinger, Dwight, 290, 324
Brown, Goold, 203
Brown, Roger, 38
Bryant, Margaret M., 335

Camden, William, 389
Cassidy, Frederic G., 133
Cassirer, Ernst, 112
Caxton, William, 398
Chaucer, Geoffrey, 395
Chomsky, Noam, 77
Coles, Elisha, 407
Costello, Donald P., 432

Davies, Hugh Sykes, 343
DeCamp, David, 247
de Laguna, Grace, 160
Dickens, Charles, 380
Dykema, Karl W., 197

Evans, Bergen, 334
Evans, Cornelia, 334

Farrar, Frederic William, 9
Ferril, Thomas Hornsby, 165
Flexner, Stuart Berg, 307, 424
Fowler, H. W., 333
Fowler, Roger, 482
Francis, W. Nelson, 211

Friend, Joseph H., 187

Garst, Robert E., 335
Gibson, Walker, 465
Gowers, Sir Ernest, 442
Guralnik, David B., 154

Hall, Robert A., Jr., 346
Harman, Thomas, 281
Hartung, Charles V., 351
Henryson, Robert, 402
Hill, Archibald A., 25
Hinton, Norman D., 286
Huxley, Aldous, 161

Ives, Sumner, 215

Jacobs, Noah Jonathan, 91
Jakle, John A., 107
Johnson, Samuel, 409

Keller, Helen, 55
Kelly, Edward Hanford, 313
Kochman, Thomas, 259
Kratz, Henry, 307
Kurath, Hans, 296

Laird, Charlton, 47
Langacker, Ronald W., 58
Langer, Susanne K., 32, 170
Liljeblad, Sven, 67
Lipton, James, 116
Locke, John, 11
Lucretius, 5

Mandeville, Sir John, 393
Marckwardt, Albert H., 337
Martin, Benjamin, 408
Mathews, Mitford M., 423

491

Index of Titles

493

E
F
G
H
I
J